LISTENING TO AMERICA

An Illustrated History
of Words and Phrases
from Our Lively
and Splendid Past

By Stuart Berg Flexner

A TOUCHSTONE BOOK
Published by Simon & Schuster, Inc.
NEW YORK

Copyright © 1982 by Stuart Berg Flexner
All rights reserved
including the right of reproduction
in whole or in part in any form

First Touchstone Edition, 1984

Published by Simon & Schuster, Inc.
Simon & Schuster Building
Rockefeller Center
1230 Avenue of the Americas
New York, New York 10020

TOUCHSTONE and colophon are registered trademarks
of Simon & Schuster, Inc.

Photo research by Cheryl Moch and Vincent Virga

Manufactured in the United States of America

10 9 8 7 6 5 4 3 2 1
10 9 8 7 6 5 4 3 2 1 (Pbk.)

Library of Congress Cataloging in Publication Data

Flexner, Stuart Berg.
Listening to America.
Includes index.
1. Americanisms. 2. English language—Etymology.
3. English language—United States—History. I. Title.
PE2831.F58   1982   427′.973   82-10319

ISBN 0-671-24895-2
ISBN 0-671-52798-3 Pbk.

To Doris, Jennifer, and Geoffrey, with love.

I hear America singing, the varied
carols I hear. . . .
   Walt Whitman, "I Hear America
   Singing," 1860, from *Leaves
   of Grass*

Contents

Preface

History teaches us a great deal about our country and our culture. In recounting the stories of great events, movements, and leaders, however, history can slight the day-to-day life of the people, our thoughts and feelings, and—that greatest monument of all—our language. This book attempts to add to history, to tell something more about our country and our fellow countrymen, by presenting some of the most common, revealing, and interesting words and expressions we have used in our daily concerns and by giving the stories behind these terms, their origins, and their use. In a small way, it is part of the oral history of the not-so-common common people.

In *I Hear America Talking* I tried to present some of the representative terms that came out of our country's great events and movements, from our wars, immigrations, ethnic groups, etc. Here I want to present some representative terms that grew out of our day-to-day life, terms dealing with food and shelter, sports and the movies, advertising and unions, and with our habits and vices. In this book, I hope you will hear the voices of the people, from Wall Street brokers, movie stars, advertising men, Philadelphia lawyers, and labor leaders through baseball and football players, golfers, boxers, smokers and drinkers, housewives, firemen, cab drivers, telephone operators, mailmen, and waiters and waitresses to hippies, pirates, prostitutes and the Mafia. Mainly, however, I hope the words may give us some insight into America and Americans, past and present, and will help tell the larger story of how we and our language became what we are.

Understanding the words, their origins, and how and when they were used can help us know and feel what it was like long ago, and not so long ago, to plant a tree, build a barn, go to the beach or a baseball game. The words can help tell us what people thought and felt about changing their hair style or deciding to grow a beard or switching from a nightgown to newfangled pajamas, of being blessed or cursed with a too-common or a too-special name or nickname, of getting up on a cold winter's morning in 1720 or 1820 or 1920. They can tell us what it was like to go into our first supermarkets, use an early telephone, send a comic Valentine, to wait for the iceman or for the return of a whaling ship, to open a can of soup or cook a steak or eat fudge cooked over a gas light, to make maple sugar or a quilt or a fortune on Wall Street. They can tell us what it was and is like to be angry or blue, to gossip and gripe, to look at the world and one's friends and say "Idiot!" or "Great!" These things, as much as great historical events, movements, and leaders, are also part of the very real world of our past and of our present lives.

This is a book about many thousands of our most common words and expressions, but it groups them together into related sections, so that the terms are shown in their historic context and the sections can be used as thumbnail histories of some of our daily activities and concerns, of our daily problems and pleasures (all terms and subjects discussed are listed alphabetically in the index). Thus this is a book about the American Language, treating that language as an important part of American history, of social history, and of the biography of us all. The story of our words is also the story of our country and our people.

Following most of the words and expressions discussed in this book are the year dates in which they were first recorded as having been in use (these dates are given in parenthesis or are set off by commas). I have relied on the usual scholarly sources for most such dates, but in some instances I have been able to list earlier dates than usually given because I have found the terms in earlier documents, newspapers, magazines, letters, diaries, etc. All such dates for the earliest known use of a word or expression can, however, be deceptive: many older terms entered the spoken language years before they were ever recorded, and many others have probably appeared in earlier writings where no researcher has yet found them. Also, of course, the mere fact that a term was recorded does not always indicate if it was still rare or already a popular term known to most people. When an exact year date for the first known use of a word or expression cannot be established, the text merely notes that it was in use in or by the time of a specific decade (the 1780s for example) or in the "early," "late," or "mid" part of that decade, by which is meant the first or last five years or the middle four years of the decade.

A fair number of words and expressions were originally spelled or hyphenated differently than they are now; indeed, some older terms have been spelled in a variety of ways over the years, especially before modern dictionaries and schooling standardized many of the spellings. Thus, though *baseball* and *fireplace* are common and proper forms to us, I have retained a few references to *base ball*, *fire-place* and other older terms to show how they appeared in their original or early written uses. Naturally, I have used our modern spellings and forms in the subsequent discussions of such terms.

Depending on the period and context, I have again used *America* and *American* to refer to the North American continent, to the various English colonies and the land areas that were later to become part of what is now the United States, and to the United States in its various expanding boundaries throughout our history as a nation.

The American vocabulary and experience are far too vast to present thoroughly in any one volume. Any one book can attempt to include only as large and representative a sampling as space and judgment provide. I have selected what I hope are among the most representative, revealing, and interesting topics and terms from our day-to-day history and language, but am sorry not to have the space, or the knowledge, to include every topic and term that any individual reader might find interesting or useful. What is contained in the book, however, is based on the most accurate, authoritative, and latest scholarship available. When details of language or history are in doubt, or when conflicting theories exist, I have tried to point that out.

Besides drawing upon such resources as the monumental *Oxford English Dictionary* and its *Supplements*, Mitford M. Mathews' *A Dictionary of Americanisms On Historical Principles*, Sir William Craigie's *Dictionary of American English on Historical Principles*, the various editions of John Russell Bartlett's *Dictionary of Americanisms*, John S. Farmer's *Americanisms*, George Matsell's *Vocabulum*, R. H. Thornton's *American Glossary*, Eric Partridge's *A Dictionary of Slang and Unconventional English*, Francis Grose's *A Classical Dictionary of the Vulgar Tongue*, H. L. Mencken's *The American Language* and its *Supplements*, and such journals as *American Speech*, the *Publication of the American Dialect Society*, and a great many other books and journals on language and history, I have used many specialized dictionaries, glossaries, books, and journals dealing with politics, sports, cooking, advertising, sailing, finance, movies, religion, the labor movement, and scores of other subjects. I have also relied heavily on official documents and archives, published letters and diaries, and on popular books, newspapers, magazines, song lyrics, radio and television programs, and movies as sources for words and expressions, as well as for background material.

I would especially like to thank: Ted Fleischaker, Operations Director of radio station WUOL, for his willingness to share his knowledge of and enthusiasm for many facets of both the past and present American scene and of the communications and entertainment fields, though his major contribution may not be apparent; Keith L. Runyon, associate editor of *The Louisville Times* for his contribution to *The Movies* section; Doris Flexner for her very professional research and editing skills; and scores of scholars, writers, friends, and correspondents who researched specific items, answered questions, and made many worthwhile suggestions. This book would not have been written without the early encouragement of Gorton Carruth, David Scott, Eugene Ehrlich, and other members of The Hudson Group, or of Walter Betkowski. It could not have been published but for the faith and energy of Dan Green. I would also like to thank my editors Erwin Glikes, Robert Eckhardt, and Jim Daly, and the picture researchers Vincent Virga and Cheryl Moch. Last but certainly not least, I sincerely want to thank the readers, those who are interested in language and history, who make such books as this both possible and worth doing.

Stuart Flexner

LISTENING TO AMERICA

This 1898 Ivory Soap *ad combined the slogan* It Floats *with an appealing drawing of a red-blooded American male at his domestic chores.*

It Pays to Advertise

Angell's 1808 tavern sign in Providence, Rhode Island, offered "entertainment," which meant that meals were served to guests.

Advertisement, literally that which causes one to turn and look (from Latin *advertere*, to turn), meant any information or advice in Shakespeare's day, though as early as 1666 the *London Gazette* relegated baser accounts of products into an "Advertisement Supplement." The British still pronounce the word as *adVERTisement*, but the American pronunciation *adverTISEment* was well enough established to appear in Webster's first dictionary in 1806. By the 1850s we often shortened the word to *ad*.

Early ads were: painted picture signs beckoning mostly illiterate customers to inns, taverns, and tradesmen's shops on nameless streets without numbers; handbills and posters; and short newspaper announcements of the arrival of shipments of coffee, tea, indentured servants, and slaves for sale; though by 1740 the *Boston News-Letter* carried ads of property for sale. In 1741, the first colonial magazines appeared, in Philadelphia, and so did the first magazine ad, a tiny notice for a runaway slave in Benjamin Franklin's *General Magazine and Historical Chronicle* (by coincidence, the first known written ad, found by archeologists at the ruins of Thebes, is also for the return of a runaway slave).

In 1841, Volney B. Palmer started the first advertising agency in the U.S.—also in Philadelphia—but he called it an *advertising broker* (he actually sold what even then was called advertising *space* for newspapers, an occupation then already called *puffing*). When Palmer expanded his firm in 1850 to the American Newspaper Advertising Agency of New York, Boston, and Philadelphia, he introduced the term *advertising agency*, which was just one year before *billboard* was recorded as meaning a roadside sign.

In the 1880s new products and new methods of packaging and marketing (people bought fewer and fewer nameless items out of barrels and stacks) led to changes in advertising and advertising media. Thus *sandwich man* (so called because the image of a man walking between two advertising boards resembles a sandwich) was in use by the 1890s, and *advertising blotter* (for a desktop blotter bearing an advertiser's name, address, and message) was in use before World War I. The merits of *electric signs* were discussed

New York City's first large electric sign appeared on the side of a building at the corner of 5th Avenue and 23rd Street in 1900. Over six stories high and topped by a 40-foot-long green pickle, it used 1,200 light bulbs and bore Heinz's slogan 57 Good Things for the Table, *used since 1898 as an alternative to the 1896* 57 Varieties, *both slogans created by Henry J. Heinz.*

in the 1890s, and the blazing glow of *neon signs* was lauded in the late 1920s. In the late 1920s, too, the public was talking about the new *road signs* (shorter and simpler than the old billboards) and even *skywriting.* In 1926 the country started chuckling over the *Burma-Shave signs,* created by Allen Odell (see BEARDS, CLOSE SHAVES, AND BARBERSHOPS for more details).

Also in the mid-1920s, *commercial* and *sponsor* took on new meanings with the wonder of home radio. The first *radio ad,* offering lots for sale, was heard over Long Island's WEAF in 1922, and the *Eveready Flashlight Hour* first introduced "intermittent commercials" during its show in 1923 (by 1928 radio advertising expenditures already amounted to $10 million a year). The term *television commercial* came toward the late 1940s, with the 1949 *Texaco Star Theater* being the first major sponsored TV program. Also by the late 1940s people were calling any man who worked in advertising a *huckster* (the word had long referred to a street vendor who shouted his wares, from Middle Dutch *hokester,* tradesman), and by the early 1950s we were using *Madison Avenue* to mean the advertising industry, because so many agencies had offices along that New York City street.

It pays to advertise has been an American business slogan since 1914. The advertising *slogan* (literally battle cry, from Scottish Gaelic *sluagh,* army + *gairm,* yell) came into wide use in the 1840s when patent medicine men, who were the first to "sell" rather than merely "announce" their wares, painted them on their wagons. Ever since, advertising slogans have been used to *whoop up* (1885) or *tout* (1924) products and have been a part of our language:

Procter & Gamble's original Ivory Soap *trademark as registered on September 23, 1879.*

Harmless as Water from the Mountain Springs, 1840s, Hostetter's Stomach Bitters, recommended for the shakes, dyspepsia, colic, dysentery, nervousness, and gloom—and containing 44 percent alcohol!

Good for Man or Beast, early 1870s, Dr. Hitchcock's Kickapoo Indian Oil.

Pink Pills for Pale People, 1870s, Dr. William's Pink Pills.

It Floats—99 44/100% Pure, 1879, Ivory Soap, introduced nine years after Procter and Gamble had perfected a hard, pure white soap to compete with the more expensive pure, white Castile soap. Procter and Gamble simply named their new product The White Soap, but when workmen left a large batch stirring too long, beating extra air into the mixture, so that the soap floated, Harley T. Procter renamed it *Ivory*, from the 45th Psalm's "out of ivory palaces they have made thee glad," and the company created its new slogan.

Eventually. Why not now?, around 1880, Gold Medal Flour, then made by the Washburn-Crosby Co., which in 1928 was to organize 127 independent milling companies into *General Mills*.

Absolutely pure, 1880s, Royal Baking Soda.

Use Sapolia, 1880s, Sapolia Soap, an early example of the pithiest of all slogans, those merely exhorting us to Use, Buy, or Drink such-and-such a product.

Let the Gold Dust Twins Do Your Work, 1880s, Gold Dust Washing Powder (*washing powder* was an 1869 term for kitchen soaps and cleansers in powder form), the Gold Dust Twins, as illustrated on the box, being two black moppets. This is an early example of ads using the magic words "you" or "your" and also of identifying a product with a personal mascotlike image.

Good Morning, Have You Used Pear's Soap?, 1880s, one of the first appeals to personal cleanliness.

Children Cry for It, 1880s, Fletcher's Castoria.

More Than One Million Copies Sold!, 1882, advertising Dr. W. H. Parker's book *The Science of Life or Self-Preservation*, published by the Peabody Medical Institute. This slogan, of course, has been used for many other books since then.

You Press the Button, We Do the Rest, 1889, George Eastman's slogan for Kodak. (See THE MOVIES for more on the 1888 name *Kodak* and why this slogan was so apt.) The Kodak became so popular that many people erroneously began to call all cameras Kodak, so, in order to prevent Kodak from becoming a generic name, Eastman soon also used the slogan *If it isn't an Eastman, it isn't a Kodak*.

If You Keep Late Hours for Society's Sake, Bromo-Seltzer Will Cure That Headache, 1895, Bromo-Seltzer, an early rhyming slogan, with snob appeal.

The Beer That Made Milwaukee Famous, 1895, Schlitz Beer, reminiscent of the 1892 Ingersoll Watch slogan—*The Watch that made the dollar famous* (see CLOCKS AND WATCHES).

The Prudential Has the Strength of Gibraltar, 1896, The Prudential Insurance Co.

Do You Know Uneeda Biscuit, 1898, the Uneeda Biscuit Co.

A Room with a Bath for a Dollar and a Half, around 1900, created by hotel entrepreneur Ellsworth M. Statler.

There's a Reason, used from 1900 to 1924 as the slogan for Charles

Post's *Grape-Nuts* and *Postum*. One could interpret the "reason" as being good nutrition and good health or the mildly laxative effect of the products (see BREAKFAST FOOD).

Shave Yourself, early 1900s slogan for the Gillette Safety Razor (see BEARDS, CLOSE SHAVES, AND BARBERSHOPS).

Good to the Last Drop, 1907, Maxwell House Coffee (see COFFEE, TEA, AND MILK for the origin of the slogan).

Constantly Imitated—Never Equalled, 1908, Onyx Hosiery.

When It Rains It Pours, 1911, the Morton Salt Co.

Ask the Man Who Owns One, 1911, the Packard Motor Car Co.

Say It With Flowers, 1912, the American Florist Association.

The Penalty for Leadership, 1915, the Cadillac Motor Co., this slogan following the original 1912 *Standard of the World*.

Pay as You Ride, 1916, Maxwell cars, introducing the widespread buying of cars on credit or paying by installments. Later phrases reminiscent of this slogan were to include *Pay as you go*, for federal income withholding taxes since 1958, and *Fly now, pay later* in airline and travel ads of the 1950s and 60s.

The skin you love to touch, 1922, Woodbury's Facial Soap. Before this romantic slogan was used, the soap was less elegantly advertised as a remedy for "conspicuous nose pores."

Thirst knows no season, 1922, Coca-Cola. This slogan, created by adman Archie Lee, first appeared with a drawing of skiers and was the first slogan advertising the beverage as a year-round treat. Coca-Cola's first advertising calendar, in 1881, advertised it "For headache or tired feeling. Relieves Physical and Mental Exhaustion," and as late as 1935 Coca-Cola still advertised itself as "A quick wholesome little lift when you need one," soon followed by the more innocent *The drink that makes a pause refreshing*, forerunner of its *The pause that refreshes*, used intermittently from the late 1930s. Incidentally, the Charles E. Hires Co., which first promoted Hires Rootbeer at the 1876 Philadelphia Exposition, claimed it was "Soothing to the nerves, vitalizing to the blood, refreshing to the brain . . . gives the children strength . . . helps even a cynic to see the brighter side of life"; and 7-Up was first sold as an "anti-acid" hangover remedy, its slogan of the early 1930s: *Takes the "ouch" out of "grouch."*

Somewhere West of Laramie, 1923, the Jordan "Playboy" car, the ad showing a spirited cowboy next to a beautiful girl at the wheel.

They Laughed When I Sat Down, but When I Started to Play . . ., 1925, U.S. School of Music, a mail order ad.

Call for Philip Morris, 1933, Philip Morris cigarettes (for details of this and other famous cigarette advertising lines see CIGARS AND CIGARETTES).

There's a Ford in Your Future, 1944, the Ford Motor Co., foretelling the upgrading of the Ford with the resumption of full production after World War II. Buick countered with its own slogan, *When Better Cars are Built Buick will Build Them*. Ford's original 1904 slogan—word of mouth had already established the product's quality—had been *A good name is better than promises*, warning prospective buyers of the many new car brands coming on the market.

Does she . . . or doesn't she?, around 1955, for Miss Clairol, meaning that one couldn't tell if the pretty model in the ad had dyed her hair or not, because the dye, now called a hair *tint*, looked so

---

Other words and phrases [after "new" and "free"] which work wonders are HOW TO, SUDDENLY, NOW, ANNOUNCING, INTRODUCING, IT'S HERE, JUST ARRIVED, IMPORTANT DEVELOPMENT, IMPROVEMENT, AMAZING, SENSATIONAL, REMARKABLE, REVOLUTIONARY, STARTLING, MIRACLE, MAGIC, OFFER, QUICK, EASY, WANTED, CHALLENGE, ADVICE TO, THE TRUTH ABOUT, COMPARE, BARGAIN, HURRY, LAST CHANCE.

"How to Write Potent Copy" in *Confessions of an Advertising Man*, David Ogilvy, 1963.

By 1939 7-Up was "real," Coca-Cola was both "delicious" and "refreshing," and Dr. Pepper was "Good for Life," as shown by these signs obscuring the Hi-Way Tavern near Crystal City, Texas.

natural. The prime example of an attention-getting double-entendre slogan, as most people knew the question was a standard one among men meaning, "Does she or doesn't she have sex with the men she goes out with?"

We Do It All For You, early 1970s, McDonald's chain of hamburger restaurants.

Alaska, Seward's Folly, and Eskimos

Alaska was first reached in 1741 by the Danish navigator Vitus Bering (for whom the *Bering Strait* is named) while he was sailing from Russia under a commission from Peter the Great. Russia established settlements in the 1780s and 90s, and Americans called the area *Russian America*. The *Aleutian Islands* got their name around 1780, the Russians taking the word from the Aleutian Chukchi word *aliuit*, beyond the shores. The Aleutian word *parka*, animal skin, comes via the Russian from a Samoyed (a language of the Siberian tundra) word for reindeer pelt; we have used the word to mean a warm outer garment with a hood since 1868 and to mean only the hood since the early 1940s, when such hoods were part of cold-weather garments issued to servicemen during World War II.

When Secretary of State William Seward purchased Russian America from Russia in 1867 for $7.2 million, most Americans called his purchase of the frozen wasteland *Seward's Folly* and the land itself either *Seward's Folly* or *Seward's Icebox*. These names stuck until the late 1890s—when gold was discovered there and suddenly Seward's purchase seemed very wise. Thus, at the turn of the century, most Americans finally began using the true name *Alaska*, which had been a formal name since the American Revolution and comes from the Eskimo word *Alakshak* or *Alayeksa*, "great land, mainland." Meanwhile, U.S. soldiers had first occupied Seward's Folly in 1867 and were forbidden whiskey—so they bought the potent liquor made by the local Hoochinoo Indians, or distilled their own and said they did, and by 1877 were calling all strong, homemade, or illegal whiskey *hoochinoo* after the Indian tribe. During the Klondike gold rush, beginning in 1896, the word was commonly shortened to *hooch*. Thus Seward's purchase and the discovery of gold in the Klondike led to Americans talking about both *Alaska* and *hooch*.

Eskimo is from an Algonquian Indian language of eastern Canada, from the Micmac *eskameege*, "eaters of raw fish." Early Americans often spelled it *Esquimaw* or *Esquimaux*. The Eskimo *iglu*, house, has been spelled *igloo* in English since 1662, taken from Eskimos in Canada and Greenland long before Alaska was known to exist (Alaskan Eskimos often built their igloos out of animal skins, driftwood, etc., using snow-block ones only for temporary or emergency shelters).

In the first decade of the 1800s we began talking of Eskimo *dog sleds* and of *sled dogs*, or *Eskimo dogs*, but it was the 1860s before we knew that dogsled drivers were supposed to shout *Mush!* to drive on their dogs. Eskimos don't shout *Mush!*: the term was originally *Mush on!* and comes from the French trappers' and explorers' *Marchons!*, "Hurry up, let's go!" We have, however, used the real Eskimo word *mukluk*, large seal, to mean a sealskin since 1868 and to mean a sealskin boot since 1902. Incidentally, Russell Stover coined and introduced the trade name *Eskimo pie* for a chocolate-covered ice cream bar in 1921 (Christian Nelson had created it in his Onawa, Iowa, candy store in 1919 but had called it an "I-Scream Bar" before becoming a partner of Stover's).

By 1810 dog sled *was in the language, but we didn't know that sled drivers were supposed to shout* Mush! *until the 1860s.*

22

Alligators and Crocodiles

Most of us can't see much difference between our native *alligators* and *crocodiles*. Neither could the early explorers and settlers in the New World: the first record of the use of both words in America was in 1682, in the same sentence, lumping them together. The true American *crocodile* was first described in 1587, but the reptile and the word had long been known (the word from Greek *krokodilos*, "worm of the pebbles," because the Greeks had first observed it basking in the sun on the shore of the Nile). By 1884 we had shortened the word to *croc*.

The ancient Greeks had first seen crocodiles basking on the pebbly shores of the Nile, thus called the reptile krokodilos, *worm of the pebbles.*

Alligator comes from the Spanish *el lagarto*, the lizard. We were talking about *alligator pears* (avocados) by the 1750s and *alligator gars* by 1821. By 1844 we had shortened *alligator* to *'gator*. Mississippi keelboatmen liked to think themselves as tough and mean as alligators, calling themselves *alligators* by 1808; the word spread from them to mean any rough-and-ready frontiersman or Indian fighter. It remained in use for any swaggering dude or sport, surfacing in New Orleans to mean a jazz musician around 1915, then a jitterbug enthusiast in the 1930s. Thus from those keelboatmen we finally got the rhyming jive farewell "See you later, alligator" of the 1930s, which had some student use into the 1950s.

Ambulance and Ambulance Chasers

Ambulance was first recorded in English in 1819; it comes from the French *hôpital ambulant*, literally "walking hospital" (Latin *ambulāre*, to walk, which also gives us *ambulatory*) and was an early form of the army mobile field hospital. During the Crimean War (1854–56) the English began using the term to refer not to such a mobile field hospital but to a covered wagon or cart for carrying the wounded from the battlefield, and the word then soon entered civilian use, to mean any special vehicle for rushing the sick or wounded to a hospital (in World War I, U.S. troops rather macabrely called a battlefield ambulance a *meat wagon*).

For a while *ambulance* had an even more general meaning in America. From the late 1850s until the early 1900s we used it to mean any large wagon, such as a *prairie schooner* (1841) or a *Dougherty wagon* (1901), a mule-drawn or horse-drawn ancestor of our modern camper, having doors in the sides, transverse seats that could be converted into beds, and canvas sides that rolled up and down.

After emergency ambulances came into being it took only about forty years for a small-time lawyer who chased them, in order to find accident-victim clients, to be called an *ambulance chaser* (1897). Calling lawyers by derogatory names was not new: we had called

In New York City there is a style of lawyers known to the profession as "ambulance chasers," because they are on hand wherever there is a railway wreck, or a street-car collision . . . with . . . their offers of professional service.
The Congressional Record, July 24, 1897

an aggressive, greedy lawyer a *shyster* since 1843 (from German *Scheisse*, shit), and a glib criminal lawyer a *mouthpiece* since 1857.

Our most interesting term for a lawyer is *Philadelphia lawyer* (1788), referring to one who is a master at discussing and using the fine points or technicalities of the law. Some say the term is merely from the prominence of Philadelphia lawyers in early America, but the first *Philadelphia lawyer* to be honored with this title was probably the distinguished colonial lawyer Andrew Hamilton, of Philadelphia, who, in 1735, successfully defended German-born printer and editor John Peter Zenger against the British government in New York after two local New York lawyers who came to Zenger's defense had been barred from the case by the pro-British judge. Zenger had been imprisoned by Governor William Cosby for seditious libel for his attacks on the governor and the Crown, in his anti-administration *New-York Weekly Journal*. Hamilton argued that if Zenger's statements were true they were not libelous. He won the right to use this defense before the jury, then convinced it

A World War I surgical ambulance *for performing operations near the battlefield.*

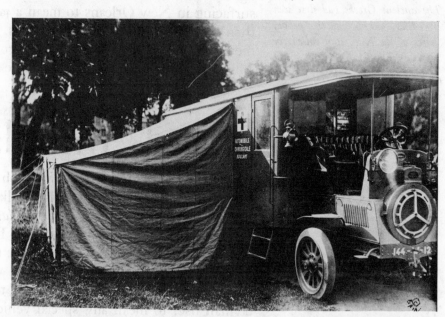

An early gallop ambulance *for rushing the wounded to hospitals behind the lines.*

24

that Zenger's statements were true. The jury's "not guilty" verdict was, of course, a landmark decision in American law, and that "Philadelphia lawyer" Andrew Hamilton had gained a major victory for freedom of the press.

American Cheese

During the Revolutionary War, Americans missed the good imported English cheese we were used to, especially *cheddar* (named after the English village where it was first made). Thus *American cheese* was a proud post-Revolutionary name of 1804, showing that we could make our own cheddar-type cheese and be independent of British products. Such homemade cheese was made and stored in the *cheese house*, an American word heard on farms and homesteads since 1759. By the 1860s our American cheddar was so common it was also simply called *store cheese* or *factory cheese;* then in the 1920s we also began to call it *rattrap cheese* or *rat cheese.* Meanwhile, bonny clabber, drained and pressed milk curd, was being made in several consistencies and for a variety of uses in America, forms of it being called *pot cheese* by 1812, *smear case* by 1829 (from German *Schmierkäse,* smearing cheese or spreading cheese—German-Americans also mixed it with sour cream and served it with chopped onions), and *cottage cheese* by 1848.

Although true *Limburger* is a Belgian product (originally from Limburg, Belgium), we have also made our native varieties. Our *brick cheese* was originally a type of Limburger, first made in 1877 by John Jossi in Wisconsin, and *Liederkranz* was first made in 1892 by Emil Frey in Monroe, New York. Emil Frey himself named his cheese *Liederkranz,* in honor of the German-American men's choral societies called *Liederkranz* (German "garland of songs") whose rehearsals and meetings often ended as social gatherings centered around beer, rye bread, and cheese.

Because of the smell of certain varieties, *cheese* was used in a pejorative way, to mean "it smells," by the late 18th century, with *cheesy* being used to mean "worthless, bad" by 1896. On the other hand, *the cheese* meant the exact thing needed or an excellent thing or person in England by 1818, with this use spreading to the U.S. by the 1830s. However, this good connotation of *the cheese* is not from our word *cheese* at all but from the Persian or Urdu *chiz,* thing, which led Englishmen in India to use *the cheese* for "the thing." This use of *the cheese* gave us *big cheese,* meaning a boss or important person, around 1890, which then became a disparaging term for a bossy or disliked person in the mid 1920s.

In the 1840s and 50s most English and American schoolgirls knew that *to make cheese* meant to twirl around so that one's skirts and petticoats flared out, then to sit down quickly and prettily in the round cheeselike wheel of garments. American males liked the girls *to make cheese* because the twirling skirts might give them a glimpse of the female ankles or legs. Thus *to make cheese* also became a vulgar term for a girl willingly exposing her legs, or more, to a boy or man (which is a possible explanation of our 1940 World War II term *cheesecake*, revealing photographs of girls in bathing suits or other scanty costumes, showing much leg).

Cheese it!, meaning "Look out!," someone is looking or listening, was a popular expression of the 1870s, when *Cheese it, the cops!* also appeared.

April Fool's Day, Arbor Day, and Valentine's Day

were more exciting terms to our parents and grandparents than they are to us, because these three special days are being celebrated by fewer people and with less fervor than they once were.

April Fool! has been shouted by small children since the 1600s, starting in England just before *April Fool's Day* was brought to America by the early settlers. The custom started in France in 1564 when that country became the first to adopt the new Gregorian calendar, changing New Year's Day from April 1 to January 1. There, and later in England, the original April Fool's trick was to pay a mock New Year's Day visit on April 1 to someone who might have forgotten the new date. Literally, *April Fool!* meant "I fooled you; it's not New Year's Day at all!"

New York City school children at a tree-planting ceremony on Arbor Day, 1908.

Arbor Day was an exciting term to millions of American school children from the 1880s until World War II. It was a day set aside "to teach the importance of forestry," and many schools observed it by parading the children to a local park to plant a tree. The idea and the name *Arbor Day* were suggested by Nebraska's J. Sterling Morton, later secretary of agriculture, and Nebraska celebrated the first Arbor Day April 10, 1872. Other states followed suit, selecting dates ranging from January in Florida to April and May in northern states. Since the late 1930s the day has become almost forgotten in many places; now children study ecology and are taught conservation as part of classroom science. Thus the excitement of that once special *Arbor Day* is now just part of the nostalgic past.

St. Valentine's Day. Several days before the February 15 feast day of Lupercalia, in honor of Juno and Pan, ancient Roman boys chose their partners for the festival by drawing girls' names from a love urn or box, the couple then exchanging gifts on the festive day. In 496 Pope Gelasius transferred this popular celebration to the feast of St. Valentine, February 14; thus *St. Valentine's Day* or *Valentine's Day* was born (the term *St. Valentine's Day* was first recorded in its secular sense in England in 1381). The early Christian church actually had three martyrs named St. Valentine, two of whom are commemorated on February 14; however, our word *valentine* does not come from any of them but from the Old French *galantine*, a lover, a gallant; hence *Be My Valentine* does not, of course, mean "Be My St. Valentine" but "Be My Love, Be My Gallant." *Valentine* meant the person whose name was picked from the box or who was chosen to be one's sweetheart or special friend for that special day by 1450; it meant the folded paper with the name on it by 1533; a gift to the special person by 1610; and finally a verse, letter, or message to that person by 1824.

The first Valentine message is said to have been sent in 1415 from the Duke of Orleans from his cell in the Tower of London to his wife, though it seems logical that in the hundreds of years before that some youths must have sent their girls a romantic message with, or in lieu of, a gift. Be that as it may, by the 16th century, young men often sent their girls poems on Valentine's Day; but since many young gallants couldn't write, much less make up poems, they often copied verses from special books, such as the very popular 1669 British *A Valentine Writer* (young men in America also used it widely). In the early 1800s young British and American men might still draw names from boxes to choose Valentine partners, just as the ancient Romans had; if the young men were truly smitten, they might wear the slips of paper with the ladies' names on them pinned to their sleeves for several days (by the early 1600s this had already given English the phrase *to wear* [one's] *heart on* [one's] *sleeve*).

I will wear my heart upon my sleeve
For daws to peck at.
William Shakespeare,
Othello, I, i, 1604

27

By the 1890s a heart-shaped or lacily trimmed box of candy was a popular Valentine's Day gift to one's wife, mother, or sweetheart. This 1953 ad appeared in such popular magazines as The Saturday Evening Post.

OH! YOU UP-ROAR SINGER
You believe yourself a prima donna
And have the world at your feet,
But all the neighbors on our block,
Say the old cat has you beat.

Comic valentines *were not the only* penny dreadful *cards; many, such as this one, could be sent at any time of year.*

By the 1800s, too, commercial woodcuts and lithographs of cupids, turtledoves, bleeding hearts, etc., began to replace or accompany the poems, with the first store selling such *valentines* opening in London in 1809. However, it was not until the introduction of penny postage and envelopes in England in the 1840s that delicately ornate or lace paper *valentines*, as we know them, came into wide use. These were soon imported from England into the U.S., and we were beginning to talk about and send *valentine cards* by the late 1840s and manufacturing them in America by 1850. By 1855 *comic valentine*, also then called a *vinegar valentine*, was in the language, followed by cartoonist Charles Howland's *penny dreadful valentines*, which cost a penny and contained "dreadful" messages (by 1873 *penny dreadful* meant any cheap, sensational novel).

28

Bad Eggs, Good Eggs, and Eggheads

The first American colonists could *egg* (each other) *on* since that had been a British slang term since 1566 (probably a pronunciation of "edge on," which had been in use to mean "incite, encourage" since the 13th century). Some thirty-five years before the Revolutionary War, the colonists could claim they had to *tread on eggs*, be extremely careful, a 1735 British term. By 1825, however, America had its own first important egg-based device and term, the *egg beater*. We then went on to introduce the term *scrambled eggs*, 1864, and *shirred eggs*, 1883 (related to the 1847 American word *shirr*, to draw or gather up cloth with bands of fabric).

Goose egg, meaning a score of zero in a sport, appeared in 1866, originally as a baseball term and probably first used in Philadelphia (though *duck egg*, meaning zero, had been a British sports term since 1863). By 1896, American women were talking about *egg-and-butter money*, their incidental money as earned from these products (also called simply *egg money* by 1935, *egg-and-chicken money* by 1941, and then reversed to *butter-and-egg money* by 1942). Then, around 1925, city slickers began referring to a prosperous farmer or businessman who spent freely in nightclubs and on chorus girls and theatrical ventures as a big *butter-and-egg man*. To *lay an egg*, be a failure, score zero with the public, originated as a 1929 theatrical term; in fact, that same year the theatrical trade-paper *Variety* announced the stock market crash with the headline "Wall Street Lays an Egg." In 1929, too, Americans began telling people who bothered them or lied or exaggerated *to go lay an egg*.

Shakespeare seems to have been the first to have used *egg* to refer to a person, in *Macbeth* (1605), where he used *egg* to mean a mere youth, one close to the egg state. In America we began calling a thoroughly rotten man a *rotten egg* or a *bad egg* in the early 1850s—a metaphor that lost some of its pungency with the advent of modern refrigeration. The opposite term, *good egg*, didn't come into use until 1918. *Hard-boiled* has meant strict or heartless since 1898, and such a person was called a *hard-boiled egg* by 1919 (said to have been coined by Jack Doyle, a keeper of a New York City billiards arcade, but first widely popularized by cartoonist "Tad" Dorgan). *Tough egg* was then popularized by detective movies and novels of the 1930s.

Though Tennyson had written of an "egg-bald head" in 1877, *egghead*, meaning a bald man, didn't appear until some forty years later. It took on a new, and usually pejorative, meaning around 1918, when some newspapermen began to use it to refer to an intellectual. This use came to the public's attention during the Presidential campaign of 1952, when syndicated columnist Stewart Alsop used it in a September column to refer slightingly to the intellectually admired, high-foreheaded Democratic Presidential candidate Adlai Stevenson (Alsop later said he was quoting his brother, John, a staunch Republican, who used it to convey an image of a head with a thin shell and mushy white insides). *Egghead* then immediately became a popular term for any intellectual or *highbrow* (itself an 1897 term), while in certain political contexts it still carries the connotation of being a liberal or even of not being tough enough to cope with hard realities.

The Barn

has a unique meaning in America, combining the concept of the British grain-storage barn (from Old English *bere*, barley + *ern*, storage) and the British stable. To save time and effort, American colonists combined the grain barn and the animal stable into one building, still calling it *barn*. Thus only in America could we speak of a *horse barn* (1854) and *cow barn* (1855) and of "closing the barn door after the horse has been stolen" (the British would say "closing the stable door," etc.). Not only were horses kept in American barns but, in the cities, so were the streetcars they pulled, with such a barn being called a *carbarn* by the 1860s.

Because of their dual purpose, American barns were big, which is why "You couldn't hit the side of a barn" became a typical American insult to a would-be marksman and "a big barn of a place" a description of any large building ("between you and me and the barn" meant "confidentially" by the mid 1850s). Big barns

This large American cow barn *would have been called a "stable" in earlier days in England.*

30

A barn raising *in Minnesota, around 1900.*

also became the first rural civic centers, being the scene of auctions *(auction barns)*, of husking bees, and of *barn dances* (which were originally based on military schottisches but had become a nation-wide pastime by the 1890s).

The term *barn raising* was often heard after 1856, when lumber (instead of logs) was in widespread use for even the most remote barns. The farmer-carpenters usually got a head start in these one-day barn raisings by cutting the lumber the day before so it would fit exactly, thus ensuring that the work could be completed in one day—so there would be time for the feast and dancing that followed.

Colonial barns were left unpainted because they were made of green wood, which paint could decay; thus the term *weather-beaten barn* has always been common in America. Even when dried wood became common after the first rush of settlement, it was considered pretentious to paint barns—until the prosperity following the American Revolution. That explains why no one spoke of a *red barn* until well into the 1780s.

Today, the American concept of the big, multipurpose barn is still going strong, as seen in the large and often rustically decorated stores called *dress barns*, *furniture barns*, *antique barns*, etc., that dot our highways, particularly in New England, where it all began.

Barnstorming was first used to describe Samuel Drake's theatrical troupe's 1815 tour from Albany, New York, to the West. This troupe was one of the first to bring melodrama and farce to the frontier—while sleeping and performing in barns. By the 1890s *barnstorming* was used mainly to refer to a political

candidate's tour of rural areas for votes, the word first appearing with this meaning in the *Congressional Record* in 1896.

From about 1915 on, *barnstorming* also referred to touring aviators who offered *joy rides* (1910) to farmers "ten dollars for ten minutes"—and to *daredevil air shows*. These pioneering aviators used farmers' fields for landing strips and barns for hangars, with the pilots often sleeping in the barns beside their plane. Thus, in a little over a hundred years *barnstorming* was used in three different ways. One wonders what thespian Samuel Drake would have thought of the men and machines who replaced him as rural entertainment.

Baseball

The term *base ball* was first recorded in 1744. It was then a name used in the south of England for the game generally known as *rounders*. This game was played by a batter against a pitcher, a catcher, and preferably two or more additional fielders, the batter hitting the soft ball with a flat-bladed bat and having to circle *(round)* two base posts to score runs. Each player tried to *stay in* at bat and score as many runs as possible, as in cricket. *Bat*, *ball*, and *base* are very old words: *bat* has meant a club since before the 10th century, *ball* is a 13th-century word, and *base* has been used in

In Hoboken, New Jersey, horse-drawn carriages surround the Elysian Fields baseball diamond in this 1866 Currier & Ives lithograph.

various children's games since the 15th century. The rounders ball had to be soft because outs were made by throwing it at the batter as he ran around the base posts. In America the game became known as *base* (an American soldier wrote of "playing at base" at Valley Forge in 1778), *stick ball* (1823), *goal ball* and *round ball* (1830s), *barn ball* (1840s), and *one old cat, two old cat, three old cat,* or *four old cat* (1850s), the number of cats referring to the number of bases.

In New England before the 1820s, the game was being played on village greens. The players paired off into two teams, used four bases instead of two base posts (the bases were still often called *goals*), and counted a circuit of the four goals as one tally. This more adult team version of the game was called *town ball* or *the Massachusetts game*. By the 1830s players were using such terms as:

out.

strike, then meaning a turn at bat, the batter being called a *striker.* *Strike* came to mean a missed swing in the 1840s, when *strike out* was also first heard (but there were no *called strikes* until 1863; in the 1840s and 50s *strike* meant only a missed swing or a fouled-off strike and a *strike out* a combination of three of these). *To fan* didn't mean to strike out until 1886.

ball club, meaning both a bat and a team, and, by 1833, a league of teams. *Team* became a popular word in the 1880s, along with *ball team* and *baseball team.*

pitcher, to pitch, and *pitcher's box.* In the 1830s the pitcher was still often just a fielder designated to put the ball into play by tossing it to the batter. He was sometimes called a *hurler,* which has been used in English to mean a "thrower" of any thing since 1532. By 1868 most teams even had a *change pitcher,* an alternate or relief pitcher. The term to be *knocked out of the box* appeared in the 1880s; *pitcher's mound, mound,* and *moundsman* (a pitcher) were first heard around 1914.

In the late 1830s someone had the bright idea of forcing the runner out by throwing the ball to the base ahead of him or by tagging him with the ball rather than throwing the ball at him. Since the runner was no longer hit with the ball, a *hard ball* could now be used—which the pitcher could throw faster and the batter hit farther. The new way of making outs and the longer hits meant that some fielders had to remain in to cover the bases while others had to play farther out to catch the long hits. In 1845 the two-year-old New York City Knickerbocker Ball Club introduced a code of rules for this new game of *hard ball:* the bases were to form a 90-foot square, balls were in play only when hit in or over this square, three strikes (missed swing or fouled-off strikes) were out, three outs retired a side, base runners could be tagged or thrown out but not hit with a thrown ball: modern baseball was born. But the players were still called *hands.* Since the rules were drawn up and popularized by the New York City Knickerbocker Ball Club the game was called the *New York game* or *New York base ball.* The first game under the new rules was played at Elysian Fields in Hoboken, New Jersey, in 1846, between the Knickerbockers and the New York Nine (the first recorded use of *nine* to mean baseball team). By 1851 New York area teams formed a *base ball association* (league) using the new rules. These new rules and the tactics made possible by the hard ball gave us many new baseball terms in the late 1840s and the 1850s, including:

fast ball, balk, 1845.

inning, from the 18th-century English cricket word *innings* (always spelled with the final *s* but considered singular in England), originally meaning a portion of a game during which a player or side is "in." A baseball inning was also called a *round* until the early 1900s.

first base, second base, third base, both as the positions and the players, 1840s. A base was also called a *base bag* and then simply a *bag* by the 1850s. The shorter terms *first, second,* and *third,* as well as the more formal *first baseman, second baseman,* and *third baseman,* were in use by the mid-1860s, as were *infield, infielder, base line, base runner,* and even *base player,* meaning a baseman. *Short stop* appeared in the 1840s, both for the position and the player, but the player was also called the *short stopper* until the 1870s.

right field, center field, left field, both as the positions and the players. The shorter terms *right, center,* and *left,* as well as *right fielder, center fielder,* and *left fielder,* were in use by the mid 1860s, as were *outfield* and *outfielder,* though these last two were also called *outerfield* and *outerfielder* until the 1890s. *Fielding average* was a late 1860s term, *right center* and *left center* were spoken of in the 1870s, and *fielder's choice* appeared in 1902.

catcher, to catch (be a catcher) also appeared during this period, though a catcher was also called a *catcher-out* until the 1870s. The term *behind the plate,* as the catcher's position, appeared in 1857, *catcher's mask* in the 1890s, and *catcher's mitt* in the 1900s.

single, run, and *home run* (1856), also then called a *home. To single*

"Honus," sometimes also called "Hans" (John Peter) Wagner, the Flying Dutchman, *played for Louisville from 1897–99 and then with the Pittsburgh Pirates from 1900 to 1917. A superb fielder and eight times National League batting champion, he is remembered as the first great shortstop.*

appeared in 1916, *homer* in 1868. *Home run* and *homer* couldn't have appeared much sooner because it wasn't until the late 1840s and early 50s that *home* was used in games to mean the place one tries to reach in order to win or score, with the baseball term *home base* then appearing in the early 1850s and becoming *home plate* in 1875.

foul, foul strike were well known in the late 1840s. In the 1860s *foul ball, foul fly, to foul,* and *foul ball line* were in use, the last being shortened to *foul line* by 1878. *Foul tip* is an 1870s term. We have called a contemptible person a *foul ball* since the 1920s.

fair and *fair ball* were used during this period to refer both to a ball hit into fair territory and to a pitch thrown in the strike zone.

on the fly also appeared during this period; bouncing balls were said to be caught *on the bound* (a bouncing ball wasn't called a *hopper* until 1905). *Fly ball, fly, infield fly, fly catch,* and *pop-up* are terms of the 1860s; *high fly* was first recorded in 1881.

the national game, 1856. Since early baseball had been called *the Massachusetts game* and the new hard-ball baseball had been first called *the New York game,* it was natural to call the latter *the national game* once it spread to other sections of the country. Note that *the national game* originally meant hard ball as played by the 1845 rules; later, people took it to mean that this game was the nation's favorite, and it grew into the popular 1920s and 1930s term *the National Pastime.*

to steal appeared in the 1860s, during the Civil War; *base stealing* in 1886; *stolen base* in 1889; *base stealer* in 1896; and *double steal* in 1900. *To pick off base* was first recorded in 1888, with the noun *pickoff* not appearing until 1939. *Lead* (from base) was first recorded in 1893 and *pitch out* (in order to catch a base stealer) in 1912.

During the Civil War, New York and New Jersey regiments spread this modern version of baseball to other Union troops, and its popularity mushroomed. During that time, too (in 1863), called strikes and walks came into existence; up to then a batter could take an unlimited number of pitches, strikes being only those he swung at and missed or fouled off, and balls not being called at all—a batter might take 10, 20, or 100 pitches until he got one he liked. Now the called strikes and walks speeded up the game and helped make it more popular. Thus, immediately after the war, between 1865 and 1869, many American men seemed to catch what was then called *baseball fever* and indulged in *baseballism,* the baseball fad. They used such new terms as *ball player, base ball player, baseballer,* or *baseballist;* went to what were then called *base ball grounds, ball fields,* or *base ball parks* (before the late 1860s these had been called *ball grounds;* in the 1890s they were to become known as *ball parks);* and read the new *base ball columns* (1869), the first of which appeared in the *Brooklyn Union* newspaper. Big cities from Boston to Chattanooga to Portland, Oregon, had *major clubs,* while small towns had *minor clubs* (forerunners of the terms *major league* and *minor league*). All the players, of course, were still

"Chuck" (Charles A.) Comiskey became a professional baseball player in 1875, at the age of seventeen, then was both a player and manager for the St. Louis Browns before becoming owner and president of the American League's Chicago team from its beginning in 1900 until his death in 1931.

amateur *gentlemen players* playing for fun, often as part of a larger gentlemen's social or sporting club. In the last half of the 1860s they heard and used such new terms as:

> *Play ball!*, now first used as the umpire's command signal to begin a game. Calling *Time!* and *Time out!* for a brief suspension of play was in wide use by 1878.
> *base ball* for the ball itself; previously it had simply been the *ball*. It was called a *horsehide* by the 1880s, a *pea* by 1908, and the *apple* in the mid 1920s.
> *ball* itself was now being used to mean a pitch outside the strike zone. *Wild pitch*, *base on balls*, *walk*, and *passed ball* are also late 1860s terms (the baseball verb *to walk* dates from about 1910).
> *battery* now came into use but meant the pitcher only; it didn't mean both the pitcher and the catcher until the 1880s.
> *double play* and *force out* were also new terms in the late 1860s. *Force play* came in the 1890s, though it was then often called a *forced play*.
> *error*, which was followed by *bobble* in 1908 and *boot* in 1940 (it had been called a *wild play* in 1857). A fielder's mental error was called a *boner* by 1912, a *bone* by 1916, and a *bone play* in 1917 (from the general 1903 term *bone-headed*, stupid, or the 1912 *bonehead*, a stupid person).
> *right shortstop*, *right short fielder*, *right short*, 1866. For ten years after the Civil War, teams experimented with this tenth player, a second shortstop playing behind the baseline between first and second. After much debate the position was eliminated.
> *to slug*, *batting average*, *batting streak*, *bunch(ed) hits*, and *clean hit* also all appeared in the last half of the 1860s, showing the increasing importance of hitting well, often, and long. *On deck* also appeared in the late 1860s. People began talking about a *base hit*, *two base hit*, *two baser*, *two bagger*, *double bagger*, *three base hit*, *three baser*, *three bagger*, *triple bagger*, *four bagger*, and being *at bat* in the 1870s. *Double bagger* and *triple bagger* were shortened to *double* and *triple* (sometimes *triplet*) in the early 1880s, when the terms *slugger*, *batting order*, and *sacrifice hit* also appeared. A *sacrifice hit* was called a *sacrifice play* by 1886 and simply a *sacrifice* by 1893, the verb *to sacrifice* not appearing until 1912. *Left-on-base* dates from 1885, *hit-and-run* from 1899, *batting practice* from around 1910, *batting slump* and *pinch hitter* (one who bats "in a pinch") from 1912, *clean up position* from 1915, and *lead-off man* and *lead-off batter* from 1922.

In 1867, players were talking about the first *base ball tour*, which had the Washington, D.C., Nationals playing other *gentlemen's teams* as far west as St. Louis. But now the gentlemen players began to grumble that *professional players* (1867) and *semiprofessional players* (1868) were ruining the game. It all began when the Rockford, Illinois, team of 1867 started paying salaries to some expert players to join their unpaid gentlemen players. Then in 1868 a *semiprofessional team* was organized in Cincinnati, hiring players for specific games, though these players didn't earn their

Grover Cleveland Alexander.

"Lefty" (Robert) Grove, Philadelphia, 1925. Left-handed pitchers had been called lefty *and a* southpaw *since the mid 1880s.*

entire living from playing. In 1869 these Cincinnati Red Stockings became the first *professional team*, hiring players to play full time and touring from New York City to San Francisco without losing a game all year (of course they were playing only against local amateur gentlemen's teams). This tour was so successful that within two years professional baseball was sweeping the country, and people were talking about such professional teams as the Boston Bostons, Brooklyn Eckfords, Chicago White Stockings, Fort Wayne (Indiana) Kekeongas, New York Mutuals, Philadelphia Athletics, Troy (New York) Haymakers, and Washington Olympics. By 1871 baseball had become America's first mass spectator sport and sports industry. This made all baseball terms more popular—and meant that future baseball terms would often be for professional tactics, ways to keep records and sell tickets, and names for new professional teams and leagues. (Also, in the late 1880s, many Americans first began spelling *base ball* in the modern way, as one word, *baseball*.) In the last hundred years millions of Americans have thus used such terms as:

clubhouse, 1869. The item and word spread with the advent of professional players who needed and demanded them.

curve, curver, 1870s. Pitchers became important in the late 1860s, developing the *curve*, which curves to the left for a right-hander and to the right for a left-hander. Within the next ten years reverse curves were developed and called *outcurves, outshots*, or *outdrops* (all 1880s words). The term *shut out* appeared in 1881, *left hander* and *lefty* for a left-handed pitcher in 1886, and *southpaw* dates from 1885—though humorist Finley Peter Dunne claimed to have coined it as a young *Chicago News* reporter in 1887, because Sox Park faced east from home plate, meaning that a left-handed pitcher threw from the south side (most ball parks do face east, so the batter won't be blinded by the afternoon sun), while *paw* had meant hand by 1840. The term *pitchers' battle* appeared in 1891 and *roundhouse curve* in the late 1890s, when it was also called a *barrel hoop curve*. Christy Mathewson's outcurve was called a *fade-away* in the early 1900s, and the New York Giants' Carl Hubbell's outcurve was called a *screwball* in the mid 1930s (he won 24 consecutive games in 1936–37). *Sinker* dates from 1928.

diamond, the base paths or infield, 1875; it meant the entire playing field by the 1880s.

The National Association of Professional Baseball Players was organized in 1871, and its teams scheduled *circuit games* with each other. It was reorganized as the *National League of Professional Base Ball Clubs* in 1876 and popularly called the *National League* that same year.

the bunt was first used in 1872 by the Brooklyn Atlantics (a player named Pearce is said to have introduced it; no one seems to know anything about him, including his first name). The word itself is just a nasalized variant of "butt," the batter butting at the ball with the bat. The term *drag bunt* appeared in 1928.

bleachers, 1880s, was originally a humorous word, referring to the

"Cy" (Denton T.) Young in his Cleveland uniform around 1910. He pitched two winning games for the Boston Pilgrims in the 1903 World Series. Baseball's Cy Young Award, *to the best pitcher of the year, is named for him.*

bleaching effect of the exposure to the sun. *Bleacherite* appeared in 1896.

home team, home club, home player, visiting team, visiting club, visiting player, visitors, 1880s.

major league, major leaguer, minor league, minor leaguer, 1882. An *American Association* (no relation to the later American League) of baseball teams existed from 1882 to 1891, becoming the *minor league*, while the National League became known as the *major league*. When this American Association merged into the National League the unified teams became known as *the major league*. The *majors* and the *minors* were terms in use by 1890, while *big league* and *big leaguer* didn't appear until 1899.

Grapefruit league, referring to the informal league of teams playing spring-training practice games in warm citrus-growing areas, such as Florida, was a popular term by 1953.

gate, the number of paid spectators at a game, 1883.

raincheck, 1884, in St. Louis.

to boo (1884) and *to root* (1889) both saw widespread use in baseball from the 1890s on, though they originated elsewhere. *Root* comes from the 1513 English *route*, meaning shout (and a similar word was even used as early as 1410 in hunting, meaning to shout directions to a hunting dog). *Boo* may have been used much earlier in the theater and elsewhere, but before the 1880s it was considered just a roaring sound and not a word. Baseball fans could *razz* a player or team by 1914 and give a *razzberry* by 1918 (spelled *raspberry* by 1920) or could express the same loud dissatisfaction with a *Bronx cheer* by 1929. Although Yankee Stadium is in the Bronx, the term didn't originate there but perhaps in the National Theater, which was also in the Bronx borough of New York City (or the term may even be from the Spanish slang *branca*, shout).

fungo, 1886, as a batting warm-up or a game in which a player tosses a ball into the air and hits it as it falls; in the game, whoever catches it on the fly becomes the next hitter (no one has ever been able to trace the origin of the word *fungo*, though some claim it's from a word "fungible," meaning substitute). By 1910 a *fungo* meant a ball tossed and hit in this way, and players were also talking about *fungo bats*, light bats with an extra-thick end for hitting fungos. Fielders began to practice or warm up by *shagging* (1902), catching batting-practice flies, and later by having *pepper games*, a 1939 term.

pennant, pennant race, 1886.

World Series. Beginning in 1884 a series of post-season games was usually played each year between the pennant winners of the National League and the American Association. These were billed as *the World Championship Series*, generally shortened to *World Series* by 1889. The teams arranged these series between themselves and split the profits. It wasn't until midseason 1903, however, that the American League (see below) was recognized as a full major league; thus, technically, the 1903 series was the first between two major league teams. In that 1903 best-of-nine series the fledgling American League's Boston Pilgrims, who soon changed their name to the Boston Red Sox, beat the National League's Pittsburgh Pirates in eight games, Boston's legendary pitcher Cy Young winning two games and his team-

John McGraw was the Baltimore Oriole third baseman from 1891 to 1899, during which time he is said to have invented the Baltimore chop. *He managed the New York Giants from 1902 to 1932.*

mate Bill Dineen winning the other three, while Pittsburgh pitcher Deacon Phillipe pitched five complete games during the 13-day series! An average of 12,500 fans saw each of the games—tickets were $1 each. Much to the players' and fans' disgust, there was no World Series the following year, as New York Giant owner John T. Brush refused to let his National League champions play Boston, claiming that the American League was still "the minor league." However, he did let his team play the 1905 World Series when, for the first time, it was sponsored not by the two championship teams but by the two leagues themselves.

Baltimore chop, a hit ball taking a very high bounce in the infield. It's said to have been purposely used (by chopping down at the ball with the bat) by its inventor John McGraw and his teammate "Wee Willie" Keeler when both played for the Baltimore Orioles, in the 1890s.

charley horse, a severe stiffness in a leg or arm muscle due to overexercise, strain, or a blow, first entered the language as a baseball term in 1888. It's almost certainly from some baseball player who walked or limped like an old horse, either because the player's name was Charley or the old, limping horse was named Charley—old horses were used by early *groundkeepers* (1903) to drag the infield and some of these baseball horses were well loved by players and fans. If it were named after a baseball player named Charley, we don't know which one (it's often said to be after Baltimore Oriole pitcher Charlie Esper, who limped, but he didn't begin playing until 1894, six years after the term was in use).

score keeper, score card, 1890s.

sandlot baseball. In the early 1880s Irish-born Denis Kearney led a San Francisco workingman's protest movement against unemployment, unjust taxes, unfair banking laws, and mainly against Chinese laborers. Since his rallies were held in a sandy lot, his followers were soon called the *sand-lot party*, and *sandlot* became a San Francisco term. Within 15 years the word had become associated with the vacant lots, sandy or not, and open fields where youths and semiprofessionals played baseball.

grandstand player, 1888, as a fielder who tried to show off making difficult catches; *grandstander*, 1891. Such players were also said to make *circus catches* by 1888.

rookie, late 1890s, from "recruit." It didn't become a widespread term until its World War I use.

bench warmer, 1892; *bench jockey* appeared in 1939; *to bench* in 1917.

double header, 1896, originally played only to make up for postponed games or games canceled by rain. In 1903 the term was used for two originally scheduled games for the price of one (general admission was then 25 cents, reserved seats 50 cents).

fan, 1896. The word is probably a shortening of *fanatic* but could be from *the fancy*, the name given sporty prizefight enthusiasts in the 1880s and 90s. *Fan mail* is a term of the mid 1920s, first heard in relation to movie stars.

American League, 1901. *The Western League* was organized as a minor league in 1893, became the major *American League* in 1901, and was accepted as an equal of the National League in midseason of 1903.

"Connie" (Cornelius McGilli-cuddy) Mack had been a catcher and a manager of the National League's Pittsburgh Pirates before becoming manager of the Philadelphia Athletics of the new American League in 1901. Beginning in 1902, his many championship teams gave the new American League status equal to that of the National League. He is shown here with members of his Philadelphia team in 1919.

the spitball was first widely known and debated during the 1904 season. The word *spitter* appeared in 1911, *spitballer* (a spitball pitcher) in 1928, even though the spitball was banned after the 1919 World Series. The original *spitball*, a chewed paper pellet for throwing, as by children, has been in the language since 1846.

bean ball, 1905 (the head had been called the *bean* since the 1880s; *to bean* someone had meant to hit him on the head since 1910). The term *dusting off* (throwing close to a batter to scare him or move him away from the plate) appeared in 1928, such a pitch being called a *duster* by 1948.

squeeze play, first consciously used, and widely talked about, in the 1905 season.

The Georgia Peach was the nickname of Ty (Tyrus Raymond) Cobb, 1886–1961, the first professional baseball player most Americans ever heard of. Son of a famous Georgia educator and senator, he was widely talked about simply because he was one of the greatest baseball players who ever lived. An outfielder with the Detroit Tigers (1905–26) and the Philadelphia Athletics (1927–28), Cobb held the records for playing more games (3,033), scoring more runs (2,244), making more hits (4,191), stealing more bases (892, stealing a record 96 in 1915), and having a higher lifetime batting average (.367; he hit over .300 for 23 straight years!) than any other major leaguer. He was the American League batting champion 12 times, nine of them in a row, and at the first election for entry into the *Baseball Hall of Fame* at Cooperstown, New York, in 1936, he received the most votes. So, baseball fan or not, you would have heard a lot about *The Georgia Peach* between 1905 and 1928. He and Babe Ruth, *The Sultan of Swat*, were the two men who got all America talking about baseball.

Texas leaguer, a weak fly hit falling between infield and outfield. Though claimed by some to have been coined in Houston, Texas, as a boasting jest, because the large size of Texas ballparks made such hits common, the term seems to have been coined in

1886 during an American Association game of Toledo at Syracuse by a Syracuse pitcher whose last name was O'Brien: three ex-Houston players who had been traded to Toledo beat him by consistently dropping hits over his infielders' heads and, in disgust, he referred to these hits as nothing but "little old dinky Texas leaguers." Such a hit was also called a *blooper* by 1937 (*blooper* has meant a mistake since 1925).

bush league, 1909.

bull pen was an early 19th-century term for a strong log pen for bulls and also for a log enclosure for prisoners (1809). These may have given baseball its *bull pen*, which term first appeared around 1910 on the West Coast. However, there is merit to the belief that baseball's *bull pen* came from the large Bull Durham billboards that once loomed above most ballpark fences, picturing a huge bull in bright red, green, and brown. Any batter hitting a ball that hit the sign received $50 and two bags of Bull Durham tobacco. Relief pitchers often warmed up near or under the shade of this outfield billboard, and thus it could well be the bull of the Bull Durham sign that gave us the baseball term *bull pen*.

night baseball, 1910, as played by amateurs and semipro teams at twilight or with the aid of primitive artificial lighting. *Night game*, the first one counting toward a (minor) league pennant was Muskogee at Independence, Kansas, in the Western League,

"Babe" (George Herman) Ruth, The Sultan of Swat, of the New York Yankees, and "Ty" (Tyrus Raymond) Cobb, The Georgia Peach, of the Detroit Tigers, in 1920.

April 28, 1930. *Under the lights*, 1935, the year major league night games began, the first being Philadelphia at Cincinnati. *Indoor game*, 1965, introduced at Houston's new air-conditioned Astrodome stadium that year.

electric scoreboard became a common term in 1912 when a huge one was erected in New York City's Times Square so that the passing crowd could follow that year's World Series.

Federal League, an "outlaw" third league that raided the two big leagues for players and conducted pennant races in 1914 and 1915. There had also been a short-lived *Players League* of dissident National League players in 1890.

iron man, 1914, originally referring to a pitcher of superior endurance.

ump, 1914. The full word *umpire* dates from the 15th-century English *a noumpire*, which slowly grew to be pronounced as "an oumpire" (from Old French *nonper*, not even, third, hence not one of a pair of contestants but a fair third party settling disputes between two others).

The Black Sox scandal had everyone talking from late 1919 to 1922. The 1919 Chicago White Sox team, one of baseball's greatest, was dubbed the "Black Sox" after eight players confessed that they had conspired with gambler Arnold Rothstein in *throwing* (an 1850s term for deliberately losing) the 1919 World Series to Cincinnati. The eight were indicted for fraud in 1920 and suspended by White Sox owner Charley Comiskey from the 1921 season but found not guilty of fraud by the jury. To give the game renewed respectability, baseball then created a *Commissioner of Baseball*, choosing the presiding judge of the Black Sox trial, Judge Kenesaw Mountain Landis, as its first *commissioner*. He immediately banned the eight players from baseball for life.

A fad expression of the 1920s, *Say it isn't so, Joe*, came into use during the trial of the eight players, when a small boy in the crowd outside the courtroom tearfully shouted it to his fallen idol, left fielder "Shoeless Joe" Jackson.

the Negro National League. The first professional black baseball team was the Cuban Giants of Long Island in 1885. In 1920 the *Negro*

Judge Kenesaw Mountain Landis in 1920, shortly after he had become the first Commissioner of Baseball.

The championship Chicago White Sox team of 1919, known as the Black Sox *after eight of the players confessed to conspiring with gambler Arnold Rothstein to* throw *the World Series to Cincinnati.*

In 1947, Jackie Robinson "broke the color barrier" and became a Brooklyn Dodger star as the first black player in the major leagues since the brothers Welday and Mosses Walker had played for Toledo in 1884.

National League was established, and the *Negro Eastern League* followed in 1921, the two pennant winners playing an all-Black World Series in 1924. These two black leagues failed during the Depression, in 1932. A new *Negro National League* was established in the late 1930s but went out of existence in 1952, five years after Jackie Robinson opened the major leagues to black players.

The Sultan of Swat, The Bambino, The Babe were all nicknames of "Babe" (George Herman) Ruth, 1895–1948, baseball's most talked-about hero. Because he was so young he was called *The Babe* and *The Bambino* (Italian for baby) soon after joining first the Baltimore team and then the Boston Red Sox, as a pitcher, in 1914. People talked about The Babe then because he was the best left-handed pitcher in the American League, pitching 29⅔ scoreless innings in the 1916 and 1918 World Series.

Ruth was called *The Sultan of Swat* soon after joining the New York Yankees in 1920 as a slugging outfielder. *Swat* because of the way he swatted the ball but the alliterative *Sultan of Swat* was a literary reference. There was a real state of Swat, now part of Pakistan. In 1878 the London *Times* published an item headed "The Akhoond [Sultan] of Swat Is Dead," which prompted George Lanigans to write a bit of doggerel:

> What, what, what,
> What's the news from Swat?
> Sad news, bad news
> Comes by the cable. . . .
> The Akhoond is dead.

Which led to the more famous Edward Lear lines:

> Who, or why, or which, or what
> Is the Akhoond of Swat?

Americans talked about our Sultan of Swat when he hit 54 home runs in 1920, the first year baseball banned the *spitball* and other tricky pitches, and put into play a tightly wound, more resilient ball, the controversial *rabbit ball* (so called because sportswriter Grantland Rice wrote that it seemed to be full of "rabbit juice"). "Babe" Ruth and the rabbit ball changed baseball from a game of strategy played in the infield to the sluggers' game that made it *the national pastime* in the 20s and 30s. People continued to talk about "Babe" Ruth because he hit a record 60 home runs in 1927 and 714 home runs in his 22 professional seasons. People also talked about this short-legged, top-heavy, 215-pound, 6-foot-2-inch player because he was a colorful, womanizing, whiskey-drinking slumboy, suspended for a month in 1922 for an unauthorized barnstorming tour, fined $5,000 in 1925 for "misconduct off the field," and earned a widely publicized, record-high $85,000 a season in 1930 and 31. And when Ruth's playing days were over we still talked about him, calling Yankee Stadium *The House That Ruth Built* with the money fans paid to see him play. Incidentally, the candy bar *Baby Ruth*, introduced in the early 1920s, was not named for "Babe" Ruth (or for Grover Cleveland's eldest daughter, who had been dead

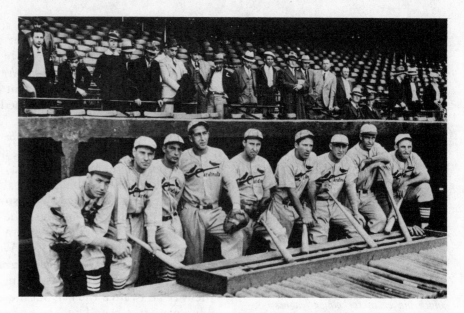

The Gashouse Gang, *the famous St. Louis Cardinal team, before the start of the 1934 World Series. Pitcher "Dizzy" (Jay Hanna) Dean, at the far left, had won thirty games that year, while his brother "Daffy" (Paul) Dean had won nineteen, the two brothers then winning two games apiece to win the Series for St. Louis.*

He slud into third base.
"Dizzy" Dean, St. Louis Cardinal pitcher, who in the late 1940s, became a popular baseball broadcaster, amusing listeners with his colorful, ungrammatical language.

Abner Doubleday.

since 1904) but for the granddaughter of George Williamson, president of the Williamson Candy Co., which originally made the candy bar.

batboy, 1925.

shoestring catch, 1926.

American Legion baseball, 1926, when the American Legion Junior League was formed for boys up to seventeen years of age. There are now 19,000 American Legion teams playing.

farm system, farm club, 1930.

send to the showers, 1931, to take a pitcher out of a game and send in another. Usually, the replaced pitcher then takes a shower and puts on his street clothes because he will take no further part in the game.

the All-Star Game was first named and played in 1933 at Chicago's Comiskey Park as a special feature of the Chicago World's Fair, as originally suggested by *Chicago Tribune* sportswriter Arch Ward.

softball, as a specific, well-organized game, 1930s.

the Little League was organized by Carl E. Stotz of Williamsport, Pennsylvania, in 1939, with three Pennsylvania teams forming it that year. There are now 15,000 Little League teams for children aged eight to twelve, playing on a field about two-thirds regulation size.

rhubarb, for a noisy argument between players or players and umpire, or the missed play leading to it, was used by baseball players as early as 1915 but was popularized by radio baseball announcer Red Barber during the 1939 season. It's an old theatrical term, from actors in mob scenes saying "rhubarb" over and over to simulate the angry, confused sounds of a mob.

Abner Doubleday, the National Baseball Hall of Fame. Legend has it that Abner Doubleday, an instructor at a local military prep school (and later a major general in the U.S. Army and a hero of the Battle of Gettysburg), invented baseball in Cooperstown, New York, in the summer of 1839 by laying out a field and conducting a game for the cadets. His field and game, however, seem to have been that of the softball town ball being played

Presidents Woodrow Wilson, Herbert Hoover, Franklin D. Roosevelt, Dwight D. Eisenhower, Lyndon B. Johnson, and Richard Nixon throwing out the first ball beginning new major league seasons.

45

When this picture was taken at the Polo Grounds in 1954, the hard-hitting twenty-three-year-old New York Giant center fielder Willie Mays was already well known as Say Hey Willie *and the Say-Hey Kid, from his frequent use of the exclamation* Say—hey!, *which then became a fad expression.*

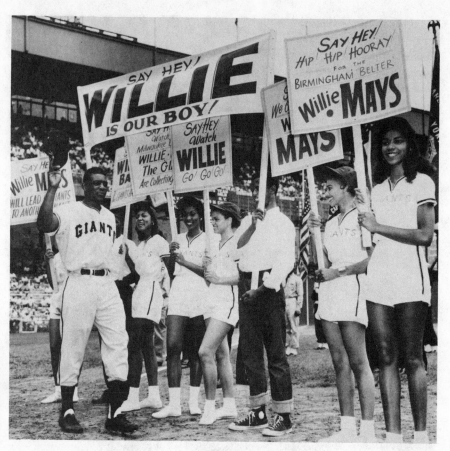

"Hank" (Henry) Aaron of the Atlanta Braves in 1973, when he was approaching Babe Ruth's career home-run record.

Pete Rose, then still with the Cincinnati Reds, on his way to setting the National League record for hitting in the most consecutive games, in 1978.

elsewhere at the time. The story that he invented modern baseball was first propagated by organized baseball in the early 1900s to give the game status, then solidified with baseball's nationwide "centennial" celebration, sponsored by organized baseball in 1939. The main ceremony of this celebration was the opening of the National Baseball Hall of Fame and Museum in Cooperstown, New York, on June 12 (the town of Cooperstown had leased the site of the original "Doubleday Field" and made it a permanent monument in 1920).

Ladies' Day appeared in baseball use in 1883 but became a popular baseball term and attraction in the late 1940s when postwar owners were looking for ways to fill up their stands again (the term had been used since 1787 to mean a day when men could bring women guests to their clubs; George Washington recorded the term in his diary that year, noting that a club at which he dined had a "ladies' day" every other Saturday). Special days on which children were given baseball-related gifts to attract them to the ball park were begun in the late 1960s, and in the 70s they proliferated with a multitude of *bat days, jacket days, cap days,* etc.

Even though baseball is no longer America's favorite professional team sport, 10 to 20 million paid spectators still watch it each year and 25 million American television sets are tuned in to the World Series annually—almost all Americans have heard the baseball terms given above. If you talk instead about football,

46

Fernando Valenzuela, then the Los Angeles Dodger rookie pitching sensation, leading his team to a victory in the third game of the 1981 World Series against the New York Yankees.

basketball, or ice hockey, you still use dozens of sport terms—such as *league, series, home team, manager,* and *post-season game*—that were first popularized by baseball. If for any reason you read your newspaper's *sports page* or *sports section* (terms of the 1920s), you are reading what grew out of the *baseball column* of 1869 and out of the *sporting columns, sporting pages,* and *sporting sections* created primarily for baseball in the 1890s. And even if you hate all sports, you have probably used the term *goose egg* (zero, no score, a baseball term of 1866) or such generalized baseball terms and metaphors as *to play ball* (cooperate, 1901), *keep* (one's) *eye on the ball* (be alert, 1907), *to have something on the ball* (have the desire and ability to succeed, 1912), *to be off base* (be crazy, be wrong, 1912), *right off the bat* (immediately, 1910), *to go to bat for* (defend or support someone, 1916), *to be in there pitching* (keep trying, keep working, 1930s), *to take a rain check* (to accept or do at another time, 1930s), or say that someone *has a strike against him* (a reason to fail or be disliked, 1940s). Thus, baseball fan or not, when you talk you probably use baseball terms, and when you listen to America you hear baseball.

Automobiles surround the New York Mets' newly built Shea Stadium in 1964.

Basketball

the only major sport of U.S. origin, was invented by a Canadian, James Naismith (1861–1939), at the International Y.M.C.A. Training School (later Springfield College), Springfield, Massachusetts, in early December 1891.

A graduate of Montreal's Presbyterian Theological College, Naismith wanted to teach "clean living" through sports and thus became a *physical education* (1858) instructor at the Springfield Y.M.C.A. Training School in the fall of 1891. The students there, studying to become Y.M.C.A. secretaries and physical education instructors, had long felt that the marching, calisthenics, and gymnastics of their gymnasium classes (to be called *gym* by 1897) were boring. The head of the department urged Naismith to invent a "gymnastic activity," a game that could be played in a gymnasium, had no bodily contact, used a lightweight ball—for the protection of both the students and the school's gym—and would give each player an equal chance to handle the ball and make plays. By early December the thirty-year-old Naismith had invented what he referred to simply as "the game." His male students tried it out, nine men to a side, with William R. Chase scoring the very first goal, ending that first game with a score of 1 to 0.

Naismith had planned on nailing an overhead box at each end of the training school's gym as "targets," but since no boxes were available, the school storeroom instead provided a half-bushel peach basket for each end of the *court*. Thus the game became *basket ball*. The term was first seen in print as the title of the article Naismith wrote introducing his new game:

BASKET BALL

> We present to our readers a new game of ball . . . It fills the same place in the gymnasium that foot ball does in the athletic field. Any number of men may play at it, and each one gets plenty of exercise.
>
> James Naismith in the January 1892 issue of *Triangle*, the publication of the physical education department of the Y.M.C.A. Training School of Springfield, Massachusetts.

By 1902 *basket ball* was often hyphenated to *basket-ball* and by 1912 was sometimes written as one word, *basketball* (if the storeroom had been able to provide those boxes, we might be playing "boxball" today).

Basketball began during the weeks before Christmas in 1891. During their Christmas vacation Naismith's Y.M.C.A. Training School students spread the word of the new game and soon local Y.M.C.A.'s were writing him for a copy of the rules. Thus the Y.M.C.A., which was first organized in London in 1844 as a club for "the improvement of the spiritual condition of young men in

James Naismith and his wife in 1926, posing with a soccer ball, such as that used in early basketball, and peach baskets similar to those that gave basketball *its name.*

the drapery and other trades" and which had opened its first chapter in the United States in 1851, in Boston, began basketball. Often called *the Y.M.C.A. game* or *Y.M.C.A. basketball*, it spread rapidly in the U.S. and around the world, to France in 1893, England, China, and India in 1894, Brazil in 1896, and Japan in 1900. In return, basketball helped swell Y.M.C.A. membership in the early 1890s, the local *Y* (a 1920s abbreviation) often being the only building in town with a gym.

Basket ball meant only the game in 1891 and not yet the ball used in the game. It was played with a soccer ball until 1894, when the Chicopee Overman Wheel Company, a bicycle manufacturer (*wheel* meant a bicycle by 1880, hence the company's name) of Falls, Massachusetts, began making a slightly larger ball especially for the game, this new ball being called a *basket ball*. A player was sometimes called a *basketballer* or even a *basketeer* into the late 1920s and wore *basketball shoes* by 1922.

Although that first score William R. Chase made in 1891 was called a *goal*, some people also called it a *basket*, with *basket* becoming the more common word for a scoring shot around 1905. In Naismith's original rules, three consecutive *fouls* by one team "counted as a goal" for the opposing team. In 1893 fouls began to result in a *free trial for goal* or a *free throw for goal*, which by 1894 was sometimes simply called a *free throw* and was taken from the *free-throw line*. Since some goals were now *foul goals*, a regular basket from the field during active team play was called a *field goal* (1895). The term *foul shot* became common in 1905, *shot* having been used in sports since the 1850s to mean an attempt to drive a ball through a goal.

Originally both field goals and foul goals were to count three points each, but in 1895 field goals were reduced to two points and foul goals to one. Until 1923 each team's best *shooter* took all the team's foul shots. Naismith's rules allowed only for "throwing" and "batting" the ball and made *running* with it a foul. The definition of running and batting led to the *dribble* (an 1830s soccer term for a series of short kicks), while what constituted *running* with the ball was precisely defined and called *walking* by 1921. Naismith also forbid "shouldering, *holding*, pushing, tripping, or striking" an opposing player, two such fouls by a player removing him from the game, with no replacement allowed, until the next basket was scored. The term *personal foul* was first used in the 1909 college rules, a player then being disqualified from a game after making four of them (increased to five in 1944); the term *foul out* became common in the early 1940s, when the success of big-time college basketball made the game much faster and rougher than before.

The original peach baskets of 1891 were joined by wood, leather, and heavy wire baskets and by wood and metal buckets over the next ten years, with teams using the latter scoring *buckets* instead of *baskets*. As early as 1893, however, the Narragansett Machinery Company of Providence, Rhode Island, made the first commercial iron hoop with a string net basket suspended from it, such a "basket" soon being called a *hoop* or the *net*. Whereas other players, including Naismith's original ones, had to use a ladder to retrieve the ball from the basket or bucket, those who used the early hoop-and-string basket could empty it without a ladder, by merely poking the ball out with a pole. Soon, of course, impatient players cut a hole in the bottom of the net basket, the open-bottomed net basket then becoming the only one allowed by the rules of 1912.

Most early baskets were fastened directly to the gymnasium walls or balcony. The balcony was a common feature of Y.M.C.A. gyms and spectators would reach over it to help or hinder a team by batting a shot in or out. In 1895, teams were instructed to construct a *basketball screen* behind the basket to eliminate such interference, with the rectangular wooden *backboard* following in the late 1890s (a nontransparent *glass backboard* was legalized in 1908, transparent ones were widely debated when first used in the mid 1930s, and the fan-shaped backboard was made legal in 1940).

Another way to prevent spectator interference, as well as to prevent the ball from going into the crowd, was to enclose the gym floor by a netting, the net-enclosed playing area being called a *cage* by 1907, basketball players and teams then being called *cagers* by 1912.

Since the early baskets were attached directly to the gym walls and balconies, some players developed the skill of running at top speed toward the wall and then up it a step or two to get a closer shot, such players being said to *climb the wall*. Even though the *up the wall* shots usually involved the infraction of running or walking, spectators enjoyed them and they were usually allowed. They were finally eliminated in 1920, when a new rule dictated that the backboard project at least two feet from the wall. In 1939 this rule was improved, dictating that the backboard project four feet from the end line; this allowed for more playing room *under the basket* or *under the boards* (the backboards), which terms then became common.

Women started to play basketball within a week or two of Naismith's original trial game. Although he had created it as a game "any number of men may play at," women teachers from the nearby Springfield Buckingham Grade School watched the curious new game during their lunch period and soon tried it, playing at the Y.M.C.A. Training School gym behind closed doors in their full floor-length dresses with leg-o'-mutton sleeves. Naismith taught them and refereed. When he called a foul on one of these young ladies she called him a *son of a bitch* (an English term of 1712

A girls' high school basketball game in Washington, D.C., in 1899.

and very common in America since the 1780s), or as the shocked Y.M.C.A. instructor put it, "she questioned my ancestry." This was the first recorded instance of a basketball player cursing a *referee* (a 1612 English legal term).

Naismith taught these young women teachers exactly the same game he had devised for his male students. *Women's basketball*, originally called *girl's basketball* and *the girl's game*, of six players per team, the three forward players in the forecourt doing all the scoring and the three backcourt players serving merely as guards, developed from a mistake made by Clara Baer of New Orleans' Newcomb College. She had requested and received a diagram of Naismith's game and mistook its dotted lines, indicating where various players might best execute plays, to be restraining lines. Then in 1895 she published her set of women's rules, restricting players to specific areas on the court.

In 1892, the year after basketball was invented, intramural *college basketball* began, being introduced to Geneva College of Beaver Falls, Pennsylvania, and to the University of Iowa by Springfield Y.M.C.A. Training School graduates and their friends. Although not officially recognized as such, the first intercollegiate basketball game was played by women's teams from Stanford and the University of California, in April, 1895. They played in high-necked shirtwaists, and full "kneelength trousers" worn over *tights* (an 1836 English word). These "kneelength trousers" were called *knee trousers* by 1899, which term was considered more ladylike than the 1830s word *shorts*. However, most women decided to play in *bloomers* (1850), which had been named after Amelia Bloomer, the women's rights, anti-hoopskirt, and temperance activist, who first published a pattern for this item, designed by Gerrit Smith for his dress-reform movement, in her temperance magazine, *The Lily*. Though considered very daring in the 1850s and 60s, by the 1890s bloomers were found suitable for bicycling, basketball, and other sports. By 1898 Vassar, Syracuse, Cornell, Wellesley, and Rosemary Hall had women's basketball teams, called *bloomer teams*.

Meanwhile, in 1894, some men's teams playing in the smaller Y.M.C.A. gyms had experimented with using five, instead of the usual nine or occasionally eleven, players to a team. Five-man teams became the rule in 1895, a team being called a *five* that same year, with some sportswriters trying to be different by using the word *quintet* by the early 1900s. The five-man team with a *center*, two *forwards*, and two *guards* filling approximately the same general functions they do now was fixed by 1922. The first officially recognized intercollegiate game, with five men on a side, was played between the University of Iowa and the University of Chicago at Iowa City, January 18, 1896, Chicago winning 15 to 12 under the coaching of its athletic director, football great Amos Alonzo Stagg, who had been a student, player, and coach at the Springfield Y.M.C.A. Training School.

While basketball was rapidly spreading and changing in the mid 1890s, some Y.M.C.A.s now found it too popular. The game and its ten to twenty players monopolized gyms, supplanting the fifty or sixty men who might otherwise be doing calisthenics and gymnastics and paying membership dues and gym-instructor fees. Many Y.M.C.A.s began to ban basketball, causing those teams that wanted to play, usually the better ones, to hire halls to play in. To pay for hiring the hall, the teams charged spectators to watch them play—and *professional basketball* was born. Many of these ex–Y.M.C.A. teams started with boys who continued playing as young men, then turned their places over to new players, the players changing but the teams keeping their identity for forty or fifty years. One of the most famous early teams, the Buffalo Germans of Buffalo, New York, began as a group of fourteen-year-olds in 1895, went through many complete player changes, and disbanded forty-four years later having won 792 games while losing only 86. The New York City 23rd Street Y.M.C.A. team won the very first national *basketball tournament*, held by the Amateur Athletic Union in 1897, then stuck together to become the very successful New York Wanderers professional team.

Though charging admission, such early teams didn't originally make a profit. The first one to do that was the Trenton, New Jersey, team of 1898, which is considered by many to be the first true *professional basketball team*, because spectators paid enough to cover the team's $25 rental fee for the local Masonic auditorium

Nat Holman was still playing for New York University when this photograph was taken in 1920, but he soon joined the Original Celtics.

and to net each player $15. The year 1898 also introduced the first professional *basketball leagues*, the New England League and the first, short-lived, National Basketball League. The latter was made up of teams from Philadelphia, Southern New Jersey, Manhattan, and Brooklyn, with players being well paid at $150 to $225 a month during the season. Then in 1905 a series of games was billed as the *World Championship* of basketball, in which Edward and Lew Wachter, Jimmy Williamson, Jack Inglis, and Bill Hardman, who played for Company E of Schenectady, New York, as well as Company G of Gloversville, New York, beat the most famous of the western teams, the Kansas City Blue Diamonds, in three straight games. This Schenectady, New York, team invented the *bounce pass* as a scoring weapon, beat the Buffalo Germans twice in one day in 1915, then took basketball's first major long-distance tour, going as far west as Montana to play 29 games, winning them all.

But it was the Original Celtics who started all America talking about basketball. They began in New York as a group of semi-professional Y.M.C.A. youngsters in 1915, traveled widely, played "every night and twice on Sunday" during most of the six-month winter playing season, and won 90 percent of their games. By the early 1920s the team was owned by the Furey brothers, played its home games at New York City's 71st Regiment Armory, and boasted such players as Johnny Beckman, Pete Barry, "Dutch" Dehnert, who invented the *pivot play*, "Horse" Haggerty, Joe Lapchick, "Stretch" Meehan, and the team's floor general and best shooter, Nat Holman. Beckman and Holman both claimed to

The Original Celtics team of 1920. In the front row the Furey brothers flank players Reich and Johnny Beckman, whose ankle is steadying the ball; in the back row in uniforms, left to right, are Whitty, "Dutch" Dehnert, Trippe, Pete Barry, and Smolick. This was shortly before "Horse" Haggerty, Joe Lapchick, "Stretch" Meehan, and Nat Holman joined the team.

Abe Saperstein and the Harlem Globetrotters *team in 1963. He first organized and named the team in Chicago in 1927.*

be the highest-paid player of the day, each reportedly earning over $1,500 a month, though it was the fast, daring Holman, who had played for professional teams while still a schoolboy, who often made half the Original Celtics' points and who was the first player to score consistently in double figures. These Original Celtics won 204 and lost 11 in the 1922–23 season, were featured in 1925 in the first basketball game ever played at New York City's Madison Square Garden (the then "new" Madison Square Garden, on Eighth Avenue between 49th and 50th streets), and finally so dominated the nine-city *American Basketball League* (formed in 1925) that when they won 109 and lost only 11 games in the 1927–28 season the team was banished from the league as "too strong" and was disbanded.

Meanwhile other professional teams were barnstorming the country, including five men Abe Saperstein piled into his old jalopy in Chicago in 1927 to play small towns, naming his team the *Harlem Globetrotters* simply because the five players were black and willing to play anywhere.

Despite such teams, basketball in the 1920s was still a much slower, lower-scoring game than it is today, the average winning score then being between 30 and 40 points. College basketball began to become a nationwide spectator sport when Edward Simmons "Ned" Irish promoted and introduced it at Madison Square Garden, presenting a double-header during the Christmas holidays of 1934, with 16,000 seeing Westminster, Pennsylvania, beat St. John's 37 to 33 (Frank McGuire and Rip Kaplinsky being high scorers with eight points each) and New York University beat

Notre Dame 25 to 18. Major annual national *college basketball tournaments* were then created in rapid succession, the *NAIA (National Association of Intercollegiate Athletics)* tournament being organized in 1937, the *NIT (National Invitational Tournament)* organized by the New York City Metropolitan Basketball Writers Association in 1938, and the *NCAA (National Collegiate Athletic Association)* tournament beginning in 1939. The term *Cinderella team*, for a winning or successful team that was thought to have little chance, was first used to refer to the University of Utah's 1944 NCAA championship team, then widely applied to CCNY's (City College of New York) 1950 team, which won both the NCAA and NIT championships.

Such widespread interest in college basketball also led to widespread betting on games and to college basketball's famous 1951 scandal. New York District Attorney Frank Hogan found that New York City players from CCNY, Long Island University, Manhattan College, and New York University had accepted bribes to win games by less than the *point spread* between the favored and nonfavored teams on which odds are based. Eventually, 49 *fixed* (a 1920s term) games in 23 cities were uncovered and players from the University of Kentucky, Bradley, Toledo, and other colleges were implicated. During the investigations and hearings of this scandal, nonbetting Americans heard the term *point spread* for the first time, as well as *point shaving* (keeping the final score closer than the point spread) and *dumping*, which then meant not neces-

Wilt Chamberlain, then with the Los Angeles Lakers, gets the ball and Jerry Lucas of the New York Knicks gets the elbow in a 1972 NBA championship game.

George Mikan (left), formally of De Paul University, scores against the College All Stars as a member of the championship Minneapolis Lakers in Chicago Stadium in 1953. Jerry West (center) of the University of West Virginia beginning a hook shot in 1958. Bill Bradley (right) of Princeton in 1965.

UCLA coach John Wooden wearing the net around his shoulders and giving the "We're Number 1" sign after his Bruins beat Kentucky in the 1975 NCAA finals, giving Wooden his tenth national championship at UCLA: his 1967–69 teams, starring Lew (Ferdinand Lewis) Alcindor, won 88 games while losing only two and had a 49-game winning streak.

sarily *throwing* (early 1930s for deliberately losing) a game but also winning it by fewer points than predicted.

Professional basketball started to become a truly national pastime when the new *National Basketball League* (formed in 1937) and the *Basketball Association of America* (formed in 1946) stopped feuding and formed the 17-team *NBA (National Basketball Association)* in 1949, with the second major basketball league, the 11-team *ABA (American Basketball Association)*, being formed in 1967.

During the 1930s and 40s the game grew ever faster and higher scoring, and the players ever taller. In the early days the two-handed *set shot*, in which the player sets his feet and takes deliberate aim at the basket, was the main shot; in the 1930s the *one-handed jump shot* became popular, when Stanford's star Angelo "Hank" Luisetti used it with spectacular success, leading to many other *one-hander* shots; and in the 1940s the *hook shot* became widely used (by the 1950s a distant set shot was called an *outside shot*). The fast *racehorse* style of play begun in the 1930s was perfected by the 1940's University of Illinois *whiz kids* (from the 1908 *whiz*, wizard, expert, plus *whiz* as the sound of a speeding object). The main aspect of this fast style was the *fast break*, which was perfected by the professional Boston Celtics in the late 1950s.

"Cooz" (Bob) Cousy, of the Boston Celtics, battling for a loose ball in 1961.

Oscar Robertson of the Royals dribbles past the Celtics' Sam Jones in 1963.

Bill Russell and 7-foot-2-inch Wilt Chamberlain ("Wilt the Stilt") fight for the ball in 1967.

The increased height of the players led to *goal tending* (1937, interfering with an opponent's shot when it was above the basket on its downward fall), which was banned from college play in 1945, after the 7-foot Bob Kurland of Oklahoma, 6-foot-11-inch Don Otten of Bowling Green, and 6-foot-10-inch George Mikan of De Paul had become famous for it the previous year. Though to *dunk* had meant to shoot the ball through the basket in any way since the 1930s, tall, agile offensive players developed the modern *dunk shot* in the mid 1960s and the *slam dunk* in the early 1970s, leaping above the basket to stuff or slam the ball down through it. The dunk was banned from college play for eight years, beginning in 1968, after UCLA's 7-foot-2-inch Lew Alcindor (who became Kareem Abdul-Jabbar in 1971) dominated the game with it in his first year of college play.

Equipment, rules, styles of play, and team names may come and go, but Naismith's Y.M.C.A. game is still giving hundreds of thousands of players "plenty of exercise," and the American language many new terms.

New York Knick's Walt Frazier in 1975.

"Dr. J.," Julius Erving of the Philadelphia 76ers, scores a one-handed slam dunk *over the New York Knicks' Bob McAdoo in 1978.*

Bill Walton of the Portland Trail Blazers and Kareem Abdul-Jabbar (Lew Alcindor in his UCLA days) of the Milwaukee Bucks in 1974.

Be Sure You're Right—Then Go Ahead

has been said by many American politicians and businessmen; it wavers between being a good motto and a bad cliché. The saying is from David Crockett's 1834 *Autobiography*, where it appears as:

> I leave this rule for others when I'm dead,
> Be always sure you're right—then go ahead.

This last line was Davy Crockett's motto in the Creek War campaign during the War of 1812.

In his own day, Davy Crockett was also well known as a rustic orator.

Let's Go to the Beach

with its image of a sun-drenched, sandy shore, is a typically American expression—in England the 16th-century word *beach* had originally meant a gravelly shore. In early colonial days, *beach* referred specifically to the Hudson River's east bank and the sandy offshore New Jersey islands. Here one might go *sea bathing* or *dipping* (the word is still found in our expression *skinny dipping*, swimming "in the skin," or naked), terms then used by refined people and by doctors, who prescribed sea bathing for ailments ranging from deafness and ulcers to asthma and consumption. Some people actually enjoyed such "sea bathing," and by 1794, Long Island residents were talking about the first American *bathing machines*, dressing rooms on wheels which were drawn from the beach into the surf by horses so that prying eyes could not glimpse the bathers as they entered the water.

Between 1790 and 1850 the old words *swimming*, *swimmer*, and *a swim* (16th century) became common. By 1810, people were

Here ladies and gentlemen bathe in decorous dresses and are very polite to each other . . . the bathing at Newport is very good.

Anthony Trollope, *North America*, 1861–62

At the beach in 1906.

By 1900 Miami was a magic name to vacationers. It still was when this photograph was taken eighty years later.

talking about *the Jersey Shore* as a *bathing resort*. Its Atlantic City became a watchword among socialites and beach enthusiasts when it had its first official season, opening July 4, 1854, with colorful Independence Day celebrations and a brand new railroad and two competing turnpikes bringing carriages full of Philadelphians to five new hotels. In 1870, Atlantic City opened its famous *Atlantic City Boardwalk*, a four-mile-long "steel and concrete" *boardwalk* which grew to eight miles in length by 1944, when a hurricane battered both the boardwalk and the city into a period of decline (the city and its beachfront became glamorous again as a gambling resort when casinos were opened in 1979). Soon after 1870, though, the term *on the boardwalk* meant only one thing—enjoying the beach and social life at Atlantic City. Elsewhere, of course a *boardwalk* simply meant what it had for generations, a mere sidewalk of boards. Talked about almost as much as Atlantic City was its rival, Long Branch, New Jersey, which was to become the favorite resort of President Grant and which was widely talked about in 1881 when President Garfield was taken there to die after being shot in Washington. Closer to New York City, a string of muddy, rabbit-infested inlets and islands, with names like Rabbit Island and Coony Island (later spelled Coney Island), became popular places to go, and wealthy Vanderbilts, Belmonts, and Lorillards rocked on the porches of the Manhattan Beach Hotel or joined the proletariat in devouring *Coney Islands* (1880s), then meaning fried clams, which preceded the hot dog as the famous Coney Island delight.

In the 1880s, Henry Flagler's Atlantic Coast Line railroad made the beaches of Florida accessible to wealthy northerners, and Florida became a magic word to all beach lovers. Tourists soon flocked to Flagler's lavish Ponce de Leon Hotel in Saint Augustine; then, by 1900, two more new names enticed American vacationers—Palm Beach and Miami.

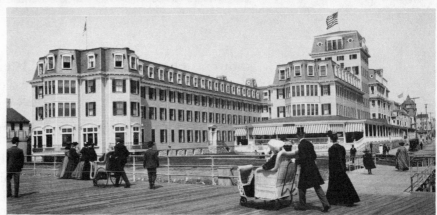

Two views of the Atlantic City boardwalk *in 1908.*

Meanwhile, more and more of the beach strollers and picnickers were actually going into the water—voluminously clad, of course. In the 1870s a fashion book listed ten yards of heavy flannel as necessary to make a woman's *bathing suit*, a term then coming into common use, replacing the terms *bathing dress* and *bathing costume*. The *bathing hat* had been a special item for women since the late 1840s, and until 1907 *bathing stockings* were required for female bathers in Atlantic City.

The skirtless *one-piece bathing suit* for women was hotly discussed when Jantzen introduced it in 1913, and by 1914 enough people were cavorting at the beach to make the song "By the Beautiful Sea" a big hit. But it was the Hollywood *bathing beauty contest* and Mack Sennett's daring *bathing beauties* (both terms common by 1920), with their bare arms and *rolled stockings*, that helped relax the rules so that enough skin could be exposed to make *sunbathing*, *suntan*, *tan*, and *suntan oil* part of the vocabulary by 1925. Men's *trunks* had been in use by professional swimmers and athletes since the 1880s (being called *trunks* by athletes even before they were

At the beach in 1980. Four Miss America beauty contestants in the surf at Atlantic City.

known as *swimming trunks*), but as late as 1935 men were arrested for wearing them without a top at Atlantic City.

Not until the 1940s were women's backs exposed and the rather skimpy *two-piece bathing suit* for women accepted. After World War II the very skimpy *bikini* bathing suit created a sensation. It was named after the Pacific island site of the 1946 U.S. nuclear tests, the name chosen and advertised to imply that the effect of a bikini-clad female was akin to that of an atomic detonation. But the bikini seemed mild in 1964 when designer Rudi Gernreich introduced his *monokini*, soon called the *topless bathing suit*, which was followed by the ultimate sensation in the early 1970s—public *nude bathing*.

Beans!

The early colonists found the Indians growing corn and beans together, with the cornstalks serving as beanpoles. Some farmers followed this custom, but most used a *beanwood*, which was called a *beanpole* by 1821 or a *beanstick* by 1823, with *beanpole* also coming to mean a tall, skinny person by 1836. The Indians also cooked the corn and beans together, in bear grease, to make what we call *succotash* (1751, from Algonquian *misickquatash*, boiled kernels of corn), which has also been pronounced *circuit hash* in parts of the South.

Bostonians have been called *bean eaters* since 1800. Their famous *baked beans* were probably based on a sweetened bean recipe of the Indians, but the dish of beans cooked with saltpork and molasses wasn't widely called *Boston baked beans* until the 1850s. This dish had been popular with the Puritans because of their strict observance of the Sabbath: it could be baked in a *bean pot* and served for Saturday supper and again on Sunday without further work on the Lord's Day. Religious families that wanted to observe the

Sabbath but still have a fresh, hot meal on Sundays could fill their bean pots on Saturday for collection by the local baker, who baked them and returned them hot with his fresh baked brown bread on Sunday, giving us the traditional combination of *baked beans and brown bread* (an early home-delivered "fast-food" meal for Sunday eating).

Green beans were called *string beans* by 1759 (from the stringlike fiber along the side of the pod) and *snap beans* by 1770 (from the sound the uncooked pod is supposed to make when broken) but were not a major vegetable on American tables until the 1870s and 80s. Since 1894, when *Beautiful Burpee*, "the stringless string bean," was developed, the term *string bean* has been heard less and less, aided by food processors who feel *green beans* is a more appetizing, salable name to have on their labels and in their advertising. The yellow variety of bean wasn't generally called a *wax bean* until the early 1900s.

Butter beans, originally a tropical vegetable, got their name in the 1820s and by the 1850s were also called *lima beans*, usually then written with a capital, *Lima beans*, after Lima, Peru. *Navy beans* (1856) got their name because of their extensive use in the Navy, and *pinto beans* (1916) got theirs from the Spanish *pinto*, spotted, painted (westerners had been calling a spotted horse a *pinto* since 1860).

Although *beanfest* sounds like original American slang, it is actually an 1806 British term, basically meaning an annual feast or banquet given for one's employees. *Beanery* has meant a cheap restaurant since 1820 and is an American word. In the 1830s we began to say someone *doesn't know beans* if he knew little or nothing and that someone *knows how many beans make five* if that person was alert or shrewd. Since beans have always been cheap and plentiful, English-speaking people have been referring to things as *not worth beans* or only *worth beans* since the 13th century, but our American expression *not worth a hill of beans* first appeared in the 1860s. We have called the head *the bean* since the 1880s and used *to bean* to mean to hit someone on the head since 1910. Children were playing with *bean-bags* by 1887 and shooting *bean-shooters* by 1889 (they were first called *pea-blowers*, in 1821, then *pea-shooters* by the 1860s).

Full of beans has meant full of energy since the 1870s, but, about 1910, people also started using it to mean full of nonsense and simply saying *beans!* to mean "nonsense!" *To spill the beans*, to give away a secret, confess, has been in use since 1919. The English use two other "bean" terms that we usually don't: *old bean*, as direct address to an old friend, which dates from around World War I, and the slang use of *bean* meaning a coin (since 1811), which did give us our hip rhyming expression of the 1950s *not to have a bean in* (one's) *jeans*, meaning to have no money at all.

*Beans, beans, the musical
   fruit,
The more you eat, the more
   you toot,
The more you toot, the better
   you feel,
Beans, beans for every meal.*
Popular American doggerel

Beards, Close Shaves, and Barbershops

General Ambrose E. Burnside, whose last name was eventually reversed to give us sideburns.

Napoleon III, whose Imperial *helped make beards popular in the U.S. in the 1850s.*

With the notable exception of the dashing Captain John Smith, most English colonists arrived in the New World with a close shave—and American men generally kept clean-shaven until the War of 1812, when small *side whiskers* began to appear (called *side whiskers* because until well into the 1820s the English word *whiskers* alone meant the hair growing above the upper lip, which we then came to call a *mustache)*. These side whiskers reached their peak of popularity and fullness during and immediately after the Civil War and were eventually called *burnsides*, reversed to *sideburns* by 1887, since it was logical that *side whiskers* became *sideburns* rather than *burnsides*. The full *burnsides* originally included not only the side whiskers but a mustache and was named after Union General Ambrose E. Burnside (1824–81), who wore them while commander of the Army of the Potomac during the Civil War and later as Rhode Island governor and senator. The fullest such side whiskers were called *mutton chops* or *mutton-chop whiskers* (both 1865), from their shape. In the 1860s they were often called *dundrearies* or *dundreary whiskers*, after the character Lord Dundreary in the English comedy hit *Our American Cousin*, that character being portrayed by the popular actor E. A. Southern as wearing mutton chops (this was the play Lincoln was attending at Ford's Theater when assassinated in 1865). From about 1882 long side whiskers were also called *side-bar whiskers*.

Beards (the word is Old English and was first recorded in the year 825) generally appeared in America in the 1850s, their heyday lasting only until the 1870s. They were often called *chin whiskers* and *chin curtains* by the 1860s. The style came to the U.S. via England from Europe, where a long mustache and a chin tuft, called the *Imperial* since 1841, was made popular by Napoleon III. The beard on the chin was the trimmed *spade* (so called since the 16th century), the related *goatee* (the word dates from the 1840s; the item first appeared on Uncle Sam in 1868, fuller whiskers on him around 1870), or the bushier *fan*. Beard styles worn under the chin or around the jaws were called *neck warmers*, *sluggers*, or *whaler's beards*.

By 1851 poet and editor William Cullen Bryant had his beard; Abraham Lincoln grew his short beard in 1860 (legend has it that a little girl, Grace Bedell, wrote him saying his thin face would look better with one); U. S. Grant had a full but trimmed beard, with mustache and side whiskers; and many other men, such as Samuel F. B. Morse and Henry Wadsworth Longfellow, sported full flowing beards. From 1860 to 1897 all U.S. Presidents—Lincoln through Grover Cleveland—wore beards.

In the 1870s there were fewer, trimmer beards and mustaches,

Artists and writers were among those who wore full flowing beards, as shown in this 1887 portrait of Walt Whitman.

The slim military mustache was considered dashing during World War I and was later worn by such romantic actors as Douglas Fairbanks, Ronald Colman, Errol Flynn, and Clark Gable.

with the mustache frequently being worn alone. *Mustache* (via French from Greek *mystax*, jaws, mustache) has been in the English language since 1585, though the British now spell it *moustache* and though, as mentioned above, it didn't fully replace the word *whiskers* until the 1820s. Mustaches were full in the 1850s and 60s, usually worn with beards, with the full *brush* being popular.

After 1880 most American men were clean-shaven again, the exceptions being some older and professional men and some college boys and sporting types. The first group mainly wore short *Imperials* or waxed and pomaded *Van Dykes* (1894, named after the 17th-century Flemish painter whose portraits show many aristocrats wearing them). The college boys and sporting types grew many varieties, including long, upward curving mustaches, which were to be called *handlebar mustaches* once the bicycle became popular, around 1890. Thus the 1880s and 90s were generally a time of clean-shaven cheeks, of mustaches without beards, the period of the *mustache cup* (an 1886 term), *mustache wax*, and *mustache comb*. By 1910 only small mustaches were generally seen, with the slim *military mustache* considered dashing during World War I and later worn by such romantic actors as Douglas Fairbanks, Ronald Colman, John Loder, and Clark Gable. After that it was every man for himself, and with the safety razor and later the electric razor, most American men reverted to being completely clean-shaven, leaving it mainly to youths to experiment with and talk about beards, whiskers, and mustaches, with sideburns becoming part of the hair style rather than being considered as whiskers.

Being clean-shaven, however, is not as easy as it sounds. As fathers have been telling their sons since the 1890s, "Women have the curse of menstruating; men have the curse of shaving." American Indians plucked their beards with clam shells or other primitive tweezers, and early colonists used a long hooked type of razor, some of which resembled small scythes. The *straight-edged razor* or *straight razor* was used and discussed as a great improvement in the early 18th century and could easily be sharpened with a *razor strop* (1750s; *strop* is just an earlier form of *strap*). Men were talking about special *shaving soap* by 1770 and were asking for the first popular *shaving cream*, Ring's Verbena Cream, in the 1830s and 40s.

In the beginning of the 19th century a *shave head* was an Indian or a frontiersman who shaved his head Indian style, leaving a challenging *scalp lock* (1826), a style considered dashing by Indian fighters, scouts, trappers, and other rugged adventurers. By 1834 a *close shave* meant a narrow escape, and by 1843 many a small boy was being called a *little shaver* ("shaver" in this expression probably being a corruption of "shaving," a small piece shaved off a larger one). In the late 1840s *razor* and *sick razor* were slang terms for a pun or a sharp wisecrack.

Despite the popularity of beards from the 1850s to the 1870s, many men continued the search for a close, comfortable shave, with the use of old-fashioned *shaving soap*, with its *shaving mug* and *shaving brush*, reaching a peak in the 1890s. Then in 1895 the modern *safety razor* was invented by the traveling salesman and inventor King Gillette, who had been seeking a product people would use once, then throw away: his Gillette Safety Razor appeared in 1901, and though only fifty-one razors and 168 blades were sold in 1903, by 1906 his razor was a huge success. Since then, men have thrown away over a hundred billion *razor blades* from half a billion safety razors. Soon, men with safety razors were using the new *brushless shaving cream*, the first brand being England's *Lloyd's Euresis*, and America's first brand *Burma-Shave* (so named because the company's original product had been *Burma-Vita*, a strongly scented ointment containing essential oils from Burma). In 1926 all America started to watch for the humorous Burma-Shave highway-sign jingles, originated by Allen Odell, son of the company's founder, Clinton Odell (that first set of 1926 Burma-Shave highway signs appeared on U.S. Highway 65 near Lakeville, Minnesota, and didn't rhyme. It read, "Cheer-Up . . . Face . . . The War Is Over").

With increasing use of the safety razor in the 1920s and 30s, *alum*, an astringent that had been used to stop bleeding from shaving cuts, began to disappear from bathroom medicine cabinets, to be replaced by the cylindrical *styptic pencil* or *styptic stick*. Also, *witch hazel*, an extract from the bark and dried leaves of the witch-hazel plant, and alcohol, both used by generations of men as an after-shave healing and refreshening solution, gave way to fancier *after shave lotions*, *after shaves*, or *skin bracers*, of which Mennen and Aqua Velva were the most frequently heard brand names. Finally in the 1930s men began to talk about the new *electric razor*, invented by retired army colonel Jacob Schick and first put on the market in 1931.

Where do the barber and the barbershop fit into all this history of shaving and beard trimming, not to mention haircutting? The words *barber* and *haircutter* weren't even used in the colonies until the 1690s, some seventy years after the Pilgrims landed. The word *barber* was then seen on signs advertising the *Barber and Chirugeon*, for early barbers traditionally offered two separate services—shaving (*barber* is from the Latin *barba*, beard) and bloodletting. The red-and-white-striped *barber pole* (also a 1690s term) represented the blood and bandages of bloodletting, and a jar of leeches for bloodletting was also usually on display. Most of the barber's work was in bloodletting and in giving wealthy men their daily shave. The average man shaved himself, though many shaved only

UNWISE AND UNFORTUNATE
IS THE MAN WHO TRIES TO SHAVE WITHOUT
WILLIAMS' SOAPS.

A Williams' Shaving Soap *ad of 1888.*

Governor Thomas E. Dewey of New York lost the Presidential election to Harry Truman in 1948. One of the few men to run for President wearing a beard or mustache after 1890, Dewey's opponents said he looked like "the groom on a wedding cake."

Fidel Castro's beard was copied by revolutionaries and revolutionary-minded students in the late 1950s and early 1960s.

once or twice a week, and had his hair cut at home—haircutting was considered a woman's job, though a brother, father, or friend might do it. Most wealthy men of the 18th century didn't need haircuts: they wore wigs over their shaved heads, following a fashion that had originated in France.

For the first thirty-five or forty years of his life Louis XIV of France had been proud of his thick hair; when it began to thin in the 1670s, he began to wear a wig. This courtly custom then spread through Europe and to England under Charles II. Thus, by the last decades of the 17th century the fashion was for educated and upper-class men to wear *false hair*. The word *wig* had entered the English language by 1675, a shortening of the earlier word *periwig*, a variant of *peruke* (from French *perruque*). Expensive wigs were made of human hair, cheaper ones of horsehair. From about 1700 to 1715, men's court wigs were long and wavy, covering the back and shoulders. Such *full-bottomed* wigs were hot, cumbersome, and liable to slip off; therefore smaller, specialized, and less pretentious *campaign wigs*, *riding wigs*, *traveling wigs*, and *nightcap wigs* slowly became popular for all occasions, these simpler styles being the preferred ones in the colonies, though still usually custom-ordered from London. However, some colonial men did favor the more formal *Ramillie* wig (as originally worn by the Duke of Marlborough, known for his victory over the French at Ramillies, Belgium, in 1706), which had a plaited tail with a bow at its top and a smaller one at the bottom.

By the 1740s, short, close-to-the-head *bob wigs* had replaced all the fancier kinds in both England and America (though some professional men, especially British judges and some clergy, retained them). Around the 1770s wigs ceased to be an indispensable article of dress to upper-class men, quickly disappearing in America during and after the Revolutionary War, along with other items of class distinction. Then many upper-class English and American men took to wearing their own hair dressed and powdered like a wig! The *hair powder* (a 1663 English term) they used was often purchased from a barber.

By the 1830s "surgeon" became a separate occupation, wigs were completely out of style, and Americans were increasingly moving to and working in towns and cities, where a good shave and a neat haircut were more important than on the farms or in the backwoods. Thus the word *barbershop* (1832) finally appeared and became common. The elegant *hairdressing saloon* appeared in the 1850s, and the grandiloquent *haircutting parlor*, *tonsorial artist*, and *tonsorialist* (from the Latin *tonsorius*, shaving) were first used in the late 1860s.

Until the 1820s and 30s barbers were almost always blacks, with the tradition of black families of barbers continuing until the 1880s, when the new *barber schools* nullified a long apprenticeship

67

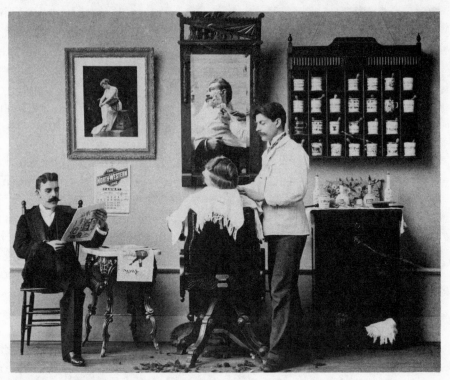

An 1896 barbershop with its magazines, picture of a pretty girl, and rack of customers' shaving mugs.

Brooklyn Dodger pitcher Sal Maglie in 1956. He was called The Barber *because he threw fast balls close to the batters' heads.*

or father-to-son training. In the 1880s, too, the traditional barbershop became fancy, with sporting magazines, calendars with pictures of pretty girls, and rows of private shaving mugs. The barbershop was the city man's counterpart of the general store, a place to joke and gossip. The barbers' own *barbershop quartets*, often called simply *barbershops*, were so popular from 1875 to 1910 that all popular close harmony was called *barbershop harmony*, and no large party, picnic, or moonlight boat ride seemed complete without them, many barbers making a good second income with their harmonizing.

Because barbers were traditionally talkative, a *barber* meant a talkative baseball player by 1925, but by 1950 *barber* had come to mean a fastball pitcher who threw close to the batter's head, giving him a "close shave" in order to make him back away from the plate.

Beds, Bunks, Pajamas, and Nighty-Night

Bed, bedstead, pallet, featherbed, and *tick* were all English words the colonists brought to America with them, with *bed* and *featherbed* dating back to the 10th century. *Bedroom* was a new word in English when the Pilgrims left England, just beginning to replace the 300-year-old *bed chamber*. In America, however, *bedroom* often meant not a separate room but merely the space set aside for a bed in the one- or two-room houses of early colonial and frontier days.

A *bed* was then usually just a pallet of blankets on the floor or a tick filled with corn shucks, straw, or wood chips, but the more demanding settler might build a *jack bed*, a platform on legs, usually placed in a corner of the room. If householders had a real *bedstead*, with ropes or straps laced across the frame to hold the tick and serve as springs, they talked of it with pride (*bed springs* were not invented until 1831). Once out of the cradle, children slept on pallets, in the same bed with their parents, or in low *truckle beds* (Greek *trakhos*, wheel) or *trundle beds*, which were rolled or pushed under the parents' bed in the daytime, the bedding being stored in a *settle*. Older children often slept in the loft. There was usually no privacy and no heat. That famous old English courtship custom *bundling* (lying in the same bed, talking and hugging but fully clothed) was recorded in America as early as 1630 and took place in the jack bed or on a bedstead. Since the bed was usually in a corner away from the family fire, bundling gave the daughter and her suitor some privacy and kept them warm.

Though *bug*, for various types of insects, was first recorded in England in 1642, Americans use the word much more than the English; thus we coined *bed bug* around 1809, with the expression *crazy as a bedbug* appearing in 1832 and *snug as a bug in a rug* in 1842.

By 1819 we were calling a rough bed or built-in sleeping platform on a ship a *bunk* (related to the Middle Dutch *banc*, bench, shelf, from Late Latin *bancus*, bench).

By the 1830s two-story houses had become somewhat common and the, now separate, bedroom moved upstairs. By the late 1830s the biggest bed in the biggest bedroom for the parents was being

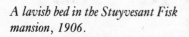
A lavish bed in the Stuyvesant Fisk mansion, 1906.

called a *double bed*. This might be a *four poster*, a term much in use in the 1820s and 30s. Such a bed was recommended because the curtains cut off drafts (*between you*, *me*, *and the bedpost*, meaning "just between us, confidentially," appeared as an American slang expression in 1830).

In the 1880s and 90s some hoboes and underworld types followed their English counterparts in calling a bed a *kip* (influenced by the Danish *horekippe*, brothel, from Old English *cip*, brothel) or a *doss* (from earlier *dorse*, back, from Latin *dorsum*). But wealthy Americans were talking about adding *sleeping porches* to their homes, a new idea that came in with bicycles, golf, and other manifestations of the new cult of fresh air and outdoor activities.

A 1905 ad. The term sofa bed *has been in the English language since 1816. Although the English* davenport, *a small ornamental writing desk, may be named after its original manufacturer or even the person who first commissioned it, the origin of the American* davenport, *a large sofa, especially one convertible into a bed, is unknown.*

Handsome and Doubly Useful

"SIMPLICITY"
Davenport Sofa Bed

Hunters, cowboys, and others who slept completely out-of-doors used a *sleeping bag*, 1856, also called a *blanket bag*, 1885.

In 1920, people were talking scandalously about the new *twin beds* for emancipated married couples who claimed to sleep better in separate beds, but by 1944 the new term was *king-sized bed*, allowing couples to have more room to sleep together comfortably. In 1970 everyone was talking about the new *water bed*, really more of a water-filled mattress, because it promised to be more comfortable and better for the back than a regular bed. Within a year, however, everyone was smirking about water beds because, when the water was heated, they offered a warm, bouncy sexual experience not obtainable on regular beds.

The original colonists brought *sheets*, *blankets*, and *pillows*, both the items and the words, with them from England and called them by the English words *bedding* or *bed clothes*, to which Americans added the term *bed clothing* in 1852. Pillows were often handed down from mother to daughter, and sheets were usually not used until the family had prospered enough to have real beds and bedrooms. People slept under *quilts*, often called *bedquilts*, or what were called *bedrugs*. The term *eiderdown quilt* was first used around the time of the Revolutionary War. *Quilting frolic* was the early name for a party to make a quilt or celebrate the completion of one, with the terms *quilting bee* and *quilting party* gaining popularity in America in the 1830s. The term *patchwork quilt* wasn't popular until the 1840s and *crazy quilt* not popular until the 1880s. Usually such quilts were named after their design, as a "rising sun quilt," a "log cabin quilt," an "American eagle quilt," or an "Adam and Eve quilt." The *comforter* appeared in the 1830s but then meant only a heavy woolen scarf, not being used to mean a heavy covering for a bed until the 1840s; *Afghan* (from Afghanistan), a knitted or crocheted wool cover, was also heard in the 1830s but didn't become a popular item or word until the 1860s. The *coverlet* was the top blanket, used both as a blanket and to spread over other blankets, with America introducing the removable *bedspread* as a new item and word around 1848.

Since *bed clothes* meant the sheets and other items that clothed a bed, the term *night clothes* was used to refer to those items that clothed people in or going to bed. However, many early colonists, especially poor ones, didn't have such night clothes but slept in the same clothes they wore during the day. The true sleeping garment was called a *night rail* (*rail* was an 8th-century word for dress or cloak), which fitted a little closer than the *night gown* (a 15th-century English term), which until the 1820s meant only a loose dressing gown and never a gown to be slept in. By 1710, women were calling their night rail a *night dress*, *night shift*, or *night smock*, and by the 1760s a *bedgown*. In the 18th century a *night cap* (an English term from 1386) was worn not only to bed but whenever one's wig was removed, so as not to expose the closely shaved head to prying eyes or cold drafts. By 1820 such caps were worn only to bed and we sometimes called them *bed caps*.

By the 1830s most men, many children, and some women were wearing *underdrawers*—and lots of people were sleeping in them. Flannel ones were the most common because the material was considered good for the health, preventing chills, absorbing perspiration, and giving the skin "a healthy rubbing" (red flannel underwear was considered even more healthy than gray). After the 1840s, however, most women slept in gowns and many men in *night shirts* (though an estimated 60 percent of American men still

Night gown *meant a loose dressing gown until the 1820s, then came to mean a gown for sleeping.*

71

This unique "table bed" was advertised in 1917.

sleep either in their underwear or in the nude, as does some smaller but uncounted percentage of women).

Pajama (Persian *pāi*, leg + *jāmah*, garment) originally referred to the loose cotton garment worn in India, which British colonials introduced into England in the 1870s, both the British and Americans originally wearing such pajamas as lounge wear. By 1900 many men and boys were sleeping in them instead of in night shirts, and some little girls and then women were wearing pajamas to bed too. Since the word *pajamas* by itself had thus now come to mean a garment for sleeping rather than lounging, those specifically for lounging had to be called *lounging pajamas* by the 1920s, with *beach pajamas* following in the 1930s. *P.J.'s*, first used as baby talk to children, was in vogue by the 1920s too. One reason everyone heard *the cat's pajamas* as an expression of up-to-the-minute approval so much in the 1920s was that pajamas were still a new enough sleeping garment to be considered somewhat daring.

Nightrobe is an English term from 1556 (*robe* dates from the 13th century), *dressing gown* from 1777, and *kimono* from 1887 (from Japanese *ki*, to wear + *mono*, thing, hence literally "thing for wearing"). *Bathrobe* is an American word of the late 1890s and originally meant exactly what it says, a robe to wear to and from the bath or from bathhouse to bathing beach.

As they had done in England, early colonists bid each other *good night*, *sleep soundly*, *have a good night*, and *God give you a good night*. Our American admonition *sleep tight* became common in the 1880s, as did our breezier *nighty-night* (1888). Until the 1690s colonists had simply slept, then some began to *doze* (probably of Scandinavian origin, related to Swedish dialect *dusa*, sleep), but it wasn't until 1848 that we began to speak of *dozing off* and the 1850s before we began to *snooze* (of unknown origin, though some believe it is a blend of *snore*, a Middle English word for hum or drone, + *doze*).

Early colonists simply would *go to bed* or *take a nap*, as they had in England, but in the 1820s our terms *40 winks* and *cat nap* grew common. In the 1870s we began to use the expression *to turn in* (1870, *turn out* had meant to get out of bed since 1805) and to tell our children "the sandman is coming," though the sandman story is an old European one. In the 1880s we began to say it was time *to hit the hay*, harking back to earlier days when on cold New England nights indentured servants and slaves slept in barns, cellars, and lofts deep in the hay. By 1907, Americans took a *flop* (*flophouse* had been common since the 1890s) and hoboes *pounded their ear* (1896). By 1915 we talked of getting some *shut-eye*, while World War I soldiers talked of *bunk duty* or *bunk fatigue*. By 1925 sailors *caulked off*, and in 1930 soldiers had *blanket drill*, but in World War II servicemen spoke of time to *hit the sack*, *sack out*, or put in *sack duty*.

Good sleepers have been saying they *sleep like a top* since the 1690s, but this has nothing to do with a spinning top; it comes from the French *taupe*, mole, and means to sleep like a mole undisturbed in its hole. Since 1895 good sleepers have also been saying they *sleep like a log*, while those who snore have been said *to saw wood* (1894). The unlucky say they *didn't sleep a wink* all night, an expression used in England since the 14th century (*wink* is related to *wince* and *winch*, a quick dodge, a turn). *Insomnia* (Latin *in-*, no + *somnus*, sleep) has been in the language since the 1750s, with *sedative* appearing in the 1790s; before that, people took *sleeping draughts*, and since the 1940s we've been taking *sleeping pills*. It wasn't until the 1880s that people commonly said they *tossed and turned all night*. The Roman god of sleep was called Somnus and his son was Morpheus, god of dreams, who appeared to people in their sleep—which gives us the expression *in the arms of Morpheus* and the drug name *morphine*.

Hit the sack *is an early 1940s term, which the couple in this 1957 ad would obviously never use.*

Big Shot, Big Deal, Big Mouth, Etc.

Big has meant important, fine, in America since the 1820s. An important person has been called a:

big bug, 1827.
big dog, big gun, big fish, big wig, early 1830s.
big man, 1855. The student term *big man on campus*, abbreviated to *BMOC*, appeared in the 1920s.
big toad in the puddle, 1877.
big cheese, 1890.
big noise, 1902.
big shot, 1910.
biggie, 1931.
big chief, 1934.
big wheel, 1941.
Mr. Big, early 1950s, originally as a leader of the underworld.

Incidentally, another American term for a big shot is a *high muck-a-muck* or *high muckety muck*. This comes from the Chinook jargon of the Pacific Northwest, *hiu* or *hiou* meaning plenty, a lot, and *muckamuck* meaning food, to eat or drink, hence the term literally means "plenty to eat." Thus a store selling food advertised in the Portland *Oregonian* in 1853 "Hiou Muckamuck [lots of food] of all kinds but Halo Lum [no rum]." Since important people ate well or saw that others did, *high muck-a-muck* was a term for a political party leader by 1856 and meant any important or pompous person by 1905.

Other terms in which "big" means important include:

big name, a celebrity, 1940.
big deal, 1940s.

Of course, *big* refers to size literally or figuratively in such terms as *big as all outdoors*, 1830s (*large as life and twice as natural* is also an 1830s expression); *great big*, 1837; *to have a big head* (swollen with conceit), 1850; *big-hearted*, generous, 1901; *big business*, early 1900s; and *big mouth*, one who talks a lot, a boaster, 1902, based on *to talk big*, to boast, brag, 1833, and *big talk*, boasting, bragging, 1874. *Big Brother* has meant omnipresent totalitarian authority or a dictator ever since George Orwell's 1949 novel *1984*, in which *Big Brother* was a Stalin-like figure watching everyone all the time via television, with the slogan "Big Brother is watching you."

Is It a Biscuit or a Cracker?

Biscuit (Latin *bis*, twice + *coctus*, cooked) still means a crisp, flat cracker or cookie in Britain. By 1818 however, *biscuit* had come to mean a softer, raised breadstuff in America; as Noah Webster noted, American biscuits were

Though biscuit *has usually meant a soft raised breadstuff in American speech since 1818, manufacturers tend to use the word in its older British sense to mean a variety of crisp flat cookies and wafers.*

"fermented" (leavened). During the first part of the 19th century, too, we began to speak of *baking-soda biscuits* or *soda biscuits*, with *beaten biscuits* not becoming common until the 1870s. *Biscuit shooter* was a facetious term for a waitress or cook from about 1890 to 1925.

Crackers (Dutch *krakelin*), as we know them, were called *soda crackers* in the U.S. by 1830. The National Biscuit Company is known for its crackers, not biscuits, but covers all American and British uses of the word *biscuit* by saying its trademark *Nabisco* (since 1901, an acronym for *Na*tional *Bis*cuit *Co*mpany) may be used on "biscuits, crackers, bread, wafers, sugar wafers . . . ," etc. It also owns the earlier 1898 trademark *Uneeda*, popularized by the punning slogan "Uneeda biscuit," which was also a cracker.

The *graham cracker* (1820s) is made from *graham flour* (1830s), named for Sylvester Graham (see BREAKFAST FOOD), who popularized this coarsely ground whole wheat flour as an aid to digestion, which is why *graham crackers* are still called *digestive biscuits* in Britain. The small, round *oyster cracker* was a latecomer, dating from 1873.

In older times soda crackers were sold by the handful from large cracker barrels in general stores, and legend has it that local politicians and wiseacres sat around them philosophizing, hence wise and witty rustics are called *cracker-barrel philosophers*, though the term didn't commonly appear until the 1930s.

Bitching, Jiving, and Dishing the Dirt

We have a lot of words for talk and talkers. Many of these words seem to fall into four general categories: gossip and idle talk; complaining, criticizing, and scolding; bragging, exaggerating, flattering, kidding, and lying; and revealing secrets.

Gossip and Idle Talk

babble has been used as a verb in English since the year 1230 and as a noun since 1460, originally referring to inarticulate sounds such as a baby makes (which is what the word *babble* was created to represent). Then, by 1510, it came to mean chatter. *Bibble babble*, 1539, empty talk. In fact there are quite a few words on this list which grew out of the sounds of people talking and also several reduplications, as *bibble babble*, *chitchat*, and *tittle tattle*, which nicely represent the sound of babbling talk.

beat (one's) *gums*, to talk idly, 1944.

bend (someone's) *ear*, to gossip or chat at great length, 1944.

blah, idle or silly talk, 1810.

blatherskite, *blatherskate*, an overly talkative man. This is a 16th-century Scottish word (from the Scottish *blather*, to babble, talk nonsense + *skate*, contemptuous man) that became common in America during the Revolutionary War because it occurs in the Scottish song *Maggie Lauder*, which was a favorite Continental Army camp song.

bull session, an informal talkfest and gossiping session among men, 1924, from the 1850s *bull* for *bullshit*, lies, exaggerated talk.

catty, spiteful, said of gossip or a gossiping woman, in English since 1885. *Cat* has meant a spiteful gossip since 1763 in English, to which we added the synonym *tabby* around 1840.

chat has been a verb in English since about 1440 and a noun since 1530 (like *babble* it is imitative of the sound). *Chitchat* dates from 1710, *chatter* from around 1800, and *chatterbox* from 1814, all first used in England.

chew the rag, an American expression of 1885, perhaps from the 18th-century English *to rag*, scold, from *bullyrag* (see below under Complaining, Criticizing, and Scolding). English also had the 16th-century *chew* (one's) *cud*, to ruminate, discuss a matter, and the 17th-century *chew* (one's) *words*, while we have added the terms *chew the fat*, gossip, chat, 1910, and *chew* (someone's) *ear off*, talk at length, 1919.

chin music, idle chatter, 1836; *to chin*, to converse, chatter, 1876; *chin-chin*, 1877, and a *chin*, 1893, both meaning a chat; *chin wag*, to gossip, 1934.

clack, idle chatter, 1833.

confabulation (from the Late Latin *confabulātiōn*, conversation; *con-*, with + *fabulari/fabula*, talk, story) was first recorded in English in 1410. By 1630 it gave us *confabulate*, to converse, to chat; and by 1741 *confab*, a talk, a conference.

dirt, gossip, early 1920s; *to dish the dirt*, to gossip, exchange gossip, 1926.

gab, an Old Norse word that entered English in the 13th century, originally meaning derision, boasting, or lying, before coming to mean idle chatter or talk in the late 1780s. *Gabby*, a foolish talker, fool, 1791 in England, but meaning talkative in the U.S. by 1899. *The gift of gab* is a 1681 English term, meaning the gift of flowery, persuasive talk and was common before the legend of the Blarney Stone became widely known (see *blarney* below).

gabfest, 1897. Our *-fest* words, such as *beerfest*, *funfest*, etc., come from the German suffix *-fest*, meaning festival; its popularity in America stems from the annual *Turner fest*, first held in 1856, of the German-American Turners men's societies. This *-fest* and the popularity of *gabfest* have also given us *talkfest*, 1910; *blabfest*, 1911; *jawfest*, 1914; *bullfest*, 1927; *chatfest*, 1934; *chinfest*, 1940; and *henfest*, 1942.

gas, has referred to idle talk in America since 1847, both as a noun and a verb; *gassy*, talkative, 1857; *gasbag* (based on *windbag*), idle talker, one who talks at length, boaster, 1873.

gossip is the Old English word *godsibb*, "god kinsman," which meant a baptismal sponsor, or godparent, when first recorded in the year 1014. By 1362 it meant any close family acquaintance or friend, such as might be a godparent; then, by 1566, one who knows and spreads personal news and secrets, as a close family acquaintance or friend might do. Thus, in a little over 500 years, the word's meaning changed from "godparent" to "an intimate" to "a spreader of intimate news." By 1811 *gossip* also meant the

The Gossips, *a watercolor rendering from the nineteenth century by Carmel Wilson.*

news or intimate talk itself. The verb *to gossip* had the same general history and changes in meaning as the noun, coming to denote talk of personal or secret things by 1611.

grapevine appeared in 1863 as meaning a Civil War rumor or unsubstantiated bit of news, sometimes being shortened to *grape* by 1864. Such news came by the *grapevine telegraph*, any surreptitious means of transmitting information so it wouldn't be intercepted, as between army units, between a soldier and his family back home, or between prisoners of war in a military prison, and stems from the construction of makeshift secret telegraph lines by army units to contact their headquarters, such lines looking like, or perhaps disguised as, vines (however the first such makeshift *grapevine telegraph* given that name is said to have been constructed before the war, in 1859, between Placerville and Virginia City, Nevada, to relay news about the Comstock Lode).

gush, to talk incessantly or sentimentally, 1860s, the term also used as a noun by 1866; *gushy*, 1889.

hen party, an informal talkfest and gossiping session among women, 1887 (*hen* has been a slang term for a woman in English since 1626).

jabber (also created to represent the sound of talking) was first recorded as a verb in England in 1499 and as a noun in 1727.

jaw has been used in English as a noun to mean talk since 1741 and as a verb since 1831, though for the first few years both this noun and verb referred to scolding and impudent talk. *Jawsmith*, a talkative person, especially a flowery or long-winded orator, is an American term of the 1860s.

kick around, discuss, talk about (something), 1947.

let (one's) *hair down*, speak plainly, gossip without reserve (said of women), 1941.

long-winded, an English term dating back to 1589.

mouthy, talkative, often with the connotation of being boastful, an English use of 1589.

palaver (via the Portuguese *palavra*, word, from the Spanish *palabra*), to talk or converse, 1733, a conversation or discussion, 1735. Seventeenth- and 18th-century Portuguese traders along the east African coast used their word *palavra* to refer to their meetings and talks with African tribesmen, mainly talks about buying goods and slaves. English traders and sailors picked up the word in Africa and brought it back to England as *palaver*. It has retained something of its original connotation of talking with someone who does not truly speak one's language or who may not understand fully.

parley (from Middle French *parle/parler*, to speak, which ultimately is from the Late Latin *parabola*, speech, parable) was first recorded in English as a verb in 1377, the noun not being recorded until 1575. It was usually spelled the French way, *parle*, until the end of the 16th century.

pass the time of day, chat, exchange pleasantries, 1836.

powwow (from the Algonquian *powwow* or *powah*, medicine man, sorcerer, from a root word meaning "he dreams") was used by colonists as early as 1624 with the original Indian meaning of "medicine man" but was also used as meaning a medicine man's or Indian conjuring ceremony or council meeting in 1625, obtaining its modern meaning of any conference by 1812. We tried to spell Indian words as they sounded, but there was no agreement; thus this word was spelled in many ways, including *pouwau*, *powah*, *powaw*, and *powwow*, with the last generally becoming the accepted one around 1850.

rattletrap, the mouth, in English use since 1824, then came to mean a talkative person by 1880 (in America *rattletrap* also meant a cheap or old car by 1915); *rattle away*, talk incessantly, keep talking, an American expression since 1914. *Rattle off* has meant to recite or repeat easily since 1884 (*reel off* has meant this since 1840).

schmooz(e), *schmoos*, to talk, gossip, used in American English since the early 1940s (via Yiddish *shmues* from Hebrew *shemu'oth*, things heard, gossip, idle talk).

spiel (from German *spielen*, to play a musical instrument) has meant a sales talk, "line," or any persuasive or colorful speech since the 1880s, originally by a huckster, sideshow barker, or the like (*barker* has meant any loud troublemaker in English since 1483 and one who stands at the entrance of a store, auction room, circus side show, etc., calling people to come in, since 1822).

spinner of street yarns, a gossip, 1816. *To spin a yarn* or *yarning* was originally English sailors' and fishermen's slang of around 1800 because they told such long, often incredible, tales while working on their nets and ropes. Until the 1890s, *yarn*, meaning a story, appeared only in the expression *to spin a yarn*. *Yarn* was first recorded as being used independently in 1897.

spout, to make a speech, brag, talk a lot, was in English use by 1756; we added *to spout off* in 1941.

talk (someone's) *arm off*, 1833; *talk* (someone's) *head off*, 1883; *talk*

TATTLE TALE
We know you carry tales to teacher.
All the whole long day.
And you make faces at her.
When she turns the other way.

(someone) *blind*, 1887; *talk the hind legs off a brass monkey*, 1927; *talk (someone's) leg off*, 1932; *talk a blue streak*, 1933; *talk the hind legs off a donkey*, 1942. *Talky talk*, excessive and trivial talk, 1902. *Talk shop*, to talk about business or one's work, 1854.

tattle was first recorded as a verb in English in 1481, then as a noun in 1529, both referring to chatter, babble, gossip; *tittle tattle*, 1583. *Tattler* appeared in 1550, as one who chatters or carries stories, and Richard Steele's famous periodical *The Tatler*, with contributions from Joseph Addison, Swift, and others, existed from 1709–11 (when it was succeeded by Addison and Steele's *The Spectator*). The English called one who was full of tattle or gossip a *tattle basket*, 1736, but we have called such a person and one who spreads secrets a *tattletale* since 1888.

twaddle was first recorded in English in 1550 and *twiddle twaddle* in 1573.

windy meant wordy, bombastic, in English by 1382, then being a new synonym for *wordy*, which had been in the language since the year 1100. *Windbag* originally meant a bellows, 1470, then came to mean a talkative person by 1820.

yack has meant a snapping sound in English since 1861 (the word created to imitate the sound), then was first used ten years later as a verb to mean to talk about. By the late 1940s *yack* also meant the sound of someone laughing, a laugh or joke, in the U.S., and by the early 1950s *yackety yack* meant both laughter and incessant talk.

yammer meant a crying out, as of birds, or a yell in English by 1320 and talk by 1792.

yap in 17th-century England meant both a barking dog and to bark or yelp; in modern slang use it was first recorded as a noun, meaning the mouth, and as a verb, meaning to talk, in 1900.

yenta, yente, a gossip, a constantly talking or scolding woman, came into American English around the mid 1960s, from the Yiddish (it may have been taken into Yiddish from the Italian *gentile*, French *gentille*, lady).

Complaining, Criticizing, and Scolding

backbiting, criticism of or gossip about people behind their backs was in the English language by 1175. The verb *to backbite* was first recorded in 1578.

bad mouth, to speak badly of, criticize, insult, was originally a black English expression going back at least to the 1930s. Though it spread from the southern U.S., it might have come to us from the British West Indies. Its opposite is to *sweet mouth*, to flatter, compliment, cajole.

ballyrag, bullyrag, to intimidate with abusive language, tease harshly, has been in English since 1807. It doesn't seem to be related to the word *bully* because the form *ballyrag* is too common and might have come first; otherwise one would assume it literally meant to bully people by *ragging* or scolding them (see *rag* below).

bawl out, to reprimand, 1907, probably a variant of the 1597 English to *shout out*, also meaning to reprimand.

beef, to complain, 1880; used as a noun, a complaint, since 1942.

bellyache, to complain, 1881 (it has meant colic in English since 1552).

bitch, to complain, late 1920s. *Bitch*, originally spelled *bicce* in Old English, has meant a female dog since before the 10th century and an immoral woman since the 15th. By 1675, *to bitch*, in England, meant to call someone a *bitch*, to curse someone, which may have given us the modern use of *bitch* meaning to complain.

bite/snap/take (someone's) *head off*, to rebuke severely, late 1920s. *Call down* has meant to reprimand in English since 1551, with a *call-down* and *calling down* meaning a reprimand or scolding since around 1900. *Call on the carpet* or *mat*, to reprimand, to call to account, late 1930s.

call (someone) *names*, to curse (someone), has been in English since 1594.

catch it, be reprimanded or scolded, 1830s; *get it*, 1867. These were probably euphemisms for *catch hell* and *get hell*, though *catch hell* wasn't recorded until 1929.

crab, to complain, an English slang use of 1812.

cussing, a scolding, 1870; *to cuss* (someone) *out*, 1880.

cutting remark, a rebuke or criticism, 1916. Such a remark is sometimes accompanied by a reproving glance or stare, called a *dirty look* since 1928.

dig, an insulting or critical remark, 1904; *dirty dig*, 1924; *dirty crack*, 1928.

the (dirty) dozens, a stream of insulting words or curses, 1960s, from the black verbal insult game in which abusive, rhyming terms are chanted, the chanting or cursing also called *joining* and *sounding*.

dressing down, a scolding, 1889, from the earlier *dressing out*, 1850, from the still earlier and English *dressing*, which meant a scolding by 1769.

get (or *come*) *down to cases*, get to the point, get down to the essential problem or criticism, 1866. *Get down to the nitty-gritty*, to get down to the hard facts or hard bargaining, 1963, when it was first popularized by black militants in the Civil Rights movement (it may have originally referred to the gritlike nits or small lice that are hard to get out of one's hair and scalp or to a black English term for the anus); it means the same as the English *to get down to brass tacks*, common only since 1900 but said to refer to the brass tacks used to install draperies, so that "Let's get down to brass tacks" originally meant that a selection had been made at the drapers and it was time to discuss price.

get it in the neck, to be rebuked or scolded, 1887; *have* (someone's) *neck*, to rebuke or scold severely, punish, 1934; *stick* (one's) *neck out*, lay oneself open to criticism or blame, 1940 (as if one's neck were on the chopping block).

get (one's) *comeuppance*, get a well-deserved rebuke or rebuff, 1869.

give (someone) *fits*, to scold or criticize severely, 1844.

give (someone) *hell*, upbraid, 1918; *give* (someone) *the devil*, 1919. To give someone hell meant that someone had to *catch hell* (see *catch it* above).

a going-over, a scolding, series of reprimands, 1884.

gripe, to complain, 1932 (it had meant to annoy since 1905); a complaint, 1934.

grouse, to complain; *grousing*, complaining, both originally British army slang of the mid-19th century.

grumble meant to complain in English by 1586 and a complaint by 1623; *grumbling* appeared around 1600.

in for it, due for a scolding or punishment, 1835.

in the soup, due for a scolding or punishment, in trouble, 1889.

jump on (someone), to berate, 1868; *jump down* (someone's) *neck*, 1888; *jump down* (someone's) *throat*, 1942.

kick, a complaint, 1839; to complain, 1870s. This may come from the 1833 English *kick up a bobbery* (*bobbery* was an Anglo-Indian term meaning a noisy disturbance or row, from the Hindi *Bāp re*, O father, O God, an exclamation of grief or surprise) or the 1836 *kick up a rumpus* (*rumpus* had meant a disturbance or uproar in English since 1764).

knock, to disparage, criticize, 1896; a disparaging remark, 1905. *Knocker*, a chronic fault finder, 1899 (*knockers* was not a common slang term for the female breasts until World War II).

lace into, scold severely, 1923. The expression had meant to beat or thrash in English since 1599: many of our terms meaning to scold severely originally meant to beat or thrash, showing that words can be used to punish and can have the force of blows, that a scolding or reprimand is often a civilized form of a beating.

lambaste and its shortened form, *baste*, to scold severely, both first recorded in 1835; *lambasting*, a severe scolding, 1846 (originally, in 1637 England, *lambaste* meant to beat or thrash, apparently from *lam*, to strike, thrash, akin to Old Norse *lenja*, to thrash + *baste*, also meaning to beat, thrash).

lathering, a scolding, 1839, which also earlier meant a beating.

lay into, to scold, 1942.

lip, impudence, since the 1820s, especially in *to give* (someone) *lip*, 1821, and *none of your lip*, 1884, meaning "don't be impudent with me."

make it hot for, make things unpleasant for by scolding, 1879 (the hotness is probably from embarrassment or anger but could be from hell; see *give* (someone) *hell*).

needle originally meant to haggle in 1812; then by 1881 it came to mean to make a minor criticism, complaint, or disparaging remark (as a buyer might have done about an item for sale in order to get the seller to lower the price). *Give the needle*, make critical or teasing remarks, 1889; *needler*, 1947; *needling*, 1949.

pick on, find fault with, criticize, 1890, probably related to the 1839 *pick-up on*, to notice and criticize.

pin the blame (or *fault*) *on*, to accuse, blame, 1924, from the 1626 English *to pin an error* (or *mistake*) *on*.

pitch into, scold or criticize severely, in English use since 1839.

pooh-pooh, to denigrate mildly, used in English since 1839, from the exclamation *pooh-pooh*, which was an 1814 reduplication of the 1602 *pooh*. In like manner, *tut tut* appeared in 1905 as a reduplication of the 1529 *tut* (representing the palatal click, sometimes represented in writing by *tsk*, or *tisk-tisk*).

put down, to rebuke, especially so as to lower the esteem of, was a fad expression of the 1960s and considered by many to be black slang but actually was first recorded in English use around 1400. The noun *put down*, a deflating rebuke, does, however, seem to be a new use of the 1960s.

put it to (someone), scold or rebuke severely, 1835.

put (someone) *in* (his or her) *place*, to rebuke by reminding him or her of one's true position, late 1920s. Though the construction is quite different, this is similar to *put down* (see above).

rag, to scold, tease, English use since 1796; we have used *ragging* to mean a scolding, teasing, since 1930.

raise Cain, to complain, especially loudly or emotionally, 1840.

rake over the coals, reprimand or scold severely, 1839; *haul over the coals,* 1880.

rap appeared in English as a noun around 1350, to mean a blow, originally a severe one, as with a sword or cudgel, and in 1377 as a verb, meaning to strike a severe blow. By 1530 *to rap* no longer meant to strike a severe blow but to strike smartly without any intent of causing serious hurt, the expression *to rap* (someone's) *knuckles* appearing in 1678. By 1733 *to rap* also had come to mean to make a formal complaint or to testify against someone, as in court, and by the late 1770s in American slang meant a prison term, blame, or a rebuke (*to beat the rap* and *to take the rap* have meant to be judged innocent or to be judged guilty of a criminal complaint, to escape or to accept blame, since the 1880s). To *rap* has meant to rebuke, criticize, since 1906; *put in a rap,* criticize, appeared in 1923.

During the Civil Rights movement of the 1960s *to rap* was used by blacks to mean to criticize whites or to demand black rights, then was widely used to mean to discuss, talk, by 1966, especially to discuss grievances or vent personal feelings (as at a *rap session*); but by the early 70s *rap* had lost many of these connotations and was merely being used to mean to chat, gossip.

ride, to harass or tease with frequent criticism, ridicule, etc., 1918; *riding,* 1936.

roast, to criticize sarcastically, has been in English use since 1726, with the noun, meaning heckling, bantering, first recorded in 1740. By the 1750s in England a *roast* was also a formal or informal gathering at which someone was *roasted,* criticized or made the butt of good-natured ridicule (this butt, or guest of honor, was also often left with the bill, having "to pay for his own roast," "roast" referring to both the criticism and the roast beef or other roast served).

row up, to scold, 1845.

rub it in, remind a person of mistakes or shortcomings, 1870.

run down, to disparage, belittle, 1855. *Bring-down,* a disparaging, belittling, or critical remark, late 1960s.

sauce and *saucy* have referred to impudence and impudent people in English since the first half of the 16th century; *saucebox,* an impudent person, 1588; *to sauce,* speak impertinently to, 1860. By the 1830s in America the dialect pronunciation "sass" was widely known and we had *sass* and *sassy,* referring to impertinent talk, with the verb *to sass* first recorded in 1871, which is the same year our *sassbox,* impertinent person, was recorded.

scorcher, a stinging rebuke, 1842 (*scorcher* has also been used since 1874 to mean a very hot day).

score, to scold severely, 1812 (from the 15th-century meaning of to mark with incisions).

shoot down, to reject with criticism or a rebuff, 1960s (from the image of shooting down an enemy warplane).

sit on, to rebuff, rebuke, as if to prevent one from being obstreperous, 1864: *sit down on,* 1887.

I scorn to rap against a lady.
—Henry Fielding, *Amelia,* 1752

slam, a stinging rebuke or remark, 1884.

sound off, express one's grievances or complaints plainly, 1936 (perhaps from or reinforced by the military command *Sound off!*, for troops to shout out in unison while marching in cadence, to call out one's name at roll call, etc.).

squawk, to complain, 1899.

squelcher, a humiliating remark, sharp criticism that settles the matter, in English use since 1866 (a squelcher was also called a *crusher* by 1887); *to squelch*, reject or humiliate with a criticism, 1893.

take it, to be able to stand up to criticism, 1920. Since 1909 to *take it lying down* has meant to take criticism, a scolding, rebuff, etc., submissively.

take it out on (someone), vent one's anger or frustrations on, blame, 1903.

take the wind out of (someone's) *sails*, to humble or check with a critical or belittling remark, 1901.

talk back, to answer a criticism or rebuff insolently or sharply, 1869, which seems to have appeared about ten years after the British noun *backtalk*.

a (good) talking to, a reprimand, warning, or stern advice, 1878.

talk out of turn, criticize when one has no right to, overstep the proper bounds of conversation considering one's position, say something insolent, 1934.

tell (someone) *where to get off*, to express anger at, rebuke strongly, 1902; *tell off*, 1919.

tongue-lashing, a scolding, 1886.

wig has meant a rebuke in English since 1804 and to scold, reprimand, since 1829; *wigging*, 1830. It's from *earwig*, to pester, insinuate, try to influence with words, from the *earwig* insect (first recorded in English around the year 1000), which was thought to enter the head through the ear.

yawp meant to shout harshly in 13th-century England and a harsh cry by 1824, then came to mean criticism by 1835 and to talk loudly or angrily by 1872.

yip meant to chirp in England in 1440, then to complain by 1910.

you should talk, a sarcastic reply to criticism or a rebuke, meaning "you're just as bad," 1931.

Though none of us likes to be criticized, rebuked, or scolded, a person who is willing to *speak* (one's) *mind* (an 1825 English expression) or *talk up* (1901) is usually admired more than one who speaks too mildly or equivocates. For such people and their words we have such condemning terms and expressions as:

beat around the bush, 1850, from the mid-16th-century English *beat about the bush*, to do something deviously or move surreptitiously.

hem and haw, 1899. This expression started out in England around 1530 as *to hum and ha* (to make the sound of "hum" or "ha" because one couldn't make a decision), which became *hum and haw* by 1749. Meantime, the 14th-century English word *to hem*, clear one's throat (as by saying "hem" or "ahem"), was used in the expression *to hem and hawk* by 1580, meaning to clear one's throat, as if to stall for time while one made up one's mind, or to express concern, disapproval, or a warning to say no more. These two closely related expressions *hum and haw* and *hem and hawk* began to be confused and melded together during the 1830s, finally resulting in *hem and haw*.

mealy-mouthed, a 1572 English expression.

pussyfoot is an American term first recorded in 1893, then meaning to have a soft tread, to walk softly; it then quickly came to mean to be lacking in forcefulness or assertion, coming to mean to hedge by 1903. *Pussyfooter*, 1934.

weasel word, a word that is purposely confusing or contradictory in context so that the speaker or writer, especially a politician, can *weasel out* (1925) of what he has said. Both terms refer to the weasel's agility, especially in sneaking through small openings. *Double talk*, purposely confusing talk, talk full of weasel words, 1943.

whiffling. To *whiffle* was first recorded in English in 1560, then referring only to the wind and meaning to veer or shift direction. By the 18th century changeable or vacillating people were said *to whiffle like a weathervane* and, soon, merely *to whiffle*, which reappeared as the popular *to waffle* in the U.S. in the 1960s.

Bragging, Exaggerating, Flattering, Kidding, and Lying

blarney, flattery, cajolery, 1819 English use, from the famous Blarney Stone in the castle near the village of Blarney, near Cork, Ireland (kissing the stone is supposed to give one the "gift of gab").

blowhard, a braggart, 1840.

blow (one's) *own horn*, praise oneself, brag, 1859.

bull, lies, exaggeration, around 1850, a shortening of *bullshit*, which, because of its taboo nature, wasn't recorded until around 1880.

butter up, to flatter, cajole, 1939; by 1946 it also meant to bribe.

card, a teaser, joker, prankster, 1835.

chaff, to tease, banter, deceive, 1827.

chaw, tease, ridicule, 1842, from the 1563 British use of *chaw* meaning to mumble (chew or chaw one's words).

cheek, impertinence, impertinent talk, an English use of 1848, with *cheeky* first recorded, in England, in 1857. *Face* has meant impertinence in English since 1607.

crap, nonsense, lies, exaggeration, 1918; *crap artist*, one known for exaggerating, lying, bragging, etc., 1934; *crappy*, mean, overly critical, 1942, as in "that's a crappy thing to say." (See GREAT, AWFUL, AND WOW! for the history of the word *crap*.)

crate, talk bombastically, orate, 1864.

gag, to hoax, lie, English use of 1777. The noun use was first recorded in America in 1805 (perhaps from thrusting one's words down the throat of a person credulous enough to "swallow" them). By 1863 *gag* also meant a joke.

get funny, to be impertinent, be too familiar, 1895. We have also called impertinence being *flip* (1847), having a lot of *gall* (1882), a lot of *nerve* (1891, *nervy* dates from 1896), or a lot of *crust* (1900).

give (or *hand* someone) *a line*, to use deceptive talk to curry favor, create a good impression, etc., 1902; to use deceptive or flattering talk to win a woman's sexual favors, 1924 (this could be from the 1882 *lines* as meaning the words of an actor's part or from the image of a fishing line used to "catch" fish).

have the laugh on, ridicule, tease, 1885; *give the laugh to*, 1895.

honeyfogle, honeyfug(g)le, to cheat, deceive, 1829; then to flatter, cajole, especially in order to gain a woman's favors; 1858. *Honeyfogle* and *hornswoggle* were both first recorded in 1829 as Kentucky words and could be forms of the same fanciful coinage. A separate but seemingly related word is the English dialect *caniffle* (1746), which became *cunniffle* (1790) and finally *connyfogle* (1890), also meaning to deceive, flatter, cajole, the change from *cani-* to *cunni-* occurring after *cunny* entered English in 1720 as a slang diminutive for *cunt*, the word *cunniffle* then taking on the added meaning of cajolery to win sexual favors.

hot air, boasting, exaggeration, 1873.

jazz, lies, exaggeration, cajolery, 1918; *jive*, with the same meaning, about 1921. The word *jazz* was first recorded in New Orleans in the 1870s both as a verb, meaning to become faster, more exciting, or frenetic, and as a noun, referring to a form of syncopated music; by 1913 it generally meant a style of ragtime (the word seems to be of West African or Creole origin, though no root form or cognate has been found).

Jive seems to have appeared in Chicago around 1921 as a black term for lies, exaggeration, or cajolery (no one knows where the word came from; it could have been a pronunciation of *jibe*). In 1928 two jazz records appeared using *jive* in their titles, Cow Cow Davenport's *State Street Jive* and Louis Armstrong's *Don't Jive Me*, the word *jive* then slowly becoming associated with such music and meaning swing music by 1937. Thus, jazz music came before jazz talk, but jive talk came before and helped name jive music.

joke in its standard meaning was in British use both as a verb and noun by 1670; we began to use it to mean to tease, make fun of, around 1881.

jolly, to kid, tease, was originally 1873 British use.

josh, to kid, tease, is an Americanism of 1845; *josher*, 1899.

kid meant to hoax in English by 1811 and a hoax or instance of joshing by 1873, with *kidder* appearing in 1896. To *kid* (oneself), lie to oneself, not face the facts, 1860; to *kid along*, an American expression of 1920. The use comes from *kid* meaning both child and young goat, hence to kid someone figuratively means either to make a child or a "goat" of that person.

latrine rumor, a soldier's rumor, army gossip, as spread by soldiers in the latrine, World War I use (see also *scuttlebutt* below).

lay it on thick, to exaggerate, flatter, 1839.

lie like a trooper (a soldier) 1885; *lie like a Spaniard*, 1899, from Spanish-American War use; *lie like a rug*, a 1942 pun.

mush, exaggerated, sentimental talk, especially of love, 1908 (*mushy* had meant sentimental, insipid, since 1839).

oil, flattery, 1919 (*oily* had meant crafty, sly, since 1879).

play up to, to cajole, humor, 1828.

poke fun at, tease, ridicule, 1835.

pull the long bow, exaggerate, lie, stretch the truth, 1833; *draw the long bow*, 1860; *draw it strong*, early 1870s.

pull (someone's) *leg*, hoax, tease, 1888.

rib, a hoax, joke, 1929; *ribber*, 1942; *ribbing*, 1944.

salve, flattery, 1859; to flatter, cajole, 1909.

scuttlebutt, sailor's rumor, navy gossip, as spread by sailors around the water bucket, 1935. When originally recorded in 1840, a *scuttlebutt* was a *butt* or cask of water with a small *scuttle* or opening for dipping out the contents; since sailors gathered around this scuttlebutt to get a drink of water and chat, the word eventually took on its modern meaning, the same as the office and factory workers' *water cooler talk*, 1940s.

shit, nonsense, lies, exaggeration, in wide use since the 1870s, probably first common among Civil War soldiers (perhaps as a shortening of *bullshit*; see *bull* above). *Chicken shit* and *horseshit*, both meaning lies, exaggeration, were first recorded in the 1930s.

snow, to lie, exaggerate, especially to curry favor or make a good impression, 1944; *snow job*, 1946. The image is of trying to "snow under" a new acquaintance with a blizzard of lies about one's past, experience, etc.

soft soap, flattery, cajolery, 1830; to flatter, to cajole, 1840; *soap*, flattery, 1891.

(soft) solder (or *sawdor* or *sodder*), to flatter, 1834; flattery, 1836, both originally English use and based on the image of making something seem better than it is by using soft solder.

spoof was first recorded in 1895 both as a noun and a verb to mean a hoax, to hoax, kidding. Though considered primarily American use, *spoof* goes back to a hoaxing game invented and named *Spoof* by the English comedian Arthur Roberts at the London Adelphi Club around 1889 and which was popular in English theatrical circles.

story has meant a lie in English since 1697 and *story teller* a liar since 1748. *Fish story* is an 1819 Americanism, referring to the stories fishermen tell of huge fish that got away. *Cock and bull story* is an English term of around 1620, originally referring to a long, rambling, tedious story or fable, there having apparently been such a story about a cock and a bull that everyone was tired of hearing by the first part of the 17th century. Not until about 1796 did *cock and bull story* come to mean an incredible story or lie.

stretch the truth, exaggerate, 1876. Though the image is apt by itself, it may be based on stretching the bow when one attempts to *pull the long bow* (see above).

string, to hoax, mislead, tease, 1848; *string along*, 1913. Again, though the image is apt by itself, this has overtones of the bowstring in the expression to *pull the long bow* (see above).

swallow it, believe a lie, exaggeration, flattery, or a hoax, 1836; *swallow it hook, line, and sinker*, 1838.

swap lies, to exaggerate to one another, to gossip or chat, 1835.

sweet talk, flattery, 1928, originally a southern expression.

taffy, flattery, "sweet talk" (from the candy), 1879.

talk big was an English expression of 1633 that became a popular American term around 1833 and gave us *big talk* (see BIG SHOT, BIG DEAL, BIG MOUTH, ETC.).

tease has been used as a verb in English since 1627, and as a noun meaning a hoax since 1693. The noun has also been used to mean one who teases habitually since 1853.

thumper, a big lie, in English use since 1677.

trade last, a compliment or opinion about oneself given or revealed in exchange or trade with another, 1896: for example, one girl might say to another, "If you tell me what you really think of my dress, I'll tell you what I think of yours," or, "If you'll tell me what Dan said about me, I'll tell you what Walter said about you"—the other girl then agreeing with, "All right, but you tell first and I'll *trade last*." *Trade*, a compliment, 1925; *T.L.*, a *trade last*, compliment, 1937.

whopper, a big lie, 1858.

wisecrack, originally meant an insulting or nasty remark in 1905, then a humorous or teasing one by the mid 1920s, which is when the verb forms *to wise crack*, and *to crack wise* appeared. The noun was shortened to *crack* by 1919. A person who makes such comments, trying to show he is wiser than others, has been called a *wisehead* in English since 1340 and a *wiseacre* since 1595 (from the Middle Dutch *wijessegger*, soothsayer).

Revealing Secrets

blab has meant a tattletale, a gossip, or an informer in English since 1374, loose talk or gossip itself, since 1400, and to talk too much, reveal secrets, since 1533. *Blabber* has meant to babble, chatter, since the late 14th century, and a person who babbles or talks too much, revealing secrets, since 1577; *blabber mouth* is an Americanism of 1925.

closed mouth, not revealing secrets, not talkative, 1872.

get (something) *off one's chest*, unburden oneself of hidden feelings, a secret or complaint, etc., 1916.

give away, to reveal, 1862; *a (dead) give away*, revelation of a secret, 1882; *give (out)*, reveal information, 1941. *Give* (someone) *the low down*, reveal the facts or confidential information, pass on the gossip, 1880.

hush (a vocalization of the sound *sh*) appeared as *husht* and *hust* around 1387 in English, by 1546 it was spelled *hush* and meant to silence, and by 1604 it was a command meaning to be silent. *Hush up* was first recorded in 1632.

in the know, knowing a secret or confidential information, 1883.

keep it dark, keep it secret, 1835, from the 1677 British *in the dark*, unknowing, not knowing a secret.

leak out, to become known, 1840; *leak*, an unofficial or improper disclosure of a military, government, or political secret, as by a spy to a foreign government or by a government official or politician to a reporter, 1955. *Plumber,* a member of the secret Special Investigation Unit Republican President Richard Nixon established in 1971 to stop or plug "leaks" he considered detrimental to the government or his administration.

let the cat out of the bag, disclose a secret inadvertently, in English use since 1760; *let out*, reveal, 1870.

loud mouth, one who can't keep secrets, one who talks constantly and without reserve, revealing secrets, personal facts, etc., 1942.

mum was used to represent an unarticulated sound, an "um" or "hum," in English by 1377; by 1399 it was a command to be silent, a way of saying "hush"; and by 1562 it meant refusal to speak. *Keep mum*, don't tell about it, keep quiet about it, 1855; *mum's the word*, 1856 (see B.O., ATHLETE'S FOOT, AND HALITOSIS for the advertising slogan *Mum's the word*).

on the Q.T. or *q.t.*, on the quiet, secretly; has been used in English since 1870, *q.t.*, of course, standing for *quiet* (*q.t.* may have been reinforced or suggested by *q.v.*, the abbreviation of the Latin *quantum vis*, "as much as you wish" and, more commonly, of *quod vidē*, "which see," used in formal writing).

open up, tell secrets, reveal one's innermost thoughts or feelings, 1921.

own, to admit, confess, 1845; *own up*, 1858.

put a bug (or *flea*) *in* (someone's) *ear*, *put a bug* (or *bee*) *in* (someone's) *bonnet*, to suggest, hint, reveal, around 1900. This seems to be a later version of to *earwig* (see *wig* above).

put (someone) *on to*, inform; acquaint with facts, insider's information, etc., 1895; *put next to*, 1896; *get next to*, become informed, 1900; *put wise*, 1901.

see through, be aware of another's motives or unstated goals, comprehend a secret through inference, 1872.

set (someone) *straight*, inform of the truth of a matter, 1925.

sh is a natural sound that probably goes back to prehistoric times. The combination *sh* didn't represent a single consonantal sound in written English until the 13th century and wasn't used in writing to stand for "hush" until the 1840s.

shoot off (one's) *mouth*, reveal secrets, say more than desired or intended, talk without reserve, 1864; *shoot off* (one's) *face*, 1927; *shoot the breeze*, chat, converse, 1941.

shutters up, an 1850s and 60s fad phrase meaning "Keep it secret; don't mention it to anyone."

slip, an inadvertent disclosure, 1919; *let* (something) *slip out*, reveal inadvertently, also 1919.

smarten up, to inform, become informed, 1930.

snitch, an informer, 1785; to inform, 1801, both then underworld use referring to informing on or giving evidence against one's confederates (perhaps a variant pronunciation of *snatch*); in general use to mean a tattletale by 1859, and to tattle, tell on, by 1891. *Snitch on* and *snitcher* were both also first recorded in 1891.

soft pedal, to say little about, deemphasize the importance of, 1919, from the 1902 expression *put on* (or *work*) *the soft pedal*.

spill the beans, 1919; *spill*, reveal, confess, 1925; *spill the works*, 1928.

spit out, to reveal, say, 1904.

squeal, inform, confess, 1821 in underworld use; *squealer*, informer, 1865.

steer, a hint, confidential suggestion, advice, 1894; *bum steer*, bad advice, 1914; *wrong steer*, 1925.

take it from me, "I'm going to enlighten you," "Believe what I'm about to say," 1908.

tattletale, see *tattle* under "Gossip and Idle Talk" above.

tell on, to inform on, 1900.

tip, to reveal, hint, 1890; *tip off*, to hint or reveal, 1893, a hint or revelation, 1901; *tip* (one's) *mitt*, 1902.

With all this talking, there have to be those who listen, who *hear tell* (a 13th-century English expression), *eavesdrop* (English use of 1606, literally to stand within the *eavesdrop* of a building, where water drops from the eaves; to listen through the wall or a window), *sit up and take notice* (1889), *get an earful* (1917), *give an ear* (1929), or are *all ears* (1938).

Some listeners may try to interrupt the speaker, *to put* or *stick in* (one's) *oar* (1734), *chime in* (1830s), *horn in* (1880), or *butt in* (1889). Other listeners will try to learn more secrets, to *worm out* (1827), *draw out* (1847), or *nose out* (1875) more confidential information, such a person being called a *Paul Pry* (1829, from the inquisitive lead character in John Poole's 1825 English comedy *Paul Pry*), a *snoop* (1832, *snoopy* appeared in 1921), or just plain *nosy* (1910), a *Nosy Parker* (1907, originally one who frequented London's Hyde Park for the vicarious thrill of spying on lovemaking couples, *parker* having meant a park keeper, keeper of game park grounds, in England since the 14th century), or *nosenheimer* (1931). If the listeners understand what they hear we say they *twig* (1815), *tumble* (1848), *savy* (1850, from Spanish *saber*, to know, understand), *catch on* (1883), *catch the drift* (1895), or *catch wise* (1934, a variant of the 1898 *get wise*). If we feel someone hears too much or is too interested in our business we can tell that person to go *hoe your own row* (1871), *tend to your own business* (1884), or *mind your own business* (1910), this last being abbreviated to *m.y.o.b.* by 1915 and with the variant *mind your own beeswax* in the early 1920s, both of which were considered very clever retorts by the flappers and sheiks of the Roaring Twenties.

Finally, if you're tired of agreeing with or indicating interest in what is being said, tired of responding with *you don't say so* (1842), *you said a mouthful* (1918), *you said something there* (also 1918), *you said it!* (1919), *you're telling me!* (1933), or *you can say that again* (1941), you can stop the talkers by saying *so what?* (1934) or by telling them to take the gossip, complaint, boast, or secret and go *shove it* or *stick it* (1952, as a short form and euphemism for *shove it/stick it up your ass*)—or perhaps it would be best to tell a speaker to Shut Your Fly Trap!

Are You Blue, All In, Jittery? English-speaking

people have said they were *downcast* (dejected, depressed, with spirits cast down) or *down* since the 14th century, *in the dumps* since the 1520s (in a state of sad reverie, depression, or perplexity, perhaps from Middle Dutch *domp*, haze, mist; *dump* didn't mean a place where refuse was dumped until 1784), *chopfallen* since 1602, *down in the mouth* since 1649, and *dished* since 1798 (used up, ruined, dejected, like food that has been cooked and dished out). Many Americans have said they wanted to *cry (their) eyes out* (1705) because they felt that others *treat (them) like a dog* (1838) or because they lead a *dog's life* (1906). They were *sick* (disgusted, 1853) or *sick and tired* (1855) or *fed up* (1899) with the way things were. So if you are *at the end of your rope* (1858) or *can't stand it* (1920), you are not alone, and never have been.

In America, people who have been sad, dejected, or despondent have been said to be or have:

> *the blahs*, late 1960s; *blah* has meant boring, dull, since 1928 and nonsense talk since 1810.
> *the blues*, 1807; *blue*, 1831. The earliest American term containing the word "blue" and meaning sad was the 1780 *to have the blue devils*. The more modern *in a blue funk*, 1895, originally meant to be frightened or confused.
> *droopy*, dejected, 1944.
> *get/have the hump*, be depressed, 1860.
> *get one down*, 1890s, literally get one "down in the dumps."
> *mope around*, be listless with dejection, 1902 (from the 1590 English verb *to mope*, be dejected, which may be related to the Dutch *moppen*, to pout, sulk).
> *sunk*, in despair, 1927.

Americans who have been tired, weary, or exhausted, physically or mentally, with work or worry, have been:

> *all in*, 1902.
> *beat*, 1834; *dead beat*, completely exhausted, 1855; *beat to the gills*, *beat to the ground*, both 1940s.
> *bushed*, 1870, probably from the earlier, 1856, use of *bushed* meaning lost in the bush, wandering aimlessly in the wilderness.
> *dogtired*, 1890.
> *fagged* or *fagged out*, often considered Americanisms but first recorded in England in 1780 and 1785 respectively, from the 1530 English verb *to fag*, to flag, droop, which may just be a corruption of *to flag*.
> *frazzled*, 1872; *worn to a frazzle*, 1894 (from the English dialect *frazzle*, to fray, wear to rags).
> *pooped*, 1880s; *pooped out*, 1934, from the nautical use of *pooped* in referring to a ship that was disabled or moving slowly because a following sea was coming over the stern or poop (*poop* is from Latin *puppis*, stern of a ship; it was also used in English to mean feces and to break wind by the 16th century and to mean buttocks in America around 1640).
> *run ragged*, exhausted from overwork or activity, 1918 (the image of *ragged* is the same as that of *frazzled*, see above, worn to rags, frayed).
> *tuckered out*, 1834 (from an Old English verb *to tuck*, meaning to torment).

Some Americans have been, like people everywhere, just plain confused or in a confused state of excitement. Like a pistol, they have tended *to go off half cocked* (1833); to them things seem as *clear as mud* (1839). They have been *in a fog* (1858), *rattled* (1869), *at sea* (1870) or *all at sea* (1890), *all of a dither* (1917, from the 1649 English verb *to dither/didder,* to tremble), and *in a tizzy* (1934, of unknown origin). Others have been *scared, scary* (frightened, 1827; the British had used the word only to mean frightening, never frightened), *scared out of* (one's) *boots* (1884), *scared stiff* (1900), *scared silly* (1905), *scared green* (1921), *scared blue* (1922), *scared pink* (1928), *scared hollow* (1934), or *scared shitless* (1947).

Worst of all is being both confused and frightened or of being nervous, even to the point of losing control of oneself, to be, have, or feel:

creepy, nervous, 1880 (the British first used it to mean a frightened feeling, a creeping of the flesh, in 1831); *the creeps,* nervousness and fear, 1898.

discombobulated, 1837 (based on "discomposed").

the fantods, a fit of nervousness or despondency, 1839 (the English dialect *fantique/fanteeg,* with the same meaning, appeared in 1825 and the English *fantads/fantodds,* nervousness, stomach ache, the sulks, appeared in 1867; all three are probably related and seem to have been suggested by "fantastic" or "phantom," but no one knows the details of their origin).

the fidgets, 1873.

flip one's wig, lose control of oneself, 1942; *flip one's lid* and *flipped,* 1950s.

go off the deep end, crazed by fear, confusion, etc., 1918.

go to pieces, lose control of oneself, 1878.

the heebie jeebies, 1910, popularized and probably coined by cartoonist William de Beck in his comic strip *Barney Google.*

in a pucker, anxious, in a hurry, 1741.

in a stew, 1806.

the jimjams, 1852 (it originally meant delirium tremens, then came to mean any feeling of nervousness); the *jimmies,* 1900.

the jitters, 1925; *jittery,* 1931; *the jits,* 1935 (*jitter* is probably based on *chitter,* a variant of *chatter,* to shiver).

the jumps, 1881 (this had meant delirium tremens since 1879); *jumpy,* 1918.

the katzenjammers, 1849 (German for "cat's wailing," originally suggesting the howling or buzzing in one's ears as an effect of overdrinking; the splitting headache of a hangover).

keyed up, as a spring wound too tightly, 1904.

lose one's grip, lose one's self-control, composure, or effectiveness, as from nervousness, 1876.

the mulligrubs, a fit of nervousness or dejection, 1838 (from the 1599 English *mulligrums,* 1619 *mulligrubs,* a mythical disease or humor causing nervousness, dejection, etc., which seems to have been a nonsense word).

on edge, 1908, nervous and irritable; *edgy*, 1931.

on the anxious seat, 1839. From at least the 1820s the *anxious seat* or *anxious bench* was the front row set aside at a revival meeting for those anxious and eager to come to the pulpit to repent or be converted.

the shakes, 1850s, originally the trembling, chills, and fever of the ague. Since about 1880, it has also meant delirium tremens.

shot (to pieces), unnerved, 1908.

the willies, 1896 (of unknown origin); *the blue willies*, 1922.

worked up, nervous, excited, distraught, 1883.

For those who are blue, all in, confused, frightened, or jittery, we can only say *cheer up* (English use since 1597; in America we have added the cheerful, fearful, *cheer up, the worst is yet to come*, 1920), *chirk up* (1837, from the 1815 *chirk*, cheerful, lively from the 14th century *to chirk*, to chirp like a bird), *buck up* (1850s), *chipper up* (1873, from the 1837 *chipper*, lively, well)—or at least *get a grip on yourself* (1896), *pull yourself together* (1900), and *take it easy* (1927).

B.O., Athlete's Foot, and Halitosis

are unknown to most of the world outside the United States—not because other people don't suffer from them but because the terms have been coined or popularized here by advertising men. Since our 1840s patent medicine men (see IT PAYS TO ADVERTISE), American advertisers have used scare tactics to sell their wares. When there hasn't been a well-known disease their products could cure they have often invented one or made a merely socially embarrassing condition sound like a dread disease by giving it a name.

In 1895, C. W. Post introduced his all-grain brew Postum, claiming not only that it made "red blood' but that it cured *coffee nerves*, a malady then unknown both to doctors and to the general public, but which we have been aware of ever since. Thus the advertisement for the cure gave birth to the term, if not the ailment.

Dandruff (1545 in English, akin to Old Norse *hurf*, scab, scurf) and *psoriasis* (1684 in English from the Greek *psōriasis*, to have the itch) are old words and ailments that have been made part of the popular vocabulary by the advertising of preparations to cure them. *Ringworm* (an English word of about 1425) of the foot is also a real ailment though it was seldom mentioned until it was widely called *athlete's foot* (1928) when Absorbine Jr. first advertised itself as a remedy for it. More recently, a manufacturer of a preparation to relieve itching in the groin area has popularized the term *jock strap itch* (mid 1970s, soon shortened by the public to *jock itch*) for

The term athlete's foot *was popularized in 1928 when* Absorbine Jr. *advertised itself as a cure for it. Before that, the antiseptic preparation had been advertised only as giving relief from muscular aches, bruises, burns, cuts, sprains, and sunburn. This ad appeared in 1930.*

SHE MERELY CARRIED THE DAISY CHAIN ...YET SHE HAS

"ATHLETE'S FOOT!"

SO fragile, so freshly feminine, so altogether lovely—the very Spirit of Youth and daintiness to all who beheld her—

Yet even as she trod the velvety green of the campus, a tiny twinge reminded her of that slight rash-like redness that she had noticed lately between her smaller toes—noticed and *worried* about, for the persistent eruption seemed such a slander upon her daintiness.

She doesn't know it, of course, but her affliction is a most common form of ringworm infection, known to millions in America as *"Athlete's Foot"!*

Many Symptoms for the Same Disease — So Easily Tracked into the Home

"Athlete's Foot" may start in a number of different ways,* but it is now generally agreed that the germ, *tinea trichophyton,* is back of them all. It lurks where you would least expect it—in the very places where people go for health and recreation and cleanliness. In spite of modern sanitation, the germ abounds on locker- and dressing-room floors—on the edges of swimming pools and showers—in gymnasiums—around bathing beaches and bath-houses—even on hotel bath-mats.

And from all these places it has been tracked into countless homes until today this ringworm infection is simply *everywhere.* The United States Public Health Service finds *"It is probable that at least one-half of all adults suffer from it at some time."* And authorities say that half the boys in high school are affected. There can be no doubt that the tiny germ, *tinea trichophyton,* has made itself a nuisance in America.

It Has Been Found That Absorbine Jr. Kills This Ringworm Germ

Now, a series of exhaustive laboratory tests with the antiseptic Absorbine Jr. has proved that Absorbine Jr. penetrates deeply into flesh-like tissues, and that wherever it penetrates it *kills* the ringworm germ.

It might not be a bad idea to examine *your* feet tonight for distress signals* that announce the beginning of "Athlete's Foot." *Don't be fooled by mild symptoms.* Don't let the disease become entrenched, for it is *persistent.* The person who is seriously afflicted with it today, may have had these same mild symptoms like yours only a very short time ago.

Watch out for redness, particularly between the smaller toes, with itching—or a moist, thick skin condition — or, again, a dryness with scales.

Read the symptoms printed at the left very carefully. At the first sign of *any one* of these distress signals* begin the free use of Absorbine Jr. on the affected areas—douse it on morning and night *and after every exposure of your bare feet to any damp or wet floors, even in your own bathroom.*

Absorbine Jr. is so widely known and used that you can get it at all drug stores. Price $1.25. For free sample write W. F. YOUNG, INC., 345 Lyman Street, Springfield, Mass.

*WATCH FOR THESE DISTRESS SIGNALS THAT WARN OF "ATHLETE'S FOOT"

Though "Athlete's Foot" is caused by the germ—*tinea trichophyton*—its early stages manifest themselves in several different ways, usually between the toes—sometimes by redness, sometimes by skin-cracks, often by tiny itching blisters. The skin may turn white, thick and moist, or it may develop dryness with little scales. *Any one of these calls for immediate treatment!* If the case appears aggravated and does not readily yield to Absorbine Jr., consult your physician without delay.

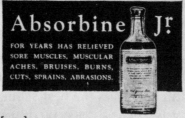

QUICK RELIEF FOR SUNBURN too! Absorbine Jr. soothes and cools; not greasy; won't stain; leaves a healthy tan

Absorbine Jr.

FOR YEARS HAS RELIEVED SORE MUSCLES, MUSCULAR ACHES, BRUISES, BURNS, CUTS, SPRAINS, ABRASIONS.

[1930]

this ailment which, now that it has a pithy, masculine name, is also talked about more than before.

Halitosis (an 1874 English word, from Latin *helitus*, breath, plus *-osis*, condition, especially a pathological condition) was a little-known medical word referring to specific breath odors that doctors could use to diagnose patients' diseases until Listerine mouthwash ads claimed it fought "insidious *halitosis*" and defined it as bad breath in general, beginning in 1921 (for the first ten years Listerine ads followed the word *halitosis* with the explanation "bad breath" or "unpleasant breath" in parentheses, knowing full well that most people had never heard of the word before).

The worst social offense, however, was not scratching one's head, elbows, feet, or groin, or even having bad breath, but underarm odor, caused by underarm perspiration—and this was indeed offensive and widespread before the routine daily shower and home washing machine. By clogging the pores, masking the odor, or combining with the perspiration, various preparations could eliminate this offense. Such preparations became available and were widely advertised in the 1920s, the advertisements then mainly being aimed at women, both because sleeveless dresses were the style, making the odor more obvious, and because many men thought their own odor was somehow manly. Thus as early as 1924 liquid Odorono was advertised as a "perspiration corrective"—for both the underarms and the feet—whose protection could last for days. Its ads popularized a blunt new term, saying that when Odorono was used under the arms it would prevent *underarm odor*. Similar liquids and creams joined the war against underarm odor and underarm perspiration stains on clothing so that during the 1930s both women and men were removing the underarm *shields* they had added to their dresses and suits to absorb perspiration and using an *underarm deodorant*, often a cream such as Mum, whose early advertising slogan was the punning *Mum's the word*. Not until the 1960s did manufacturers call the all-too-vivid yet somewhat passive sounding *underarm deodorant* by the more active, scientific sounding name *anti-perspirant*, and now that almost everyone took daily showers, deemphasized underarm odor in favor of emphasizing that the product stopped *wetness*, a new euphemism for underarm clothing stains.

The hallmark of scare ads against underarm and other body perspiration odors, however, was Lifebuoy Health Soap's campaign. In 1933, millions of Americans began to laugh at and use the abbreviation *B.O.* to mean *body odor*, as popularized by the advertising of this orange-colored, peculiar-smelling (the ads said it had a "crisp odor"), oddly shaped bathsoap. Soon the two-note foghorn warning $^B{}_O$ was known to everyone through radio ads—and Lifebuoy was the best-selling soap in America. By 1935, *body odor* was such an accepted term that Lux laundry soap was

Lifebuoy soap ad of 1947. Its B.O. *campaign was then in its fourteenth year, and the term* B.O. *was so common that the ad didn't even need to explain that it stood for "body odor."*

advertising that women should "Lux underthings after each wearing to wash away stale body odors."

With the success of *halitosis* and *body odor*, modern advertising continued to coin and popularize terms for both real and imaginary ailments and embarrassing conditions. In the 1930s and 40s there were ads for products which would help prevent everything from *irregularity* (a euphemism for constipation) to *pink toothbrush* (caused by bleeding gums), followed by ads for products that could prevent that horror of horrors *tattletale gray* (left on laundry from using too mild a laundry soap), *dishpan hands* (in general use by 1944, red hands from using too strong a dishwashing soap), *tired blood* (from not having enough iron in one's diet), and, echoing the earlier "tattletale gray," *ring around the collar* (mid 1970s, from not using a liquid detergent that removed collar grime from shirts in a home washing machine).

If there was any doubt after the 1920s, 30s, and 40s that advertising could popularize a term, the history of *chlorophyll* set it to rest. Only scientists had heard of *chlorophyll* (from the Greek *chlor/chloro*, light green, greenish yellow, plus *-phyll/phyllo*, leaf), the green coloring matter in plants essential for photosynthesis, until the late 1940s, when the substance was first claimed to be able to "fight unwanted odors." Soon there were Nullo pills, advertised as a product that "kills body odors and bad breath . . . Safe as a lettuce leaf . . . contains nature's chlorophyll." Next came the 1951 ads for the lozengelike Clorets "makes breath kissing sweet . . . contains chlorophyll," and by 1952 a torrent of products advertising chlorophyll as their special ingredient, including at least 30 tablets and lozenges sold as breath sweeteners, 11 toothpastes and tooth powders, 9 chewing gums, 8 brands of dogfood, 4 mouthwashes (for humans), and one brand of cigarette. The chlorophyll fad began to fade the following year, though some of the products are still with us and the word has become a part of the general vocabulary, now found in all desk dictionaries and known to almost every school child from basic science classes.

Bohemians, the Left Bank, and the Lost Generation

The first gypsies arrived in Western Europe from Bohemia in the 15th century and were called *Bohemians*. The word then slowly changed from meaning a true gypsy to meaning a gypsy of society, as shown in Thackeray's 1848 novel *Vanity Fair*, in which Becky Sharp's wild, roving nature is attributed to her parents, "who were Bohemians by taste and circumstances." The concept had also come to include poor, nonconforming artists, as in Henri Murger's romanticized account of the poor and passionate artist's life in Paris in his 1849 *Scènes de la Vie de Bohème*. Thus in America *Bohemian* was used by the 1850s to mean a wandering or homeless adventurer; in the 1860s–80s to mean a hard-drinking, loose-living roving reporter, as one covering the Civil War or roaming the far West; and by 1910 was widely used to refer to poor, nonconforming, and scandalously immoral writers and artists, and soon to any avant-garde nonconformist.

The student quarter of Paris has been called *the Latin Quarter* since the Middle Ages, because students at the University of Paris learned and were required to converse in Latin. Bohemian artists and writers have long been associated with this student quarter, because student-style rooms and restaurants are cheap; thus by the

Gertrude Stein said she first heard the term the lost generation *from a French garage owner. After hearing it from her, Ernest Hemingway used it as the epigraph of his 1926 novel* The Sun Also Rises.

96

1870s *Latin Quarter* had come to mean any poor, Bohemian neighborhood in a large city. Around World War I *the Left Bank*, referring to the left bank of the Seine, became something of a synonym for a *Latin Quarter*. By the 1890s in America the name *Greenwich Village* already conjured up an image of a native Latin Quarter, being known as a section of New York City where artists and writers could live cheaply. However, its bohemian reputation didn't really flower until after World War I, and by 1930 most of the famous writers and artists had left.

Gertrude Stein said she had heard the term *lost generation* in a conversation with a French garage owner. After hearing it from her, Ernest Hemingway used it in the epigraph to his 1926 novel *The Sun Also Rises*, which became something of a bible to the rootless, disillusioned young adults who came to maturity during World War I. This *lost generation* became a landmark term, being the first to name and identify a young generation considered separate from the general population by its age and special experience, leading to such later concepts and terms as *the Beat Generation* (see Hep, Hip, Hippie, Cool, and Beat). Besides "the lost generation," poet, novelist and critic Gertrude Stein left one other major memorable phrase to the American language, "Rose is a rose is a rose," from *Sacred Emily* (1922).

Booze and Bars
Yes, this section is about *liquor, spirits, booze, alcohol*—all words the first colonists brought to America with them:

> *liquor* meant any liquid to the first colonists; it didn't come to mean alcoholic liquid until about a hundred years after the Pilgrims landed. *Hard liquor* was first recorded in America in 1890.
>
> *spirits*, when 12th-century alchemists first distilled alcohol they thought they had distilled the mysterious *aqua vita* (Latin, "water of life"). The Scandinavians still drink *aqua vit*, and our *whiskey* literally means "water of life." Such water or essence of life was called *distilled spirits* by the 14th century; by colonial days *ardent spirits* were the strong rum, gin, and brandy while *spirits* by itself often meant the less potent beer, wine, and cider.
>
> *booze* (Middle Dutch *bosen*, to drink, tipple) has been in English as a verb (*to booze*, drink) since the 13th century; the noun *booze*, liquor, has been in the language since the 16th century—but *booze* didn't become a popular American word until the 1880s.
>
> *alcohol*, a 17th-century English word (from Latin *alcohol vini*, spirit or essence of wine, fine powder, from Arabic *al-kohl*, powdered antimony, used to tint the eyelids). The short U.S. form *alky* dates from 1844.
>
> *strong water* was the term preferred by some early colonists.
>
> *rum*, a 1667 English word, shortened from the 1640s *rumbullion* or *rumbustion*, but no one is sure where these came from: some theories are that the words referred to distillation, to the French

chateau town of Rambouillet, or to "rum booze" (English slang for "excellent booze"). The colonists used *rum* to refer both to the specific drink and to liquor in general. It was so common on the Atlantic seaboard that "spirits" and "rum" were synonymous (until the 1930s, temperance workers continued to use "rum" or "demon rum" to mean all alcoholic beverages).

The early colonists had never heard of *whiskey*, *rye*, or *Bourbon*, much less *Scotch* or *vodka*. They talked about their three most common alcoholic beverages—beer, cider, and rum—and also about the less common wine, brandy, and gin. The history of American hard drinking thus really starts with rum and goes to whiskey and rye, then to Bourbon, Scotch, and vodka, in that order. Here's what we talked about:

rum was made in the Caribbean almost as soon as the Spaniards landed and planted sugar cane. By 1639 our colonists were calling rum by the West Indies name *Kill-Devil*. New Englanders soon imported molasses and sugar from the West Indies to make their own rum, drank lots of it, and had a thriving business exporting the rest to the other colonies, Africa, and elsewhere. New England ships traded rum for slaves on the African Gold Coast, then brought the slaves to the West Indies and traded them for molasses and sugar, which they brought back to New England to make more rum—making huge profits at each point on their triangular trips. This New England–made rum was called *Yankee rum* and *stink-a-bus*. It was the basic colonial liquor, and a dram or tot at breakfast was a common preventive against the malaria that plagued the southern colonies (the rum didn't help).

Then the British got nasty with the independent American colonists and imposed high taxes and import duties before the Revolutionary War, passing the restrictive Molasses Act in 1733 and the Sugar Act in 1764, then later imposed embargoes and closed harbors. Thus New England's rum industry was crippled. There wasn't as much cheap rum to drink or talk about as there had been.

whiskey and rye. Fortunately, by that time the Scotch-Irish immigrants had arrived in force and were old hands with the *pot still* (*still* is a 16th-century word, the formal *distillery* came later, in the 18th century, both from the verb *to distill*). By 1722 these Scotch-Irish had reached Pennsylvania, especially the Shenandoah Valley, distilling their home-grown rye into *usquebaugh* (an Irish Gaelic word meaning "water of life"). This soon was pronounced as *whiskybae*, then shortened to *whiskey* (whiskey with the *-e-* is the American and Irish spelling, thus the way we spell our products *Bourbon whiskey* and *Irish whiskey*—whisky without the *-e-* is the British spelling, thus the way British products are spelled, *Scotch whisky*, *Canadian whisky*). From the mid 1730s through the Revolution, as the British made West Indies molasses and sugar more difficult to obtain, we turned from rum to this *whiskey* made of native rye. By 1785 *whiskey* had become a general term for all liquor, and if you wanted whiskey made

98

In 1871 this Oregon distillery was making bourbon *a long way from Bourbon County, Kentucky.*

> *. . . when you absorb a deep swig of it you have all the sensation of having swallowed a lighted kerosene lamp.*
>
> Irvin S. Cobb (1876–1944), definition of *corn licker*

from rye, you had to specify *rye whiskey*, which was not commonly shortened to *rye* until the 1890s. Some easterners, however, still have "rye" in mind when they say "whiskey."

Rye whiskey soon met its own political fate. Money was short after the Revolutionary War, and the very first Secretary of the Treasury, Alexander Hamilton, persuaded President Washington to levy an excise tax on domestic whiskey. Those Pennsylvania Scotch-Irish resisted paying the tax, tarred and feathered some tax collectors, and in 1794, 13,000 militiamen were sent to quell the riots, which were called the *Whiskey Rebellion*. After that, some Pennsylvania rye-making farm families moved out of the tax collectors' reach, over the Appalachian Mountains into the new state and tall corn of Kentucky.

Bourbon. When their rye crop was a little short these new Kentucky settlers started mixing some corn in their mash. This soon made *corn spirits* (a term first used in 1764) a common drink all the way down the Ohio and Mississippi rivers to New Orleans. It was called *mountain dew* by 1816, *corn* by 1820, and formally known as *corn whiskey* by the 1840s. By the 1850s, however, most people were calling it *Bourbon County whiskey, Bourbon whiskey,* or simply *bourbon,* after Bourbon County, Kentucky, where the Pennsylvania immigrants first made it famous in their log-cabin distilleries (*Bourbon County* had been named for the French, and Spanish, royal family). Later, corn whiskey, especially when made by small stills or illegally, was also called *moonshine* (1877), which was sometimes shortened to *shine* (1890) or *moon* (1920s). Today true corn whiskey must be made from mash containing 80 percent corn, bourbon from 51 percent. Many southerners still mean "bourbon" when they say "whiskey."

gin. Americans have been drinking gin since colonial days (French *genièvre* from Dutch *jenever,* juniper berries, which give gin its distinctive basic flavor). It had been created as a medicine (many of our after-dinner liqueurs were also created as medicines or tonics) by a chemist and doctor, Professor Sylvius, in Holland. William of Orange introduced it into England in the 17th century as a substitute for the imported brandy made by his enemy the French. Since it was easy and cheap to make, it soon became the workingman's drink, being called "the workingman's curse" and "mother's ruin" on both sides of the Atlantic in the

99

18th century. Since it is so easy to make, even in bathtubs (*bathtub gin*, 1920s), it became very popular during Prohibition and has retained its popularity and improved its social status ever since.

Scotch, which, of course, is made from malted barley, began to dribble out of the Scottish Highlands after the English conquered the Scots at the famous battle of Culloden in 1746 and built a road into the region. But it was not until the 1850s, when the new "patent still" produced the simpler, lighter, blended Scotches, that the rest of the world heard much about *Scotch whisky*. Except for travelers to England and a few wealthy people, Americans generally did not drink or talk about *Scotch* until the mid-1890s. Expensive to make and import, it gained further status during Prohibition, then became the sophisticated drink between World War II and the 1960s. "Scotch" is still what the British mean when they say "whisky."

vodka (diminutive of Russian *voda*, water, literally "little water") was originally made from potatoes and originated in imperial Russia, with the rest of the world first hearing of it during the Crimean War (1853–56). More and more Americans began to drink it and talk about it after World War II (our Russian allies were always drinking vodka toasts), and it became a sophisticated drink. In 1975 vodka replaced Scotch as America's best-selling booze.

The colonists also had *brandy* (a 17th-century word, originally *brandewine* or *brandywine* from Dutch *brandewijn*, burnt wine, distilled wine), but not *brandy snifters*, that term being first recorded in 1848.

Besides the more formal *liquor*, *spirits*, etc., we have also called liquor, especially strong, cheap, or illegal liquor, many things, including:

> *Jersey lightning* (applejack), 1780; *lightning* (gin), 1891; *white lightning* (corn whiskey), 1900s.
>
> *phlegm cutter*, 1806.
>
> *blue ruin*, 1810; *blue rum*, 1831, for cheap gin or whiskey; *blue pig*, 1840.
>
> *firewater*, 1817, from the burning sensation it causes in one's throat and stomach.
>
> *rot gut*, 1819, implying it rots one's guts or stomach.
>
> *red eye*, 1819, because habitual drinkers would have bloodshot or red-rimmed eyes; *red-eye special*, 1922, as very cheap, very strong whiskey sold in speakeasies and by bootleggers during Prohibition.
>
> *lush*, 1840, from the 1790 English use meaning liquor, drink (in 15th-century English it meant "juicy").
>
> *coffin varnish*, 1845.
>
> *forty rod*, 1858 (you can smell it or get drunk on it 40 rods away).
>
> *tanglefoot*, 1859.
>
> *bust skull*, *bust head*, 1860s.
>
> *tarantula juice*, 1861.
>
> *sheep dip*, 1865.

snake medicine, 1865. (These 1860s terms grew with the Civil War and are just a few of the Northern Army's many colorful words for the cheap or illegal whiskey the soldiers bought or made.)

nose paint, 1881 (referring to the red nose of some habitual drinkers).

hooch, hootch, 1898, originally *hoochinoo*, 1877 (see Alaska, Seward's Folly, and Eskimos for details).

smoke, 1904, meaning cheap whiskey. During and after Prohibition *smoke* meant denatured alcohol, assumedly with most of the poisonous denaturants removed. *Canned heat* generally meant the same denatured alcohol but specifically alcohol or paraffin originally meant for cooking and heating.

mule, 1900s; *white mule*, 1920.

juice, 1920.

the sauce, 1920s.

panther sweat, 1929; *panther piss*, 1941 (*panther piss* is probably the older term, perhaps even very old, but its taboo nature prevented it from being recorded sooner).

We have also called a drink of liquor:

hair of the dog (*that bit* you), 1546 in England; first recorded 1842 in the U.S. It's a drink of the same kind that gave one a *hangover* (1912) used to cure the hangover.

slug, 1762.

eye opener, the first drink in the morning, and *nightcap*, a drink taken before going to bed, both 1818.

finger, 1856, an amount equal to the width of a finger laid against the bottom of the glass.

pick me up, 1867.

snort, 1889; *snorter*, 1891.

nip, 1891.

jolt, 1905.

shot, 1906.

belt, 1921. *To belt* (to have a drink, to drink) is an 1846 term; both the noun and the verb go back to the 1830s expression to have a drink *under* (one's) *belt*.

Americans have been drinking all this liquor at home, in inns and taprooms. We have also *wet* (our) *whistle* (14th-century England, 1840 U.S.) or *bent* (our) *elbow* (1880s) and asked the bartender to *set 'em up* (1851) in the local:

tavern, a 13th-century English word (from Latin *taberna*, shed, booth, and in Roman days a wine shop; the same word for shed gives us *tabernacle*, where Christians house the Eucharist and Jews the Ark of the Covenant).

bar, a 16th-century English word, from the bars or grating pulled over the serving counter at closing time (law courts had similar bars, hence lawyers have been practicing "before the bar" since the 16th century too). *Bar room*, 1797; *bartender*, 1836; *bar keep*, 1846; *barfly*, 1910. Incidentally, the expression *mind your P's and Q's* is said to have originally been an admonition to bartenders when they were measuring out *p*ints and *q*uarts for customers.

Perley McBride's Shop. Liquor Shop *was an 1809 British term,* spirit shop *an 1837 American term, both then meaning saloon or tavern.*

rum house, 1730s (sometimes shortened to *house* and may be the origin for *on the house*, meaning free); *whiskey house*, 1835.

rum shop, 1730s.

drinking booth (a shop or stall), 1796; *drinkery*, 1840.

rum hole, 1834; *whiskey hole*, 1889.

exchange, 1835.

saloon, 1841.

rum mill, 1849; *whiskey mill*, 1856; *gin mill*, 1865.

gin palace, 1846; *rum palace*, 1890.

joint, as any low place, 1887; *whiskey joint*, 1901; *drinking joint*, 1902.

café (French *café*, coffee), a 19th-century term for coffee house; first used for a saloon, 1893. *Café society*, 1930s, referring to wealthy people who frequented the best nightclubs, bars, and restaurants.

cocktail lounge, *lounge*, after 1934. In the battle to end Prohibition, promises were made that the "saloon" would not be revived; thus after Prohibition the word *saloon* was out and terms such as *cocktail lounge* and the older *bar* (now sometimes *bar and grill* if food is served), *tavern*, and even *taproom* and the British *pub* were used.

juice joint, 1934.

juke joint, 1940s, a bar or roadhouse where jukebox music is available.

Incidentally, the custom of *making toasts* while drinking goes back to medieval days (though this has been called a *toast* only since the 17th century; originally toast was dipped in the wine and then eaten). Our more modern, less elegant toasts include:

Bottom's up, before 1860.
Here's how, Here's to you, Here's looking at you, 1890s.
Here's mud in your eye, 1930s.
Down the hatch, first recorded in 1942.

For how we Americans have drunk our booze and what we have mixed it with, see COCKTAILS, HIGHBALLS, GROG, ETC.

Boxing, Prizefighting, and Pugilism

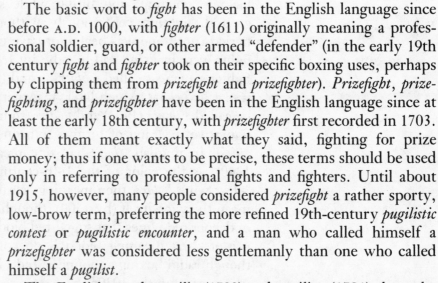

mean the same to most Americans. *To box* has meant to hit with the fist in English since 1519 but didn't mean to fight in a formal match until almost two hundred years later. *Boxing*, fistfighting, was first recorded in English in 1711, *boxing match* in 1714, and *boxer*, a skilled fistfighter, in 1742.

The basic word to *fight* has been in the English language since before A.D. 1000, with *fighter* (1611) originally meaning a professional soldier, guard, or other armed "defender" (in the early 19th century *fight* and *fighter* took on their specific boxing uses, perhaps by clipping them from *prizefight* and *prizefighter*). *Prizefight*, *prizefighting*, and *prizefighter* have been in the English language since at least the early 18th century, with *prizefighter* first recorded in 1703. All of them meant exactly what they said, fighting for prize money; thus if one wants to be precise, these terms should be used only in referring to professional fights and fighters. Until about 1915, however, many people considered *prizefight* a rather sporty, low-brow term, preferring the more refined 19th-century *pugilistic contest* or *pugilistic encounter*, and a man who called himself a *prizefighter* was considered less gentlemanly than one who called himself a *pugilist*.

The English words *pugilist* (1790) and *pugilism* (1791) show the sport's origin, coming from the Latin *pugil*, a fighter with a protective leather hand-cover; it is related to the Latin word *pugnus*, fist, from the Greek *pygnē/pux*, fist, with the clenched fist. The Greek gladiators originally stood toe to toe and clubbed each other with fists and forearms wrapped in leather thongs to soften the blows, fighting without rest until one man admitted defeat. By 900 B.C., however, the fighters sat on flat stones facing each other and the protective leather thong had evolved into a weapon, a *cestus* (belt) covered with metal studs and spikes for battles to the death. Theagenes of Thasos was the all-time cestus champion: he is said to have obliterated 1,425 opponents, killing many of them with his first hammerlike blow. By the first century A.D. the Romans were forcing slaves to kill and maim each other in similar fights as part of their arena spectacles, though the Romans allowed the fighters to stand and move within a restricted area, which made the fights

prizefighter. One that fights publicly for a reward.

The first definition of *prizefighter* to appear in a dictionary, Samuel Johnson's *Dictionary of the English Language*, 1755 more exciting. The famous Greek and Roman pugilists won the *crown* of a champion (*crown* has been used since the 12th century in England to refer to the wreath awarded victors in Greek and Roman games) and were rewarded with long after-dinner orations, elaborate and expensive cups and belts, beautiful women, and, according to Homer, at least one received "a jackass in good condition" (in our day fighters never receive jackasses). Fighting with mailed fists or weighted gloves became part of the historic Greek Olympic contests in 688 B.C.; there were no weight divisions and only the largest and strongest participated. Boxing was added to the modern Olympics in 1904.

Modern boxing began to develop in London toward the end of the 16th century. The word *bout* meant a fight, and also any part or division of a contest, by 1591; *fist fight* appeared in 1603; *fisticuffs* appeared in 1605 (from *fisty*, fistic + *cuff*, cuffing with the fists). The early bouts were brawls, the fighters wrestling, hitting, kicking, gouging, and biting while standing or rolling on the ground, fighting continuously without gloves, rounds, or rest periods until one was beaten or gave up. From the beginning the fights were bruising and bloody: by 1604 a discoloration around a fighter's eye was called a *black eye* and blood flowing from a fighter was called *claret*. Much later, in America, a black eye was also to be called a *shiner* (1904) and *to give* (someone) *a black eye* took on the figurative meaning of to give someone a bad reputation (around 1905). In English, *claret* had first meant light red or amber (by 1440), as the color of the 14th-century wine *vin claret* (literally "clear wine," *claret* then meaning "clear" in French), then came to mean the wine itself (by 1500), though, of course, it was the color of deeper red wines that suggested blood be called *claret*. The 1604 use of *claret* meaning blood is one of our oldest boxing terms, though radio boxing announcer Ted Husing popularized it again, in America, in the 1930s.

Although the first all-punching bout, with no wrestling allowed, was reported in England in 1681, it was a London boxer, wrestler, swordsman, and cudgel fighter, James Figg, who first made punching more important than wrestling in prizefighting. Acclaimed best fighter in England in 1719, Figg remained unbeaten in over thirty fights until his retirement in 1730, amply demonstrating his claim that a well-timed, well-aimed punch to the jaw was the surest way to win a bout. His bareknuckle style of punching without wrestling became known as *Figg's Fighting*, which he taught at Figg's Academy for Boxing and later at Figg's Amphitheatre. His students had opened over a dozen such *boxing academies* by 1729 (the 1535 term *fighting school* referred to military training).

Figg was soon followed by the equally honorable 200-pound Jack Broughton (1704–89, the only prizefighter buried in Westminster Abbey), who became English champion in the late 1730s. Broughton not only relied on boxing more than on wrestling but imposed a set of rules on prizefighting which lasted almost a hundred years, until the revised London Prize Ring Rules of 1839. His written rules for *Broughton's fighting* were first used in an August 10, 1743, bout, with Broughton himself acting as boxing's first formal *referee* (in English legal use since 1621 but not a common boxing term until the 1860s), assisted by two *umpires* (see *ump* at BASEBALL for details on this word), these being the forerunners of today's referee and judges. *Broughton's rules* called for a "stage" with a one-yard square chalked or scratched in the middle: after a fighter had been knocked down or been beaten against the "rails," his "friends" had thirty seconds to help him get up and toe this square opposite his opponent to begin the next *set to*. Broughton's "stage" and "rails" were, of course, his version of the modern ring and ropes; the "friends" who could help a fighter get up and back to the center square developed into boxing's *handlers* (first used in England to refer to trainers of fighting cocks and dogs around 1825) and *seconds* (an English dueling term of 1613, used in boxing by 1897). *Set to*, a term Broughton coined for his 1743 rules, not only was used to mean a fight itself but also part of a fight and was the precursor of our modern *round* (first used in English boxing in 1812). The thirty seconds allowed a fighter to get up, recuperate, and return to the center of the ring was called *time* in American fighting by 1812. Broughton's rule requiring fighters to begin each set to by facing each other across his one-yard square in the middle of the ring eventually gave English *to square* (1820), *to square at* (1827), *to square off* (1837) and *to square up to* (1873), the last two terms in particular being widely used both in and out of boxing to mean to assume a fighting position or face up to an adversary or an adverse situation.

Broughton's 1743 rules were also the first to forbid professionals to hit or fall upon an opponent who was down, to seize an opponent "by the hair, the breaches, or any part below the waist," and the first to forbid "hitting below the belt" (*to hit below the belt* became a nonboxing idiom in 1928, meaning to take an unfair advantage).

Broughton's rules allowed for *by battles* on the "stage" by other fighters before the *main battle* among the *principals*. A "by battle" wasn't called a *preliminary* in boxing until the 19th century, sometimes shortened to *prelim* by 1906; a "main battle" was usually called the *main event* by the 1920s in America, when fifteen-round limits were put on fights, meaning that several fights were usually scheduled to replace the hours of fighting the spectators were used to seeing from one long bout. Broughton's rules even provided that two-thirds of the money collected from spectators for each fight be given to the winner and be publicly distributed on the stage after

Hitting below the belt was a term widely used by boxing fans in 1930 when, as shown in this series of photographs, during the fourth round of the June 12 fight for the heavyweight title vacated by Gene Tunney, Jack Sharkey delivered a low blow to Germany's Max Schmeling. Sharkey was disqualified after the round, although only one of the three officials admitted to having seen the blow.

the fight, a concept of honesty and fairness new at the time, and still more honest than what is done in many modern boxing circles. Thus Broughton's 1743 rules pointed toward the modern ring with its ropes, the modern referee and judges, preliminary and main bouts, modern rules against hitting below the belt, and giving knocked-down fighters time to recuperate—which also meant a fighter could be counted out when this time elapsed. Also, the fact that after each knockdown the fighters had to return to the chalked or scratched square on the stage for the next set to gave us our concept of rounds.

Beginning in the late 1740s Broughton opened his own boxing academy, teaching "the mystery of boxing" to English gentlemen. Such classes were now advertised as instruction in *the manly* (or *noble*) *art of self defense*. Broughton was the first to believe in practice sparring to keep in shape and train for his bouts. His insistence that his students *spar* made the term a popular one in boxing, which is why Samuel Johnson's 1755 *Dictionary of the English Language* was the first to define *to spar* as "to engage in practice boxing; make motions of attack with arms and hands" (*to spar* had meant to strike rapidly in English since 1400 and had been used in cockfighting to mean to strike with the feet or spurs since the 16th century). *Sparring lessons* then became a term for boxing lessons in England by 1847 and a boxing academy was also called a *sparring academy* by 1853.

Beginning in 1734, Broughton used a type of padded glove in his practice or sparring bouts, then at his Haymarket Academy in 1748 devised what he called *mufflers*, larger, more padded gloves, for his gentlemen students, assuring them that these would prevent them from getting bruised hands and faces (not until 1875 were such gloves commonly called *boxing gloves*).

Despite Broughton's rules, much prizefighting was still brawling. In his only defeat, the forty-six-year-old Broughton lost his title in 1750 to the crude, old-fashioned *bruiser* (1744 in England, for a prizefighter) Jack Slack, who broke Broughton's nose and injured both his eyes with what we today would call a *backhand blow* (an 1813 English term, called a *backhander* by 1836 and simply a *backhand* in all sports by 1850).

The first truly *scientific* (1678 in this sense) *fighter* was 160-pound Daniel Mendoza, who consistently beat bigger men during his reign in the early 1790s, then opened his own London boxing school for young gentlemen—the only way for an honest 18th-century fighter to make a good, consistent living. Mendoza's speed allowed him to dodge blows and *beat* (opponents) *to the punch* (*beat to the punch* took on its nonboxing figurative meaning, to do what another person plans before he does it, by 1823). Although many of the terms were not used until much later, he seems to have perfected a variety of punches and boxing techniques, including the:

> *chop*, a 14th-century word for an overhand blow or strike. In the early days of boxing such an overhand landed on the opponent's head, face, or shoulders with the heel of the fist, like a hammer blow. Figg, Broughton, Mendoza, and their imitators and students used this hammerlike blow less than other fighters, but Mendoza effectively used a modern short chop.
>
> *infighting*. Mendoza developed this style of boxing at close quarters in England in the 1790s, though the term wasn't used until 1816 (since 1948 we have also used *infighting* in America to mean contention or rivalry within a group). The light Mendoza perfected this style to avoid the smashing blows by his heavier, slower opponents; he was one of the first fighters who did not try to knock down his opponent with every blow (*belt*, to deliver a strong blow, 1846; as a noun meaning a strong blow, 1896) but knew he had to wear them down with many series of blows, to *take the fight out of them* (an expression that first appeared in English boxing circles in 1812).
>
> *one-two*. In relying on a series of blows rather than knockout punches, Mendoza also developed combination blows, and the term *one, two*, for any punch with one hand followed immediately with a punch by the other, appeared in England in 1820. In

modern boxing the *one-two* usually means the classic combination of a left jab or hook followed by an overhand right.

jab. This may have been Figg's famous blow to the jaw, though we don't know how he delivered his punch. Mendoza definitely had perfected a straight jab. *Jab* meant a prod or poke in England by the 1820s but didn't take on its specific boxing use until the 1880s, some ninety years after Mendoza perfected it. In the 1920s many fighters believed that a jab was more effective if one twisted or ground one's fist into the opponent, this twisting jab then being called a *corkscrew punch*.

hook didn't become a common boxing word for a sidearm punch until the 1890s though, again, Mendoza developed such a blow in the 1790s.

upper cut, a boxing term of 1897. In the 1930s a three-quarter, somewhat sidearm, uppercut was popularized by fighter Ceferino Garcia, who called it a *bolo punch*, saying he had learned the motion while wielding a single-edged machetelike *bolo* in the sugar-cane fields of his native Philippines. This punch was later used by and became associated with welterweight champion "Kid" Gavilan (real name Gerardo Gonzalez) in the 1950s.

Well before the 1790s, British boxing had developed regional and class rivalries, but since Mendoza was a Jew his reign was the first in which ethnic rivalry played a major role. Thus many English gentlemen were more than pleased when "Gentleman Jack" (John Jackson, sometimes also called "Gentleman Jackson") beat Mendoza in 1795, by holding him by his hair with one hand while clubbing him with the other. Despite this tactic, then completely legal, Jackson was a gentleman boxer, a college champion and medical school graduate who at nineteen had knocked out Birmingham hoodlum Bill Fewterell with the Prince of Wales cheering him on. A social climber, as well as a skilled boxer and boxing teacher, Jackson had upper-class friends and students who helped give English boxing new respectability. Although the short, somewhat stout, clubfooted Lord Byron was probably not one of Jackson's better gentlemen students, he did take boxing lessons from him and called Jackson "the emperor of pugilism."

Though boxing and boxing terms were mainly English well into the 19th century, an occasional Irishman or American came to London to try his luck, including two American-born former slaves, Bill Richmond (1763–1829) of Staten Island and Tom Molineaux (1784–1818) of Virginia. Richmond was discovered by British General Earl Percy, then stationed in New York, who took Richmond to England when the army transferred him home in 1777 during the Revolutionary War. Richmond then fought the top English prizefighters, including a loss to title aspirant Tom Cribb in 1805, and became the first American we would consider a professional. Molineaux, who had been given his freedom by his owner after whipping a bully on a neighboring plantation, became the first American to fight for a professional championship title.

Billed as "the Yankee Nigger," he also lost to Tom Cribb, who by then was British champion, before a crowd of 20,000 spectators in England on December 10, 1810, having made a punching bag out of Cribb for the first thirty rounds, before fracturing his own skull against a ringpost (Cribb beat the still ailing Molineaux again in 1811 at Wymondham, England, before a record-breaking crowd of 40,000). These two American ex-slaves fought many "unknowns" in England, actually well-known English fighters who refused to use their real names in condescending to fight the two American blacks, each of whom earned less than $350 during his career.

Big money was, however, soon to be made by English fighters. In 1824 the first *boxing stands* were erected for a fight between English heavyweight champ Tom Spring, whose "punch could not dent butter" but whose quick left jab and skill wore down opponents, and Irish champion Jack Langan. The stands, on the outskirts of Worcester, England, seated 4,000 fans, who paid ten shillings a seat (about $2.50 then), with over 20,000 added standees also watching. Spring wore Langan down, then knocked him out in the seventy-seventh round, winning $27,000, including $5,000 as his share of the grandstand seat sales.

In 1839 the revised London Prize Ring Rules were created, based on Broughton's rules, and governed British and American boxing for the next 50 years. As most formal rules before them, they were created to make boxing less of a *knock down and drag out* (an 1827 English use for any rough, anything-goes fight) in order to attract more reputable Englishmen to *the fancy* (1811 as meaning those sporting gentlemen who frequented prizefighting, though by 1820 it also meant the art of boxing). Though a stage or "ring" marked off by "rails" or ropes had long been used in many fights, the 1839 London rules were the first official rules to require a square *ring* (then 24-feet square, still the maximum professional size) bounded by ropes.

> *ring* had meant the informal circle of spectators surrounding a fight in England since 1659; *the ring* meant the prizefighting profession in England by 1770. *Ringside*, the seats closest to the ring, was an American word of 1866, with the English then first calling the people who sat in such seats *ringsiders* in 1901. Broughton's rules had made the informal circular ring of spectators into a square "stage" and we Americans called the square prizefight ring a *square(d) circle* by 1927.
>
> *the ropes*. Even though the 1839 London rules called for ropes around the ring, *the ropes* and *on the ropes* didn't become common boxing terms until the 1850s, with the nonboxing, figurative use of *on the ropes*, meaning in a difficult or hopeless situation, first appearing as an American slang term in 1924. (Incidentally, *to know the ropes* was originally a seafaring term, first recorded, in America, in 1840.)

Since the enclosed 24-foot-square ring made defense and mobility more important, by the 1850s, too, *feint* was a new boxing term.

By the new London rules a round still ended only when a fighter went down, but after the *knockdown* (an 1809 English boxing term) he could be helped to his *corner*, rest for 30 seconds, then had to go unaided to a line drawn or scratched in the center of the ring and resume fighting. If a fighter could not *toe the scratch* or *come up to scratch* 30 seconds after he was knocked down he was declared *not up to scratch* and beaten, these new 1839 boxing terms giving us our figurative *toe the scratch* and *(not) up to scratch* (*scratch* had meant a starting or boundary line in English cricket since 1778 and the starting line in horse racing since 1821). By the 1840s we were also using the terms *toe the line* and *toe the mark* figuratively, with *toe up* being a now forgotten 1901 slang term for meeting the requirements, being able to do what was required. The new rules also declared as a *foul* (an English sports term since 1797) such tactics as kicking, biting, butting, *gouging* (a 1779 English term), and *low blows*.

Boxing was now less bloody and more organized and it soon became the custom for a badly beaten fighter's sponsors or friends to end a fight by throwing the sponge, used to wipe his face and body between rounds, into the ring. This gave English prizefighting the expression *throw up the sponge* or *throw in the sponge* by 1860.

Meantime in America, fighting remained less professional and less formal, with fewer rules. From the earliest colonial times local brawlers had fought in clearings, barrooms, or streets, some winners declaring themselves local champions or even champion of all the colonies or all the United States. Thus in 1816 Jacob Hyer beat Tom Beasley in a grudge fight in New York City and somewhat jokingly claimed to be the American champion, though others took his claim seriously. In the 1840s Hyer's twenty-two-year-old, 205-pound, 6-foot-2½-inch son, Tom, who seems to have had about five formal fights, claimed to have succeeded his father as the American champion, then in 1849 strengthened his claim by beating the visiting British fighter James Ambrose, who fought in the U.S. under the name "Yankee Sullivan." Though such American brawlers were not true professionals, beginning in the 1830s a few Irish and English immigrants had begun to spread the more formal *English-style boxing* to America by becoming itinerant fighters, wandering from town to town and barroom to barroom fighting for bets and whatever money spectators would contribute. As with fighting dogs and fighting cocks, there were famous winners and money earners. In fact, the human fighters were sometimes part of illicit, inhumane shows held in barns, locked barrooms, or secluded fields which included fighting dogs, cocks, and men on the same card.

[Prizefighting is a] disgrace formerly confined to England.
Philip Hone, *Diary*, 1842. Hone was an auctioneer, mayor of New York, and an early leader of the Whig party.

Such itinerant fighters were called *pugs* by 1858 (from *pugilist*, many people then pronouncing *pugilist* with a hard *g* as *pug-ilist*) and any fight they won easily over a local amateur was called a *walkover* (1859). Such a pug was the handsome 195-pound self-proclaimed champion of the United States, John C. Heenan, "the Benicia Boy" (from Benicia, California), who, unable to find enough challengers in America, went to England in 1860 and managed to fight the 140-pound English champion Tom Sayers to a 42-round *draw* (used in England since 1839 for an even or undecided contest or game) when toughs favoring the losing Sayers, and probably resenting the 55-pound weight difference, broke into the ring and disrupted the fight. Such disruptions occurred frequently in those days, if police didn't break up the fight and arrest the fighters first (though bribed or sympathetic police in the U.S. and Britain often ignored professional prize-fighting, it was illegal; "Bendigo," William Thompson, three times English champion between 1839 and 1851, was arrested 28 times for fighting). Since there was then no such thing as a decision or point scoring, the only way a fight could end in a *draw* was if both fighters quit or the fight was interrupted.

Though completely illegal, this Heenan-Sayers fight was the first widely touted international bout featuring an American: the 2,500 spectators included not only Prince Albert, Charles Dickens, and William Makepeace Thackeray but also four American reporters. Each side put up $2,500, the winner to take all and to receive a *championship belt* (by 1889 *to hold the belt* meant to hold the championship).

Thirty rounds, 42 rounds, 77 rounds—the number of rounds in the old bareknuckle days awes us today, until we remember the number of rounds was not always due to the boxers' stamina but to the fact that a round ended every time a boxer went down, giving him 30 seconds' rest before the next round began. Thus a losing or tired boxer often fell down as soon as the next round started, doing this over and over again, gaining 30 seconds' rest each time, until he felt ready to carry on; many boxers were down as much as they were up and many rounds passed without a single blow, while the crowd booed and jeered and called at the downed fighter to "get up and fight like a man." But this began to change in 1867 when the well-educated athlete and lightweight boxer John Graham Chambers of the English Amateur Athletic Club devised a new set of rules to encourage boxing (he had also been the first to define *amateur* in the formal sport's use of the word, though it had first been loosely applied to less experienced boxers in 1801). Chambers' Amateur Athletic Club rules followed the London Rules in many ways but forbade all wrestling, required all fighters to wear "padded gloves," redefined a *round* by making it not dependent on a knockdown but a specific three-minute period with a minute's rest between each, and required a downed fighter to get up unaided within ten seconds or be declared *knocked out of time*. The rules forbidding wrestling and requiring gloves are closely related because fighters can't wrestle effectively while wearing gloves, which is why many early fighters were against wearing them. Most of us have never heard of Chambers' rules because, in order to attract a better class of patron to boxing, the young John Sholto Douglas, eighth Marquis of Queensberry (1844–1900) lent his name to them so they would be associated with the upper classes. Thus, since their introduction in 1867, John Graham Chambers' English Amateur Athletic Club boxing rules have been called *the Marquis of Queensberry rules* or simply the *Queensberry rules*. The new rules popularized some existing boxing terms and were to lead to some new ones, including:

clinch. The term had been used in English since 1652 to mean to close and struggle, as wrestlers. In absolutely forbidding any form of wrestling, the Queensberry rules forbade clinching, which thus took on its specific boxing meaning. In American slang *to clinch* was also used to mean to embrace, as lovers, by 1899.

boxing gloves. As described above, the original Greek pugilists had worn protective leather thongs on their hands and forearms, and Jack Broughton had worn padded gloves in sparring matches from 1734 and devised more padded *mufflers* to protect the hands and faces of his students in 1748. A few other fighters had also worn tight-fitting *gloves* or "padded mittens" since 1818. Thus, although the 1867 Queensberry rules first made *boxing gloves* (1875) mandatory in amateur fights, the term *put on the gloves* had meant to fight since 1847 in England (*to take the gloves off*, to set to in earnest, is an American expression of 1928, but refers to taking off dress gloves and getting one's hands dirty).

knockout. The Queensberry rules said a fighter who was knocked down had to get up unaided within ten seconds or be declared *knocked out of time*. This was replaced by to *knock out* in the early 1880s. The noun a *knockout* appeared in the late 1880s and *knockout punch* in the 1890s; *haymaker*, for a knockout punch, appeared in 1912, perhaps from the 1880 *hit the hay*, go to sleep. *Knock cold* appeared in 1896. In America we have used *knockout* to mean an outstanding or beautiful person or thing since 1894 and spoken of *knockout drops* since 1896.

Other expressions based on "knock" as hitting hard have included the English to *have* (one's) *brains knocked out* (1591) and our American *knock* (someone) *into the middle of next week* (1821), *knock into a cocked hat* (1833), *knock the socks off* (someone) (1844), *knock the spots off* (someone) (1850), *knock* (someone) *galley West* (1875, from the English dialect term *colly-West* or *colly-Weston*, in the opposite direction), *knock the stuffing out of* (someone) (1883), *knock silly* (1884), *knock for a loop* (1918), and *knock the hell out of* (someone) (1930).

the count. A fighter *knocked out of time*, unable to get up in ten seconds after being knocked down, was said *to take the (full) count* by the 1890s, the counting off of the ten seconds being called simply *the count* by 1913. *To count out*, however, goes back to the early 1800s, before the Queensberry rules, and was originally used in English cock fighting.

the bell. Though a *stopwatch* (1737, in English) had been used in timing the 30-second interval allowed knocked-down fighters under older rules, signaling the beginning and end of a round by hitting a gong or bell became common as the Queensberry three-minute round was accepted. This also meant a downed fighter could be *saved by the bell*, since counting for the knockout ended when a round was over. The boxing bell most of us have heard today is that of the *automatic timekeeper*, a ringside clock that automatically rings the bell and tolls the minutes of a round, this device being first used in the James J. Corbett–Peter Jackson heavyweight fight in San Francisco on May 21, 1891.

The Marquis of Queensberry rules were first fully used in an 1872 London amateur tournament, which was also the first to award *trophies* to modern boxers and the first to separate fighters by weight *class*, these original amateur classes including only *lightweight* (then up to 140 pounds), *middleweight* (140 to 158 pounds), and *heavy class* (over 158 pounds). Up to then there were no formal weight classes in fighting and a 50-pound difference between opponents was not unusual. Even when the idea of formal weight classes was first introduced into professional prizefighting, a champion had quite a bit of leeway in determining exactly what the limits of his weight class were, changing the limits to match his own weight loss or gain or to avoid dangerous challengers by claiming they were *not in his class*. In general, however, early champions were pleased to fight lighter men for the money and heavier ones for the glory. We now have the following classes, in order of increasing weight:

flyweight, the weight division of the lightest boxers (now up to 112 pounds), was created and named in England in 1910 and recognized later that year in the U.S. Frankie Mason then outfought two others to claim the U.S. championship of this new division, with Johnny Buff being the first to win it, by beating Mason in New Orleans in 1921.

bantamweight (now the division of boxers weighing 113 to 118 pounds) first appeared in U.S. boxing use in 1894, though *bantam* itself had then already been used in boxing for many years. *Bantam* had meant a small fowl in English since 1749 and had been used as an adjective meaning "small" since 1782 (from the village of Bantam in Java, site of the first Dutch settlement in the East Indies, where a breed of small fowl was supposed to have originated). By the 1850s any of the smallest fighters had been simply called a *bantam* (some weighed as little as 105 pounds), with Charlie Lynch then being the best such American fighter and claiming the unofficial "bantam championship" after beating England's best in 1859. After Lynch's retirement no one claimed the bantam title until Tom Kelly did in 1887 (both Lynch and Kelly would now be considered flyweights).

featherweight (now the 119- to 126-pound division), like *lightweight*, *welterweight*, and *heavyweight*, comes from English horse racing in the days when gentlemen riders were not small jockeys but were average-sized men rated by their weight. The word was first used in English racing in 1812, by 1838 was in general English use to mean both light in weight and trifling or unimportant, then came into English boxing in the 1880s. Scotsman Ike Weir, "The Belfast Spider," was the first boxer to be considered world featherweight champion, in the 1880s, then came to America and was defeated in San Francisco by Billy Murphy of New Zealand in 1890, Murphy then being regarded as champion of the new division. In the early days, however, there were often two claimants to the featherweight title, because some fighters claimed the top weight of the division was 122 pounds while other, slightly heavier fighters claimed it was 126 pounds.

lightweight came into wide boxing use in the mid-19th century, originally in England, to refer to any fighter under 154 pounds, then by the 1870s to refer to the weight class of all those under 140 pounds (now it is the 127- to 135-pound division). The word was first used in English horse racing in 1733 to refer to lightweight gentlemen riders, by 1809 was in general use to mean light in weight, and by 1882 was used to refer to an unimportant or mediocre person. The first recognized, but unofficial, U.S. lightweight champion was 130-pound Abe Hicken, who defeated Pete McGuire to claim the title in Perrysville, Missouri, in 1868, this being the first recorded fight between American boxers who called themselves "lightweights." For a brief time after World War I there was a *junior lightweight* division of up to 130 pounds.

welterweight (now the 136- to 147-pound division) goes back to Middle English *welt*, to roll (from Latin *volvere*), with *welter* generally being used to refer to somewhat less than heavyweight racehorse riders by the late 18th century. *Welter* was then first used in prizefighting in 1792, when several English boxers started calling themselves "welters," including 145-pound "Paddington" Tom Jones, who defeated all challengers. Not until the 1870s did some U.S. fighters start calling themselves *welters*, with Paddy Duffy being the first to claim to be American champion, beating all challengers in the 1880s, followed by "Mysterious" Billy Smith (real name Amos Smith), who claimed the championship in 1892. Thus *welter* is older than *welterweight*, which appeared around 1850 in English racing and in 1896 in American boxing to replace it. However, *welterweight* was originally a very vague term in boxing, applied to any fighter who considered himself too heavy to be a lightweight but too light to be a middleweight. For a brief time after World War I there was also a *junior welterweight* division of 131 to 140 pounds.

middleweight (now the 148- to 160-pound class) was called *the 150-pound class* (vaguely up to 158 pounds) when Tom Chandler beat Dooney Harris in a bareknuckle fight in San Francisco in 1867 to claim the title. Then, for a brief period after Chandler's victory, it was called *Chandler's class*. George Fulljames seems to have been the first to insist on calling this the *middleweight class* and challenged all comers in it beginning around 1883. The division was officially recognized in 1884 and Jack Dempsey, "the Nonpareil" (real name John Kelly, he was no relation to the later heavyweight champion Jack Dempsey), then accepted Fulljames' challenge, beating him in Toronto on August 30, to become the first official champion.

light heavyweight (now the 161- to 175-pound division) was created and named in 1903 when Chicago boxing promoter and newspaperman Lou Houseman claimed there were many fighters too heavy for the middleweight division (which then had a 158-pound limit) but still too light to compete with heavyweights and advocated a new *light heavyweight* class (called *cruiserweight* in Britain). Houseman had his own reasons for wanting this new division: his boxer, Jack Root (real name Janos Ruthaly), had recently eaten his way out of the middleweight division. On April 22, 1903, Root outpointed Kid McCoy (real name Norman Selby) in 10 rounds in Detroit to claim the title, but the first light-heavyweight championship belt was awarded to George Gardner after he knocked out Root later that year.

heavyweight (now the over-175-pounds division) didn't become a common word until the 1850s, when it appeared in both English horse racing for the heaviest riders and in boxing for the heaviest fighters. Until then it was generally considered a boxer's own business to determine how big a man he would fight, though a fighter could call himself a *welter* (see *welterweight* above) or by some other weight designation if he chose not to fight the heaviest men. In America we used *heavy* as a slang word to mean "wealthy" or "important" since 1842 and our 1879 use of *heavyweight* to mean an important or consequential person stems from this earlier use of *heavy* as much as from the boxing term *heavyweight*.

Since both the 1867 Marquis of Queensberry rules and the 1872 division of fighters into rigid weight classes were created for amateur boxers, most professional fighters considered them effete and stuck to the old London rules until the 1890s. In fact, the 133-pound Chambers himself fought by the old professional bareknuckle rules in his professional fights in England, Canada, and the U.S. in the 1870s and became bareknuckle lightweight champion in 1879, twelve years after he devised the Queensberry amateur rules requiring gloves and three-minute rounds. However, the excellent 160-pound English heavyweight champion "Jem" (James) Mace, who had first won the title under the bareknuckle London rules in 1861 and continued fighting until 1890, found he had a better chance of beating heavier opponents under the Queensberry rules. As were other British prizefighters of the Victorian period, he was deplored by the public and hounded by the police; thus, in 1868, the *champ* (1868), like many other English boxers, came to America to fight, helping to introduce boxing gloves and Queensberry rules here. Our own undefeated lightweight, Jack McAuliffe, who had been the American amateur champion before becoming the professional champion in 1885, retained the amateur's gloves and rules in his professional bouts whenever possible and his fights were often billed on *fight cards* (a late 19th-century term) as being under "the new Queensberry rules." Incidentally, by now in the U.S. a prizefight was often called a *mill* (1819) and prizefighters were said *to scrap* (1874) and were often called *scrappers*. America's "Nonpareil" Jack Dempsey, middleweight champ from 1884 to 1891 (though he fought in several weight divisions), also often fought under the new rules. Good as these fighters were, however, it remained for heavyweight John L. Sullivan to create major boxing interest in America and put all professional fighting under the Marquis of Queensberry rules.

Though the exodus of boxers such as Jem Mace from Victorian England had spread English-style fighting to the U.S., Canada, Australia, and Europe in the 1850s and 60s, such superior English fighters often fought exhibition fights among themselves or whipped our unskilled challengers with boring ease before small crowds. English champion James Burke had had the same problem in finding worthy opponents, when in 1835 he became the first champion to visit the U.S., fighting a few dull and unprofitable fights from New York to New Orleans. In 1880, however, the 200-pound Irish-born American Paddy Ryan, who seems to have had about four fights in his entire professional career, beat the visiting heavyweight champion Joe Goss in 87 rounds near Colliers Station, West Virginia, and became the first American heavyweight *world champion*. Ryan was then completely outclassed and outpunched, being knocked out in 9 rounds by the 195-pound, 5-foot-10½-inch Boston-born John L(awrence) Sullivan, "The Boston Strong Boy," in Mississippi City, Mississippi, in 1882. This made Sullivan "champion of the universe"—a celebrity who could fill small-town arenas with workingmen and Madison Square Garden with 10,000 socialites in formal evening wear—although police stopped three of his illegal fights in Madison Square Garden between 1882 and 1884.

Sullivan had frequently boxed with gloves in legal "pugilistic exhibitions" in Boston theaters, and after he won the heavyweight title, "Professor Sullivan" gave many completely legal "illustrated lectures on pugilism" (demonstration fights) and traveled with a theatrical group exhibiting "the art of boxing," wearing strips of leather over his knuckles and following the Queensberry rules, giving "nice people" their first chance to witness boxing bouts in America. When these bouts with his "sparring mates" from the theatrical troupe proved too tame an attraction, Sullivan offered $100, and later $500, to any man he could not knock out in four rounds. His famous *all-comers* challenge filled the theaters in the mid-1880s as men, women, and children paid to see this new American champion demolish rural braggarts and *local prides*. Of course, Sullivan slipped away from his gentlemanly theatrical

The last bareknuckle, London Rules heavyweight championship fight in America: John L. Sullivan vs Jake Kilrain in Richburg, Mississippi, July 8, 1889. Kilrain was unable to toe scratch for the 76th round.

troupe "exhibitions" and "illustrated lectures" now and then to continue his illegal bareknuckle championship fights. Thus at 10 A.M. on July 8, 1889, when the temperature was already 100 degrees at the secret ring site in Richburg, Mississippi, Sullivan beat Baltimore's Jake Kilrain in the last bareknuckle heavyweight championship fight, London Rules, held in America. The 3,000 fans from nearby New Orleans saw Sullivan, in his green breeches and flesh-colored stockings, *nail* (hit hard, 1886) Kilrain many times in the two-hour, sixteen-minute fight, Kilrain being unable to "toe scratch" for the 76th round.

Three years later, the thirty-four-year-old Sullivan, slowed by years of bourbon-gulping dissipation, accepted the championship challenge of "Gentleman Jim" (James J.) Corbett but insisted on full Marquis of Queensberry rules, including boxing gloves, to avoid police harassment (the public and the police tended to accept illegal prizefights if they were fought under Queensberry rules). Sponsored by the New Orleans Olympic Club as one of three illegal fights in a three-day "Championship Carnival" of boxing, this September 7, 1892, *go* (an 1890 word for a fight) saw the 187-pound, 6-foot-1-inch San Francisco-born Corbett knock out Sullivan in the 21st round, winning the title, the $35,000 *purse* (first recorded as a boxing term in 1891, from the 1724 English horse racing use), and the $10,000 side bet. After this defeat, Sullivan continued touring as a boxer, actor, and vaudevillian for over 20 years—but was never defeated for the bareknuckle London Rules heavyweight championship. That championship title died with him. Corbett reigned from 1892 to 1897 as the first heavyweight champion under the Marquis of Queensberry rules and proved what Sullivan had known all along: that prizefighting could be an exciting, highly lucrative sport under the Queensberry rules, the fighters avoiding arrest while attracting larger, more respectable crowds than ever before.

During his five-year championship reign Corbett also proved that a big man could be a quick and clever fighter. He and the widespread acceptance, and later legalization, of prizefighting under the new rules made such boxing words as *hook*, *jab*, and *upper cut* (see above for details) much more commonly known and eventually led to widespread use of such terms as:

> *solar plexus*. This term had been in English medical use for the network of nerves behind the stomach since 1771, but in the 1890s Corbett and other fighters began to use it in a general way to mean the pit of the stomach. The term became even better known when Bob "Fitz" Fitzsimmons, also known as "Ruby Robert," knocked out Corbett with "a blow to the solar plexus" to win the heavyweight championship in 1897.
>
> *fighting clip*, an 1881 term for the short, clipped haircut some fighters wore but which became something of a fad hairstyle for the many young men who imitated Corbett during his reign.
>
> *decision*. Some early fights in England and America had been decided by a referee when the fighters agreed not to accept a draw if the fight were stopped by the police or an unruly crowd. However, the idea of limiting a fight to a specific number of rounds and then declaring a winner if there had been no knockout developed slowly after the Civil War. Many such early decisions resulted when one fighter had bragged that he would either knock out his opponent by a certain round or openly admit defeat, and was forced to do just that. One of the first major *decisions* in the modern sense was Tommy Burns over Marvin Hart after the mutually agreed upon 20 rounds had elapsed in their 1881 fight in San Francisco.
>
> *Newspaper decision* became a common term in New York State in 1916 when a new law allowed ringside boxing writers to score prizefights and reveal their decisions in their newspapers the next day. The New York State Walker Law of 1920 then made *decision* common in boxing by limiting bouts to a maximum of 15 rounds, the winner to be declared by a "decision" if there was no knockout.

punching bag, an 1897 American term (the English have also called it a *punch bag* since 1899) which Corbett helped popularize. By the early 1900s there was the separate *heavy bag* of 60 to 80 pounds and the smaller, round *speed bag*, which some fighters called the *punching ball*.

footwork, as agile movement of the feet, early 1900s.

weigh in, 1909 in boxing use, from the 1868 horse-racing use (meaning the weighing of a winning jockey, his saddle, and assigned weights after a race).

shadow boxing, an English boxing term of 1919.

Until Sullivan and Corbett brought nationwide attention to Marquis of Queensberry prizefighting, professional fights in the United States had mainly been for the rough entertainment of lumberjacks, miners, and factory workers, with many fighters being from these backgrounds or strong, hungry immigrants and farm boys seeking quick fame and fortune in the ring. Regardless of skill, local and ethnic champions continued to draw the biggest crowds for many years, and still do in many local fights. Many of the early American fighters had earned local reputations in *free fights* (1856) or *free-for-alls* (1902) or while *fighting drunk* (1890) or were simply *fighty* (pugnacious, 1843) or *fighting fools* (1918, probably from wartime army use) who loved *to mix it up* (fight, 1905). Some took so much punishment in the ring that the term *cauliflower ear* (1909, for an ear deformed from the repeated swelling of many blows) became common, while some boxers became *punch drunk* (1915), which was later sometimes shortened to *punchy* (1942) and also called *slap happy* (1941). Some never had a *fighting chance* (1889) and were a *pushover* (1906) for any skilled boxer who made them look like a mere *palooka* (a big, dumb, inept fighter, the word said to have been coined by sportswriter Jack Conway in *Variety* in the 1920s) or even like a *stumble bum* (1934). A few were dishonest and were paid to be a *set up* (1923, from the 1848 verb use meaning to plan to defraud), to *throw* (lose intentionally, 1860s) a fight by *pulling* (one's) *punches* (1934) or by agreeing *to take a dive* or *go into the tank* (both meaning to pretend or allow oneself to be knocked out, 1930s).

Though ethnic fighters contributed few words to our language, they helped create a nationwide awareness of ethnic names and added some colorful nicknames. Before 1915 Irish-Americans were dominant in most divisions with many skilled and colorful fighters such as "Irish" Bob Cassidy (many Irish-American fighters put "Irish" in front of their names to show they were proud of their ethnic origin), Packey McFarland, Terry McGovern, "Philadelphia" Jack O'Brien (real name Joseph Hagen), and Jack and Mike "Twin" Sullivan. Such fighters were said to put on a good *Donnybrook* (a 1900 English term for an action-filled fight, from the village of Donnybrook, near Dublin, Ireland, whose annual fair was once known for its brawls) and their names sold a lot of *ducats*, tickets to an event, a word first popular in boxing around 1910 (from various 14th-century European coins called *ducati*, because they bore a likeness of a *duca*, or doge, on them).

Before World War I, German-Americans dominated the middle-weight division and there were such German-American fighters as Frank Klaus, Frank Mantell, Billy Papke, and Ad Wolgast. Polish Americans rooted for Michigan's Stanley Ketchel, "The Michigan Assassin" (real name Stanislaus Kiecal), who lost the middleweight championship to Billy Papke in 1908 and won it back from him in San Francisco that same year, beating Papke so bad his own sister didn't recognize him. Danish Americans had Battling Nelson (real name Oscar Nielson), who dominated the lightweights. Jewish fighters of this period included Abe Attell, Joe Choynski, Ruby Goldstein ("The Jewel of the Ghetto," referring both to his origin on Manhattan's Lower East Side and his name), who later became a famous referee, and Battlin' Levinsky (real name Barnard Lebrowitz). From 1915 through the 1930s such Jewish fighters were in the ring as Max Baer, "The Livermore Larruper" (he lived in Livermore, California; *larrup* had meant to beat or thresh since 1839, from the Dutch *larpen*, flail), who became heavyweight champ in 1934 by knocking out the 6-foot-5¾-inch "Italian Alp," Primo Carnera, after knocking him down twelve times in eleven rounds, then lost to James J. Braddock in 1935; Benny Leonard (real name Benjamin Leiner), who also later became a referee; "Slapsie Maxie" Rosenbloom (known for his slaplike punches, scoring only 18 knockouts in his 289 professional fights), who was light-heavyweight champion from 1932 to 1934, then played in movies and became a nightclub comedian; and others such as Al Singer, Lew Tendler, and Sid Terris.

In the 1920s Italian-American fighters began to emerge, eventually giving us lightweight Billy Petrolle, "the Fargo Express" (he was from Fargo, North Dakota, and was known for his constant offense); featherweight and lightweight champ Tony Canzoneri; featherweight John Dundee, "the Scotch Wop" (because although his ring name seemed Scottish, his real name was Joseph Carrora); middleweight champion Rocky Graziano (real name Rocco Barbelo); heavyweight "Two-Ton Tony" Galento, who was built like a beer keg and knocked down Joe Louis in their 1939 title fight, before Louis knocked him out; heavyweight Rocky Marciano, "the Brockton Blockbuster" (real name Rocco Marchegiano, from Brockton, Massachusetts—*blockbuster* had been a World War II word of 1942 for an 8,000-pound bomb, big enough to destroy a city block), who became heavyweight champion in 1952 by knocking out "Jersey Joe" Walcott and retired undefeated in 1956; light-heavyweight Joey Maxim (real name Joseph Berardinelli); and featherweight champion Willie Pep (real name William Papaleo).

Just as they were discriminated against in other fields, American blacks were discriminated against in boxing. Thus John L. Sullivan said he would "draw the color line" (originally a southern reconstruction expression of 1875) in refusing to risk his title against Peter Jackson, and Jack Dempsey refused to fight Harry Willis. Nevertheless, blacks had begun their boxing climb in the 1900s with Baltimore's Joe Gans (real name Joseph Gaines), who was lightweight champion from 1902 to 1908 and was the first to be called the best fighter in America *pound-for-pound*, and reached the top when 215-pound, 6-foot-1-inch Jack "Li'l Arthur" (John Arthur) Johnson of Galveston, Texas, became the first black heavyweight champion. The thirty-year-old Johnson whipped Tommy Burns (real name Noah Brusso) so badly on the day after Christmas, 1908, in Sydney Stadium in Australia that the police stopped the fight in the 14th round. This should have made Johnson the champion, but he had to win it again by knocking out James J. "Jim" Jeffries, who came out of retirement to try to beat him, in Reno, Nevada, on the Fourth of July, 1910, in 15 rounds.

Although Johnson was now the undisputed heavyweight champion, boxing promoters, newspaper reporters, politicians, celebrities, and most other white Americans seemed to consider his prowess and fame a racial affront, especially since he seemed to be laughing at all white boxers and mocking the white middle-class world—and seemed to have had a penchant for white women.

Jack Johnson vs *James J. Jeffries, Reno, Nevada, July 4, 1910. Johnson, the first black heavyweight champion, knocked out Jeffries in the 15th round, and many white Americans began looking for a* white man's hope *to beat him.*

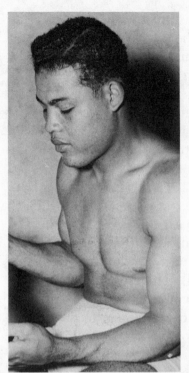

Handsome twenty-three-year-old Joe Louis, the Brown Bomber, won the heavyweight championship in 1937 after knocking out James J. Braddock in eight rounds. Louis kept the championship until 1949, defending it twenty-six times.

Thus white America began looking for and talking about the *white man's hope* (1911) or more commonly a *(great) white hope*, a white fighter who would give this first black heavyweight champion his comeuppance (by 1912 *great white hope* was also used to mean any promising white leader). However, it was five years before Johnson was knocked out by the 250-pound, 6-foot-6¼-inch Jess Willard, "the Potawatomie Giant" (from Potawatomie County, Kansas, and the tallest heavyweight most people had ever seen) in 26 rounds in Havana, Cuba, in 1915. Not until 1937, when 200-pound, 6-foot-1½-inch, 23-year-old Joe Louis (real name Joseph Louis Barrow), a former Golden Glove star from Lexington, Alabama, and Detroit, Michigan, knocked out James J. Braddock in 8 rounds in Chicago to become our youngest heavyweight champion, did America fully accept a black as a title holder.

During his long and popular heavyweight reign, from 1937 to 1949, Joe Louis was a fighter and an American most of us talked about with pride, especially after he avenged an earlier defeat by knocking out the German Max Schmeling in the first round of their 1938 rematch in the anti-German days before World War II. However, America still had Louis' color on its mind when we condescendingly called him, as many Americans did, "a credit to his race," and in giving him the name "the Brown Bomber" (which also reflected our wartime preoccupation with bombing planes). Louis had emerged as a fighter during the Depression years of the mid 1930s, which is when black fighters began to dominate boxing, as the Irish, Germans, Jews, and Italians had before them. We soon had nonstop puncher "Hurricane" Henry Armstrong

"Sugar Ray" Robinson knocks out Bobo Olson in their 1955 middleweight title bout. Walter Smith began his professional career before he was old enough to obtain a fight card and fought under the name of an older friend, Ray Robinson, who did have one. Later, a Watertown, New York, sports editor dubbed him "Sugar Ray"; thus was the name "Sugar Ray" Robinson created.

(real name Henry Jackson), who held the featherweight, light-weight, and welterweight titles simultaneously (heavyweight Tommy Jackson of the 1950s had the same nonstop attacking style and was called "Hurricane Jackson"); light-heavyweight champion Archie Moore (real name Archibald Wright); and welterweight and middleweight champion "Sugar Ray" Robinson, who demonstrates the growth of a boxer's name. He was born Walter Smith; then, when he was a teenager, still too young to fight, he used the Amateur Athletic Union fight card and name of an older friend, Ray Robinson, in order to enter the ring. He was then nicknamed "Sugar" by sports editor Jack Case of Watertown, New York, who wrote that the young amateur was "sweet as sugar" in the ring and thus became "Sugar Ray" Robinson throughout his 25-year, 202-bout professional career (1940–65), during which he won the middleweight championship five times and the welterweight championship once. After Joe Louis, we had such black heavyweight champions as Ezzard Charles, New Jersey's "Jersey Joe" Walcott (real name Arnold Raymond Cream), Floyd Patterson, "Sonny" (Charles) Liston, "Smokin' Joe" Frazier (he came out "smokin'," or throwing many blows), and, of course, Muhammad Ali (see JOHN AND MARY: COMMON FIRST NAMES and MR. AND MRS. SMITH: COMMON LAST NAMES for more on the names of Americans both black and white and see FATS, SHORTY, RED, AND BALDY: COMMON NICKNAMES for more common American nicknames).

But despite the famous American fighters from Sullivan and Corbett on, it was the ex-cowhand, sheriff, saloon keeper, Klon-

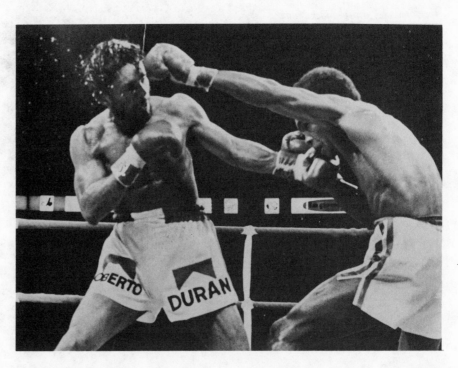

"Sugar Ray" Leonard vs Roberto Duran in their 1980 fight in Montreal. Leonard took his boxing name because of his admiration for "Sugar Ray" Robinson.

dike goldrush prospector, and natural-born showman George Lewis "Tex" Rickard (1871–1929), the fight *promoter* (in general English use since the 15th century; *matchmaker* appeared in general English sporting use in 1704, though at that time especially in horse racing), who made boxing big business and *leather pushers* (boxers, 1920) millionaires. After staging the lightweight fight between Battling Nelson and Joe Gans in Goldfield, Nevada, in 1906, in order to promote that mining town, and the Jack Johnson–Jim Jeffries fight in Reno in 1910, in which Rickard was also referee, Rickard knew the financial possibilities of prizefighting as a 20th-century spectacle. Selling tickets was especially easy if a fight could be touted as a *grudge fight* (a 1920s term) of black against white, as were the first two fights Rickard promoted; or of an American against a foreigner, as his Dempsey–Carpentier and Dempsey–Firpo fights; or even of an alleged World War I slacker, Dempsey again, against "The Fighting Marine," Gene (James Joseph) Tunney (who had been a member of the Marine Corps during World War I).

Rickard, who had exclusive rights to Dempsey after promoting the fight in which Dempsey knocked out Willard in Toledo in 1919 to win the heavyweight championship, created the much-talked-about first *million-dollar gate* (*gate*, 1886, as the total gate receipts of a sports event) in Dempsey's title fight against the French light-heavyweight Georges "Orchid Man" Carpentier, in an arena Rickard built on Boyle's Thirty Acres in Jersey City, New Jersey. Dempsey won in four rounds; ticket sales grossed $1,789,238. Rickard then promoted four more fights for Dempsey and his

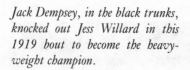

Jack Dempsey, in the black trunks, knocked out Jess Willard in this 1919 bout to become the heavyweight champion.

Luis Firpo, the Wild Bull of the Pampas, *knocks heavyweight champion Dempsey out of the ring in the first round of their 1923 fight at New York City's Polo Grounds. Dempsey went on to win this fight, boxing's second* million-dollar gate.

famous *manager* (a 17th-century English word), Jack Kearns, which drew over one million dollars in receipts: Dempsey against Argentinean Luis Firpo, "the (Wild) Bull of the Pampas," 1923; his two fights against Gene Tunney, in 1926 and 1927; and against Jack Sharkey (real name Joseph Paul Zukauskas), also in 1927. Tunney won both his fights with Dempsey by 10-round decisions. It was the second Dempsey–Tunney fight in Chicago, on September 22, 1927, in which Dempsey was trying to win back the heavyweight title before 100,000 spectators, that added the term *long count* to our boxing vocabulary. In the seventh round Dempsey knocked Tunney down and referee Dave Barry delayed beginning the count until Dempsey went to a neutral corner: when Tunney got up at the count of 9, 14 seconds had elapsed, and Tunney then went on to win.

Born in Manassa, Colorado, the 190-pound, 6-foot-1½-inch Jack (William Harrison) Dempsey, "the Manassa Mauler," had begun his fighting career in Colorado and Utah mining camps before taking the title from Jess Willard in Toledo, Ohio, on the Fourth of July, 1919, knocking Willard down seven times in the first round, Willard's seconds finally *tossing in the towel* (see *throw up the sponge* above) before the fourth round began (this the first widely reported instance of tossing in a towel rather than a sponge to signify giving up in a fight). Though a quick and skillful defensive fighter, Dempsey is best remembered for his powerful close-in, hooking attack and smoothly moving style. His fame, style, and imitators helped popularize many boxing terms:

mauler. Dempsey was called "the Manassa Mauler" because he was born in Manassa, Colorado. *Mauler* had been in the English language, meaning one who mauls or uses a maul, since the 17th century and to *maul* had meant to beat or thrash since 1841. The Manassa Mauler was so famous that by 1920 *mauler* was used in prizefighting to mean any hard-hitting fighter. A hard-hitting fighter had been called a *slugger* since 1877 and a bout full of heavy hitting a *slugfest* since 1916.

fighting out of a crouch. From the earliest days of English boxing, most fighters had assumed a *stand-up* (1821) style of not flinching or crouching to avoid blows. Dempsey preferred using short hooks out of a crouch and soon many other fighters were following his style and *fighting out of a crouch* (though Dempsey's crouch was more extreme than that of most modern boxers).

Break! Relying on his short, hard hooks thrown from his crouch, Dempsey liked close-in fighting, which led to many more clinches. Thus referees saw more clinches during and after Dempsey's time and it was in the late 1920s that many of them first began shouting *Break!* to the clinching fighters.

K.O. Rickard and Dempsey knew the million-dollar crowds wanted to see knockouts and tried to give the crowds what they wanted; thus knockouts became more common and more talked about during Dempsey's championship period and a knockout was often called by the abbreviation *K.O.*, which might then be re-spelled *kayo* (1923). Incidentally, to *put to sleep* had meant to knock someone out since 1891.

on the button. Dempsey was known especially for his knockout blows to the chin; *button* came to mean chin around 1920 and a hard, solid Dempsey-like blow on the chin was said to be *on the button* by 1928. Fighters with a *glass jaw* (1914) couldn't stand up to Dempsey or his imitators and during the early 1920s it was often said that, in order to win, a fighter had to be able to *take it on the chin*.

headgear. Not until Rickard and Dempsey made boxing and the knockout punch such a big money business did most professionals start wearing a leather head protector, the *headgear*, while sparring in the gym, both for basic protection and to avoid getting hurt and having to cancel or postpone a major fight with its major payday. Almost all fighters now also began wearing a *mouthpiece* while in the ring, this item said to have been perfected by a fight-loving dentist named Brad Levin around 1912.

Golden Gloves. The new popularity of boxing during Dempsey's time, and of all sports during the 1920s, led the *Chicago Tribune* to sponsor an annual amateur boxing tournament beginning in 1923. The *New York Daily News* organized a similar annual tournament and called it the *Golden Gloves* in 1927 (the Amateur Athletic Union had begun its annual competition in 1888).

By now, prizefighting was becoming legal in many states, though some still outlawed it or couldn't make up their minds, passing and repealing various laws for and against it. Rickard, with Dempsey's fame to help him, had changed prizefighting from an event usually held outdoors in makeshift arenas or baseball stadiums to *indoor boxing*, mainly because Rickard's copromoter, Fred Armstrong, had a lease on New York City's Madison Square Garden. The two men practically had a monopoly on New York boxing under the state's new boxing law (Rickard's accounts included money for "political overhead"). In 1920 the *Walker Law* was pushed through the New York legislature in Albany—while Rickard and Armstrong and Rickard's original employer, a British boxing promoter who had "spent a great deal of money in Albany," eagerly waited offstage. It was pushed through the legislature by state senate Democratic leader Jimmy Walker (who became the very popular mayor of New York City in 1926 and finally resigned under charges of graft and corruption in city government in 1932). This Walker Law had again legalized prizefighting in New York, and Rickard soon had Dempsey in Madison Square Garden, knocking out Bill Brennan in 12 rounds.

Madison Square Garden was originally located across from New York City's Madison Square Park, at the northeast corner of Madison Avenue and 26th Street, where a New York and Harlem railroad horsecar barn had once stood. In 1873, P. T. Barnum built his $35,000 Barnum's Monster Classical and Geological Hippodrome there, also called Barnum's Great Roman Hippodrome, for scientific and freak displays, chariot races, and cowboy-and-Indian shows. The famous military bandleader Patrick Gilmore bought the property in 1875, added statues, fountains, and gravel walks, and presented more genteel athletic and other events, renaming it *Gilmore's Gardens*. Commodore Cornelius Vanderbilt took over the property in 1879, and his son William K. Vanderbilt then named it *Madison Square Garden*, "Madison Square" from its location and keeping the "Garden" from *Gilmore's Garden*.

The second Madison Square Garden was built in 1890 on the same site. The new block-square building cost $3 million, had a main arena seating 15,000 and included the Hippodrome theater, a ballroom, restaurant, and a summer garden. The building, designed by Stanford White, was topped by a 320-foot tower supporting a 13-foot-high revolving copper statue of a nude Diana the Huntress, bathed in searchlights at night (the nude statue was later removed as being of "depraved taste"). This second Garden opened on June 16, 1890, with a concert by Eduard Strauss; its new roof-garden theater and supper club opened the night of June 25, 1906, this high-society event being interrupted when the thirty-five-year-old Pittsburgh industrialist Harry K. Thaw shot Stanford White for his "exotic housekeeping," as the newspapers termed it, with Thaw's beautiful twenty-two-year-old wife, the Floradora girl Evelyn Nesbit.

Farewell to thee, O Temple of Fistiana,
Farewell to thee, O sweet Miss Diana.
Poem by ring announcer Joe Humphreys which he recited at the last fight before the closing of the second Madison Square Garden, May 5, 1925. "Miss Diana" was the statue of the nude Diana, goddess of the hunt, which was originally on top of the building's 320-foot tower.

The "New Madison Square Garden" on 8th Avenue between 49th and 50th street was built in the 1920s with $6 million raised by Tex Rickard and was sometimes called The House That Tex Built.

The second Madison Square Garden was built on the site of the original one, near Madison Square Park on Madison Avenue and 26th Street in New York City. Note the famous nude statue of Diana the Huntress on top of the building.

The next "New Madison Square Garden," the present one, was completed in 1968 on top of the new Pennsylvania railroad station between 7th and 8th avenues and 31st and 33rd streets.

This ornate building was razed in 1925 to make way for a 40-story office skyscraper, but Tex Rickard raised $6 million to build a "New Madison Square Garden," sometimes called *The House That Tex Built*, on 8th Avenue between 49th and 50th streets. Though Rickard built it primarily for prizefights and the circus, it opened with a six-day bike race. The new arena was a long way from Madison Square and had no garden but was still named *Madison Square Garden*. The current incarnation, also called the "New Madison Square Garden," was built in 1968 atop Pennsylvania (railroad) Station between 7th and 8th avenues and 31st and 33rd streets. Madison Square itself is still where it has always been, at Madison Avenue and 26th Street.

The $100 ringside seats for the 1946 Joe Louis–Billy Conn fight at Yankee Stadium helped make it a million-dollar bout.

After Rickard, Mike (Michael Strauss) Jacobs, who had been a ticket broker under Rickard, was the next great promoter. While Rickard had Dempsey, Jacobs had Joe Louis fighting exclusively for him beginning in 1935 and, by 1937, Jacobs was also promoting for Madison Square Garden. Louis had three fights grossing over a million dollars in ticket sales (against Max Baer, 1935; Max Schmeling, 1938; and Billy Conn, 1946) and defended his title 26 times. A dozen of these fights were against relatively unknown fighters between 1938 and 1941, these unknowns soon being called *the bum of the month*. One of these was Jack Roper, whom Louis knocked out in the very first round of their fight at Los Angeles on April 17, 1939. After the fight, Roper, who had hoped to evade Louis's punches, told the radio audience that he was hit by Louis' knockout punch because, "I zigged when I should have zagged," and the expression immediately entered the general language (the German *zickzack*, sharp point, first entered English in the term *in zic-zac*, in a switchback pattern, with the modern spelling *zig-zag* appearing in 1822 and the verb *to zig zag* still being new in the 1930s).

With the end of Louis's and Max Jacobs's reign, the best fight promoter since the 1950s has been television. When heavyweight champion Rocky Marciano knocked out challenger Archie Moore in 1955 the largest part of the just under $2,500,000 gross came not from the gate but from television rights. Television's importance in boxing had begun in 1944 when its Friday night *Fight of the Week* (broadcast until 1964) made Friday night *fight night* with Don Dumphy's *blow-by-blow* account. It also made such prizefighters as Beau Jack (real name Sidney Walker), who had been undisputed lightweight champion twice, famous to millions of viewers because of the frequency with which they appeared on the television fight card (Beau Jack fought three times in televised bouts in March 1944). Television made boxers who could hit hard and move gracefully, especially if they were also good-looking or publicity-wise, even more in demand and made nationwide enthusiasm for a fighter more important than his local or ethnic following. As had radio before it, television and its announcers brought old boxing

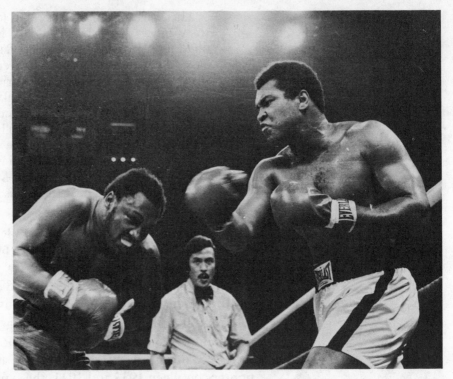

Though no longer able to float like a butterfly, sting like a bee, *a strong, experienced Muhammad Ali pounded Joe Frazier into a 14-round TKO in their 1975 bout in Manila to retain the heavyweight championship. Ali won the championship three times from 1964 to 1978.*

terms into the national vocabulary and quickly spread new and often faddish ones, for example:

peekaboo style, Floyd Patterson's early 1950s style of fighting with his gloves in front of his face (he held the heavyweight championship 1956–59 and 1960–62, being the first to win it twice). This protective style was devised for Patterson by his manager, Cus D'Amato, because Patterson had been easy to hit in the head and knock down (it was named after the game of *peekaboo* as played with young children, which was first known as *peek-boo* in 1599 in England).

rope-a-dope, Muhammad Ali's style of leaning back against the ropes with his arms and gloves protecting his body and face while his opponent futilely punched at him until fatigued. The aging Ali first used and named this style in his October 30, 1974, fight in Kinshasa, Zaire, when he regained the heavyweight title from George Foreman (because Ali, on the ropes, was "roping" the "dope," who would thus wear himself out). The young, fast-moving, hard-hitting Ali of the mid 1960s had said his boxing style was to "float like a butterfly, sting like a bee"; because he could outtalk most interviewers and opponents with his egotistical remarks of being "the Greatest," he was sometimes called "the Mouth."

Heavyweight champion Larry Holmes training in 1981.

Thus, as in so many fields, television became the major form of communication in spreading both old and new terms. Now every home with a television set is part of the arena and all can watch and cheer the gladiators—and expertly use the boxing terms we see in action.

130

Breakfast Food

can, of course, be anything taken for breakfast, from "just a cup of coffee," as preferred by Lincoln, to the large old-fashioned American breakfast of fruit and oatmeal, followed by steak, eggs, fried potatoes, and biscuits, followed by flapjacks, doughnuts, or pie. Many colonials and early Americans ate *porridge* (oatmeal or other meal boiled in milk or water), but most made it out of cornmeal and called the dish *mush* (1671), *Indian mush, cornmeal mush*, or *mush and milk*.

Although *Cream of Wheat* had been packaged as a hot-cereal or porridge mix as early as 1894, *breakfast food* took on a new, specific meaning when a packaged cereal, *Ralston's Health Club Breakfast Food*, was advertised in 1898—it was meant primarily for the 800,000 members of Ralston's Health Club, which had been founded by Dr. Ralston of Baltimore, Maryland (he was soon to give his endorsement and name to the Purina Company of St. Louis, Missouri, and to its product *Purina Wheat*). Within the next ten years *breakfast food, breakfast cereal*, and *cereal* had all come to mean packaged, ready-to-eat cold cereal.

It had all begun years earlier with *Grahamism* (1830s), the regimen prescribed by the Reverend Sylvester Graham (1794–1851). A Connecticut eccentric who had once been in ill health, Graham had married his nurse and had become a food faddist, temperance leader, and self-styled physician known for his impassioned lectures for temperance and against white bread. Graham advocated many healthy things—meatless, spiceless, dry dishes; frequent bathing and exercise; and even brushing the teeth regularly—but Americans generally associated him with his main belief, that bread or other cereal products made from coarse-ground, unbelted flour and eaten slightly stale aided digestion (Graham also thought it would help prevent the further deterioration of "the Yankee race" and bring man back to God). Thus to "Doctor Graham" do we owe not only the terms *graham flour* and *graham cracker* (both terms common since the 1830s), but the development of our cold breakfast cereals as well. The prototype of such cold packaged cereal was developed and named *Granula* by one of Graham's New York State followers, Dr. James Caleb Jackson, and health seekers were soon talking about other hard, cold cereals with such names as *Gluten Grits, Barley Crystals*, and *Hazel Cereal*.

But it was Dr. John Harvey Kellogg and C. W. Post in Battle Creek, Michigan, who, in the late 1890s, truly changed America's breakfast eating habits and started us all talking about *breakfast food* and brand names for it. Various health food movements had been centered around Battle Creek since 1866, when Mother Ellen Gould White, wife of Elder James White and a leader of the Seventh-Day Adventist Church, established the Western Health Reform Institute there (she advocated meatless days and the *ovo-*

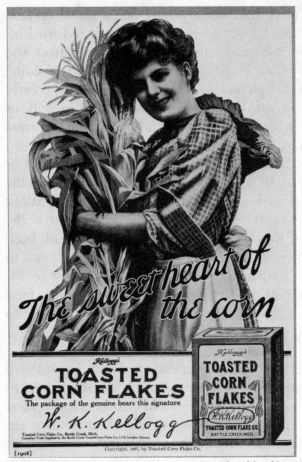

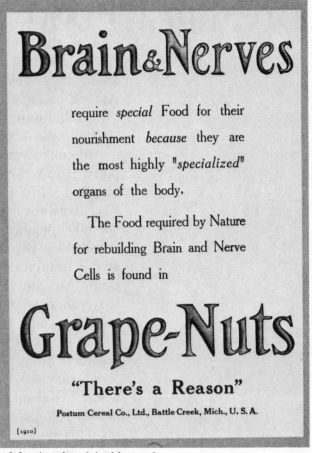

Kellogg's Toasted Corn Flakes *was introduced in this 1907 ad showing the original box and the slogan* the sweet heart of the corn. Grape-Nuts *was introduced in 1898.*

lacto-vegetarian diet—eggs, dairy products, and vegetables). The Whites awarded a medical scholarship to the young Seventh-Day Adventist named Kellogg, who as a medical student in New York City breakfasted daily on seven graham crackers and an apple, then, after his graduation, put him in charge of nutrition at their institute. Dr. Kellogg later headed this institute, then became its owner in the mid-1870s and renamed it the Battle Creek Sanatorium, which thousands of health seekers and food faddists affectionately called "the San." Besides prescribing large doses of bran for everyone and his own "Battle Creek health foods" (the first was *Granola*), Kellogg prescribed zwieback to keep teeth healthy: when one patient objected to eating zwieback Kellogg developed as a substitute his first true cereal, *Granose*. Probably his best-known cereal is *Kellogg's Corn Flakes*, introduced in 1907 with the punning slogan "the sweet heart of the corn."

Earlier, C. W. Post, a salesman of land, farm implements, and his own brand of suspenders, who had come to Battle Creek in 1891 as an ulcer patient at "the San," had offered to help Dr. Kellogg promote Kellogg's new coffee made from cereal and, when he was refused, began manufacturing his own on January 1, 1895. Post first sold his health-food coffee substitute from carts in the streets of Battle Creek, calling it *Postum Cereal Food Coffee*, and "Postum Cereal, the hot food drink," which became known to millions as *Postum*. He formed the Postum Cereal Company on October 1, 1896, its slogan, "Postum—it makes red blood." Post then introduced *Grape-Nuts* in January 1898. Though it contained not a single grape or nut, he claimed that grape sugar was formed when the wheat and malted barley were baked during processing (which never did explain the "nut" part). Each package contained a copy of his pamphlet "The Road to Wellville." Post then introduced his corn flakes, *Elijah's Manna*, in 1906, the picture on the box showing a raven dropping food into the hands of the prophet Elijah. Soon tens of thousands of people all over the country heard outraged clergymen denounce from the pulpit the use of this Biblical name (Great Britain even refused to register the trademark). So in 1908 Post changed the name from *Elijah's Manna* to *Post Toasties*. (Incidentally, Postum Cereal Company merged with *Jell-O* in 1925, and in 1929 became another name we all know, General Foods.)

Thus Ralston, Kellogg, and Post gave the term *breakfast food* (not to mention the word *boxtop*) a new, specific meaning. Since *Ralston*, *Granose*, *Grape-Nuts*, and *Corn Flakes*, Americans have talked about a great many packaged cold cereals, with such names as *Puffed Rice* and *Puffed Wheat* (introduced in the early 1900s with the slogan "Shot from Guns"), *Shredded Wheat* (invented by Henry Perky, who ran a vegetarian restaurant in Denver, Colorado), *Wheaties* ("The Breakfast of Champions," introduced in 1922 by the Washburn Crosby Co. and named by Jane Bausman, the wife of one of the company's executives, in a contest among company employees and their families), *Rice Krispies, Cheerios, Kix, Special K* (the "K," of course, for Kellogg), *Alphabits, Cap'n Crunch, Frosted Flakes, Most*, and on and on *ad nauseam*. At least such "breakfast food" is cheap and has increased milk consumption in the U.S.—but one wonders whether anyone eats mush any more and whether the Reverend Sylvester Graham and Mother Ellen Gould White would be laughing or crying.

Butter and Margarine
Butter (from Greek *bous*, cow + *turos*, cheese) has given us several common expressions. *To butter* meant to flatter as early as 1850 but didn't become *to butter up* until the late 1930s. Since 1888, *butterfingers* (as if one's fingers are greasy) has meant a person who drops things. *Butterballs* were first used around 1910—they were a fancy way of serving butter, but *butterball* didn't come to mean a

fat person until the 1930s. *A big butter-and-egg man* appeared around 1925, during the speakeasy era, and meant a big out-of-town spender, such as a farmer or small-town businessman who spent lavishly on nightclubs, chorus girls, etc.

Oleomargarine (Latin *oleum*, oil + Greek *margaron*, pearl, from the pearllike luster of a glyceride erroneously thought to be an ingredient) was in the American language by 1873, though originally it was a processed suet-and-milk mixture developed at the request of Napoleon III as a cheap butter substitute for his troops. It was simply called *oleo* by 1888—but it wasn't talked about widely until the late 1930s and early 40s, when millions of American housewives, trying to save money and avoid World War II butter shortages, were using it for the first time. The product then still had to be sold under the full name of *oleomargarine* owing to the successful lobbying of the dairy industry, which also required restaurants to serve it in triangles (instead of in butter's traditional square pats) and retailers to sell it in a white rather than in butter's yellow form. A common kitchen scene during World War II was of women squeezing and kneading plastic bags of the white oleo to mix it with the yellowish-orange coloring packet included with it. During this period *oleo* took on a distasteful connotation and by the war's end the word *margarine* had taken over.

Can It!—Freeze!

In American slang, *can* has meant a toilet since 1900, a jail since 1910, a cheap car since 1929, and the buttocks since 1930. *To can* has meant to fire a person from a job (1885) or expel him from school (1905) and *can it* has meant stop or shut up since 1906. Recorded music has been called *canned music* since 1917, the same year a type of solid alcohol or paraffin fuel packed in small cans and used to heat food was commonly called *canned heat*, or by one of its brand names, *Sterno*.

All this came from the basic word *can* (Old English *canne*, cup), which meant a container for liquids long before tin cans were invented. We still use *can* in this general way, as well as to mean a sealed, filled tin can—the British don't like this confusion between the two types of cans, so they call the latter a *tin*, especially if it contains solid food. Americans have been using the term *tin can* for a large open tin container since 1770, but it wasn't until 1812 that the sealed *tin can* as we know it was invented and not until 1847 that a new stamping process was perfected that produced such tin cans cheaply, starting a whole new food industry. By the 1850s *to can* was a verb and California gold miners were eating the new mass-produced *canned food*, especially their two favorites, *canned oysters* (oysters were then still cheap and common in America) and *canned tomatoes* (a good thirst quencher). But it was the Civil War that made canned food common: since it didn't spoil, such food was supplied to troops fighting in the hot southern summers. Thus most American men first ate and talked about canned food while serving in the war. They were supplied with Gail Borden's new condensed *canned milk* (see COFFEE, TEA, AND MILK), Van Camp's new *canned pork and beans* in tomato sauce (created by a grocer and ex-tinsmith, Gilbert Van Camp of Indianapolis, just before the war), and the Libby and McNeill brand of canned foods (founded during the war, in 1863). After the war the soldiers returning home asked their wives for such early varieties as *canned corn*, *canned beans*, *canned peaches*, *canned cherries*, *canned pineapple*, and *canned strawberries*. *Canned soup* started to become a popular term in 1869 when the Campbell Soup Co. was established.

Many American men first ate canned food while serving in the Civil War, as shown by the used cans on the ground in this scene of Northern troops celebrating Thanksgiving Day in camp in 1862.

Home canning in rural Utah, 1940.

By 1870 *canner* and *cannery* were common terms, 30 million cans of food were sold annually, *home canning* was popular, and the term *can opener* was known to all. Home canning, of course, was usually done in the screw top, porcelain-capped *Mason fruit jar*, patented in 1858 by John Mason, just in time for the Civil War and postwar canning boom, and simply called the *Mason jar* from the 1880s.

To freeze was an American slang term of the 1840s–90s, meaning to have a strong yen or desire for something; thus people spoke of "just freezing for a steak." By 1855, poker players were talking of the game of *freeze* or *freeze-out*, in which each player started with the same stake and dropped out when it was lost, until one player had won all. From this game *to freeze out* soon came to mean to exclude someone, as in business, and by 1876 *to freeze* (someone) or *to give* (someone) *the freeze* meant to ignore or neglect him, a new synonym for *to give* (someone) *the cold shoulder* (1816). *Freeze!* has meant to remain motionless, as if in a state of suspended animation, since 1865.

All these terms referred to natural freezing. As early as 1626,

The can and its label as art: (right) a label from the Campbell Co.; (above) Andy Warhol's 1964 Campbell Soup Can.

Francis Bacon had experimented with freezing meat (he died from exposure suffered during the experiments) and in the 1840s some meat, fish, and poultry were frozen with natural ice for storage and shipping. However, it wasn't until after 1917 that practical *quick freezing* to preserve the flavor and texture of foods was achieved, by Clarence "Bob" Birdseye, an explorer and scientist who had observed how Eskimos froze food in Labrador. The first that most people heard of *frozen food* (1920s) was his *Birdseye Sea Foods*, *Birds Eye Frosted Foods*, or finally *Birds Eye Frozen Foods* (his name became the two-word *Birds Eye* brand; his patents and the trade name were sold to General Foods in 1929). In the 1930s the top compartment of the new refrigerators was called a *freezer* (which had meant ice cream freezer since the 1840s), *freezing compartment*, or often *ice cube compartment*. This compartment became the forerunner of the separate *home freezer* of the 1940s.

Just as the Civil War was the proving ground that made canned foods common, World War II was the proving ground that made *frozen food* common. Lighter than canned goods, frozen foods were shipped to American servicemen all over the world. Within five years after the war *frozen food, frozen food locker, deep freeze,* and *home freezer* became popular terms, especially after *flash freezing* was perfected. Beginning with Swanson's frozen Chicken Pot Pie in 1951, *precooked foods* were also frozen and sold, leading to complete frozen-meals-on-a-tray that could be heated, served, and eaten with little attention, the first being Swanson's 1953 *heat-and-serve* frozen turkey dinner, complete with mashed potatoes and gravy,

all packed in an aluminum tray. Since the appearance of such frozen meals coincided with the introduction of cheap, mass-produced television sets, for a few years all America seemed to be heating and eating such meals while watching television —and the C. A. Swanson company obtained its trademark name for such a meal—*TV Dinner*. Now, too, the earlier *frozen peaches* were joined by scores of frozen foods and food terms, from *frozen orange juice* to *frozen peas* to *frozen cheesecake;* whatever the food was, raw or cooked, it seemed that the word *frozen* could be put in front of it. The frozen juices were often preserved with some of the water removed, to be re-added when the *concentrate* was thawed. In the late 1960s, new *dehydrated frozen food*, needing no refrigeration and called *freeze-dried*, was much talked about. Although such food is used mainly by hikers and campers, *freeze-dried coffee* did become a rival of the older instant coffee in the early 70s.

Candy and Chewing Gum

Candy is short for the redundant 14th-century *sugar candy* (Arabic *qandī*, made of sugar). Early colonists talked about their *sugar plums* and *maple syrup candy* or *maple candy*, about the New Amsterdam *marchpane* (later called by the German name *marzipan)*, and in the 1720s about the new British *caramels* (Latin *canna mellis*, sugar cane). American children were asking for *lollipops* (British dialect *lolly*, tongue + *pop*, the noise) soon after they became popular in England in the 1790s. *Pralines*, originally almonds coated with white sugar, were created for and named after French diplomat César du Plessis Praslin (1598–1675); but Americans began to make them in the 1800s and the Creoles of French New Orleans substituted native pecans and brown sugar.

By 1817, *lemon drops* and *peppermint drops* were popular, and by the 1820s any larger piece of hard candy was called a *sucker*, with *sourball* not appearing until 1900 (the term *all-day sucker* wasn't used until around 1906). In the 1840s *Pease Horehound Candy*, developed from a bitter cough syrup, was becoming very popular, and people also began calling peppermint drops *peppermint candy*, with *peppermint sticks* following in the 1850s. In the 1840s, too, *candy pulls* became popular, being called *taffy pulls* by the 1870s, when *taffy* also came to be a slang word for flattery. *Taffy* (British *toffee*) was simple to make, from molasses or brown sugar and butter, and the taffy pulls entertained young and old alike and were a suitable face-to-face pastime for courting couples. *Salt water taffy* became associated with the Atlantic City Boardwalk by the 1880s, and the box of neatly wrapped pastel rows of taffy became its typical souvenir.

One of the many praline women *who used to sell their own home-made pralines on the streets of New Orleans.*

138

Hershey's chocolate wrapper, 1916.

Meantime, England was using *sweetmeats* to refer to fancy, soft, or filled candies; but we kept using the word *candy* to refer to all kinds. This was particularly noticeable after fancy French confections were made popular at London's 1851 Great Exhibition and called "French-style candy" in the U.S. This new French-style candy made the 1820s word *bonbon* (French *bon*, good, baby talk "good-good") popular by the mid-1850s and by the 1860s had Americans talking about *chocolate creams (butter cream* appeared in 1952, as a filling).

In the late 1850s, too, people were talking about *peanut candy*, *peanut and molasses candy*, or *peanut brittle* (though the last term didn't become truly popular until about 1900). By 1860, children were asking for *gumdrops* and in the late 60s for *jawbreakers* (which had meant a hard-to-pronounce word since the 1830s) and *vinegar candy*. This last, a vinegar and sugar taffy, was made extremely popular by its frequent mention in the children's stories of Rebecca Clarke, especially her *Dotty Dimple Stories* of 1867–69. With all this variety and with white sugar replacing molasses and brown sugar, by the 1870s the time was ripe for every general store and grocery to offer lollipops, peppermint sticks, vinegar candy, licorice whips, and many others as *penny candy*.

By the 1880s, adults were talking about the new *milk chocolate*, invented in Switzerland in 1875. By the 1890s dark, herb-flavored, baby-shaped *nigger babies* were known (originally this was a Confederate army term for the enormous shells fired against Charlestown), but the new candy that college girls were talking about was *fudge*. *Fudge* had meant to cheat, a hoax, or nonsense since at least 1833, and *Oh fudge!* was a common expression in the mid 1850s. This may or may not be where the candy got its name, but it was first popularized at women's colleges where making it was often an excuse, or fudge, used by the girls to stay up late, talk, and keep the lights on (fudge could be made over a gas light) after "lights out." In fact, early recipes usually were named *Vassar fudge*, *Wellesley fudge*, *Smith College fudge*, etc. White *divinity fudge* wasn't heard of until around 1910.

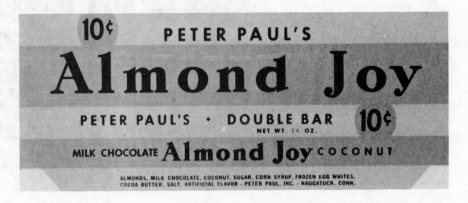

By 1905 all children spoke of *jelly beans*, and *jelly bean* meant any weak or inferior person by 1915, any girl to World War I soldiers, and any person in the jive talk of the 1930s. *Candy bars* became an American institution during World War I when they were mass produced for "the morale, health, and even survival of the dough-boys," according to the National Geographic Society. New types, names, and brands of candy continued to emerge, including *cotton candy* in 1926, and there are many famous success stories and names associated with American candy, as: the *Tootsie Roll*, which first appeared in 1896 as the original paper-wrapped penny candy; *Hershey Bar* (caramel manufacturer Milton Snavely Hershey began to make America's first milk-chocolate bars in Lancaster, Pennsylvania, in 1903); *Life Savers* (Cleveland chocolate-candy manufacturer Clarence Crane, father of poet Hart Crane, invented them, marketed them unsuccessfully as "Crane's Peppermint Life Savers—5¢—for that Stormy Breath," and sold out to others in 1913); *Charms; Russell Stover; Whitman Samplers*, etc. All this goes to prove one point: Americans have a big sweet tooth, which is shown by all the types and names of candy we have talked about throughout our history. Today we eat over 3.5 billion pounds of candy a year, almost 18 pounds for every man, woman, and child.

Chewing gum is an American term—and an American craze. Early colonists saw Indians chewing the resin of the sweet gum tree and many chewed it themselves. Then around 1805 *spruce gum* from the spruce tree became the first commercially sold *gum (gum for chewing)*. It wasn't until the 1870s that the longer term *chewing gum* became popular, because by then such gum wasn't always true gum but was made of chicle.

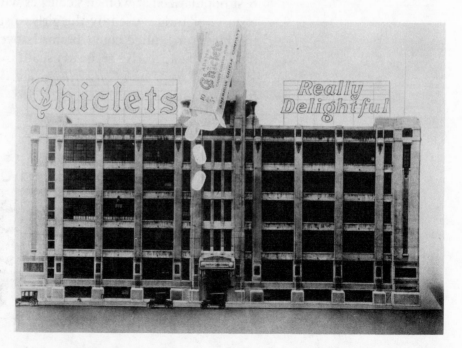

Though Henry Fleer created and named Chiclets, *Adams' American Chicle Co. soon became the best-known manufacturer.*

A Wrigley's Spearmint ad of 1914.

Chicle (Aztec Nahautl *chictli*, the milky juice or latex of a tropical evergreen) was introduced into the U.S. in the 1860s, perhaps by the exiled Mexican General Santa Ana, who often chewed it in public. Around 1872 part-time photographer, part-time inventor Thomas Adams of Staten Island, New York, tried and failed to make a synthetic rubber out of it: after he failed, he remembered that his own son, Horatio, as well as Santa Ana, liked to chew this tasteless substance, so he mixed it with hot water, rolled it into balls and persuaded a Hoboken, New Jersey, druggist to sell his chewable chicle balls at one cent each, and had another son, Thomas Adams, Jr., a traveling salesman, sell it all the way to the Mississippi. Later Adams, Sr., packaged his gum as "Adams' New York Gum—Snapping and Stretching." Since chicle will also carry a flavor, Adams next introduced the first flavored gum, flavored with sassafras; when that failed he introduced the very successful licorice-flavored *Black Jack. Peppermint gum* was introduced in the 1880s by a former popcorn salesman, William White: named *Yucatan*, this brand was the first to contain corn syrup, which made the gum softer and sweeter. White soon became wealthy, then a U.S. congressman, then a frequent companion of actress Anna Held, who repaid his largess by chewing and complimenting his gum in public. Meantime Adams also introduced the term *vending machine* in the 1880s, using the device to sell his *tutti-frutti gumballs* on New York City elevated-train platforms (these vending machines were, of course, also called *gumball machines*).

It was in the late 1890s and early 1900s, however, that modern processing, packaging, and advertising made chewing gum truly popular. Soap salesman William Wrigley, Jr., who had promoted nonchicle chewing gum as early as the 1860s, founded the Wrigley, Jr., Company in 1898. It is now the world's largest manufacturer of chewing gum and has given us such popular brand names as Wrigley's *Spearmint*, *Juicy Fruit*, and *Doublemint*. In the early 1900s Frank Fleer, who had been making chewing gum since 1885, introduced *bubble gum* with his too-sticky *Blibber-Blubber*; then, in 1928, he successfully produced the nonsticky *Double Bubble*, which was an immediate success. Meanwhile his brother, Henry, had created and named *Chiclets*, candy-coated chicle pellets, in the early 1900s (the first *Sugarless gum* was introduced in 1969). Thus chewing gum started in the 1840s and became a major preoccupation in the 1890s. Today when we listen to America we're also likely to hear America chewing.

A Chicken in Every Pot

I wish that there would not be a peasant so poor in all my realm who would not have a chicken in his pot every Sunday.
Henry IV of France when he was crowned king in 1589.

A chicken in every pot, and a car in every backyard.
Attributed to Herbert Hoover in 1928 Presidential campaign.

Herbert Hoover actually never said "a chicken in every pot." It was attributed to him by his Democratic opponent, Al Smith, in a speech Smith made in Boston during the 1928 Presidential campaign. Smith got the line from a Republican campaign flyer and newspaper ad titled "A Chicken for Every Pot" and used it to lambaste Hoover, claiming that the average working man couldn't afford a chicken dinner every Sunday. But people still think Hoover used the slogan and made the promise of a chicken in every pot to Americans during the Depression.

Chicken on the table did represent prosperity to many earlier Americans. On the frontier and in the West, domestic chicken represented fancy civilized food as opposed to game, and suggested that farmers and homemaking women had at last arrived. By 1838 *chicken fixings* meant any fancy or superior meal; thus a traveler at an inn might order the more expensive "white bread and *chicken fixin's*" as opposed to the cheaper basic "corn pone and *common doin's*." Poor immigrants of the late 19th and early 20th centuries associated roast chicken with the upper classes back home, and being able to afford it as Sunday dinner in the New World was a great comfort and mark of success (American Jews ate it on Friday night, as part of their Sabbath). Thus chicken every Sunday was part of America's good life, as well as a popular 1943 book, *Chicken Every Sunday: My Life with Mother's Boarders*, by Rosemary Taylor.

Southerners had been talking about *fried chicken* since 1710, originally fried in the South's ubiquitous bacon grease or in lard, which also added something to the accompanying cream gravy. *Southern fried chicken* and such variants as *Kentucky fried chicken* and *Maryland fried chicken*, however, didn't become popular terms until millions of Americans saw them advertised on the signs of roadside restaurants in the 1930s. Our American dish and term *chicken salad* has been around since 1841, and *chicken (pot) pie* since 1845, while southerners have been bragging about their *chicken gumbo* since 1867 (*gumbo* is a slave word, from Bantu *Kingombo*, okra, though recipes seem to have come via the West Indies). *Chicken à la King* was introduced in the 1880s, one story being that it was suggested at Delmonico's restaurant by Foxhall Keene, son of the famous Wall Street operator and sportsman J. R. Keene, and

A Chicken *for* Every Pot

THE Republican Party isn't a *"Poor Man's Party:"* Republican prosperity has erased that degrading phrase from our political vocabulary.

The Republican Party is *equality's* party—*opportunity's* party—*democracy's* party, the party of *national development*, not *sectional* interests—the *impartial* servant of every State and condition in the Union.

Under higher tariff and lower taxation, America has stabilized output, employment and dividend rates.

Republican efficiency has filled the workingman's dinner pail—and his gasoline tank *besides*—made telephone, radio and sanitary plumbing *standard* household equipment. And placed the whole nation in the *silk stocking class.*

During eight years of Republican management, we have built more and better homes, erected more skyscrapers, passed more benefactory laws, and more laws to regulate and purify immigration, inaugurated more conservation measures, more measures to standardize and increase production, expand export markets, and reduce industrial and human junk piles, than in any previous quarter century.

Republican prosperity is written on *fuller* wage envelops, written in factory chimney smoke, written on the walls of new construction, written in savings bank books, written in mercantile balances, and written in the peak value of stocks and bonds.

Republican prosperity has *reduced* hours and *increased* earning capacity, silenced *discontent*, put the proverbial "chicken in every pot." And a car in every backyard, to boot.

It has *raised* living standards and *lowered* living costs.

It has restored financial confidence and enthusiasm, changed *credit* from a *rich* man's privilege to a *common* utility, *generalized* the use of time-saving devices and released women from the thrall of *domestic drudgery.*

It has provided every county in the country with its concrete road and knitted the highways of the nation into a *unified* traffic system.

Thanks to Republican administration, farmer, dairyman and merchant can make deliveries in *less* time and at *less* expense, can borrow *cheap* money to re-fund exorbitant mortgages, and stock their pastures, ranges and shelves.

Democratic management *impoverished* and *demoralized* the railroads, led packing plants and tire factories into *receivership*, squandered billions on *impractical* programs.

Democratic mal-administration issued *further* billions on mere "scraps of paper," then encouraged foreign debtors to believe that their loans would never be called, and bequeathed to the Republican Party the job of *mopping up the mess.*

Republican administration has *restored* to the railroads solvency, efficiency and par securities.

It has brought the rubber trades through panic and chaos, brought down the prices of crude rubber by smashing *monopolistic rings*, put the tanner's books in the *black* and secured from the European powers formal acknowledgment of their obligations.

The Republican Party rests its case on a record of stewardship and performance.

Its Presidential and Congressional candidates stand for election on a platform of sound practice, Federal vigilance, high tariff, Constitutional integrity, the conservation of natural resources, *honest* and *constructive* measures for agricultural relief, sincere enforcement of the laws, and the right of *all* citizens, regardless of *faith* or *origin*, to share the benefits of opportunity and justice.

Wages, dividends, progress and prosperity say,

"Vote *for* Hoover"

Contributed by a Friend of Mr. Hoover   Advertisement

---

served as *Chicken à la Keene* (another story says the dish was created at Claridge's in London for J. R. Keene himself).

Our familiarity with, and concern over, raising and eating chickens has given rise to many "chicken" words and expressions, including the obvious *chicken farm* in 1887 and *chicken wire* in 1920, as well as:

she's no chicken, 1827 (an old expression in England by the 1730s); *she's no spring chicken*, 1906, referring to a woman no longer young.
chicken feed, small change, a little money, 1836.
chicken fit, temper tantrum, 1845.
chicken, any person, 1846; meaning a girl "of easy familiarity," 1859; *chick*, a girl, 1927; *hip chick*, 1937; *slick chick*, 1941.
chicken-hearted, cowardly, 1848; *chicken-livered*, 1872; *chicken*, cowardly, 1930s; *to chicken out*, be a coward, back out, 1950.
as scarce as hen's teeth, 1863.
chicken shit, disagreeable rules, pettiness, lies, 1948.

Cigars and Cigarettes

Cigars (Mayan Indian *sikar*, to smoke, from *sik*, tobacco) were made in Connecticut when it was first settled in the 1630s. Until about 1810 "seegars" were often made by women and children at home, then peddled door-to-door. Then cigar factories appeared in Connecticut, New York, and Conestoga, Pennsylvania, home of the famous *Conestoga wagon*. The large, strong cigar made in Conestoga became a favorite of the wagon drivers and was called the *Conestoga cigar*, soon shortened to *Conestoga*, then to *'stogy* or *stogie*, which by the 1880s came to mean any cigar, especially a strong, cheap one.

Cigars are given descriptive names indicating their size and shape. Some of the names most often heard in America are:

> *corona* (Latin "crown"), a large cigar, usually about 5 ½ inches long, with blunt ends or with a rounded top.
> *ideal*, a slender, torpedo-shaped cigar, about 6 ½ inches long.
> *panatela* or *panetella* (Spanish for "long thin biscuit," from Latin *panis*, bread), a thin, straight cigar about 5 inches long, now open at both ends but formerly having a finished top that had to be cut off before smoking.
> *cheroot* (from the Indian and Ceylon Tamil word *shurutta*, roll, cigar) a thick, stubby panatela. The word also came to mean any cigar, especially a small one, and has sometimes been used to mean a cigarette.

Cigars enjoyed their greatest popularity between 1850 and 1900. In that half-century desktop *ashtrays* and chairside *cigar stands* for ashes, *cigar stores* (1840) and hotel lobby *cigar stands* (1870s) for selling cigars—all became common terms. By the 1870s large carved *wooden Indians*, *cigar store Indians*, or *cigar sign Indians* were common sights in front of tobacco stores, often holding flames for lighting the newly purchased cigar. But as it turned out, the cigar was mainly a 50-year bridge between the chewing tobacco era and the cigarette era. By 1920 cigarette sales pulled abreast of cigar sales and have been drawing ahead ever since.

The conquistadors took the Latin American Indian's cigar to Spain, where street beggars collected the discarded butts, ground them up, and made the first paper-wrapped cigarettes. British and French soldiers then discovered the cigarette in Spain during the Napoleonic campaign of 1814, the French giving them the name *cigarette*, "little cigar." By the late 1820s Americans were talking about the new *paper cigarettes* and the "actresses" and society women who were affecting them. British troops then discovered and popularized Turkish and Russian cigarettes in the 1854 Crimean campaign, and by the 1860s Americans were talking about the fancy *Turkish cigarettes* and the women, "foreigners" (mainly immigrants), and cosmopolitan or effete men who smoked them.

> *. . . a woman is only a woman but a good Cigar is a Smoke.*
> "The Betrothed," a poem in which a man must choose between his love and "the great god Nick o' Teen," Rudyard Kipling, in *Departmental Ditties*, 1886

Vice President Thomas R. Marshall while presiding over a Senate debate on the needs of the country (during Woodrow Wilson's Administration, 1913–21); in 1918 *Owls* were six cents each and *White Owls* were seven cents. Cheap two-cent cigars had been called *two centers* by 1834 and two-for-a-nickel cigars had been called *twofers* ("two for") since 1892, *twofer* later meaning two theater tickets for the price of one by 1948.

Hand-rolled in small factories, these cigarettes were also called *tailor mades* by the 1880s.

Meanwhile, also by the 1860s, another style of cigarette had evolved for American he-men. They were talking about the *roll-your-own* cigarettes, *hand rollers*, or *hand mades*, made with *the fixin's* or *the makin's*, for which a drawstring pouch of *Bull Durham* was essential. Such he-men cigarettes were also available as *factory mades*, produced in factories by *cigarette girls* (1870), who rolled 15,000 to 18,000 a week and earned 50 cents a thousand.

In the late 1870s machine rolling came in with James Bonsack's *cigarette-making machine*, creating the first cheap mass-produced brands (a box of 10 for 5 cents, 20 for 10 cents). Between 1880 and 1910 Americans were talking about such popular *machine mades* as:

American Beauty
Bon Ton
Cameo (an 1886 brand aimed at the women's market)
Cloth of Gold
Cross Cut
Cycle (popular in the bicycling Gay 90s)
Duke's Best and Duke of Durham
High Life
Home Run (cheap at 20 for 5 cents)
King Bee (another cheapie)

Melrose
Old Gold (taken from the "golden tobacco belt" of Virginia, the name was resurrected in a modern brand in 1926)
Our Little Beauties
Piedmont
Sweet Caporal ("Sweet Caps" the best-selling Gay 90s brand and one of the cheapest)
Three Kings
Vanity Fair

There were also some generally more expensive "all-Turkish" factory brands being widely talked about, as *Egyptian Deities*, *Helmar*, *Melachrino*, *Mogul*, and *Murad*; and around 1900 some cheaper Turkish-Virginia blends, as *Fatima*, *Hassar*, and *Mecca*. Many of these early brands were offered "cork tip or plain" and "regular or in boxes."

Boys were smoking *cornsilk* (1853) behind the barn or saving up to buy the cheap, tobaccoless *Cubebs*, made of and named after the crushed dried berries of an East Indian pepper plant, *Piper cubeba*. These *Cubebs* were first sold widely in the 1870s as a medicated cigarette, a coughdrop to be smoked: "No tobacco or habit forming drugs—12 for 5¢ at any drugstore."

In 1879 the *Marquis of Lorne* brand printed a picture on the pack's cardboard stiffener and soon men and boys were talking about and trading *cigarette cards*, pictures of famous postage stamps, Indian chiefs, actresses, athletes, generals, birds, flowers, etc. Baseball players were first pictured on cigarette cards by *Old Judge Tobacco* in the 1880s, such cigarette cards then being called *baseball cards*, with over 2,000 *baseball card sets* (series of cards distributed by one company in a single year) being distributed since then, though later ones have been distributed by soft-drink and chewing-gum manufacturers as well (Topp's chewing gum

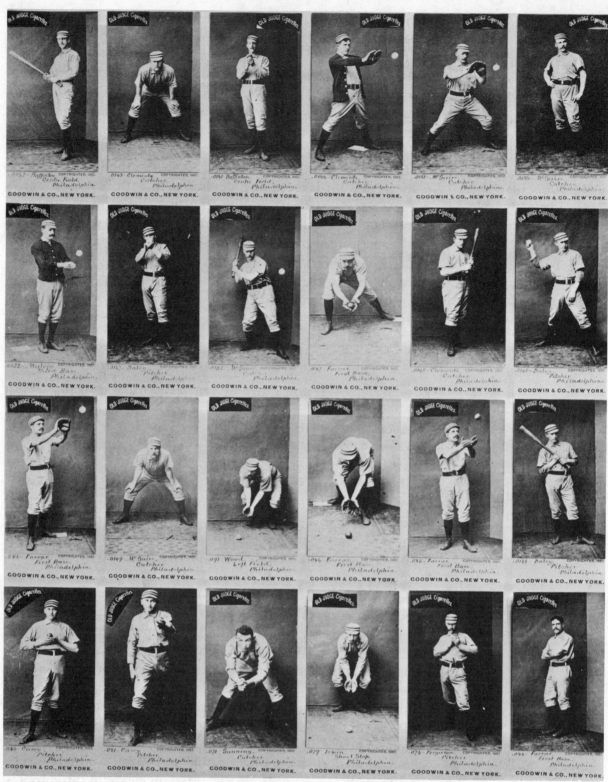

A set of Old Judge *cigarette baseball cards of 1887.* Hassan *featured cigarette cards showing baseball players and, later, auto-racing drivers;* Mecca *cigarettes presented a series of boxing champions and of billiard players, and* Fatima *and* Sweet Caporal *had a series of actresses, the pin-ups of the period. In 1910, Pittsburgh Pirate shortstop "Honus" Wagner, who disliked cigarette smoking, threatened to sue* Sweet Caporal *unless production of a baseball card of him was discontinued. The card was withdrawn, making it one of the rarest and most valuable to collectors.*

alone printing 250 million baseball cards a year in the late 1970s). In the late 1870s and 1880s, too, many cigarette packs began to carry the magic words "Valuable Coupon Enclosed" and the words *premium* and *coupon* took on new meanings (one cheap cigarette was even named *Coupon*). These were redeemable for photo albums for the family, pennants for college boys, or silk stockings for the ladies.

In 1890, James Buchanan ("Buck") Duke of William Duke and Sons had cigarette smokers talking when he won "the cigarette war," merging "the Big Four" (the cigarette manufacturers Allen & Ginter, Goodwin, Kimball, and Kinney) into his *American Tobacco Co.* By 1899 he had also acquired the 1760 snuff, pipe, and chewing tobacco firm of *P. Lorillard*, the 1875 plug manufacturer *R. J. Reynolds*, and merged again with the rival combine, the *Union Tobacco Co.*, which gave him *National Cigarettes*, an option on the largest plug tobacco producer in the world—*Liggett and Myers*—and control of Blackwell's *Bull Durham*. This last, the most talked-about *roll-your-own*, was named after its home region, the area around Durham, North Carolina (where in 1925 Trinity College agreed to change its name to *Duke University* in order to receive a $40 million trust fund from the Duke family's "machine made" cigarette fortune).

Everyone, including Theodore Roosevelt, had been talking about Duke's *tobacco trust* when the government finally broke it up into four companies in 1911. These became four of the best-known company names in America, still much talked about today: *American Tobacco*, which put George Washington Hill, young son of the firm's president, in charge of promoting *Pall Mall*; *Liggett and Myers*, which continued *Fatima* and *Piedmont* cigarettes and in 1912 introduced *Chesterfields* (a brand name the American Tobacco Company had absorbed with the Drumond Tobacco Company); *P. Lorillard*; and *R. J. Reynolds*. The last retained only plug and pipe tobacco lines and in desperation in 1914 turned its seven-year-old *Prince Albert* pipe tobacco blend (Turkish, Virginia, and burley) into a new cigarette named *Camel*, the name chosen to suggest the Oriental names of fancier all-Turkish cigarettes. Within a year American men were calling Camels *humps*.

The new competition plus the newly developed, milder *bright* or *Virginia leaf* tobacco led to new cigarette *blends*, which gave us some of the brands we still smoke and talk about today. In 1917 American Tobacco countered the *Camel* blend with its own *Lucky Strike* (first used as the name of a plug tobacco in 1856, when would-be gold and silver miners were flocking to the far West); Lorillard answered with *Old Gold* in 1926; and *Philip Morris* entered the competition in 1933. These brand names and their various advertising slogans became a major part of the American language.

As late as 1914, however, roll-your-owns or hand mades still far

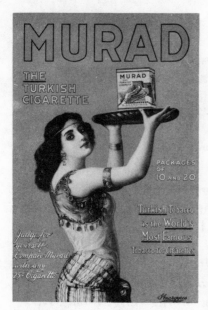

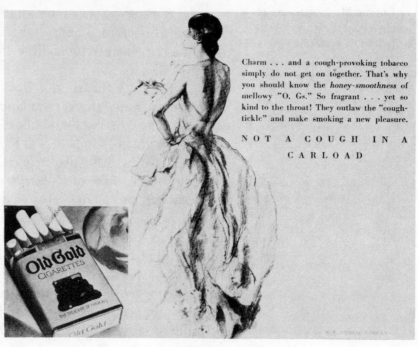

"All Turkish" factory-made cigarettes had a higher-class appeal
than those made from native
American tobaccos. The Murad ad
(above) is from 1910.

In 1929 Old Gold Cigarettes promised honey-smoothness and asserted that there was
"not a cough in a carload."

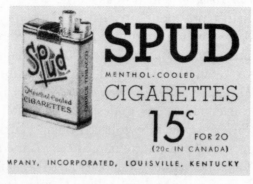

People had been talking about
menthol cigarettes *in rural Ohio
and Kentucky ever since Lloyd
"Spud" Hughes of Mingo Junction,
Ohio, had found a way to impreg-
nate tobacco with menthol in the
mid 1920s. He sold his Spuds
door-to-door before selling out to
Axton Reed for $90,000, which he
spent on racing cars, airplanes, and
the stock market crash. As this
1935 ad shows,* Spuds *became a
major nationwide brand in the
1930s, the forerunner of such later
menthols* as Kool *and* Newport.

In 1914, R. J. Reynolds introduced the first blend, Camel cigarettes, which captured 40 percent
of the market by 1918. The beloved
Barnum and Bailey dromedary
"Old Joe" was featured on the pack.

In 1917 the American Tobacco Co. introduced its blend Lucky Strike with the slogan "It's Toasted" (all cigarette tobacco is toasted). Other famous Luckies' slogans created by George Washington Hill, the aggressive head of American Tobacco from 1925 to 1946, and by Albert Lasker's advertising agency, were to follow. The 1928 slogan "Reach for a Lucky Instead of a Sweet" helped make Luckies the best-selling brand by 1930. The 1930s slogan "OK America" implied that it was OK to smoke Luckies as they were "kind to your throat." The 1940s slogan "With Men Who Know Tobacco Best . . . It's Luckies 2-to-1" referred to tobacco auctioneers, as typified by the rapid-fire auctioneering radio ads with auctioneer L. A. "Speed" Riggs, which ended with his shout "Sold American," meaning that the best tobaccos were auctioned to American Tobacco for use in Lucky Strikes. The 1942 wartime slogan "Lucky Strike Green Has Gone to War" made the company's change from a green to a white pack seem patriotic (wartime shortages and increased costs of the metallic printing inks needed on the green pack had caused the change). In 1944 the new slogan was "L.S./M.F.T.," the abbreviation of Lucky Strike Means Fine Tobacco. This 1950 ad shows several of these and other Lucky Strike slogans.

Scientific tests prove Lucky Strike milder than any other principal brand!

These scientific tests, confirmed by independent consulting laboratory, prove Lucky Strike mildest of 6 major brands tested!

MARLENE DIETRICH says:

"I smoke a smooth cigarette—Lucky Strike!"

Let your own taste and throat be the judge! For the rich taste of fine tobacco — for smoothness and mildness . . .

THERE'S NEVER A ROUGH PUFF IN A LUCKY!

Chesterfield was introduced by Liggett & Myers in 1912, then made into a milder blend in 1915 to become the number-two best-selling cigarette after Camels. This World War II ad of 1942 emphasizes "mildness" and "taste," while reminding us that we should send our troops cartons of cigarettes to "Keep 'em smoking'."

It's CHESTERFIELD

KEEP 'EM SMOKIN'
Our fighting men rate the best . . . . See that they get plenty of milder cooler-smoking Chesterfields. Everybody who smokes 'em likes 'em.

THEY TREAT YOU RIGHT . . . They keep you happy because they're *Milder* . . . they let you know how good a cigarette can be because they *Taste Better*. You'll like them these hot days because Chesterfields smoke *Cooler*.

TODAY'S MILDER BETTER-TASTING CIGARETTE

Virginia Slims' *"You've Come a Long Way, Baby"* slogan introduced in the 1970s followed a long tradition of cigarette brands and ads aimed at the women's market. Some women began smoking cigarettes in the late 1820s, and cigarette makers have encouraged them to smoke ever since. (Left) American women are not unique in smoking cigarettes, as shown in this 1931 British ad for Craven "A" cigarettes. (Right) A 1940 ad for the short-lived red-tipped Debs cigarettes, which were supposed to leave lipstick unsmeared.

outsold factory mades; during World War I the government bought the entire Bull Durham supply "for the Doughboys." The postwar Roaring Twenties saw a huge increase in cigarette sales, and not just to sheiks and flappers. By the 1930s new signs appeared in the new movie houses, "Smoking in the Balcony Only." In the 30s, too, *menthol cigarettes* became a nationwide term when a large company obtained the rights to *Spuds*.

"Roll your own and save your roll" was a popular slogan of the Depression (a 5 cent sack of tobacco made about 33 cigarettes). The Depression also saw new, cheap factory-made brands like *Twenty Grand*, named after horse racing's famous 1931 Triple Crown winner, while Brown and Williamson reduced the price of its *Wings*, which then became a best seller.

World War II saw cigarette consumption double, and after the war *king-size* was the popular new cigarette term. The concept wasn't new, however, as *Viceroy* had a *king* with a *filter* in 1936, *Pall Mall* had "kinged" in 1939 (going from the standard 70- to the king-size 85-millimeter length) and soon doubled its sales; *Herbert Tareyton* also was a king; and in 1940 a *Little King* had been introduced, named after Otto Soglow's comic strip of that name. By 1953, 25 percent of cigarette sales were of the "longer smokes"

and a new "crushproof, flip-top box" was being talked about (a hinged improvement on the sliding pasteboard cigarette box introduced by William Duke and Sons in the 1880s). In the late 1960s a new longer *100* (100-millimeter cigarette) was advertised, and in 1975 a 120-millimeter drive began with even longer cigarettes, bearing names such as *More, Long Johns*, and *Max*.

But in 1953 everyone was talking about medical research that showed "a relation between throat cancer and cigarette smoking." Cigarette manufacturers dubbed this "the cigarette scare" and combatted it by advertisements emphasizing such words as *mildness* and *smoothness*—and by having actors dressed in doctors' white smocks recommend their brands on television commercials. Mainly, however, manufacturers introduced new *filtered cigarettes*, soon called simply *filters. Kents* (named after one of Lorillard's best-remembered executives, Herbert A. Kent) became the first major filter brand name, introducing its "Kents with the Micronite filter" in March, 1952. Filters were not new, however; some premium brands, such as *Parliament* and *Viceroy*, had advertised filters or "filter-tipped mouthpieces" for years. By the mid 1950s *kings* were combined with *filters* to give us the popular term *filter kings*.

Cigarette smoking seemed mature, sophisticated, and romantic from the late 1930s into the 1950s. Clockwise: a tough Humphrey Bogart, a cynical Lana Turner, the reflective news commentator Edward R. Murrow, and the worldly Marlene Dietrich.

After January 1, 1971, Americans heard less advertising talk about cigarettes: cigarette advertising was banned from radio and TV, almost seven years after the 1964 Surgeon General's 387-page *Smoking and Health* report that linked cigarette smoking to lung cancer, heart disease, and other ailments. But through 150 years of war and peace, Turkish and Virginia leaf, short and long cigarettes, good times and bad, good health and cancer, Americans have been puffing away and talking about cigarettes. We have called them:

smokes, 1830s.

coffin nails, 1880s. This term and the British *gaspers* were very popular with the 1914 anticigarette campaign, supported by such personalities as Edison and Ford, and by many temperance groups; a dozen states also banned cigarettes during Prohibition.

cigs, 1890s.

weeds, 1904. Tobacco has been called *the weed* since 1947.

fags, 1908; before that, to a cigarette smoker, "fag" had meant a burned-down stub.

butts, since World War I.

pimp sticks, 1925.

It's a Cinch

Not until after the War of 1812 did American terms for easy and difficult appear with any frequency; before that, most people expected life and its necessary tasks to be hard. Our early popular terms for "easy" or "requiring little effort" were usually gentle, homey, and passive, things were as *easy as pie* or as *easy as rolling off a log*, while later popular terms tend to use more active verbs and images and suggest taking advantage of another, *as easy as taking candy from a baby*. Our terms for easy include:

cinch, meaning both certain and easy by the early 1890s, as sure as if secured by a *cinch*, which had meant a saddle girth since 1859 (via Spanish *cincha* from Latin *cingula*, girth). *Dead cinch*, 1895; *lead pipe cinch*, 1898, with *pipe* itself then being used to mean a certainty or an easy task by 1902.

duck soup, 1912.

easy as falling/rolling off a log, 1840; *easy as pie*, 1891; *easy as shooting fish in a barrel*, 1939; *easy as ABC*, *easy as taking candy from a baby*, both 1942.

peaches and cream, 1920.

a picnic, 1870.

pie, 1889 (first recorded two years before *easy as pie*).

pushover, 1906.

soft snap, 1845; *soft*, 1867; a *snap*, an easy thing, 1877.

tear off, to do easily, 1923.

153

We also have our American terms for difficult or complicated tasks or situations, including:

ball buster, *ball breaker*, first common with World War II troops, then in wide civilian use by 1944 (*balls* has been a slang term for the testicles since the 1880s).

bitch, first recorded in 1928 as meaning a difficult or complicated task or problem, *son of a bitch* having been used with this meaning since World War I (*son of a bitch* has meant a despicable man since 1712).

large order, 1884.

plaguing, difficult, 1815; *plague*, a difficult or perplexing task or problem, 1818.

sticky, complicated, requiring finesse, 1915.

tough, 1883. *Tough* had meant hard luck since the early 1870s, with *tough luck* first being recorded in 1890, *tough titty* in 1929, and *tough shit* in 1946, though this last was probably in use much earlier but wasn't recorded until changes in attitudes and morality after World War II began to allow such terms in print.

Some things are not so difficult as they are perplexing or embarrassing, leading us into trouble. Thus a task, problem, or situation can be a *stumper* (1807) or something *to stump* us or leave us *up a stump* (both terms 1812) or *up a tree* (1825), in a *tight place* (1841), *tight hole* (1918), or *tight spot* (1931), or *on the spot* (1928) or *in a spot* (1930).

Clipper Ships, Windjammers, and Steamers

America's *China trade* or *tea trade* began in 1784 when the new *Empress of China*, named for its destination, sailed to the Orient, bringing back tea, silk, porcelain, and cotton. Three years later two patriotically named ships, the *Columbia* and the *Washington*, sailed around Cape Horn, traded tools and knickknacks with Pacific Northwest coastal Indians for sea-otter pelts, and then sailed to Canton, where they traded the sea-otter pelts for Chinese goods. The *Columbia* continued sailing westward from Canton, arriving home in Boston on August 10, 1790, as the first American ship to sail around the world. On her second three-year voyage to China and around the world, the *Columbia*, again visiting the Pacific Northwest for pelts for the China trade, discovered and sailed into the *Columbia* River, which her captain, Robert Grey, named in honor of his famous vessel.

More New England ships were soon sailing to Canton, some westward around the Horn, some eastward via the West Indies, the Cape of Good Hope, India, and Indonesia. Any such trading vessel was called a *merchant* (a 1585 English use), *merchantman*

> *Never, in these United States, has the brain of man conceived, or the hand of man fashioned, so perfect a thing as the clipper ship. . . .*
>
> Samuel Eliot Morison, *The Maritime History of Massachusetts*, 1921

The Columbia *attacked by Indians. This was the first American ship to sail around the world (1787–90) and the ship that discovered the river that her captain, Robert Grey, named after her.*

(1627), or *merchant ship* (1747). A dockworker who loaded and unloaded such ships was now called by our new term *stowadore* (1788, from Dutch *stuwadoor*, storer, stuffer), which was to be pronounced and spelled *stevedore* by 1828 (influenced by the Spanish *estivador*). Such a worker was also soon called a *longshoreman* (1811, because he worked on the docks "alongshore").

As the lucrative China trade grew, American shipbuilders constructed ever sleeker ships to reduce the sailing time to the Orient—ships with longer hulls, sweeping bows, and towering tiers of canvas, faster ships designed to reduce pitching in tropical storms, to slice through the awesome seas of Cape Horn, and to catch the slightest breeze in the horse latitudes.

Seeking such vessels, shipbuilders began to look again at the *schooner*. This type of ship had first been launched in 1713 in Gloucester, Massachusetts, and was a two-masted fore-and-aft-rigged vessel with the larger sail on the aft mast (this arrangement was called *schooner-rigged* by 1804). According to legend, a bystander watching the launching shouted, "Oh, how she *scoons*" (from Swedish dialect *skunna*, *scoon*, to skim over the water), and the captain of the new ship had responded, "A *schooner* let her be." The only flaw in this story is that the word *scoon* never seems to have been used in English. At any rate, America introduced the schooner and its name, just as it had introduced *scow* (1669, from Dutch *schouw*, pole boat) and would later introduce *catamaran* (1848, as a raft with an outrigger; 1884 as a twin-hulled boat, from a Tamil word of India and northern Ceylon, *kattamaran*, tied wood).

Regardless of the truth of the story of how the schooner got its name, it soon became the most common coastal vessel in American waters. In the early 1840s the name *prairie schooner* was given to the large covered wagons crossing the prairies to Oregon, and by 1877

155

a tall beer glass was also called a *schooner* (getting its name, perhaps, from the ship's tall masts).

Schooners and other ships developed narrower underwater lines for the increased speed they needed when used as fast *packet ships* (1782, a fast ship on a regular route, from the river *packet boat*, 1709, which carried packets of mail as well as passengers and cargo, from the French word *paquebot*), as *slavers* (1820s), as *privateers* (see PIRATES, PRIVATEERS, AND BUCCANEERS), and in trying to outrun blockading British men-of-war during the War of 1812. By the early 19th century, Baltimore had become the shipbuilding center of the long, fast schooner and such a ship was called a *Baltimore flyer* (1814), *Baltimore schooner* (1818), and finally a *Baltimore clipper* (1823, from *clip*, a 1710 English word meaning trim, shipshape, which by 1820 had come to mean "to move fast" in America). Such sleek American-built ships, with their American captains and Irish crews, soon dominated such trans-Atlantic routes as New York to Liverpool and were noted for their "elegant and large" cabins, some as long as 7½ feet! Thus American *ship lines* (1818) and *liners* (1836, both from the 1781 stagecoach use of *line*, to mean a transportation system and its vehicles) were in their ascendancy. By 1834 *clipper-built* had come to mean light and clean-lined and was applied not only to ships but to everything from buildings to plows and sleds, in the same way we have used the word *streamlined* since the late 1890s.

Throughout the 1820s and 30s *Baltimore designs* or *clipper designs* kept reducing time on the long voyages to the Orient, finally producing the first full-sized *clipper schooner* or *clipper ship*, both terms from 1845, the year that the first one, the *Rainbow*, designed by New York's John W. Griffiths (1809–82), was launched (though some naval historians consider the smaller 1833 *Ann McKim* the first true clipper ship). Now *clipper* became a magic word and every ship owner, captain, and seaman wanted a fast, sleek clipper; America was caught up in the grasp of *clipper fever* (1852). Between 1842 and 1855 such new terms as *clipper bark*, *clipper brig*, *clipper brigantine*, *China clipper*, *tea clipper*, and even *opium clipper* appeared.

When gold was discovered in California in 1848 scores upon scores of additional new clipper ships were added to our merchant fleet, now called the *merchant marine* (1850s), to rush supplies, freight, mail, and complete households, as well as many *49ers* (an 1853 term) themselves from the East Coast around Cape Horn to San Francisco. By 1850 as many as 30 of these *California clippers* a month were sailing around the Horn for California, the average clipper now making the 15,000-mile Boston or New York to San Francisco voyage in just a little over five months, about the same length of time it took a prairie-schooner wagon train to cross the 2,000 miles of prairie, desert, and mountains from Independence, Missouri, to the Pacific.

The Sea Witch.

Then in 1850–51 the clipper ship the *Sea Witch*, designed by Griffiths, reached San Francisco from New York in 97 days, the *Sword Fish* sailed from the East Coast to San Francisco in 90 days, and finally the *Flying Cloud* made the journey in 89 days. If these clipper-ship speed records didn't impress shipowners, their profitability did, especially when the *Surprise* netted her New York owners $650,000 from her first three-month voyage to California. The speed records and the profits didn't end in San Francisco: after unloading in California many clipper ships continued for another three months to China to carry tea back to Europe and the U.S., sailing from China around Africa to London in another three or four months, circling the globe and returning a huge three-way profit in less than a year.

Thus the 1840s and 50s was the age of the clipper ships, the period when they were being built in shipyards from Baltimore to Maine, the *Baltimore clipper* having grown into the ever faster and larger *Yankee clipper*, the 4,555-ton, 325-foot, four-masted 1853 *Great Republic* being the largest clipper ship ever built.

Griffiths and Nova Scotia–reared Donald McKay (1810–80) of Boston were the designer geniuses of clipper ships, many of whose poetic but descriptive names became as well known as those of the most popular celebrities of the day. Besides the *Flying Cloud*, the *Flying Fish*, and the *Great Republic*, McKay designed the spectacularly large and fast 2,421-ton *Sovereign of the Seas*, with a top speed of 18 knots. He also designed four of the world's fastest clippers

Six days shalt thou labor and do all thou art able,
And on the seventh—holystone the decks and scrape the cable.
Richard Henry Dana, *Two Years Before the Mast*, 1840. *Before the mast* was an English seafaring term dating from 1627; officers' quarters were toward the stern of a ship, behind the mast, while crew's quarters were at the bow or "before the mast."

157

The Great Republic, *the largest* clipper ship *ever built*.

The Sovereign of the Seas.

for the Australian Black Ball Line, including the *Lightning* (which made a top speed of 21 knots), the *Champion of the Seas* (which made a record run of 465 nautical miles in one day), and the *James Baines* (Boston to Liverpool in 12 days, 6 hours). America, which had been discovered in the search for a short route to the Orient, finally provided not the route but the best sailing ships to reach the Orient or any other distant part of the world.

But even as they became the fastest, largest, and most beautiful sailing ships the world had ever known, American clipper ships were competing with the rapidly improving British *steamers* (an 1825 British word). Our *greyhounds of the sea* (1880s) were writing the last glorious chapter of the age of sail as the age of steam began.

The *steamboat* (1785) had proved itself on calm rivers and lakes since Robert Fulton's *The Steamboat* (also known as *Fulton's Folly* and officially as the *North River Steamboat* or the *Clermont*) made its first successful trip on the Hudson in 1807. By 1809, American and European paddle-wheel steamboats were making coastal trips and British paddle-wheelers were crossing the English channel. These open-water steamboats were always *side-wheelers* (1836) for the sake of stability in ocean seas and quite different from the shallow-draft, boiler-above-deck *Mississippi riverboat*, which appeared in 1816 (and was to be called simply a *Mississippi steamboat* by 1832). Then in the early summer of 1819, barely a hundred years after the first schooner and while the Baltimore clipper was still evolving, a little sailing packet, the *Savannah*, built for the New York–Le Havre route, crossed the Atlantic from Savannah, Georgia, using a steam-driven *paddle wheel* (1779) as an auxiliary to her sails. She used her engine for a total of only 3½ days of the 29-day voyage to Europe, having run out of coal, then made the return trip on sail alone—but she had proven that steam-driven paddle-wheelers could be used on the open seas.

Since America had clipper fever and the best clipper ships, it was Britain that took the lead in developing oceangoing steamships. In 1821–22 a British steamer crossed from England to Chile; in 1825 the British *Enterprise* steamed to India in 113 days, including 10 days spent in *coaling* along the way. In the 1820s also, other British, French, and Dutch steamers went to the West Indies and Central and South America. Then in 1830 the first specially designed *marine steamship engine* drove a wooden paddle-wheeler completely across the Atlantic, with the first primitive *propeller-driven steamboat* crossing just three years later, from England, of course.

In 1833, too, the same year the little clipper the *Ann McKim* was built, a forty-six-year-old Nova Scotian by the name of Samuel Cunard sent the *Royal Williams*, a paddle-wheeled tug that had failed in the Canadian coastal trade, from Canada to England in order to sell it at a better price than he could get at home. It crossed the Atlantic in 25 days on 324 tons of coal and eventually became the Spanish navy's first steamship; it also gave Cunard his first taste of trans-Atlantic success. Soon British ships were using steam-driven paddle wheels no longer as an auxiliary to sails but as the prime power, with the ever present sails now being the auxiliary source. The British-owned British and American Steam Navigation Co. then started regular trans-Atlantic steamship runs in 1838, when it sent the overloaded *Sirius* from London to New York with mail, cargo, and forty adventuresome passengers, then sent the larger 1,320-ton *Great Western* from Bristol to New York. Built and named with the idea of adding trans-Atlantic steamship service to Britain's *Great Western* Railway system, the *Great Western* made the crossing in just 15 days, while America's crack sailing vessels took a full three weeks. Soon British steamers demolished most of the trans-Atlantic records our best sailing packets had held.

Then in 1843 the six-masted British steamer *Great Britain* crossed the Atlantic not with her sails and not using a paddle wheel or a primitive propeller, but using the new *screw propeller*, invented by the Swedish John Ericsson in England in 1836. The *Great Britain* was also the first large commercially successful *iron ship* (Ericsson moved to America in 1839 and later designed the screw-propeller ironclad *Monitor* of Civil War fame).

Now the British gave profitable mail contracts to Cunard, who in 1840 had formed a *trans-Atlantic line* and brought about a shipbuilding revolution by building four almost identical mail-and-passenger ships, which the British immediately called *sister ships*. These first four sister ships were small, ugly, Scottish-built wooden side-wheel steamers with a tall funnel belching smoke between their auxiliary masts—but their two-cylinder, 740-horse-power engines could drive these 1,150-ton, 200-foot ships at 8 to 10 knots. Though such steamers couldn't match the top speed of fast sailing-packets or of clipper ships in a good wind, it was a case of the tortoise and the hare: the steamers raced on day in, day out, good wind or not, and on the shortest, port-to-port routes. Thus by 1847 the consistent steamers were beating sailing ships around the Horn and the British *Cunarders*, as the Cunard steamers were then called, were on regular schedules from Europe to Boston and New York, taking the wind out of the sails of America's trans-Atlantic shipping.

To meet this British competition the U.S. government began subsidizing our own wooden side-wheeler *trans-Atlantic steamers* in 1847. Soon our Ocean Line's 11-knot *Herman* and *Washington* were on the New York-Southampton-Bremen route, our Collins Line's *Humboldt* and *Franklin* were on the New York-Le Havre route, and our own 1850 sister ships, the *Atlantic*, *Arctic*, *Baltic* and *Pacific* were in service. At 2,860 tons, these last four were the largest steamers of their day and so "extravagantly" fitted out that, along with the Collins Line's 1856 13½-knot *Adriatic*, they became the pride of our *paddle steamer* fleet. America's steamers seemed about to supersede the clipper ships in the public's mind and the names of our famous steamers, though always more prosaic than those of the clipper ships, were well known. But no matter how fast, large, or well fitted out these steamers were, the combination of wooden-sided ships and steaming boilers was a dangerous one. After the *Arctic* collided with a French steamer in a fog and sank with the loss of 200 lives and the *Pacific* disappeared without a trace in mid Atlantic in 1856, the U.S. government quickly withdrew its subsidy for trans-Atlantic steamers, and oceangoing steamship development came to a halt here for the next thirty years. We had had clipper fever for too long and, except for brief periods, as during a war, would never again have true maritime supremacy on the seas.

The sister ships *the* Atlantic *(top) and the* Pacific *(middle) and "the largest ship in the world," the* Adriatic *(bottom), were the pride of the American paddle steamer fleet in the 1850s.*

Thus in the late 1850s and the 1860s it was the foreign steamship lines Inman, North German Lloyd, Hamburg-American, and Cunard that turned to fast *packet steamers* (1863), with screw propellers assisted by a full spread of sail. They grew wealthy hauling shiploads of emigrants to America, leaving the least profitable cargoes and routes as the last stronghold of our once proud American sailing packets.

The British introduced the *Great Eastern* in 1860, an 18,914-ton iron behemoth designed for the England-to-India run and having both a paddle wheel and a four-bladed screw propeller, run by separate engines, plus six masts with 6,500 square yards of canvas. It was so long it was launched broadside on the Thames, where it stuck fast for three months, bankrupting the original owners. It was then purchased for the North Atlantic route, where it was a failure except for the work it did laying 1,200 miles of new *Atlantic cable* in 1865, replacing Cyrus Field's 1858 system, which had almost immediately broken down.

The first *steel ship* to cross the Atlantic was American, the steel-hulled 1862 paddle steamer *Banshee*, but it was built in Liverpool, as a *blockade runner* (an 1863 Civil War term) for the Confederacy. A great many of our clipper ships ended their days during the Civil War as fast but vulnerable Union naval ships blockading the South—such wartime use demonstrating conclusively the superiority of iron and steam over wood and sails. Both John Griffiths and Donald McKay had turned to steamship design in the late 1850s, with Griffiths designing the first successful *twin-screw* ship in the early 1860s. However, a few clipper ships were built after the Civil War, McKay designing one last clipper in 1869, the spectacular *Glory of the Seas*, which set the San Francisco to Sydney record of 35 days and was in service until 1923. Meanwhile, the large *Grand Admiral* logged almost three-quarters of a million miles between 1869 and 1897.

Thus clipper ships died slowly, continuing to work on some routes until well after the Civil War, not because clippers were still a bit faster than steamers under optimum conditions but because they could still be more profitable: wind was free and their holds could be filled with cargo, while steamers had to give valuable space to large bunkers full of costly coal. Clipper ships could also make the long runs along and around South America and Africa and across the Pacific where coaling stations were still few and far between.

After the Civil War, too, the slow, square-rigged New England *downeaster* (1835, from the regional phrase *down east* as meaning New England) was perfected for carrying heavy and bulk cargo. Though not as fast as clipper ships or steamers, these wide, squarish American ships could carry more cargo for their size than either of the others. Thus, after the Civil War hundreds of two-, three-, four-, and even six-masted sailing ships still plied the East Coast and the Caribbean and crossed the Atlantic, Pacific, and Indian oceans with lumber, grain, granite, and coal, including coal for distant steamship-fueling stations. Such slow cargo vessels had been called *freighters* since 1836; by the 1880s a freighter that wandered from port to port as cargo dictated was called an *ocean tramp* or, if it used steam, a *tramp steamer*, both terms being shortened to *tramp* by the late 1880s.

But marine engines, steam routes, and coaling stations were improving. England opened the Suez Canal in 1869, reducing the need to sail around Africa and bringing the East into the range of many more steamers. That same year the British National Line's *Holland* was launched with a new *compound-expansion engine*, in which the steam was used in a second cylinder at a lower pressure after it had done its work in the first. The British and French then invented the high-pressure *triple-expansion marine engine*, first used in 1873, which reduced the amount of coal used to one-tenth of that needed by earlier steamers. This opened even the longest Pacific routes to steamers, reduced the number of time-delaying coaling stops, and made all steamers more profitable, not only because less coal need be bought but because more space was freed for cargo. Thus such steamers as our Pacific Mail Line's 5,000-ton *City of Peking* and *City of Tokyo* cut the San Francisco to Yokohama run to sixteen days.

In 1871, Britain's beautifully outfitted White Star liner *Oceanic* (3,700 tons, 15 knots), on the Liverpool to New York route, introduced the term *luxury liner*. Such liners grew to 8,000 tons with a mean speed of 19 knots in the 1880s and made the *steamer chair* (a British term of 1886) the symbol of comfortable life aboard ship, with Americans adding the terms *steamer rug* in 1890 and *steamer trunk* in 1891. America regained the trans-Atlantic speed record (less than six days) when the foreign built *City of New York*

Crewmen of a cargo ship taking in sail off the East Coast in 1869.

and *City of Paris* were transferred to the American Line in 1893. But all was not luxury and speed. Specially designed steamers were now carrying bulk liquids, introducing the term *tank steamship* in 1891, which was to become *tanker* by 1905. Also, disgruntled sailors, who had few luxuries aboard any ship, were now said to *jump ship* (1897, from the earlier, 1883, *jump the boat*) when they abandoned their ship in a port.

The age of sail was now past: by the mid 1890s the United States had more shipping tonnage in steam than in sail. In 1899 steamship sailors, sailors without sails, men whose seagoing fathers had once clamored for berths on clipper ships, derisively began to call any merchant sailing vessel a *windjammer*, referring to the high spread of sails needed to *jam* or capture enough wind to move.

The *quadruple-expansion engine* was just being introduced when the reciprocal steam engine was supplanted by the *steam turbine* (1894, shortened to *turbine* that same year). Britain's first small, experimental 44-ton, 2,000-horsepower turbine-driven ship, the *Turbinia*, with three propeller shafts and three screws, was built in 1894, then amazed shipbuilders with a speed of 34½ knots in 1897. Turbines were then used on the 1905 Cunard *Carmania* and on the 1906 *Lusitania* and *Mauretania*, the last two then being the largest, fastest liners the world had ever seen, the *Mauretania* (31,900 tons, 760 feet, with a top speed of 29 knots) holding the trans-Atlantic speed record for the next twenty-two years.

Both the first successful *motor ship*, using an internal combustion engine, and the first *electric motor ship* were built in England in 1903. The first *diesel ship* was built in 1906 (*diesel* from the German engineer Rudolph Diesel, who invented his engine in 1892), with the Swedish-American Line's 1925 *Gripsholm* being the first large diesel ship put into regular service between Europe and America.

After World War I, England, France, and Germany vied for the trans-Atlantic speed record, as well as income and international prestige, with such patriotically, or nationalistically, named passenger liners as France's 1926 *Ile de France* (43,450 tons, 52,000 horsepower, mean speed of 24 knots), which was superseded as queen of the Atlantic by North German LLoyd's 1928 *Bremen* and *Europa* (each 50,000 tons, mean speed of 28 knots). France countered in 1932 with the *Normandie*, the first of the 1,000-foot vessels (83,000 tons, 160,000 horsepower, mean speed of 31 knots, and accommodating 2,170 passengers), with England regaining supremacy with Cunard's 1934 *Queen Mary* (similar to the *Normandie* in size and horsepower but with a mean speed of 31.7 knots) and the slightly larger 1938 *Queen Elizabeth*, which accommodated 2,288 passengers. America's lighter 1952 *United States* (53,000 tons) finally regained the record for us by crossing New York to Southampton with a mean speed of 35.59 knots. As with the

Left to right: The Queen Elizabeth, *the* Queen Mary, *and the* Normandie *at Hudson River piers in New York City in 1940.*

clipper ships and innovative steamers of earlier days, the names of these huge, fast liners became part of everyone's vocabulary. But the fast luxury liners were to be overwhelmed by their competition too. Increasingly after World War II, and especially in the late 1950s, busy travelers looked to the air again, not now to fill sails but toward the ever faster and larger *airliner* (1915), which crossed the ocean so easily and timed its trips not in days but in hours. Now, only a few ocean liners are left, most of the old ones and almost all the new ones being designed or redesigned as slow, sunseeking *cruise ships* (a British concept of the 1720s), serving as oceangoing sightseeing buses and resort hotels.

The most strikingly new shipbuilding term since World War II has been *nuclear-powered ship*, with the United States launching the first *nuclear-powered submarine*, then often called an *atomic-powered submarine*, the *Nautilus*, on September 30, 1954. The first nuclear-powered cargo and passenger liner was our 1959 *Savannah*, named in memory of that little 1819 paddle-wheeled sailing packet that had started the oceanic age of steam.

Though the age of sail has long been gone, its images and terms are embedded in our language. Besides those ancient nautical terms still used by the navy, the merchant marine, and weekend sailors, we still use many old sailing terms that have taken on metaphorical or general meaning. Some of these common terms were originally British, some American. In the list below, a year given indicates not only when the term came into its nonnautical or informal use, but also that it originated in America.

all at sea, 1890s.
the bitter end, 1800. In nautical use the term referred to the end

portion of a rope belayed around *bitts* (timber crosspieces), especially to the end of the anchor rope attached to the massive bow bitt or *bitter*.

chock-a-block, originally referring to a tackle's being pulled up as far as it would go, until its two *blocks* or pulleys were drawn together. *Chock full* is an American term of 1830.

the cut of one's jib, 1825.

the devil to pay probably comes from the many old stories of people making a bargain with the Devil and having to pay him in the end; however, some people believe it comes from the nautical use of *devil* to mean the seam where the keel of a ship is attached to the sides and the word *pay* meaning to smear or paint thickly, as in the nautical expressions *the devil to pay and no hot pitch*.

give a wide berth to, 1794, from the sailors' term for not approaching dangerous shoals, shorelines, etc., too closely.

fag end, in its original nautical use the end of a rope that has become unraveled or *fagged out*, this last having meant worn out in English since 1785.

half seas over, 1737, and *three sheets to the wind*, 1821, both meaning "drunk," the latter term from the fact that when a ship is "in the wind" it is in a position where the sails are not filled but are flapping and impeding progress (this had to originate as a land-lubber's term, because *sheet* means sail to nonsailors but working rope to a sailor).

hand over fist, originally referring to hauling on a rope, as when hoisting a sail.

hard and fast, from its nautical meaning of solidly aground, so that a ship cannot be freed from the bottom, rocks, etc.

hard up, 1820s, meaning short of money. A ship is "hard up" when the rudder is turned as far to one side as it will go.

keel over, 1896, to faint, fall unconscious, from the nautical use of to *keel over* (1840, originally to *keel up*, 1832), to turn a ship over for repairs or maintenance of the hull or bottom. *Overhaul* has somewhat the same meaning.

know the ropes, as a good sailor must.

mainstay, from the huge tarred rope that served as the chief stay supporting the mainmast.

to lose one's bearings. In sailing use this originally meant to sail at an angle at which a ship did not have its best stability, then later came to mean to lose knowledge of one's ship's position.

plain sailing, originally from 16th-century navigation using Mercator's projection, assuming that the earth's surface is a flat plane, hence originally "plane sailing."

sailing under false colors, sailing under a flag other than a ship's true one, in order to avoid a fight or capture in time of war, or to avoid an embargo, tax, etc.

shipshape, 1860.

squared away, from the nautical meaning of having changed a sailing ship's position to that of the prevailing wind, with the yards turned at right angles to the deck.

stand by, from the nautical meaning of "be ready," as when preparing to weigh anchor, put up sail, etc.

take the wind out of one's sails, 1901, from the nautical use in referring to one ship blanketing another from the wind, as when in close quarters or as a tactic in a battle or race.

Clocks and Watches

In 15th-century England, *timepieces* were divided into two categories, large *clocks* that struck the hour (Latin, *cloca*, bell) and the newer, small, spring-driven *watches* that had only hands and dials for "telling" time (one had to *watch* or look at them). We retain something of this distinction today, as in speaking of *wristwatches* but of *alarm clocks*.

Until the 19th century, only the wealthy owned their own clocks. Most people depended on sun and stomach to tell them time, or told time from *sundials*, simple *sun marks* or *noonmarks* on windows, windowsills, and doorsills, and used *sandglasses* to time sermons, classes, and cooking. A man might also step into an inn or tavern to check the time, these establishments usually having a prominent clock, often a large *Parliament clock*, the name harking back to the days when the British Parliament taxed clocks heavily. Although Boston was talking about its new *public clock* in 1660, it wasn't until the 1770s that the term *town clock* was in use. Then the town clock, usually on the city hall or other conspicuous public building, became the local pride and time standard of cities and towns all over America, and remained so throughout the 19th century and into the early 20th century.

In the 1780s *cuckoo clocks* brought from Germany were conversation pieces (they had been invented by Anton Ketterer in Schönwald, Germany, in 1730 but had just gotten their popular name). In the 1800s *banjo clocks* were in demand, being patented in 1802 by Simon Willard and named for their shape. However, it was Connecticut clockmakers who put clocks into the average American home, often peddling their own wares as prototype "Yankee peddlers." In 1807 the Connecticut firm of Terry, Thomas, and Hoadley was established to manufacture clocks by mass production. After 1814 many people were thus talking about the new *Terry clock* or *shelf clock* of Eli Terry, cheap because it was mass-produced with wooden works. People also talked about the "Seth Thomas clocks." The spread of these good cheap Connecticut clocks coincided with the growth of cities, offices, and industry in the 1820s and 30s, which made it important to get to work, meetings, and appointments on time. Thus more and more people were asking "What time is it?" and were able to find the answer at home. By 1837 enough people owned reliable clocks so that the term *like clockwork* came into use. By the 1840s, time was so important and clocks so common that Americans began to talk of arriving at places *on time*—a brand-new experience and term—the pace of modern industrial life had begun to quicken.

Although Americans began to talk about *alarm clocks* around 1875 (the first one, a large brass clock and bell in a pine cabinet, seems to have been made by clockmaker Levi Hutchins in Concord, New Hampshire, in 1787, to wake himself up at 4 A.M. every day) and *electric clocks* in the late 1880s, the clock Americans spoke of with pride in the 1870s and 80s was their *grandfather clock*, an old type of clock with a new name and new popularity. The name is said to have been popularized by Henry Clay Work's 1876 song "My Grandfather's Clock," with its often heard lyrics:

Pennsylvania German settlers considered large floor clocks, such as this one of 1830, a symbol of family stability and prosperity. By the mid 1870s many American families had such clocks, calling them grandfather clocks.

> My grandfather's clock was too long for
> the shelf,
> So it stood ninety years on the floor.

In 1887, workers began to complain about the new *time clocks*, which gave rise to the 1890 term *clockwatcher*, a worker interested mainly in how soon work would be over. But the Industrial Revolution had finally made clockwatchers of us all. In fact, between the 1860s and 1900 most men decided they couldn't wait until they saw or heard a clock to know the time and began to wear and talk about their own *pocket watches* (a British term dating from 1696).

In 1864 the Elgin National Watch Company of Elgin, Illinois, was established, and made popular the old 1804 term *jeweled movement*. By 1867 Elgin had many people talking about its revolutionary *stem-winding watch*, often simply called a *stem-winder* (setting and winding a watch by a simple stem, rather than by a key, made the pocket watch, and later the wristwatch, practical—Rolex invented the *self-winding watch* in 1931). The popularity of the pocket stem-winder led to the popularity of the *watchfob* in the 1860s (*fob* from German dialect *fuppe*, pocket; a *watchfob* originally meant a small watch-pocket in the waistband of trousers). Soon *stem-winder* was slang for any superior person or thing.

An 1894 stem-winder. *Although the $2.50 price included a free watch chain (a 1739 English term) with a charm, its price couldn't compete with the $1 In-gersoll watch.*

By 1890, Americans were talking about the first truly cheap watch, the *Waterbury watch*, produced first in 1880 by D. A. Bush of the New Haven Company and later by the Waterbury Clock Company, both of Connecticut. Then, in 1892, Robert Hawley Ingersoll, who helped develop the mail-order and chain-store systems, introduced his famous one-dollar *Ingersoll watch*, using the slogan "The watch that made the dollar famous." Suddenly every man could afford to wear a pocket watch and for the next thirty years *Ingersoll* was used as a generic term to mean any pocket watch. But even in Ingersoll's heyday time was catching up with the pocket watch: in 1896 people were beginning to talk about the new stem-wound *strap watch*, which became a popular novelty. It was soon called a *wristwatch* and replaced the pocket watch in popularity during World War I, when soldiers found it much more convenient than the pocket variety (still selling his pocket watches, Ingersoll went broke in 1922 and sold out to the Waterbury Clock Company).

New technology led to the popular digital watch *and* digital clock *in the late 1970s, such timepieces displaying the time—and often the day, date, an alarm setting, and elapsed time—directly in digits formed by an* LED *(light-emitting diode) powered by a minuscule battery. Since the exact digits are shown with the hour first, such terms as "eight minutes after ten," "quarter after ten," "half-past ten," or the vague "almost ten after ten" are not used with such timepieces but are replaced by the exact digital "ten-o-eight," "ten-fifteen," and "ten-thirty." Thus changing timepieces are leading to a change in telling the time.*

Cocktails, Highballs, Grog, Etc.

The American *cocktail* (1806) has spread around the world, many countries having adopted both our word and our drinks. The word almost certainly comes from French *coquetier*, egg cup, dating back to the 1790s when a French-born New Orleans apothecary, Antoine Peychaud, dispensed tonics of Sazerac du Forge cognac and his own *Peychaud bitters* in egg cups, the concoction then being called, after its container, a *coquetier*. Other theories are that *cocktail* is (1) from the old British *cock tailings*, a mixture of the tailings from various liquor kegs, sold cheaply; (2) from the British *cock ale* (1648), a mixture of chicken broth and ale; (3) from *cock's ale*, an ale-and-liquor mixture given fighting cocks; or (4) from a colorful mixed drink the French introduced into America during the Revolutionary War and which was pronounced something like "cocktail" or looked like or was decorated with cock feathers.

True cocktails originally had to be made of liquor, sugar, water, and bitters. In fact, in the early 19th century, cocktails were often called *bitter slings*, and the *Old-Fashioned* is so named because it is an "old-fashioned whiskey cocktail" made with bitters (it was invented, or reinvented, by a bartender at the Pendennis Club in Louisville, Kentucky). The word *cocktail* also gives us such combined terms as *gin cocktail* (1845), *rum cocktail* (1861), *whiskey cocktail* (early 1870s), and finally *champagne cocktail* (1870s). Everyone stirred these drinks or shook them in a makeshift shaker until the 1860s, when both the item and the term *cocktail shaker* first appeared.

We Americans also drink our liquor *straight* (1855, the British have said "neat" since 1579) or with a *chaser* (1897), or we *lace* (1677, England) or *spike* (1889) our punch, fruit juices, or soft drinks with it. We have been asking for a *long drink* since 1828 and for various kinds of *whiskey and soda* since commercial soda water became common in the 1840s and 50s. Southerners have been asking for *bourbon and branch* since the 1850s, when both *bourbon* and *branch*, meaning branch water, entered the language (*branch* has been an Americanism for "small stream" since 1624, first taking hold in Maryland, Virginia, and North Carolina). When the word *highball* appeared in 1898 (*ball* was bartenders' slang for a glass in the 1890s, a "high ball," a tall glass) it meant a Scotch and soda—Scotch and the highball becoming popular together—but soon *highball* meant any kind of whiskey and soda. During Prohibition some soda-water manufacturers curtailed production and some new, hitherto innocent, drinkers opted for sweeter drinks—thus ginger ale became an acceptable substitute for soda.

The mixed drinks Americans have talked about include:

> *the Bogus, the Bombo, the Meridian,* and *the Sampson,* all colonial concoctions whose recipes are unknown today. They merely show that early Americans had fanciful names for their drinks too (the Indians even had a rum drink they called *coow-woow,* the sound of their war whoop!)
>
> *black strap,* rum and molasses, a favorite colonial drink. When water was added to dilute it, this drink was called a *switchel.*
>
> *a stone fence,* cider laced with rum or applejack in colonial times. Later it became cider spiked with brandy or bourbon.
>
> *punch,* popular in early America as a mixture of wine, liquor, milk, and hot water. *Punch* was first recorded in England in 1632 (from Hindi *panch,* Sanskrit *panchan,* "five," referring to the five original ingredients: arrack, tea, sugar, lemon, and water).
>
> *juleps* (from Arabic *julab,* Persian *gulab,* rosewater) entered English around 1400 as minted, nonalcoholic fruit drinks. Rum and brandy juleps were served in colonial days; *mint julep* is an American term of 1809 (forty years before Kentucky's bourbon became well known).
>
> *bounces* and *shrubs* were made by pouring brandy or rum over fruit, sugar, and water, sometimes with citrus slices and spices, then allowing the mixture to sit or ferment for at least a week. *Orange-*

brandy bounce, *orange-rum bounce*, and *cherry shrub* were esteemed by the colonists. Benjamin Franklin's recipe for his orange-rum bounce was a gallon of rum, two quarts of orange juice (instead of the oranges), and two tablespoons of sugar; cherry shrub might call for a quart of dark rum over five pints of cherries. *Shrubs* (probably from Arabic *shurb*, drink) had also been popular in England and sometimes differed from bounces only in that they were strained and sweetened with brown sugar before serving.

grog is named after British Admiral Edward "Old Grog" Vernon, who in 1740 ordered his sailors to take rum and water daily, instead of "neat spirits," to prevent scurvy (it didn't prevent scurvy). He was called Old Grog because he was famous for wearing a shabby old *grog*ram coat in foul weather. His drink became "Old Grog's drink," "Grog's drink," and then simply *grog*. Americans loved it so much that forge and mill workers expected employers to serve it to them at midmorning and midafternoon (what we would call a "grog break" today).

Incidentally, George Washington's estate *Mount Vernon* was also named after this same Admiral Vernon. Washington inherited the estate from his older half-brother Lawrence, who had served under "Old Grog" and named Mount Vernon after him.

eggnog was made in England with ale (*nog* meant strong ale) or dry Spanish wine. The word was first recorded in America in 1775, by which time it was made with local rum or hard cider by most people, and with imported brandy by the rich.

syllabub (from Sillery, in the champagne region of France, + *bub*, an Elizabethan word for "bubbling" drink) became a wine eggnog in America, popular at Christmas and served to women and children at family gatherings in place of stronger eggnog. One assumes the British originally made it with *champagne*, a word that entered English in the 17th century. That Elizabethan word *bub* probably contributed to our calling champagne *the bubbly* by 1895; we had called it *fizz* by 1860 and called it *gigglewater* in the 1920s.

toddies (from Hindi *tārē*, palm tree sap, which is distilled into a strong liquor) have been popular since the 18th century. Earlier Americans made them with more nutmeg, cinnamon, and/or cloves than we do.

san garee (French *sang*, blood, from Latin *sanguis*, because the drink is dark red) is what the colonists called their drink of red wine, fruit slices, citrus juice, sugar, and spices. We have known it as *sangría* (Spanish for "bleeding"), since it was reintroduced into America from Spain by commercial bottlers in the 1960s.

flips were originally hot drinks for cold New England days. First a mug was filled with hot ale, liquor, or a combination of both, and sugar and spices were added. Then a red-hot poker would be thrust into it. The poker was called an "iron flip dog" (hence the name *flip*) or a *loggerhead* (all early Americans had these hung by their fireplaces). If a beaten egg had been added, the drink was called *a yard of flannel*, the egg and bubbling liquid having a fleecy appearance. Today's *sherry flips* usually contain an egg, sugar, and spices but are served over ice.

slings (*sling* had been English slang for any drink since 1788) have

> *The inhabitants [of Maryland] . . . were notoriously prone to get fuddled and make merry with mint julep and apple toddy.*
> Washington Irving in Diedrich Knickerbocker's *History of New York*, 1809

171

been popular since the early 1800s; *gin sling* was first recorded in 1800, six years before the word *cocktail* itself; *bitter sling* meant any cocktail in the early 19th century; *whiskey sling* appeared in 1880. Today they are usually made with gin or rum, to which brandy, sugar, and lemon juice are added; earlier Americans also added nutmeg.

Sazerac. Because Antoine Peychaud had used Sazerac du Forge brandy in his *coquetiers*, some people called any cocktail a Sazerac in the early 19th century. The specific drink we now call a *Sazerac* (made of bourbon, sugar, orange extract, Peychaud bitters or Angostura bitters, and a dash of absinthe or an absinthe substitute such as Pernod) dates from the 1820s and was later made popular at the Hotel Roosevelt bar in New Orleans.

cobbler's punch was the last of the ale, liquor, sugar, and spice drinks to be popular, still drunk and talked of fondly in the 1840s (assumedly it was a favorite of cobblers in earlier days). While still in vogue it gave us the simpler *cobbler,* in which sugar and spices were added to rum, cider, brandy, or wine. The drink was then decorated with fruit slices and, if possible, served chilled or over ice. By the 1830s *sherry cobblers* were popular; the term *whiskey cobbler* appeared in 1862. Incidentally, midwesterners began to call a deep dish pie a *cobbler* in the late 1850s; thus the drink the *sherry cobbler* was popular almost thirty years before the *cherry cobbler* got its name.

sours were first popular in the 1850s. They were really simple *slings,* without the brandy. We still make them the same way, with liquor, sugar, and citrus juice. *Brandy sour* dates from 1861, *whiskey sour* from 1891.

fizzes became popular in the 1860s and are sours with soda water added (commercial soda water became common in the 1840s and 50s). New Orleans' *Ramos gin fizz* became famous after 1888, when Henry Ramos bought the Imperial Cabinet saloon and introduced his complex, tasty gin fizz there.

the Manhattan was first recorded in the 1880s and was named, of course, for the New York City borough. It is basically whiskey and vermouth with bitters. *The Bronx* substitutes gin for the whiskey and appeared in 1919.

gin ricky, 1895, is said to be named after a Washington, D.C., imbiber, but no one knows which Mr. Ricky this was. A drink of gin, soda water, and lime (hence also sometimes called *lime ricky*), it's really a gin fizz without the sugar. If we put the sugar back in, or a syrup, and pour in a little more soda we have a *Collins* (a Collins is thus actually a fizz with more soda, a little less sugar, and a little more citrus juice—a tall, sour fizz). The original *Tom Collins* is said to be named after the bartender who invented it.

martini was first recorded in 1899, but people were drinking something called the *Martinez* (about half gin, half dry vermouth) in the 1860s. If the martini grew out of the Martinez it might be named (1) after a famous hotel, restaurant, or bar by that name (there were several famous ones) or (2) by "Professor" Jerry Thomas, who, in his book *The Bon-Vivant's Companion,* claimed to have invented it at San Francisco's Occidental Hotel while tending bar there in 1860–62, first making it for a thirsty traveler on the way to Martinez, California. The more prosaic story, but not therefore necessarily true, is that the martini

1 dash of bitters
2 dashes of maraschino
1 jigger of gin
1 wineglass of vermouth
2 small lumps of ice
Shake thoroughly and strain into a large cocktail glass. Add 1/4 slice of lemon and serve.

"Professor" Jerry Thomas's recipe for a "martini" in 1862 (actually this drink was then called a Martinez)

¹/₄ ounce dry vermouth
2¹/₂ ounces gin
3 to 4 ice cubes
1 strip lemon peel
Combine in a mixing glass, place a shaker on top of the glass and shake quickly 5 or 6 times. Rub the cut edge of the lemon peel around the inside rim of a chilled cocktail glass. Strain, pour the martini into the cocktail glass and add the lemon peel.

Modern martini recipe (note that the ratio of gin to vermouth is 10 to 1 here)

emerged in the 1890s under the auspices of Martini and Rossi brand vermouth, taking its name from the brand. The 1899 martini called for two parts gin to one of vermouth (strengthening the story that a vermouth manufacturer was behind the whole thing). As a general rule of thumb, the martini has become one part more gin (or later vodka) during every twenty-five years of its history, being today five or six to one against the vermouth: let's face it, *martini* is, for all practical purposes, now the polite name for a straight gin or vodka.

the Gibson is named for a Mr. Gibson (perhaps the illustrator Charles Dana Gibson) who liked his martinis very dry and with a pearl onion instead of a lemon twist or olive.

the Rob Roy is sometimes called a "Scotch Manhattan" since it is a Manhattan made with Scotch. It's named after Scotland's own Robin Hood, Robert MacGregor (1671–1734), popularly known as Rob Roy (Roy being a Scottish nickname for men with red hair). This is the same person about whom Sir Walter Scott wrote his 1817 novel *Rob Roy*.

Bloody Mary, 1934, was originally called a *Red Snapper* when it was brought to New York City by a bartender from Paris's famous 1920s expatriate hangout *Harry's Bar*. Mary I, Queen of England and Ireland, 1553–58, had been called Bloody Mary since the 16th century, so the name was not especially original (though the drink was probably named after some less regal Mary).

The list and the names go on and on. The *Alexander* isn't named for any czar or pope but probably for some forgotten bartender or patron of that name; the *blue blazer* is another drink Jerry Thomas (see *martini* above) claimed to have invented, named from the pouring of the ignited Scotch back and forth from one mug to another; the *daiquiri* was originally made with rum from Daiquiri, Cuba; the *Moscow mule* of vodka and ginger beer was named for the capital of Russia (when we still associated vodka with Russia) plus the "mule's" kick; the *orange blossom* is orange from the orange juice added to the gin and sugar; the *pink lady* is pink from the grenadine, cream, and egg white added to the gin; *planter's punch* is supposed to have been a favorite of 19th-century Caribbean and southern planters, drunk daily to cool off after returning from surveying the work on the plantation; the *Tom and Jerry* is yet another drink "Professor" Jerry Thomas claimed to have invented, this time at San Francisco's El Dorado bar, but others say the name came from Jerry Hawthorne and his buddy Tom, characters in an 1821 book about London by British boxing writer Pierce Egan, who liked this hot milk-and-egg punch with rum and brandy. (For more about American drinking terms see BOOZE AND BARS.)

Coffee, Tea, and Milk

MAX MAYER CO.
TEA & COFFEE

OOLONG

KEE WUNG

JAPAN TEA

COPY-RIGHTED FEB. 1878.

D. H. HOUGHTALING & CO.
IMPORTERS AND JOBBERS OF
TEAS,
39 BROADWAY, NEW YORK.

Coffee and *tea* are comparatively recent English words, both first recorded in 1598, just 22 years before the Pilgrims sailed to America. *Coffee* gets its name, via Turkish and Arabic, either from the Abyssinian port of Kaffa, from which it was shipped (Abyssinia, now Ethiopia, is the native home of the coffee plant) or from Arabic *quhiya*, Turkish *kahveh*, originally meaning a wine tonic, as for those who had no appetite, then applied to any beverage, such as coffee, thought to have tonic effects. *Tea* gets its name, via Dutch and Malay, from the Ancient Chinese *d'a*. Our early colonists preferred *hot chocolate* (a 17th-century term) to either.

The colonists talked widely about tea in 1767 when the British passed the Townshend Acts levying a three pence per pound import tax on tea coming into the colonies (as well as levying an import tax on paper, paint, glass, and lead). They talked even more about tea after the 1773 Tea Act, passed by Parliament in an attempt to give the British East India Co. a monopoly on tea. Such acts, of course, led to the December 16, 1773, Boston Tea Party in which certain Boston citizens disguised as Indians threw cases of tea overboard from three newly arrived ships in Boston harbor, thereby enforcing the nonimportation resolve of the colonies (this incident wasn't generally called *the Boston Tea Party* until the 1830s). Cases of tea were soon being tossed overboard by *tea mobs* in other coastal cities, and then on March 1, 1775, the colonists actually banned tea to protest the British tea tax—and removed or obliterated the word *tea* from many signs and ads. Many colonists then drank *liberty tea*, a tea substitute made of dried loosestrife leaves, but tea had become a fighting, unpatriotic word, and many more colonists turned to drinking coffee. Thus coffee became a patriotic, but very expensive, American beverage: by the end of the Revolutionary War coffee sales had increased 600 percent.

Even after the Revolution, coffee was too expensive to become our true national drink. Tea again grew in popularity, and, besides regular tea, American women talked about a wide variety of tasty or health-giving teas, such as *ginger tea*, *sassafras tea*, *elderbark tea*, *camomile tea*, and especially in the 1880s, *cambric tea*, weak tea with lots of hot milk, so named because it was as white and "thin" as the fabric. However, we have never had the custom of the British *afternoon tea*, even in colonial days, mainly because this British custom didn't begin until around 1840, established by Anna, the wife of the 7th Duke of Bedford, to take the place of the midday meal. This British use of the word *tea* to mean a meal, however, goes back to 1738; *low tea* in Britain is simply one of tea, toast, cakes, etc., to sustain one until dinner and can be eaten at a *teashop* (a British term of 1745), while *high tea* is more filling, usually a *meat tea*, and has in the past served as the evening meal for British

Sir Thomas Lipton opened a grocery store in Glasgow, Scotland, in 1876, which grew into a chain of British grocery stores before he acquired tea, coffee, and cocoa plantations in Ceylon. He passionately enjoyed yacht racing and considered it a good advertisement for his business. All five of the yachts with which he unsuccessfully tried to win the America's Cup were named Shamrock, *not only for good luck but also in honor of his Irish parents.*

workers who still ate large, hot noonday meals. Though such edible teas are British, *tea cake* is an American term, of 1829.

After the Revolution, British tea merchants still dominated the tea market, including Joseph Tetley, who established his British company in 1836 (giving us *Tetley tea*) and the Scot, Thomas Lipton, whose firm grew big in the 1880s and 90s (giving us *Lipton's tea*). But in 1859 the Americans George Huntington Hartford and his partner George Gilman pioneered the buying of tea directly off ships to sell cheaply to consumers, eliminating the middleman and retailing their tea at 30 cents a pound, as opposed to the then going price of $1 a pound. This was the beginning of their Great Atlantic Tea Company, which became the Great Atlantic and Pacific Tea Company, which became our familiar *A&P* (see SUPERMARKET).

Meanwhile, coffee still remained expensive, so much so that many people boiled their used *coffee grounds*, 1754, over and over or drank such substitutes as *barley coffee*, 1758; *rye coffee*, 1769, also called *Boston coffee* by 1830; *Canadian coffee*, 1851, made from roasted peas; and *crumb coffee*, 1866, made from burnt bread crumbs. Then in the early 1860s Hartford and Gilman finally made real coffee cheap enough to become America's overwhelmingly popular hot beverage. Following their success with tea, they organized the American Coffee Corporation to buy coffee directly from Brazilian and Colombian growers, soon retailing their best *Sultana* at 35 cents a pound, and their *Eight O'Clock Breakfast Coffee* brand at 25 cents a pound, as compared to the $2 per pound some other coffees then cost, especially on the western frontier. Ever since, Americans have been talking more about coffee than tea.

Our other tea terms include:

> *iced tea*, in the language since the 1860s; novelist Owen Wister even found it available at the Can Can Saloon in Benson, Arizona, in 1894. However, it became truly popular as the result of the 1904 St. Louis World's Fair, when an English tea salesman, Richard Blechyden, added ice so he could sell his tea on hot days. The temperance movement helped spread the drink as a competitor to the many iced alcoholic drinks then popular.
>
> *tea parties* became an American afternoon pastime in the 1870s, especially among society women. They were sometimes then called *kettledrums*, either referring to the din of the chatting guests or perhaps harking back to colonial times when British officers' wives made the kettledrum a popular tea table.
>
> *tea bag* was a new term in 1902, when tea merchant Thomas Sullivan distributed samples of his blends in small hand-sewn bags for his customers to try. Instead of opening the little bags, his customers brewed the tea in them and asked for more. Also in the early 1900s perforated metal *tea balls* were used as a sort of tea bag.
>
> *tea dance*, a late afternoon dance at which tea is served, popular 1915–25.
>
> *instant tea* was first widely heard in the 1930s.

175

Other American coffee terms include:

java, since about 1850, from the Indonesian island, where much coffee is grown. *Mocha* is also an 1850s generic word for coffee, from the Yemeni coffee port of Mocha. By 1914 we had combined the two words into *jamoke*. We have also called strong or bitter coffee *mud* and *embalming fluid* since about 1910.

Maxwell House Coffee was a blend concocted by Joel Cheek in the 1880s and then served at the famous Maxwell House hotel in Nashville, from which it got its name. Its slogan is attributed to Theodore Roosevelt, who while a guest at the Hermitage in Nashville was asked if he would like another cup of this Maxwell House blend and is supposed to have replied, "Delighted! It's good to the last drop."

Kaffee-klatsch (German for coffee chitchat) began to be Americanized in the 1880s, which is also when *coffee cake* (1879) became a common term.

drip coffee pot, an American term of 1897. *Percolator* (from Latin *per-*, through + *colare*, to strain) and *coffee pot* had been English terms, though we Americans sometimes called it a *coffee boiler* by the 1850s.

coffee and, meaning coffee and doughnuts, the word "doughnut" being understood, dates from around 1900.

Sanka, from French *san(s) ca(ffeine)*, was developed in 1903 but wasn't talked about much in the U.S. until General Foods began to distribute it in 1928.

Though java *and* mocha *have referred to specific types of coffee, they have also been used generically to refer to any brewed coffee since about 1850. This is from an 1898 ad.*

instant coffee became a popular term in the 1940s, though various forms of coffee powder had been made and sold since the 18th century.

Milk, as every baby knows, is a much older beverage than coffee or tea; our word (Old English *milc)* goes back to the 10th century, give or take a hundred years or so. However, early Americans considered cow's milk suitable only for babies, for cooking, and for use in hot chocolate, tea, and coffee. In fact, until the Civil War, when people spoke of milk they often sadly spoke of *milk sickness, the milk evil, milk poison, the slows,* and *the trembles* (which killed Lincoln's mother), all ailments caused by drinking milk from sick cows or from cows that had eaten the wrong things, such as white snakeroot.

It wasn't until the 1850s that *milk ranches* (to be called *dairy farms* in the 1870s) were shipping milk by *milk trains* to the cities (*milk car* wasn't a railroad term until 1919), while *milk men* delivered milk on *milk routes* in *milk wagons*. Until the 1860s the milk was always poured into the customer's *milk can* (1830s), left outside his door. In the 1860s various bottles were sometimes used, but the special *milk bottle* wasn't patented until 1894, by Harvey Thatcher. His bottle had a top held in place by a wire handle, and had a picture of a cow being milked by a man on a stool, above which were the words "Absolutely Pure Milk." The disposable paper milk container was also patented in the 1890s, but it wasn't until the 1930s that people began talking about the new *milk cartons*. Though milk, as most other beverages, was served from pitchers, the term *milk pitcher* wasn't recorded until 1863. Our other milk terms include:

condensed milk, evaporated and sweetened for preservation, was patented by journalist-turned-scientist Gail Borden in 1856.

A label from a can of condensed milk, 1867. Unlike most condensed milk, this brand had no sugar added.

Duchess County Condensed Milk.

Purity Brand.

Prepared by the United States Condensing Company of N.Y.

Borden developed it after seeing one child die and others become sick from bad milk produced by two cows carried on a ship on which he was returning from England to the U.S. in 1853. It became a commercial success during the Civil War when the Union ordered it as a field ration for its troops. It was very popular with the troops because it was sweet, originally having a strong caramel flavor, being whole milk and sugar cooked under vacuum until 60 percent of the water was removed. It was also popular with both the troops and the government because the heat of the canning process actually pasteurized it and made it safe to drink, though this was before Louis Pasteur came up with the idea of *pasteurization* in the 1860s, leading to the term *pasteurized milk*.

milk toast, toast soaked or served in a bowl of warm milk, often sprinkled with sugar and cinnamon, seems to be an American dish, first recorded in 1857. It has given us the pejorative *milquetoast*, meaning a *milksop*. (See SISSY! CRYBABY! YELLOW-BELLY! for more on both of these words.)

malted milk was created by William Horlick and was an 1887 trademark of Horlick's Food Company. It was originally sold as a tonic or "food preparation for infants and invalids."

milk shake also appeared in the late 1880s, but the term then usually meant a sturdy, healthful eggnog type of drink, with eggs, whiskey, etc., served as a tonic as well as a treat. Since *malted milk* (see above) was also considered a tonic, the combined *malted milk shake* was a logical step and in the early 1900s people were asking for the new treat, often with ice cream, and before 1910 were using the shorter terms *shake* and *malt* (the longer word *malted* being somewhat more common in the Eastern states). *Malt shop* was a term of the late 1930s, usually being a typical soda fountain of the period, especially one used by students as a meeting place and hangout.

evaporated milk, evaporated to half its original bulk and canned unsweetened (see *condensed milk* above), appeared in the early 1920s.

Daylight Saving Time, Eastern Standard Time, Etc.

Greenwich time was first adopted by British astronomers in 1850 and the term was soon well known in America. However, each American city and hamlet from New York to San Francisco had its own *sun time*, leading to great confusion, especially in railroad schedules and telegraph messages. In 1872 the U.S. railroads proposed the nationwide adoption of *railroad time*, a system of four *time zones* that were finally adopted by the federal government in 1883. Though the boundaries of these time zones have changed, since twelve o'clock noon on Sunday November 18, 1883 (when the railroads and much of the rest of the country adjusted clocks and watches to the new system), Americans have been qualifying time by saying *Eastern Standard Time*, *Central Standard Time*, *Mountain Time*, or *Pacific Time*, or, later, using such terms as *Eastern Daylight Saving Time*, etc.

Daylight Saving Time, abbreviated as *DST*, has been cursed by farmers ever since Congress first adopted it in 1918 to save coal and electricity during World War I. Although the idea of adjusting clocks forward to make better use of summer's daylight hours goes back to the 18th century, farmers and others felt it was unnatural and wanted to stick to God's own sun time. They forced the repeal of DST in 1919, Congress then leaving the decision to have it or not up to local authorities. Lack of uniformity caused confusion, and finally in 1966 Congress passed the Uniform Time Law, requiring uniform time, either *Standard Time* or *Daylight Saving Time*, within each state (officially, however, the term "Daylight Saving Time" is not used, as all time, including the summer when clocks are set forward, becomes the nationally accepted "standard" time). Why didn't farmers prevent the passage of the bill in 1966? Because there were fewer of them to protest: America had become an urban nation since 1919. Thus our common use of the term *Daylight Saving Time* today is a result of the urbanization of America.

Dinner or Supper?

Colonists ate their big hot meal of the day, actually served lukewarm in the style of the times, between noon and 2 or 3 P.M. This meal was called *dinner* (a 13th-century English word, via French *diner*, from Latin *dis-*, away + *jejunus*, fast) and the hour at which it was eaten was called *dinner time* (a 14th-century English term). On eastern farms and southern plantations family and fieldhands might be summoned to dinner by a large *dinner bell* (1809) or *dinner horn*

Calling the hands to dinner with a dinner horn.

(1836), and later, on western ranches, the hands might be summoned by either a dinner horn or a *dinner gong* (1900).

Until the late 1820s and early 1830s the last meal of the day was always called *supper* (also a 13th-century English word, via the French, and related to *soup* and *sip*). This supper was much humbler than dinner and originally was a farm laborers' meal of bread dunked in soup or milk.

Lunch and *luncheon* both originally meant a hunk or thick piece of something in the 16th century (perhaps from Spanish *lenja*, slice, hunk), but in the 17th century, *luncheon* came to mean only a slice or hunk of something to eat as a midmorning snack. Americans began to talk of eating *luncheon* (soon shortened back to *lunch*) as the midday meal in the 1820s and 30s, when the increasing number of city workers began to find it necessary to eat a quick, cheap midday meal at or near work rather than going home for a large dinner or buying one in an expensive restaurant. Of course, some workers managed to eat a hot dinner at work by taking one along in a *dinner pail* (1856) or *dinner bucket* (1901), which always held hot dinners (cold lunches were carried in *lunch pails*, which became the *lunch box* of the late 1850s). Thus, during the six-day work week the big hot midday dinner gave way to the quicker lunch (see RESTAURANTS, LUNCH COUNTERS, DINERS, AND DRIVE-INS), but Americans continued to eat a big midday dinner on the one day a week they could, calling it *Sunday dinner*. However, the quick workingman's lunch of the 1820s and 30s put off the main meal or "dinner" of most days until suppertime—and it could now be called either *supper* or *dinner*, with working-class families being more apt to call it *supper*. In fact, if you're like most American families, you eat *breakfast*, *lunch*, and *supper*, but when guests come or you have something extra fancy, and use the best silverware, etc., you call that "supper" dinner.

Grant Wood titled his painting of a large midday meal in rural Iowa Dinner for Threshers.

Incidentally, *snack* (Dutch *snacken*, to bite) meant the bite of a dog to early colonists, a dram of liquor in the late 17th century, and not a light meal or something eaten between meals until the 18th century. *Leftovers* is an 1890s concept and word: by then ice boxes were very common (so leftover food could be stored longer), families were already a bit smaller (so there was apt to be more food left over), and our post-Victorian families were becoming more frank (so they admitted using leftover food for a second meal).

By 1897 Oxford University students who liked to sleep late on Sunday and combine breakfast and lunch were calling the combined meal *brunch*, the word becoming popular in America in the 1920s. In the late 1920s the expression *from soup to nuts* appeared, long after a last course of fruit, wine, and nuts was a thing of the past at even the most formal dinners.

The Almighty Dollar

The word *dollar* comes from the German *t(h)aler*, a word the Germans got from shortening *Joachimstaler*, a silver coin first minted in Joachimstal, Bohemia, in 1519 (*Joachimstaler* itself literally means "of the Saint Joachim valley," *t(h)aler* meaning "of the valley"). This original *t(h)aler* became such a common European coin that *t(h)aler* or *da(h)ler* soon became the general name for any large silver coin in various German states and the name of the basic coins of Denmark and Sweden, with the word being spelled *dollar* in England by 1581.

The first *dollar* widely circulated in America was a Dutch coin bearing the likeness of a lion. Brought here by the original Dutch settlers around 1620, it was a favorite of European merchants and sailors and continued to be brought to America and to circulate widely long after the English took over the Dutch lands in 1664 and turned the Dutch colony of *New Netherland* (so named by the Dutch in 1621) into *New York* and *New Jersey*. We called this Dutch dollar a *lion dollar* or *lion* by 1725. This Dutch dollar was not the only dollar the colonists had. The Spanish peso was also in wide use in all the American colonies and called a *Spanish dollar* from at least 1684. By the early 1750s any peso, whether from Spain or Spanish America, was called a *Spanish dollar*, *Spanish mill(ed) dollar*, or simply a *dollar*. (Calling a peso a *dollar* is a habit we have retained: we started calling the Mexican peso a *Mexican dollar* in 1831, when it was the major currency in the far West, which was then still Mexican territory, and began calling it an *adobe dollar* in 1909.)

Thus when the second Continental Congress began issuing *Continental money* in 1775, the year before the Revolutionary War

> . . . *the almighty dollar, that great object of universal devotion throughout our land* . . .
> Washington Irving, "A Creole Village," in the November 12, 1836, issue of *Knickerbocker Magazine*. Irving coined the term "almighty dollar" and used it here for the first time.

> *We Americans worship the almighty dollar! Well, it is a worthier god than Hereditary Privilege.*
> Mark Twain, *Notebooks*

The Joachimstaler *coin, first minted in Joachimstal, Bohemia, in 1519, gave us our word* dollar.

began, it was issued in terms of the well-known *dollar*. So much of this money was put into circulation during the war that *Continentals* became almost worthless, but *dollar* was by then well on its way to becoming the basic American monetary word. Besides issuing its temporary Continental money, the second Continental Congress knew that it had to prepare for a permanent American monetary system. Thus, even while appointing Washington Commander in Chief, moving toward the Declaration of Independence, and then coordinating the Revolutionary War effort, from 1775–77 it drafted the Articles of Confederation (not ratified until 1781), which, among many other vital things, gave Congress the jurisdiction to coin money. But what should our money be? The task of preparing a report suggesting a specific new American monetary system fell to Gouverneur Morris (1752-1816), the assistant to the superintendent of finances of the United Colonies from 1781–85. His report, suggesting a decimal coinage using *dollars* and *cents* (see the list of U.S. currency below for more details and specific bills and coins), was then improved, simplified, and proposed to Congress by Thomas Jefferson and became the basis of our monetary system.

Morris and Jefferson agreed that English units and terms, such as *pounds*, *shillings*, and *pence*, should not be used, and defended their new system successfully against bankers who wanted to keep the English system. They also agreed that the word *dollar* should be kept, because Americans had become so used to it with our use of the Dutch, Spanish, Continental, and other "dollars." (Since it was Jefferson who suggested that the dollar actually be the basic unit of our currency and sent the official 1784 memorandum to Congress which proposed the new dollars-and-cents system, it is Thomas Jefferson rather than Gouverneur Morris who is called *the*

So much Continental money *was put into circulation beginning with the second Continental Congress in 1775 that it became almost worthless. Note that these bills were redeemable in* Spanish milled dollars *as well as gold and silver.*

father of the American dollar.) Thus the dollar was the basic American currency even before the very beginning of our nation. It was a major relief finally to have a monetary system and currency of our own, because since the earliest colonial days we had suffered from the lack of a uniform system and enough money to go around.

Money was always scarce in the American colonies. England drained away the few silver and fewer gold coins in circulation by demanding that its duties and taxes be paid in them and kept all English money in circulation in the colonies at a minimum. Even that minimum was often old, worn-out, and unwanted coins: among other abominations the colonists were forced to use were badly minted coins the Irish had rejected and special brasslike imitation pence, two-pence and half-pence *Wood's money*, manufactured especially for the colonies by William Wood in England during the early 1720s. Thus, though they kept accounts in British pounds, shillings, and pence, many colonists saw precious few of them and relied on barter, a confusing variety of local colonial money, and any foreign coins they could get their hands on.

Barter was called *country pay. Country pay* had originally meant good home-country English money in 1643 but soon came to mean barter and the axes, barrels of cider, cheeses, chickens, hay, loads of firewood, salt, sides of meat, tallow, wool, and other valuable country-grown and homemade products that could be traded for other goods. Such goods for bartering had also been called *truck* since 1637 (from Old French *troquer*, to exchange). As the country became less dependent on hunting, trapping, and homemade products, such truck was increasingly farm and garden produce. Thus *truck* came to mean such produce by 1809 and eventually we began to speak of the gardens where vegetables were grown as *truck gardens* (1866), which, of course, have nothing to do with the modern trucks that take produce to market.

With or without British authority, the colonists also struck desperately needed coins and printed paper money. The first coins made in North America were silver *pine tree shillings*, also called *Boston shillings* and *Bay shillings*, struck by silversmiths John Hull and Robert Sanderson in Boston by order of the Massachusetts Bay Colony from 1652 to 1682. They bore a picture of a pine tree encircled by the word *Masathusets* and every one of them made during this thirty-year period bore the original year of issue, 1652—to conceal from the authorities in London that the coins were being made continually. Sixpence and three-pence *pine trees* and *oak trees* were also made in Boston during the same period.

Massachusetts also printed the first paper money in the colonies with its 1690 *bills of public credit*, but all the individual colonies repeatedly issued notes in a variety of pound, shilling, or dollar denominations (such as the Massachusetts ten-shilling *angel*, first

The silver pine tree shilling of 1652, the first coin made in North America.

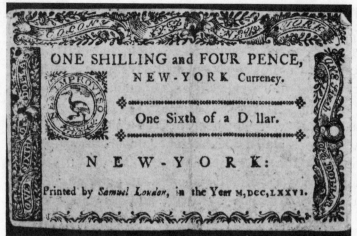

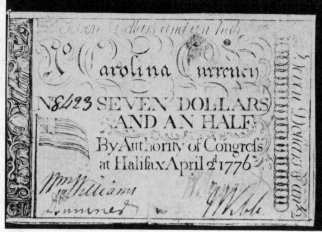

A New York one shilling four pence bill, equal to one-sixth of a Spanish milled dollar, and a North Carolina 7¹/₂ dollar bill, both issued by provincial congresses in early 1776. The bills of one colony were not always accepted or fully valued in other colonies.

issued in 1713) until Parliament prohibited the issuance of paper currency in New England in 1751 and in all the colonies in 1764. Though colonial bills were in wide use (Benjamin Franklin printed many of them in the 1730s and 40s), in the long run most of them were disastrous. Their value was seldom certain, some were backed by gold and silver or by British or other coin, and some were not, and a *South Carolina pound* might be worth half as much as a *Pennsylvania pound*, depending on how far one was from South Carolina and on what people thought about its politics and fiscal stability.

With English money in short supply and colonial money uncertain, the most prized and trusted money was often gold and silver coins from Spain, France, Holland, Mexico, Portugal, Brazil— from just about every European country, possession, island, and even mission (the Spanish Jesuits in Tuban, Arizona, minted coins as early as 1707). Such gold and silver coins were brought to America by its original Dutch, French, Spanish, and German settlers and continued to come in through merchants, sailors, and pirates from all the Western world. Since no busy money changer, banker, or shopkeeper could know all the denominations and values, each had a trusty scale on which coins were weighed and then exchanged for their exact metallic value. Thus, besides British guineas, pounds, shillings, and pence, Dutch and Spanish dollars, and colonial bills and coins, early Americans used and talked about such coins as the:

doubloon. This Spanish gold coin, worth from $5 to $16 at various times, was a major cash asset in the colonies, especially in the South, many of the coins reaching us from South America and the West Indies. Our English word *doubloon* is from the Spanish word for the coin, *doblón* (from Spanish *doble*, double, because it was double the value of a pistole).

johannes. This Portuguese coin was worth $8.81. It was so common in the colonies that we called it a *Johnny* or *Johney* by 1766 and also a *Joe* by 1772.

peso. The Spanish *peso* (literally weight, from Latin *pēnsum*, something weighted) was worth eight Spanish *reals* (see below) and marked with a figure 8; it was the famous *piece of eight* (so called in England since 1610). We called this Spanish coin and its value *peso*, *eight reals*, *piece of eight*, and, of course, *dollar*.

picayune. This French coin (from French *picaillon*, a small copper coin) was widely circulated in Louisiana and Florida in the late 18th century and was still in wide use at the time of the Louisiana Purchase in 1803. By 1855 we used *picayune* to mean trifling, of small value.

pistole. The Spanish gold *pistole* (from Middle French *pistolet*, coin) was worth 2½ pesos. It also circulated freely in the colonies and was associated not only with Spain but with pirates, who seemed to prefer it for its gold content, size, and weight—and for use as an earring.

real or *bit*. The small silver Spanish *real* (Spanish for "royal," from Latin *rēgāl*, regal) was worth one-eighth of a peso or 12½ cents. By 1683 we also called it a *bit* (from Old English *bite*, bit, morsel), which was an English term for any small piece of money, as in "six-penny bit," though this monetary use of the word *bit* was reinforced in America by the Spanish word *pieca*, piece, bit, which sounded like "bika" to many colonists. Of course, our *two bits* meaning 25 cents (two Spanish bits of 12½ cents each) comes from this Spanish *bit* (see *quarter* in the list of U.S. currency below for details on *two bits*, *four bits*, etc.).

sou markee or *sou marqué*. This small 18th-century French copper coin once circulated freely in America. It is important only because by 1836 we used *sou markee* to mean trifling or of little value, the same way we still use *picayune*.

Of course, the many foreign coins in America didn't disappear overnight when the Revolutionary War was won and we began minting our own United States currency. In fact, in 1793 foreign coins were declared a legal part of the U.S. coinage system, and not until 1857 did Congress finally pass a law removing foreign coins from circulation. Spanish coins continued to be plentiful and in use in the Southwest long after we acquired that region in the Mexican War of 1846–48 (Spain once occupied what are now twenty-six states), and many Americans, East and West, were using and hoarding the *Spanish quarter*, then worth about 20 cents, during the coin shortage of the Civil War (see *shinplasters* below).

Such foreign coins began to be replaced by our own money, however, when the Continental Congress, on July 6, 1785, adopted the dollars-and-cents system of decimal coinage devised by Gouverneur Morris and Thomas Jefferson, created the *Department of the Treasury* in 1789, and put our coinage system into use with the Coinage Act or "Mint Act" of 1792, which also established the *Mint of the United States* (reorganized as the *Bureau of the Mint* and put under the Department of the Treasury in 1873).

Our own new United States currency was called *federal money* (1806), *lawful money* (1809), and *specie dollars* (1821) to distinguish it from the foreign coins still in circulation.

The first three coins made directly under the auspices of the United States government (but see *fugio* at *cent* in the list of U.S. currency below) were the silver 1792 *half disme* (see *half dime* in the list of U.S. currency below) and the 1793 copper *cent* and *half cent*. These were all made from dies created by Robert Birch and Joseph Wright and first struck in John Harper's cellar, a short distance from the first U.S. mint, which was then being built in the new nation's capital, Philadelphia (this mint produced its first coins in 1794). However, such U.S. coins were not the only ones in circulation; in addition to all the foreign coins still being used in all parts of the country, the early United States allowed private coinage as long as the coins contained full weight and purity and didn't copy or imitate any official government issue (see *slug* in the general list of terms below).

Since the individual colonies and then the Continental Congress had fared so badly with paper currency, and individual states continued to fare badly with it, the U.S. government itself issued no paper money as legal tender until the Civil War (see *greenbacks* in the general list of terms below), creating the Treasury Department's *Bureau of Engraving and Printing* in 1862 to print it. However, the U.S. Treasury did issue its first *treasury notes* or *treasury bills* in 1812 to meet expenses of the War of 1812 (*treasury note* was a 1756 term, then referring to an interest-bearing certificate issued by the treasury department of a colony). Even without U.S. legal-tender paper money, there were plenty of paper bills around in the early days of the Republic because most states allowed banks to issue paper money up to the amount of their gold deposits—many banks, of course, issued more paper money than their gold or gold-coin assets could cover and failed when enough holders of the paper bills demanded the gold the banks didn't have, making such paper money worthless.

The Coinage Act of 1792 also established a standard of bimetallism in the U.S., defining the dollar in terms of both gold and silver. Thus until 1873 the U.S. used both gold and silver as a basis for our money and the U.S. mint purchased both to be coined. It ceased purchasing silver during 1873–79 (see *free silver* under *dollar* in the list of U.S. currency below) and during that time *bimetallism* (an 1876 English word) first became a major political issue. Bimetallism and the *silver standard* (an 1896 term) were rejected in the elections of 1896 and 1900, in both of which the *silver Democrats* and their Presidential candidate, William Jennings Bryan, were defeated. Thereafter the U.S. was effectively on the *gold standard* (an 1857 term), made official by the Gold

Standard Act of 1900, and it was not taken off this standard until 1933.

From 1865 until 1933 the U.S. issued not only gold coins but paper *gold certificates* (an 1863 term, the year Congress first authorized them) which certified that the U.S. Treasury had deposited gold for their redemption. In 1933, when the U.S. was taken off the gold standard, gold coins were removed from circulation, gold certificates were called in, and our coins and paper money were declared legal tender. From 1878 until 1963 the government also issued *silver certificates*, paper money backed by silver dollars. Today, about 90 percent of our paper money is in *Federal Reserve Notes* issued through the twelve *Federal Reserve Banks* or "bankers' banks" created by the Federal Reserve Act of 1913 to establish a unified banking system.

Before discussing our own specific bills and coins, let's look at some general words and expressions, both formal and slang, having to do with money. *Money* itself has been in the English language since 1330: we get the word, via Old French, from the Latin *monēta*, coin, mint, after the temple of Juno Monēta, on the Capitoline Hill, where Roman money was coined. Juno Regina, the wife of Jupiter, was one of the busiest Roman goddesses; queen of the heavens and goddess of the moon and war, she also watched over women, virginity, and marriage rites, and was the goddess of warnings—the name Juno *Monēta* (from Latin *monere*, to warn) means "Juno of the warnings." Our 1413 English word *mint*, where money is coined, also comes from *monēta*, but via Old English *mynet*.

Some General Terms

> *banknote*, 1695 in England, originally as made out by a specific bank to a specific person. The shortened form, *note*, was first recorded in 1696.
>
> *bean*, any coin, 1810. It came to mean specifically a $5 gold piece in 1859, then meant $1 by 1905.
>
> *bill* meant a letter or a legal document in English by the 15th century (from Latin *bulla*, official seal, then a document bearing such a seal, which we still use in the term *papal bull*). By the late 16th century in England this "official document" meaning led to *bill*, which was used as a word for paper money.
>
> *bogus* first appeared in an 1827 newspaper account in the *Painesville (Ohio) Telegraph* as a name for an apparatus that made counterfeit money (probably being related to the word *bogie*, devil, ghost, goblin). By 1839 it was used as an adjective to refer to counterfeit bills and coins themselves. Incidentally, *counterfeit* itself is a 700-year-old English word, first recorded in 1291 (from Middle French *countrefaire*, to copy, imitate, from *countre*, opposite + Latin *facere*, to make).
>
> *bread*, 1935 as slang for money, then widely used by the Beat Generation in the 1950s (see HEP, HIP, HIPPIE, COOL, AND

187

BEAT). This use of *bread* is said to be from the Cockney rhyming slang *bread and honey*, meaning money, but it certainly shares the same image as *dough* (the idea that money is as basic and as necessary as bread is also shown in the Spanish *pan*, bread, being used as a Spanish slang word for money).

cash, 1596 in England, when it also still meant money box, case (via French *caisse*, Italian *cassa*, cash box, merchant's case, from Latin *capsa*, box). *Cash article*, valuable or worth an amount of money, 1835; *cash crop*, 1868.

change meant smaller denominations exchanged for an equal amount of money by 1622 in England (via Anglo French from Latin *cambium/cambere*, exchange); then by 1691 in England *change* meant any coin of a low denomination. We Americans have used *small change* since 1819 to refer to coins of less than a dollar and since 1908 to mean insignificant or trifling (the English had referred to coins of small value as *small money* since 1561; we have also called such pieces *small coin*, 1879, and *small silver*, 1891).

In America we began speaking of *loose change* in 1827, referring to both coins and bills of small denominations carried loose in the pocket. *To short-change* someone is an American term of 1903 and our term *short-change artist* dates from 1922.

check, 1717 in England, originally as a bank draft with a counterfoil, or especially the counterfoil itself, to "check" or prevent alterations and forgeries. Americans liked *to check* money into and out of banks by 1809 and were using the term *checking account* by the 1920s.

coin originally meant a die or wedge in English (via French from Latin *cuneus*, wedge), then by 1386 meant a piece of gold, silver, or other precious metal of a specific weight and value made into money by being stamped with an official device (the first known coins date from about 700 B.C. in Lydia, now part of Turkey). Since all money was originally coin, *coin* was a general word for money too, though it appeared as a slang word for money (both coins and bills) in America in 1846. Not until the wide acceptance of our paper money after the Civil War did *coin* come to have the connotation of a small coin worth less than a dollar.

Commemorative coin, 1892, when Congress authorized the first one to help finance the World's Columbian Exposition in Chicago, the special 50-cent piece selling for a dollar as a souvenir and raising over $5 million to help pay for the fair.

currency, 1699 as money in England, because it is the current, generally accepted medium of exchange (from Latin *currentia/currere*, to run).

dinero, late 19th century, the Spanish word for money. We have also taken many other foreign words for money or monetary units to use as slang words for money, as *gelt* (see below), *ruble*, *yen*, etc.

dough, 1840, almost certainly from considering bread dough as the necessary, basic staff of life. *Do-re-mi*, as a pun on *dough* and the musical *do*, 1925; *oday*, Pig Latin for *dough*, 1926.

easy money, easily obtained money, 1836; *easy dollars*, 1890s. *For my money*, as far as I'm concerned, 1840. *To pay one's money and take one's choice*, 1864. *Money talks*, money has influence, 1910. *Money from home*, easily obtained money, 1913.

The 1892 World's Columbia Exposition commemorative 50-cent piece, the first U.S. commemorative coin.

Lincoln's Secretary of the Treasury, Salmon P. Chase, who decided that the first United States legal-tender banknotes have their backs printed green, giving us greenbacks.

filthy lucre, used in England to mean "dishonorable gain" since 1526, then in America to mean "money" by 1830 (from the New Testament's "Not greedy of filthy lucre," I Timothy iii, 3). The *filthy* of *filthy lucre* contributed to our 1940 term *filthy rich.*

folding money, 1930.

gelt, 1889, though it may have been in English underworld use since 1698 (from German *Geld*, money).

greenbacks, Lincoln's secretary of the treasury, Salmon P. Chase, strengthened the Union's banking system during the Civil War and, in 1861, also issued the first United States legal-tender banknotes (not then redeemable in gold or silver), deciding himself that the backs of these new U.S. Treasury *demand notes* be printed green. The Union issued about a half-billion dollars' worth of these new green bills, inflation making each dollar of them worth about 39 cents in gold by the end of the war. Union soldiers, among the first to receive such bills from the government, are said to have given Chase's green-backed bills the name *greenbacks.*

The Confederates had their own paper currency, their bills called *Confeds, bluebacks,* and *graybacks,* issuing a billion dollars' worth without any gold or silver behind them. These Confederate bills were considered so worthless they were also called *shucks* (which had been a slang word for worthless, no account, literally as worthless as corn shucks, since 1843). By the war's end a dollar of these Confederate bills was worth 1.7 cents.

After the war the U.S. also had *gold backs* (1873), which were banknotes redeemable in gold and bearing a gold-colored emblem on the back, and *yellow backs* (1880s), which had backs printed in a yellowish color.

hard money, 1831, then meaning coins as opposed to paper money, probably because the Spanish silver peso had been called a *hard dollar* (1780), which seems to have been a translation of the Spanish *peso duro*. By the early 1840s, however, *hard money* meant ready cash in any form, coin or paper, which was soon superseded by the term *hard cash*. From the first, however, *hard money* took on a wider financial and political meaning, referring to those who favored the use of gold and silver coins over paper money that could be printed at will and had no intrinsic value.

jack, 1859 as money, but at first usually used to mean only a small coin or a small amount of money (*jack* had been English slang for a farthing since 1700).

An original Civil War green-back.

legal tender, an English term of 1740, being bills or coins that must be accepted in payment of a debt when tendered.

long green, our green paper money (see *greenbacks* above), 1891. Since this earlier paper money is somewhat leaflike in color it has given us such slang words for money as *kale* (1911), *lettuce* (1929), and *cabbage* (1942). However, the earliest of these vegetable terms, *kale*, could very well be from the 1673 English slang *cole*, meaning money (*cole*, coal, from the 15th century interjection *precious coals!*), which, once misunderstood or pronounced as *kale*, could have led to our slang use of *lettuce* and *cabbage*. (With *dough*, *bread*, and *sugar*, these slang words for money show the close relation in our minds between food and money).

loot, late 1940s as money.

mad money, 1920, originally as money a girl carried on a date in case the boy made a pass at her, or otherwise made her mad at him, so that she could return home via streetcar, bus, or cab on her own. By 1946, however, it meant a small sum of money a woman keeps to splurge on any items she might want to buy on impulse.

mazuma, 1880, via Yiddish from Hebrew *mēzumān*, ready, fixed, from the Chaldean term meaning "the ready necessary," which the Chaldeans used in exactly the same way we use *the ready* and *the necessary*, to mean money.

the means, used in England since 1630 to mean resources, especially monetary, for obtaining some result.

moola(h), 1930; occasionally shorted to *moo*, 1943. No one knows how this slang word for money originated.

paper money, first recorded in 1691 when the famous Congregationalist clergyman Cotton Mather criticized his fellow colonists for not wanting to accept it as pay and for demanding "Spanish gold" instead.

paper currency, 1723, in Pennsylvania. The earliest paper money (actually more of a personal promissory note that could be passed from person to person) seems to have been used in China in the eighth century A.D., while in the West the Bank of Sweden printed banknotes from its founding in 1656. The first true English paper currency appeared in the late 17th century and was then called *running cash*, being a note against money that could be drawn from a bank in favor of *the bearer*.

   Though it varied in size, most of our own early paper money was considerably larger than it is now. In 1929 new bills began to be printed that were approximately two-thirds the size of the old, all bills being the same size regardless of denomination. For a while after 1929 the old, larger bills still in circulation were called *large size bills* or *blanket bills*.

piece has meant a piece of money, a coin, in England since 1526. Between 1829 and 1875 all U.S. coins of less than a dollar were also given the name *piece*, as a *5-cent piece* (1829), *10-cent piece* (also 1829), *50-cent piece* (1836), *3-cent piece*, and *25-cent piece* (both 1875). Larger-denomination coins were often called a *piece* too, as a *$5 piece* (1834) and a *$20 piece* (1867).

ready cash, 1712, in England, where *ready pennies* had appeared in 1300 and *ready money* in 1548. *The ready*, as slang for money, first appeared in general use in the United States in 1890, but seems to have first been a late 17th-century English underworld term.

rock, 1846 as a piece of money, a gold or silver coin, especially in the expression *to have a pocketful of rocks*, to be carrying or worth a lot of money (*rock* was first used to mean a diamond in 1908).

sandwich coin, 1965, for a coin made with a layer of one metal or alloy clad on both sides with a layer of another, the three layers resembling a sandwich. To save precious silver, the U.S. began making dimes and quarters in this way in 1965 and half dollars in 1970. The more formal term for such a coin is *clad coin*.

scratch, 1929, for money, because one scratches around to get it as a chicken does for food; the basic expression behind this term, *to scratch for a living*, goes back to 1847.

shekel, a piece of money. Though known from its Biblical use for centuries and used by Shakespeare in his 1602 *Measure for Measure*, Act II, Scene 2, this word was first used as a general slang term for money, coins or bills, in 1871. It's from the Hebrew *sheqel*, weight, coin, from a Babylonian unit of weight and a silver coin weighing about two-thirds of an ounce.

shinplasters. Silver was scarce and silver coins so widely hoarded during the Civil War that business suffered because shopkeepers soon found it almost impossible to make change. Thus the Union first declared postage stamps legal tender, then, in 1862, issued stamplike *postal currency* or *fractional (paper) currency* of 3-, 5-, 10-, 15-, 25-, and 50-cent denominations. These were also called *paper coins*, *three cent bills*, *ten cent bills*, etc., even though they looked more like stamps than bills (for example the 25-cent bill bore a reproduction of five 5-cent stamps).

These flimsy, ugly little bills were most contemptuously called *shinplasters*, because they resembled the little pieces of paper people soaked in vinegar, tobacco juice, or some other home remedy and applied to their shins, feet, and other parts of the body to help soothe and heal small rubbed spots and cuts. This fractional paper currency continued in use until 1876, when confidence in our paper money was strong enough so that people stopped hoarding silver.

silver has been used as a medium of exchange since the 9th century and has thus been used to mean "money" for over a thousand years. In the late 1860s and early 1870s, when few silver dollars were in circulation, we began to use *silver* to mean small change, coins worth less than a dollar (*coppers* had been slang for small change in English since the late 17th century).

slug has referred to any small counterfeit coin since 1929, originally usually a counterfeit nickel or blank nickel-sized disc, later often a dime one, especially as used in a pay phone or turnstile slot. The word first appeared during the California gold rush in 1849, meaning a gold nugget; then in the early 1850s it came to mean any privately minted California gold coin, originally the 1851 octagonal $50 gold piece minted by Moffat & Co. which had no picture or words on the back but only a closely knit pattern of geometric swirls. It is this meaning of "privately minted," plus perhaps the blank side of that Moffat coin, that has come down to us in the modern use of *slug*.

soft currency and *soft dollar*, both 1776, and *soft money*, 1844, all originally meant paper currency as opposed to coins or hard money but were especially used to refer to paper money not backed by gold or silver. By 1926 *soft money* was also a slang term

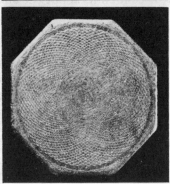

A privately minted 1852 octagonal $50 gold piece or slug *with a "blank" pattern of swirls on the back.*

for money easily obtained, *soft* having come to mean "easy" around 1920.

sound money, 1895, as money having a stable value, probably because such money is financially "sound" or secure (though some people claim it is from the sound heard when one drops a coin to test its ring of authenticity).

spondulic(k)s, 1856, as a slang word for money, also spelled *spondulix* by 1890. No one knows where this word comes from.

spot cash, cash that can be paid here and now, on the spot, 1879.

sugar, 1859, as a slang word for money (see PROSTITUTES, BROTH-ELS, AND LEWD WOMEN for *sugar daddy*).

wad, 1814, as any large or small wad of money carried in a pocket or purse, then in the late 1860s as a large amount of money or all of one's stake. *To lose one's wad*, 1891. *Tightwad*, 1900 (*tight* has meant tightfisted or stingy since the 1820s).

wampum, first recorded in 1638 as the Algonquian word for Indian shell money (literally "string of white" shells); it has been considered as general American slang for money since 1904.

the wherewithal, 1809, in England, originally as the necessities or supplies to accomplish a desired end. This more formal term is not as old as our similar American slang words for money, *the needful* (1771) and *the necessary* (1772). *What it takes*, meaning money, dates from 1929.

Now let's look at the major words and expressions our own monetary system has given us, including the names of our specific bills and coins, starting with the lowly mill and ending with the larger amounts.

U.S. Currency Terms

mill, 1791, when it was first used by Thomas Jefferson to mean a thousandth part of a dollar or a tenth of a cent (from Latin *millēsimum*, a thousandth part). *Mill tax*, 1848, as a tax of one mill per dollar of assessed valuation (the United States has never minted a mill, but some states have, as for payment of sales taxes in stores).

half cent, 1786, when this large copper ½-cent coin, about the size of today's quarter, was authorized by the Continental Congress. It was minted from 1793 to 1857 and was also called a *half copper* (1825).

cent. It was the assistant to the superintendent of finances of the United Colonies, Gouverneur Morris, who first proposed, in his report outlining a new American monetary system in 1782, that the word *cent* (from Latin *centum*, a hundred) replace the English word *penny*. Morris, however, suggested our cent be silver and our basic unit of value. Thomas Jefferson approved the new word *cent* but, in improving Morris's monetary plan for the Continental Congress, suggested the coin be made of copper and the dollar itself be our basic unit. Thus, thanks to Gouverneur Morris and Thomas Jefferson, we have the *cent*, but linguistic habits are hard to break and, although we speak of "one cent" or "ninety cents" in referring to value, we have long ago reverted to

The 1793 one-cent coin, the first such issued by the U.S.

calling the coin by that old English word *penny* (for more about our use of *penny* see below).

The original 1793 U.S. one-cent copper coin was issued until 1857. The cent has also been called *red cent*, 1839 (from the copper's reddish color), which sometimes has been shortened to *red* since 1849. *One-cent piece*, 1873.

copper has been used since the late 16th century in England to refer to various small copper coins. Between 1774 and 1789 several colonies and states minted *coppers*, all of which were eventually driven out of circulation by clandestine imitations and an immense quantity of British copper tokens made expressly for American use. Many of these British tokens somewhat hypocritically bore portraits of George Washington and, along with a great many buttons, medals, and other coinlike souvenirs bearing Washington's likeness, were called *Washington pennies* by early Americans.

Since so many penny copper coins had been called *coppers*, the first U.S. copper cent was immediately called a *copper* and *copper cent*. *Not worth a copper* is an American term of 1788, followed by *not worth a cent* (1820s), *not to care a cent* (1839), *not to care a Continental copper* (1841, shortened to *not to care a Continental* in 1882), *not to care a copper* (1843), *not to care a dime* (1849), and *not to care two cents* (1856)—but all these originated in our colonial expression *not to care a farthing* (1709). Incidentally, the English *shilling*, like the *farthing* and the *copper*, was used with the connotation of "cheap." This colonial use persisted long after independence: the west side of New York City's Broadway, where cheaper goods were sold, was called the *shilling side* or the *shilling sidewalk* from 1849, while the more expensive east side was called the *two-shilling side*.

fugio, fugio cent (or *coin*), 1787. In 1776 the Continental Congress authorized a pewter dollar to provide support for the inflated Continental paper currency. Designed by Benjamin Franklin, this dollar featured a sundial, a chain of thirteen links representing the United Colonies, the word *fugio* (Latin for "I fly," in allusion to *tempus fugit*, "time flies"), and the motto "Mind Your Business." In 1787 Congress licensed James Jarvis in New Haven, Connecticut, to mint copper cents of this same design, this coin becoming the first ever issued by the U.S. government and called the *fugio* and the *Franklin cent*.

penny is a much older word than our 1782 *cent*. It's an Old English word in use for over a thousand years and was once spelled *pen(d)ing* and *penig*, after Penda, an 8th-century Mercian king for whom the coin was first made. Our patriotic resolve to call our U.S. one-cent piece a *cent* (see *cent* above) could not break our long English colonial habit of calling such a coin a *penny* and by 1831 many Americans were calling our coin a *penny* again (however, patriotic New Englanders then still frequently criticized the rest of the country for reverting to the old English word and continued to use *cent* more often than Americans from other regions). That *penny* is the name most Americans use for the coin is shown by such American terms as *penny ante* (poker), 1855; *penny pitching*, the game, 1871; and *penny pincher*, a thrifty person or miser, 1920s. We have also continued to use English "penny" expressions, based on the English penny, without changing the

E Pluribus Unum
This Latin motto ("One out of many") was chosen by Thomas Jefferson, Benjamin Franklin, and John Adams in 1776 to be the motto of the United States and appear on the face of the Great Seal of the U.S. In 1873 a law was passed that all U.S. coins bear this motto.

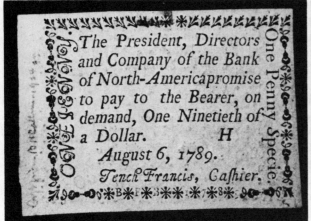

The Bank of North America still used the British word penny on this 1789 bill.

word *penny* to *cent*, including: *a penny for your thoughts* (1546 in England), *a pretty penny* (1768 in England, meaning a good sum of money), *penny-a-liner* (1834 in England, as a hack journalist), and *a penny saved is a penny earned* (1899 in England, though the original *a penny saved is a penny got* was an English expression of 1695).

nickel cent, 1857, when our original large copper cent was replaced by one made of copper and nickel. This coin was issued until 1864 and was also called a *nickel.*

Indian head penny, issued from 1859 to 1909 (our original 1793 one-cent coin also bore an Indian head but seems not to have been called an *Indian head penny*). The model for the Indian depicted on our 1859 Indian head penny was not an Indian at all but was Sarah Longacre, the daughter of an official of the mint.

Lincoln penny, first issued in 1909, the hundreth anniversary of Lincoln's birth.

steel penny and *shell-case penny,* 1940s, for the World War II pennies made from steel or from melted-down shell casing to conserve scarce or strategic metals. All such coins were called *emergency coins* because they were made during the wartime "emergency."

two-cent piece, 1864, for this bronze two-cent coin, first issued that year (though the adjective *two-cent,* meaning sold or bought for the sum of two cents had been in use since 1850). During the second half of the 19th century there were several experiments with coins of odd denominations, including this two-cent piece, the three-cent piece, and a silver twenty-cent coin. This two-cent coin was the first to bear *In God We Trust,* because during the Civil War, Secretary of the Treasury Salmon P. Chase received many requests to have a reference to God on U.S. currency.

three cents, 1829, as a coin of this value issued by some local banks.

Three-center, 1848, as an adjective meaning cheap or low class, as a saloon selling drinks for three cents each (such a saloon would be called a *two-bit saloon* by the late 1850s, showing the effects of inflation).

three-cent piece, 1851, when the U.S. three-cent coin was introduced, mainly as a coin people could use to pay the new, reduced, three-cent postage rate that went into effect on several types of mail. The three-cent coin was silver until 1865, then nickel until it was discontinued in 1890. Thus for a while people spoke of the *silver three-cent piece* and, later, of the *nickel three-cent piece* or *three-cent nickel*.

half-dime, 1792, the year this five-cent silver coin, the first ever struck under the auspices of the U.S. mint, was first issued (it was issued until 1873). Thomas Jefferson and other early proponents of our monetary system originally called it a *half disme* (see *dime* below). It was also called a *five-penny bit* (1799) and was even called by the British term *five pence* as late as 1849. (Incidentally, some American colonists pronounced the English "five-penny bit" as *fi'penny* or *fipenny bit*, from which they coined the slang word *fip* for this coin and the sum of five pence.)

five-cent piece, 1829, as another term for the half dime.

five-center, 1880s, both as a five-cent piece and something sold or bought for five cents, especially a five-cent cigar.

nickel didn't refer to our five-cent coin until 1881. The first U.S. coin to be called a *nickel* was the copper and nickel one-cent piece of 1857 and the next U.S. coin to be called a *nickel* was the three-cent nickel coin of 1865 (see *nickel cent* and *three-cent piece* above). In 1875 we began to talk about our new *five-cent nickel* (actually made of one part nickel and three parts copper) and had shortened the name of this five-cent coin to *nickel* six years later. The five-cent nickel has given us such expressions as *nickel novel*, 1896 (a cheap novel, the term based on *dime novel;* see under *dime* below) and *nickel nurser*, a tightwad or miser, 1924.

Liberty (head) nickel, a five-cent piece coined from 1883 to 1913 and showing the goddess of Liberty bordered with stars. This coin was a favorite of confidence men and other crooks who, with or without gold plating it, passed it off as a $5 piece, the V (Roman numeral for 5) on the original design not being followed by the word "cents."

jitney, a nickel, 1901 (see TAXI! for the origin of this word); occasionally shortened to *jit* by 1915.

not worth a plugged nickel is an American expression first recorded in 1908. A plugged coin is one from which the center, valuable gold, silver, etc., has been removed and replaced by a plug of base or cheaper metal. Dishonest colonists had been caught *plugging* English, Spanish, French, and other coins as early as 1694.

buffalo nickel or *Indian-buffalo nickel*, minted from 1913 to 1938. The Indian head depicted on this coin was a composite of three Indian models.

Don't take any wooden nickels, 1915, literally meaning "You're so innocent I even have to warn you against this obvious counterfeit," but usually having an affectionate connotation of "goodby, good luck, and keep out of trouble." Though counterfeit coins of wood were being passed at least as early as the 1850s in America, the *wooden nickels* in this expression are probably a more general and humorous reference to the many outlandish counterfeit wooden items long said to have been sold to rustics by conniving Yankee pedlars, there being many early 19th-century jokes about those who unsuspectingly purchased *wooden nutmeg* (1825), *wooden cucumber seeds* (1831), and even *wooden hams* (1832). Thus *don't take any wooden nickels* most probably originated as a general warning or joke about such items (though there is the rather

An 1864 two-cent piece, *the first year the coin was issued. It was the first U.S. coin to bear the words "In God We Trust."*

The original U.S. quarter of 1792. Quarter *had meant one quarter of a Spanish or of a Dutch dollar since 1704.*

A standing Liberty quarter *of 1917.*

The Washington quarter, *first issued in 1932.*

remote possibility that *wooden nickels* came from the term *Wood's money,* which see above).

Jefferson nickel, minted since 1938.

dime, 1786, when it was first proposed as a name for the tenth part of a dollar in reports prepared for the Continental Congress (from the Latin *decimus,* tenth, via Middle French *disme;* Thomas Jefferson and other early proponents of this unit and coin called it a *disme). Dime novel,* as a cheap, sensational novel, 1864 (Erastus F. and Irwin P. Beadle began publishing the Dime Book Series in 1860 with Ann S. Stephens's novel *Malaeska, the Indian Wife of the White Hunter,* which thus became the first dime novel); *dimer,* 1910, both as a 10-cent piece and something sold or bought for a dime; *dime a dozen,* so plentiful as to be cheap, not valuable, 1930.

During the Depression we had the new terms *thin dime* (1931) and *Brother, can you spare a dime?,* which was the title of a popular 1932 song, after which it was considered the panhandler's typical request (*brother* had been used in English to mean friend and as a term of address to a stranger since the 17th century).

ten-cent piece, 1829. *Ten-cent Jimmy,* 1856, meaning a politician advocating low tariffs and low wages, implying advocacy of a wage of ten cents a day (the *Jimmy* almost certainly comes from James Buchanan, to whom the term was first applied during his successful 1856 campaign for the Presidency). *Ten-center,* something sold or bought for ten cents, 1873.

hog, hogg, 1859 as a dime, from the English slang use of *hog* to mean a shilling (which was first recorded in 1676, soon after Charles II issued a coin with the picture of a boar on the reverse side for use in Bermuda). *Not to have a hog in* (one's) *jeans,* having no money, broke, late 1940s, *hog* in this expression meaning any coin or even a dollar. Our 1828 expression *to go the whole hog* may or may not be related to *hog* as a piece of money. I believe it refers to the *hog* as a shilling, in which case it literally means to spend the whole amount, the whole shilling. Others believe that the expression comes from William Cowper's 1779 poem "The Love of the World Reproved; or Hypocrasy Detected," which contains the lines "But from one piece they thought it hard/From the whole hog to be debarred," referring to hypocritical followers of "the prophet of the Turk," who can't decide which part of the pig makes it unfit to eat but nevertheless decide to eat the rest, thus eventually eating the whole pig.

Mercury dime, issued 1916 to 1945. It does not bear a picture of Mercury but of Liberty with wings on the cap, which most people took to be Mercury.

Roosevelt dime, first issued in 1946, a year after President Franklin D. Roosevelt's death.

quarter, 1704 as one-quarter of a Spanish or of a Dutch dollar. By the time of the Revolutionary War, *quarter* was in wide use to mean a quarter of any dollar, foreign or Continental, or any coin worth 25 cents. *Quarter of a dollar,* 1789; a *quarter-dollar,* 1794. (When the first colonists came to America, *quarter* was just becoming somewhat archaic English slang for a farthing; *quarter* then reappeared in English slang in 1903 to mean five shillings, a quarter of a pound).

two bits (see *bit* at *real* in the short list of foreign coins above). Being worth one-eighth of a Spanish peso or Spanish dollar, the

A 1794 silver half dollar, *the first year this coin was issued.*

original Spanish real or *bit* was worth 12½ cents. Not only was this bit itself a coin, but the peso could be cut into halves, quarters, or pie-shaped wedges of eights, so a *bit* was both the coin and a cut-off section of a peso worth the same amount. This *bit*, being 12½ cents, gave us our term *two bits* (1730, originally as two separate bits or the sum of 25 cents, then as our own 25-cent coin in 1792), *four bits* as 50 cents (1836), and *six bits* as 75 cents (1840). In the past we have even used the terms *three bits* to mean 37½ cents (1839) and *half a bit* to mean 6¼ cents (1723, though this term was also sometimes used to mean half a penny).

Since we had also used *bit* to mean any coin by 1705, in the San Francisco area around 1854 a *short bit* was 5 cents and a *long bit* a dime, but *bit* still then meant 12½ cents to too many people for these uses to prevail, so by 1879 in the far West a *short bit* meant a dime, as a little less than a full 12½ cents bit, and *long bit* meant 15 cents, as a little more than 12½ cents. *Two-bit*, as an adjective meaning cheap, especially in referring to a saloon where drinks were to be had for two bits, 1856 (the adjective also originally had a disparaging connotation of rural or rustic, less elegant and expensive than in the big city).

twenty-five-cent piece, 1875.

Liberty quarter or *standing Liberty quarter*, issued from 1916 to 1930. This coin immediately became an object of debate and much snickering because the goddess of Liberty was shown with a bare breast, which the Treasury Department soon covered in a more modest design.

Washington quarter, first issued in 1932 to commemorate the two hundredth anniversary of Washington's birth (Washington had refused to let his likeness appear on the first U.S. coins, claiming that such veneration was not consistent with the principles of democracy).

half dollar, 1786, in the *Journals of the Continental Congress*, reporting the authorization of this U.S. 50-cent silver coin, which was first issued in 1794 (the *Spanish half dollar* had been in wide use in colonial times, so the term *half dollar* was not new to Americans).

Half-a-dollar, 1844; *half*, 1859; *half case*, 1878.

fifty-cent piece, 1836.

Liberty (walking) half-dollar, issued from 1916 to 1947, the wife of poet Wallace Stevens posed as the model for the goddess of Liberty on this coin.

Franklin half-dollar, issued from 1949 to 1963.

Kennedy half-dollar, first issued in 1964, a year after President John F. Kennedy's assassination.

A 1964 Kennedy half dollar, *issued the year following President Kennedy's assassination.*

dollar (see the discussion of *dollar* in the introductory paragraphs of this section). *Dollar bill*, 1774 (referring then to a bill of credit issued by a colony); *one-dollar bill*, 1838. *One dollar*, as a piece of money, 1785; *a one*, 1821.

Our dollars have come in gold, silver, paper, and even pewter. The Continental Congress authorized the *pewter dollar* in 1776, which also was called the *fugio dollar* (see *fugio* under *cent* above for more details). *Silver dollar* was first recorded in 1781, then referring to the Spanish silver peso. In 1792 Congress authorized the minting of U.S. silver dollars, these first *United States dollars* being issued on October 15, 1794—which means that any "silver dollar" George Washington might have thrown across the Potomac as a younger man would actually have been a Spanish peso. Our own silver dollar was also called a *wheel* (1807) or, more commonly, a *cartwheel* (1855) because of its large size. The *gold dollar* was the U.S. one-dollar gold piece issued from 1849 to 1890.

free silver, the *trade dollar*, and the *Morgan dollar*. The Coinage Act of 1873 ended the minting of silver dollars for domestic use, but from then until 1885 a special *trade dollar* or *silver trade dollar* was issued for use in the Oriental trade only. Owners of western silver mines and mining stocks hadn't complained when the minting of the domestic silver dollar ended, because commercial users of silver paid more for it than the government had. However, when new silver discoveries lowered the market value of silver, these mining interests joined with cheap-money advocates in denouncing the demonetization of silver as *the Crime of 1873* and made *free silver* (late 1870s as the free and unlimited coinage of silver) and *bimetallism* a hotly debated political issue until the end of the century. Free-silver advocates claimed that if more money were put into circulation because of the minting of silver dollars, prices would rise, which would help farmers and laborers pay off debts more quickly. By 1878 such interests forced Congress to pass a law requiring the Treasury to buy from two to four million dollars' worth of silver every month and coin it into silver dollars. This newly authorized silver dollar, issued from 1878 until 1904, was sometimes called a *standard silver dollar* or *standard dollar* (1878, to distinguish it from the silver trade dollar which contained slightly more silver), a *Morgan dollar* (they were designed by George T. Morgan), and a *buzzard dollar* (1879, in derisive allusion to the eagle on it, since it was less valuable than the silver trade dollar).

Peace dollar, 1921, a silver dollar with the word "peace" on it, commemorating the peace treaty ending World War I.

Eisenhower dollar, first issued in 1971, two years after the death of President Dwight D. Eisenhower (he was probably put on the coin because of his fame as a general rather than for having been President, but we don't put mere generals on our coins and bills).

Susan B. Anthony dollar, first issued in 1979, following a decade of the women's liberation movement and advances in women's rights, this was the first U.S. coin with a woman on it, other than goddesses from classical mythology (and made Susan B. Anthony and Benjamin Franklin the only two famous Americans shown on our coins who have not been President). The small, round Susan B. Anthony dollar with an octagonal design did not

A *silver* trade dollar.

An 1878 Morgan dollar, *the* standard silver dollar *newly issued that year.*

The Peace dollar.

The Eisenhower dollar.

A 1979 Susan B. Anthony dollar, *the first year this coin was issued.*

gain popular acceptance, because most people found it too easily confused in size, shape, and weight with the quarter.

The dollar has also given us many common terms and expressions, including: *sound as a dollar,* 1841 (see *sound money* in the list of general monetary terms above); *bet your bottom dollar,* late 1850s, referring to the last dollar at the bottom of one's pocket or purse; *dollar-a-day,* 1902, cheap, especially as a boardinghouse charging this rate; *Boston dollar,* also 1902, not a dollar at all but a jocular western term for a penny, alluding to the supposed stinginess of New Englanders; *dollar diplomacy*, 1910, originally as diplomacy conducted by Secretary of State Philander Knox for the benefit of overseas United States commerce; and *dollar-a-year man*, 1918, originally referring to any executive working for the World War I War Industries Board, which, under Bernard Baruch, mobilized industry and labor for the war effort, such an executive being paid a dollar a year because it was illegal to pay them nothing.

The almost forgotten terms *dollars-to-buttons* and *dollars-to-dumplings* appeared in the 1880s, meaning "almost certain" and usually used in "I'll bet you dollars-to-buttons/dumplings" or "you can bet dollars-to-buttons/dumplings." They were replaced by 1890 with the more popular *dollars-to-doughnuts* (a 1904 variation, *dollars-to-cobwebs*, never became very common, perhaps because it didn't alliterate).

We also have many slang words for dollar, most of which, like dollar itself, when used in the plural also mean money or a sum of money. These include:

ace note, 1926, a dollar bill, from the ace in playing cards as representing a "1."

berry, 1900.

bone, 1865.

buck, one of the oldest and most common slang words for dollar. *Buck* meant a male deer (as well as a male goat) by the year 1000 in England, with *buckskin* and *buck hide* both coming into the language between 1430 and 1450. Between 1700 and 1750 a quarter of a million to half a million buckskins were traded each year on the American frontier and by 1720 many hunters and traders were calling these buckskins *bucks* and reckoning earnings and rates of barter and exchange in terms of such bucks. Thus, though *buck* wasn't recorded as meaning a dollar until 1856, a buck or buckskin had long been used as a unit of exchange and a measure of wealth in America.

case note, 1859, originally meaning one's last dollar (probably from faro's *case card*, 1856, as the last card of any denomination in the dealer's box or case).

clam, 1930s. No one knows the origin of this use of the word (a tentative suggestion might be that it comes from the 1890s beggar's use of *to clam*, meaning to beg for money, go about trying to grab some money).

simoleon, 1881. This may have come from the now long-forgotten slang word for a dollar, *Simon*, 1859 (which had been English underworld slang for sixpence since 1700, using the proper name *Simon* because it alliterates with *six*), though the shift in accent from the first syllable in *Simon* to the second syllable in *simoleon* may point against this origin.

sinker, 1894, for a silver dollar, at which time *sinker* was also slang for a pancake and a round breakfast roll, coming to mean a doughnut, especially a heavy one, by 1925.

two-dollar bill, 1813. *A two*, 1842; *two-case note*, 1859 (see *case note* under *dollar* above); *two spot*, 1904 (from the pips on playing cards and dice being called *spots*, 1843). *Two-dollar word*, a long word, especially as used to impress rather than to communicate with a reader or listener, 1929.

deuce, 1930, from calling a two of cards or the two on a die or dice a *deuce* (1846, via French from Latin *duos/duo*, two).

three-dollar note, issued by the Continental Congress in 1776, each note backed by three Spanish silver dollars. *Three-dollar bill*, 1842, as issued by various local banks (for *queer as a three-dollar bill* see GAY MEN AND LESBIANS). *Three-dollar coin*, a gold coin issued from 1853 to 1890.

five-dollar bill, 1778; *five-dollar bank note*, 1779; *a five*, 1821 as a $5 bill; *fiver*, 1840; *five case note*, 1885 (see *case note* under *dollar* above); *five spot*, 1903 (see *two spot* under *two-dollar bill* above).

half eagle, the U.S. $5 gold piece, first mentioned in 1786 during the planning and discussions of the first U.S. coins, then issued from 1795 to 1929 (see *eagle* under the *ten-dollar gold coin* below).

finnif, 1859 for a $5 bill (via Yiddish *finif* from German *fünf*, five); shortened to *fin*, 1929 (perhaps reinforced by *fin*, being slang for hand, suggesting five from the five fingers, since the late 18th century).

The eagle *or* ten dollar gold coin. *This design was created by Augustus Saint-Gaudens in 1907.*

the *ten-dollar gold coin* was also called an *eagle* (from the American eagle stamped on the reverse side of it) even during the 1786 planning of our new currency; with various modifications it was minted from 1794 to 1933. Hence *half eagle* and *double eagle* as the $5 and $20 gold pieces and *quarter eagle* as the $2.50 gold piece (this last coin authorized by Congress in 1792 and minted from 1796 until 1929). *To make the eagle scream* meant to indulge in high-flown patriotic oratory by 1847 (referring to the American eagle and having nothing to do with the coin), but by 1911 it meant to be stingy or miserly, as if holding on to those golden eagle coins too tightly. *The day the eagle shits* (or sometimes, euphemistically, *the day the eagle screams* or *flies*) was a common World War II serviceman's term for payday, though this expression may go back to the Spanish-American War and the late 1890s (the eagle in this expression referring both to our national symbol and to its widespread use on U.S. currency).

ten-dollar note, 1807; *a ten*, 1821; *ten spot*, 1848 (see *two spot* under *two-dollar bill* above); *tenner*, 1926 (tenner has been used in England to mean a ten-pound note since 1848, which may have suggested our use of the word).

sawbuck, 1850 (from the Roman numeral X for 10, which was on many $10 bills, this X resembling the cross support of a *sawbuck* or sawhorse); sometimes shortened to *saw* by the 1920s.

ned, a $10 gold piece, 1859 (this had been English slang for a guinea since 1753 and for a gold sovereign since 1846, from the proper name).

The original 1796 quarter eagle *or $2.50 gold piece.*

201

The double eagle *or* twenty dollar gold piece. *This is the* flying eagle *designed by Augustus Saint-Gaudens in 1907.*

twenty-dollar bill, 1829; *a twenty,* 1839, for a $20 bill.

double eagle was, from the very beginning, a common term for the $20 gold coin issued from 1849 to 1933 (see *eagle* under *the ten-dollar gold coin* above); *twenty-dollar gold piece,* 1867. Augustus Saint-Gaudens's new designs for our $10 and $20 gold pieces were introduced in 1907. Many people consider his $20 gold piece the most beautiful of all U.S. coins.

double sawbuck, a $20 bill, 1859 (see *sawbuck* under *the ten-dollar gold coin* above); sometimes shortened to *double saw* by 1931.

a fifty, a $50 bill, 1838; *fifty spot,* 1868, but never common. *L,* 1839, but never common (from the Roman numeral L for 50).

half a century, 1908, and *half a C,* 1934 (see *century* and *C* at *a hundred* below).

a hundred has meant a hundred dollars in America since the first half of the 18th century.

C note and the much less common *C spec* were both first recorded as meaning a hundred-dollar bill in 1830 with *C* alone following in 1839 (all from C as the Roman numeral for 100). *Century* appeared in 1859, originally as a gambler's term, with the longer *century note* following in 1905 (both from *century* as representing a hundred, probably reinforced by mistaking the C of *C note* or *C* alone, for hundred dollars, as an abbreviation for *century* rather than the Roman numeral for 100).

yard, 1929 (because this is a three-digit bill and the yard represents a unit of three feet).

Since 1969 all U.S. currency in denominations over one hundred dollars has been withdrawn from circulation as the bills have come in to Federal Reserve Banks. A thousand dollars has been called a *thou* since 1869, a *grand* since 1900 (which was sometimes shortened to *G* by 1920), and a *big one* by the 1950s. The *$10,000 Federal Reserve Notes* were the highest currency ever in general circulation and, although the last ones were printed in 1944, about four hundred are still in private hands. The *$100,000 gold certificates,* with President Woodrow Wilson's likeness, were first issued in 1934 and were the highest denomination ever authorized in the world; however, they were never in general circulation, being for official transactions only (twelve of these are still in Federal Reserve Banks). Although U.S. currency has never come in larger denominations than this, it is, of course, possible to amass and talk about still larger amounts (see MILLIONAIRE).

English *vs* American

This subject could, and does, fill many volumes, but the most obvious and representative differences between English English and American English include:

Differences in American and English Vocabulary

It's easy and fun to point out the differences between the American and the English vocabulary: the differences seem quaint and there are comparatively so few that we can easily spot them. Many of the differences are merely a matter of preference: we prefer *railroad* and *store* while the English prefer the synonyms *railway* and *shop*, but all four words are used in both England and America. In addition, we know or can easily guess what *braces*, *fishmonger's*, or *pram* means, just as the English know or can figure out what *innerspring* mattress, *jump rope*, and *ice water* mean. Finally, many of the words that once separated American English from English English no longer do: our *cocktail* (1806), *skyscraper* (1833), and *supermarket* (1920s) are now heard around the world, and the English increasingly use *radio*, *run* (in a stocking), and *Santa Claus* instead of *wireless*, *ladder*, and *Father Christmas*. The following list gives some of the most interesting and typical differences between the American and English vocabulary, differences that may especially interest tourists and those who enjoy both American and English books and movies (many such differences are pointed out throughout this book and I haven't repeated them all here).

> *God save the king, that is lord of this language.*
> Geoffrey Chaucer, "Prologue" to *Astrolabe*, 1380.

airfield—aerodrome.
annual (a plant)—*bedder, bedding plant*.
antenna—aerial.
apartment; *apartment house, apartment building*, all 1870s—*flat; block of flats* (to an Englishman an *apartment* means a room). Our *high-rise apartment* (building) is the English *tower block* (of flats).
attic—loft.
baby carriage, 1870s, *baby buggy*, 1880s—*pram*, 1884 (short for *perambulator*, literally one who walks).
    stroller (for an infant)—*push chair*.
baggage—luggage.
       baggage car (on a train)—*luggage van*.
       to check baggage—to register luggage.
bangs (of hair)—*fringe*.
bank account—banking account. The English frequently use *-ing* to end the first word of a compound term when we do not, as in *dancing hall, dialing tone, ingrowing toenail, rowing boat, sailing boat*, and *washing day*. However, they say *swing door* where we add the *-ing* to get *swinging door*.

barbershop—barber's shop. The English frequently use the possessive -'s or -s' where we do not, as in *doll's house, ladies' room,* and *tailor's shop.*

baseboard—skirting board.

beet—beetroot.

bill (paper money)—*note.*

billboard—boarding.

billfold, 1900 (originally called a *billfolder*)—*notecase, (folding) wallet, pocketbook.* The English call a lady's *handbag* just that, or sometimes a *bag,* but never a *pocketbook.*

bobby pin, late 1920s—*hair grip.*

bookmaker, bookie, 1880s—*turf accountant, commission agent.*

bouncer, 1865—*chucker out.*

bowel movement, movement—motion.

briefcase—portfolio, dispatch case.

broad jump—long jump.

buddy—mate.

bulletin board, 1820s—*notice board.*

business suit, 1870—*lounge suit.*

can (of solid food)—*tin.* In England a *can* is still only for containing liquids.

    can opener—tin opener.

candy—sweets

    candy store—sweet shop.

    hard candy—boiled sweets.

car, automobile—motor car. Many terms having to do with cars, driving, and roads are different in America and England, such as:

    battery—accumulator.

    bumper—fender.

    dash(board)—fascia (panel).

    driver's license—driving licence.

    fender—wing, mudguard.

    gas(oline)—petrol.

    gear shift—gear lever.

        high (gear)—top gear.

        first or *low (gear)—bottom gear.*

    glove compartment—glove box, cubby, cubbyhole.

    hood—bonnet.

    horn, siren—hooter.

    license plate—number plate.

    light—lamp.

        backup light—reverse lamp, reversing light.

        dome light—roof lamp.

        headlight—head lamp.

    moving van—pantechnicon.

    muffler—(exhaust) silencer.

    parking lot—car park (here the English do prefer *car* to *motor car*).

    pass—overtake.

    rest area, repair area (at side of road)—*lie-by.*

    roof, top—hood, especially a convertible top, which the English also call a *drop top.*

    rumble seat—dickey (seat).

    shoulder (of a road)—*verge.*

    spark plug—sparking plug.

sports car—two-seater.

station wagon—estate car (note again the more American use of *car*).

superhighway, interstate—motorway.

tailgate (of a station wagon)—*tailboard.*

traffic circle—roundabout, circus.

traffic jam—traffic block.

trailer—caravan.

tread—track.

truck—lorry for a large one, *van* for a small one, even if it has an open bed. Our *truck stop* (restaurant) is the English *transport café.*

trunk—boot

windshield—windscreen.

carnival—fun fair.

checkers—draughts.

checking account, 1926—current account.

savings account—deposit account.

checkout counter (in a supermarket)—*cash desk.*

chocolate chips—polka dots.

cigar store—tobacconist's (shop).

clerk (1771), *salesperson—*(shop) *assistant.*

closet—cupboard.

clothespin—clothespeg.

common stock—ordinary shares.

preferred stock—preference shares (see *stocks—shares* below).

cookbook—cookery book.

copy editor—subeditor.

corn (field corn)—*maize.*

corner (of a street), *turn* (of a road)—*turning.*

corporation (abbreviated *Corp.*)—*(limited) company* (abbreviated *Ltd.*).

cot, 1840s—*camp bed* (to an Englishman a *cot* is what we call a *crib,* for babies).

cotton candy, 1926—candy floss.

counterclockwise—anti-clockwise.

cracker—biscuit (see Is It a Biscuit or a Cracker?).

cream, coffee cream—single cream.

whipping cream—double cream

cuff (on trousers)—*turn-up* (the English use *cuff* only in referring to sleeves).

dance hall, 1858—palais (from *Palais de Danse*).

Dacron—Terylene.

diaper, 1714 (before that it meant a type of linen)—*nappy* (from *napkin,* little cloth).

dinette, 1930, breakfast room—morning room.

dish towel—washing-up cloth, tea towel.

do the dishes—wash up.

dish cloth, 1828; dish rag, 1839—washcloth (when Americans say *washcloth* we mean a *face cloth*).

dish pan, 1872—washing pan.

dishwasher (machine)—*washing-up machine.* In Great Britain *dish* means only a platter or serving dish, not a plate; thus a "dish towel" or "dishwasher" would apply only to platters.

doctor's office, dentist's office—surgery.

dormitory—hall of residence. To an Englishman a *dormitory* is only a bedroom for several students.

drugstore, 1819—*chemist's (shop).*
>   *pharmacist, druggist*, 1816—*chemist, dispenser.*
dry goods store, 1776—*draper's (shop).*
editorial (in a newspaper)—*lead article, leading article, leader.*
eggnog—*egg flip.*
electric outlet—*power point, point.*
elevator, 1853—*lift* (short Englishmen who want to appear taller put *elevators* on their shoes; we call these *lifts*).
employ, hire (a person)—*engage* (the English *hire* cars, we *rent* them).
eraser—*(India) rubber.*
excelsior (wood shavings for packing)—*wood wool.*
executive, 1890s—*director.*
fedora, late 1880s—*trilby.*
fire department, 1825—*fire brigade.*
fish store—*fishmonger's.*
flashlight, 1890s—*torch.*
floor lamp, 1920s—*standard lamp.*
floor walker, 1876—*shop walker.*
flophouse, 1890s—*doss house.*
foreman—*chargehand.*
french fried potatoes, french fries—*chips.*
>   *potato chips*—*crisps.*
>   *mashed potatoes*—*creamed potatoes, mash.*
>   *baked potato*—*jacket potato.*
fruit and vegetable store—*greengrocer's.*
furnace—*boiler.*
garbage can, 1906—*dust bin.*
>   *(garbage) dump*—*tip.*
>   *garbage man*, 1888—*dustman.*
>   *garbage truck*, 1920s—*dustcart.*
garter (a vertical one suspended from a band around the leg, as worn by American men since the 1880s)—*(sox) suspender* (the English use *garter* only to designate a round, horizontal one).
gelatine (dessert, such as *Jell-O*)—*jelly.*
general delivery—*poste restante* (French for "remaining mail," mail left at the post office until claimed).
grab bag—*lucky dip.*
grade (of a road), 1808—*gradient.*
grade (division of a school or the pupils in it)—*form, class, standard.* Our *grade school* is the British *primary school.*
green thumb (knack for gardening)—*green fingers.*
ground (of electrical circuit)—*earth.*
ground beef—*minced meat, mince.*
>   *ground round*—*best minced meat.*
hair spray—*lacquer.*
half-past (the hour)—*half.* Thus the English say "half-twelve" when we would say "half-past twelve"; however, they usually use "past" in telling time where we use "after"—for example, the English say "twenty past ten" when we would usually say "twenty after ten."
hall, hallway—*passage.*
hardware store, 1789—*ironmonger's.*
hassock—*pouf, pouffe.*
ice cream—*ice.*
>   *sherbet*—*water ice, sorbet* (via French and Italian from Turkish

sharbet from Arabic *sharbah*, drink; thus *sherbet* and *sorbet* are different forms of the same word).

ice water—iced water. The English frequently add *-ed* to end the first word in a compound term when we do not, as in *six-roomed house*, *stockinged feet*, and *wheeled chair*.

information (telephone use)—*directory inquiries*.

innerspring (mattress)—*interior spring*.

installment plan, 1876—*hire-purchase system*, *hire system*, the "never-never."

janitor, 1868—*caretaker* (the person we would call a *caretaker* of an estate would be called a *gardener* in England; the person an Englishman calls a *janitor* we would call a *doorkeeper* or *doorman*).

jelly roll—Swiss roll.

jump rope—skipping rope.

kerosene, 1855, *coal oil*, 1858—*paraffin* (what we call *paraffin* the English call *white wax*).

key punch—card punch.

kindergarten—infant school.

ladybug—ladybird, golden knop.

lawyer, 1707—*solicitor*, one who does general legal work; *barrister*, a trial lawyer.

lemonade—lemon squash.
 orangeade—orange squash

letterhead (stationery)—*headed paper*.

lifeguard, 1896—*life saver*.

line (file of people waiting)—*queue* (via French from Latin *cōda*, tail).

lint—fleck (the English use *lint* to mean surgical dressing).

living room, 1860—*sitting room*; loosely, *drawing room*.

long distance (telephone call)—*trunk call*. Our long-distance *direct dialing* is the English *subscriber trunk dialing*.

lumber (boards), 1662—*timber*. In England *lumber* refers to superfluous household items of the kind stored in the attic.

mail—post. Our street-corner *mailbox* is the British *pillar box*.

martini—gin and it, gin and French. If you order a *martini* in England you will get a glass of vermouth.

megaphone, 1878—*loud hailer*.

merry-go-round—roundabout, giddy-go-round. We both also use the word *carousel*.

molasses—treacle.
 sulphur and molasses—brimstone and treacle.

move (from one house to another)—*move house*.

movie—cinema, flick. We both also use *film* and *picture*.

mucilage, glue—gum.

mutual fund—unit trust.

nail polish—nail varnish.

(newspaper) clipping, 1838—*press cutting*.

nightstick, 1893, *policeman's billy*—*baton, truncheon*.

on the cuff (on credit)—*on the slate*.

orchestra seat (in a theater)—*stall*. Our American use of *orchestra* to mean the first floor of a theater or the seats nearest the orchestra dates from 1786.

package—parcel.

pantry—larder.

pants—trousers (these two words mean the same to most Americans, but many English still use *pants* only to mean underpants).

Here will be an old abusing of God's patience and the king's English.
 William Shakespeare, *The Merry Wives of Windsor*, I, 4, 1600

pantyhose—tights.

parka—anorak.

part (in hair), 1871—*parting.*

period (punctuation mark)—*full stop.*

personal (business)—*private.*

pour, pour down (rain)—*pour rain.*

powdered sugar—icing sugar.

private detective—inquiry agent.

property taxes—rates.

pry (open or apart)—*prise.*

pullover (sweater)—*jersey,* and a woman's *jersey* is often called a
 jumper.

> *turtleneck* (shirt or sweater)—*roll neck, polo neck.*

racetrack, 1866—*racecourse.*

radio—wireless.

> *(radio) tube—(wireless) valve.*

railroad—railway. Many of the terms having to do with railroads are
 different in America and England, such as:

> *bill of lading—consignment note.*
>
> *car* (for passengers)—*carriage.* We both also use *coach.*
>
> *car* (for freight, cattle, etc.)—*wagon.* Thus our *boxcar* is the
 English *goods wagon.*
>
> *conductor—guard.*
>
> *cowcatcher—plough* (which we spell *plow*).
>
> *engineer—(engine) driver.*
>
> *freight train—goods train.*
>
> *freight yard—goods yard.* In England *freight* still applies only
 to that which is transported by water (it's from the Dutch *vrecht,*
 cargo, fee for a transport ship).
>
> *grade crossing—level crossing.*
>
> *one way* (ticket)—*single.*
>
> *rails—metal.*
>
> *right of way—permanent way.*
>
> *roundhouse—running shed.*
>
> *round trip* (ticket), 1868—*return.*
>
> *ticket agent—booking clerk.*
>
> *tie—sleeper.*
>
> *track—line.*

raincoat, 1907—*mackintosh, mac.*

raise (in salary)—*rise.*

rare (meat)—*underdone.*

ready-to-wear (clothes)—*off the peg.*

> *custom made,* 1847, *made to order—bespoke.*

real-estate agent—estate agent.

repairman, plumber, mechanic—fitter.

reversible (overcoat)—*turnabout.*

roller coaster, 1892—*scenic railway;* less frequently called a *switchback.*

row house—terrace house (a row of such houses is called a *terrace*)

rubber band—elastic (band).

rummage sale—jumble sale.

run (in a stocking)—*ladder.*

sandbox—sandpit.

Santa Claus—Father Christmas (not an exact equivalent but a slim-
 mer, less jolly version of our Santa).

scrambled eggs, 1864—*buttered eggs.*

scratch pad, 1900s—*scribbling block, scribbling pad.*

shopping bag—*carrier bag.*

sidewalk (the cement walk by the side of a road), 1851—*pavement*, and still sometimes called a *footway.*

sled (as children use in snow)—*sledge.*

slingshot, 1849—*catapult.*

slippery—*greasy.* Thus in England a wet road can be *greasy.*

smoked herring—*kipper* (originally the Old English *cypera*, male salmon, perhaps meaning "copper," referring to its color).

sneakers, 1895—*plimsolls.* We both use the term *gym shoes* (the English *plimsoll* is from Samuel Plimsoll, who caused the adoption of the Plimsoll marks on cargo ship hulls to indicate the depth to which they may be legally loaded; the shoes were worn by sailors and have a mudguard resembling a Plimsoll mark).

soda fountain—*soda bar.*

soft drinks—*minerals* (because they were originally flavored mineral water).

solitaire (a card game for one player)—*patience.*

spool of thread, 1873—*reel of cotton.*

stenographer, 1796—*shorthand typist*, formerly *shorthand writer.*

stock—*shares.* The British do speak of the *stock exchange* and *stockbrokers* as we do, but they sell *shares* to *shareholders* in the *shares market.* When the British speak of *stocks* they often mean what we call *bonds*; thus our "stocks and bonds" would be the British "shares and stocks."

storage room—*box room* (literally a room for trunks, since the English say *box* where we say *trunk*) or *lumber room* (for miscellaneous and superfluous household items; see *lumber* above).

store, 1721—*shop.* *Store* originally meant warehouse in both England and the colonies, but colonial shops had to stock a great deal of merchandise because cargo vessels couldn't always be depended upon. Thus a shop became something of a warehouse or "store." The British still use *store* only to refer to a large shop.

    department store—*departmental store.*

strip mine—*open cast mine.*

subway—*underground, the tube.* In England *subway* means a pedestrian underpass.

suspenders—*braces.*

swim—*bathe.*

taffy—*toffy.*

Thermos (bottle), 1908—*vacuum flask.*

thumbtack, 1884—*push pin, drawing pin.*

tic-tac-toe—*noughts and crosses.*

toilet (meaning bathroom)—*lavatory.*

    toilet paper—*lavatory roll.*

toilet kit, shaving kit—*sponge bag.*

tote bag, 1960s—*holdall.*

transom (a small window above a door or another window), 1880—*fanlight.* We both use *transom* to mean lintel (from Latin *transtrum*, crossbeam) and a crosspiece at the stern of a ship or boat.

traveling salesman, 1878, *drummer*, 1880s—*commercial traveller.*

union suit, 1890s—*combinations.*

unlisted (of a telephone number)—*ex-directory.*

vacation (from work), 1844—*holiday.*

    vacationer, 1890—*holiday maker.* The English use *vacation* only to mean a university recess, the summer recess being called the *long vacation*.

vaudeville—music hall.

vest, 1809—waistcoat. What we call an *undershirt* the English call a *vest*.

wall-to-wall carpeting—edge-to-edge carpeting, fitted carpeting.

warden (of a prison)—*governor*. *Governor*, pronounced "gov'ner" in England, is also used to mean "sir" and "Dad" and is also an informal form of address. Thus the London cabbie's "Where to, gov'ner?" is akin to our "Where to, Mack?"

washcloth, face cloth—flannel (when an Englishman says *washcloth* he means what we call a *dish rag;* see *dish towel* above).

water heater—geyser (*geyser* is from *Geysir*, the name of a hot spring in Iceland, from Icelandic *geysa*, to gush: the English use of the word refers to the hotness of the water; our American use refers to its spouting from the ground).

wax paper—greaseproof paper.

weather bureau—meteorological office.

whole wheat—whole meal.

Windbreaker, 1920s—wind cheater.

wrench (a tool used to tighten a nut, pipe, etc.)—*spanner*.
  monkey wrench, 1850s—adjustable spanner.

yard, lawn—garden (an English *garden* need not always have flowers or vegetables growing in it).
  backyard—back garden.

zero—nought.

zucchini, 1920s—courgette.

There are, of course, hundreds of more terms that differ in American English and English English. The English don't use *mean* for "nasty," *dumb* for "stupid," *mortician* for "undertaker," or *Realtor* for "real-estate agent," and many of them might not know what our *to bawl out, bonehead, boob, bootlegger, commuter, dirt road, enlisted man, go-getter, graft, intern, roomer, scrubwoman, sea food,* or *tuxedo* mean. Similarly, many Americans wouldn't know how heavy a man is who weighs 12 *stone* (a *stone* equals 14 pounds), that a *coalfish* or a *coley fillet* is black cod, or that an *Albert* is a watch chain.

Our use of prepositions sometimes also differs: we live *on* a street, the English live *in* it; we chat *with* people, the English chat *to* them; we speak of an increase *in* something, the English of an increase *on* it; we get snowed *in*, they get snowed *up*; we get nervous *about* something, they get nervous *of* it; we say something is different *from* something else, the English say it is different *to* it; we buy *at* auction, the English buy *by* auction.

Differences in American and English Pronunciation

The major differences in American and English pronunciation is in intonation and voice timbre. We speak with less variety of tone than the English: this may be due in part to our matter-of-fact American attitude and is definitely due in part to the teaching of generations of American students to repeat and articulate every syllable in a word as given in Noah Webster's spelling book. Our voice timbre seems harsh or tinny to the English, their's gurgling or throaty to us. English conclusion: Americans speak shrilly, monotonously, and like a schoolboy reciting. American conclusion: the English speak too low, theatrically, and swallow their syllables. The more precise differences include:

(1) In general (but not always), we use flatter, shorter *a*'s and less rounded *o*'s. Thus we pronounce the *a* in such words as *ask*, *brass*, *can't*, *dance*, *fast*, *grass*, *half*, *last*, and *path* as a short, flat *ă*; the English pronounce it more as the broad *ä* in *father*. Our shorter, flatter *a* is just a continuation of the way our first colonists from Southern England pronounced it; the English dropped this pronunciation in the 18th century and began to use the broad *a* (this same change took place in parts of New England and the South, giving some Americans the pronunciation of *aunt* as "ahnt" and *vase* as "vahz").

On the other hand, most Americans sound the short *ŏ* in such words as *box*, *hot*, *lot*, *not*, *pot*, and *top* almost as the broad *a* in *father*, while the English (and some New Englanders) give it a more open sound, with the lips rounded.

One might overgeneralize and say we tend to make all vowels shorter or flatter than the English (we say *ĕvolution*, the English *ēvolution*), but this isn't true (we say *prīvacy* and *vītamin* and it's the English who say *prĭvacy* and *vĭtamin*).

(2) We Americans are more scrupulous about clearly articulating certain unaccented syllables, especially *-ary*, *-ery*, and *-ory*, and certain *d*'s, *g*'s, *h*'s, *l*'s, *r*'s (following vowels) and *t*'s than the English. Thus the English say *melanc'ly*, *monast'ry*, *necess'ry*, *preparat'ry*, *secret'ry*, etc., when we fully articulate the final syllables. Also, except in parts of New England and the South, we articulate the first *l* in *fulfill*, the *h* in *forehead*, the *r* in *lord* and *there*, and the final *t* in *trait*, rather than pronounce them as the English do: *fu'fill*, *for'rid*, *laud*, *theh*, and *trai*.

On the other hand, we Americans tend to slight the final *-ile* of such words as *fertile*, *missile*, and *sterile*, which the English pronounce as *fer-tile* (to rhyme with "aisle"), *mis-sile*, and *ster-ile*.

(3) We frequently move the accent or stress to the first syllable of a word, thus say *ALly*, *DEfect* (the noun), *EXcess*, *INquiry*, *LAB'ratory*, *MAma*, *PApa*, *REcess*, and *REsearch* while the English say *alLY*, *deFECT*, *exCESS*, *inQUIRY*, *laBORat'ry*, *maMA*, *paPA*, *reCESS*, and *reSEARCH*.

On the other hand, there are certain words in which we accent a later syllable than do the English: we say *gaRAGE* and *adverTISEment*, they say *GARage* and *adVERTisement*.

Other pronunciation differences don't fall into such easy categories; some resemble a general shift in vowel sounds, some show the different pronunciations of diphthongs, some use the initial English pronunciation of *sch-* as *sh-* instead of the American *sk-*, etc., and some are just unique pronunciations of individual words. Such miscellaneous differences in pronunciations include:

ate, we say "eight"—"et" is an accepted English pronunciation.
been, we say "bin"—the English say "bean."
clerk—"clark."
either, *neither*, most Americans say, "ē-ther, nē-ther"—"ī-ther, nī-ther" is the English pronunciation.
figure, we say "fig-yur"—the English say "figgar."
issue, we say "ish-you"—the English say "is-sue."
leisure, most Americans say "lē-sure"—the English say "lāysure."
lieutenant, we say "lew-tenant"—the English say "lef-tenant."
nephew, we say "nef-hew"—the English say "nev-hew."
schedule, we say "sked-ule"—the English say "shed-ule."

Differences in American and English Spelling

When the colonists came to America, spelling was not a problem—if a man could write at all he was lucky. English spelling was not yet rule-ridden: *i* and *j*, as well as *u* and *v*, were often used interchangeably; *y* was not a common letter; and redundant final *e's* were often sprinkled on the ends of such words as *half(e)* and *year(e)*. Not until 135 years after the Pilgrims landed did English spelling have a guide in Dr. Johnson's *Dictionary of the English Language*. This monumental work froze much of English spelling and, among other things, decreed that such words as *critick*, *logick*, *musick*, and *publick* end in a final *k* and such words as *colour*, *honour*, etc., end in *-our*.

England, including its colonies, began to follow Johnson's spelling; but, in 1758, three years after Johnson's dictionary was published, Noah Webster was born, in Hartford, Connecticut, and 21 years after Johnson's dictionary the American Revolution began—two events that were to help separate English English and American English. After graduating in law from Yale, Webster couldn't make a living doing legal work, so he became a teacher. He then found English schoolbooks hard to obtain, and unsatisfactory, so he compiled his own three-part *Grammatical Institute of the English Language*, including an elementary spelling book (in 1783), a grammar (in 1784) and a reader (in 1785). Part I became the fantastically successful *The American Spelling Book*, which went through edition after edition and sold 80 million copies in its first hundred years, 1783–1883. It was one of the most influential books ever published in America: from the time America became a nation, past the Civil War, and almost into the Gay 90s, generations of Americans learned to spell and pronounce from it, spelling and pronouncing each syllable in every word over and over again under stern teachers. It was known to millions as *Webster's Speller*, the *Blue-Backed Spelling Book* (1853) and the *Blue-Backed Speller*.

The success of his spelling book gave Webster the financial

Noah Webster (1758–1843). His spelling book and dictionary did much to separate British English and American English.

freedom to devote himself to a variety of language projects, including his 1806 *Compendious Dictionary of the English Language*, which was to be the forerunner of his monumental 70,000-entry 1828 *American Dictionary of the English Language*. This was the predecessor of all modern American dictionaries. Its subsequent editions were called *Webster's Dictionary* or simply *Webster's* by the 1840s (upon Webster's death in 1843 the brothers George and Charles Merriam, printers, booksellers, and publishers, acquired the publishing rights to the dictionary, bringing out the first *Merriam-Webster Dictionary* in 1847).

Noah Webster grew to manhood during the period of increasing American patriotism preceding the Revolutionary War; he then served in the war and became a staunch Federalist. He and other Americans of his generation wanted to create a new civilization different from anything ever known in England, and he and some others were determined that the English language in America be a unique "national language" that would weld the thirteen states into a unified nation. By 1789, in his *Dissertation on the English Language*, Webster challenged Samuel Johnson's English rules and practices. His friend Benjamin Franklin had convinced him that spelling reform was necessary, though Webster's reforms didn't go as far as Franklin's, which included six new characters, the dropping of all silent letters (*giv*, *wil*, *rong*), and a confusing array of respelling such as *obzerv*, *reezon* (reason), and *tong* (tongue). Webster's dictionaries were based on his beliefs that he had to outdo Johnson and that America needed its own language and hence its own dictionary. The Webster's dictionaries were the first to contain such American words or meanings as *Americanism*, *applicant*, *appreciate* (to increase, 1778), *barbecue*, *Congressional* (1775), *coop* (for chickens), *corn*, *crib* (for corn), *druggist*, *land office* (1781), and *lot* (piece of land). Webster also dropped the *k* that Johnson had added to such words as *critic*, *logic*, *music*, etc., and gave us many other differences between American and English spelling that still exist today (most of these differences are merely in word endings). These differences include:

(1) Ending certain words with *-er* instead of *-re*. Thus we spell *center*, *fiber*, *meter*, *scepter*, *theater*, etc. The English spelled them our way from about 1550 to 1700, which is how the colonists brought them to America. Then in the 18th century the English went back to the 14th century *-re* ending for these words: some Americans followed the English and some didn't. In his 1806 dictionary Webster printed all such words with the *-er* ending, settling the matter for Americans.

(2) Ending certain words with *-or* rather than the English *-our*. Thus we spell *color*, *favor*, *honor*, *humor*, *labor*, etc., while the English spell these words *colour*, *favour*, *honour*, *humour*, *labour*. Johnson's 1755 dictionary had imposed the Middle English *-our* ending on the English; in his 1806 dictionary Webster went back to the Latin *-or* ending. However, we do follow the English *-our* in our spelling of *glamour* and *Saviour*.

(3) Ending or spelling certain words with a *-k* instead of the English *-que*. Thus we spell *check*, *lackey*, *mask*, *risk*, etc., while the English spell these words *checque*, *lacquey*, *masque*, *risque*. This change also appeared in Webster's 1806 dictionary.

(4) Ending certain words in *-ense* rather than the English *-ence*. Thus we spell *defense*, *license*, *offense*, *pretense*, *recompense*, etc., while the English spell such words *defence*, *licence*, *offence*, *pretence*, *recompence*. The American spellings were also given in Webster's 1806 dictionary.

(5) Ending certain words in *-ize* instead of English *-ise*. Thus we spell *agonize* and *criticize*, etc., while the English traditionally spelled these *agonise* and *criticise*. Since the 1911 edition of Henry W. and Frank G. Fowler's *Concise Oxford Dictionary of Current English*, however, the English have increasingly accepted the *-ize* ending.

(6) Ending certain words in *-ction* instead of the English *-xion*. Thus we have *connection* and *inflection* while the English spell such words *connexion* and *inflexion*.

(7) Using a slightly different rule as to when to double a consonant at the end of a word before a suffix beginning with a vowel, our American way gives us a single consonant in some situations where the English use a double consonant. Thus we have *jeweler*, *traveler*, and *traveling* while the English spell these *jeweller*, *traveller*, and *travelling*. Webster stated the American spelling rule in his 1828 dictionary.

In addition, there are smaller categories and other individual words we Americans spell differently from the English, including:

alarm—alarum.

aluminum—aluminium. Our spelling, found in the 1828 *Webster's Dictionary*, is the way the English chemist Sir Humphrey Davy originally spelled it; the English later changed their spelling to *aluminium* to match the *-ium* ending of *potassium* and *sodium*.

ax, jail, wagon—axe, goal, waggon. These three American spellings were among the many simplified spellings that Franklin, Webster, and others recommended by the late 1780s.

catalog—catalogue. In 1935 the *Chicago Tribune* published a list of words that it recommended be shortened and began to use the new spellings. *Catalog* is the major word on this list whose simplified spellings caught on.

cider, siphon, tire—cyder, syphon, tyre. The American *i* spellings have also been acceptable in England since the Fowlers' 1911 *Concise Oxford Dictionary*, but many Englishmen still prefer the *y* spellings. On the other hand, we Americans use a *y* as the first vowel in *gypsy* while many English spell it *gipsy*.

curb—kerb.

czar—tzar or *tsar.*

forever (one word)—*for ever* (two words).

maneuver—manoeuvre.

medieval—mediæval.

mustache—moustache.

naught—nought.

pajamas, story (of a building)—*pyjamas, storey.* These are two more words whose American spellings are now acceptable in England since the Fowler brothers' *Concise Oxford Dictionary* of 1911.

plow—plough.

today, tonight, tomorrow—to-day, to-night, to-morrow (hyphenated in England).

In addition, the English are more apt to use Latin and other foreign plurals for the words they borrow from foreign languages, while we tend to give foreign borrowings the simple English *-s* or *-es* plural form. Thus many Americans say and write *formulas, indexes, librettos, nebulas,* and *sanatoriums* while the English are more apt to say and write the plural forms *formulae, indices, libretti, nebulae,* and *sanatoria.*

The English are also more conservative in using fewer abbreviations and more capital letters and commas than we do. They capitalize such words as the *Bar,* the *Church,* the *Government,* the *Press,* and *Society.* By doing away with such capital letters, we are closer to the fashion of the 18th century, when the months, the days of the week, and the names of religions were often not capitalized. In fact, in the first draft of the Declaration of Independence, Jefferson even wrote *god* with a lower-case *g*. We don't do that any more, but we still use fewer capital letters than the English.

Fats, Shorty, Red, and Baldy: Common Nicknames

The English word *nickname* comes from *ekename* (1303, literally "additional name," from *eke*, meaning in addition to, as when one ekes out a living doing additional jobs) with the *n* of "a*n* ekename" becoming attached to the second word and appearing as "a *nickname*" by 1440. Descriptive nicknames, be they serious appellations or facetious sobriquets, have always abounded, as witness the 10th-century French kings *Charles the Bald* and *Charles the Fat* or the Norse navigator *Eric the Red*, who explored and named Greenland during the period of 982–85.

In early America such descriptive names flourished because family names often meant little to roving pioneers in a democracy that said a man was what he made himself. The East had many a *Wood-chopper Joe* and *Deermeat John* and the West its *Frisco Kate*s and *Gold Dust Pete*s. Names were often given for a man's occupation, place of origin or work (as the many cowboys called *Tex* to this day, or *the Cimarron Kid*, from the Cimarron Territory, now the Oklahoma panhandle), or from a famous exploit (as *Christmas Tree Murphy*, who once killed a man with a Christmas tree, or the men called *Bear* because they had wrestled one or killed many).

By the 1880s, however, an important change had taken place. Many nicknames now referred not to a man's occupation, place of origin, or exploits but merely to his appearance or a distinguishing physical feature, especially to his weight, height, hair, or age—appearance had become more important than what a man did or who he was. Thus among the most common nicknames heard in the last hundred years have been *Fatty* and *Fats*, both of which have seen some use since 1825; *Slim* and *Shorty*, both of which had rather wide rural and cowboy use before moving to the cities in the late 1880s; the nicknames for hair or lack of it, especially *Red*, *Whitey*, and *Baldy*, which were all common by the late 1880s; and the nicknames referring to age, as *Pop* and *Kid*, which were in use by the mid 1880s, and *Sonny* and *Babe*, which became popular around 1910 (after the mid 1940s *Babe* usually referred to a pretty girl rather than a young man). Of course, all *Fats*, *Slims*, and *Shorties* are not necessarily fat, slim, or short, because our American love of humor and hyperbole often turns an expression inside out, so that *Slim* can be a standing joke for the fattest man around. Also, because of men's respect for women, and a lack of the masculine type of camaraderie among women, women have seldom been called or called each other by such descriptive names.

Even among men, descriptive epithets seem to have been most common from 1910 to 1950, being heard less and less since then, hanging on mainly in the world of sports, where an occasional *Red*

"Duke" (Edward Kennedy) Ellington in 1943. "Duke" has been used to refer to a dapper man since the 17th century.

216

"Casey" (Charles Dillon) Stengel as manager of the New York Mets in 1962. He was originally called "K.C." because he came from Kansas City.

"Old Hickory" (Andrew Jackson).

or *Whitey* still appears and where young prizefighters may still be named *Kid* or *Sonny* (for more on specific boxer's nicknames see BOXING, PRIZEFIGHTING, AND PUGILISM). Somehow, such nicknames now seem too brassy, too exuberant, and rather old-fashioned for our contemporary tastes.

In addition to short, common nicknames that have been applied to many, we have applied unique and often longer nicknames to many of our best-known and most colorful generals and politicians. Successful generals are first talked about by their troops, then by the general public. Thus the nicknames the troops use often become well known. Many generals have "old" in their appellations because generals do seem old to their young soldiers, because *old* has been a term of familiarity since early colonial times, and because *the old man* has been a term for both a ship's captain and a military commander since the War of 1812. Here are the popular nicknames for some of our most talked-about generals:

Mad Anthony Wayne was so called from his reckless heroism in the Revolutionary War, especially after his successful surprise attack on the British garrison at Stony Point on the Hudson in 1779.

Old Hickory was the name given Andrew Jackson by his soldiers in 1813 during a battle against the Creek Indians in which he proved himself "tough as hickory" wood. The public got to know and use the name when Jackson became a national hero after his successful defense of New Orleans (1814–15) during the War of 1812, the name then becoming common throughout his political life and Presidency.

Old Rough and Ready was the sobriquet for Zachary Taylor, beloved by his troops during his 40 years of army service. It was used widely during the Mexican War, 1846–48, when he was the commanding general in the field, capturing Matamoros and Monterrey and defeating Santa Anna at Buena Vista. The name stayed with him when he stepped almost directly from the battlefield into the Presidency in 1849.

Old Fuss and Feathers was General Winfield Scott's best-known appellation, referring to his vanity and pomposity. This hero of the War of 1812 was also called *Old Chippewa*, after his successful 1814 battle at this village above Niagara Falls, and later called *Old Chapultepec* for winning the Battle of Chapultepec, Mexico, and occupying Mexico City in 1847 during the Mexican War. (As Mexico City tourist guides to Chapultepec Park point out, Chapultepec, an Aztec name meaning "grasshopper hill," was a military academy for youths, some of whom jumped to their death rather than surrender and are remembered by Mexicans as "the Boy Heroes of Chapultepec.")

Stonewall Jackson is still the only name we use in talking about Confederate General Thomas J. Jackson, a West Pointer who resigned from the Union army to fight with the Confederacy. He earned this appellation by having his brigade hold its ground at the First Battle of Bull Run, July 21, 1861. It is said to have been given to him by one Bernard Bee, who, before being killed in the battle, said, "See, there is Jackson, standing like a stone-wall."

"Old Fuss and Feathers" (General Winfield Scott).

"Stonewall" Jackson (General Thomas J. Jackson).

"Old Blood and Guts" (General George Patton).

(After leading the Confederate troops brilliantly in the Shenandoah Valley Campaign, Jackson, too, died in the war, from wounds received accidentally from the fire of his own troops at Chancellorsville.)

Old Three Stars is the almost forgotten nickname of General U. S. Grant, who was also called *the American Sphinx* for his uncommunicative, enigmatic command of the Union forces in the Civil War.

Black Jack Pershing is what most people called General John Joseph Pershing, the commander of the American Expeditionary Force in World War I. He got his nickname from leading black troops early in his career in Cuba and the Philippines.

Old Blood and Guts was the way most of us referred to General George Patton, commander of the U.S. Seventh Army in Sicily and of the Third Army in the World War II invasion of Western Europe. It was usually a tribute to, but sometimes an angry criticism of, his aggressive determination. Patton probably got the name while commanding the Second Armored Division in 1940.

Vinegar Joe was the name given General Joseph Stilwell because of the acidity with which he expressed his opinions. It was borne out when he was recalled from his command of Chinese troops and of all U.S. forces in the China-Burma-India theater in World War II after his vinegar tongue caused friction between him and China's Chiang Kai-shek in 1944. He was also called *Old Turkey Neck* because his face and neck were usually red from the sun during the long marches of retreat and counterattack in Burma.

Ike was the way everyone referred to General Dwight Eisenhower, commander in chief of U.S. forces and later of all the Allied forces of World War II. He said that boyhood classmates called him and all his brothers "Ike," from the name Eisenhower,

218

Dwight being called "Red Ike" to distinguish him from the others. The name Ike stuck throughout his 30-year military career and into the Presidency. It was made even more popular with the political buttons bearing the slogan "I Like Ike" which first appeared in 1947 when it seemed he might be a possible Democratic Presidential candidate: when he finally declared he was a Republican, "I Like Ike" became the successful slogan of his 1952 and 1956 Presidential campaigns.

We have given almost every well-known political leader and politician at least one nickname, ranging from mere shortenings of first names to uniquely descriptive, rhetorical, or even poetic phrases. Politicians also often seem to have more than one nickname, different ones being used by those who like or dislike them or being applied during different periods of their political careers. Among the most memorable, and typical, of such nicknames from our earlier history are these five:

To the memory of the Man, first in war, first in peace, first in the hearts of his countrymen.
From Henry "Light Horse Harry" Lee's resolution presented to the House of Representatives on the death of George Washington, December 26, 1799

the Father of His Country, the appellation we still often give to George Washington. It was first used on a 1778 calendar, published by Francis Baily in Lancaster, Pennsylvania, showing a medallion of Washington with a trumpet blaring in German "Das Landes Vater," then appeared in English on a 1799 almanac.

Washington had other appellations as well. The founding fathers liked to see in themselves and the new nation the freedom, dignity, and grace traditionally associated with ancient Greece and Rome, as witnessed by the style or design of many of the new nation's buildings, coins, and symbols. Thus our first President was also called the American Cincinnatus because, like the legendary 5th-century B.C. Roman hero Cincinnatus, he had left his farm to serve his country. Washington's critics did not consider him so noble, calling him the Old Fox and the Stepfather of His Country.

Honest Abe was Abraham Lincoln's first widely known sobriquet (used since 1858) and is still the one heard most today. He became the Rail Splitter after a log he had split was presented to the Illinois Republican State Convention in 1859. The South often called him Old Abe (a familiar nickname first given him by friends in 1847 but used in a much less friendly way in the South), Ape (corrupting "Abe" and mocking his appearance), and the Tycoon (see tycoon at MILLIONAIRE). Blacks called him Uncle Abe; the Great Emancipator was never a common term, being used mostly by politicians and historians since the 1880s. The frequently bad-tempered Mrs. Lincoln seems to have had no affectionate nicknames; the only common epithet for her was the She-Wolf.

the Mill Boy of the Slashes was always a popular reference to Virginia-born Kentucky Congressman Henry Clay, because his boyhood chores had included driving a donkey loaded with bags of meal from the local mill to his home in the slashes (in the early 1800s, when Clay was first in Congress, most people still knew that a slash or the slashes meant low, marshy ground). Clay also became known as the Great Pacificator for his role in advocating the

"The Rail Splitter."

219

"*The Mill Boy of the Slashes*"
(Henry Clay).

You shall not press down upon the brow of labor this crown of thorns; you shall not crucify mankind upon a cross of gold.

Concluding sentence of William Jennings Bryan's speech before the National Democratic Convention, Chicago, July 10, 1896

"*The Boy Orator of the Platte*"
(William Jennings Bryan).

Missouri Compromise in 1820, then was called *the President Maker* for his support of John Quincy Adams in the Presidential election of 1824. By 1843 Clay was affectionately called *the Great Commoner* (a name later applied to William Jennings Bryan), which became a very popular sobriquet for Clay during his unsuccessful bid for the Presidency on the Whig ticket in 1844. Clay's last popular appellation was then *the Great Compromiser*, for his crowning achievement, the series of resolutions known as "the Compromises of 1850," seeking to resolve the slavery issue and avoid the Civil War. Thus the names by which Henry Clay was known sum up his forty-six-year career (1806–52) as senator, representative, Speaker of the House, and secretary of state, and show how he dominated the politics of the period as a leader of his party and of the West.

the Plumed Knight.

> *Like an armed warrior, like a plumed knight, James G. Blaine marched down the halls of the American Congress and threw his shining lance full and fair against the brazen forehead of the defamers of our country and the maligners of his honor. . . .*

Thus did Robert Ingersoll saddle James G. Blaine with the name *the Plumed Knight* in presenting him as a Republican Presidential nominee in 1876. Thus, too, began a tedious tradition, because this speech of Ingersoll's was the first of the long, flowery nominating speeches that have since become the custom at political nominating conventions. Perhaps it was poetic justice that Blaine lost the nomination that year (he finally did win the Republican nomination in 1884 and was defeated in the election by Grover Cleveland).

the Boy Orator of the Platte, often shortened to *the Boy Orator*, became the popular nickname of the powerful speechmaker William Jennings Bryan soon after he entered the House of Representatives in 1891 (he was thirty-one at the time and represented Nebraska's Platte River region). The boy orator became an adult orator with his historic "Cross of Gold" speech advocating the free coinage of silver at the 1896 Democratic Convention, which speech won him the Presidential nomination (McKinley defeated him that year). Bryan's oratory, imposing appearance, and fierce integrity attracted many followers throughout his life and when he outgrew the name *the Boy Orator* he was known as *the Great Commoner*, the appellation that had earlier been given to Henry Clay. After resigning as Wilson's secretary of state in 1915, Bryan continued to orate, spending much time speaking on the Chautauqua Circuit and at Fundamentalist religious meetings, drawing large and appreciative crowds. His oratory finally failed him at the famous 1925 Scopes Monkey Trial in Dayton, Tennessee, when chief defense attorney Clarence Darrow exposed his ignorance of modern science. Bryan, who was one of the prosecuting attorneys, died suddenly in Dayton shortly after the trial ended. Despite his final defeat, William Jennings Bryan had earned his place as one of America's foremost orators—a man who could talk to America and often had America talking.

Fire!

was first recorded as being a shout of warning of a conflagration in 1682. However, the exclamation is probably much, much older than that, since *fire* has meant the accidental burning of a building since the 12th century.

Many ancient cities seem to have had fire watchers or fire brigades, including Rome under Augustus Caesar in 32 B.C., but as late as 1666 England's largest metropolis had no organized fire protection system when the Great Fire of London destroyed much of that city. As early as 1648 in America, Peter Stuyvesant, the governor of The New Netherlands, outlawed thatched roofs in New Amsterdam (later known as New York City), appointed four men to inspect chimneys for fire hazards (such a man called a *schoorsteenschouw*, Dutch for "chimney viewer"), and required all able-bodied men to take turns serving on an eight-man fire watch. In 1658 Stuyvesant began the *rattle watch*, so called because it patrolled New Amsterdam's streets at night and alerted the Dutch colonists to fires by shaking wooden rattles. Elsewhere in colonial days a *fire bell* (a 1626 English term), horns, or drums were used to give the alarm, the bell on a town's church, town hall, or school eventually becoming the most common device used to rouse the citizens to come help put out a fire. In 1679, Boston established the first paid fire department in the colonies, a small crew of men with one hand-operated pump; and in 1697, New York City, then under British rule, appointed two *viewers of chimneys and hearths* in each ward, these inspectors having the power to levy a 40-shilling fine on any householder whose chimney and hearth were not kept clean and in proper repair.

Except for those who lived near Boston's small hand-operated pump and its crew, early Americans could expect no professional help in putting out or escaping from fires. Cities and towns burnt and so did forest and prairie. The terms *brush fire* (1777), *forest fire* (1779), and *prairie fire* (1824) were coined and often used in America. We attempted to halt the progress of such fires by setting a *backfire* (1784) or by plowing or clearing a strip of land called a *firebreak* (first recorded in Canada, in 1841) around a farm or even around an entire settlement.

On the frontier and in the growing cities each family kept its own ladder; a *fire hook* (an English term of 1487) for pulling down burning roofs and walls and scattering burning embers; several *fire buckets* (an English term of 1585); and often a *fire bag* (1769) for carrying small items from their burning home. Using these simple devices, families depended on themselves and their neighbors to put out a fire and save what they could.

When a fire started in a city or town the cry "Throw out your buckets" was sounded up and down the street. After the buckets were thrown out, all who could help came running to the fire and formed a two-line *bucket brigade* to the nearest pond, river, well, or

221

other water supply, one line passing the buckets full of water to the fire, the other passing the empty ones back to be refilled. If there was more organized help against fire in early colonial times it was usually only from the *fire watch* (an English term of 1694), *fire ward* (1711), or *fire warden* (1714) assigned to patrol the streets to watch for fires or enforce fire laws. The word *fireman* itself was not even recorded as meaning one whose job it is to put out fires until 1714, in England (*fireman* had, however, been used in English since 1626 to mean a user of firearms and since 1657 to mean one who tends a fire or furnace).

Not until 1736, after a major fire had destroyed much of Philadelphia, did Benjamin Franklin found the first organized volunteer fire brigade in America, Philadelphia's Union Fire Company. By the early 1800s such untrained volunteer units existed in most American cities but were still mainly bucket brigades and, indeed, were called *bucket brigades*. As time went on, however, more and more of these volunteer bucket brigades stopped throwing water directly on the fire and instead, following Boston's earlier example, used their leather buckets to fill the reservoir of a cartlike hand-operated pump that the men hauled to the fire with hand ropes. Some of the men then formed a bucket brigade while others worked the two opposed barlike pump handles, half a dozen men on each side.

Such volunteers units were made up of civic leaders and other hard-working men who pledged to drop everything and come running with ladders, hooks, and buckets to work together when the fire warning sounded. Beginning with the Philadelphia Contributorship, founded in 1752, the volunteer groups were joined by

This 1784 "green tree" fire mark identified buildings insured by the Mutual Insurance Company.

equally untrained units paid by *insurance fire companies* (1792, the term *fire insurance* didn't appear until 1796) to protect only those buildings they insured. Each insurance company then put its *fire mark*, usually a plaque or symbol, on the buildings it insured, people often buying fire insurance to have the plaque and fire protection as much as for the insurance itself. Any volunteer or insurance company group that fought fires might variously be called a *fire company* (1736, in the name of Franklin's original Union Fire Company), *fire club* (1744), *fire department* (1825), *fire society* (also 1825), *fire brigade* (early 1830s), or *fire guard* (1833).

By the early 1800s firemen were hauling not only the *fire pump* to fires but also separate carts or wagons containing hose or hooks and ladders, with the water buckets now attached to hooks on these hand-drawn vehicles. The equipment was now usually owned by the fire company and the buckets, wagons, and other items were often elaborately decorated not only with the company's name or symbol but also with patriotic and mythical motifs. The cart or wagon with the hose might be manned by a *hose company* (1806), each member being a *hoseman* (1825). Eventually the hose was put on a reel on wheels, a *hose reel* (1837), which grew into a specially designed, sometimes horse-drawn, *hose cart* (1865) and then the heavier horse-drawn *hose wagon* (1876) or *hose carriage* (an 1890s term), all of which the firemen called a *jumper* by the 1870s. The cart or wagon with the hooks and ladders might be manned by a special *hook and ladder company* (1821) of *hook and ladder men* (1825) and grew into a *hook and ladder carriage* (1831) or *hook and ladder truck* (1830s) operating from a *hook and ladder house* (1834) or

The Great Chicago Fire *of 1871 burned for three days (October 8–10), killed 120 people, destroyed 18,000 buildings in a 3.5-square-mile area, and left 10,000 families homeless.*

truck house (1854), these terms appearing when all equipment was still hand-drawn to the fire. The hooks were considered less important, or at least less obviously necessary than the ever-lengthening ladders by the 1880s, when all equipment was horse-drawn, as shown by the fact that "hook" was dropped from "hook and ladder," giving us the simpler terms *ladder company* (1887) and by 1889 *ladder house, ladder truck,* and *ladder man.* The 1889 *ladder man* was, however, still called a *shepherd* by his fellow firemen, because he still carried the hook, which resembled a shepherd's staff (this image of a protecting shepherd was reinforced, of course, by the ladder man's job of rescuing people from burning buildings).

Because the hand-operated fire pump, the largest of which took sixteen men to pump, was an "engine" for pumping or throwing water on a fire, it had been called a *fire engine* since the first 23-pound one appeared in England in the late 1670s. By 1820 in America the men who pulled this "fire engine" to the fire and worked the two pump bars were called an *engine company* and their leader the *chief engineer.* By the 1840s, as buildings and hence fire ladders had grown still taller, forcing the ladder wagons to grow longer, the hook and ladder men who pulled the ladder wagon or ran beside it to guide it and keep it from turning over were said to *run with the wagon,* while the members of the engine company who pulled or ran beside the fire engine were said to *run with the machine.* Thus, saying that firemen who responded to a fire were making a *run* (1887) once meant exactly what it said: firemen ran to a fire alongside their equipment.

Some firemen still pulled their equipment to the fire while others ran with the machine in this 1895 lithograph. Though it's been a long time since a fireman had to run to a fire, we still say a fireman makes a run when he rides to a fire in modern equipment.

A high-pressure fire hydrant *in use in 1908.*

Though the early fire pump "engines" were filled with water by bucket brigades, as time went on and more and more cities had piped water supplies, the engines more and more often drew their water from a *fire plug* (a 1713 English term, which we often shortened to *plug* by 1727). *Fire plug* was originally a very descriptive term: early water mains had holes drilled in them every 150 to 200 yards, with wooden plugs stopping up these holes, so that when a fire brigade got to a fire it had only to pull out the plug to reach the water supply. The more sophisticated *hydrant* (1806, from the Greek combining form *hydr/hydor*, from *hýdōr*, water + the suffix *-ant*), an upright pipe with an outlet for drawing water from a main, was originally intended for public use, a device from which householders could draw their drinking, cooking, and washing water. However, a special hydrant was soon introduced for firemen to attach a hose to; this special hydrant was called a *fire hydrant* by 1839 (once these special fire hydrants began to outnumber those for public use, *hydrant* came to mean "fire hydrant" and any still designated for public use were then called *public hydrants*, 1850). *Fire plug* illustrates the persistence of language—it is still a more common term than *fire hydrant*, even though true fire "plugs" haven't been in use for some 150 years. A fire hydrant has also been called a *fire cock* (1829), *stand pipe* (1850), and *fire pipe* (1865), the last two terms being first recorded in England.

From the early days of the bucket brigade to the first decades of the fire hydrant, membership in the volunteer fire companies was by invitation: one had to be accepted by the members of the company and joining a fire company was, for many, a masculine rite of passage. The livery stable, shed, or barn where the "engine" and hose carts were kept became the firemen's clubhouse. Though the early volunteer companies included a town's most respected civic leaders, merchants, and workingmen, by the 1830s and 40s many big city volunteer companies were made up of lower-class laborers, often from one ethnic group, especially Irish and German, plus assorted neighborhood rowdies. In many cities firemen were now called *red shirts*, from the bright-red shirts they wore, and *fire eaters* (1828), not only because of their volunteer job but because, since 1804, *fire eater* had meant a tough, pugnacious person (probably harking back to the 1672 English use of the term as meaning a magician or juggler who "ate" or pretended to swallow fire or burning coals).

Bitter hostility often existed between companies from rival ethnic neighborhoods or companies that owed allegiance to rival politicians. Each raced to reach a fire first but then might fight over whose engine had the right to be closest to the fire or whose hoses had the right to a particular fire hydrant. Each volunteer company chose its own captain, usually the most reliable, popular, or toughest man but sometimes the greediest vote-getter. In some big city precincts the men were led by politicians, ward heelers, or local gangsters who used the neighborhood engine house as their own social and political club and the firemen as personal followers and henchmen. Thus New York City's Boss Tweed got his start as head of a fire engine company, ordering his firemen about through a silver-ornamented speaking trumpet, and the famous gangster and ward heeler "Butcher" Bill Poole was a leader of the notorious Bowery Boys fire company (and was killed by another Bowery Boy, in 1855). With or without Poole, New York City's Bowery Boys were among the most notorious of all the volunteer fire companies:

> *the Bowery*, a New York City street extending from Chatham Square to East Fourth Street, got its name from the Dutch word *bouwerij*, farmstead, estate, as granted to a Dutch settler. The area was originally given the name *the Bowery* because it was the farm, or *bouwerij*, of Governor Stuyvesant. By the 1670s, after the English had taken over New York City, it was a popular rural area for summer picnics and winter sleigh rides but was eventually absorbed into the growing city and became a crowded, bustling neighborhood which slowly degenerated until, by the 1830s, it was notorious for its beer halls, brothels, and ferocious street gangs, including the Bowery Boys (finally, during the Great Depression of the 1930s, it became the most famous skid row in America). By the late 1840s *Don't act like you were born in the Bowery* was already a common expression, meaning "don't act so vulgar" or "use some good manners."
>
> *the Bowery Boys* was originally the name for a gang of Bowery toughs that existed from about 1835 to 1845. Its members were almost always volunteer firemen, which kept the gang strong and out of trouble, because the Bowery Boy firemen were strong supporters of and henchmen for the ward heelers of Tammany Hall, and Tammany Hall took care of its friends. The gang was so notorious that by the 1840s the term *Bowery Boy* was in general use to refer to any tough, vulgar youth. These Bowery boys were not as mean as the original gang members but were flashily dressed, swaggering punks. When one referred to such a *Bowery Boy* the fad was then to use a contemptuous or humorous mock Irish pronunciation of "Bowery B'hoy." A Bowery Boy's girlfriend or female counterpart was called a *Bowery Girl* (1856), often pronounced "Bowery Ga'hal."

The Bowery Boys were known for their fights with rival fire companies. The first Bowery Boy at a fire was supposed to claim or put a barrel over the nearest fire plug and defend it against rival fire companies until the Bowery Boys' own fire engine arrived, often leading to a free-for-all while the fire blazed out of control (an 1835 New York City fire destroyed 600 buildings at a loss of $20 million and an 1845 fire did $7.5 million worth of damage).

It was such volunteer firemen who scoffed at the first portable soda-ash *fire extinguisher* (1837) and at the *fireproof* (1804) chests

*The Bow'ry, the Bow'ry!
They say such things, and they do strange things
On the Bow'ry, the Bow'ry!
I'll never go there any more!*
"The Bowery," 1891, lyrics by Charles H. Hoyt, music by Percy Gaunt for their musical *A Trip to Chinatown*

226

called *fire safes* (1845) in which some people kept their valuables. It was also often such tough, intimidating men who collected the most money for the local *firemen's fund* (1841) for disabled fellow firemen and their families and for the "widows and orphans" brave firemen had left behind. But the way most volunteer fire companies raised money for such a fund was by selling tickets to the *firemen's ball* (1842), which capped the annual *firemen's anniversary* (also 1842) celebration, this ball usually held on the eve of Washington's birthday as part of that patriotic celebration. Such firemen may have laughed at the first *fire boat* (1849) but answered the first electromagnetic *fire alarm* (1847) and the first *false alarm* (also 1847: once there is a fire alarm can a false alarm be far behind?). However, this was merely a new, specialized meaning for the term *false alarm*, which had been in military use in English since 1594; by 1900 in America it had also come to mean an impostor or a person who doesn't live up to one's expectations or his own promises or braggadocio.

Not until municipal water supplies and the horse-drawn *steam pumper* both became common in large cities, beginning in the 1850s, did such large city volunteer fire companies end and the era of the professional paid fire department begin. Not only did cities not trust the volunteers with such expensive equipment as the steam pumper, but they realized that to gain full benefit from its horse-drawn speed they would have to have firemen always on duty in the firehouse to man it instantly. Many volunteer companies fought the introduction of a professional paid fire company and its new horse-drawn equipment, though some volunteers did become full-time paid firemen. Cincinnati bought its first steam pumper in 1853 and hired a tough ex-volunteer fireman to drive it and to recruit a paid fire department to work it. These paid firemen, with the help of 250 bodyguards, had to beat off a mob of volunteer firemen who tried to wreck the pumper and prevent them from putting out fires. Not only did Cincinnati thus become the first American city to have a modern paid fire department, paying each man a salary of $60 a year, but it soon became the first to issue each man the newly developed *fire hat* (1851).

Once the professional paid fire department proved its worth, the days of the big city volunteer fire company were soon over. Thus when the Prince of Wales visited New York City in 1860, some 6,000 volunteer firemen honored him with a torchlight parade, pulling their huge gleaming fire engines and brightly painted hose carts and ladder wagons in review, but just five years later, in 1865, New York had not a single volunteer fireman left, depending now on a *paid fire department* (1858). Since all fire departments had once been volunteer ones, the word "volunteer" hadn't been necessary in their names, but by 1876 "fire department" meant a paid fire department to so many people that the

Fire horses *pull a* steamer, *1909*.

smaller communities that still retained volunteer units called them by the full name *volunteer fire department*. Firemen were, however, still called *red shirts* and their officers *white shirts* or *white hats*, since officers usually wore white shirts and many wore white hats as part of their summer uniform.

The horse-drawn steam pumper that became common in large cities before the Civil War was almost always called a *boiler* (a 1757 word for the iron tank in which water is boiled to create steam in a steam engine), though sometimes, following the British usage, it was later referred to as a *steamer* (1872). It had an engineer who rode the rear platform and stoked the boiler, hoping that by the time the fire was reached there would be enough steam pressure built up to operate the pumps, which in the case of the very popular Hurp steam pumper were under the driver's seat and could pump about 600 gallons of water a minute. The *fire horses* (a term not recorded until 1883) were the biggest and strongest that could be found. They were often white or gray and—with their eyes wide, manes flying, and hooves thundering, harnessed two or three abreast to pull the smoke-belching red and brass steam pumper—came to symbolize the excitement and fear of fires and the fast efficiency of the paid fire departments. Soon horses were used to pull all the equipment, including the extra water hose wagon and the hook and ladder wagon, the largest of which had a second steering seat and steering gear for the rear wheels at the rear end.

The increasing size of the cities and of their paid fire departments necessitated a well-organized chain of command. Thus, though the term *fire commissioner* had appeared in 1840, *fire marshal* first appeared in 1861 and *fire chief*, meaning the one in charge of all a municipality's fire departments, was used in 1889, with *battalion chief* and *deputy chief* also appearing in the 1880s.

Meanwhile, the first outside iron-stairs *fire escape* was added to an apartment house in 1860 (the term *fire escape* was first used in England in 1680 but until the last half of the 19th century had referred only to rope or chain ladders kept for making an emergency escape from a building). By the 1870s we were calling an arsonist a *firebug* and by the 1880s a few buildings had primitive *sprinklers* or sprinkler systems. Soon a building without fire escapes, a sprinkler, or enough stairs and exits for safe egress was called a *fire trap* (first recorded in England in 1887). In the 1890s some schools and factories had their first *fire drill* (1893), while the possessions or goods damaged by fire in burning homes, stores, and factories might be sold cheaply in a *fire sale* (1891) or, soon, a *fire auction* (1904). Early in the 20th century, especially after the 1903 Iroquois Theater fire in Chicago killed 602 people and the 1908 Rhode's Opera House fire in Boyertown, Pennsylvania, killed 175 more, there was a demand that theaters place a fireproof *fire curtain* (1912) at the proscenium.

Though the first steam-propelled steam pumper had appeared in 1852, it was the 1890s before anyone saw a gasoline-powered fire engine, such a piece of equipment often being called an *automobile fire engine* until around 1920. The gasoline-powered fire engine was often a big Reo, using tire chains all year round to pull it through muddy dirt roads. It was kept in a *fire house* (1906). Such engines were so fast that by the 1920s the expression *Where's the fire?* was the clever way of asking anyone, "What's the hurry?"

Chemicals were now also used to fight fires, the term *chemical company* having appeared in 1887, such a fire company then using a horse-drawn *chemical hose wagon*, with the term *hose and chemical truck* appearing around 1910. The early gasoline-powered chemi-

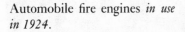
Automobile fire engines *in use in 1924*.

Boston firemen using deck guns, *such gunlike hoses having been called this since the 1940s.*

Hartford, Connecticut, firemen using an aerial ladder, *the term being used since the 1950s.*

cal hose truck was usually a 40-horsepower vehicle specially fitted with a 200-gallon chemical tank, 100 feet of hose, a 16-foot extension ladder, siren, and searchlight.

Fires have always drawn spectators. By 1903 one who came to watch fires was called a *buff*, which by 1931 came to mean any devotee or amateur expert. Some say such spectators were called *buffs* because they once watched fires on winter nights while huddling under buffalo robes; others say it was because firemen once slept under buffalo robes, wore waterproof buffalo-skin clothing, or wore buff-colored shirts. Any—or none—of these may be the origin of *buff* meaning devotee; we just don't know. What we do know, however, is that the first *buffs* were fire buffs.

By 1897 the putting out of fires was called *firefighting* and by 1903 firemen were *firefighters* (the slang term *smoke eater* didn't appear until around 1930, a gentler term based on that 1828 *fire eater*). *Firefighter* has had a surge in popularity since the late 1970s when liberated women began to join fire departments, some then considering the term *fireman* sexist (actually a few women had served on volunteer fire departments since the early 19th century and the term *fire woman* was recorded in 1899).

In recent times fire engines have grown larger and more sophisticated. Though the common fire truck carries a 35-foot extension ladder and a 500-gallon water tank, many cities and towns have trucks with a turntable-mounted *aerial ladder* (1950s) that reaches about 100 feet, or eight stories. Other trucks have elevating cagelike platforms attached to a boom, often with a built-in hose that can extend 150 feet, both the platform and boom assembly and the entire piece of equipment being called a *snorkel*, having first been given this name by Chicago firemen in 1958 (the original German *Schnorchel*, air intake, spiral, was a retractable tube for ventilating World War II submarines as they cruised slightly below the surface; by the late 1940s in America *snorkel* had come to mean a breathing tube for a swimmer swimming face-down in the water or near the surface). Some cities also now have a *super pumper* (mid 1970s), a tractor and semitrailer that can pump 8,000 gallons per minute through a 4.5-inch hose.

As in the days of Peter Stuyvesant's "chimney viewers," however, the best fire protection is still fire prevention. Thus our annual *Fire Prevention Week* was begun October 8, 1922, the anniversary date of the Great Chicago Fire of 1871, which burned from the eighth through the tenth of October. Thus, too, since there are still 2.5 million fires and some 8,000 fire deaths a year in the U.S., the two most recent major fire-related terms have been *smoke detector* and *heat detector*, both in common use in the home since the mid 1970s in order to prevent that horrifying shout of "Fire!"

Just Plain Folks

Folk had meant a people, nation, and even the common people, before the year 1000, with *folks* first appearing as the plural in the 14th century and becoming the ordinary plural in the 17th century. American colonists began calling their parents and other relatives their *folks* around 1715 and by 1750 were using the word to apply to friends and neighbors. By the 1830s many democratic Americans liked to refer to themselves as *just plain folks*, and were also using such combinations as *men folks*, *country folks*, and *old folks*. By the 1860s *folksy*, meaning plain or neighborly, was common in America, as was the expression *poor white folks*, especially in the South, though this term saw its greatest popularity after the Civil War.

Meantime, in 19th-century England, rural ways were beginning to disappear and city people and intellectuals began to examine with nostalgia, and some superiority, such newly quaint things as *folklore* (a term W. J. Thomas, the founder of *Notes and Queries*, first suggested in an article in the August 22, 1846, *Athenaeum*), *folkfaith* (1850), *folklife* (1864), and, eventually, *folktales* (1891). Such interest and pride in the old ways came later to America. Not until the Depression did a new pride in being *just plain folks* develop here, often with social and cultural overtones against capitalists and high culture. Thus in the 1930s the adjective *folk* took on fresh connotations, leading to the popular post–World War II interest in *folk songs* (an 1870 English term, a translation of Johann Herder's 1773 German coinage *Volkslied*), *folk music*, *folk stories*, and *folk customs*.

Grant Wood's American Gothic, *1930.*

Way down upon the Swanee Ribber, far far away,
Dere's wh' my heart is turning obber,
Dere's wh' de old folks stay.
All up and down de whole creation,
Sadly I roam.
Still longing for de old plantation
And for de old folks at home.
Stephen Foster, "The Old Folks at Home," popularly called "Swanee River," 1851.

Dover, Delaware, July 4th, 1938.

Football

developed as a terrifyingly brutal game in England soon after the Roman conquest of A.D. 43. Best known in such Roman centers as Chester and Derby, it was similar to the Roman game of *harpastum* ("handball"). By A.D. 217 it was a wild free-for-all in which scores or even hundreds of youths from two places would meet at some midway point and kick, push, shove, and fight an air-filled bladder or other object in the rival group's farm, town, or district, often miles away. This mass-riot game became part of special annual celebrations, market days, and fairs, with Shrove Tuesday eventually becoming *football day* in England, the local shoemaker making an annual leather ball for the occasion.

In England the game was first called *kicking the bladder*, then, after the early-11th-century Danish invasion, *kicking the Dane's head* (though legend has it that the skulls of Danish soldiers were used, it is more likely that an air-filled cow's bladder was called a *Dane's head*). The name *fut balle* was given the game in the 12th century, when the game was first played on a large *field* with boundry lines, there then being approximately fifty men to each side, depending on the size of the field. Between 1314 and 1603 it was banned by Edward II, Edward III, Henry II, Henry IV, Henry VIII, and Elizabeth I of England, and James I, James II, and James IV of Scotland. Some of the monarchs banned the game because it kept men from archery and other military pursuits, others because it created so much havoc and so many injuries. That it was banned so often merely shows that none of the bans succeeded. In fact, James IV himself instructed his own treasurer to buy two *fut balles* in 1497, which is the first recorded use of the term to mean the ball rather than just the game. During this time, the 12th-century *fut balle* game was also spelled *fut ball* (1424), *footballe* (1457, the first time it appeared as one word), *foteball* (1486), *foote ball* (1508), and *foote balle* (1531), with the modern spelling *football* finally appearing in England in 1650.

The earliest games had few rules, though it does seem that clubs and other weapons were not permitted. One could kick, hit, shove, and wrestle the ball and opposing players at will. Tame by comparison, the modern game closest to the original is *Gaelic football* (1894), which stems from a 16th-century Irish version. In the 1820s some schools still played a free-for-all game close to the original, the best-known American one being the traditional *Bloody Monday* game between Harvard freshmen and sophomores, in which as many players from these classes as desired tried to push a ball over a line. This and a similar freshmen hazing game at Yale were banned by the schools in the 1830s.

Football started to become respectable in 1603 when James I of England succeeded Queen Elizabeth I and lifted the ban against it, after which rules against mayhem slowly evolved. Physical contact was reduced and eventually the ball could not be wrestled across

> *"I'll not be stricken, my lord."*
> *"Nor tripped, neither, you base football player."*
>
> *King Lear*, Act I, William Shakespeare, 1605; this is the first recorded use of *football player* (though Shakespeare did not use the modern spelling for the game).

the goal but had to be kicked through two sticks, or *uprights*, at each end of the field. By 1711 the new term *football match* was a respectable sporting term in England. The English football game was, of course, developing into what we Americans now call *soccer* but which most of the rest of the world still calls *football* (*football* in Great Britain and France, *fussball* in Germany, *futbol* in Brazil, etc.). For football finally developed into at least three major games: soccer, Rugby, and our own American football.

The English game, depending on kicking and butting the ball, grew in popularity as an informal campus pastime at the great English "public" schools. Then, in 1823, young William Ellis of Rugby School in Warwickshire, England, out of a reflex action, exuberance, or frustration, picked up the round ball and ran with it down the field, a maneuver that had been unthinkable for generations. Though Ellis's captain apologized profusely to the other side for this unsportsmanlike conduct, some English players thought this play was a good idea and began to allow a player to run with the ball if he caught it on the fly or on the first bounce. This carrying of the ball, of course, again led to the opponents wrestling the ball carrier to the ground to stop him. To *tackle* was first defined in Noah Webster's 1826 dictionary, as to grip or lay hold of "as a wrestler his opponent."

Since William Ellis had begun this new type of running-with-the-ball football game at Rugby, it was first called *Rugby's game* or *Rugby football*, then became simply *Rugby* by 1839. Now when someone spoke of *football* in England he might be asked, "Which kind, regular or Rugby?" Players of the regular no-ball-carrying kind drew up its rules for their London Football Association in 1863 and then said they played *association football*, which was soon shortened to "assoc football" and then to " 'soc," to which the standard -*er* ending was added, giving us the word *soccer*. By a somewhat similar process, *Rugby* was also called *rugger* in England by 1893.

Some form of soccer has been played in the United States since 1820, when Princeton students played a form they called *ballown*; New Haven forbade Yale students to play it on the "public green" in 1858; the First Maryland Regiment played its version of soccer during the Civil War; and complete rules for the game appeared in an 1866 *Dime Library* booklet.

Thus when Rutgers beat Princeton 6 goals to 4 at New Brunswick, New Jersey, on November 6, 1869, in America's first intercollegiate *college football game* or *varsity football game* (*varsity* is an 1845 colloquial shortening of *university*, from English university sporting slang), it was a form of soccer using a round ball (called a *leather* since 1868). The twenty-five men on each side could advance the ball by foot, head, shoulder, or by batting it with their hands, and goals were made only by kicking the ball under the

While a few Union soldiers continue to play a soccerlike form of "foot-ball," most consider it an excuse for a free-for-all in this 1865 illustration from Harper's Weekly.

I will not permit 30 men to travel 400 miles merely to agitate a bag of wind.

President White of Cornell University in 1873, forbidding Cornell's first planned intercollegiate football game, with the University of Michigan at Cleveland, Ohio. The teams had agreed on soccer rules with 30 men to a side.

crossbars. In that very first intercollegiate game, played four years after the Civil War, Princeton players used a blood-curdling Civil War rebel yell, which they called their *scarer,* to accompany important plays. This was the first *football yell,* but it took so much of the Princeton players' breath that in the return match on November 13 they turned the yelling over to the handful of Princeton supporters on the sidelines, which first *cheering section* may have helped Princeton win, 8 goals to zero.

A year after those first two intercollegiate football games, Columbia played Princeton and Rutgers and in 1872 Yale played its first intercollegiate game. These four schools met in 1873 and agreed to play football by soccer rules—soccer seemed on its way to becoming the major American football game. But Harvard, which in 1871 had begun playing its own form of the game, called the *Harvard game* or the *Boston game,* in which the round inflated rubber ball could be picked up at any time and the *holder* could run if pursued, held out for its Rugby type of game and refused to join the new soccer-playing league—ultimately preventing soccer from becoming *football* in America.

Not being able to play its game against Columbia, Princeton, Rutgers, or Yale, Harvard gladly accepted a challenge by Montreal's McGill University to play three games in 1874. On May 14, using its own *Boston rules* and on its home field, Harvard beat McGill 3 goals to zero. On the next day the two teams played to a scoreless tie, using McGill's Rugby rules. This was the first Rugby game played in the U.S., the first in which an "egg-shaped ball" (as the Harvard players called it) was used, and the first formal game in which Americans had occasion to use such British Rugby terms as *drop kick, free kick, fair catch,* and *off sides.* After playing the third game in Montreal, Harvard decided to adopt McGill's Rugby game. Yale soon agreed to play Harvard by these rules and the first of the now traditional *Harvard-Yale football games* (still then a form of Rugby) was played on November 13, 1875, Harvard winning 4 goals to 0. Harvard also made three *touchdowns* in this game, but by the rules then in effect a touchdown served only to give one's team a free kick or *try* at the goal. Two Princeton team observers liked this Harvard-Yale game so much that Princeton dropped soccer and, with Columbia, Harvard, Rutgers, and Yale, formed a new Intercollegiate Football Association in 1876, using the Rugby-type rules and the egg-shaped ball. For their own convenience, these teams adopted a fall schedule for 1876, making football *the fall game* and, eventually, every traditional game a *fall classic*. They also immediately began the tradition of allowing the winning team to keep the *game ball*, both as a trophy and to use in its next game (Yale bragging it could go through an entire season with one battered ball). City College of New York, Pennsylvania, Stevens, Trinity College of Hartford, Connecticut, Tufts, and Wesleyan joined the Rugby-rules bandwagon in 1877, with Michigan being the first *western team* to do so, in 1878 (the first college football league to be called a *conference* was to be the seven-team *Western Conference*, formed in 1896, which eventually grew into the *Big Ten*).

In 1877 the Intercollegiate Football Association rules were still for a tough, Rugby, kicking game: only kicked *goals* counted in the scoring; players ran with the ball mainly to get it in position for an easier kick. The fifteen men on each side, nine on the *rush line* and six behind them, kept the ball in play on a field 140 by 70 yards for two continuous 45-minute *halves* separated only by a *halftime* (an 1871 English soccer term). There were no quarters, huddles, or numbered down (games weren't divided into *quarters* until 1910, which, of course, is the year the terms *first quarter*, *second quarter*, *third quarter*, and *fourth quarter* first appeared). A team kept the ball until it scored a goal or the other team took it away, players had free use of their hands and arms, and substitutions were allowed only when an injury prevented a player from playing any more that day. Names for the players, plays, parts of the field, etc., were mainly English soccer terms of the day, as *halfback*, *three-quarter back*, and *fullback*, *boot* (to kick), *blindside*, and *midfield*. In fact, new soccer and Rugby terms were to be added to American football for many years, soccer adding the *linesman* as an official in 1891 and American football then adding that official and adopting the term in 1894.

These 1877 teams usually played two games a week, on Wednesday and Saturday, and even more when on a *trip*, in order to make full use of expense money. Practice was already every afternoon, mainly in kicking and in running down the field to catch *punts* (an English dialect form of *butt;* to punt a ball originally meant to butt it). Such things as a special separate *training table* (1893) or a *training camp* (1913) were in the future for both collegiate and professional athletes, no matter what the sport. The best training for football was still in wrestling and boxing and many of the better football players were college champions in these sports.

Though 1878 and 1879 saw no major changes in our football rules or vocabulary, they saw a major change in our football clothing. Each team had begun to wear distinctively colored soccer-style *football uniforms* in 1875, the usual outfit then being *tights* (1836) worn under *shorts* (1830) and a *jersey* (1857 as a tunic worn in sports, all three terms originating in England). But in 1878 the tights and the loose easy-to-grab shorts and jerseys were replaced by canvas *football pants* and *football jackets*, mainly for protection. The few players who by now were wearing homemade *football padding* or *pads* were considered sissies by their teammates. In 1880, beginning with Yale, players took to wearing their hair long as a mark of distinction, the fad becoming a tradition among most players during the next twenty years, during which time their fellow students called the hairy players *gorillas* (which wasn't too imaginative; see WILD ANIMALS).

In the early decades of football the *Yale Blue* was the most feared and influential team. Its unbeaten 1882 team outscored its opponents 482 to 2 and its unbeaten 1888 team outscored its opponents 698 to zero in fourteen games, while eight of its players, whose average weight was 169 pounds, later became famous college coaches, including the team's smallest player, 5-foot-4-inch Amos Alonzo Stagg, as well as Charley Gill, William "Pudge" Heffelfinger, and George Woodruff. But Yale's most talked about and influential football man was Walter Chauncey Camp, who was a star halfback of the unbeaten 1882 team and coach of the 1888 one. He was a 157-pound Yale *footballer* or *footballist* (both 1870s words for player) from 1876 through 1882 (four years as an undergraduate and three as a medical student), then returned to Yale in 1888 at the age of twenty-nine as its athletic director and *football coach* (an English soccer term of the 1840s). As a player, coach, and member of the Intercollegiate Football Rules Committee for forty-eight years, from his playing days until his death at one of its meetings in 1925, he was instrumental in many of the changes that transformed our Rugby game of the 1870s into American football in the 1880s, which is why he was already called the *Father of American Football* by the 1920s.

Many of these major changes were made in 1880 and 1882. In 1880 the eleven-man team was introduced and the field was reduced to 110 by 53 yards (the 100-yard-long field with a 10-yard *end zone* in which passes could be caught behind the goal line, wasn't adopted until 1912). The new rules of 1880 gave us:

Footballer *Walter Camp posing in his* football pants *and* football jacket *as captain of the Yale team in 1878.*

237

eleven-man team. Yale had played the first eleven-man game in America, using English soccer rules against a visiting Eton soccer team in 1873, then in 1880 finally persuaded other American schools to adopt a team of this size. Although the British had called both cricket and soccer teams *elevens* since the first half of the 19th century, we didn't commonly call a football team an *eleven* until the early 1920s.

substitute. Though earlier fifteen-man teams might have inexperienced replacements for injured players, the new eleven-man teams continued to carry and practice with fifteen players, now considering the extra four an integral part of the team, as valuable *substitutes* for the injured. The 1830s *sub* for *substitute* was originally used for substitute workers, especially printers, then came into sports use in 1889. Not until 1910 could a player removed from a game return to play, and then not until the next quarter; thus football teams didn't use the term *bench* or *bench warmer* until the early 1920s.

snapback. In the 1870s the man who put the ball into play did so by *heeling* it back, in a backward kick to a teammate, this then being called a *kick-off* (the modern use of *kickoff*, to the other side, dates from 1916). Beginning in 1880 he was allowed merely to touch or *baby* the ball with his foot, then toss the ball back quickly, this *toss-back* soon developing into the modern *snapback* or *snap*. The toss-back not only created the modern center as we know him but also brought the quarterback in closer to the line to receive the ball, creating the specialized job of the modern quarterback. The early toss-back was rare, as play was still continuous, being interrupted only when a goal was scored, the ball went out of bounds, etc.

scrimmage. With the new 1880 toss-back to the quarterback at the line, our *scrimmage* (a 1776 word for *skirmish* and first used in English Rugby) replaced the *scrummage* or *scrum* (a later form of the word *scrimmage* and which had become the popular word in England). In the scrummage both teams would battle for possession of the ball as it was put into play, while in the scrimmage it was snapped back by one side to begin play. Once the scrimmage entered football in 1880, the term *scrimmage line* (also a 19th-century Rugby term) began to replace the term *rush line*. From 1880 until 1888 the two lines stood almost bolt upright at the scrimmage line, with constant crowding and shoving, waiting for the toss-back, then wrestled each other to get at or protect the kicker or the ball carrier. To eliminate this crowding and shoving before the snapback, Bert Williams, a former Harvard football captain, introduced the idea of the *neutral zone* between the opposing lines in 1903.

The eleven-man team of 1880 already contained all the modern positions and players:

rush line of the 1870s had been reduced from nine to seven players in 1880. It was simply called the *line* by 1887; the line was said to *line out* to its positions by 1893 and to engage in *line play* by 1894. The individual *line rusher* (1870s) or *rusher* (1883) was called a *line man* by 1905. (By 1896 we were using *line* in an additional way, in *line-up*, meaning a list of the players in a game; *roster* has meant a list of members, as of a club or team, since 1891.)

right and *left end rush* or *rusher*, simply called an *end* by 1892.

right and *left tackle*, 1880s. Some plays were said to be run *off tackle* by 1900.

right and *left center guard*, 1880s (so called because they were to guard the center rusher during the toss-back), shortened to *guard* by 1893.

center rusher or *center rush*, both 1887 terms, shortened to *center* by 1893, by which time he was also called a *snapper back* and a *snapback*.

back. The 1880 eleven-man team reduced the players behind the line from six to four, eliminating one of the fullbacks and the three-quarter back, leaving one fullback, two halfbacks, and the quarterback, who, though he had now moved up to the line to receive the snapback from the center rusher, was not yet allowed to carry the ball himself. The *halfbacks* and *fullback*, of course, had been named in English soccer from the comparative distances they played behind the rush line and the comparatively recent *quarterback* had evolved from soccer's *center halfback*. The ending *-back* from these terms wasn't used separately until the late 1890s, when people first began to talk about a *back* without specifying which one; the backs weren't collectively called the *backfield* until 1923.

Despite the modern team, the toss-back, and the scrimmage of 1880, play was still continuous and football a kicking game. In eliminating the free-for-all scrummage, teams could retain possession of the ball for long periods of time and in 1880–81 the slow, dull *block game* developed, each team trying to keep the ball for an entire half so the opponent wouldn't have a chance to score, then trying to kick a goal in the closing minutes. To end this, Walter Camp determined to mark off the field every five yards and establish a system of *downs*, each team having to advance the ball five yards in three downs or turn it over to the other team. That was adopted as a rule in 1882, truly transformed football into our modern game, and gave us such terms as:

yard mark, yard line, 1882.

down, first down, second down, and *third down*, 1882. Originally a down was also often called a *scrimmage down*. The distance needed for a new first down was increased from five to ten yards in 1906, the number of downs allowed increased to four in 1912, giving us the new term *fourth down*.

In his 1893 *Walter Camp's Book of College Sports*, Camp said the word *down* was used because when a ball carrier was tackled he ended the play by shouting "down." That was the ball carrier's way of admitting his forward progress was at an end, so opposing players would stop tackling and wrestling with him. The ball was then *dead*, a word first used in sports in English lawn bowling in 1658, then used in cricket, soccer, and Rugby by the late 1820s.

gridiron. That the field was marked off with yard lines led to its being called the *gridiron* by 1897, sometimes shortened to *grid* by 1928. *Gridiron* referred solely to the striped pattern the yard lines made on the field, as *gridiron* meant a series of stripes (*the gridiron* was a nickname for our striped American flag from 1812 to about 1900). The field was marked off into a 5-yard-square checkerboard pattern from 1906 to 1910 (when passes had to be thrown from 5 yards behind the line and at least 5 yards to either side of the center), but the striped football field had been called a *gridiron* nine years before this checkerboard field appeared.

signals. The new 1882 system of downs revolutionized the game, breaking it up into specific plays that could be planned in advance and in which every player had to do his part. Thus coaches were soon giving players *chalk talks* (1881, as any lecture with a blackboard) and teams began to call *signals* (1882). These signals were originally sentences, phrases, and names, then changed from words to numbers in 1885. Calling or changing plays at the line of scrimmage, after seeing the defensive team's formation, came into wide use in the late 1960s, such a signal then being called an *audible*, *automatic*, or *checkoff*.

With the introduction of signals, *hike* (to hoist, in general use by 1867) became the quarterback's command to the center to snap the ball to begin each play. After World War II, *hut* often replaced *hike*, *hut* having originally been a command for a horse to start or go faster and then used in the military as the count of "one" in marching, as in "hut-two-three-four."

blocking. When many of the old soccer rules were discarded in the early 1880s, offensive players were allowed to run ahead of the ball without being called offside, and thus *guarding* developed, to be called *blocking* by the late 1880s. Between 1888 and 1891 Yale guard "Pudge" Heffelfinger became the game's first memorable *blocker*, as well as the first guard to *pull out of the line* to lead offensive plays.

Chicago Bears' Whizzer White holds the ball for quarterback George Blanda's 48-yard field goal kick to beat the San Francisco 49ers in the last minutes of this 1952 game. When he ended his professional career as an Oakland Raider in 1979, Blanda, then the oldest player in the league, had kicked more than 300 field goals and scored more than 2,000 points.

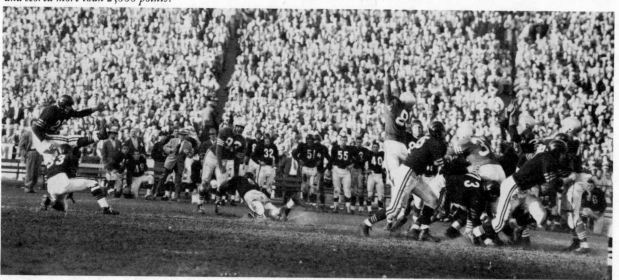

In 1883 numerical scoring was introduced, with a kicked *goal* from the field (which had also been called a *kick over* and a *kick out* since the late 1870s and was to be called a *field goal* by 1902) counting as five points, a goal kicked after a touchdown (then called a *kick from touchdown)* four points, the *touchdown* (originally a Rugby word) itself two points, and a *safety* (also called a *safety touchdown* in the 1880s and 90s) one point. This numerical scoring meant the word *goal* was used less: instead of winning a game "two goals to one," a team now won it by the numerical score of "10 to 5." These scoring values still kept football a kicking game and a touchdown was still most valuable for the try at the free kick after it. Finally, in 1884, a touchdown was counted as four points and the kick after touchdown only two, making the runner and his score more important than the kicker and his effort after it. The kick after touchdown was reduced to its present one-point value in 1897 (creating the term *point after touchdown*, which was made into the acronym *PAT* in 1979), the field goal was reduced to three points in 1909, and the touchdown was increased to six points in 1912. The most recent scoring term is the 1958 *two-point conversion*, successfully running or passing the ball into the end zone after a touchdown for two points instead of trying for the one-point kick after touchdown.

In 1888, *tackling* below the waist was first allowed, changing our definition of *tackle* from to lay hold of "as a wrestler his opponent" to the modern meaning of to throw a person down by grabbing his legs. Downs and tackling below the waist made football less of a wrestling game, so the backs moved in closer to the ball carrier to give him protection from tackling and the line men began to crouch at the line of scrimmage, to charge low and hard.

Besides all the other influence Walter Camp had on American football and its language, his list of the best players each year popularized the term *All-American*. He acted as consultant to Casper Whitney, part owner of *The Week's Sports*, in choosing the first widely publicized *All-American* football teams in 1889 and 1890 and for Whitney's *Harper's Weekly* column in 1891. Camp soon took over Whitney's column, then later picked his All-American team for *The Spalding Football Guide* and *Collier's*. For the first seven years all the All-American players were from what we would now loosely call the Ivy League, or at least from major eastern schools, few other schools playing football in its early days. However, Camp and the students of his day never heard the term *Ivy League;* it was coined by the *New York Herald Tribune*'s Caswell Adams in the 1930s to refer to the old, ivy-covered eastern colleges, with football's official Ivy League not formed until 1956. Camp's yearly selection of All-American football players was so eagerly awaited and widely discussed that rival publishers tried to steal them, forcing Camp to compile his list in three separate segments and guard them like military secrets. Thus the term *All-American* became widely known and came to mean the best in any sport by 1904. The terms *college football poll* and *top ten* emerged in 1936 when the Associated Press first conducted a poll of experts to determine the ten best college teams. Incidentally during World War I, Camp coined the term *daily dozen* as the title of his specific "Daily Dozen" exercise routine, which he created in Washington in 1917 for naval personnel and government officials.

The next major football innovator was Amos Stagg (1862–1965), who, while attending Yale Divinity School, had played under Walter Camp and had been on the original 1889 All-American team, before going on to the Y.M.C.A. Training School at Springfield, Massachusetts, as a student, player, and coach (and where he also became involved in another new sport; see BASKET-BALL). Stagg then became a coach and head of the physical education department at the University of Chicago in 1892 and made the University of Chicago *Maroons* a great football power of the early 1900s. Stagg introduced many things to football and his presence at the University of Chicago also helped popularize or establish many football traditions and terms, including:

> *practice dummy*, which Stagg seems to have invented in 1889, before his coaching days at Chicago. His first practice dummy was a rolled-up mattress suspended from a chain for indoor practice (*dummy* had meant a mannequin since the 1840s). It was also called a *tackling dummy* and a *tackling bag* by 1892.

Coach Amos Alonzo Stagg with his University of Chicago football team in 1893.

pigskin. Stagg's 1894 University of Chicago team seems to have been the first to call a football a *pigskin*.

end-around run was an innovation of Stagg's during the late 1890s. It was simply called an *end run* by 1902.

cheerleader, 1909. The first official ones were at the University of Chicago, leading the cheering of Stagg's teams.

shift. Stagg initiated a *line shift* for his University of Chicago line in 1902 and a *back shift* for the backs two years later, soon adding the first *man in motion*. John W. Heisman (see *the Heisman Trophy* below) further developed *the shift* at Georgia Tech in 1910 and Knute Rockne made an art of the precise, complicated shifts he devised for Notre Dame in the 1920s.

single wingback. Stagg introduced this in 1910; the term was almost immediately shortened to *single wing*. Within the next ten years Glenn "Pop" Warner, who coached at Carlisle, Georgia, Cornell, Pittsburgh, and Stanford during his own long career, refined the single wing at Pitt and combined it with his own *unbalanced line* and *slant plays*, then much later invented the *double wingback* at Stanford, first using it to beat Army 26 to 0 in 1928.

letter. Stagg began the custom of awarding monograms of the first letter of a school's name to athletes who had accumulated a specific amount of playing time in a sport, such a monogram being called a *letter* by 1914 and an athlete who received one being called a *letterman* by 1926.

Jim Thorpe, All-American left halfback of Carlisle (Indian) Institute of Pennsylvania in 1911–12, favored the hidden-ball trick and sometimes wore "slightly illegal" shoulder pads of sheet metal that destroyed opposing ball carriers. After leading Carlisle in upsets over Harvard, Army, and Penn in 1912, he went to the Olympics in Stockholm and won both the decathlon and pentathlon, then played professional baseball in 1913–14.

Stagg is also sometimes credited with introducing the *hidden-ball trick* and the *huddle*. However, the hidden-ball trick seems to have first been used by "Pop" Warner when coaching at Carlisle (Indian) Institute of Pennsylvania in a 1903 game against Harvard, just to liven things up, since Carlisle was already ahead 40 to 0. The play became a Carlisle tradition and a favorite of its great left halfback Jim Thorpe in 1911–12. Though Stagg may have initiated the huddle at Chicago, it was Bob Zuppke of the University of Illinois who made it a standard part of the game in the early 1920s, *huddle* then coming into general use to mean any conference by 1929. The time a team took for the huddle and to get the ball into play was originally unlimited, then kept being reduced, with the penalty and term *delay of game* being introduced in 1942.

At Chicago from 1892 to 1933, Stagg won six Western Conference titles and had five undefeated teams and a won-loss record of 269–141. In 1934, at the age of seventy-two, he became coach of the College of the Pacific at Stockton, California, where he was called *the Grand Old Man of Football* even before he was named college coach of the year in 1943, at the age of eighty-one, after which he continued to be an active football coach and advisor until he retired at the age of ninety-eight.

Walter Camp and Amos Stagg were proud that their teams' innovations and victories shaped football and created widespread interest in the game—because both considered football as a way to build character, with Stagg, a divinity school graduate with a

Y.M.C.A. background, always insisting that the game was a way to clean living. Yet their very successes in creating winning teams and building the game's popularity led to an emphasis on winning which kept football brutal, and eventually created big-time college football with its commercialization, including football-oriented, money-making athletic departments—and college alumni, trustees, budget directors, and public-relations men who demanded and depended on winning teams.

Even in Camp's and Stagg's early days players would *pile on*, while *clipping* was such a common act it wasn't even given a name until 1925. Two of the most exciting and dangerous plays from the 1880s to the early 1900s (on the average, a half-dozen players were killed on the field each year during this period) were *bucking the line* and running *V-formations*. In the first the *line bucker* (1893) was pushed, yanked, or otherwise propelled forward by his teammates, serving as both ball carrier and battering ram, some players even attaching straps to their uniforms to give their teammate *pushers* a better grip. The V-formation originally took place only on the old-fashioned "kick-off" when, instead of heeling the ball back, the player who was to put it into play would merely touch it to his toe and then pick it up and run with it inside a V-shaped wedge of his own teammates, this being called the *V trick*, the *Princeton wedge*, and the *Lehigh V* in the early 1880s.

In the very early 1890s, while still at the Y.M.C.A. Training School, Amos Stagg developed his *ends back* play, in which the two ends pulled back to protect the ball carrier, the three players forming a V; then at Chicago in 1894 Stagg invented his similar *tackles back* wedge. But the most spectacular and brutal wedge formation was the true nine-man *flying wedge* invented at Harvard for kick-off returns in 1892, Harvard gaining 45 yards on the play the very first time it used it and beating Yale 6 to 0. This was called the *flying wedge* because the nine offensive players who were to make the wedge formed two Indian-file lines about twenty yards behind the receiver and ran at full speed to converge in front of him as he received the ball, starting the play with full speed and tremendous momentum. In 1894, Pennsylvania modified this flying wedge to a four-man *flying interference* from scrimmage, pulling back both ends and tackles to form a smaller wedge, in effect combining Stagg's ends-back and tackles-back plays. This *flying interference* formation added the term *interference* to football and blockers were soon said to *run interference* for the ball carrier. A variation of this flying interference was the *hurricane charge*, a mass formation that charged through or around the opponent's flank.

Although big, strong defensive men, called *wedge busters*, could successfully hurl themselves against such mass formations, some of these formations were almost unstoppable and all caused many injuries. Thus some teams and leagues—but not enough—banned mass formation plays by the beginning of the 1895 season. Such teams began to look for players who could run well in the *broken field* (1899), though *broken-field runner* didn't become a common term until the 1920s. The wedge and other mass formations continued in use at many schools, however, and by emphasizing brawn opened up expensive and sometimes snobbish colleges to poor youths from farms or from many immigrant and minority groups because many colleges were now willing to accept such lower-class youths—as long as they were big and strong and willing to play mass-formation football. College teams were said to be *recruiting* such high school youths with bribes and promises by 1897. Those players who were recruited or who changed from school to school because they were promised special consideration and favors were called *tramp athletes* by 1907.

Brutality in football finally became a nationwide issue after a 1905 game in which the University of Pennsylvania's players tried to *get* (1860s as meaning to hurt or retaliate against) Swarthmore's main hope to win, 250-pound defensive lineman Bob Maxwell. Although receiving a merciless beating on almost every play, Maxwell managed to survive the entire game, but when a photograph of his bloody, beaten face appeared in newspapers the

Don Hutson, the first great pass-catching end and star of the 1935 Rose Bowl game. He is shown here catching a pass for Green Bay in the championship game against the New York Giants in 1938.

245

country was horrified. Some schools, such as Columbia, abandoned football, and President Theodore Roosevelt even called representatives of Harvard (his alma mater), Princeton, and Yale to the White House to tell them that if such brutal play wasn't ruled out he would abolish the game by executive order! Finally, at the end of the 1906 season, football leaders and rules committees everywhere outlawed mass formations and such dangerous plays as *hurdling* (vaulting over players still on their feet), reduced the game from 90 to 60 minutes, increased the yardage needed for first down from 5 to 10 yards, added a second referee (who was replaced by a *field judge* in 1907), and—to open up the game further—legalized the forward pass.

The *forward pass* had been used as a trick play in informal games for years and since 1903 had been advocated by John Heisman when he was coach at Penn State, but even after it was officially accepted in 1906 it still was little used. This was partially because until 1910 it had to be thrown from 5 yards behind the line and 5 yards to either side of where the ball had been put into play, resulting in the field's being ruled off into a checkerboard pattern to aid the officials. Then from 1910 to 1912, passes were limited to 20 yards maximum, and there was a 15-yard penalty for a forward pass that failed (the terms *incompleted forward pass* and *completed forward pass* didn't become common until 1926, with the first term dropping its final -ed to become an *incomplete forward pass* by the early 1930s).

Wesleyan threw the first legal forward pass, against Yale, in the 1906 season, impressing Mrs. Walter Camp, who then convinced her husband to add it to Yale's repertoire. Yale then used one of its rare forward passes in a desperate attempt to beat Harvard that year, winning the game on it, 6 to 0. But for years the pass was still considered merely part of a team's *deception* (a word Harvard coach Percy Haughton added to football's vocabulary in 1908).

Then in 1913 everyone heard about the *forward pass*. The overpowering Army team had chosen a weak, unknown team from a little midwestern institution named Notre Dame as an easy target in its otherwise strong schedule. But Notre Dame's coach Jesse Harper, quarterback Charles "Gus" Dorias, and end Knute Rockne had prepared a surprise, with Dorias and Rockne practicing their "passing routine" while working together at their summer jobs on the beach at a vacation resort at Cedar Point, Ohio. During this time Dorias referred to himself as the *pitcher* and Rockne as the *catcher* (after the game, newspapers referred to Dorias as the *forward passer* and Rockne as the *pass receiver*, the shorter *receiver* not becoming common until the 1930s). In the game at West Point, Army players stood around helplessly as Dorias whipped successful passes over their heads to end Rockne or back Pliska for long gains, Notre Dame winning a tremendous 35 to 13 *upset* (used in

Knute Rockne with Notre Dame's mascot Terry, in 1924. Rockne had five undefeated seasons and a record of 105 wins, 12 losses, and 5 ties in his twelve years of coaching at Notre Dame. His backs sometimes shifted into an oblong box *toward his* strong side *or* weak side *offense.*

this sense in English since the early 1800s). This game not only started Notre Dame's rise from an obscure little college as its team became a football *powerhouse* (1890 in the literal sense, 1920s as applied to an overpowering team), but it encouraged other smaller schools to field their own lightweight teams, using the pass to beat bigger, more powerful teams, spreading football's influence and vocabulary to smaller schools and communities all over the country.

Sportswriters were soon calling forward passes *aerials* and a team that used many passes an *aerial circus* (from the barnstorming pilots' *flying circus* and *aerial circus*, well known after World War I), with the Southern Methodist University team of the early 1920s being the first to be so called. Soon, too, the once fat, "egg-shaped" ball, meant for kicking, began growing more sleek and streamlined, for better passing.

The forward pass also helped put *numbers* on the players' uniforms. Since the early days, the fans, officials, and especially newspaper reporters had complained because they didn't know which player had made a play or if an injured player had been replaced or by whom. Borrowing the idea from track athletes, Washington and Jefferson put numbers on its players' backs in one game in 1908; then the University of Chicago experimented with this system in 1913. Once the forward pass became important, however, everyone, including the quarterback, wanted to know who that was waiting for a pass downfield. Thus, in 1915, Pitt became the first team to make numbers a permanent feature of its players' uniforms. However, the idea was promoted there by Karl Davis, who was in charge of Pittsburgh's football program sales—and he changed the players' numbers every week so regular fans would have to buy a new program for each game! All teams were wearing numbers on their backs by 1920; numbers on both back and front have been required since 1937. *Retiring a number* of a famous player began with "Red" Grange's "77" at the University of Illinois in 1925.

Another aid to fans and reporters was the introduction of *hand signals* by the referee to indicate penalties. The first ones were created by referee Ellwood Geiger at a Syracuse-Cornell game in the late 1920s, for a radio broadcaster who had asked to be kept better informed so he could describe the game in more detail.

As football grew more popular, the *football field* very quickly grew into a *stadium* (from Greek *stadion*, a unit of length, eventually one-eighth of a Roman mile, then a race course of that length, and finally any athletic field, including an elaborate one with many seats, this use in English by the 1740s). Harvard built a 30,000-seat concrete *football stadium* in 1903, Syracuse had its 35,000-seat Archbold Stadium, and Princeton its 80,000-seat Palmer Stadium even before football's "first major stadium," the beautiful 25-acre,

The University of Pennsylvania team plays on Franklin Field in 1904. This was still basically a football field, though Harvard had built a 30,000-seat football stadium in 1903.

71,000-capacity *Yale Bowl*, was completed in 1914. Since such huge stadiums could hold more than the combined total of a school's students, faculty, and living alumni, the colleges that built them knew that football was already a highly profitable spectator sport, one that was going to pay for public relations, athletic departments and, in some cases, new academic buildings and improvements.

After World War I, all sports mushroomed in popularity, including both college and professional football, and in the 1920s many half-million-dollar college football stadiums were built. The *pep demonstration* (1915; *pep* was an 1850s word but became very popular around 1912) grew into the gigantic *pep rally* (1924). Alumni, flappers, and sheiks filled the stands, the college boys in *coonskin coats* (a 1649 term) with a *hip flask* in their pocket, their dates wearing chrysanthemums or other corsages matching their team's colors. By 1935 many colleges were holding an annual *homecoming* featuring a *homecoming game* for alumni. College recruiters and alumni were now offering prospective players not only tuition, board, and acceptance into the best fraternities but also pocket money, flashy *sports cars* (1925), and a good job after graduation. The trickle of big, brawny players who were sons of poor immigrants became a flood, a standard joke of the 1930s being that the names of Notre Dame's "Fighting Irish" players read "like a page out of the Warsaw phonebook."

The *Yale Bowl* of 1914 made *bowl* a synonym for football stadium, even horseshoe-shaped ones. *Bowl* then soon had another meaning, that of an annual postseason game played at a major stadium between outstanding teams. Though one of coach "Hurry Up" Fielding Yost's University of Michigan's *point-a-minute* Wolverine teams, with halfback Willie Heston leading the offense, had beaten Stanford 49 to 0 in a special game played during Pasadena's Tournament of Roses on January 1, 1902, there was no Tournament of Roses game during the next thirteen years. Then in 1916, Washington State, the Pacific Coast Conference champion, was given the honor of inviting an eastern team to play as a feature of the rose festival, beating Brown 14 to 0 at the *Pasadena Bowl* on January 1, 1916, in *the Tournament of Roses Association Game*, as it was then officially called. In 1917 Oregon State beat Pennsylvania in the same Pasadena Bowl, which had now been renamed the *Pasadena Rose Bowl*. This 1917 game popularized the terms *Rose Bowl*, *bowl game*, and *postseason* game. The game was not officially named the *Rose Bowl Game*, however, until 1923, when a new, larger stadium was dedicated and simply named the *Rose Bowl*, as suggested by Pasadena's Harlan Hill.

The success of the Rose Bowl led to many other annual postseason bowl games, and to postseason charity games, many of them originating in the 1930s. Thus we have had such games and names as:

> *the North-South Game*, 1932, also called *the Shrine All-Star Game*, because proceeds go to the Masonic Shrine. A somewhat similar game, *the East-West Game*, also called *the Shrine Game* and *the Shrine Classic*, began at San Francisco in 1925.
>
> *the College All-Star Game*, 1934, a charity game between the best college seniors, called *the College All-Stars*, and the National Football League champions. It was the brainchild of *Chicago Tribune* sports editor Arch Ward, created as a counterpart to the All-Star baseball game (see BASEBALL).
>
> *the Orange Bowl*, at Miami, 1933. Patterned on the *Rose Bowl* name, this made a tradition out of naming a bowl game after a local product or item and, incidentally, punning on the word *bowl*.
>
> *the Sugar Bowl*, at New Orleans, 1935.
>
> *the Sun Bowl*, at El Paso, Texas, 1936.
>
> *the Cotton Bowl*, at Dallas, 1937.
>
> *the Blue-Gray Game*, at Montgomery, Alabama, 1938, also called *the North-South College All-Star Game*.
>
> *the Gator Bowl*, at Jacksonville, Florida, 1946.
>
> *the Blue Bonnet Bowl*, at Houston, 1959, officially *the Astro-Blue Bonnet Bowl* after it moved into Houston's Astrodome in the late 1960s.

Such special games attract much attention and have helped disseminate football terms. Thus the *flea flicker*, invented by Bob Zuppke at the University of Illinois as a forward pass followed by a lateral followed by another forward pass, became well known when California's *Wonder Team* of 1920 used it in its defeat of previously unbeaten Ohio State 28 to 0 in the Rose Bowl on January 1, 1921 (the play named for the quick flealike jumping of the ball as it is flicked from player to player). Similarly, *goal line stand* became well known in 1934 because Lou Little's Columbia team made a famous one against Stanford to win that year's Rose Bowl 7 to 0, Columbia making its touchdown on a *fake reverse*, which then also became a play and term known to millions.

College football was, of course, no longer the only attraction. No sooner had the colleges created American football than small semi-professional and professional teams took it up. Pro football (*pro* is an 1887 shortening of *professional*) seems to have developed in western Pennsylvania, especially around Pittsburgh, in the early 1890s, with teams sponsored by local athletic clubs, Y.M.C.A.s, and business firms. The first player to *play for pay* (a late 1950s term) is said to have been Yale's famous "Pudge" Heffelfinger, who was reported to have been paid $500 by the Allegheny Athletic Association to play against the Pittsburgh Athletic Club in 1892. The first professional game was played August 31, 1895, between two Pennsylvania teams, a team from Jeannette and a Y.M.C.A. team from Latrobe, Latrobe winning 12 to 0. It is called a professional game because all the Latrobe players shared in the profits (Latrobe also paid an outsider, quarterback John Brallier of Indiana Normal and the University of West Virginia, a fee of $10). Other Pennsylvania teams, such as the Pittsburgh Duquesnes and McKeesport Olympics, began to pay players in the next two years and their opponents in adjacent regions of Ohio followed suit in the early 1900s.

The early "professional" players were paid by the game or sometimes put on the payroll of the sponsoring athletic club, Y.M.C.A., or business firm. Many paid players were college stars who played in as many paid games and for as many teams as they could. Besides Yale's "Pudge" Heffelfinger, such college stars as Princeton's Arthur Poe, Michigan's Willie Heston, Pennsylvania's Lou Little, and Cornell's Glenn "Pop" Warner combined college and semi-pro careers, with Knute Rockne being most in demand, playing not only for Notre Dame but for as many as six semi-professional teams in one year. In fact, some complete college backfields played for professional teams, some of whose rosters

"Bronko" Nagurski of the Chicago Bears.

"Red" Grange in action.

read like a college All-Star list. In 1914, when college football was becoming big business, so many small-time professional and semi-professional teams existed that college coaches and alumni complained of the unfair competition and for many years were to claim that professional players could never be as honest as the clean-living, idealistic students who played only for the love of the game and the glory of their schools. This attitude helped keep college attendance up and professional attendance down for decades.

Nevertheless, the *American Professional Football Association* was created at a meeting in Ralph Hay's Hupmobile showroom in Canton, Ohio, on September 17, 1920 (which is why the professional *Football Hall of Fame*, dedicated in 1963, is in Canton). The area businessmen and football enthusiasts at that first meeting agreed that each of the franchises in the new league should cost $100, though none of them could afford to pay anything. One franchise went to George Halas, the player-coach of the *Decatur (Illinois) Staleys*, named after the local Staley Starch Co., which sponsored the team. Jim Thorpe was made president and titular head of the league, which collapsed before the season ended but was reorganized in 1921 with Joseph F. Carr, a Columbus, Ohio, businessman and promoter, as president. Carr immediately reduced the price of franchises to $50 (in 1925 Tim Mara bought the New York Giants' franchise for $500 and in 1933 Art Rooney bought the Pittsburgh Steelers' franchise for $2,500, such franchises being worth $25 million by the late 1970s). The *Decatur Staleys* had been playing their home games in Chicago so George Halas renamed his Decatur team the *Chicago Bears* in 1921, won the league championship that year, then actually moved the Chicago Bears to Chicago in 1922—sometimes playing before as few as eighty fans. Also in 1922 the American Professional Football Association changed its name to the *National Football League* (the abbreviation *NFL* didn't become common until the boom in abbreviations during World War II and the boom in professional football after it).

Though the NFL was well on its way in the early 1920s, the star who made pro football a national pastime was shy, retiring ex–University of Illinois halfback "Red" (Harold) Grange. His sobriquets were "Red," 77 (his number at the University of Illinois), *the Wheaton Iceman* (he was an iceman in his hometown of Wheaton, Illinois, throughout his high school and college days and even at the beginning of his professional career, though he then drove his $6,000 Lincoln to work), and *the Galloping Ghost*. This last, and most famous, name was first applied to him by sportswriter Grantland Rice after Grange's spectacular game on the warm Saturday afternoon of October 18, 1924, in Urbana, Illinois. In that game Grange ran for five touchdowns and passed for a sixth against previously unbeaten Michigan. His first touchdown was

The opening lines of Grantland Rice's October 19, 1924, *New York Herald Tribune* write-up on Notre Dame's 13 to 7 defeat of Army at New York City's Polo Grounds the previous day. One of the most famous sports pieces ever written, it immortalized the four players in Notre Dame's backfield. Rice got the idea of calling them *the Four Horsemen* from George Strickler, then student publicity director for Notre Dame, who had seen a Four Horsemen movie, starring Rudolph Valentino, and told Rice the four players were "just like the Four Horsemen."

his 95-yard kickoff return, his second a 67-yard return of the next kickoff, his third a 56-yard punt return, and his fourth a 44-yard run from scrimmage—these four touchdowns being made the first four times he handled the ball and in the first twelve minutes of play. He scored a record 31 touchdowns in three college seasons (24 games), then left college in 1925 to become pro football's first major *gate* (1880s in this sense) attraction, playing with the Chicago Bears until 1932. During his first two years with the Bears his barnstorming tours attracted crowds of up to 70,000 per game.

Since Red Grange had left college to sign with the Bears before graduating, the NFL was accused of *kidnapping* him, this 1925 use of the word then immediately coming to mean any professional team's recruiting of a college player (because of the furor over Grange's leaving college, the NFL declared college players ineligible until they finished school). In 1947, Grange helped popularize another term, *television football announcer*, when he became one of professional football's first major television announcers, again for the Chicago Bears.

The success of big-time college football, bowl games, and professional football in the 1920s and 30s made all football terms much more common; the advent of televised games following World War II made football and its terms a part of American life. New terms for players, new plays, and new offensive and defensive formations now seem to appear each season. Since the 1930s we have heard and used such new football terms as:

watch-chain guard, 1930, a small, fast guard who led end sweeps, a term created for Notre Dame's 153-pound Bert Metzger.

T formation, 1931. Though Knute Rockne's Notre Dame backs sometimes lined up in a T in the late 1920s, they shifted into an oblique *box* toward his *strong side* or *weak side* offense before the play began. The true *T formation*, operating behind a *balanced line* and with the backs staying in the T until the ball is snapped, was introduced by coach Ralph Jones of the Chicago Bears in 1931, using Sid Luckman as the first *T-formation quarterback*. The term *T formation* then became very common in the 1940s when such college teams as Stanford, Notre Dame under Frank Leahy, and Army under Earl Blaik used the *T* with tremendous success.

The T formation soon led to other new terms. Playing out of the T, one of the fullbacks could be used as a *flanker* (late 1930s). The *split T* was developed by Don Faurot at Missouri in 1941, giving the running quarterback the option of tossing the ball to another running back or continuing to run with it himself, this being called the *option play* by the 1950s. In the 1950s, too, the professional *pro set* became popular, using three backs in the T with the fourth out to the side as a *wide receiver*, with some professional teams adding the *slot T* by the late 1950s. Another term the T formation created was the *four-man line*, used to defend against it.

play-off, 1933, when the enlarged National Football League divided

Notre Dame's Four Horsemen *backfield, known for their Rockne-designed* shifts *and* laterals, *were (left to right in this 1924 photograph): Don Miller, Elmer Layden, Jim Crowley, and Harry Stuhldreher. They were given the name the* Four Horsemen *by sportswriter Grantland Rice, which led to the name the Seven Mules for the seven linesmen on the team. The Four Horsemen played their last game together in the 1925 Rose Bowl, beating Stanford 27–10.*

We are just the seven mules. We do all the work so that these four fellows can gallop into fame.

Notre Dame center Adam Walsh, October 1924, expressing the Notre Dame linesmen's resentment of all the publicity given its *Four Horsemen* backfield. His statement led to calling the Notre Dame line *the seven mules.*

The Heisman Trophy *was named for John W. Heisman, the New York Downtown Athletic Club's first athletic director. He had played at Brown and Pennsylvania and coached at Clemson, Georgia Tech, and elsewhere. The player on the trophy was modeled on University of Chicago back Jay Berwanger, its first recipient.*

into an Eastern and a Western division, the winner of each meeting in a postseason game or *play-off* to determine the league championship.

the Heisman Trophy, 1935, awarded by the New York Downtown Athletic Club to "the most outstanding" college player of the year. The trophy, officially the *John W. Heisman Trophy,* was named for the club's first athletic director (who had played at Brown and Pennsylvania from 1887 to 1891, then coached for thirty-six years at Clemson, Georgia Tech, etc.). The first winner was University of Chicago back "Jay" (John Jacob) Berwanger, who then served as the model for the player on the trophy.

football draft, 1935, when the NFL decided to end expensive bidding among teams for the best college players by holding a *draft* for them (*draft* was first used in sports in 1889 when A. G. Spalding proposed one for baseball). When the first football draft was held, in 1936, the Philadelphia Eagles, as the weakest team, had the first *draft choice.* It chose the University of Chicago's Jay Berwanger, winner of the first Heisman Trophy, then sold the rights to him to the Chicago Bears, but the Bears and Berwanger couldn't come to contract terms: thus the first player drafted by the pros, and the first Heisman Trophy winner, never played professional football.

the seven blocks of granite, 1937, referring to Fordham University's line, which allowed no running touchdowns all season.

A formation, 1938, when the New York Giants made it famous. In this offensive alignment a halfback, the quarterback, and the fullback form an A behind the line, the fullback at the apex; the center can snap the ball to any of them, and the fullback is sometimes used as a passer.

hand off, early 1940s. Originally an English Rugby term, it became common in American football with the popularity of the T formation, in which a running back, who has gained momentum by starting at the snap, takes the ball from the quarterback as he approaches the line. A hand off was also called an *exchange* by the late 1940s.

two-platoon system, 1945, when college teams were allowed to use separate *offensive* and *defensive units;* Michigan immediately used it with great success that year. Since this system depends on large teams and coaching staffs, it was considered unfair to smaller schools and was not allowed from 1953 to 1965, when *unlimited substitution* (first tried in 1941) went into effect. Between 1959 and 1965, however, *wild-card substitution* was allowed, in which certain players could be put into and removed from a game at any time.

quarterback sneak, 1940s, as a T-formation play in which the quarterback does not hand off the ball to another back as expected but runs with it himself, now usually straight into the line to gain short yardage needed on a third or fourth down.

The All-American Football Conference was organized in 1946, played four seasons, then merged with the NFL. In the years during which the two leagues competed for college players, salaries soared. Thus in 1947, star University of Georgia halfback Charles Trippi accepted a Chicago Cardinal's offer of $100,000 for four years, then making him the highest-paid player in the game.

Coach Paul Brown's *Cleveland Browns,* which had been among the first teams to sign black players, such as fullback Marion Motley and guard Bill Willis, dominated the All-American Football Conference, winning all four championships. Then, in 1950, the first year after the merger, the Browns won the NFL championship.

taxi squad, late 1940s, for the extra available players under contract to, and practicing with, a team but for which it had no room on its active-player list. The term originated in Cleveland, where the original owner of the Cleveland Browns, Art McBride, used such extra players as drivers for a fleet of cabs he owned.

tee, 1948 in football use, as a three-pronged stand for holding the ball during kickoffs (the name, of course, comes from the *golf tee;* see FORE!).

Jay Berwanger leaping for yardage against Wisconsin in 1934. The first Heisman Trophy winner and the first college player ever drafted by the pros, he never played professional football.

umbrella defense, 1950, when the New York Giants introduced this pass defense of a *six-man line* with one linebacker and the four defensive halfbacks fanned out behind them like an open umbrella.

bootleg, around 1950, when this play, in which the quarterback fakes a hand off before hiding the ball on his hip and running with it himself, was perfected by quarterbacks Bob Waterfield of the Los Angeles Rams and Frank Albert of the San Francisco 49ers. In its original meaning the word first appeared in 1850, referring to carrying or hiding a bottle of illegal whiskey in one's boot leg.

Pro Bowl, 1951, when the NFL's all-professional *All-Star Game* (first played in 1938) between the stars of its two divisions was established in Los Angeles, the *Los Angeles Times* being the first to rename this All-Star Game the *Pro Bowl*.

clothesline, mid 1950s. This tactic of stopping a ball carrier short by sticking out one's arm to catch him around the neck, as if he were running into a clothesline, became well known from its use by the Kansas City Chiefs' Fred Williamson and the Los Angeles Rams' Dick "Night Train" Lane.

Alley-oop, late 1950s, as a lob pass over the heads of the defenders to a tall receiver, first used in pro football to refer to such passes by San Francisco 49er quarterback Y. A. Tittle to 6-foot-3-inch ex-basketball player R. C. Owens. It's from the late 1920s interjection *allez-oop!* (pronounced and often spelled "alley-oop"), said upon lifting something, reinforced by the comic strip *Alley Oop*, named for its main character, a large, friendly caveman. The interjection *allez-oop* itself sounds very much to be the French *allez*, you go + a French pronunciation of our "up"; hence "you go up," as if coined by French and American servicemen trying to communicate during World War I.

game plan, late 1950s, as the strategy and specific tactics a team plans to use in a game, based on its strengths and the opponents'

Johnny Unitas played for the University of Louisville, then earned $7 a game as a semi-professional player for the Bloomfield, Pennsylvania, Rams before getting a tryout with and then becoming the star quarterback for the Baltimore Colts in the late 1950s. Here he's shown passing the 1959 Colts to their second consecutive National Football League championship, beating the New York Giants 31–16.

255

Joe Namath (number 12), after starring as the University of Alabama quarterback, received a $400,000 bonus in 1965 for signing with the New York Jets. He led the Jets to the first American Football League Super Bowl victory, over the Baltimore Colts.

weaknesses. The term took on political and economic use, meaning strategy, tactics, or just "plan" in 1969, when it became a favorite of President Richard Nixon and several members of his Administration. They had gotten this football term as avid fans of the capital's hometown team, the Washington Redskins.

wide end, split end, 1958.

the American Football League (AFL) was formed in 1959–60, became a successful rival of the NFL, and agreed to merge with it in 1966. The two leagues then became part of a greatly enlarged NFL, playing an interlocking schedule as the National and the American Football Conferences since 1970. This new, merged NFL with its increased number of teams and spectators immediately made professional football the major American spectator sport, surpassing baseball in both its number of ticket-buying fans and television viewers in 1970.

bonus player, early 1960s. From 1960 to 1966 the NFL and AFL teams were competing for "talent," bidding against each other for, and offering large bonuses to, the best college players for signing contracts with them; thus the term *bonus player* became common. In 1965 University of Alabama quarterback Joe Namath received $400,000 for signing with the New York Jets and the following year Texas Tech halfback Donnie Anderson received $600,000 from the Green Bay Packers. It was only the size of such bonuses that was new: the first college player to receive a bonus for signing to play with a professional team was probably University of Michigan halfback Willie Heston, who received $600 for signing with the Canton, Ohio, team in 1905.

I formation, early 1960s. College coaches Tom Nugent of the Virginia Military Institute and John McKay of the University of Southern California popularized this formation in which the quarterback, halfback, fullback, and tailback line up in a straight line behind the center, forming an I. By the late 1960s the *power I* was in vogue, with only three backs in a straight line behind the center, the fourth off to one side.

blitz, red dog, 1960s, as a pass defense in which the defensive backs rush the quarterback to *sack* him (tackle or throw him to the ground behind the line of scrimmage) before he can throw a pass. Though *red dog* had been an 1830s term for a *wildcat* (1838) business, such as a hastily formed and financially precarious, or speculative, bank, the football term seems to come from *red* as a defensive signal word warning to beware of or guard against the pass plus the verb *dog*, meaning to pursue or hunt down as a dog does (this verb used in English since 1519).

Blitz was our 1940 shortening of the 1939 *blitzkrieg* (taken directly from the German *Blitzkrieg*, which is *Blitz*, lightning + *Krieg*, war), first used to refer to the Nazis' fast armored conquest of Poland which was launched September 1, 1939, and began World War II. All competitive sports have their share of warlike terms, as the basic *offense, defense*, etc., with the rougher sports having the most. After World War II, football used several new warlike terms including *blitz, bomb* (late 1950s, as any pass over 30 yards, though especially a long touchdown pass), and *sack*, which has meant to loot or pillage a captured city in English since 1547 (though the football use is reinforced by our other verb *sack*, to put or tie up in a sack, used in English since 1386).

the wishbone, 1960s, when this formation was the specialty of Darrell Royal's University of Texas teams. It got its name from its shape, the fullback lining up behind the quarterback and the two halfbacks lined up deeper and to the sides, forming a Y, or wishbone, shape.

moving pocket, mid 1960s. This method of protecting the quarterback as he moves to either side to pass, by surrounding him with a "pocket" of the other backs who move with him, was an innovation of coach Frank Stram of the Kansas City Chiefs. Around this same time Stram's teams also introduced the *bump and run*, in which a defensive cornerback bumps a prospective pass receiver to slow him down as he runs by him and then turns and runs after him to further guard against his receiving a pass.

synthetic turf, artificial turf, artificial grass, were first widely heard in 1965 when the 66,000-seat *Astrodome* stadium (officially the Harris County Domed Stadium) was opened in Houston, Texas, being the first domed stadium. The best-known synthetic turf was the trademark *Astroturf*, developed specifically for use in the new Astrodome and named for it. The Houston *Astrodome* itself got the *Astro-* because Houston was well known as the headquarters of the National Aeronautics and Space Administration (NASA), which was then very much in the news for sending our *astronauts* into space.

Though the *Astrodome* was our first domed stadium (and set the pattern for later ones using *-dome* as the last element in their names), the first *indoor football game* had been played long before, being Pennsylvania *vs* Rutgers in 1887 in the original Madison Square Garden in New York City, and the first indoor professional game had been Syracuse *vs* the Philadelphia Nationals in Madison Square Garden in 1902.

monster man, late 1960s, as a roving defensive back, this term being first applied to defensive back George Webster of Michigan State during 1965. Other college teams were soon calling their roving defensive back gorilla man or similar monster names.

Green Bay Packer coach Vince Lombardi smiling as his team beats the New York Giants 16–7 at Yankee Stadium to win the 1962 NFL championship for the second straight year. His team also won the first Super Bowl, *on January 15, 1967.*

Winning isn't everything. It's the only thing.
Attributed to Green Bay Packer coach Vince Lombardi in the 1960s, but delivered by actor John Wayne, playing a football coach, in the 1953 movie *Trouble Along the Way.*

the *Super Bowl.* Once the NFL and AFL agreed to merge, in 1966, fans got their wish to see a one-game championship play-off between the championship NFL and AFL teams (later between the National and American Conference champions of the merged NFL). The first was held in the Los Angeles Coliseum on January 15, 1967, after the end of the 1966 season, the NFL's Green Bay Packers, under coach Vince Lombardi, beating the AFL's Kansas City Chiefs 35 to 0. Legend has it that this climactic postseason "bowl" game was named the *Super Bowl* by AFL founder Lamar Hunt after hearing his daughter call her toy rubber ball a "super ball," his mind then jumping to *Super Bowl* since professional football was then searching for a name for this annual game. The Latin prefix *super-,* above, over, in addition, has been used to form new English words since the 15th century; it was first used as a slang word for *superior* around 1925.

DEEfense (the noun *defense* with a strong accent on the first syllable) appeared as a cheer of encouragement to and appreciation for one's defensive team's players in the early 1970s, making this secondary and dialect pronunciation more common (the usual pronunciation is deFENSE). This cheer and pronunciation was first heard by millions of nationwide TV viewers as Dallas fans cheered Tom Landry's Dallas Cowboys' exciting *doomsday defense* in the late 1960s and early 70s.

jock, late 1960s, originally a big, dumb college football player, by mid 1970s any athlete, always implying an excess of brawn and a lack of brains and sensitivity. It is, of course, related to the horse-racing *jockey* (1825) and the aggressive athlete called a *jockey* in the 1940s because he would often *ride* (1918 as taunt, heckle) an opposing player, but it mainly carries the connotation of *jock strap* (1915, *jock* having been a slang word for penis in English since the 16th century, because *Jock* was long a common nickname for *John,* the most common masculine name).

scramble, early 1970s in football use. It had originally meant to mix and cook, as eggs (1864), then in World War II referred to waiting fighter pilots rushing to their planes and taking off as quickly as possible, in no specific order, to intercept approaching enemy bombers. This connotation of speed and disorganization made *scramble* yet another World War II term taken into football, referring to the quarterback's frantic efforts to evade onrushing tacklers. The term was first widely used to describe the evasive running of the best-known *scrambler* of all, Fran Tarkenton of the Minnesota Vikings, especially in the early 1970s.

flake, as an eccentric person, and *flaky,* as eccentric, are claimed by both football and baseball. However, *flaky* was a late 1950s slang term which was clipped to form the noun *flake,* which appeared in professional baseball in 1964 and then in professional football in the early 1970s, especially then referring to Joe Don Looney (who couldn't, after all, be called merely a *looney,* 1869, from the 1845 *crazy as a loon),* who attacked tackling dummies in anger and seldom heeded signs, and Fred Dryer, who lived in a minibus instead of in a house or an apartment.

sudden death (overtime), early 1970s, referring to an overtime or fifth period of no more than fifteen minutes allowed in professional football if the score is tied at the end of the fourth quarter. It is called *sudden death* because the extra period is suddenly over when either team scores, winning the game (the term had been used in golf since at least the 1950s; see FORE!).

spike, early 1970s, to throw the ball down hard in the end zone, as if driving in a spike, after one has crossed the goal line and scored a touchdown, then by the mid 1970s also applied to any impromptu victory dance or braggadocio gesture or antic performed by such a scoring player.

front four, early 1970s for the two guards and two tackles on a team's defensive unit.

three-man front, mid 1970s when the Houston Oilers and the New England Patriots adopted a three-man defensive line, putting eight men behind the line as linebackers and defensive backs. At the beginning of the 1970s the *nickel defense*, named for the five men in the defensive backfield, was widely used and discussed.

The World Football League (WFL) was formed as a rival to the NFL in the 1974–75 season. Several of its teams soon went bankrupt and the league collapsed, its better players joining, or rejoining, NFL teams, a few of its franchises serving as the nuclei for NFL *expansion teams* (league use for new and struggling teams).

the shotgun, was used by coach "Red" Hickey of the San Francisco 49ers in 1959, became part of the Dallas Cowboy offense in 1972, and became widely known when used with tremendous success by Cowboy quarterback Roger Staubach in 1976. In this passing formation the quarterback is protected because he is positioned about eight yards behind the line when he receives the ball from the center. Originally, the other backs never gave the quarterback protection, but rushed downfield and spread out, like shotgun pellets, to confuse the defense and give the quarterback a wide range of possible receivers.

With strong nationwide interest in professional football since World War II, especially as televised since the 1950s, the names of many teams have become well known. Some, especially in the early days, were named after a sponsoring business firm, the color of the uniforms, or even after a baseball team in the same city (as the All-American Football Conference's *Brooklyn Dodgers*, and the *New York Yankees*). However, most team names refer chauvinistically to their city's image (its history, location, or industry), to an animal, or to an aggressively masculine term. Sometimes, of course, team names combine these elements: animal names are usually chosen from the more aggressive animals (as the Chicago *Bears*) but can refer to an animal also suggestive of the city's image (as the Miami *Dolphins*). Some team names even combine all three elements: the Philadelphia *Eagles* are named after a bird, and an aggressive one, but the American eagle is implied, reflecting Philadelphia's history as the cradle of the Declaration of Independence.

Professional football teams named to reflect their city's history, location, or industry have included the: Dallas *Cowboys* and Dallas *Texans* (Dallas grew from its land and ranches for its *Cowboys*), Green Bay *Packers* (for the local meat-packing industry), Houston

---

If Jesus were alive today, he would be at the Super Bowl.
Norman Vincent Peale, referring to the 1981 Super Bowl game, quoted in *Time* magazine, January 1982.

Dallas Cowboy *Tony Dorsett scoring in the 1978 Super Bowl.*

Oilers (Houston grew from its oil and industry for its *Oilers*), Minnesota *Vikings* (suggesting the Scandinavian settlers of the area, though *Viking* is also a strong male explorer-warrior name), New England *Patriots* (from Boston), New Orleans *Saints* (not a religious name but from New Orleans's jazz tradition, exemplified by the song "When the Saints Go Marching In"), Pittsburgh *Steelers*, and San Francisco *49ers*.

Teams named after animals have included the: Atlanta *Falcons*, Baltimore *Colts*, Buffalo *Bisons* (also, of course, referring to Buffalo, named for the American bison), Canton *Bulldogs* (the 1922 and 1923 NFL champions; there has also been a Cleveland *Bulldogs* and a Chicago *Bulldogs*), Chicago *Bears*, Chicago *Cardinals*, Cincinnati *Bengals* (Bengal tigers), Denver *Broncos*, Detroit *Lions*, Los Angeles *Rams* (there has also been a Cleveland *Rams*), Miami *Dolphins*, St. Louis *Cardinals*, and Seattle *Seahawks* (and an old Miami *Seahawks*).

Team names chosen for being masculine and aggressive (though some have a local connotation, as places where Indians once lived, etc.) include the: Buffalo *Bills* (a pun on Buffalo Bill, the nickname of William Cody, the rugged pony express rider, cavalry scout, buffalo hunter, and Wild West showman, who had no connection with Buffalo, New York), Kansas City *Chiefs* (the Washington *Redskins* and the old Cleveland *Indians* also refer to the American Indians), Los Angeles *Dons* (more courtly than aggressive and referring also to the city's Spanish heritage), New York *Giants* (and the old New York *Titans*), New York *Jets* (who with the old Chicago *Rockets* and Providence *Steamrollers*, the 1928 NFL champions, take an aggressive name from technology), Oakland *Raiders*, San Diego *Chargers* (Los Angeles once had a *Chargers* too, the

Houston Oiler *running back Earl Campbell is stopped by* Pittsburgh Steeler *Ron Johnson in a 1980 game (yes, Johnson was "called" for* facemasking *and the Steelers penalized 15 yards).*

260

connotation now more of a charging player than of a warhorse), and Tampa Bay *Buccaneers* (also referring to the city's early history).

This mix of team names primarily from local chauvinism, animals, and aggressive masculine images seems to apply to all American sports teams, not just football. The animals are chosen from among the aggressive, tenacious, or swift—no major team has been named the *Lambs* or the *Canaries*, though there are *Cardinals* and *Orioles* (local chauvinism when from Baltimore) and *Wrens*. Baseball seems to have less aggressive team names than those sports with more physical contact, but this may merely be because it carries an older tradition of names from less violent times, as that of naming teams *Athletics* (from the Athletic Clubs that originally sponsored some teams) or from their uniform's color, especially the color of the uniform's socks (as the Boston *Red Sox* and Chicago *White Sox*).

Buffalo Bill *O. J. Simpson leaps for a short gain against the* Miami Dolphins *in a 1969 game.*

Fore!

Golf may be played on Sunday, not being a game, within view of the law, but being a form of moral effort.
"Why I Refuse to Play Golf," in *Other Fancies*, Canadian humorist, Stephen Butler Leacock, 1923.

Men have probably been hitting stones, nuts, and other small objects along the ground with a crooked stick since before the dawn of history, eventually developing many games from this simple pastime, including field hockey and golf. The ancient Romans played *paganica* (Latin *paganus*, countryman, hence "a game played by countrymen"), in which a ball stuffed with feathers was driven over the fields with a club. Roman legions may have introduced this game, or may have encountered similar games, as they moved through Europe. Thus there were such medieval games as *het kolven* in the Netherlands, *jeu de mail* in France, and *cammock/cambuc(a)/caman* in Britain (the British words originally referred to a bent stick, then, beginning in the 13th century, also meant a game played with a curved club and a small wooden ball).

Evolving from such early games, golf first appeared in Scotland, being so popular there by 1457 that King James II banned "golf" and "footballe" (see FOOTBALL) as interfering with the archery practice necessary for defense. This 1457 Scottish decree against *golf* contains the first written instance of the word, though it was later to be spelled in a variety of ways, especially as *goiff* and *goff* in the 16th and 17th centuries (*golf club*, as the club used to hit the ball, was first recorded in 1508, *golf ball* in 1545). The word *golf* is almost certainly from the Middle English Scottish dialect word *gowf*, meaning to strike or hit (a few sports historians think it comes from a Dutch word *kolf*, club, via that old Dutch game of *het kolven*, but the early Dutch never used *kolf* to mean either the game or the club used in it).

261

Despite the royal decree against golf, James IV of Scotland (1473–1513) was an avid player; his son, James V, played at East Lothian; James V's daughter, who was to become Mary Queen of Scots (1542-87), played at St. Andrews; and her son, who was James VI of Scotland and later James I of England (1566-1625), played at London's Blackheath common. Here, in 1608, an "Honourable Society of *Golfers*" (this is the first recorded use of *golfer*) formed the Royal Blackheath Club, just five years after James I began his reign as king of England. Thus, beginning in the late 15th century, golf was popular with four generations of the royal family of Scotland and came to England with them in the early 17th century.

Legend has it that Mary Queen of Scots was not only an avid player but was actually the first woman player, and that while being educated with the royal children of France she introduced the French word *cadet* (from Gascon *capdet*, little chief, from Latin *capit*, head) into England, this French word eventually becoming the English *caddy*. Whether she introduced it or not, the French word *cadet* was first recorded in English in 1610 (twenty-three years after her death), then meaning a younger son of a nobleman, who, not being first in line to inherit wealth or titles, was without prospects (since such younger sons often entered the military, a *cadet* meant a student at a military school in English by 1775). By 1630 in Scotland the English *caddy* often meant any young fop or ne'er-do-well and by 1730 had degenerated even further to mean a street youth serving as an errand boy or porter—this last meaning fully taking on its specialized golf use by 1857, to mean a youth who carries a player's clubs. Legend also has it that Mary was playing golf that day in 1567 when she received the news of the murder of her cousin and husband, Lord Darnley, and then calmly continued playing the round. Many historians now consider it quite likely that she knew of the murder beforehand, and perhaps even helped plan it; nevertheless, this story is probably the basis for many of golf's oldest jokes about those singleminded golfers who happily play despite bereavement or the inconvenience of funeral processions.

Though golf had been popular in Scotland since at least the mid 15th century, the first known society or association of golfers there, the Royal Burgess Golfing Society of Edinburgh, was not founded until 1735, with the Company of Gentlemen Golfers of Edinburgh following in 1744 (the first Ladies' Golf Club was formed at St. Andrews in 1872, though women had long played golf in Scotland). This Company of Gentlemen Golfers, who played the five holes of the Leith links, played for the first known *golf trophy* in 1745, the city of Edinburgh's *silver club*. Such a silver club then became a common trophy in early golf and the expression *to win the silver club* soon meant to win any golf tournament or game and is still occasionally heard to mean to make a spectacularly good shot. Each winner of Edinburgh's early silver club trophy became "Captain of Golf" during his reign as champion and his interpretation of the rules and decision on all disputes was final.

On May 14, 1754, twenty-two of Edinburgh's golfers founded its third golfing group, the Society of St. Andrews, now the Royal and Ancient Golf Club of St. Andrews, to compete for their own silver club. St. Andrews, which is 33 miles northeast of Edinburgh and originally had a twelve-hole course (see *hole* in the list of Scottish, English, and Canadian golfing terms below) based its silver-club tournament rules on those of the Company of Gentlemen Golfers, but the Royal and Ancient Golf Club of St. Andrews, now the oldest golf club in continuous existence, eventually became the most important club in the world, developing many of the rules and traditions of the game. In fact, the Royal and Ancient Golf Club of St. Andrews became so well known that it and its rules have long been referred to in golfing circles merely as the *Royal and Ancient* and even by the initials *R and A*.

Thus from the 1740s through the 19th century, Edinburgh's leading golfers, many of whom we would call professionals today, developed the game and served as its arbiters and teachers. In addition, many of them were highly skilled craftsmen who designed and made the clubs and balls used in the game. Like the Romans who had played *paganica* before them, the Scottish golfers had always used balls that were small handmade bags of softened bull's hide tightly packed with an enormous quantity of boiled goose feathers and hammered round before being painted. This ball was called a *feathery* throughout its history. Good ball makers,

In this photograph of some of Scotland's best 19th-century golfers, fourth from right at ground level is Old Tom Morris, the green keeper *and then patriarch of St. Andrews, who won the Prestwick Golf Club open championship in 1861, 1862, 1864, and 1867. Above him, in the dark jacket, on the top step, is his son, Young Tom Morris, who picked up where his father left off, winning the Prestwick championship in 1868, 1869, 1870, and 1872, there being no championship tournament in 1871, partially because the Morrises' domination had made it a dull affair.*

such as members of the Gourlay family of Leith in the mid 18th century or Allan Robertson in the mid 19th, could make fewer than a dozen of these handmade balls a day. However, even the best featheries were never perfectly round, and they cut easily, became soggy and flew apart in wet weather—and could be driven only about 150 yards. These feather balls demanded long, graceful clubs with thin, whippy shafts and thick grips and were best played with a long, full, graceful swing, the famous *St. Andrews swing*.

The earliest known professional golf-club maker was Edinburgh's William Mayne, who was listed as being both royal spearmaker and royal *golf-club maker* to James VI in 1603. He made three types of club, a *play club*, which was a driver with very little loft, a hand-forged *irone* (iron), and a *bonker* (we're not sure what this was, but it was probably for hitting a ball out of a bunker or natural sand trap; see *bunker* in the list below). By the mid 18th century, Scotland had a half-dozen famous clubmakers who refined *irons* and *woods*, giving its golfers a wider range of clubs and strokes, and by the first half of the 19th century there were already a dozen clubs in use in Scotland: two *drivers*, three *irons*, five *spoons*, and two *putters* (see the list of clubs below).

Then in 1845 the Reverend Robert A. Paterson made the first *gutta-percha* ball. Each of these was made from a single lump of brown, hand-rolled gutta-percha, the coagulated juice or latex of various Malaysian trees (from Malay *gĕtah*, gum + *pĕrcha*, the tree producing it). Incidentally, this gutta-percha substance was also used as a dental filling and to insulate early telegraph wires in the 19th century; the gum was sometimes simply called *gutta* by 1852 and a gutta-percha golf ball was itself simply called a *gutta* or *gutty* by 1881. Reverend Paterson's *Paterson patent balls* were rapidly replacing the feather balls by 1848, as they were easier to make, cheaper, held their shape, were virtually indestructible (even in wet weather), putted truer, and soon could be driven farther. The early gutta-percha ball dropped too quickly, not "sailing" like the old feathery had, but it was soon found that putting it into a mold to give its surface little knoblike *brambles* (early 1850s in this golf use) made the ball *carry* (1636 as used for a projectile) as far as 175 yards.

The gutta made golf a much more accessible and pleasant game, attracting many new players in Scotland and England. This harder ball did not demand the long, thin clubs of the feather ball and thus led to new clubs and new club designs: woods became shorter and less whippy and had squatter heads, sometimes with leather inserts. Soon Scottish craftsmen were making seven different woods and six different irons. This increase in the number of clubs led to the introduction of a new British golf item and golf term, the sailcloth *golf bag* (1870s) needed to carry all the clubs (before the 1870s a player or caddy simply carried the few necessary clubs under his arm). Most clubs were still handmade in Scotland and most were still used only in Scotland and England. The wooden heads were still cut and shaped out of a single block of wood, as they had always been, then leaded and sometimes stained; iron heads were still hand-forged; but shafts for both woods and irons were now almost always seasoned hickory from Tennessee and the clubmaker's real art was in making these shafts the right shape and length and with the right amount of flexibility. Grips were varnished strips of untannd leather wound over a cloth foundation and bound to the shaft with twine.

Up to now, the 1880s, golf had been a British, mainly a Scottish, game. Thus long before Americans took up golf, most of its basic terms existed and we borrowed them from Scottish players and immigrants or from Americans who had visited Scotland and learned the game there. As was true of most sports until the late 19th century, golf received little attention from writers, historians, newspapers, or magazines. Thus the earliest dates given for the Scottish and English golf terms below should be suspect—many of the terms had probably been used much earlier but just weren't recorded until, beginning in the 1870s, the rising middle-class and its increasing prosperity and free time led to a greater interest in and awareness of games and sports, including golf. This lack of awareness of golf before the late 19th century also means that many more of golf's words are probably of Scottish origin than we realize, because by the time many of the terms were first recorded they had already spread south to England, entering general British use. Besides *golf*, *caddy*, *feathery*, *gutta-percha*, and other terms discussed above, we have:

Golf Terms from Scotland, England, and Canada

address the ball, 1867. *Address* had been used to mean "to prepare oneself" since 1485 and "to set in order" since 1375.

approach (shot), 1879. The noun *approach* had meant both a passage and a route of drawing nearer since 1633; the verb *to approach* had meant to come nearer since 1305.

bogey. In 1890 Hugh Rotherham of the Coventry Golf Club in England devised a golf game, *Rotherham's game*, in which each hole was assigned a *score*, *ground score*, or *scratch*, all meaning the number of strokes a moderately good player would be expected to take and which each player tried to equal or better, after adding his or her individual handicap. Then in 1891, the song "The Bogey Man" appeared and became very popular in Britain (*bogey* or *bogy*, goblin, ghost, hobgoblin, is from the Middle English *bugge*, demon, which may have come from the Welsh *bwg*, ghost; the Scots had used *bogey* to mean goblin since around 1500). Golfers who were trying to beat the *score* on each hole or round felt as if they were playing against a mythical bogey who had made that score and, by 1892, said they were trying *to beat bogey* or at least *make bogey* (tie the expected score for a good golfer).

After the rubber golf ball was invented in America in 1898 (see below), the bogey that had been established for the old gutta-percha ball became too easy and the British lowered their bogies by about one stroke per hole and kept the term, but Americans began to use the word *par* instead, keeping the old British word *bogey* to mean the older, easier expected score of a good player, usually one stroke more than the new par. Thus around 1898 Americans began to use *bogey* to mean one over par.

Incidentally, the British who tried "to beat bogey" may have further personified the mythical player who had set that score by naming him *Colonel Bogey*, that name and expression coming to mean a typical plodding Englishman, probably originally a retired army officer, who could be depended upon to do his duty (make the good average score expected of him) though never being a brilliant player or person.

bunker, from the Scottish *bunker/bonkar*, bin, chest, box, has long been used to mean a bin or receptacle, as the coal bunkers on steamships. In Scotland it also meant the sandy binlike areas grazing sheep made by eating away the grass or rooting it out and making hollows for themselves as protection from the coastal winds. The early Scottish links all had such hollowed-out sandy bunkers, and by 1824, golfers were talking of man-made *bunkers*, it then being assumed that such hazards should be a normal part of all golf courses. A bunker was also called a *sand trap* by 1842.

club has meant a thick stick since the year 1200 and a stick or bat with a knobbed or curved end for use in games since 1450. The term *golf club* was first recorded in 1508. Our other word *club*, an association of people with similar interests, originated with friends and associates who, in 17th-century London, began to meet regularly in taverns to drink and talk while *clubbing* (that is, each paying for his own food and drink); by 1648 a *club* meant such a group and by the 1660s it meant any group who met to share interests, whether in a tavern or not.

divot has been a Scottish word for a slice of ground with grass growing on it since 1536, such pieces of turf then being cut out of the earth to roof cottages and top stone fences.

dogleg has been in common golf use since 1907. The adjective phrase *dog legged*, bent like a dog's leg, appeared in 1703, with the shorter form *dogleg* appearing in the 1880s (originally both forms were used only to refer to zigzag staircases; then they were finally generalized to refer to any sharp bend or turn).

drive has meant to propel forward since before the year 1000. To *drive* was first recorded as a golf term in 1801; the noun a *drive* was a common golf term by 1867.

dub, meaning to hit the ball poorly, a poorly executed shot, and an unskilled or inexperienced player, all appeared in the late 19th century. The word had meant any blow or thrust since the 16th century and had come to mean to poke or hit weakly by the 1830s.

duffer seems to be from the Scottish word *duffar*, dullard, stupid person, from the earlier *dowf*, dull, perhaps related to an earlier

Arnie's army *looking at the shot that cost Arnold Palmer the 1961 Masters championship at Augusta, Georgia. Needing only a par to beat Gary Player, Palmer blasted this shot from the sand trap completely across the 18th green and into the* gallery, *chipped back, then took two putts for a double bogey.*

Germanic word for *deaf*. In golf use it had spread south to England by the 1840s, with the Scots later shortening it into a verb, *to duff* (1897), to hit the ball badly, make a bad shot.

fairway. Fair has meant unobstructed since 1523. *Fairway* first meant an open or navigable channel for ships (1523), then took on its golf meaning around the 1840s (before that the entire fairway had often been called the *green;* see below).

follow-through was first recorded in golf use in 1897.

Fore! has been in common golf use since 1878, probably being a shortened form of *before*, which has meant "in front of" since the year 971. During the centuries of feather-ball golf, being hit by a golf ball was not so dangerous, which is probably why *Fore!* became a common golf term only after the harder gutta-percha ball came into wide use. The polite "Fore, please," as a request for spectators at a tournament to be quieter or move back, probably dates from the 1890s.

foursome, match foursome, 1867 for the four players of a match in which two players alternate in playing one ball against the other two.

gallery has meant the spectators at a golf match since 1891, but then usually referred to those fans who came to see and cheer on a specific player; thus each golfer might have his own "gallery" (the best known such "gallery" in America has been Arnold Palmer's cheering supporters, who were first called *Arnie's army* in the mid 1950s). *Gallery* itself originally meant a covered walkway, around 1500; then by 1630 came to mean a balcony, as in a church or theater. This last use then also came to mean the audience in the balcony by 1649, which is how golf's spectators came to be called the *gallery*, even though not seated in one.

green has meant grassy ground since 1300. From at least the late 17th century it was used in golf to mean both the entire course and that mowed part of it we now call the *fairway* (see above). This older, wider golf meaning of green gives golf *green keeper* (1705) and *green committee* (first recorded in 1896, at St. Andrews), a committee concerned with the entire course, not just the putting area. *Green* was then restricted in use by some players to mean only the putting surface around a hole by 1849, though other golfers still prefer the more precise 1847 term *putting green* so there will be no confusion over which "green" is meant, the entire grassy course, the fairway, or just the special area around the hole.

grip has meant a person's hold or grasp since the year 1000. Not until the 1880s, however, was there much concern about various golfing *grips* or ways to hold the club. The most commonly used modern grip, the *overlapping grip*, is generally attributed to Britain's great golfer Harry Vardon, who said he began using it in the 1890s (many golfers used to call it the *Vardon grip*), though some say Vardon's famous contemporary J. H. (John Henry) Taylor used it first. Golfers who found this Vardon's grip awkward or uncomfortable soon began to say they used the *interlocking grip*, which has been preferred by players with small hands or short fingers, such as Gene Sarazen and Jack Nicklaus.

handicap was first widely used in golf in the early 1890s by those who tried to beat *bogey* (see above). However, *handicap* has been in general sports use since the 1870s and in British racing use as

Harry Vardon demonstrating the Vardon grip, *as well as how to address the ball, 1920.*

267

early as 1754. The word is supposed to come from an old swapping game "hand in cap" or "hand i' cap" in which two people put objects or objects and money in a cap and a referee then put his hand in the cap to group or remove them until satisfied that each player had items or items and money of equal value. A golfer who plays at par has no handicap and is said to be a *scratch player* (1890s, for more on the sporting uses of *scratch* see BOXING, PRIZEFIGHTING, AND PUGILISM).

hazard, as a bunker or any stream, pond, inlet, or other body of water that a golfer must hit over or around, 1837. The word has meant peril or jeopardy since 1548, via Middle English and Old French *hasard*, an early form of the dice game craps, from Arabic *az-zahr*, the die. In golf a hazard formed by water has been called a *water hazard* since about the 1870s. Fearful amateurs often save their old or scuffed golf balls to use in attempting to hit across water hazards, such a ball being called a *water ball* in America since about 1925.

Any temporary body of water on a course, as a large puddle after a heavy rain, is not a true, designed hazard and is called *casual water* (a British golfing term of 1899).

hole has been a word in general use since before the year 1000, though it was 1808 before anyone pointed out that the Scots were using this old word in a rather specialized way in golf (a golf *hole* is now 4½ inches in diameter and at least 4 inches deep). *Hole* has also been used since 1891 in golf to mean the distance from the tee to the hole. *To hole a putt* and *to hole out* both date from the 1850s; the term *hole high*, even with the hole, neither short of nor beyond it but to the side, appeared in 1897.

Pin was first recorded as meaning the flagstick or pole in Scotland in 1901, while *cup* appeared in the 1930s (technically, the *cup* is not the hole itself but the metal or plastic liner inside it).

Many early golf courses had only three holes; the first Leith course had five holes, in 1744; and St. Andrews originally had twelve holes, in 1754, though the concept of playing eighteen holes as a round originated there ten years later (see *round* below). Any nine-hole course was still spoken of with pride in the 1890s and the *eighteen-hole course* was still a novelty in the first decade of the 20th century. Our American term *the 19th hole*, meaning a drink back in the bar after the game, dates from 1921.

honor, as the right or privilege of teeing off first, was first recorded as a golf term in 1896. However, *honor* (spelled *honour* in Britain) had meant the respect or courtesy due royalty or rank since 1388, and I would assume that the Scottish sovereigns who played the game in the 15th and 16th centuries were always accorded the "honour" of going first.

hook, to curve the ball widely to the left, was first recorded in golf use in 1857 (at that time *draw* had the same meaning, but now it means only the drift of the ball toward the left at the end of its flight, a common occurrence among right-handed players). The use of the words *hook* and *slice* (see below) only after the harder, faster gutta-percha ball replaced the feathery probably means that earlier golfers using the softer, lighter, less round feather-filled ball considered such wildly curving shots as a natural part of the game.

lie, as the situation of the ball as it rests on any part of the course, 1807.

links is a Scottish word for grass-covered sandhills or sandy ground rising from the sea (from Old English *hlinc/hlincas*, rising ground, slope). The first playing area to be called a *links* was at Leith, Scotland, in 1575. Technically, only such a sandy, rising, seaside area can be a true *golf links*, all others being a *golf course* (a term first used in the early 17th century).

loft has been used as a verb in golf since the 1840s and as a noun since the 1880s (meaning both the height a hit ball reaches and the backward slant or angle of a club face—a driver has almost no loft; a wedge has a great deal of loft). From the 1840s until the 1900s, *loft* and *loft shot* also meant any short, high shot, what we have called a *pitch* (when it has backspin) or a *chip shot* (without backspin) since.

match play, in which the score is kept by holes, each hole being won by the player who holes his ball in the fewest strokes, is the oldest form of golf, so old that golf meant this form to most amateur golfers until the 1880s, when *stroke play* (see *stroke* below) began to grow popular; thus there was no need for the term *match play* until then (it was first recorded in 1893). In match play a hole is said to be *halved* (golf use, 1857) when each side plays it in the same number of strokes. After one side has won more holes or is more holes *up* (golf use, 1894) than remain to be played, the remaining holes—which will have no effect on the outcome—are called *bye holes* (1887). When a side is ahead by as many holes as remain to be played, so that it still can be tied but can no longer lose, that side is said to be *dormie* (1887), with *dormie one* meaning one up with only one hole left to play, *dormie two* meaning two ahead with two holes left to play, etc. (*dormie*, sometimes spelled *dormy*, is from the French *dormir/dormi* from Latin *dormire*, to sleep, assumedly because the leading side or any spectators may at this point find the game boring and could go to sleep).

Mulligan is a late 1920s term for a second drive from the first tee, which some friendly amateurs grant each other if a first drive is a bad shot, discounting that first one. This second-chance drive is said to be named after a David Mulligan of St. Lambert Country Club in Montreal, Canada, who was granted this privilege because he always drove the car carrying his regular foursome to the club, driving over a very rough road and a bridge surfaced with crossties near the club entrance. According to this story, the extra shot accorded him was both in appreciation for his driving and to compensate for any shakiness he still might have from holding the steering wheel tightly during the bumpy drive.

open has meant open to all, with everyone being admitted, since before the year 1000. The first truly national golf championship was held in Scotland in 1860 as an annual tournament limited to well-known golfers, whom we would call professionals today. In 1865, however, this Scottish tournament was declared "open to all the world" and grew into the *British Open;* the first U.S. open championship tournaments were held in 1895, the first Canadian one in 1904. *Open* still has two connotations in golf, open to players from all countries and open to both professionals and amateurs. Since the mid 1970s we Americans have sometimes used the name *Pro-Am* to mean a golf or tennis tournament open to both *pro*fessionals and *am*ateurs, usually to invited professionals and celebrities who are amateur players and often with the tournament being sponsored by a charity, large corporation, etc.

penalty (stroke) first appeared as a golf term in 1902. The word *penalty* has generally been used in sports only since 1885.

pitch is a Scottish golfing term of 1901. For sixty years before that the more general term *loft* (see above) was used.

putt, both as a verb and as a noun, was first recorded in 1743. It is merely a Scottish variation and pronunciation of "put"; hence to putt the ball into the hole is to put it into the hole (though some sports historians believe *putt* is from a Dutch word meaning the hole itself).

rough, the long grass bordering the fairway, sometimes with bushes and trees, has been considered a golfing term since 1901, first appearing in Scotland.

round has meant a circular course or route since 1590, then also came to mean a continuous series of events, turns, etc., during the next century. As late as 1879 a *round* of golf was still considered a peculiarly Scottish term, from St. Andrews. The original 1754 St. Andrews course had twelve holes, ten of which were played twice, for a total of twenty-two holes for a round. Because the St. Andrews players were dissatisfied with two of the holes, however, in 1764 the course was reduced to ten holes, of which eight were played twice for a total of eighteen holes per round, this number then becoming the standard. The first nine holes at St. Andrews were then called the *left-hand*, *out*, or *front nine;* the second nine, played over much of the same course, became the *right-hand*, *in*, or *back nine.*

sclaff, to hit the ground behind the ball, was first recorded in 1893. It's an old Scottish word meaning both a slight blow or slap and to shuffle along.

short game is an 1858 term for approach shots and putts. This term then led to a term for strokes in which distance is more important than control, being called the *long game.*

Putt, *first recorded as a golf term in 1743, is merely a Scottish variant of the word* put. *Cary Middlecoff (above) crumples and grimaces as he misses a birdie putt in 1956; Jack Nicklaus (left) glares as he misses a birdie putt at the 1974 Pebble Beach par five 11th at Spyglass Hill; Jan Stephenson (right) squats to coax her ball for her fourth consecutive birdie in the final round of the LPGA tournament in Dallas, Texas, in 1981.*

slice first meant a slicing, downward stroke with the club (1886), then came to mean to curve the ball wildly to the right (1890). A ball that drifts to the right toward the end of its flight is now said to *fade* (probably 1930s). *Hook* (see above) is older than *slice*, probably because hooking the ball has always been much more common than slicing it, at least among right-handed players.

stance was first recorded as a golfing term in 1897, as the position of a golfer's feet in playing a stroke, then slowly also came to mean the position and posture of a player's entire body when addressing the ball.

stroke has been used as a term in various stick-and-ball games since 1400. *Stroke play*, in which scoring is by the total number of strokes players take to complete a round or tournament (rather than scoring the number of holes each side wins, as in *match play;* see above), seems to have emerged in the first half of the 18th century, the first tournament using *stroke play* being in 1759 in Scotland. Because match play was long considered the amateur game and stroke play mainly for professionals who played for trophies or medals, in America we have also called stroke play *medal play* (1890).

stymie was first recorded in 1857, both as a noun meaning a ball blocking another ball's path to the hole on the green and as a verb meaning to block a ball in this way. By 1902 the word had generalized in America to mean to thwart, block, or put one in a quandary. The word may very well come from the 14th-century Scottish expression *not to see a styme*, not to see at all, which by 1616 in Scotland led to the use of *stymie* to mean a person who does not see well. However, as with *putt, tee,* and *golf* itself, those who hold that modern golf had its beginnings in the Dutch *het kolven* believe that *stymie* comes from an old Dutch expression *stuit mij* (pronounced "stytmy") meaning "it stops."

swing has been used as a noun and verb in the sports sense since the 14th century.

tee first appeared as the word *teaz* in golf, in Scotland, in 1673, when it was already used both as a noun and a verb. By the 1720s it was already spelled *tee*, because people mistakenly thought *teaz* was the plural form and clipped off the final *s* sound to get *tee* as the singular (the same thing happened to *pease* in the 17th century, the word that had been both the singular and plural was mistaken as the plural form only and shortened to *pea* to get a more obvious singular form). Until the 1920s a teaz or tee was always just a pinch of sand or dirt on which the ball could be placed for the first stroke on each hole, but then a golf-loving New Jersey dentist, Dr. William Lowell, invented and marketed the modern peglike device we call a *tee* today. *Teaz* as used in golf came from an earlier Scottish *teaz/teise* meaning to poise or hold at the ready, as a spear before throwing (there is no evidence that *tee* came from a Dutch word for the mound on which the ball was placed, *tuitje*, pronounced "toytee," or from the Greek letter *tau*, the Greek T, which was once used as we use the letter X today, to mark the spot).

Though Scotland and England developed golf and contributed its basic terms, America did finally get into the game. As early as

1657, Dutch settlers played *het kolven* in America, at Fort Orange, New Netherlands (now Albany, New York), this game being played in fields, streets, and on frozen ponds and rivers and seeming to combine elements of both hockey and golf. A South Carolina golf club was formed by wealthy planters of English background in Charleston in 1786, just ten years after the American Revolution began, and another golf club was founded in Savannah, Georgia, in 1795, though both these seem to have been primarily social organizations sponsoring dinners and dances. In fact, there is no record that golf was ever actually played at these first two American golf clubs and they may have used the name *golf club* to mean what we now call a *country club* (an 1867 U.S. term) rather than a true golfing association. Both these clubs ceased to exist around the time of the War of 1812, when wealthy planters with British manners did not fare too well (the South Carolina Golf Club was rechartered by the Sea Pines Plantation on Hilton Head Island in 1969).

The first permanent golf club on the American continent was the Royal Montreal Golf Club, organized in 1873 as a governing body to lay down the rules for the game (both Montreal and Quebec had had three-hole courses since around 1860). The first permanent golf club in the United States was the Foxburg Golf Club, founded in 1887. It grew out of games played near the Foxburg, Pennsylvania, summer home of Joseph Mickle Fox of Philadelphia, who had learned the game and acquired his left-handed clubs while visiting Scotland in 1884. Also in the 1880s, two Scotsmen living in New York began to introduce golf to the United States. They were John Reid, from St. Andrews, and Robert Lockhard, who had shipped golf balls and clubs to the U.S. during his annual trips back to Scotland. Introducing the game to four or five friends and taking turns using the few clubs and precious golf balls they had, they began to play on a large lot near Reid's home in 1887, then in 1888 moved their game to a 6-hole, 30-acre Yonkers pasture. Though their neighbors considered the game a "ridiculous folly" and local preachers criticized them for playing it on Sunday, Reid and several of the other players formed their St. Andrews Golf Club of Yonkers in November, 1888. The club grew to ten or twelve members in 1889, the same year Mrs. Reid and another woman played in what the members called a *mixed foursome* (a man and a woman on each side). In 1889, too, a group of English immigrants formed the Middlesboro (Kentucky) Golf Club and opened a full 9-hole course. This is now the oldest permanent nine-hole course in the United States.

By the mid 1890s the game introduced here from Scotland and England had taken firm root. There were nine-hole courses in Lakewood, Montclair, New Brunswick, and Paterson, New Jersey; five or six in Westchester County; one in Greenwich, Connecticut; two on Long Island; one on Staten Island; and courses in Newport, Brookline (Massachusetts), and Chicago. The location of most courses in wealthy suburban areas was no accident, most Americans considering golf a pastime for wealthy businessmen and socialites.

The St. Andrews Golf Club of Yonkers played a major role in developing and popularizing golf in America, inviting other U.S. clubs to an amateur tournament in 1894 (the same year the Newport, Rhode Island, Golf Club held its first amateur championship) and calling for a "general meeting of golf clubs" which formed the *Amateur Golf Association of the United States* that same year. This association then held the first official U.S. open men's and women's amateur championships and the first men's U.S. open tournament in 1895. (Thirty-two men played in that first men's amateur championship, at the Newport Golf Club, and thirteen women played in the women's amateur, at the Meadow Brook Club on Long Island.) The Amateur Golf Association of the U.S. eventually became the *United States Golf Association (USGA)* of private and public golf clubs, the main controlling body that establishes and oversees golf rules and conducts tournaments in the United States. By 1899 there was the regional *Western Golf Association*, then covering all the country west of Buffalo, New York. The game that city toughs laughingly called *cow pasture pool* (1890s; city slickers were later to call the game of horseshoes *barnyard golf*, 1929) was spreading across the country.

Though the gutta-percha ball revolutionized golf, it had only a fifty-year history. In 1898 Coburn Haskell, a Cleveland, Ohio, golfer, and Bertram G. Work, of the B. F. Goodrich rubber company, invented the *rubber golf ball*, winding rubber thread under tension on a solid rubber core, though some early rubber balls kept a gutta-percha core and many had a gutta-percha covering. The lively and light Haskell rubber balls, briefly known as *bouncing billies*, gained complete acceptance when Walter J. Travis won the U.S. amateur championship with them in 1901. A. G. Spalding and Brothers began mass-producing its rubber *Spalding Wizard* in 1903. Soon a Chicago professional, Dave Foulis, put the mass-produced rubber ball, like the gutta-percha before it, in a mold to give it bramble markings, with England's William Taylor reversing the brambles into *dimples* in 1908, which gave the hard rubber ball a meshlike surface and made it carry even farther, up to 200 yards (*dimple* has meant a small hollow in the cheek since 1400 and any small surface depression since 1632; the modern golf ball has 360 dimples). Since mobile cores were found best for resilience and a heavy core best for distance, manufacturers experimented with different cores. The Kempshall Golf Ball Co. produced its *Kempshall water core* and others tried a core of "liquid lead" (which was good for golfers but poisonous to

273

curious children), zinc oxide (which eventually settled in one place and unbalanced the ball), and mixtures of glue, glycerin, and water, increasing the weight of the ball by about one-fifth of an ounce. Finally the USGA and the R and A agreed in 1921 that balls used in tournament play must weigh no more than 1.62 ounces and measure no less than 1.62 inches in diameter, but a slightly lighter and larger *balloon ball* became standard in the U.S. in 1930–31, with U.S. golfers liking the slightly larger ball so much that a ball of not more than 1.68 inches in diameter became our standard (making our golf balls slightly larger than the British ones). The modern rubber ball has about thirty yards of rubber thread wound around a core of water or castor oil and liquid silicone, and a good drive will go about 230 yards. The *molded ball* was introduced in 1960.

Beginning in the late 19th century, at about the same time the rubber golf ball was introduced, new technology and materials, factory production, and the increasing popularity of golf began to bring about a revolution in clubs, especially in the U.S. By 1894, A. G. Spalding and Brothers was making clubs in America; by the first years of the 20th century shoe-last manufacturers were mass-producing wooden club heads, and foundries were drop-forging iron ones; grips began to be made of composition material (and later of molded plastic); carbon steel and then stainless steel club-shafts were developed (*steel-shafted club*, 1910), with carbon steel replacing hickory shafts in the 1930s (Sam Snead became the first professional to make his reputation as a power golfer with the steel-shafted clubs), with aluminum and fiberglass being introduced later. Such developments and precision manufacturing led to an almost endless variety of mass-produced clubs: clubs with minor gradations of loft and head thickness and with a variety of shaft material and flexibility for every conceivable distance and lie. Soon there were more types of clubs than there were traditional names for them. The solution was obvious to American golf-club manufacturers: they began to number rather than name their clubs in the 1920s (numbers were also more specific and took up less space on a club's sole). Since mass-produced clubs of different types could be manufactured with the same "feel" and with precisely graduated flexibility, manufacturers also now began to sell *matched sets*. The number of individual clubs was carried to such a confusing extreme (there were even $5^{1}/_{2}$ and $7^{1}/_{2}$ irons) that in 1938 the USGA limited the number of clubs that could be used in a round to fourteen. Thus most regular players now carry three or four woods and nine or ten irons, though beginners can still get by with seven or eight clubs.

The various clubs, of course, are each designed for specific distances, lofts of the ball, and for hitting a ball from certain lies by differing in weight, shaft length, and suppleness, size and shape of the head, and the angle of the club face from the vertical. The lowest-numbered clubs have the least loft and send the ball longer distances over the flattest trajectory (about 230 yards for a Number 1 wood), while the clubs with the highest numbers loft the ball into the highest trajectory over the shortest distance (up to 90 yards for a Number 10 iron). The clubs are divided into *woods* (with wooden heads; *wood* has been in use since 1683 to mean something made of wood), which are generally used for distance, and *irons* (clubs with iron or metal heads, as James VI's *irone* of 1603), which are generally used for shorter approach shots, from bad lies, and to obtain more loft and accuracy. By the middle of the 19th century there were three woods, a *long, middle,* and *short wood* (there are now five woods) and six irons (there are now twelve). Since at least the 1930s the Number 1, 2, and 3 irons have been called *long irons*, the Number 4, 5, and 6 irons the *middle* or *medium irons*, and the Number 7 through 10 irons the *short irons*. Even though we began to call clubs by their standardized numbers in the 1920s, many of their older names are still known and used, and some modern numbered clubs have also been given familiar names.

Clubs

Number 1 wood. The *driver* (first recorded as a British golf term in 1867, though the use is probably at least sixty or seventy years older than that), so called because it is used *to drive* (1801) the ball far, as from the tee. It was originally called the *play club* (1603, in Scotland). During most of the 19th century a *grass driver* was also popular, having more loft than the usual driver.

Number 2 wood. The *brassie* (first recorded in 1888, in Scotland), often spelled *brassy/brassey* in the first decades of the 20th century, so called because the sole of the club was covered with a brass plate. Expert golfers now often omit this club from their fourteen-club set and carry an extra wedge, giving them both a pitching wedge and a sand wedge (see *Number 10 iron* below).

Number 3 and *Number 4* woods. These both developed out of the *spoon* (1814 golf use), which originally meant any wood with a slightly concave head (after various clubs with concave faces brought several golfers to sudden success and prominence, concavity was banned in 1931). Today it is only the *Number 3* wood that is called a *spoon*. The *Number 4 wood* has no modern name, though it had developed from the spoon into what was called a *baffy spoon* during the middle decades of the 19th century; then from about 1888 to 1914 was generally just called a *baffy* (probably from the Scottish *baff*, a blow, hit), though some 19th-century golfers also seemed to call this club a *wooden cleek* (see *Number 1 iron* below).

Number 5 wood, a comparatively recent club for players who play woods better than irons, using it to replace the Number 3 or 4 iron.

Number 1 iron. This is the *driving iron* (1890) which, earlier, had been called a *cleek* (1877, from Scottish *cleyke*, large hook). *Cleek* was first recorded as a golf term in the 1820s, when it seems to have been used to refer to any iron.

Number 2 iron. This seems to have developed in the U.S., where it was first called a *mid-iron* (1905).

Number 3, 4, 5, and 6 irons. These were originally known as the *mid-mashie, mashie iron, mashie,* and *spade mashie* respectively. *Mashie* (1881) was often spelled *mashy* in the first decades of the 20th century. Though no one is sure, *mashie* seems to come from the French *massue,* club (via Vulgar Latin *mattea* from Latin *matteola,* mallet, club), and be related to *mace,* perhaps reaching English through the French billiard term *coup masse* or the *masse/mace* billiard stroke made with a heavy macelike cue. The basic *mashie* (now the Number 5 iron) was introduced into golf as a type of squared-off niblick and, along with the Number 7 iron, has also been called the *mashie niblick* (1909).

Number 7, 8, and 9 irons. These have been known as the *mashie niblick,* the *pitching niblick* or *lofter,* and the *niblick,* respectively. The origin of *niblick* (1862) is unknown, the three usual guesses being that (1) it is related to the Dutch *kneppelig,* German *Kneppel,* club, (2) it is related to Germanic *nibbelen,* to peck, pick up in the beak, (3) it is based on our word *nibble*—the last two because the club is used to make short, nibblelike pitch shots, putting backspin on the ball to stop it from rolling once it hits the ground. The basic *niblick* was also called a *tracking iron* (also first recorded in 1862).

Number 10 iron. This is the *wedge,* of which there are now two types, the *pitching wedge* for the shortest pitch shots, and the *sand wedge,* for use in bunkers, this last replacing a club that had been called a *sand iron* (1857). After the *concave sand wedge* of the late 1920s had been banned, the modern *straight-faced sand wedge* was developed, and simply called the *sand wedge,* in the U.S. in the 1930s, with Gene Sarazen getting most credit for its development and introduction into golf, winning both the USGA and British Open with it in 1932, revolutionizing bunker play. This sand wedge is designed to slice through the sand under the ball to *pop* it out of the bunker. Before its use, many golfers, such as Bobby Jones, used a 9 iron to hit the layer of sand behind the ball, to *blast* (1927 in golf use) both sand and ball out of the bunker—a shot that was not very pleasant when the wind was blowing in the golfer's face.

Texas wedge does not refer to a wedge at all but is a late 1950s humorous American term for a putter when it can be used for a short approach shot over very flat, rather bare ground, as might be found in Texas.

putter, first recorded in 1743 for the club and in 1857 for a player who putts (see *putt* in the list of Scottish, English, and Canadian golf terms above). Technically, the putter should be the *Number 11 iron* (even though it may have an aluminum head), but the club is so important and such a personal friend or enemy to golfers that it has kept its name rather than becoming known by a number.

A. W. Knight of the General Electric Co. of Schenectady, New York, developed the aluminum-headed *Schenectady putter*

Eighteen-year-old "Bobby" (Robert Tyre) Jones shaking hands with Harry Vardon during the National Open in 1920. The greatest "amateur" golfer of modern times, Jones dominated golf from 1923 to 1930, winning the U.S. Amateur five times, the U.S. Open four times, the British Open three times, and the British Amateur once. He won all four of these tournaments in 1930, the feat then becoming known as the grand slam of golf (today, the professional grand slam of golf is the U.S. and British Open, the PGA championship, and the Masters). Jones retired from tournament play after his grand slam and concentrated on designing and building golf courses, including Augusta National, built in 1932, the Masters tournament beginning there in 1934.

Patty Berg, first president of the LPGA.

(with the shaft attached near the center) around 1900. The American golfer Walter Travis then won the 1904 British amateur with such a club, straddling the ball and putting from the new *croquet stance* (such putters were banned by the R and A in England in 1908 and this method of putting was banned by both the R and A and the USGA in 1968).

As golf grew in America during the 1890s, 1900s, and 1910s, it created a growing number of American professionals. Our *Professional Golfers Association (PGA)*, to promote golf and improve the standards and welfare of the professionals, was initiated by multimillionaire merchant Lewis Rodman Wanamaker, son of the founder of the Wanamaker department stores, at a luncheon in New York City's Taplow Club in 1916. It held its first tournament that same year. The *Women's Professional Golfers Association (WPGA)* was formed in 1946, with Patty Berg as its first president, and conducted its first annual U.S. Women's Open that same year. Then in 1949 a reorganization of this group resulted in the formation of the *Ladies' Professional Golfers Association (LPGA)*, again with Patty Berg as first president, and continued the Women's Open through 1952, after which the USGA assumed responsibility for this tournament so the LPGA could concentrate on conducting the women's professional tour.

As amateur and professional golf became increasingly important

(Left) Mrs. Glenna Collett Vare receiving the Cox trophy in 1928. She won the U.S. Woman's Amateur title six times between 1922 and 1935. (Middle) "Babe" (Mildred) Didrikson Zaharias in 1947. She was a track and field star in the 1932 Olympics, then began playing golf, dominating woman's golf from the late 1930s until the early 1950s, winning the U.S. Women's Open in 1948, 1950, and 1954. (Right) Nancy Lopez as the LPGA "rookie sensation" in 1978, here shown relaxing after winning her fifth consecutive tournament.

President Dwight D. Eisenhower keeping his eye on the ball in 1954.

to Americans, we began entering international competitions, now usually no longer for a silver club but for such trophies as:

the *Walker Cup*, for the winner of the biennial men's amateur team match between the U.S. and Great Britain, first held in 1922 (the cup was given by G. Herbert Walker, president of the USGA in 1920).

the *Ryder Cup*, for the winner of the biennial men's professional team match between the U.S. and Great Britain, officially begun in 1927 (the cup was given by the English golf patron Samuel Ryder).

the *Curtis Cup*, for the winner of the biennial women's amateur team match between the U.S. and Great Britain, officially begun in 1932 (the cup was donated by Harriet and Margaret Curtis, who between them had won four USGA Women's Amateur Championships between 1906 and 1912).

the *America's Cup*, for the winner of the biennial men's tournament between the U.S., Royal Canadian, and Mexican golf associations, begun in 1952 (the cup was donated by Jerome P. Bowes, president of the Western Golf Association in 1950–51, but refreshingly, rather than being named "the Bowes Cup," was named after the geographical location, North America, of this tournament).

the *Hopkins Cup*, for the winner of the annual tournament between U.S. and Canadian professional men's teams, begun in 1951 (the cup was donated by John Jay Hopkins).

the *Eisenhower Cup*, for the winner of the World's Amateur Golf Council men's tournament, organized by the USGA and Scotland's R and A in 1958 and holding its first tournament at St. Andrews that same year (Dwight D. Eisenhower, in his second term as President of the U.S. in 1958, had not only been Commander of the Allied Expeditionary Force in Western Europe in World War II and Supreme Commander of the Allied Forces occupying Europe after the war, but was also then the world's best-known golf enthusiast).

As golf became increasingly accessible and Americans had more leisure time after World War II, the game began to achieve its present dual status of a very popular game for the average person and a big-money sport for professionals *on the tour* (a term common by the late 1940s). Soon the average player didn't even have to walk after his ball down the fairway but could ride in a motorized *golf cart* (early 1950s).

As with other sports, golf's presence and vocabulary became part of millions of lives in the 1950s through television, when those who didn't play or attend tournaments began to watch professionals at work in front of network cameras, the first nationally important tournament to be televised being the 1947 U.S. Open from St. Louis. Between the 1950s and 1970s the number of spectators attending PGA tournaments tripled, with television adding millions of distant fans. By the early 1980s professionals played for PGA purses totaling over $10 million a year, and 18 million American amateurs played golf, spending $700 million each year on clubs, balls, bags, and other golf equipment. Thus, via television, golf has become a major spectator sport in America and, on our 12,000 private and public courses, a major outdoor game. Now, too, we Americans have added a few terms of our own to the vocabulary of golf, including:

Golf Terms from the United States

birdie, one stroke under par for a hole, 1921. It comes from our 1839 slang use of *bird* to mean anything excellent or first rate (a golf *birdie* is still sometimes called a *bird*); some claim the word was first used as a golf term at the Atlantic City Country Club shortly after World War I.

chip (shot) was first recorded in 1909, in the U.S., though it could be an older British use. A chip differs from a pitch in that it has no backspin, the ball thus rolling after it lands.

eagle, two strokes under par for a hole, was in U.S. golf use by 1922, an *eagle* being even bigger and better than a regular *birdie* or *bird* (see above). *Eagle*, of course, almost immediately led to the term *double eagle*, three under par for a hole. Many Americans probably first heard the term *double eagle* when Gene Sarazen made his famous one on the par five, 520-yard fifteenth hole of the 1935 Masters tournament (on a long drive followed by a 230-yard Number 4 wood "drive" into the cup), which tied him with Craig Wood for the lead, Sarazen then going on to win the playoff. Incidentally, this famous *double eagle* was made in the second *Masters*, the tournament and term both originating in 1934.

four ball, a 1904 U.S. term for a match game in which two partners each play a ball and count their better ball or score on each hole against that of the rival twosome (this game also later being called *best ball*).

gimmie, in a friendly amateur game, a putt, usually less than about 18 inches, so easy to make that it is conceded without the player having to "tap it in." *Gimmie* was first recorded as a slang pronunciation for "give it to me" in 1888 and has been used as an informal golf term for a "concession" since the early 1940s.

Nassau, a system of match play in which one point is awarded for winning the first nine holes, one point for the second nine, and a point for the full eighteen (or, often, a three-part bet of equal money on the first nine holes, the second nine, and the total). This scoring and betting system got its name from the Nassau Country Club at Glen Cove (in Nassau County), Long Island, around 1900, when, it is said, some match players devised it so they could not lose by embarrassingly high scores (in Nassau scoring the worst drubbing is 3 to 0). Incidentally, *Nassau* on Long Island, as well as *Nassau* in the Bahamas, comes from the original *Nassau*, the ancient Duchy, associated with the House of Orange, now part of Hesse in West Germany.

par, an 1898 U.S. golf term (from Latin *par*, equal, that which is equal). The original golfing term for this concept had been *bogey* (see *bogey* in the list of Scottish, English, and Canadian golf terms

Sam Snead at the 1948 U.S. Open. There were 5,000 spectators, and this was the second U.S. Open to be nationally televised.

above), which is still used to mean "par" in Britain. According to the USGA, *par* is the score an expert is expected to make on a hole or course, playing without errors or flukes in ordinary weather. Par always includes two putts on each green plus the stroke(s) needed to reach the green; thus it is computed on the distance from the tee to the hole:

men's par	women's par
par 3 up to 250 yards	up to 210 yards
par 4 251 to 470 yards	211 to 400 yards
par 5 471 yards and over	401 to 575 yards
par 6 (none in men's play)	576 yards and over

smilie, 1970s for a cut made by the club on the cover of a ball (since the ball is round the cut looks like a smile).

sudden death, a hole-by-hole playoff between players tied at the end of a tournament, the first player to win a hole being the winner (the others then suddenly being "dead" or losing players). The term has been in golf use since at least the 1950s, then came into football use (see FOOTBALL).

Ben Franklin and *Poor Richard's Almanack*

Poor Richard, 1733.

AN

Almanack

For the Year of Chrift

1733,

Being the Firft after LEAP YEAR:

And makes fince the Creation   Years
By the Account of the Eaftern *Greeks*   7241
By the Latin Church, when ☉ ent. ♈   6932
By the Computation of *W.W.*   5742
By the *Roman* Chronology   5682
By the *Jewifh* Rabbies   5494

Wherein is contained

The Lunations, Eclipfes, Judgment of the Weather, Spring Tides, Planets Motions & mutual Afpects, Sun and Moon's Rifing and Setting, Length of Days, Time of High Water, Fairs, Courts, and obfervable Days.
Fitted to the Latitude of Forty Degrees, and a Meridian of Five Hours Weft from *London*, but may without fenfible Error, ferve all the adjacent Places, even from *Newfoundland* to *South-Carolina*.

By *RICHARD SAUNDERS*, Philom.

PHILADELPHIA:
Printed and fold by *B. FRANKLIN*, at the New Printing-Office near the Market.

Franklin's first Poor Richard's Almanack.

Benjamin Franklin, 1706–90, said many things we still say today (as shown by the accompanying quotes), did many things we still talk about today, and created many things that called forth new American words. This practical, tinkering, mobile American who had so many interests was the son of a Boston soap and candle maker. Apprenticed to a brother, a printer, Benjamin ran away to Philadelphia at seventeen, owned his own printing shop at twenty-four, and retired at forty-six to devote himself to science, philosophy, and politics.

We still talk about his semiweekly *The Pennsylvania Gazette*, the most valuable newspaper property in the colonies between 1730 and 1748; his 1727 "Junto" discussion club, which evolved into *The American Philosophical Society* in 1743; and his *Poor Richard's Almanack* (Richard Saunders was Franklin's pen name, used as the author of the almanac's maxims) from 1733 to 1757, the most widely read and quoted almanac in the colonies at a time when the almanac served as a family guide, popular encyclopedia, and home entertainment center. Franklin helped establish the first American "hospital," the Philadelphia Hospital in 1751, and that same year was widely talked about for his famous "kite-key experiment" that demonstrated that lightning is electricity. But he is most frequently talked about for his place in American history: for representing the colonies in England (1757–62, 1766–75); for being a member of the Second Continental Congress and helping to draft the Declaration of Independence (1776); as our popular representative to France (1776–85); as one of our negotiators at the Treaty of Paris (1783, in which Britain recognized U.S. independence and our western border as the Mississippi); and as a member of the Constitutional Convention (1787).

In addition to what he said and did, Franklin created or popularized many new terms in America, including:

circulating library. He organized the first one in America in 1731 (it became the Philadelphia Library in 1742).

postmaster. Franklin was appointed postmaster of Philadelphia in 1737; the British appointed him *co-deputy postmaster general* of all the colonies (1753–74); and he was appointed the first postmaster general of the American Postal System by the Continental Congress in 1775.

academy. He founded the first one in America in 1749, the Academy and College of Philadelphia.

the Franklin stove, so called since 1787; when he first introduced it in 1744, it was called the *Pennsylvania-fireplace*.

armature, battery, condenser, positive, negative. Franklin began his experiments with electricity around 1746 and was an early user of these words (in fact he probably coined them, but the evidence is not clear).

lightning rod, so called since the late 1780s. Franklin invented it in 1749 and for the next 50 years it was often called the *Franklin rod*.

street-cleaning service. He initiated the first colonial one in Philadelphia in 1752, which he described as "a poor industrious man . . . keeping the pavement clean . . . for the sum of sixpence per month, to be paid by each house."

rocking chair. No one is sure who invented this American item; some say Franklin invented it around 1760.

bifocals. Franklin invented them in 1785 and for the next hundred years they were often called *Franklin spectacles* or *double spectacles*.

By the 1760s scientists also spoke of the *Franklin system* of electricity; a *Franklinist* was one who followed his precepts, and a *Franklinism* meant any pithy proverb. John Paul Jones's "I have not yet begun to fight" ship, the *Bonhomme Richard*, was named in Poor Richard's honor; from 1784 to 1788 there was even the unofficial state of Franklin, set up on land North Carolina ceded to Congress (now part of Tennessee); and there are still at least thirty-one cities and towns named *Franklin*. The first U.S. adhesive postage stamp (a 5-cent one) bore his likeness and was called a *Franklin* (the 10-cent stamp was a *Washington*). Of course people still read and talk about his autobiography (first published in a complete edition in 1868), and he also has his share of American plants named after him, as well as his share of savings banks (no, the innovative *Franklin* car was not named after him but after its designer, Herbert Franklin). Thus because of his importance in so many facets of American history, when we hear America talking we still hear many sayings Benjamin Franklin first said and talk about many things he did or created.

Gadget

was first used by British sailors in the mid 1850s (probably from the French *gachette*, small hook or catch, or the French dialect *gagée*, tool, contrivance) and had become part of American naval slang by 1906. To sailors, the word meant any small mechanical contrivance, but when the word spread to the general American population in the 1920s, it took on the additional meaning of anything whose name was unknown or temporarily forgotten. We've had a lot of synonyms for these uses, including:

> *what-d'ye-call-em*, 1639 (in England); *what-d'ye-call-it*, 1871; *what-is-it*, 1882; *whassit*, 1931.
>
> *thingumbob, thingamabob*, 1750; *thingamajig, thingumjig*, 1880s (the original such word was the English *thingum* of 1680).
>
> *gilguy*, like *gadget*, was a British sailors' term (of 1867) that became American naval slang (by 1880). It also had some general non-naval use but never became as popular as *gadget* (*gilguy* originally meant any rope or cable used in hoisting or fastening, especially a troublesome or ineffective guy or guy line).
>
> *dingbat*, 1861 (from the Dutch *ding*, thing); *dingus*, 1870s. By 1940 *dingbat* also meant a stupid person, especially a dumb girl or woman; this meaning was popularized in the 1970s TV situation comedy series *All in the Family*, whose lovable, bumbling, narrow-minded character Archie Bunker called his wife *dingbat*.
>
> *doodad*, 1908; *doodinkus*, 1911; *doohickey*, 1925 (also used to mean a pimple or skin blemish by 1930).
>
> *gimmick*, late 1920s. This was originally a carnival grifters' word for the secret device, also called a *gaff*, used to control a crooked

prize wheel. By 1930 *gimmick* was already being used to mean any plan or device to increase sales or appeal.

gismo, gizmo, 1941, probably originally a World War II Navy word.

Why were *gadget, gilguy,* and *gizmo* all originally sailors' terms? Simply because standard and makeshift lines, knots, riggings, and hoists called for them.

Gay Men and Lesbians

have suffered all the stigmas and verbal abuse of other minority groups. If one had listened to America throughout our history, however, one would have heard little about homosexuals and homosexuality, because the subject was often taboo and most of us were more than happy to ignore it. In fact, *homosexual* (from Greek *homo-,* same) and related words, or any references to homosexuals and homosexuality, were censored from most family newspapers, radio stations, and movies (by the Hays office, see THE MOVIES) until the mid 1940s. In private conversation, most men used the words with anger, loathing, or laughter until that time, then often with disgust or studied nonchalance—women and children often knew of the subject and its words only by derogatory winks and whispers.

When they felt it absolutely necessary, as in sermons and laws, the early colonists might use old English words, such as *sodomy* and *sodomite* (from the Bible's wicked Sodom), *buggery* and *bugger* (literally heresy, heretic, from Latin *Būlgaris,* Bulgarian, because Bulgaria adhered to the heretical Eastern Church), and later *pederast* (Greek *paiderastēs,* lover of boys). Many would not have known, or admitted knowing, what homosexuality was or that it existed, and, as these words show, those who did often associated it only with men. Nineteenth-century Americans also used the terms *uranism* (Greek *Ouranos,* heaven), *unnatural* acts, and *pervert,* all of which could be applied to both men and women, and first heard the word *lesbian* (Latin *Lesbius,* birthplace of the 6th-century B.C. homosexual poetess Sappho).

By the 1880s *effeminate* men, only some of whom were homosexuals, were an acceptable topic of conversation but were often spoken of merely as grown-up sissies or were laughed at or cast off with such terms as *goody-goody,* followed by *Willie boy* in 1896, *la(h)-de-da(h)* around 1900, *lizzie boy* and *lizzie* around 1905, and *Percy boy* in the 1930s. In the 1840s, however, the first informal derogatory terms for true homosexual men came into common use, to be followed by many other offensive terms during the next hundred years:

Miss Nancy, 1842; *Nancy, Mary,* 1870s; *Nance,* around 1910.

faggot, fag, 1905, probably from the 1830s British *fag,* a schoolboy

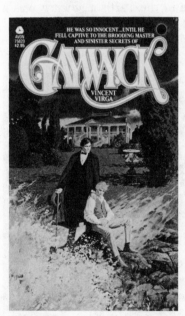

Attitudes, and language, change. In 1980 the successful Gaywyck *was the first gay gothic novel to be published, and the New York State Council on the Arts helped sponsor the 1981 Gay Film Festival.*

serving an older student as a lackey, perhaps reinforced by *fag* meaning a cigarette, considered effeminate by some men until World War I.

fairy, 1908. It had meant a pretty girl since the 1880s.

queer, 1920s. *Queer as a $3 bill* could refer both to male homosexuals and anything unusual or suspicious, *queer* having meant counterfeit money since at least the 1870s.

pansy, fruit, fruitcake, queen, 1930s. *Fruit* had meant any eccentric person since around 1910, with *fruitcake* coming to have the same meaning in the 1930s, giving us the 1935 *nutty as a fruitcake*, combining this use of *fruitcake* with the 1880s *nutty*, crazy, eccentric.

swish, 1941.

In the 1940s, after World War II, with a relaxing of taboos, plus a growing understanding of psychology and the varieties of sexuality (the first Kinsey report was published in 1948), there was a surge of words by, for, and about both male and female homosexuals and homosexuality (many of these terms known to insiders before the 1940s) including:

limp wrist, referring to male homosexuals and homosexuality.

homo (which had been in restricted use since 1925) and *lesbo* (in use since 1940).

gay. This had first been used with a special meaning in the colonies in 1680, the Pennsylvania Dutch and Quakers calling themselves *the plain people* and the more worldly Calvinists and Lutherans *the gay people*. In the Gay 90s, *to be gay* meant to take liberties, and a *gay woman* was a prostitute, while in the 1920s a *gay dog* was a woman chaser. Thus *gay* referred to flaunting oneself and had sexual connotations before it came to mean homosexual.

Members of the Gay Activists Alliance demonstrate for "homosexual rights" in Times Square in 1978.

A Gay Liberation Movement parade in Greenwich Village in 1974, encouraging not only gays but their parents to come out of the closet.

drag, a transvestite rather than a homosexual term, referring to dressing in the clothing of the opposite sex. It was an 1850s word for a petticoat worn by male actors playing female roles, because it created an unfamiliar "drag" when they walked.

camp, camp it up, to flaunt one's homosexuality (from Italian *campeggiare*, to stand out). *Camp* was also used in the 1960s to refer to ostentatious display, a self-conscious flaunting of oneself, or even vulgarity as a style, the use spread among intellectuals by Susan Sontag's 1964 article "Notes on Camp" in the *Partisan Review*.

dyke, bull dyke, an aggressive, masculine lesbian, perhaps from the 1850s *diked out*, dressed up, "all decked out" in fancy clothes.

butch, meaning the same as *dyke* and also often used as an adjective (this is primarily a heterosexual term for lesbians, seldom used by lesbians themselves). *Butch* had long been a nickname for the youngest son in a family, then came to mean a tough guy, then in the 1940s was a name for a man's very short haircut, which some lesbians adopted.

AC/DC, bisexual (from the two types of electric current).

straight, not homosexual.

In the 1950s the combination *drag queen* (literally a transvestite homosexual) often replaced *queen*, homosexuals began talking about *closet queens* (homosexuals who deny their sexuality or who pass as heterosexuals), and to *swing both ways* meant bisexual. All homosexual terms have become much more widely known since the late 1960s, when organizations such as the Gay Activists Alliance and the Gay Liberation Front were formed, creating what became popularly known as the *Gay Liberation Movement* (1969) or *Gay Lib* (1970), which encouraged homosexuals to *come out of the closet* and to work for equal rights for homosexuals. Such new attitudes were reinforced by the American Psychiatric Association's decision in 1973 to remove homosexuality from its diagnostic and statistical manual after finding that homosexuality per se was not an indication of mental illness. Indeed, no one has ever been able scientifically to find the ultimate sexual attraction between the sexes, much less what causes a preference for members of the same sex. Thus, the greater visibility and awareness of homosexuals and homosexuality has led to our increasing, but still uneasy, acceptance of *gay men* and *lesbians*, which are the terms by which they now prefer to be known.

Georgia Cracker

has nothing to do with the crackers we eat but is from *corncracker*, one who cracks or pulverizes corn to make hominy grits or cornmeal. Such corn cracking was a common chore in all the colonies, and *cracker* meant a braggart or liar by 1766. Corn remained a basic cereal in the South long after the North had turned to other grains—that's why *cracker* had come to mean a southern backwoodsman by 1836 and a poor white from Georgia or Florida by 1891 (Georgia has been called *the Cracker State* since soon after the Civil War). Thus the *cracker* in *Georgia cracker* literally means a person who still cracks corn because he is too countrified or too poor to buy cornmeal or to use wheat or other flour.

A poor, rural southern white has also been called a *red neck* (1830s, originally a farmer or other outdoor laborer with a sunburned neck) and *peckerwood* (1932, probably from reversing the elements in "woodpecker"). On the other hand, rich or poor, a loyal southerner, with all the charm and prejudice the term conveys, has been widely called a *good ole boy* since the mid-1960s, the term becoming popular then to refer to the Texas cronies of President Lyndon B. Johnson (*old boy* has been a familiar term of address in England since the 17th century and has been used in the U.S. since 1846, while *old* itself has been widely used with an affectionate connotation in referring to things and people in the U.S. since the 1870s, especially in the South).

> *. . . a good ole boy . . . is somebody that rides around in a pick-up truck . . . and drinks beer and puts 'em [the empty beer cans] in a litter bag. A redneck's one that rides around in a truck and drinks beer and throws 'em out the window.*
>
> Billy Carter, a Georgia gas-station owner, peanut grower, and the brother of President Jimmy Carter, quoted in *Redneck Power: The Wit and Wisdom of Billy Carter*, 1977.

Goose, To Goose, and Gooseberries

Although *goose* has meant a silly person in English since 1547, most of our "goose" terms originated in the 19th century. The hissing sound of a goose gave us the theatrical term *to goose* by the 1850s, meaning to hiss or boo a play or performer, and the play or performer so hissed was said *to get the bird* by 1859 and *to get the goose* by 1865. *To goose* someone took on a new

"Goose" (Richard Michael) Gossage, New York Yankee relief pitcher, 1981. Men known for their goosing or for reacting violently to it are sometimes nicknamed "Goose," as are some who look or waddle like a goose.

meaning in the early 1890s, when it came to mean to poke a finger between someone's buttocks, because it makes the victim hiss or cry out like a goose; because of this use, *a goose* meant any practical joke in the 1900s. We also use *goose* in many expressions, including:

> *a wild goose chase* was defined by Dr. Johnson in 1755 as "a pursuit of something as unlikely to be caught as a wild goose" but actually has nothing to do with that catching-a-goose image. A *wild goose chase* was originally the name of a follow-the-leader horseback riding game in Elizabethan England, so called from the way geese fly, following the leader in an evenly spaced line (thus Shakespeare's " . . . if thy wits run the wild-goose chase, I have done," *Romeo and Juliet*, Act II, Scene 4, means "my mind will not be able to follow or keep up with yours").
>
> *goose step*, 1806 in England, when it referred to a military exercise in which recruits stood on one leg while swinging the other back and forth, a form of calisthenics used in most European armies in the 19th century (called the *goose step* because it resembled the stiff-legged walk of a goose). By the end of the century *goose step* referred to a slow, straight-legged marching step and in the early 1930s became associated with the Nazi marching step. *Goose-stepper*, 1923, meaning a chauvinist or follower of militarism.
>
> *a gone goose*, a person sure to be ruined, defeated, etc., 1830.
>
> *goose grease, goose fat*, especially used humorously to refer to any very slippery grease, 1836.
>
> *to be sound* (or *right*) *as a goose*, have sound opinions, originally used in reference to those favoring slavery in Kansas in 1857, and used a little throughout the Civil War by pro-slavery people to mean "he agrees with us."
>
> *goose egg*, zero, 1850s, a common term in baseball by 1866 (from the shape of a goose egg, which resembles a zero).

Nazi troops goose-step *through the streets of Vienna in 1938.*

the goose hangs high, all is wonderful, 1866. Sometimes said to be from "the goose honks high," referring to the fact that geese fly higher in good weather, but there is no evidence that this is the origin of the term.

goose bumps, 1867; *goose pimples*, 1914 (because they resemble the bumpy skin of geese).

goosey, silly, dumb, 1871; sensitive to being "goosed," 1906.

to cook one's goose, to ruin, beat, or get revenge on someone, 1879.

to kill the goose that laid the golden egg (from the Aesop fable of the woman who did so), 1890s.

The *gooseberry* got its common name in England in the first half of the 16th century: like a great many plants named after animals, there is no apparent relation between the animal and the plant and we assume that, sometime in the distant past, people saw geese eating or living among gooseberries and hence gave the plant and berry the name. Gooseberries were eaten in 18th-century colonial America in the new English dish *gooseberry fool*, 1719, *fool* being a 16th-century word for clotted cream and by the 18th century for crushed or puréed fruit mixed or served with clotted or whipped cream, sometimes topped with macaroons. Gooseberries were also popular in the American *gooseberry tart*, 1785, as well as in *gooseberry pie* and *gooseberry jam*, until our taste for tart dishes began to wane around the end of the 19th century.

Great, Awful, and Wow!

When we listen to America or ask how one thing will *stack up against* (1903) another, we find that very few things are merely *so-so* (from the 1583 English expression *neither so nor so*, neither this nor that), *betwixt and between* (1830s), *six of one and a half-dozen of the other* (1843), a *toss-up* (1872), *fair to middlin'* (1896, especially in regard to someone's health), or *the same difference* (1945). Few things are *sort of* (1840s) or *pretty near* (1926): most things seem all good or all bad. We tend to think and speak in terms of *black and white* (an English expression since 1599, then also sometimes given as *white and black*, and originally meaning written down, in black ink on white paper, so there would be no mistake) rather than in shades of gray.

We express our likes and dislikes, our tastes and opinions, with a steady stream of words for "great" and "awful," with new, sometimes faddish, slang synonyms appearing every few years. In a sense, the words are true American superlatives; there is nothing better than "great" or worse than "awful" and very little in between. The words are often just catch words and counterwords, used quickly and without much thought, almost as automatic responses, because they are easily available current words and quickly show where we stand and who we are—what our group, mold, image, or stance is. The words are not always precise, which is one reason we like them so much and use them so frequently. We save time and effort in not seeking more precise words and also avoid arguments and fine distinctions we would rather not make. The blurred word, the blurred world, can be a happier, friendlier one. "Great" and its synonyms can mean such diverse things as: admirable or merely pleasing or liked; full of grandeur and beauty or merely attractive; delicious; exciting; superior or excellent or merely fairly good; large; successful; or merely unusual—mainly they mean that we accept and approve of something. "Awful" and its synonyms can mean: badly done; boring; disgusting or merely ugly; disliked or merely displeasing; flimsy or shabby; wicked or merely mischievous; completely worthless, inferior, or merely insignificant—mainly they mean that we do not find something acceptable or worthy of our approval. "Awful" things are those we *have no use for* (1887) or will *have no part of* (1935).

Though we may not want such words to be precise, we do want them to be forceful. They are often strong words and show our love of hyperbole and understatement (two ways to add force to what we say), as shown by such reverse terms as *evil, mean, nasty,* and *tough* to mean "great" or wonderful, as well as *no slouch of a . . .* and *not half bad*—and of *no great shakes, not so hot,* and *nothing to write home about* for "awful" (see the list below for more on these terms).

For "great" we have had:

A number 1. In 1834, Lloyds of London began classifying and rating ships for insurance purposes, *A number 1* being the highest rating in the highest category, hence the best or most insurable ships. By 1841 *A number 1* was in general use as meaning the best, sometimes shortened to *A 1* by 1844. Incidentally, *A 1* was melded with *OK* in early aerospace use as a verbal response that all electronic circuits were functioning properly and a spaceship was ready for launching, *A-OK* first being heard by the general public during the televised launching of Alan Shepard's space flight in 1961.

aces, the best, 1901; *ace*, 1931; both, of course, from poker, where aces beat lower cards. To *stand ace high* was an 1896 term, meaning to be highly esteemed.

amazing, amazingly good, 1805.

bang up, excellent, exceedingly well done, as "a bang-up job," 1830.

a bear, an outstanding person or thing, 1934. This stems from the 1840s use of *a bear* as meaning a person with emotions, appetites, strength, etc., as strong as a bear's, as in *as cross as a bear*, or *a bear for work*.

a beaut, a prime example, a wonderful specimen, 1848; *beautiful*, excellent, 1940s.

the berries, the best, wonderful, 1908.

a bird, something excellent, 1839.

boss, the best, first recorded as a slang word in the 1870s, but the Dutch, who gave us the noun *boss*, also used it as an adjective to mean "the best" in colonial America in the 17th century.

bound to shine, among the best, outstanding, 1865.

the cat's pajamas, remarkable, first used around 1920, when *pajamas* were still somewhat shockingly new (see BEDS, BUNKS, PAJAMAS, AND NIGHTY-NIGHT); the *cat* in this expression could come from *the Cheshire*, a 1770 English slang term meaning the correct or desired thing, because such a thing makes one grin like a Cheshire cat (there had also been an unrelated American expression *as high as a cat's back*, 1833, meaning exceedingly, very much). *The cat's pajamas* was given such variants as *the cat's meow*, 1922, and *the cat's whiskers*, 1923, and shortened to *the cat's*, 1928.

It was joined by such similar expressions and constructions as *the duck's quack*, 1920; *the bee's knees, the clam's garters, the elephant's wrist, the eel's ankles, the gnat's elbow*, all 1923; *the elephant's arches* and *the sardine's whiskers*, both 1924; *the bullfrog's beard, the cuckoo's chin, the leopard's stripes, the pig's wings, the snake's hips*, and *the tiger's spots*, all 1925. All these terms were considered satisfyingly modern, clever, and slangy by the flappers and sheiks of the 1920s, and there were many similar nonce terms combining animals, fish, and fowl with unlikely parts of the body and clothing (one could almost make a game of it, "the fish's feet," "the worm's fingers," etc.). However, such constructions may not have been new in the 1920s, as there was an 1844 expression, *to a gnat's heel*, meaning exactly right, down to the last detail, which gave us *to a gnat's bristle* in 1903 and *to a gnat's ear* in 1905.

the checker, the exact thing, 1850.

the cheese, the exact thing, an English use of 1818, then recorded in America by the 1830s (see AMERICAN CHEESE for the etymology of this term, which has nothing to do with edible cheese).

class, superior, in the best taste, 1850; *classy*, 1890.

a clinker, an outstanding person or thing, 1842; *clinking*, outstanding, first rate, 1850s (this use is from the sound of something that clinks, especially a gold coin known to be genuine from the way it clinks; our other *clinker*, meaning a failure or awful thing, comes from the furnace *clinker*, whose story is told at THROW ANOTHER LOG ON THE FIRE).

cool, real cool, crazy, far out, gone, real gone, nervous, weird, wild, in general use around 1950 (see HEP, HIP, HIPPIE, COOL, AND BEAT).

copacetic, satisfactory, 1933, with some later use meaning excellent. This word was popularized by the tap dancer Bill "Bojangles" Robinson, who used it heavily in his vaudeville and stage appearances in the 1920s and 30s. Though the origin of the word is not certain, it could come from the Creole French *coupersètique* (from Old French *couper*, to strike), able to be done or coped with.

a corker, something or someone remarkable, 1891; *corking*, also 1891.

cracking, excellent, 1830, from the 1790 *crack*, first rate, excellent.

creamy, excellent, 1880s.

cunning, charming, attractive, 1854 (from the 1355 English use meaning learned, which by 1423 also meant skillful and by 1671 also meant clever).

cute, charming, attractive, almost always with the connotation of being small, 1868 (from the original 1731 English meaning of "acute" or clever). *Cute as a bug's ear*, 1930; *cute as a bug in a rug*, 1942; *cute as a button*, 1946. *Cute* and *keen* were two of the most overused slang words of the late 1920s and the 1930s.

a daisy, the English used this as an adjective, meaning first rate, charming, since 1757 (from the flower, which has been called a *daisy* since around the year 1000, though then spelled *daegesēage*, day's eye); we have used it as a noun to mean a first-rate person or thing since 1835.

dandy appeared in English in 1780 as meaning a fop or swell, then by 1784 in England and 1787 in America it was also used as a noun meaning a wonderful person or thing and as an adjective

Daisy *has been used as an adjective meaning excellent since 1757 and as a noun referring to a first-rate person or thing since 1835.*

meaning fine, excellent. It seems to have entered general English from the 1690 Scottish *Jack-a-Dandy*, fop, which would mean that, in Scotland at least, *dandy* came earlier and is from *Dandy*, a Scottish form of the name Andrew, or "Andy," as we would say.

a darb, an expert, 1900; an excellent person or thing, 1915, from the 1691 English *dab*, expert (perhaps from a pronunciation of a*dept* or *dap*per).

devastating, beautiful, excellent, 1935.

a devil of a . . ., a remarkable example of a . . . , 1848.

a dilly, an outstanding person or thing, 1935, earlier used also as an adjective (probably from shortening *delightful* or from the 17th-century English *dilling*, darling).

a dinger, something excellent, 1809 (this word is thus older than *humdinger*, see below).

divine (via Middle French from Latin *divinus/divus*, divine, god) has meant of or pertaining to God in English since the 1370s, then came to mean excellent, great, a hundred years later. Both *divine* and *divinely* saw widespread flapper use in the 1920s.

a dream, something or someone beautiful, handsome, or wonderful, 1880s; *dreamy*, wonderful, 1940.

ducky, fine, wonderful, around 1830 (from its 1818 English slang use as a term of endearment; in Shakespeare's time *ducky* was slang for the female breast).

elegant has meant tasteful, dainty, refined, in English since 1475; we have used it to mean first rate, excellent, since the 1790s.

evil has meant morally depraved, wicked, in English since the year 971; we have used it in American slang to mean great, wonderful, since the 1960s, with the connotation of being so bad or unique as to be good, so attractive as to be sinful. In similar fashion we have used *bad* to mean extraordinary, great, since the late 1960s.

excellent meant superior, excelling, preeminent, when it entered English in 1382 but by 1604 was already being used more generally to mean very good, personally pleasing.

fabulous has meant of, or of the nature of, a fable in English since 1546 and astonishing, incredible, wonderful, since at least 1611. *Fab* (from *fab*ulous) and *gear* were the typical teenage slang words for wonderful during the 1960s, imported from English teenage use via popular music and musicians, as the Beatles.

famous has meant celebrated, much talked about, in English since 1385, and first rate, wonderful, since the 1790s.

fantastic has meant existing only in the imagination, unreal, in English since 1387, but has been common in informal American use to mean wonderful only since the late 1940s.

first-rate goes back to 1666 when the English classified warships into various ratings, the *first rate* being the largest and best equipped; by 1681 *first rate* was in general use and meant of the highest class, excellent. *First class* first appeared in English in 1807 as a specific class of passenger accommodation on ships, was applied to similar accommodations on trains and horse-drawn coaches by the 1830s, and had its general meaning of the best quality, excellent, by 1858. *Of the first order* appeared in England in 1794, then applied to diplomats and other dignitaries of the first rank. *Of the first water* is an old diamond-grading term; until the mid-

19th-century, diamonds were graded as *first water* (white stones of the highest quality), *second water*, and *third water* (of lower quality).

George has been an American slang word for excellent since around 1900, as in "Everything is George" or as an exclamation, *George!* The word was made popular again in the 1950s because it was the catch word of comedian Jerry Lester on the popular early 1950s TV show *Broadway Open House*.

grand (via Middle French from Latin *grandis*, large, great, full-grown) meant preeminent, of chief importance, when it entered English in the 15th century; during the first half of the 18th century it also came to mean magnificent, splendid, in a formal sense (the Alps or a royal pageant could be "grand"); then by 1815 *grand* was used in an informal way to mean wonderful, great, personally pleasing.

great was an Old English word, first recorded as meaning massive, thick, coarse, in the year 909; it meant distinguished, important, by 1297, excellent by 1709, and was used informally to mean wonderful, personally pleasing, by 1809. The interjection *great!* appeared in America in 1848. We have used the slang *the greatest* since the 1950s in an attempt to use the superlative to laud something better than "great," but *the greatest* is merely hyperbole and not a true superlative.

heavenly, wonderful, 1903.

heavy, important, then wonderful, early 1960s; *hefty*, a late 1960s variant.

a honey, something excellent or well liked, 1888; *a honey of a . . .* , 1942.

hot stuff, attractive, excellent, 1895; *hot*, attractive, 1910; *hot sketch*, a remarkable or amusing person, 1920; *hotsy-totsy*, fine, 1926; *hot shot*, an expert, 1943, as an adjective meaning exciting, ostentatious, late 1940s.

Huge! a slang interjection for "Great!," 1883.

a hummer, something or someone wonderful, 1888; *humdinger*, also 1888 (from *hummer* + *dinger*; see *dinger* above).

hunkum-bunkum, excellent, great, 1842; *hunky-dory*, fine, pleasing, 1866 (from *hunk*, a New York dialect word for home base, from Dutch *honk*, goal).

immense, splendid, 1841.

jake, satisfactory, 1900.

Jim Dandy, excellent, satisfactory, 1887; *Joe Dandy*, 1890; *Joe Darter*, 1851, an outstanding person or thing.

keen, wonderful, 1925; there was also an 1839 noun *keener*, meaning a superior person or thing, perhaps from *keen hand*, an English term for a shrewd person. *Keen* was an Old English word (spelled *cēne)* that first appeared in the 9th century and then meant brave and skilled in war; by the year 1000 it meant fierce and also wise, learned; by 1225 it meant sharp, having a fine edge (as a weapon); by 1350 it meant eager; by 1398 it meant intense, piercing, pungent; and by 1704 it meant shrewd, clever.

a killer-diller, a remarkable thing or person, 1939. *To kill* has been used as an adverbial phrase meaning to a great degree, since 1831, and as a verb meaning to overwhelm, since around 1910. *To slay* has meant to overwhelm, since 1927.

knobby, excellent, 1889; *with knobs on*, doubly, very much, around 1910 (also then used as a retort to an insult, meaning "the same to you in double measure").

a knockout, an excellent or very beautiful person or thing, 1894. *Knock* (someone) *cold*, overwhelm with excellence or beauty, 1896; *knock* (someone's) *eyes out*, 1901; *knock* (someone) *dead*, 1917; *knock* (someone) *for a loop*, 1918; *knock* (someone) *for a row*, 1920.

lovely, pleasing, excellent, 1869; *a love of a . . .* , 1866.

a lulu, a remarkable or wonderful person or thing, 1886; *a lulu of a . . .* , 1896 (from the girl's name).

magnifique, magnificent, wonderful, 1913 (from the French); *magnifico*, late 1940s (from the Italian).

marvelous has meant wonderful, astonishing, in English since the 14th century. We added the exclamation *Marvelous!* in 1920, the short *marvy* in 1934, and *marv* in the late 1930s.

mean, wonderful, early 1960s.

nasty, wonderful, 1834. Although the use of a "bad" word to mean "good" has been most obvious in black slang and cool use since the 1950s, *nasty* demonstrates that the concept of emphasis by opposites is much older.

nice originally meant simple-minded, foolish, when it entered English in 1290 (via Old French from Latin *nescius/nescire*, ignorant, not to know); by 1325 it meant wanton, loose-mannered; by 1430 extravagant or flaunting of dress; by 1483 elegant, fashionable; by 1551 fastidious, refined; and by 1769 delightful. *Nicely* meant attractive, agreeable by 1714 and satisfactorily, very well, by 1829. In America, we added *nice going* as an expression of approval by 1941.

nifty, splendid, 1865. When Bret Harte used the word in an 1869 piece he said it was short for mag*nifi*cent, which may or may not be true.

no slouch of a . . . , good at . . . , a good example of a . . . , 1796.

not half bad, quite good, very good, 1896, a prime example of understatement for emphasis.

numerous, excellent, a slang use of 1841.

the nuts, the best, wonderful, around 1910, probably based on *the berries* (see above), but *nuts* had meant a wonderful or agreeable thing in English dialect slang since 1589.

out of sight, remarkable, wonderful, an 1840s Bowery term, very popular in student slang of the 1950s.

a peach, something or someone wonderful, 1870 (a pretty girl has been called *a peach* since the Civil War, from having a "peaches and cream complexion"). *A peach of a . . .* , 1896; *peachy*, fine, wonderful, around 1900; *peacherine*, also around 1900; *peacherino*, 1905; *peachy keen*, humorous for "peachy," 1955.

a phenom, a phenomenal person or thing, 1896.

a pippin (from Old French *pepin*, seed, seedling apple) meant the seed of certain fruit in England by 1300, and gave us the shortened form *pip* for such a seed by 1598. By 1432 *pippin* also meant certain varieties of apple grown from seeds, some of which were considered excellent for eating, and by 1664 meant a remarkable person. In America we have also called a remarkable or good-looking person or thing a *pip* or *pipp*, 1912, and a *piperoo* or *pipperoo*, 1942.

a pisser, an extraordinary person or thing, figuratively so astonish-

I'm stuck on yer shape. It's outa sight. . . .
    Maggie: A Girl of the Streets, Stephen Crane, 1896.

ing or amazing as to make one piss in one's pants, first recorded in the 1940s (*piss* entered English as a verb, meaning to urinate, in 1290 and as a noun, meaning urine, in 1377; *pisser*, as one who urinates, was first recorded in 1386, all these from the Old French and going back to Vulgar Latin *pisiare*, to urinate, ultimately imitative of the sound).

prime, has meant the best in English since the 16th century; we have used it generally to mean great, wonderful, since 1910.

prize has meant a trophy, reward, in English since around 1300, something worth striving for since 1606, and something worthy of winning a prize, something excellent, since 1803. We have used the term *a prize package*, a wonderful person or thing, since 1941.

a pulse quickener, an exciting or extraordinary thing, 1920.

a rattler was a 1630 English term for a coach, especially a fast one, then by 1841 meant a remarkably good horse, as might draw such a coach; this use gave us our 1886 use of *rattler* as meaning any remarkable thing. *Rattling* has been English slang for wonderful, thoroughly, since 1690.

that rings the bell, that is satisfactory, just what was wanted, 1904 (probably from the circus and carnival use of testing one's strength by trying to drive a weight up a pole with a mallet, winning if the weight reaches the top and hits the bell there).

ripping, excellent, splendid, in English use since 1826. We added *riproarious*, 1830, and *riproaring*, 1834, as well as *ripsnorter*, 1840 (see *snorter*, below).

a roarer, something excellent, 1829.

a rouser, an extraordinary person, 1859.

royal has meant magnificent, splendid, since around 1386 in English, only twelve years after it first appeared in its basic meaning of connected with or of a sovereign or line of sovereigns. The adverb *royally*, magnificently, splendidly, also appeared in 1386.

a screamer, a person or thing of remarkable size, quality, etc., 1818; *screaming*, excellent, first rate, 1859 (*a scream* didn't mean a funny of ridiculous person or thing until 1906).

scrumptious, excellent, especially stylish, 1830 (perhaps from *sumptuous* or from an early word such as *scrimp*, meaning fastidious).

sensational, wonderful, great, 1870; *sensash*, early 1960s.

skookum, excellent, 1918 (from Chinook jargon of the Indian tribes of the Pacific Northwest, originally meaning large, powerful).

slick has meant easy or "smooth" in speech or manner since 1599 in England and by 1815 meant skillful, deft, in the U.S. We then also used it to mean excellent by 1835, though by the early 1840s it also meant attractive, well groomed. The use meaning "smooth," glib, crafty, has given us *slick as (bear's) grease*, 1811; *slick as oil*, 1834; *slick as goose grease*, 1836; and also the 1830 *slick as a whistle* and 1844 *slick as an Indian*. *Slicker* has meant a crafty or "smooth" person since 1880.

a smasher, something excellent, 1794.

smooth, superior, especially sophisticated, modern, well designed, etc., 1893.

a snorter, an extraordinary person or thing, 1824.

a sockdolager, something extraordinary, 1869, from its 1836 use as meaning a heavy or knockdown blow.

solid, great, from jive use of around 1935.

some, used emphatically to mean remarkable, 1843, as in "That's some pig!" *Some pumpkins*, an extraordinary person or thing, 1846.

something else, beyond compare, 1950s.

spiffy, excellent, 1872. Though this meant well dressed, stylish, in English from 1864, not until 1913 was this use dominant in the U.S.

a standout, an outstanding person or thing, 1941.

super, wonderful, 1925; *super-dooper*, early 1940s.

supreme, wonderful, 1934.

sweet, excellent, wonderful, 1880.

swell meant to become distended or large in English before the year 1000, then was used to mean pompous, arrogant (having a swelled head) by 1724, a fashionably dressed person by 1804, and came to mean first rate, excellent by 1811. In America we added *swellegant (swell + elegant)* in 1913.

take the shine off (something), surpass, excel, 1834; *takes the rag*, 1840, from the 1835 *take the rag off the bush*; *takes the cake*, after the 1860s, when cakewalk dance contests became popular, the winner taking or winning the cake.

terrific, wonderful, 1888 (originally it meant terrifying, 1667, and by 1809 meant severe, excessive).

too much, extraordinary, early 1960s.

topping, splendid, English use since 1822, to which we added *top notch*, the best, 1833, and *tops*, 1933. *(Out of the) top drawer*, 1909 English use; *top flight*, 1946. *Tip top*, first rate, excellent, 1851 (from the basic 1702 English meaning of the very top).

tough, wonderful, the connotation being that something has a unique existence and is strong or tough enough to stand alone, early 1970s.

a whale of a . . . , an extraordinary example of a . . . , 1890.

wonderful has meant full of wonder in English since 1100, but by that time, when it was first recorded, it already had taken on the additional meaning of fine, excellent.

a wow. Wow! has been an exclamation of surprise, admiration, disappointment, etc., in English since 1513. We have used *wow* as a noun, meaning a great success, something excellent, since 1910, with *wower* appearing in 1928 (*to wow*, gain great approval, overwhelm, was first recorded in 1927). Other exclamations of joy or approval, as for something great, include *Whoopee!* (1904), *Whee!* (1920), and *Yippee!* (1930).

yummy, excellent, delightful, 1940, especially said of, but not restricted to, food (from the 1940 *yum-yum*, from the exclamation over delicious food, *Yum!*).

For "awful" we have had such terms as:

appalling, very bad, 1890 (when it entered English in 1824 it meant dismaying, shocking).

atrocious, very bad, 1830s; *atrocity*, 1871 (when it entered English in 1669 it meant something extremely cruel or wicked).

awful originally meant causing dread, inspiring awe, when it entered English in the year 885; we were using it to mean very bad in America by at least the 1820s. We were also using *awful* as an adverb to mean "very" by 1818 and *awfully* to mean very, exceedingly, by 1830. Our phrase, *gosh awful*, "very awful," appeared in 1897.

beastly, disgusting, English use since 1603; we have used it to mean awful since 1880.

cheesy, worthless, bad, 1896 (see AMERICAN CHEESE for details).

crappy. *Crap* (from Middle English *crappe*, residue, rubbish) has long meant feces in English, then was used to mean nonsense, lies, in America by 1910 and something awful by the early 1940s, which is when *crappy* also became common, meaning awful. Old English *scītan*, to defecate, was spelled *shite* by the 14th century and *shit* by the 16th, then began to take on its various figurative uses in the 1870s. *Shitty*, meaning worthless or awful, was common slang use by the 1940s.

cruddy, disgusting, awful, early 1940s, originally popular World War II servicemen's use, from the mid 1920s use of *crud* to mean dried semen, as on the body or clothing after sexual intercourse, or a discharge from the penis as caused by a venereal disease. *The crud* also meant a venereal disease, especially syphilis, by the mid 1920s.

crummy, inferior, worthless, 1931.

dinky, *dinkey* (perhaps from Scandinavian *dink*, neat), unimpressive, insignificant, 1887.

disgusting has meant repulsive in English since 1754.

dreadful meant full of or inspiring dread or awe when it entered English in the early 13th century; it came to mean exceedingly bad by 1700.

foul has meant offensive, loathsome, in English since the year 800.

frightful meant full of fright or terror when first recorded in English in 1250, had taken on the meaning of causing fright by 1607, and by 1700 meant dreadful, loathsome, unpleasant. *Frightfully* meant terribly, very, by 1817, as in "I'm frightfully sorry."

(strictly) from hunger, very bad, awful, 1946.

ghastly has meant frightfully, horribly, with a deathlike look, in English since 1593. We have used it to mean awful, terrible, since 1860.

godforsaken, wretched, awful, 1885.

grotty, disgusting, awful, 1960s (from *grot*esque), probably introduced into the U.S. from English teenage use via popular music and musicians, such as the Beatles.

grungy, disgusting, awful, 1950s.

gummy, disgusting, awful, 1902 (the exclamations and intensifiers *Gummy!* and *By gummy!* appeared in 1848, the latter shortened to *By gum!* by 1873).

horrible meant causing horror, repulsive, frightful, when first recorded in English in 1303. By 1400 it was used as an intensifier to mean excessive and since 1908 has been used in America to mean awful, very bad.

the limit, *that's the limit*, the worst, around 1908.

loathsome has meant disgusting, sickening, since the 14th century.

lousy meant full of lice in English by 1377 and very bad, awful, by the mid 16th century.

mouldy had been a slang term for worthless, awful, in America since the 1890s. In cool jazz use of the early 1950s a *mouldy fig* was a "square," a person who didn't understand or appreciate modern jazz.

n.g., since 1839 a slang abbreviation for *no good*, and perhaps *no go* (meaning "completely unacceptable," 1835).

no great shakes, not very good, pretty bad, 1815.

not so hot, not very good, pretty bad, 1925.

not worth shucks (corn shucks), 1840. *Not worth a tinker's damn*, 1825 British use, because tinkers, itinerant menders of metal household utensils, were known for their cursing. There is a myth that *not worth a tinker's damn* refers to a small dam of material used to hold a tinker's solder in place; this was first suggested in 1877 but is baseless; in fact, a variant of the phrase is *not worth a tinker's curse. Not worth a damn*, 1918; *not worth a cuss*, 1851; *not worth a hill of beans*, 1860s, *not worth beans*, 1903; *not worth a Continental*, 1882; *not worth a jigger*, 1928; *not worth a hoot, not worth two hoots in hell*, 1942, all meaning worthless.

nothing to write home about, not very good, pretty bad, 1930.

the pits, the worst, the worst possible condition, late 1970s (the reference is to armpits).

putrid has meant in a state of decomposition, rotten, since 1598; we have used it to mean awful since 1833.

revolting has meant disgusting in English since 1806; we have used it to mean very bad, awful, since 1927.

scuzzy, disgusting, awful, 1979 (from di*sgust*ing).

seedy has meant shabby in English since 1739 (in allusion to a plant that has "gone to seed"); we have also used it to mean cheap, ugly, bad, since 1915.

sleazy has meant flimsy in English since the mid 17th century; we have also used it to mean bad since the 1940s.

stinking has meant smelling bad in English since the year 1000 and has been used since 1225 to convey general disgust and contempt. *To stink, stink on ice*, and *stink out loud* are American expressions of the 1930s; *to smell*, be awful, dates from 1938.

terrible has meant causing terror in English since 1430, has been used to mean very great, excessive, since 1596, and awful, very bad, since at least the mid 18th century.

Hairdos and Beauty Parlors

There was a little girl
Who had a little curl
Right in the middle of her forehead,
When she was good
She was very, very good,
But when she was bad,
She was horrid.
   "There Was a Little Girl," 1883,
   Henry Wadsworth Longfellow.

Although most women didn't have the time, inclination, or audacity to *friz* (an English word of the 1660s, from French *friser*, to curl) their hair until the early 1800s, enough early colonial women did so that Congregational clergyman Cotton Mather

(1663–1728) fulminated against the "apes of fancy, friziling and curlying their hair." Thus some American women were using and talking about *curling irons* as early as 1680, calling them *beaucatchers* in the 1750s and *curling tongs* in the early 1800s.

Cotton Mather also spoke out against the "tower and comet" hairstyles and wigs worn by wealthy women of his day, hairstyles so high that it was said some women could not ride in a coach without kneeling on the floor or sticking their heads out the window. This "tower and comet" hairstyle was more elegantly called a *fontange* (said by some to have been named after a French "court lady" but perhaps from the French *fontanelle*, little fountain), a towering fountain of frills and complex, lacy intertwinings shaped around a wire frame and considered the height of fashion from the 1690s to around 1710. After this elaborate style, women wore their hair, either their own or a wig, closer to the head, the wealthy and more style-conscious frequently powdering it white or gray from about 1760 to 1820 (men's and women's hair fashions often are in tandem, after 1740 style-conscious men were also wearing shorter, simpler wigs and began to powder their hair, see BEARDS, CLOSE SHAVES, AND BARBERSHOPS).

Those curling tongs finally became quite common in the early 1800s because *side curls* (an English term of 1780) reappeared and then the new, somewhat daring *spit curls* (1831) became the rage. However, now women were also recommending *curl papers* to each other, as well as the new *hairpins* (an English word of 1818). In the late 1840s and in the 1850s Elizabeth Barrett Browning's long side curls were much copied and often called *spaniel's curls* in America. Some side curls had also become thicker and had grown into the Victorian hairstyle of *pads* over the ears by the late 1830s, the pad or coil of hair next moving to the back of the head and being called a *Grecian knot* or *psyche knot*. For reasons of simple change or to match wartime austerity, the next major hairstyle was the *chignon* (Old French *chiagnon*, chain), which many, many women wore during the Civil War. In the 1860s, too, women first began using *hair washes* and *hair oils* and saying they were going to *shampoo* their hair rather than "wash" it (*shampoo* is from Hindi *chāmpo*, to press, massage, and from the 1760s to the 1860s had meant "massage" in English).

Immediately after the Civil War some women wore *kiss curls* (ringlets of curls on the cheeks or forehead), but *hair waving* became the fashion, the wave often appearing as a *fringe* of crimped or frizzed hair worn low on the forehead by the early 1880s, though the fringe could also be a straight one and reverted to a line of curls in the 1890s. Women who helped other women dress their hair in the home had been called *hair dressers* since 1770: now, in the 1870s, with the advent of new waving methods and the new *hair dryer*, some hairdressers began to work in the first *hairdressing*

Louisa May Alcott began wearing a chignon *while a nurse in a Union hospital during the Civil War.*

An early Miss America getting her hair done.

Our New Radium $5⁰⁰ Home Permanent Wave Bathing Beauty

salons. By 1900 these hairdressing salons were called *beauty shops* and by 1910 *beauty parlors*, though it wasn't until about 1920 that the hairdressers who worked in them were called *beauticians.* The complete beauty parlor also offered its customers a *manicure* (an 1880s English word, via French from Latin *manus*, hand + *cura*, care) and, later a *facial*, an American word of 1914. (As hairdressing, shampooing, and dyeing moved out of the home, they became part of big business and new terms were apt to come from manufacturers and their advertisements; see It Pays to Advertise).

By 1910 the *Marcel wave*, created by the French hairdresser Marcel Grateau in the 1870s, was what most women were asking for in beauty parlors, though they could give themselves one at home by using Marcel's 1897 invention the "Marcel waving iron," an elaboration on the curling iron that became a huge success because it created natural-looking undulating waves. In 1915, Charles Nestle, who had introduced his *Nestle wave* in his London beauty shop in 1905, was forced to leave England as an alien and moved to New York City, where he opened a beauty parlor that became an overnight sensation (Charles Nestle was originally Karl Ludwig Nessler from Bavaria, but German names weren't very popular in England and America before and during World War I). Inspired by the Marcel wave, which he had learned to give as an apprentice hairdresser in Paris, Nestle became famous giving his long-lasting "Scientific Everlasting Wave," better known as the *Nestle wave* and also called a *Nestle permanent*, an expensive, uncomfortable 6- to 12-hour process in which strands of hair were wound around rods, covered with a paste, inserted into asbestos tubes, and steamed in an iron-pipe contraption. Then in 1915, the same year he opened his New York shop, Nestle invented his quicker, cheaper, mass-produced Nestle wave, called simply the *permanent wave*. Thus, thanks to the French Marcel Grateau and the German Charles Nestle, in the 1920s American women were talking about *Marcels, waves, hot waves, cold waves* (steaming by chemical action and finally perfected around 1930), *permanents*, and *sets*. In the 1920s, too, Americans were using another new word, *hairdo*, the older French *coiffure* (literally "headdress," from Latin *cofea*, cap) now seeming too formal and stilted.

The permanent wave grew very popular with the vogue for short hair in the 1920s. Then the *bob* (from the verb *to bob*, to crop a horse's tail) swept the country. Introduced around 1915, the bob was also called *the shingle bob, the shingle*, and *the Eaton crop*. It was the typical hairdo or haircut of the flapper of the Roaring 20s, scandalously said to have been a style worn by French whores and first seen and approved by our World War I doughboys "over there." It was also popularized by ballroom dancer Irene Castle and made part of our literature in F. Scott Fitzgerald's 1920 short story "Bernice Bobs Her Hair," which was about the great decision of the times, to bob or not to bob.

In the next two decades, although short hairdos continued, such as the *shortcut* or *feathercut* (1939), some long hairstyles became popular again, such as the shoulder-length *pageboy bob* of the late 1930s and early 40s (so called from the wig worn by English pageboys) and the *shaggy sheepdog* and *over the eye* look of the 40s, popularized by such movie stars as Greta Garbo and Veronica Lake. The *upswept hairdo* of 1946 was a way to make long hair look short! In the early 1950s short, shaggy styles, somewhat similar to bobs, became popular again, called *poodle cuts*, *pixies*, and *Italian cuts* (featuring ringlets over the forehead), the last as originally seen in such widely talked-about postwar Italian realistic movies as *Shoe Shine* (1946) and *The Bicycle Thief* (1948). These were followed by the *bouffant* (French for puffed, full), in the mid 50s, achieved by *back combing*, called *teasing* in the 1960s, and the keeping of the hair in place with the new grooming aid called *hair spray*. Such longer styles created a vogue for wigs again, or for the new *wiglets*, especially the new *fall* (a word borrowed from dog fanciers, describing the hair falling over the face of a dog). Thus in the 60s, women could enjoy several hairdos at once, by changing wigs between morning and evening, or by combining a simple or short styling of their own hair with a fancier wig for special occasions.

All this hair was not always its natural color. A few colonial and pioneer women did dye their hair, usually with berries and herbs, elderberry juice for black, butternut extract for brown. It wasn't

This official 1961 White House photograph of Mrs. John F. Kennedy shows her modified bouffant hairstyle, which many American women imitated in the early 1960s.

until after the Civil War, however, that, along with the wave, golden hair became something of a fashion, at first among upper-class women. By the 1870s women were talking about *hair dyeing* for the first time. By the early 1920s the term *blonde chorus girl* was common, and in 1925 Anita Loos's novel *Gentlemen Prefer Blondes* appeared. In the late 1930s *peroxide blonde* (having used a peroxide bleaching agent) was a new term and by the 1950s the euphemisms *tint* and *rinse* were in use, for hair dye (until World War II, however, most hair dye was used to conceal white or gray hair, not to change from one color to another). Thus new terms for hair-styles and coloring come and go—though some never disappear completely. We still see and talk about *spit curls*, *chignons*, *permanents*, etc., as modern women wear a variety of styles or change their hairdos and color to suit the occasion, their mood, and their changing concepts of themselves.

Hash, Stew, Chowder, Chili, and Burgoo

entered our cooking language in that order. *Hash* was a brand new English word when the early colonists brought it to America (from Old French *hacher*, to chop, which is also the root of the word *hatchet*). It never did mean any specific dish but a mixture of any leftover meat heated with vegetables; thus Samuel Pepys's *Diary*, written between 1660 and 1669, uses *hash* as a synonym for the English *shepherd's pie*, which is now a meat and mashed-potato casserole. *Corned beef hash* is an American dish and term, dating from 1902; it was also called *corned Willie* by World War I.

By the 1860s in America *hash* was a slang word for any food or meal and we have called a cheap restaurant a *hash house* or *hashery*, and a person who worked in one a *hash slinger*, since the late 1860s (see Restaurants, Lunch Counters, Diners, and Drive-Ins). *I'll settle your hash*, do you in, take out my aggression on you, has been in use in America since 1809 and was joined by the variant *I'll fix your hash* by the 1900s. Military service stripes, one for each period of enlistment, were called *hash marks* by 1907. We have *hashed over*, talked over, things and been *hashing out* our differences since 1931, and *making a hash of things* since 1934.

Stew (from Old French *estuver*, to steam) meant a stove, a heated room, a hot bath, and a brothel in the 14th century. It didn't get around to meaning a dish of stewed meat and vegetables until the 18th century, about the same time we were beginning to use *stewed* to mean drunk (1737), with *stewed to the gills* appearing in 1925. American stews include:

Making Mulligan stew.

Mulligatawny, Mulligan stew. Mulligatawny was originally a meat and curry soup from India (from the Indian Tamil word *milagu-tannir*, pepper water). In 18th-century England and America it contained chicken, carrots, apples, green peppers, curry, cloves, and mace. *Mulligan stew*, made of meat, potatoes, and onions, may be named after some long-forgotten hunter or cook named Mulligan or it may just be a condensed form of *Mulligatawny*— both names have been used since 1900 in America to mean any hearty stew. The basic meat-and-potatoes *Irish stew* dates from 1834.

Slumgullion, slum. Slum originally meant slime (probably just a variant pronunciation of slime), especially the disagreeable soupy residue left after processing whale blubber or fish or the muddy residue from colonial iron mines. By 1847 *slum* was used to mean a rather watery stew of salt pork and potatoes and by the 1880s to mean beef stew or any rather unappetizing mess of food. *Slumgullion* was an 1849 California gold rush term, used by the 49ers to mean the slum of sluicing (*slum + gullion*, an English dialect word for mud); by 1902 it had come to mean a meat and vegetable slum or stew.

son of a bitch stew, called *son of a gun stew* in front of ladies, was a chuck-wagon specialty of the old West, made for cowboys from brains, kidneys, hearts, and other less desirable parts of slaughtered steer. However, it had to include gut (part of the stomach—tripe) leading to the expression "A son of a bitch might not have any brains and no heart, but if he ain't got guts he ain't a son of a bitch."

Chowder, like many other stews and soups, goes back to the fishermen's and hunters' custom of throwing an assorted catch into

a big pot for cooking. The word comes from the French *chaudière*, kettle, cauldron, and moved down the Atlantic Seaboard from Newfoundland and Nova Scotia, via the French Canadians, being given its American spelling *chowder* before the 1750s. *Clam chowder* was talked about by 1822 and called *New England clam chowder* or *Cape Cod chowder* by the 1880s to distinguish it from the pinkish, tomatoey *Rhode Island chowder* or *New York chowder*, which had recently appeared with the new popularity of tomatoes (see TO-MAYTO OR TOMAHTO?). We have called the type with tomatoes *Manhattan clam chowder* since the 1930s. Also, by 1848 *chowderhead* meant a stupid person, one whose brains were as mixed up as chowder, and in the 1870s *chowder* itself was used to mean any mixture or confusion.

Legend has it that Jesse James refused to rob the bank at McKinney, Texas, because his favorite *chili parlor* was in that town. Until the late 1820s *chili* (from the Aztec Nahuatl language) meant only the pepper itself. Then it came to mean various Mexican dishes and sauces using the pepper, especially a dish of the peppers stuffed with meat. Around 1828, Mexicans living in what is now Texas invented *carne con chili*, meat chunks with chili, which by the 1850s had evolved into a stew of meat, chili peppers, beans, and tomatoes, with the turned-around name *chili con carne*, or *chili* for short. This was sold from large kettles by Mexican street vendors in the main plaza of many towns in Texas and the Southwest, where both the pepper and the dish were often then called *chili Colorado* (after the Colorado River of Texas). A bowl of this chili contained meat chunks and diced chili pepper and was probably the spiciest, hottest dish Americans ever ate. At any rate, *chili* now meant three things: the pepper, various Mexican dishes and sauces (*chili sauce* is an 1882 term), and this Texas-Mexican stew. The completely tame bowl of chili that you and I know didn't emerge until 1902, at which time both ground beef and commercial *chili powder* were widely available. Incidentally, real chili lovers never, never add beans.

Burgoo and *Brunswick stew* were both basically squirrel stews served chiefly at political rallies, church suppers, cockfights, horse sales, etc., in the South. *Burgoo* (via Turkish *burgu*, porridge, from Arabic *burghul*, grain) was originally a sailor's porridge or mush. During the 1820s–50s it became a spicy American stew of game, usually squirrel (now often beef), corn, tomatoes, and onions, especially as made in the southern hill regions, where it has to be cooked in a copper kettle. It is still talked of fondly in rural Kentucky and Tennessee and has been traditionally served at Kentucky Derby parties. People from Virginia, Maryland, and North Carolina talk fondly of *Brunswick stew*, said to have first been created in 1828 by a member of the Virginia State Legislature, Dr. Creed "Uncle Jimmy" Haskins of Brunswick County,

Virginia, who wanted something special to serve at a political rally. It too was made of game, usually squirrel (now often chicken), corn, tomatoes, and onions. So what it boils down to is that southern hillbillies were eating *burgoo* and Maryland and Virginia aristocrats were eating *Brunswick stew*—both good names for what appears to have been substantially the same squirrel stew.

Hawaii: Aloha, Hula-Hula, and Ukulele

King Kalakaua in 1874.

In 1778 British sea captain James Cook discovered and named the *Sandwich Islands*, after the fourth Earl of Sandwich (see THE SANDWICH AND THE SANDWICH ISLANDS for more about him). Between 1782 and 1810 Kamehameha I unified the islands by conquest and by 1820 New England whaling ships were bringing in rum and syphilis, and New England Congregational missionaries were bringing in Christianity. However, most Americans weren't really aware of the islands until 1893, when poet-composer Queen Liliuokalani was deposed and the Sandwich Islands requested U.S. annexation. By then, Honolulu-born Sanford Dole (1844–1926), the son of American missionaries, had become the dominant political figure of the islands and leader of the movement that overthrew the monarchy. Because of Dole's intervention, President Cleveland withdrew the annexation treaty from the Senate and, in 1894, Dole became President of the Republic of Hawaii. Thus the Sandwich Islands became *Hawaii* to America and the rest of the world (from the native word *Hawaiki* or *Owykee*, "homeland").

During the Spanish-American War the U.S. suddenly realized the strategic importance of Hawaii and did annex it, in 1898, then made it a territory in 1900, with Dole as the territorial governor. Thus the question of annexation had Americans talking about Hawaii during the 1890s, and Hawaii, and the South Sea Islands in general, became something of a rage. Many Americans first talked about *Honolulu* (literally "sheltered bay") and the beach at *Waikiki* (literally "spouting water") and saw or sampled the dances, dress, and food of Hawaiians and other South Sea Islanders at the Chicago Columbia Exposition of 1893, which had a "Samoan Village," or during the St. Louis Fair of 1904, which had a "picturesque South Sea Islanders" exhibit. Soon Joe Kikuku brought Hawaiian music to the U.S.; Laurette Taylor gained fame in the popular melodrama about the South Seas, *The Bird of Paradise*, and Jeanne Eagels scored her great success playing the missionary-baiting South Seas tart Sadie Thompson in *Rain* (1922). Thus from the 1890s through the 1920s the word *Hawaii*

Sanford Dole.

gained its stereotyped image of palm trees, thatched huts, moonlit beaches, hula-hula dances, and ukuleles.

Hawaii retained this image until December 7, 1941, when the Japanese attacked Pearl Harbor, bringing the United States into World War II. During the war Americans talked about Hawaii and many other South Seas places as bases were supplied, battles raged, and thousands of Americans fought and died on once unknown Pacific islands. We debated whether or not Hawaii should become a state in the late 1950s; it became the 50th state in 1959, the only "overseas" state, 2,387 miles from San Francisco.

Statehood for Hawaii made Hawaiian part of the American language. It's a soft, vowel-filled Polynesian language containing only 12 letters, the five vowels plus seven consonants: *h, k, l, m, n, p,* and *w*. These combine into only 40 possible syllables (a syllable being a vowel or a consonant followed by a vowel) and the language has a vocabulary of only 20,000 words. Since the Hawaiians had not "discovered" writing, its written form was first developed by missionaries in 1822. Hawaiians also spoke some Beach-la-Mar, a trading patois of the western Pacific, and their speech also reflects the population's polyglot makeup: the population being about one-third Japanese (now rapidly decreasing); one-third Caucasian (increasingly from the American mainland); and the rest Hawaiian (now less than 2 percent of whom are pure-blooded), Filipino (some groups still speak Tagalog), Chinese (including a banker and merchant class), and blacks (imported long ago to work in the sugar cane fields). This mixture of peoples and languages, plus the fact that English has been taught in Hawaiian schools since 1853, has meant that Hawaiian has had but little effect on the American language in general. In fact, the only words most mainland Americans associate with Hawaii are:

aloha (Hawaiian for "love"), used both as a greeting and to mean "farewell." Hawaii is called *the Aloha State* (1959), and the song considered Hawaii's anthem is "Aloha 'Oe" ("Farewell to Thee"), its lyrics written by Queen Liliuokalani.

hula-hula (the Hawaiian word for this pantomime story dance is *hula*), first recorded in the U.S. in 1869. By 1910 it was sometimes simply called the *hula* or the *hula dance*.

lei, the Hawaiian word for garland of flowers, wreath.

luau, the Hawaiian word for feast.

mainland, Hawaiian use for the continental United States.

muumuu (Hawaiian for "cut off," because the garment has no yoke), the typical long, loose, beltless Hawaiian dress, modeled on the 19th-century *Mother Hubbard*, which was introduced to Hawaiian women by missionaries. This Hawaiian dress was something of a fad among American women in the 1950s.

pineapple is associated with Hawaii by most Americans, but pineapples are not native to Hawaii. The plant is called *pineapple* because the fruit resembles a giant pine cone; English got the word in the 14th century probably from the Dutch *pi jnappel*,

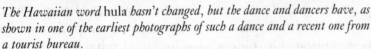
The Hawaiian word hula hasn't changed, but the dance and dancers have, as shown in one of the earliest photographs of such a dance and a recent one from a tourist bureau.

Lovely is Hawaii, the island of Keawe,
Adorned with brilliant lehua and fragrant maile of Panaeua.
Grand is Maui with Haleakala And 'tis for thee alone the beauteous rose will e'er be sacred.
Thus ends my song of fair Hawaiian isles,
And as we call to you, oh, let your answer echo far and near.
"Na Lei O Hawaii" ("Song of the Islands"), by Charles King, 1915.

pine cone; Columbus rediscovered the plant in the West Indies and called it *piña de Indes*, "Indian pine (cone)." Pineapples were first planted in Hawaii in 1790 and large-scale production began in the 1880s. The Hawaiian Pineapple Co. has dominated the Hawaiian pineapple industry; it was founded by James D. Dole, a cousin of Sanford Dole, in 1921, giving us such brand names as *Dole Pineapple Juice*. *Pineapple* came to mean a small bomb or hand grenade in the 1920s because of similarities in shape and exterior shell design.

poi is the Hawaiian word for a native dish made of cooked taro root pounded to a paste and then fermented.

ukulele is the Hawaiian word for "flea," and the instrument's name is usually said to come directly from it, from the jumping flealike movements of the player's fingers. However, *ukulele*, flea, was the Hawaiian nickname for British army officer Edward Purvis, a small, lively man who loved to play this new four-stringed instrument and, as a member of King Kalakaua's court, helped popularize it in Hawaii—thus the name of the instrument probably comes from Purvis's nickname. The instrument itself evolved from a small guitar Portuguese laborers brought to Hawaii in 1879, but less than thirty years later Americans already considered it the typical "native" Hawaiian instrument. All Americans heard the ukulele in 1915, playing the year's favorites "Song of the Islands" and "On the Beach of Waikiki." By the mid 1920s the easy-to-play ukulele was the college boy's favorite instrument, the most popular piece then being "Ukulele Baby."

307

It's Not the Heat—It's the Humidity,

a truism and semi-wisecrack, and the equally annoying summer's conversational gambit "Is it hot enough for you?" made many sweltering Americans want to throttle their friends and neighbors who uttered them—until the mid 1960s, when office and home air conditioning became the norm.

Of course, handheld *fans* had been used and talked about by even the earliest colonists (the word *fan* appeared in England around 1555) and large steam-driven or water-driven fans with rotating blades appeared in the 1830s in some factories, with smaller household *electric fans* being first seen and talked about in the late 1890s, but these never really seemed to cool enough and did nothing about the humidity. Large *window fans* and *attic fans* were in wide use and were common terms in the 1940s and 50s, but these also only moved the air, or brought the cooler nighttime air inside, rather than cooling the air itself.

The heat had actually been taken care of by Florida's Dr. John Gorrie's pioneering 1830s *air-cooling* system, which blew air over ice to ease his hospital's malaria and yellow-fever patients. To supply his invention, Dr. Gorrie also invented what he called an *icemaking machine*, about which a New York newspaper jeered, "A crank down in Florida thinks he can make ice as good as Almighty God," as indeed he could. The humidity was taken care of in 1902 when Willis H. Carrier designed a humidity-control unit as part of an *air-cooling system* for a Brooklyn, New York, printing plant (today the Carrier Corp. is the world's largest manufacturer of air conditioners).

By the late 1930s the magic words "It's cool inside" were waving from large white banners in front of movie houses, enticing soggy customers to seek respite if not entertainment, and introducing the masses to *air conditioning*, a term that had first been used in 1907 (in a paper discussing humidity control in textile mills and read by Stuart Cramer before the American Cotton Manufacturers Association). Today, over 50 million American homes and apartments have *central air conditioning*, over 50 million American cars have *car air conditioning*, and about 5.5 million *window units* are manufactured in America each year, these three terms all appearing in the mid 1940s.

Since the mid 1960s the popularity of air conditioning has changed the sound of the land, the hum of window units replacing the nighttime whirl of window and attic fans. Without air conditioning, such names as *Miami, St. Petersburg, Atlanta, Houston, Las Vegas, Phoenix, Tucson, Palm Springs*, and hundreds of other unbearably hot and/or humid cities and towns would seldom be talked about as a place to move, work, vacation, or retire. They would still be much smaller places, places where people would always be asking, "Is it hot enough for you?" or wetly remarking, "It's not the heat—it's the humidity."

Hep, Hip, Hippie, Cool, and Beat

Keep cool: it will be all one a hundred years hence.
"Montaigne," *Representative Men*, 1850,
Ralph Waldo Emerson

A bearded Allen Ginsberg in 1966 with his longtime friend, roommate, and fellow poet Peter Orlovsky in the East Village, *a late 1950s term for the Lower East Side section of New York City nearest to and east of Greenwich Village.*

Some Americans were using *hep* to mean informed, in the know, as early as 1903, *get hep* appeared in 1906; *hep to the jive*, hep to jive musicians' talk, was popular by 1925 (see *jive* at BITCHING, JIVING, AND DISHING the DIRT). In the early 1920s jazz and jive musicians began calling each other *cats*, meaning well-dressed sports, hep tomcats whose howling was their music. *Hep* and *cats* were then seemingly combined to form *hepcats*, the word everyone was using in 1935 to describe frenetic dancers to jive music. A few insiders, such as Cab Calloway, however, called these dancers not *hepcats* but *hepsters*.

By 1931 *hep* was occasionally being pronounced *hip*. This led to calling hep girls *hip chicks* and calling *hepsters* (jive dancers and fans) *hipsters* by the late 1930s. Thus it seems that the 1903 *hep* became the 1931 *hip* and that *hep + cat* became *hepcat* by 1935. It seems, and probably is, this way, but no one knows for sure, because no one knows where *hep* comes from: some say it comes from an all-knowing Chicago bartender of the 1890s, Joe Hep (which seems unlikely), some say that *hip* was the original word (coming from the opium smoker's *on the hip*, smoking opium, which was done lying on one's side or hip), and there is even the possibility that *hep*, *hip*, and *hepcat* come from the African Walof *hipicat* (meaning "one who has his eyes wide open").

In any event, by 1945 *hip* had completely replaced *hep* in informed circles, *cat* had come to mean any aware person (by the 1950s it was to mean any person at all), and *hipster* was beginning to mean a devotee of the new "progressive jazz" from the West Coast. This intellectual, nonemotional jazz was also called *cool jazz* as opposed to the *hot jazz* of the 1920s. It was *cool* or *beat*, both meaning unemotional, aloof. *Beat* had meant exhausted, physically and emotionally drained, since 1834; as a verb *to cool* has meant to calm down since the year 1000 and, as an adjective, cool has meant unemotional since the 1830s (Americans have used the expression *cool as a cucumber* since 1836).

During the decade of 1945–55 *hipster* drifted away from its jazz meaning and was applied to any hip or cool youth. The cool jazz fan's vocabulary also moved into general student use, so that some of the youthful catch terms most frequently heard were *cool*, *real cool*, *crazy*, *far out*, *gone*, *real gone*, *nervous*, *out of sight*, *wild*, and *weird*—all vaguely meaning great, wonderful, satisfying, exciting, or unique. Other terms of the era included *nowhere* and *Squaresville* for nonhip, "awful," or disliked things, and *Coolsville* for good ones.

By 1957 we began to talk about a new American type, *the Beat*, originally with a capital B. He seemed an extension of the *super cool* college-age youth, not only repelled by post–World War II, atomic-age American materialism but rejecting bourgeois career-oriented life and withdrawing from traditional American values, emotions, and rationalism to seek his own amoral identity. He was talked about as leading a spontaneous, roving life (on his motorcycle, by hitchhiking, or from an old car or vividly painted converted bus) while searching for nirvana with the aid of drugs, jazz, poetry, and casual sex. There were few such real *beats*, but the press found them sensational and the beats' own writers expressed themselves well and loudly, as in Allen Ginsberg's long 1955 poem *Howl* and Jack Kerouac's 1957 novel *On the Road*. *Beat* became a widely used word in 1957; the beats were said to be *beat*, to lead a *beat life*, and to make up *the Beat Generation*. Then on April 2, 1958, they were first called *beatniks*, in Herb Caen's popular "Bagdad-by-the-Bay" column in the *San Francisco Chronicle* (*beatnik* being one of the *-nik* words based on the suffix contained in the name of the first man-made space satellite, the Russian *Sputnik*, launched in October, 1957).

By 1957 the true beats had followers, a growing number of *hipsters* who, that year, were first called *hippies*, younger, watered-down versions of the beats, often merely *anti-establishment* kids from affluent middle-class homes who had become *dropouts* from school and society. The beats looked down on them as not being true free spirits but merely college kids living a unique but still consciously patterned life. Such a me-too beat was also called a *rebel without a cause*, a pop psychology term from Robert Lindner's 1954 book *The Fifty-Minute Hour* and the name of the popular 1955 James Dean movie (this modern romantic concept of "rebel" going back to Albert Camus's 1951 novel *The Rebel*).

By the early 1960s everyone was talking about these hippies, their attitudes and *life-styles*, their colorful dungarees, sandals, long hair, *granny glasses* and *love beads*, their temporary *crash pads* and their permanent *pads* (apartments, rooms, originally an opium addict's term for a couch or bed, then in jazz musician's use by 1915). Parents talked about ways to prevent their teenagers from becoming hippies, from running away to the hippies' mecca *the*

310

Some members of a hippie commune *at their Pennsylvania farmhouse in 1968.*

Don't trust anyone over thirty. Although often attributed to Jerry Rubin, this popular hip, beat, and radical student slogan of the 1960s and 70s was first uttered by Jack Weinberg in 1964, on the steps of Sproul Hall at the Berkeley campus of the University of California during a demonstration of the Free Speech Movement.

Haight, or, more popularly, *Hashbury*, the Haight-Ashbury section of San Francisco (*Hashbury* from blending the two street names, reinforced by the slang *hash* for hashish), or to New York's suddenly blossoming East Village, and of keeping them out of the hippies' rapidly spreading *drug culture*. If you liked hippies you called them *flower children* and approved of their *flower power* and *love is* slogans; if you hated them you called them *beatniks*, but it was the word *hippies* that most people used most often, and beats, hipsters, and hippies had all become one in the public mind. By the end of the 1960s a few hippies had settled in *hippie communes*, some had completely disappeared into the world of drugs, some had returned to a more traditional life—and all had been a major influence on our language, fashions, and attitudes of the 1960s and 70s.

Hoboes, Tramps, and Bums The American hobo

was created by the railroad and the Civil War. The war uprooted many men and enamored some of camp life; when it was over some "homeward bound" soldiers took to aimless wandering, soon *pounding the rails*, walking the railroad right-of-way, because there were no laws against trespass on it. From here it was but a jump to riding in boxcars, where at first the men were accepted as worthy war veterans. But as the years went by, pilferage and damage to

railroad property caused the railroads to order train crews to get rid of them and to hire special *bulls* (1893, from Spanish *bul*, policeman), also called *cinder bulls* and *yard bulls*, to keep them out. This drove the wanderers from the boxcars to more dangerous ways to *bum a ride* (1896), by *hopping a freight* (1880s) and:

> *riding the rods*, *riding the rails*, 1880s, riding the connecting or draw rods below the body of the cars, right above the wheels and track.
>
> *riding blind baggage*, 1887, riding in the doorframe or niche of the locked or doorless front end of the *blind baggage car* (1883), the baggage or mail car right behind the engine tender.
>
> *trucking it*, 1890s, riding or clinging to the trucking hardware between the wheels. This may have contributed to the jitterbug's use of *trucking* (also meaning to leave or move on in the 1930s) and to the 1960 students' phrase *keep on trucking*, keep moving, keep trying, keep "doing one's (own) thing" with good cheer.

By now the train-riding veterans had been joined *on the road* (1890s) by other chronic wanderers, by itinerant misfits and criminals, and by migratory harvest workers and lumberjacks. By 1905 there were 60,000 men on the road. We had many names for them:

> *bindle stiff*, 1890s, *bindle man*, 1900, and also *bundle stiff*, *blanket stiff*, *jungle stiff*, and *railroad stiff*. They were called *bindle stiffs* because they carried a *bindle* (1880, from "bundle"), a blanket roll or bedroll containing one's possessions (*bedroll* didn't enter the language until 1916). *Stiff* had meant a rough, clumsy person since 1876 and a hobo by 1893.
>
> *bum* (from German *Bummler*, loafer), a drunken loafer, 1855, first recorded in Oregon, which suggests it might first have been applied to leftover wanderers from the California gold rush or to migratory workers and lumberjacks; it came to mean a vagabond or tramp by 1862. *To bum*, to loaf, 1836; it meant to wander, beg, by 1857. The original wanderers had still also been called by the full term *bummer*, loafer, since 1855, which had come to mean a foraging soldier by 1861; this Civil War use was then applied to the wandering Civil War veterans and contributed greatly to our present use of *bum*. *Stew bum*, 1918 as a drunkard (*stew* had meant a drunkard since 1908).
>
> *hobo*, first recorded in Washington State in 1889, by which time *bo* was already in use as a short form for it. Like *bum*, *hobo* seems to have come from the Pacific Northwest, again suggesting its original use as a name for migratory harvest workers and lumberjacks. In fact, as late as 1913 the IWW (Industrial Workers of the World) defined *hobo* as a migratory worker, such men forming a large part of its membership. By 1910 many hoboes carried the little red IWW membership card to show trainmen and housewives they were honest workingmen worthy of a free ride or a backdoor handout; thus this card became known as a *pie card* (which had also meant a meal ticket since 1908).
>
> No one knows the etymology of *hobo*. Some theories are that it's (1) from the vagabonds' old sarcastic greeting to each other

Knights of the road *may sound romantic and chivalrous, but hoboes and their life usually are not.*

"Ho! Beau"; (2) from the Civil War's wandering veterans' pretense of being "*ho*meward *bound*"; (3) from those young wanderers who were runaway "hoe boys" from the farm.

knight of the road, 1880s, may sound romantic but is straight out of the underworld. By the 1560s in England *knight* was thieves' cant for any vagabond who lived by his wits and by 1698 a highwayman was called a *knight of the road*, *knight of the post*, or *knight of the blade*.

In the 1840s, the humorous or sarcastic use of *knight* became popular in America with such terms as *knight of the buskin*, an actor; *knight of the cleaver*, a butcher; *knight of the quill*, a reporter or writer; *knight of the rifle*, a hunter; *knight of the needle/shears/thimble*, a tailor; and *knight of the whip*, a horse-cab driver. After the Civil War we used *knight*, without intentional humor, in the names of many organizations that considered themselves highminded, as the benevolent *Knights of Pythias*, founded in 1864; the workingman's *Knights of Labor*, 1869; the white supremists' *Knights of the White Camelia*, 1870; the Catholic *Knights of Columbus*, 1882; and the reorganized post–World War I Ku Klux Klan's *Knights of the Invisible Empire* and *Knights of the Ku Klux Klan*.

tramp, British use since 1664, meaning one who tramps from place to place, as a wandering vagabond, beggar, or thief (*tramp* meant to tread heavily by the 14th century and to walk by the 16th).

vagabond and *vagrant* are both 15th-century English words for a homeless wanderer or itinerant beggar (from Latin *vagābundus/ vagus*, wandering), the difference in the forms of the two words being that *vagabond* entered English from Old French, *vagrant* from Norman French. *Vag*, American use, a vagabond, 1859.

yegg man (probably from German *jäger*, hunter), 1901 as a tramp or hobo (see SNEAK THIEVES, YEGGS, AND MUGGERS for later meanings of *yegg*).

Is there a real difference between a *hobo*, a *tramp*, and a *bum*? *Hobo* probably started out meaning a migratory worker; *tramp* originally meant a migratory nonworker; and *bum* meant a drunken nonmigratory nonworker. In fact, there's an old saying:

> The hobo works and wanders;
> the tramp dreams and wanders;
> the bum drinks and wanders—but not far enough.

In modern use, however, *hobo* has lost its meaning of migratory worker and stands for the aimless tramp, while the *tramp* and *bum* are often lumped together on a lower level.

Call them what you will, these hoboes, stiffs, bums, tramps, and knights of the road added many terms to our language and helped popularize and spread others. In cold weather they slept in rows on the floors of cheap rooming houses, which they called *flop houses* (1890s), *flops* (1913) or *flea bags* (1920s; originally a *flea bag* meant a bed or mattress, 1835). They were *moochers* (1857, from Middle English *mowche*, to lurk about) who knew the best places *to*

313

mooch (1890, to beg, sponge; in the 17th century it meant to loaf or play truant). They were *panhandlers* (1890, probably from the 1847 slang *pan*, meaning both money and bread, from Spanish *pan*, Latin *pānis*, bread) who preferred *to panhandle* (1900) on what they called the *main stem* (1890, main street or best street to beg) or *main drag* (1900; this had been called the *main road* since 1687, and we have called any major city street *Main Street* since 1855). They called law-abiding citizens *scissor bills* (1871; some say this is an older term for a knife and scissors grinder) and when things were really tough, as during the Depression, they begged more aggressively and *put the arm on* (1930s) the passers-by.

Besides begging money, hoboes had other ways to *rustle up a meal* (beg, scrounge, 1871); *to get a rustle on*, to move or work energetically, dates from 1892, both referring to the rustling sound of movement. One way was to ask for a *handout* (1832) of leftover scraps at backdoors (by 1941 *handout* also meant a prepared public relations statement given to the press). They also called a handout a *poke-out* (1899 for food handed out in a bag) or a *lump*, a *bald lump* if it were given to them unwrapped. Much of this food was literally *crummy* (1910; hence by 1931 the word meant inferior).

They carried some of the food back to their *hobo jungle* (1908), that waste area near the railroad yard, where they added it to their *Mulligan stew* (1900, see HASH, STEW, CHOWDER, CHILI, AND BURGOO), unless they were *jungle buzzards*, hoboes who scrounged from other hoboes but didn't contribute to the pot. These *jungles* (1910) were the hoboes' base, where they ate, swapped stories about stealing chickens from home coops and shirts from clotheslines, talked about which towns had the best begging or the meanest police, and made fun of the *gay cats* (1907), those inexperienced or dilettante hoboes who would soon return home.

In the jungle, too, the older hoboes broke in the *road kids* (1890), those runaway teenagers who had gone *over the hill* (1870, originally West Coast use, perhaps meaning over the Sierra Nevada, headed east) and *hit the road* (1894, to become a tramp). Most road

A small hobo jungle in St. Louis, 1936.

kids were soon under the "protection" of an older bo, a *prushun* (1880s, from "Prussian," because of the discipline he demanded, but by 1900 *prushun* meant the youth himself, at first humorously). The older bo taught the youth how to beg, scrounge, steal—and usually taught him pederasty. The bo who had a catamite road kid was called a *wolf* (about 1912), a *jocker* or *jock* (1915, a sodomite, coming from the British *jock*, to copulate, 1698, from *jock/jockum*, the penis, 1566). *Road kid* helped give us *roadie*, another term for hoboes by the 1930s, then used in the 1950s to mean a wandering hippie and in the late 60s to mean a close friend or companion. *Jocker* and *jock* contributed to our late 1960s use of *jock* meaning athlete, though its later emphasis is on masculine virility (see *jock* at FOOTBALL).

When the road kid had outgrown his subservient usefulness or was abandoned by his jocker he became a *punk kid* or *punk* (both terms around 1890), a worthless conniving young hobo seeking another protector or an easy way to prove himself. This use of *punk* may have come from: (1) the 1596 British use of *punk*, meaning harlot; (2) the 1880s southern schoolboy use of *punk*, meaning a box of goodies from home; (3) the earlier, 1880s, hobo use of *punk* meaning bread, because the stale bread given tramps as handouts often had the color and texture of punk, decayed wood used as tinder. The hobo use of *punk* for the ex-road kid gave us our general uses of *punk*, meaning "young thug" by 1896 and "inferior" by 1905. A punk kid was also called a *pipsqueak* (1900, an insignificant person, later to be used by World War I soldiers to name a small German shell) and *squirt* (which had meant a brainless fop since 1839). Not until the Depression years of the 1930s did some women and girls become hoboes, being called *road sisters.*

Hoboes also gave us the word *moniker* (1899, as a tramp's nickname or alias; originally the word was pronounced "monikey," but no one knows where it comes from). They used railroad water tanks as their bulletin boards, writing notes, directions, comments, and their monikers on them. In the 1890s and 1900s some famous monikers on the nation's water tanks included *Buffalo Smith, Burley Bo, Cinders Sam* (literally "Sam from Pittsburgh," that city being called *Cinders* and *The Burg* by hoboes), *Minnie Joe* (meaning "Joe from Minneapolis"), *Mississippi Red, Ohio Fatty, Syracuse Shine* (there were a good number of blacks on the road and *shine* meant a black by 1902, probably originally a hobo term), *Texas Slim,* and *Yellow Dick.* A few hoboes still ride the rails, of course, but today they ride in boxcars and freight cars, between cars, and on top of the cars, there being no more blind baggage cars or true rods to ride. But their era ended when the Depression did, when their wanderlust was satisfied by World War II, and when fast freights gave way to the highways' trucks.

Husking Bees, Quilting Bees, and Spelling Bees

The *bee*, a social gathering for work, games, or entertainment, was an American institution for two hundred years, a welcome get-together on the frontier and farm. This word *bee* was first used in New England and New York and may have originated merely as a reference to

This caricature of a quilting bee *amid other family activity appeared in* Gleason's Pictorial Drawing-Room Companion *in October 1854.*

This caricature of what happened when an ear of red corn was husked at a husking bee *appeared in* Ballou's Pictorial Drawing-Room Companion *in November 1857.*

This drawing of an apple bee *appeared in* Harper's Weekly *in November 1859. Most of the* bees *were indoors and considered activities of the fall social season.*

the combined labor of bees in a hive, but it may also have come from the Yorkshire dialect word *bean*, day, hence a special day for doing something.

Husking bees, first called *cornhusking bees*, were the earliest, first mentioned in 1693, and the youth who found he had husked an ear of red corn got to kiss the girl of his choice, a gleeful custom adapted from the Iroquois (the Indian prize was much more than a mere kiss and probably originally meant to be symbolic of fertility and seed planting). By the mid 1700s there were *spinning bees*, *road building bees*, and *church building bees;* indeed, almost any work could be and was made into a *bee* at times. *Quilting bees*, later also called *quilting frolics* and *quilting parties*, began to get very popular in the early 1800s and reached a peak of popularity in the 1830s and 40s. *Raising bees* were what men enjoyed in the 1830s, gatherings to raise a log cabin or a log barn in one day (the term *barn raising* became common after 1856).

Spelling bees were a New England invention, very popular after the Civil War. The *National Spelling Bee* was inaugurated by the *Louisville Courier-Journal* in 1925 and continued under the Scripps-Howard newspapers after 1939, with local newspapers sponsoring schoolchildren under the age of sixteen and the national championship being held in Washington, D.C.

The Ice Man, the Icebox, and the Refrigerator

> *A hundred Irish, with Yankee overseers, came from Cambridge every day to get out the ice [off Walden Pond]. They divided it into cakes. . . . They told me on a good day they could get out a thousand tons. . . . The sweltering inhabitants of Charleston and New Orleans, of Madras and Bombay and Calcutta, drink at my well. . . .*
> Henry David Thoreau, *Walden*, 1854.

Thus, somewhat poetically, was Thoreau aware of the ruthless, flamboyant Frederic Tudor of Boston, the "Ice King," who pioneered and monopolized the ice industry from 1806 into the 1850s. Tudor designed or commissioned the development of ice cutting, handling, shipping, and storage equipment, including the first horse-drawn *ice cutter* (a sleigh with toothed runners for cutting uniform blocks of ice from ponds) and efficient commercial ice houses to store the blocks for years. He had the rights to the ice from most New England *ice ponds* (1851, also called *ice quarries*, 1860, and *ice farms*, 1889), including Walden Pond, had a monop-

317

Ice wagon *was a common term by 1865.*

oly on ice houses in such places as Charleston and Havana, and shipped thousands of tons of his "Cambridge Fresh Pond Ice" yearly in his own fleet to the West Indies, South America, Europe, and eventually even to India and China. And, of course, he had a virtual monopoly on the *icebox* (1839)—which when it had been invented in 1803 had originally been called a *refrigerator!*

To increase business, Tudor convinced much of the world that *iced drinks,* including *iced water* (which had been spoken of as a curiosity since the 1790s), were healthy; that *ice cream* (1744 but known even to the earliest colonists) was a fancy dessert; and that *ice bags* and primitive *water coolers* were desirable in every household. He revolutionized our eating and drinking habits, improved our health, and made *ice, icebox, ice cold,* and scores of other *ice-*words part of the everyday language.

Until Tudor's major successes in the 1830s, people spoke proudly of storing food in *springhouses* (over cooling springs or brooks), in *ice cellars* (1771, a root cellar in which winter ice and snow were shoveled over perishables to preserve them into summer), or of hanging food in the coolness "down the well." Winter ice, cut with *ice saws,* was kept in double-timbered, stone-floored ice houses under straw and sawdust. By the late 1830s and early 1840s, when *to break the ice* came to mean to introduce something, Tudor was on his way to changing all that for the increasing numbers of city dwellers. Many were beginning to talk about their *iceboxes* or *ice chests* (1841) containing the uniform blocks of ice which had been stored in a commercial *ice house* or *ice depot,* sold to them by an *ice company* (1834, also called an *ice dealer* by 1851), and delivered in an *ice cart* (1842, called an *ice wagon* by 1865) by an *ice man* (1844).

From the late 1830s to the 1930s the icebox kept growing in size and popularity. Many families kept it in the kitchen, the pantry,

318

the basement, or on the porch (so the ice man could put in ice without knocking), emptied the *drip pan* from under the icebox daily, used *ice picks* (1860s) to chip off small pieces of ice, and kept ice water or small pieces of ice in an *ice pitcher* (1865) or *ice cooler* (1892). By the 1890s people spoke of preserving or postponing something by *keeping it on ice*, and the ice man making his deliveries carrying huge blocks of ice on his shoulder, and small boys snitching pieces of ice from his wagon to suck, were common sights. By 1895 *to cut no ice* meant to make no difference, have no importance; *to chop one's own ice* meant to be independent; and *on ice* meant sure, certain. By 1906 *ice* was a breezy word for diamonds. *Artificial ice* and the *ice plants* that made it were talked about since the first artificial ice plant had been built in New Orleans in 1865; people talked with awe and national pride of the first railroad *refrigerator car* (1868, an icebox on wheels); of restaurant *ice machines* or *ice makers* by 1875; and of the steaming, finger-burning carbon-dioxide *dry ice* when it became commercially available in 1925.

Now, what about that *refrigerator*? Back in 1803 a Maryland farmer, Thomas Moore, had invented an effective, double-walled boxlike affair for storing perishables with ice; he called it a *refrigerator* (Latin *re-*, thoroughly + *frigerare*, to cool). By the late 1830s most people had come to call it an *icebox* (usually spelled as two words or with a hyphen, *ice-box*, until the 1930s), but a few continued to call any superior icebox a *refrigerator*, which was sometimes shortened to *frigerator* by 1886. What we call a *refrigerator* today was first sold to the public as an *electric refrigerator* in 1916; its price was around $900. General Motors' *Frigidaire* refrigerator appeared in 1918 and eventually became so popular that many people erroneously used this trade name as the generic term, calling all electric or gas refrigerators "frigidaires" (the Electrolux Refrigerator Sales Company of Evansville, Indiana, introduced a

319

"household gas refrigerator" in 1926). Not until about 1930, however, were such refrigerators cheap and dependable enough for most families to talk about buying their first one, usually the familiar round-motor-on-the-top General Electric model introduced in 1927. When they did buy their first refrigerator, many families simply kept their old icebox in the basement or on the back porch, or moved it there, for storing extra beer and watermelon for summer parties.

Though an *icebox* now meant a box with a block of ice in it for storing food and beverages and a *refrigerator* meant the electric appliance, many people used the word *icebox* for the appliance—and were frequently reminded by their children to call it a *refrigerator*. The old term was so persistent that the new cookies made from dough chilled and stiffened in refrigerators were called not "refrigerator cookies" but *icebox cookies* (1929), and many older people still call an electric *refrigerator* an *icebox*. Thus the refrigerator came to most American homes in the 1930s, in fact if not in name, and most housewives were soon keeping an empty milk bottle of *ice water* in the new *box*, proudly serving drinks over *ice cubes* (1920), and making quick, homemade ice cream in the *ice cube trays*.

Idiots, Blockheads, and Dumb Doras

People seem to delight in calling other people stupid. It's the smart thing to do, a way of saying we ourselves are *nobody's fool* (1923), that though we may *play dumb* (1905) when it suits us, we are not about to *buy the rabbit* (be a dupe, 1825) or be a *chump* (1883 in English use; the word had previously meant a thick butt of wood) or *umpchay* (Pig Latin for *chump*, 1930s), *mark* (1896), *pigeon* (British use since the 1590s), *patsy* (1909, perhaps from the Italian *pazzo*, fool), or *sucker* (1831, one as innocent as a suckling).

Many terms for stupid people and stupidity are based on metaphors suggesting that the head or brain is like a thick, solid object or substance (*beetlebrained*, see below for its origin, *blockhead*, *bonehead*, *muttonhead*, etc.), that the brain is weak, deficient, numb, broken, or scrambled (*dimwit*, *imbecile*, *lamebrain*, *numskull*, *scatterbrain*, etc.), or that the person or brain resembles one of the dumber of the dumb animals (*ass*, *birdbrain*, *dodo*, *harebrained*, etc.). However, the most striking thing about our words for stupid people and stupidity is how old so many of them are, that so many that seem brash and contemporary are actually Old English words used for generations on both sides of the Atlantic. Our delight in calling other people stupid is an old English delight, and indeed an old German, French, Italian, Spanish—and worldwide—delight.

addlebrained, addlebrain, in English since 1591 and 1674 respectively. The English also have *addlepated,* 1601, and *addleheaded,* 1641 (basically, *addle* means to become spoiled or rotten, "an addled egg," from Old English *adela,* liquid filth, akin to German *Adel,* Swedish *adel,* liquid manure, urine).

ass has meant "jackass" in English since about the year 1000 and a stupid person since 1400. Until World War II it was assumed that *ass* for a stupid person referred to jackass, but since 1940 it has increasingly referred to *ass hole,* which by then was also a common term for a stupid person (this confusion doesn't exist in England, where *ass* refers to the animal, *arse* to the part of the body).

beefbrained, a 1627 English term; *beefhead,* a 1775 English term; *beefheaded,* an 1828 American term.

beetlebrained, a 1604 English term. Though our image is now often that of having a brain as small as the insect's, the original reference was to another *beetle,* from Old English *bētl,* hammer, a tool with a large, heavy wooden or stone head and a long handle affixed to its center, used for tamping down paving stones, crushing, ramming, and compressing earth, etc. Thus, a *beetlebrained* person had a head as solid as a *beetle.*

birdbrain, 1943; *birdbrained,* 1944, these appearing in America over a hundred years after the somewhat similar English *featherbrain, featherbrained.*

blockhead and *blockheaded* were both first recorded in England as meaning a stupid person, stupid, seventy-one years before the Pilgrims landed here. The original "blockheads" were wooden heads or blocks on which hats and wigs were made, displayed and stored, the term *blockhead* then used by 1549 to refer to a person whose head had no more intelligence than one of these wooden blocks.

boneheaded, 1903; *bonehead,* 1912.

booby was recorded as meaning a stupid person in English in 1599; *booby prize* is an American term of 1893; *boob,* meaning a stupid person, is an Americanism of 1909. Thus it took over three hundred years for *booby* to be shortened to *boob. Booby* is probably from the Spanish *bobo,* fool, from the Latin *balbus,* stammering, though it could be from the German *Bube,* fool. Incidentally, the *booby* bird, a species of gannet, has been so called since 1634 in English, because it was considered stupid and easy to catch. (*Boobie* or *boob* meaning breast has a completely different etymology; it is related to the German *Bübbi,* French *poupe,* meaning teat, and has been in the English language, originally spelled *bubby,* since at least 1686.)

cabbagehead has meant a stupid person since 1682, when it was first recorded in English.

calabash has meant "empty head" in the U.S. since 1848 (from the name of the gourd, which comes to us via French and Spanish *calabaza,* from the Arabic *qar 'ah yābisah,* dry gourd, empty gourd).

chowderhead, an 1819 British term, has nothing to do with fish chowder but was originally a Scottish dialect form based on the 1748 English term *cholterheaded/jolterheaded,* having a head or brain that has been "jolted."

chucklehead, 1731, and *chuckleheaded,* 1764, were originally English terms that had nothing to do with chuckling; they are based on the 17th-century noun *chuck*, lump, and its 18th-century adjective *chuckle*, like a lump, big and clumsy.

clown originally meant a rustic or bore in English, in 1563, then came to mean a jester (the clowns in Shakespeare's plays were still usually country bumpkins), a character in pantomime, etc. We've used *clown* to mean a stupid person in America only since 1942 but often with that 16th-century connotation of an unsophisticated, boorish person.

cluck, 1928, shortened from *dumb cluck* (see below).

crackbrain, 1570, and *crackbrained*, 1634; these English terms have implied both stupidity and insanity.

dead from the neck up, 1920s; *dead between the ears*, 1932.

dimwit, 1922; *dimwitted*, 1940; *dim bulb*, 1934, when it was recorded as meaning both a stupid person and a bore. Although the "dim bulb" image is from the light bulb, *dim* has meant dull in mental perception since 1729 in English.

dizzy, then a verb spelled *dysegan*, originally meant to be stupid, foolish when first recorded in Old English in the year 880 (it didn't come to mean to be giddy or to cause the senses to reel until the 16th century). In America we've used *dizzy* to mean scatterbrained since 1878, which is the same year *dizzy blonde* was first recorded.

dodo appeared in English in 1628, then meaning the large, clumsy, flightless bird (from Portuguese *doudo*, fool, silly); by 1874 in England it was used to mean a stupid or senile old man or one who, like the bird, would not change or learn new tricks, being used in politics to refer to a staunch conservative. In America we've used it to mean any dumb person since the 1890s. The alliterative and redundant *dumb dodo* dates from the 1930s.

donkey has meant "jackass" in English since 1785 and a foolish person or "ass" since 1840.

dope and *dopey* have meant a stupid person and stupid in America since 1896, originally referring to a person as stupefied or mentally confused as if drugged or under the influence of dope (from the Dutch word *doop*, dripping sauce).

doughhead, 1838; *doughheaded*, 1908.

dumb. The Old English word, first recorded around the year 1000, meant "mute," then came to mean stupid in the early 16th century, with *dummy* meaning a stupid person in English by 1736. Since the early 1820s, however, we have used *dumb* to mean stupid much more frequently than the British, our American use perhaps coming from or being reinforced by the German *dumm*, Dutch *dom*. *Dumb ox* is said to be a translation of the sobriquet given to St. Thomas Aquinas around 1250 when he was a young monk at the Cologne, Germany, Dominican monastery—because he was so profound others didn't understand what he said. In America we have also called a stupid person a *dumbkopf*, 1809 (literally "dumb head," from German *Dummkopf* or the Dutch *domkop*); *dumbhead*, 1820s (the translation of *dumbkopf*); *dumbbell*, 1850s; *dumb Dora*, 1941 (a scatterbrained young woman, originally the name of a "Tad" Dorgan cartoon character); *dumb Isaac*, 1916 (a dull-witted man); *dumb cluck*, 1920s; *dumb bunny*, 1922, a somewhat affectionate term, but combining "dumb" with the connotation of *harebrained* (see below); and *dumb-dumb*, popularized by insult comedian Don Rickles in the late 1960s, probably suggested by *dumdum*, 1897, a bullet with the soft core exposed through the metal casing at the point, to expand on impact (named after Dumdum, the British military station and arsenal where such bullets were first tested, in the town of Dumdum, India, near Calcutta).

dunderhead, 1625; *dunderheaded*, 1825 (these English words are probably based on the Dutch *donderbol*, cannonball, literally "thunder ball," but since *-bol*, ball, is also Dutch slang for head their *donderbol* was also used to mean "cannonball head").

empty-headed, a 1650 English term, though the English had spoken of heads as being "empty" of brains or knowledge since 1611.

fathead, an 1842 English term, which we in America converted into the adjective *fatheaded* by 1889.

featherbrained, 1820; *featherbrain*, 1839, both originally English terms.

feebleminded, an English term of 1534, with the literal sense of being mentally deficient, though *feeble* itself had originally meant lacking in mental or moral strength since its appearance in Old English around the year 1200.

flathead first appeared in English in 1537 as a somewhat scientific description of certain American Indian tribes. We have used it since 1884 to refer to a stupid person.

flibbertigibbet was originally *flybbergyb/flibbergib* when it first appeared in England in 1549, then meaning only a gossipy woman. It has had its modern form and spelling since the 1890s. The word is intended as an imitation of the flighty chattering sound of a scatterbrained gossip.

fool entered English as *fol* in 1275, though it was for centuries used more in compassion than contempt. It came to English via Old French from Latin, *follis*, bellows, which was also Late Latin slang for an empty-headed person or one who talked foolishly (our 1890s *windbag*, a boring, talkative person, has exactly the same image as this Latin *follis*).

gazook, 1928, as any fellow, especially a clumsy, somewhat dull-witted one, probably from the 1866 *galoot*, with the same meaning (English sailors had used *galoot* as a contemptuous word to refer to a dumb, awkward, or inexperienced soldier since 1812).

goof is probably a form of the 1570 English dialect word *goff* (akin to French *goffe*), meaning dolt, simpleton. We have used it widely in America since 1917, adding *goofy* around 1920, and *goofer* and *goofus*, both meaning a silly person, around 1925. To *goof off*, waste time, shirk, was a World War II term, first appearing in the early 1940s.

gooney or *goony* is probably from the 1580 English dialect word *gony*, stupid man (which, in turn, may be from the Scottish *goynel* with the same meaning). It has been used in America since 1837. Sailors have called various large birds, especially the albatross, *goonies* or *gooney birds* since the 1850s. Our World War II troops called a native of the Pacific Islands, and sometimes any Oriental, a *gooney*.

goop, meaning a stupid person, seems to have been coined by humorist Gelett Burgess (1866–1951), who used the word in the title of his 1900 book *Goops and How to Be Them*.

> To never see a fool you lock yourself in your room and smash the looking-glass.
> Carl Sandburg, *The People, Yes*, 1936.

goose has meant a silly person in English since 1547 (see GOOSE, TO GOOSE, AND GOOSEBERRIES).

gump has meant a fool in the U.S. since 1825 (it may be taken from the Scottish verb *to gump*, to grope).

halfwitted, 1645, and *halfwit*, 1755, are both of English origin, with America adding *halfwittedness* in 1832. Incidentally, *halfwit* had an earlier literary use in England, meaning a poor or half-funny humorist since 1678.

harebrain, and *harebrained*, are English terms dating from the 1550s.

have no smarts, 1960s.

hockey puck, another insult term popularized by comedian Don Rickles, in the early 1970s.

idiot (via Latin *idiota*, ignorant person, from Greek *idiōtēs*, layman, private person) has meant a mentally deficient person in English since 1300. In more recent times it has been used technically to refer to one with the most extreme mental retardation, having a mental capacity of no more than a three- or four-year-old.

ignoramus, the Latin word for "we do not know," was first used in English as a 1577 legal term for a grand jury's finding of insufficient evidence for a case to go to a jury trial (the jury members actually wrote the word "Ignoramus" on the back of the indictment, indicating they did not know or have enough evidence to warrant a trial). In 1615, George Ruggle's play *Ignoramus* appeared, its main character a lawyer named Ignoramus, the word then being used to refer to an ignorant and arrogant lawyer, figuratively one who could not find enough evidence, or present the evidence well enough, to convince a jury. By the next year, 1616, *ignoramus* meant any stupid person, though for some time it was especially used to refer to a stupid lawyer or to any person who was stupid though well educated.

imbecile (via the French from Latin *imbecillus*, weak) has been an adjective meaning weak, feeble, in English since 1549, taking on the special meaning of mentally weak or feebleminded around 1755 (as in "an imbecile person"), but not being used as a noun until 1802 ("an imbecile"). In more recent times it has been used technically to refer to a person having a mental capacity of no more than a seven- or eight-year-old, between that of an idiot and a moron.

jackass has meant a stupid person or *ass* (see above) in English since 1823 (it was first used to mean a male ass or donkey in 1727).

jelly bean, about 1915, used *bean* to mean "head" (a slang use since the 1880s), hence a head or brains full of or soft as jelly, but punning on the candy *jellybean*.

jingle brains, 1889, an Americanism having somewhat the same image as the earlier British *chowderhead* (see above).

judy, an American term for fool, usually in the phrase *to make a judy of oneself*, 1824. This may come from the 1810 British slang use of *Judy* meaning any girl (in the same way we use *Jane*), the Judy of the Punch and Judy show, or the American use of *Judy* as a common name for a donkey or mule, in which case *to make a judy of oneself* would be a variant of *to make an ass of oneself*.

lamebrain, 1934; *lamebrained*, 1942.

leatherheaded, an English term of 1668, with America adding *leatherhead*, 1839, and *leatherheadedness*, 1876.

> *Idiot. n. A member of a large and powerful tribe whose influence in human affairs has always been dominant and controlling.*
>
> Ambrose Bierce, *The Devil's Dictionary*, 1906.

lummox, a clumsy, stupid person, 1825 (the origin is not known, but the word sounds as if it might be built on "dumb ox").

lunkhead, 1852; *lunkheaded*, 1885 (the lunk is either from the dialect *lunk/lunker*, large, large and clumsy, or is based on "lump").

moron was created (from the Greek *mōros*, foolish) and adopted for use by the American Association for the Study of the Feebleminded in 1910. It has been used technically to refer to a person having a mental capacity of an eight- to twelve-year-old, being the most intelligent of the feebleminded.

muff was used in England as a contemptuous name for a German or Swiss as early as 1590 and came to mean any stupid person by 1812; *to muff* meant to make a mistake, bungle, by 1857. (Our standard word *muff*, for the tubular covering used to keep the hands warm, comes from the French *moufle*, mitten, but the use of *muff* to mean a stupid person could have a different and unknown origin.)

mug meant a stupid, insignificant person in English by 1859, probably from the 1840s slang use meaning face (faces were a part of the design of many drinking mugs of earlier days). *Muggins* also meant a fool in America by 1870, used almost as a mock surname based on *mug*, though *muggins* had also been a card game in the 1860s.

mushhead, 1888.

muttonheaded, 1768; *muttonhead*, 1804, both originally English terms though the Scots had used *mutton* as a contemptuous term for a man since 1508. In America we shortened *muttonhead* to *mutt* by 1901, adding the connotation of commonplace, so that *mutt* meant an average stupid man; then by 1904 we were also calling any nondescript dog a *mutt*.

narrow-gauge, dumb, small-minded, with a narrow view of life, 1872 (from the 1841 railroad use).

nincompoop first appeared in England as *niconpoop* (1676) and *nickumpoop* (1685), the modern spelling and pronunciation of *nincompoop* not appearing until 1706. Not knowing that the word was originally *niconpoop*, the great English lexicographer Samuel Johnson (1709–84) suggested that *nincompoop* came from the Latin *non compos*, not competent, not capable (as in *non compos mentis*, mentally incapable, not of sound mind)—but that early *nic-/nick-* element at the beginning of the word disproves his theory. One now has to speculate that, since *poop* has meant feces since the 16th century (see *pooped out* at ARE YOU BLUE, ALL IN, JITTERY?), the origin of *nincompoop* may not have been a polite one.

ninny has meant a simpleton in English since 1593. It is easy to jump to the conclusion that this comes from *nincompoop*, until one realizes that *ninny* is the older term; *ninny* probably comes from *innocent* or from a quick, shortened way of saying "an innocent."

nitwit was an Americanism of 1926 and seems to come from the German *nit* (a German dialect variant of *nicht*, not) plus our word *wit*, hence "not having any wits."

nobody home, with no brains, having an empty head, 1910.

not all there, meaning both stupid and crazy, 1821; *not to know beans*, 1830s (see BEANS!); *not to know enough to come in out of the rain* and the variant *not to know enough to go in when it rains*, 1840; *not to know (one's) ass from (one's) elbow*, 1851, and *not to know (one's) ass from a hole in the ground*, 1880s (for early uses of *ass* as meaning ass hole rather than jackass, see *ass* above); *not to have all* (one's) *marbles*, 1927; *not to know from nothing*, 1945.

numskull, an English term of 1724. The more obvious but variant spelling *numbskull* appeared in America in 1855. *Numheaded*, about 1850, and *numhead*, 1876, are Americanisms.

out to lunch, meaning both dumb and crazy, 1950s (based on the *not all there* image); *lunchy*, 1960s.

pinhead, 1896; *pinheaded*, 1901.

playing with half a deck, not having normal intelligence, lacking in brains, late 1960s (also based on the *not all there* image).

pudding headed, a 1726 English term from which we formed *pudding head*, 1849.

pumpkin headed, 1835; *pumpkin head*, 1841. In 1781 Yale University (then still Yale College) students started calling New Englanders *pumpkin head* because some religious-oriented laws required men to have their hair cut evenly all around, as if a cap, bowl, or half a hollowed-out pumpkin had been used as a guide; thus *pumpkin head* became a late-18th-century term for a New Englander (this use seems not to have influenced our 1841 use of *pumpkin head* for a stupid person).

putty head, 1868.

rattlehead, 1641; *rattleheaded*, 1647; *rattlebrain*, 1709; *rattlebrained*, 1716. These English terms were based on the 1627 British slang use of *rattle*, meaning foolish talk; thus the original connotation was of a foolish talker or talking foolishly, of words rattling out of one's mouth, rather than having one's brains rattling around in one's head.

retard, from "mentally *retarded*," a dumb person, 1976.

sao, stupid, late 1960s, a Vietnamese word used by American servicemen during the Vietnam War.

sapheaded, *sappy*, and *sapped* were 17th-century English terms, with *sapheaded* first recorded in 1665. *Saphead*, 1798, and *sap*, 1815, however, were first recorded in America. The image is not of undermining or sapping a fortification but of tree sap, as if one's head were full of sap, as is immature or unseasoned wood.

scatterbrained, 1747, and *scatterbrain*, 1790, were both originally English terms, perhaps from the 1719 English *shatterbrained*, which was never common in America.

silly originally meant innocent, feeble, with a connotation of helplessness and deserving of pity; it meant ignorant by 1547 and feebleminded later in the 16th century. In America we have used *silly* as a noun meaning a foolish person since 1858, often with an affectionate connotation ("you old silly, you"); our *silly Billy* dates from the late 19th century.

simple appeared in English in the year 1220 and meant free from guile, innocent; by 1340 it meant unlearned, unknowing; and by 1604 it meant dumb. *Simpleton* is an English word of 1650; *simp* is an Americanism of 1916.

slow has meant dull-witted, sluggish, since it first appeared in Old English in the year 880, making it, along with *dizzy*, one of the two oldest English words on this list.

softhead, 1650, and *softheaded*, 1667, were both originally English terms; we added *soft in the head* in 1938.

solid ivory, referring to the head, as if it were a billiard ball, 1906.

stiff, a stupid, commonplace person, 1890.

stupid and *stupidity* (from Latin *stupidus/stupēre*, numbed, senseless) were both first recorded in English in 1541. *Stupid* was used as a noun in England by 1712 ("a stupid" meaning a stupid person) with *stupe* appearing there in 1762. The American expression *stupid as a nun* appeared in 1774, *stupid as a pump* in 1843, and *stupid as a loon* in 1891 (based on our 1845 *crazy as a loon*).

thickheaded, 1801, and *thickhead*, 1871, were originally English terms, though in America we added *thickheadedness*, 1889. Long before the English used *thickheaded*, however, we had used *thick-skulled*, 1653, one of the earliest American uses of a word meaning "dumb."

weak in the intellectuals was used in English in 1661 and *weak in the brain* by 1831. *Weak in the head* is a 19th-century Americanism and *weak in the upper story* a mid-20th-century one.

yahoo has meant a dumb, brutish person or ignorant rustic since Jonathan Swift coined *Yahoo* as the name of a race of manlike brutes in his 1726 *Gulliver's Travels*.

yap, 1894 (a *yap* had meant a yelping dog in English since 1603).

yo-yo (from the name of the toy) meant a vacillating person, one who couldn't make up his mind, in the 1940s; then came to mean a dumb person, one who had no mind to make up, in the 1950s.

John and Mary: Common First Names

The term *first name* is an Americanism dating from the 1830s; before that we spoke only of Christian names and given names. *John* has been the most frequently heard first name in America ever since the English landed. In fact, *John* (from the Hebrew for "God is gracious, gracious gift of God") has easily been the most common name in the English-speaking world since the 11th century—and the equivalent German *Johann* and *Hans*, French *Jean*, Spanish *Juan*, Italian *Giovanni*, Russian *Ivan*, Gaelic *Ian* and *Sean*, etc., make "John" one of the most common names in the world (a man named *John* has been familiarly called *Jack* by English speakers since the 13th century or by the Scottish *Jock* since the 16th). *John* also gives us two of our most frequently heard family names, *Jones* and *Johnson*, both of which mean "son of John" (see MR. AND MRS. SMITH: COMMON LAST NAMES for the most common American family names).

Since *John* was such a common English name, it came to be used as the name of the average, typical fellow by the 14th century. By then *John Doe* and *Richard Roe* were already used as substitute names on legal documents in England to protect the identities of the two witnesses needed for every legal action (such witnesses were first required under the Magna Charta in 1215). Later these

Father calls me William,
Sister calls me Will,
Mother calls me Willie,
But the fellers call me Bill!
Eugene Field (1850–95), "Just 'Fore Christmas." (*Bill* is an early-18th-century London or southern English dialect form of *Will*.)

two names were used in standardized court proceedings in which *John Doe* stood for the plaintiff protesting eviction by a hypothetical *Richard Roe*, the landlord defendant. Thus *John Doe* became the common man. *John* and *Richard* were common first names in England, but where did the hypothetical last names *Doe* and *Roe* come from? Some say from *doe* (venison) and *roe* (fish), since these were the foods the typical Englishman liked best—but it could be that *Doe* and *Roe* were what landowners called men who poached deer and fish, and who would be just the kind of men willing to witness legal documents against the landowners and their landed rights.

Before the word "Yankee" became common, British soldiers disdainfully called the rustic colonists *Brother Jonathan;* colonial farmers were sometimes called *John Farmer;* and by 1810 the average American family man became *John Family.* We called Congress *Johnny Congress* around 1817; a Frenchman *Johnny Crapeau* by 1839; a Chinese laborer *John Chinaman* by 1853; and an Indian *Johnny Navajo* in the 1860s and 70s. A Confederate soldier was called *Johnny* or *Johnny Reb(el)* by the North in the Civil War, but *Johnny* also meant any soldier on either side, as shown by the Northern marching song "When Johnny Comes Marching Home," composed by Union Army bandmaster Patrick Gilmore. *John Hancock* has meant a signature only since 1903 (from his signature on the Declaration of Independence, written large as a gesture in defiance of England), while *John Henry* has also meant one's signature since 1914. We have referred to *John Q. Public* and *John Q. Citizen* since about 1940.

By 1907, itinerants and criminals were calling a policeman and the police *John Law,* thus *John* came to mean a policeman by 1924. However, by the 1920s, when hoboes and criminals used the word *John,* they usually meant the average, law-abiding sucker, and in the 1930s *John* came to mean a man who was keeping a girl—and also a prostitute's customer.

Johnnie meant fellow, chap in English by the 17th century and a man-about-town in the 1880s. *Johnny-come-lately* was in use in America by the 1830s, *Johnny on the spot* by the 1890s, and *stage-door Johnny* by 1912.

That about covers the extended uses of our most common first name, *John,* except for our use of it to mean bathroom, men's room, toilet. This use goes back to England, where a privy was called a *john* by the 1650s; some say this is after one of Queen Elizabeth I's courtiers, Sir John Harrington, who invented an indoor flushing toilet in 1596, but there is no scholarly evidence that his name was given to the device, and privies had already long been given men's names. Before that a privy had been called a *jake* (1530), and even before that had been referred to as *Jake's house.* We also called it a *cuz John* by 1735.

(Clockwise) John Winthrop, first governor of the Massachusetts Bay Colony; John Adams, second President of the United States; John Brown on his way to being hanged for treason in 1859 for leading the anti-slavery raid on Harpers Ferry; "John-John" (John Kennedy, Jr.) at the funeral of his father, President John F. Kennedy, in 1963. John Paul Jones, our first naval hero.

Jane, though not the most common female name, is the female equivalent of *John* in its metaphorical uses. A woman has been called a *Jane* in America since the 1900s; a man's sweetheart has been his *Jane* since the 1920s; a *jane* has been a ladies' *john*, bathroom or toilet, since the late 1920s; and *Jane Doe* was the female counterpart of *John Doe* by the late 1930s.

The first name *Joe* has also had increasingly extended use in America. *Joe Bunker* meant any American soon after 1776; *joe* meant a john, privy, water closet, by 1847; a *joey* was slang for a banjo by 1884 (it means a young kangaroo in Australia, not from the name *Joe* but from a native word for young animal); *joe boat* was the name of a flat-bottomed skiff by 1874, seeming to predate its being called a *john boat* (1905); and by the turn of the century *Joe Dandy* (1890) was a variant for *Jim Dandy* (1887), referring to any remarkable or excellent person or thing. However, *Joe* didn't begin to rival *John* in meaning an average or typical man until the 1920s. Then a *Joe boy* meant a typical, faddish youth of the Roaring 20s and *Joe Zilch* (*zilch*, nothing, zero, no one) a typical college youth, who was also called a *Joe College* by the mid 1930s. *Joe Blow* was common by the late 1930s, first among tough-talking types (it may have originated as a jazz term for an average hornplayer), while a *good Joe*, an *ordinary Joe*, and *Joe Doakes* enjoyed great popularity in the 1940s (perhaps *Joe Doakes* comes from the old British *John-a-Nokes*, "John from I don't know where; John from nowhere"). The culmination of this common use of Joe in the 1940s was, of course, in the term *GI Joe* for any American soldier, first used in Dave Berger's comic strip for the weekly soldier's paper *Yank* on June 17, 1942.

John, *Jane*, and *Joseph* have not, of course, been the only common American first names. Here, in decreasing order of popularity, is a list of the most common American first names since the Pilgrims landed.

Most Common American Male Names	Most Common American Female Names
John	*Mary*
William	*Elizabeth*
James	*Barbara*
George	*Dorothy*
Charles	*Ann*
Robert	*Margaret*
Thomas	*Helen*
Henry	*Ruth*
Joseph	*Jane*
Edward	*Virginia*
Richard	*Jean*

From early New England colonial records it seems that *John* and *William* accounted for 40 percent of the men's names and *Mary* and *Elizabeth* for 40 percent of the women's names. Of the 99 males of

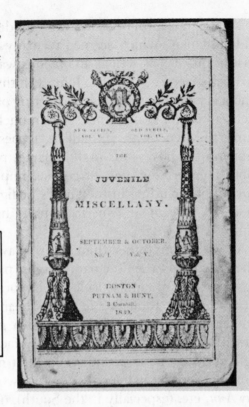
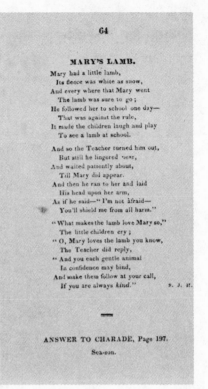

Mary had a little lamb,
  Its fleece was white as snow,
And every where that Mary
  went
  The lamb was sure to go.
  Sarah Josepha Hale,
  "Mary's Lamb," 1830.

Mary Cassatt, a self-portrait of around 1880.

Raleigh's 1587 "Lost Colony," 23 were named *John* and 15 *William*. *John* was also the most common, and *William* the second most common, first name of the 68 men and boys who came to America on the *Mayflower*. Of the women listed in official records of the Massachusetts Bay Colony until 1670, more than 20 percent were named *Elizabeth*. However, throughout our history *Mary* has been about twice as common as *Elizabeth*, and *Ann* and *Jane* have had periods of tremendous popularity not reflected fully in the long-term list above.

In the long run, our male names have been strongly influenced by the Catholic and Protestant custom of giving boys saints' names, thus keeping certain names toward the top of the list. In the short run, what parents name their children often depends on current events or fads. Though Biblical names have always been among the most popular, the Puritans strongly favored Old Testament names for boys and religious qualities for girls, thus in early New England such names as *Abraham, Moses, Daniel, Samuel,* and *Joshua,* and *Grace, Hope, Faith, Charity, Mercy, Constance,* and *Prudence* were among the most common. After the Revolution the trend was to name boys after heroes; thus there were many *Georges* and *Thomases* as well as first names of *Washington* and *Jefferson*.

During the 19th century a trend began of officially giving girls names that had earlier been only affectionate diminutives, as *Betty* instead of the full Elizabeth, *Molly* or *Polly* for Mary, and *Sally* for Sarah—though *Nancy* had become an accepted replacement for Agnes (and sometimes for Ann) since the 1770s.

The 19th century also saw a sudden trend for giving boys middle names, which seemed to many people to add a touch of class or quality, as well as an obvious way to distinguish between, or apologize for, all the John Smiths, William Joneses, etc. Though some boys might have a string of saints' names or be given their father's, a grandfather's, or an uncle's first name as a middle name, the trend was, and still is, to bestow the mother's maiden name on the boy as his middle name, perpetuating it for at least another generation and, of course, implying that it was a name worthy of including in the child's pedigree. Since the Civil War, about 80 percent of American males have been given a middle name.

As with many other things, girls have generally been slighted when it comes to middle names, most parents evidently considering this touch of family pride not important to a girl or her future success. Thus, though a few girls bear their mother's, a grandmother's, or an aunt's first name as a middle name, even fewer carry their mother's maiden name. In fact, any middle name given a girl is apt to be a second-choice first name, giving some girls a combination first name either as two words or one, as *Betty Jane*, *Kay Ann*, etc. (especially in the South), or *Maryann*, *Rosemary*, etc. Whether it reflected disappointment in not having had a boy or a desire that the girl be more competitive and athletic than most other girls of the period, the early 19th century also saw the creation of new girls' names by adding a feminine ending to boys' names, giving us *Georgia* (or *Georgina*), *Roberta*, etc.

In general, the first names of black Americans have differed little from that of whites. Early slaves certainly kept their African names and passed them and others on to their children, but slave owners and the removal from African life and customs soon had most slaves bearing the same first names as other early Americans. The main differences were that slaves who were brought to America via the Spanish Caribbean islands might bear Spanish first names for a generation or so, and that a few plantation owners, impressed with their own learning and life-style, bestowed classical names on their slaves, especially their house slaves. Most of the African names that survived the first few generations were "day names," the traditional African names indicating the day of the week on which the child was born. Thus a girl born on a Monday was called *Juba*, while a boy born on Monday was called *Cudjo*. Besides *Juba*, two of the African first names white Americans knew best were *Cuffy*, an African Gold Coast name for a boy born on Friday, and *Sambo*, a north Nigerian name meaning "second son," these last two being rather widely used by many whites to refer to any black man around 1820.

However, most slaves born in America were given common

American first names by their masters or parents, these names then often being preceded in actual use by *Black* or *Nigger* to distinguish the slave from any local white with the same name. Thus, from the earliest colonial days until several decades after the Civil War, blacks might be called by such names as *Black Joe*, *Nigger Jim* (as the character in Mark Twain's 1884 *The Adventures of Huckleberry Finn*), *Black Sarah*, etc. Since no slave, no matter how old, faithful, and beloved, could ever be given a title of respect, the informal *Uncle* (which had been used in English since the 16th century as a term of address to an elderly man) and *Aunt* were sometimes used before such a black's first name, starting in the 1820s and 30s. Thus we had many a name such as *Uncle Remus*, *Uncle Tom*, *Aunt Jemima*, etc.

Because they were especially common in the South, first names that have been more common among blacks than whites in general have included *George, Amanda (Mindy), Dinah,* and *Elizabeth (Liza, Lizzie)*. *George* was a term of address to any Pullman-car porter from at least the 1880s, perhaps because it was such a common black first name, or perhaps because Pullman cars were invented and made by George Pullman, who decided to staff them solely with black porters. *Elizabeth (Liza, Lizzie)* was such a common black first name it was used by whites from the 1880s until the late 1920s as a generic word to refer to any black woman, especially a black servant, as a cook or maid. Early in this century, whites even joked that black domestic servants had *Elizabeth clubs* on their day off to gossip about their employers, compare wages and working conditions, etc. Also, calling a Model T Ford ("any color as long as it's black") a *tin lizzie* (1915) is from this common name for a black maid, the usual explanation for the term being that the car, like the maid, worked hard all week and prettied up on Sunday. Because such first names were common, it's not at all surprising that in Harriet Beecher Stowe's 1852 *Uncle Tom's Cabin* the mulatto who, with her babe, is pursued over the Ohio River's ice floes is named *Eliza* and her husband is named *George*. (For the more recent use of Islamic names, such as *Muhammad*, by some American blacks, see Mr. and Mrs. Smith: Common Last Names.)

Since World War II, the breakdown of the large extended family and the greater freedom to do what one wants have resulted in the choice by white and black parents alike of less traditional first names for their children than previously. Yet many old favorites are still common. The most common names given babies in the 1940s were:

Boys	Girls
Robert	*Linda*
John	*Mary*
James	*Barbara*
Michael	*Patricia*
William	*Susan*

333

During the 1970s there was an even greater shift away from tradition. Though there are no official census figures on first names, various records, school enrollment lists, etc., indicate that the most common first names for that decade were:

Boys	Girls
Michael, David (each with about 5% of the total)	Jennifer, Susan (about 3% each)
John (about 3 1/2%)	Deborah, Karen (about 2% each)
Mark, Christopher, Steven, Jeffrey (about 2%–3% each)	Cynthia, Kim, Elizabeth, Linda, Sharon, Sarah (a little under 2% each)
Kevin (2%)	
James, Donald, Paul (slightly under 2% each)	Amy, Christine, Kimberly, Lisa, Melissa, Michelle, Stephanie (1%–2% each)
Bruce (about 1 1/2%)	

The major successes in the 1970s were *Michael* and *Jennifer*. *David* (which has been moving up steadily during the 20th century, especially since the 1940s), *Mark, Christopher, Steven, Jeffrey, Kevin, Paul,* and the unlisted *Brian, Scott,* and *Todd* also rose sharply in popularity on the boys' side, with *James, John, Robert,* and *William* losing out. On the girls' side, *Jennifer, Cynthia, Deborah, Karen, Kim,* and *Sharon* made amazing gains in popularity, with *Ann, Elizabeth,* and *Mary* losing out. The major trend, however, is the increasing variety of the most common first names, the greater number of names in the first-name pool from which parents feel they can happily choose. This has been a continuing trend throughout our history, first as immigrants added Dutch, German, Irish, French, Spanish, Polish, etc., names, often Americanizing them to English names; then the trend toward variety accelerated with the relaxation of strong family and religious ties and the emphasis in the 1960s and 70s of "doing one's own thing," including naming one's children. Thus, whereas originally in the colonies the four most common names (*John* and *William* for males, *Mary* and *Elizabeth* for females) accounted for almost 40 percent of American men and women, and whereas by the early 20th century the ten most common men's and ten most common women's names still accounted for about 50 percent of the population—in the 1970s the ten most common boys' and girls' names accounted for only 20 to 25 percent of each group. It is interesting to note, too, that the most common boys' names are bestowed more frequently than the most common girls' names: girls are given a greater variety of names than boys. Parents seem to feel more freedom, or to use more imagination, in choosing girls' names, indicating there is still a rather sexist attitude that it is more important to be conservative or carry on a first-name tradition on the male side, to aid the boy's future success and carry on family pride. Thus a boy's name is still more often chosen for reasons of tradition while a girl's name is still more apt to be chosen merely because somehow it sounds pretty to the parents.

Laissez-faire, Inflation, and Bread Riots

were all added to the American language during the Panic of 1837 (1837–40). People were talking about the collapse of the wildly inflated prices of land, cotton, and slaves; the failure of many canal companies and their bonds; and the folding of many state banks and the Bank of the United States owing to "inflated money."

When *inflation* caused the price of flour to rise to $12 a barrel in February and March 1837, poor people broke into New York warehouses to get it and the state militia was called out to quash the *bread riots.*

President Van Buren expressed his attitude toward the panic by saying:

> The less government interferes with private pursuits, the better for the general prosperity.

This was called his *laissez-faire* (French "allow to do") attitude, a let-business-alone attitude, which helped William Henry Harrison defeat Van Buren's reelection bid in 1840.

Throw Another Log on the Fire

> The happiness of the domestic fireside is the first boon of Heaven. . . .
>
> Thomas Jefferson, letter to John Armstrong, 1813.

Mankind has been burning wood to keep warm for over 200,000 years. Wood still provided 90 percent of America's fuel a hundred years ago—and still provides 90 percent of the fuel of many poorer nations today. Although the English word *wood* (then spelled *wudu/wuda*) meant tree when first recorded in the year 725, by 888 it meant firewood. Since wood was basically fuel for so long, the word *firewood* itself, implying there were other types of wood, was not even necessary until some six hundred years later, being first recorded in English in 1496 (*kindling* is a 1513 English word, originally meaning only the material for lighting a fire).

Thus for untold centuries, heating depended on wood logs for fuel. The words *heating,* *log* (from Middle English *logge,* tree limb, fallen tree), and *fuel* (via Old French *feuaile* from Latin *focālis,* hearth) were inseparable. In fact, all three words were first recorded in English in the same 1398 manuscript.

Until the 11th century most European dwellings had dirt floors with a fire burning on a hearth in the center, this *hearth* (an English word dating from the year 700) being nothing more than a flat stone or stone platform or a pit, the smoke from the fire escaping through the uncovered window openings or chinks in the walls and roof. Then, beginning in the 11th century, the first multi-

storied castles were built, their fortresslike walls and upper stories preventing smoke from escaping from a room with a simple hearth. This was no problem in the smaller rooms, which were heated only when occupied and then only by individual metal heating baskets, braziers, or fire pans in which charcoal or wood was burned. But something better than a large smoking hearth in the center of the floor had to be devised for the castle's great halls. They were heated by something new, large hearths actually built into the thick outside walls which, in turn, were specially constructed with tunnel-like openings through which the smoke could escape. Such hearths and wall tunnels finally led to the introduction of the *chimney* in the 14th century. Spelled as *chimenai* (via Latin *camīnus*, fireplace, from Greek *hámīnos*, heating chamber, furnace), the word was first recorded in English in 1330 and then meant both the hearth or *fire hearth* (a 1440 English term) and the special opening through wall or roof to let the smoke out. Not until 1513 did this word *chimney* mean only the smoke-funneling structure, especially that part of it above the roof (the chimney was also called a *flue* in English by 1582). The word *fireplace* then eventually appeared in England in 1655, thirty-five years after the Pilgrims had landed in America. Thus our earliest colonists spoke of chimneys, hearths, and fire hearths, but not of fireplaces.

Until well into the 18th century almost all American colonists heated their dwellings as the English at home did, by burning firewood in some type of fireplace with a hearth and chimney. There was usually a *grate* (a 1605 English word, from Latin *grāta*, grating) and *andirons* to hold the logs (*andiron* is an English word dating from 1300, perhaps formed by melding the word *iron* into the Gaulish word *andera*, heifer, since early ones were often in the shape of or decorated with figures of animals, which may be why they have also been called *fire dogs* since 1840). We also tended the fire with *fire tongs* (an English term dating back to the year 1100) and a *poker* (an English word of 1534), though as early as 1637 we also called the poker a *firestick* and the tongs *firesticks*. By 1758 the English were using and talking about the *fire screen* in front of the fireplace; we were soon using this term and, as late as 1874, also began calling it a *fire fender* and a *fire guard*. A poorer family might not have such an item, but both rich and poor would close off their fireplace in the summer with a *fireboard* (1855), the rich having an elaborately decorative one and the poor using a plain one.

As did the English at home, we had a variety of names for the timber or long stone supporting the masonry above the fireplace or the shelf it made or supported, using the English terms *mantel tree* (1482, *mantel* is just a variant of *mantle*, cloak, hood), *mantel* itself (1519), *mantelpiece* (1686), *mantelboard* (1825), and *mantelshelf* (1828). In America *mantel tree* was considered to be a New England term, *mantelpiece* was seldom heard west of the Mississippi, and *mantelboard* was considered a rustic southern term. We also added our own American terms to these English ones, coining *mantelplace* (1870) and *chimney shelf* (1881).

In America we also had the often fringed or lacy *chimney cloth* (1744) valance around the mantel or chimney piece, both for decoration and to keep some of the fireplace smoke out of the room; spoke of our native *chimney swallow* (1789, which is actually a swift that nests in chimneys and which John J. Audubon more accurately was to call a *chimney swift* in 1849); and called a natural rock formation in the shape of a chimney a *chimney* (1832) or a *chimney rock* (1847).

After 1776 in America many fireplaces also had a rifle hanging above the mantelpiece, the weapon slung there by soldiers returning from the War of Independence, not to use but as a symbol of victory and peace. A rifle over an American family fireplace was then not a mere decoration but proudly proclaimed that one or one's father or grandfather had fought in the war (as hunters and farmers still know, the best place to keep a rifle intended for ready use isn't over the fireplace but near or over a door).

With or without a mantelshelf, chimney cloth, or rifle, the fireplace was a good and very necessary family focal point—but it wasn't a very effective device for warming a person or a room, much less a family or a house. By definition and tradition this fireplace, which had developed in those 11th-century castles, was built into the wall of a house, warming best one side or area of one room only. The bigger the fire the more heat possible. Thus many early colonial fireplaces were as large as six feet high and ten feet wide, sometimes taking up an entire wall, and burned huge quantities of wood—most of the heat going right up the chimney. Many colonial homes had only one fireplace, in the kitchen for

The fireplaces were of a truly patriarchal magnitude, where the whole family, old and young, master and servant, black and white, nay even the very cat and dog, enjoyed a community of privilege, and each had a right to a corner.

Washington Irving, in Diedrich Knickerbocker's *History of New York,* 1809.

both heating and cooking. Thus, in winter, the kitchen served as a one-room house for most activities and people with small one-room cabins were as warm or warmer than those with larger houses, as extra rooms and sleeping lofts were cold.

Even some of the earliest colonial houses did, of course, have more than one *fireroom* (1708, a room containing a fireplace), the second one usually being a sitting room with a fireplace back-to-back with the kitchen fireplace, the two fireplaces sharing a common chimney. Any extra fireplaces, however, meant that extra wood was needed and extra *wood cutting* (1683) had to be done or extra money available to pay someone else to cut and haul it. If one didn't want to keep the wood piled outdoors, additional fireplaces and their extra wood also meant that a larger *wood house* (an English term of 1274), *woodshed* (1844), or *wood room* (1855) had to be built. Though later Americans might recall the woodshed as the place father whipped or spanked the sons out of earshot of the women of the house, or where youths could retreat to their first forbidden pipes or cigarettes or to exchange the latest communiqués from the world of sex, early colonists knew the wood house as a frighteningly dark and bitterly cold place where snakes and spiders lurked, as well as, perhaps, Indians, bears, and ghosts.

Feeding even one hungry fireplace took much time and hard work: men chopped the trees, women and children helped trim them and cut and split the wood into proper size. Trees were felled in an ever growing circle around frontier cabins, farms, and towns. The land was full of trees, but within a few decades there weren't enough trees left near the towns to feed the fireplaces, and buying a winter's supply of wood was to most families prohibitively expensive. Thus it was best to own one's separate *wood lot* (1643), later sometimes called a *wood patch* (1856) to ensure there would be enough inexpensive fuel. The large supply needed for churches, schools, or an elderly or sick householder was often provided by a community gathering to chop wood, such a gathering called a *wood bee* (1857; see HUSKING BEES, QUILTING BEES, AND SPELLING BEES for other, similar community gatherings), *wood spell* (1864), *wood chopping* (1872), or *wood frolic* (1889). The late date of these terms shows how long wood was our major fuel. However, early New England meeting houses didn't need any wood, because they had no fireplaces at all. The Puritanical congregations endured the cold with wraps, foot warmers, boxes of hot coals, and heated soapstones, perhaps basking in the vivid sermons about the hot fires of hell.

Early New England churchgoers were used to the cold because even their homes were chilly. To get warm from a fireplace one has to stay close to the fire, for the heat radiates only from the fire itself and the hot stones or bricks at the back of it. During New England winters one couldn't even write any distance away from the fire,

What matter how the night behaved?
What matter how the North wind raved?
Blow high, blow low, not all its snow
Could quench our hearth-fire's ruddy glow.
John Greenleaf Whittier, *Snowbound*, 1866.

because hands numbed and ink froze. The coldness indoors determined fashions in clothing, interior design, and living habits. Everyone needed layers of wool clothing or ruglike robes of thick wool or buffalo or other animal skins; most people slept long hours in well-blanketed beds, washed but seldom, ate huge hot meals and drank hot, often alcoholic, drinks. In all but the smallest rooms, any tables or chairs intended for use were clustered around the fireplace, leaving the rest of the room bare.

The early colonists knew from bitter lifelong experience that a fireplace didn't heat even one room well. Even when the first colonists landed at Jamestown and Plymouth, however, something existed that heated much better and used less wood than the fireplace. It was called a *stove* (from Old English *stofa*, hot-air sweating room, probably from a Latin word *extufa*, referring to steam or smoke, from the Greek *typhein*, to give off smoke). This English word *stove* had been in use since 1456, first meaning a sweating room, then meaning a box or enclosed brazier for burning fuel by 1552, an oven by 1640, and finally an enclosed fireplace, which is what a modern stove is, by 1702. The object had been around much longer than the English word for it: stoves had been used in China since 600 B.C.; the first European wood-burning cast-iron stove for heating a room was made in Alsace, France, in 1475 (and one of brick and tile was made there in 1490); with other stoves being built in Germany, Holland, and other parts of Europe—though they were not to be manufactured in quantity in Britain until 1754.

Our original colonists didn't use stoves because a stove couldn't be built by oneself as a fireplace could and because, in the 17th century, stoves were little known and less loved by traditional Englishmen. Yet our early colonists did know that stoves existed, and some of the Pilgrims, who had spent twelve years in Holland, had probably been well acquainted with Dutch stoves. A few of the early colonists actually did experiment with and build stoves. The first *cast-iron stove*, actually just a boxlike brazier with no grate, to be given that name in America, was made in Lynn, Massachusetts, in 1642; a larger boxlike cast-iron stove, probably based on an enclosed stove the Pilgrims had seen in Holland, was manufactured in Saugus, Massachusetts, in 1647; and a patent on such a stove was issued to John Clarke by the General Court of Massachusetts Bay Colony in 1652.

Other American colonists were trying to improve the fireplace itself, first by building fireplaces narrower and lower, then, around 1700, by putting a large cast-iron plate, called a *firebank*, behind the fireplace fire to reflect more heat into the room, and finally by adding not only firebanks but also hearths and sides of iron. This last development led to detached iron fireplaces, not built into the wall but set into the old fireplace opening and using its chimney; then, between 1700 and 1740, some of these iron fireplaces were built on legs and placed in the middle of the room. Thus between 1700 and about 1740 a few innovators were gradually turning the American fireplace into a stove while others were copying or adopting Dutch and German stoves for American use. During this forty-year period we had the:

> *fire frame*, a four-sided iron box on legs, but with no front or back, and set into the fireplace. Its popularity increased even after Benjamin Franklin invented his five-sided Pennsylvania fireplace in 1744, the fire frame selling very widely especially around 1800, mainly because, having no back, it was cheaper and was easier to install than the Franklin one.
>
> *German fire-place*, a five-sided box on legs, having a back but no front. At first it had no smoke pipe and was set in the fireplace, using its chimney; later some versions of it had a smoke pipe so that it could sit in the middle of a room. The Pennsylvania Dutch (who, of course, were Pennsylvania Germans, the *Dutch* being from *Deutsch*, German) introduced this *German fire-place*, also then called a *German stove*, to America in the early 1700s and it was manufactured in quantity in Pennsylvania from 1741 to 1768. It was called a *German fire-place* or *German stove*, not because the Pennsylvania Dutch first introduced and made it, but because, following their tradition, most such stoves were decorated with illustrations of Biblical subjects with titles in German, which the Pennsylvania Dutch still used; thus "German" referred to the words on these stoves.
>
> *Holland fire-place*, a six-sided iron box, usually about three feet high and on six-inch legs or a foot-high stand. The sixth side or front was an iron fuel door and the top had a hole for a smoke pipe. Though this completely enclosed stove was to be eclipsed by the open-front German stoves and Franklin stoves until almost the mid 19th century, it was constantly improved and constantly useful, also being called the *close stove* (1725, closed stove), *box stove* (1820), and *six-plate stove* (also 1820), because, of course, it was a closed box of six iron plates bolted together. When made of brick, with an iron door, it was called a *brick stove* (1809).

The German fireplace and Holland fireplace could stand in the middle of the room, radiating heat from all sides, heating a larger area and using less wood than a conventional wall fireplace. When they stood in the middle of the room with their own smoke pipes they were also called *draft stoves* and *wind stoves*, since they then provided their own draft instead of relying on that of the fireplace. Being completely closed, the Holland fireplace was the most efficient for heating: occasionally one was piled on top of another for added heat, and a few were even provided with elaborate long flue pipes to increase the heat flow and heat a larger area. However, the completely enclosed fire of the Holland fireplace or six-plate stove meant it could not be used for light or for many types of cooking. Thus, since the open-faced German stove filled all three necessary fireplace functions of heating, lighting, and cooking, it was for many years more successful than the Holland one.

Were such cast-iron devices fireplaces or stoves? By 1740 some Americans were calling them both "fire-place" and "stove" but seemed to prefer "fire-place" if they were set directly on a stone or brick hearth or floor and "stove" if they were set on legs, especially if on legs and moved out from the old fireplace opening. Thus a "new invented iron fire-place" was advertised for sale in the *Pennsylvania Gazette* in 1741, the first recorded use of the term *iron fire-place*. The most famous and certainly one of the best designed and made iron fireplaces was the one Benjamin Franklin introduced in 1744. It was a large cast-iron box with an open front which had a tonguelike grate extending out from it to hold andirons and the small logs used. Being without legs, it was meant to be set in a fireplace or on a stone or brick hearth, with a flue pipe running up through the chimney opening, the rest of the regular fireplace and chimney to be closed off. This, Franklin's own improved version of the German fireplace, did not have Biblical scenes on it, but his original fireplaces had an ornamental design of a sun with sixteen rays surrounded by leafage and streamers with the motto *Alter Idem*, "Another like me," as this open stove gave off both warmth and light as did the sun. Except for the flue pipe, it had a flat top, on which Franklin suggested owners could "boil the tea kettle, warm the flat irons, keep warm a dish of victuals." He wrote his own testimonial for his invention, claiming that it made his own room "twice as warm" while using only "a quarter of the wood" he had formerly burned in his traditional fireplace (later scientific tests showed that Franklin's invention was over three times as effective as a traditional fireplace).

Franklin himself always called his invention, which originally had no legs and was meant to be placed inside the traditional wall fireplace, the *Pennsylvania fire-place* (1744), but others were to call it or later versions of it the *Franklin stove* (1787), *the Franklin* (1818), and even the *Franklin heater* (1839) and the *Franklin furnace* (1846). Other stove makers also used Franklin's German fireplace design—and his name—in patents and to sell a variety of stoves, some with added ornaments and superstructures, some with more complex flues to extend the amount of metal that was heated, some even enclosing the fire by adding a sixth side and a fuel door, calling their stoves by such names as the *Franklin fireplace stove*, *pipe Franklin stove*, *closed Franklin stove*, *fold-door Franklin stove*, and *side-door Franklin stove*. Many of these later "Franklin stoves" had little relation to Franklin's original Pennsylvania fire-place and many people tended to use "Franklin stove" as a general name for any wood-burning cast-iron stove.

Other Pennsylvanians, usually of German descent, also introduced stoves new to America around the mid 18th century. There

We keep fires to sit by seven months of the year . . . wood, our common fuel, which once might be had at everyman's door, must now be fetched near 100 miles in some towns, and makes a very considerable article of expense.

Benjamin Franklin, "Account of the New Invented Pennsylvania Fire-Place," 1744.

341

was the large, 450-pound *five-plate stove* (1744, also later called a *jamb stove*, 1830) that first appeared in the German district of Philadelphia and consisted of a five-sided iron box projecting into one room with the open front built through a brick or stone wall into an adjoining room, so it could be fueled from one room but projected into the next, heating both. The open end served as a fireplace itself or, more frequently, was built next to one, so coals from the fireplace could be shoveled into it easily. During the 1750s and 60s Germans in Pennsylvania also made a tall, slim, cylindrical cast-iron closed stove whose top tapered into a smoke-pipe cap. Based on a cylindrical sheet-metal stove made in Germany, its rounded shape helped radiate the heat. Because it looked like a cannon barrel stood on its breech it was called a *cannon stove* (1764; this term also first recorded in the *Pennsylvania Gazette*, the newspaper in the heart of the stove area) and was especially used to heat large areas, such as public rooms and churches.

By 1766 there was the large, expensive *ten-plate stove*, which was a closed six-sided stove with a second box of three sides and a back attached to it to be used as an open-fronted oven. Thus the stove could now heat and do most forms of cooking; if one could afford enough candles or lamps for light, the fireplace was unnecessary. Not until April 26, 1815, however, was the James Custom *Cookstove* patented, by William T. James of Union Village, New York, this stove soon being made in Baltimore, Maryland (as well as in Troy, New York) and thus sometimes called a *Baltimore cook stove*. The cookstove was also called a *cooking stove* by 1823, with the term *cooking range* appearing in 1846, referring to an elaborate cookstove, usually with more than one oven and a top with holes or indentations and removable covers for heating pots and pans. Thus soon after the War of 1812 there were specialized wood-burning stoves for both heating and cooking.

Some of the inventors who tried to improve the fireplace and perfect stoves had, of course, experimented with burning *coal* (first recorded in English, in the year 825, then spelled *colu/colum* and meaning charcoal, burnt wood or coals that could be reburnt, then recorded as meaning the mineral in 1236). The American Indians had used coal in pottery making and colonists had found it along the James River in Virginia in 1649 and mined it there since about 1750, as it was in demand by blacksmiths and iron makers. Early experimental coal-burning stoves often used *soft coal* (a 1789 English term), or *bituminous* (from Latin *bitūmen*, mineral pitch, asphalt; *bituminous* had been used to mean such pitch or asphalt, and even petroleum, in England since 1620 but wasn't to be widely used to refer to soft coal until around 1830). Such soft coal was dirty and needed constant attention. What was needed was a stove that burned *hard coal* (also a 1789 English term), or *anthracite* (from Greek *anthrakítēs*, coallike, from Greek *anthrax*, coal; *anthracite* had

The word cookstove *appeared in 1815 and* cooking range *in 1846. In 1851, during the Presidency of Millard Fillmore, the first iron kitchen range was installed in the White House, all meals for earlier Presidents and their families having been cooked over an open fireplace.*

This 1872 stove could burn either wood or coal.

been used in English since 1604 to mean a rubylike stone but wasn't to be used to refer to hard coal until 1820). Such hard coal was cleaner than soft coal and burnt slower, longer, and more completely, leaving fewer ashes. An easy-to-tend, relatively clean coal stove was necessary before coal-burning stoves were to be admitted into the kitchen and sitting room.

In 1821 the Lehigh Valley Coal Mine Company sent a small sample of coal to the Reverend Dr. Eliphalet Nott (1773–1866) asking him to design a stove to burn it efficiently and cleanly. Nott was the perfect man for the job. His intellectual fame and moral reputation could lead to public acceptance of any coal stove he invented, for not only was he a leading combustion expert with several patents on heating devices, but he was also a leading Presbyterian clergyman, president of both Union College of Schenectady, New York, and of Rensselaer Polytechnic Institute of Troy, New York, a well-known supporter of public education, and a prominent temperance worker and abolitionist. Nott succeeded, developing his first base-burning coal stove, which contained a special coal grate, a firebox made of *firebrick* (a 1793 English term), an ashpit, and even a mica window. He called his first coal-burning stove the *Saracenic grate* (probably for the connotation of the Saracens and hot Arab climates) and by 1839 had fourteen patents on coal stoves. Nott's Union College installed coal stoves for students in the 1820s and by the late 1820s and early 30s the few coal stoves to be seen were often called *Nott's patent stoves* or simply *Nott stoves*.

Coal stoves became truly popular, however, only after Jordan L. Mott, Sr., of New York City improved and simplified Nott's base-burning design, obtaining a patent on a pyramid-shaped stove with a slanting coal grate in 1833, the coal sliding down from the upper part to be burned at the bottom. Mott's stove and grate were designed to burn *nut coal*, which was then very cheap, costing $3.50 a ton, making coal stoves possible for the average home. He made his stoves, which the public called *Mott stoves* by 1838, at his J. L. Mott Iron Works at Mott Haven, New York (now part of the Bronx in New York City), and they quickly gained the reputation of being as well made and reliable as the old Franklin wood-burning stoves. Mott's stoves soon came in five sizes and various models, including his original *Mott's Defiance* (it defied the coldest weather), a line of Mott's Parlor Cook Stoves, including the "Electra Cottage Parlor" model, the oval "Sirius," the round "Scorcher," and even an "Empire Franklin." His stoves and those of his imitators and competitors were so successful that soon *stove* didn't automatically mean "wood stove" any more and we had to distinguish between wood-burning and coal-burning by using the full terms *coal stove* (1834) and *wood stove* (1847).

Although some early coal stoves were open-grate ones, most

This elaborate 1874 stove used soft coal and was topped with an urn for holding water, perfume, or aromatic spices to relieve the stuffiness of the room.

were designed as completely closed stoves, which then became the accepted design for all stoves, whether coal-burning or wood-burning. Thus by the 1840s the front plates of many stoves were meant to be closed, and by the time the Civil War began, most stoves were designed with no hearth opening at all but only with a hinged door for feeding and tending the fire (closed coal stoves are six times more effective than a wood-burning fireplace and two or three times as effective as open-faced wood-burning stoves). Thus it took some one hundred and twenty years for Franklin's 1744 German-style "Pennsylvania fire-place" to close its hearth completely and become a closed stove. No longer could one read by or even see the cozy fire, except perhaps through a mica window, and some Americans first began to speak with nostalgia of the "open parlor grate."

Wood was, of course, still used in many stoves, especially cookstoves, long after the Civil War, as shown by such late-occurring terms as *stove wood* (1867), *stove length* (1881, as wood cut to the size of a stove's fuelbox), and *stove stick* (1888, a stick of stove wood). However, such terms as *stove board* (1875, a protective metal plate or mat on the floor under a stove, especially found under parlor or sitting-room stoves), *stove lid* (1876, the usually round metal plate for covering the opening on top of a cookstove), and *stove lid lifter* (1886, for picking up the hot stove lid) might apply to either a wood or coal stove.

Though stoves were an obvious improvement over fireplaces and a blessing to many Americans from the early 1700s into the early 1900s, the first wood-burning ones were mainly used in the Middle Colonies, especially in Pennsylvania (where they were developed), New Jersey, and the Shenandoah Valley. Many of the more solidly British New Englanders continued to depend on the fireplace for generations, out of preference, stubbornness, or a desire to rise above such sissified creature comforts as a well-heated room or home (they were later to resist furnaces and central heating too, as some British still do). Other Americans, especially less affluent frontiersmen, continued to use the fireplace because they were not able to buy or transport a stove. Many people who could afford stoves in all parts of the country also resisted them, regarding them as dangerous "redhot monsters" (Charles Dickens' term for the stoves that overheated him on a visit to America in 1842) that made the room too hot, dry, and stuffy, causing headaches. This complaint, which was also later to be made against central heating, led many people to put pans of water on their stoves to get more water vapor into the room, though many later and fancier stoves were designed with their own urns to hold water. In addition, closed coal stoves in particular were accused of robbing the room air of its oxygen and of creating poisonous byproducts of combustion that could lead to death, or at least

A chimney fireplace is preferable to a stove which is apt to give the air a close or disagreeable smell and produce headache.

The Practical Housekeeper, 1857.

Redhot stoves in close rooms are among the abominations of the age.

New York Tribune, 1860.

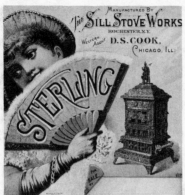

The Sill Stove Works of Rochester, New York, seemed to feel its "Sterling" model heated so well that a lady might need a fan.

could lead to a variety of ailments ranging from scrofula to insanity.

Despite such criticism, stoves grew more common and were manufactured in large quantities. As they became part of American family life they were less frequently called by such plain generic "six-plate stove" and "ten-plate stove" names. By the mid 1840s many stoves, following the tradition of the first "German stoves" with their Biblical illustrations, were heavily decorated, often covered with or featuring cast-iron fruit, flowers, animals, birds, or profiles of George Washington, and frequently topped with an urn or urns for water, perfume, or aromatic spices to relieve the stuffiness of the room or to replace the smell of hot cast iron, and sometimes of smoke and ashes, with a pleasant aroma. Such stoves were often called by names referring to their "artistic" shape and decorative motifs, as the *lyre stove*, which was shaped like a lyre; the *jew's-harp stove*, similar to the lyre stove; and the *dolphin stove*, which had vertical structures in the shape of dolphins. There was also the *little cod stove*, a tiny box stove, about 1 foot by 1½ feet, made for warming a bedroom, and having a codfish design on each side. Any small, often charcoal-burning, bedroom stove was called a *four o'clock stove*, since it was lit about four in the afternoon to warm the room by bedtime.

Following Mott's lead, other stove manufacturers began giving their various models either practical descriptive names or almost poetic names invoking homey or traditional American images. Thus in the 1840s the *two-column stove* was first advertised, this design having two vertical flues connected by a horizontal pipe with a chimney pipe in the middle. The Littlefield Stove Company of Albany, New York, which had been founded in 1853, introduced its very successful base-burning "Pioneer" model in 1855, then the "Morning Glory," followed in 1863 by its famous "Our Pleasant Home" model, which had two mica windows, a shelf for a tea kettle, and an American eagle on top. Other companies offered stoves in many models and sizes and with much ornamentation too. The "Seavey" stove was manufactured in Boston in twenty-three sizes, the smallest meant to heat a small parlor, the largest meant to heat a large one-room general store; while Bussey, McLeou, and Co. of Troy, New York, introduced its "Gold Coin" model in 1878, which had shining nickel-plated panels, railings, urn, hinges, and turnkey.

The round or cylindrical stove had the best shape for heating a large room evenly. The cannon stove had been the first round stove in America, and Isaac Orr made a squat rounded stove in Philadelphia and Washington during the first three decades of the 19th century. Mott's early rounded stoves were called *pot-bellied baseburners* and *pot-bellied stoves* by the late 1840s (*pot-bellied* had first been used in England in 1657, to refer only to people, with the

adjective being applied to bottles and other rounded objects by the 1820s); however, such a rounded stove was more apt to be called a *globe stove* during the late 19th century and was sometimes called a *barrel stove* (1904) during the early 20th century. The most famous pot-bellied stove was actually a globe stove made for schools, stores, and railroad stations, with the "Station Agent" being for years the most common stove found in railroad stations. It was usually around such a large pot-bellied stove that the *stove league* (1914) or *hot stove league* (1915) gathered, these terms referring to those rustic or neighborhood idlers who sat around the stove in a general store, basking in its warmth while discussing baseball, politics, and local news and gossip.

Famous stove models and homey stove names persisted for years; the "Station Agent" was in use in some of New York City's Sixth Avenue elevated railroad stations until 1939 and the U.S. Army used a "Warm Morning" baseburner in some of its camps during World War II. There were also specialized stoves, as the small, portable coke-burning *salamander stove* (1852) used for heating small rooms, drying plaster, etc., and so named because the salamander is supposed to be able to withstand extreme heat; and the *Yukon stove* (1898), a small sheet-iron box stove and oven with a telescoping smoke pipe, as carried by prospectors to the Yukon during the Klondike gold rush, which began in 1897. All coal stoves burned *nut coal*, as had Mott's first coal stove (it was also called *chestnut coal* by the 1880s), the slightly larger *egg coal* (1859) or the larger *lump coal* (also 1859) or *stove coal* (1880s).

A few fireplaces, stoves, and *heaters* (a 1688 English word) had been designed to heat more than one room, such as: the back-to-back fireplaces heating two rooms; the five-plate stove fed from one room and projecting into another, heating both; the *Russian stove*, developed in Russia and first mentioned as being used in the U.S. in 1811, which had multiple flue pipes radiating heat to as many as four rooms; the American *drum stove* (1833), which heated a ground-floor room in the normal way but which also had a flue pipe running through a sheet-iron drum in a second-floor room or sleeping loft to warm it also (such a drum stove was also called a *dumb stove* by 1851, because people confused "drum" and "dumb" and the upstairs heating drum was "dumb" in that it had no fire of its own); and the *Latrobe Heater*, invented by John Latrobe in the 1850s, and *Sanford's Challenge Heater*, first manufactured by the National Stove Works in New York City in 1858, which were stoves with stovepipes for heating several rooms. Such stoves were mainly curiosities, however, and none was very effective. Thus, though the stove was a vast improvement over the fireplace, most stoves shared one major flaw with the fireplace: they could heat just one room or part of a room. Pipes carrying hot water, steam, or air were needed to heat several rooms from one source, and that was the next step in heating.

Hot-water heating was developed in France in the early 18th century, where it was first used in a greenhouse and then in a chicken hatchery, word of its success spreading so that by 1792 it was used to heat the Bank of England in London. Meantime, James Watt (1736–1819), the Scottish inventor of the modern steam engine in 1765, experimented with heating by steam in 1784

Though long flue pipes helped spread heat, it was difficult for a stove to make an entire school or store comfortably warm.

and a Halifax, Nova Scotia, inventor had patented a *steam-heating* unit in 1791, such units being used to provide *steam heat* in some British factories by 1822. Both hot-water and steam-heating systems were introduced into the U.S. in a few theaters and in public rooms of a few of the more plush hotels in New York City and Boston in the 1830s and 40s, with Boston's Eastern Exchange Hotel of 1846 being the first to have every room heated by steam. However, it wasn't until the 1870s, 80s, and 90s that new valves, return-line piping systems, and other components were perfected that the terms *hot-water heating* and *steam-heated* (1884) became well known.

Both systems used a *boiler* (meaning a vessel for boiling water since 1725 and a vessel for boiling water to steam for a steam engine since 1752, both meanings first recorded in England) to produce the hot water or steam which is fed via a *hot-water pipe* (1842) or a *steam pipe* (1857, both first recorded in England) to a room *radiator* (1851) or a *steam radiator* (1879). Since a valve is needed on each radiator, to allow air to escape when the heated water expands in a hot-water system or when the steam enters in a steam-heating system, there could be a loud *knock* (1869 as the sound of mechanical parts striking together, the word first recorded in the year 1000 in English to mean the sound of a blow or rap). The two systems evolved almost simultaneously, with each having its own advantages. Since hot water holds its heat longer than steam, a hot-water system can keep the temperature of a room or building more constant with less fuel, but the lighter steam is easier to move through pipes and radiators and thus has advantages over hot water in larger apartment houses and office buildings.

At the same time as boiler-fed hot-water and steam-heating systems were developing, so was the hot-air furnace. For just as the fireplace had been enclosed in iron and moved to the center of the room to become a stove, the stove was to be fitted with hot-air pipes and moved to the basement to become a *furnace* (first recorded in England in 1223 as meaning a device in which metals are smelted, then recorded in 1691 to mean an enclosed fireplace or stove, from Latin *fornax,* oven, kiln, related to the Latin *formus,* warm). The term *hot air furnace* was first recorded in America, in 1841, *warm air furnace* in 1846, and *furnace fire* in 1859 (though it had been used in English since 1645 to refer to a fire in a smelting furnace). Thus, just as hot-water and steam-heating systems began to appear in the 1830s and 40s, so did the very first, often wood-burning, basement hot-air furnaces, with hot air welling up through brass *registers* (1845 with this meaning) in the floor.

While some families were installing full-sized basement furnaces, others who did not have the money or inclination to do so installed small furnacelike *heaters* in their fireplaces, these units releasing hot air through a register over the mantel or to rooms

A turn-of-the-century coal-fueled hot-air furnace.

above via multiple flues or hot-air pipes through the ceiling. Thus in the 1870s and 80s some families installed the *Baltimore Heater* or *Baltimorean*, a fireplace heater made by Bibb and Son of Baltimore, Maryland, while others installed such pseudofurnaces in their fireplaces as the *Dimmick Heater*, introduced in 1877; the *Lawson Fire-Place Furnace*; the *Jackson Fireplace*, made by Edwin Jackson & Brothers of New York City beginning in 1880; and the *Sunnyside Fire-Place Heater*; while many offices used the large *Fire-in-the-Hearth Heater*.

Despite such heaters, it was the full basement furnace that gained the most popularity. By the 1890s most new homes and apartment buildings for the upper and middle classes were being built with boilers and steam or hot-water radiators or with *coal furnaces* and hot-air registers, with owners of older houses and apartment buildings installing them when the structures and their pocketbooks allowed. Thus *central heating* came to America, though the term itself was not recorded until 1906. Central heating was a new and wonderful thing—though it wasn't as new as most people thought, since some 2,000 years earlier the ancient Romans had furnaces or enclosed fires under some buildings whose floors were raised on pedestals, the heat flowing through and radiating from hollow terra-cotta channels in the floor and walls (such a system is called a *hypocaust*, from Greek *hypōkauston*, room heated from below, from *hypo-*, below, under + *kauston/kaustōs*, heated).

Not only did central heating change the way we kept warm, but by heating the entire house it changed home design and construction, interior design, dress styles, and living habits. The size and shape of houses and rooms now no longer needed to be determined by how many fireplaces or stoves one could keep going. Each new home, now with a basement for the furnace, could have as many windows and doors as desired, without the previous limitations on size, since drafts were no longer as important as before, though such new terms as *heat loss* and *heat insulation* were being discussed by the 1880s and *heat flow* entered the language by 1902, showing that new concerns had to be taken into account. One could now wear lighter clothing indoors, eat meals in a separate dining room away from the kitchen stove and without its own fireplace, enjoy less hearty and even cold foods and drinks all year, and sleep under fewer blankets or even stay up late in a warm house to read, talk, or play games. One could also wash, bathe, and shave in a warm room and hence did so more frequently—and in a separate bathroom, complete with its own sink and tub, instead of near the fire (*hot running water* from a *hot-water pipe*, 1897, was, of course, often a companion to central heating and many families began to rely on both at the same time). Where chairs and tables had once been clustered near a wall fireplace and later around the stove in the center of a room, central heating not only allowed full use of all

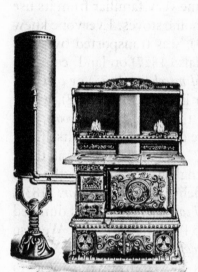

Although hot running water *was a companion to* central heating, *some of the more elaborate kitchen stoves had a tank for heating household water, as did this 1898 Columbia Newport stove, which cost $32.25 when bought direct from the manufacturer.*

heated rooms for family activities but, since it warmed the entire room from wall to wall, allowed furniture to be spread out, even into corners or against all four walls, immensely changing interior and furniture design. The family had gained a larger, fully usable house, but it had also lost its hearth—the fireplace or stove around which the entire family gathered and shared its life, the focal point that kept the family and its various generations, activities, and interests together, had disappeared. The American family would never be the same again.

By the time the *coal-fed furnace* (1880s) started to become a common home feature, coal had become very familiar from its use in steam locomotives, factories—and home stoves. Everyone knew that coal came from a *coal mine* (1613), was transported by a *coal barge* (1827) on water or a *coal wagon* (also 1827) on land, could be bought in a *coal sack* (1632) from a *coal merchant* (1677) or *coal man* (1707), was kept in a *coal shed* (1719) or in a *coal cellar* (1838), which might be filled via a *coal chute* (1813, then spelled *coal shoot*), and carried to the *coal box* (1729) beside the fire, or to the fire itself in a kettle or bucket called a *coal scuttle* (1771) or *coal hod* (1825), all these terms, and the dates shown, being English. In the U.S. the coal mine might be in a *coal field* (1813), delivered in a *coal cart* (1839) from a *coal yard* (1851) owned by a *coal company* (1852) and dumped into the cellar through a *coal hole* (1854) in the sidewalk. We also were often calling a coal scuttle a *coal bucket* by 1887. As coal increased in use in America it was moved from the mine to factories and towns in a special railroad *coal car* (1858; this term had meant any cart or wagon for transporting coal since 1830), a train of such cars being called a *coal train* (1861) and a railroad devoted to such trains being called a *coal road* (1887). The increasing use of coal created wealthy *coal barons* or *coal kings* (both 1887) who owned coal mines, coal roads, and coal companies, though the humblest man could look for *coal land* (1750) where he might find a *coal hill* (1781) or an exposed *coal bank* (1805) or a *coal seam* (1850), which could result in a profitable *coal diggings* (1882) for a *coal prospector* (1888) who owned such a *coal claim* (1891).

Though the coal furnace made life much easier than the wood-burning fireplace and stove, it was by no means automatic. During the fifty-year period from the mid 1890s until the mid 1940s coal was delivered to most homes by wheelbarrow, cart, horse-drawn wagon, or truck, carried to the coal cellar or shoveled or dumped down the chute into the basement *coal bin* (1864), each such home delivery leaving a trail of broken coal on streets, yards, and driveways and a fine film of *coal dust* (a 1597 English term) over the furniture. Father or an older son rose early every winter morning to walk down cold basement steps to *shake down* the ashes from the furnace grate to the ashpit (*shake down* meant to dislodge by shaking in English by 1500 and to cause to settle by 1611) and

Coal is a portable climate.
Ralph Waldo Emerson,
The Conduct of Life, 1860.

Coal miners, 1922.

remove the *furnace clinkers* (1853) or *clinkers* that wouldn't fall through the grate (*clinker* had been used in English since 1641 to mean a paving brick, from the Dutch *klinker*, a type of kiln-hardened brick, then by 1769 was used to mean a piece of slag formed from impurities in coal). Then he stirred the fire with a long poker and carried buckets or shovelfuls of coal from the coal bin to the furnace, stoking the fire to a roaring pitch to warm the house before the rest of the family rose to dress. Women and older children would feed the furnace coal as needed during the day, with father taking a turn when he came home from work, removing the day's ashes and clinkers, perhaps getting a roaring fire going again before the children undressed for bed and then, before going to bed himself, *banking* the fire for the night (since 1860 to *bank* a fire has meant to heap compact fuel around it to keep it burning slowly for a long time, to *bank* having meant to pile up in English since 1712, from the English noun *bank* first recorded in the year 1200 to mean a raised ridge). Wealthy families, of course, might pay an odd-job laborer or poor or ambitious youth as a *furnace man* (1880s as one who tends a furnace) to come to the house several times a day to perform these chores.

By the late 1930s, however, some lucky homes had furnaces fed by an automatic *stoker* (originally used in English in 1660 to mean one who stokes a furnace, then first recorded in 1884 as a mechanical device for doing this). This stoker was usually a large screw or *worm* that carried small lumps of coal, usually specially shaped *briquettes* (also an 1884 English word), from a specially filled hopper in the basement coal bin directly into the furnace. It and the flue draft were automatically activated, when the temperature fell below a predetermined level, by a *thermostat* (an English word dating from 1831, from Greek *thermē/thermo-*, heat, hot, + Greek *statēs/-stat*, constant, set, something that stops or steadies; the first thermostat used in home-heating systems had appeared on Elisha Foote's airtight stove of 1849 and was a bimetallic rod that expanded with heat to close the draft automatically).

Even though automatic stokers and thermostats made feeding the furnace a simple job, and the stoker kept the basement, and entire house, freer of coal dust, the most advanced coal furnaces, like the fireplaces and stoves before them, were still burning fuel that left ashes that had to be removed, stored temporarily, and eventually disposed of. In the early days ashes and other refuse might be kept in an *ash house* (1807) until taken away by the *ash man* (1836), who later collected or emptied the *ashes barrel* (1846) or, still later, the *ash can* (1899).

Besides the stoker and thermostat, there was another major advance in furnaces around 1930. Until then, since warm air is lighter than cool, the warm air from the furnace was simply allowed to float up through the large, usually circular *furnace pipes* (a 1664 English term) from the basement through the hot-air registers. Such pipes had to be large, and second- and third-floor rooms were often not warm enough. Though various methods to create a *forced draft* (1865) or *forced air* (1880) had been attempted in stoves and early furnaces, not until 1930 did *forced warm air heating*, as it was then widely called, begin to come into use. It used a motor-driven fan to force the warm air through smaller, usually rectangular *ducts* (the word used in England since 1713 to refer to a channel for liquids, then used in America to refer to furnace pipes since 1884). Such forced warm air systems, of course, heated upper floors and distant rooms better.

The smaller, neater furnace ducts meant that the basement was no longer cluttered with big, cumbersome pipes but could be a neat usable area, even paneled to serve as a *rumpus room* (late 1930s) or *family room* (which term had been used to mean an informal living room or second parlor since 1853).

Forced warm air heating had many other advantages: the warm air could be forced through a *filter* to clean it, which made homes much cleaner and kept much more coal dust out of the house (*filter* was first recorded in English in 1563, referring then only to a device for filtering liquids; it had been used to refer to a device for filtering impurities from the air since 1874, which is the same year that the longer term *air filter* first appeared). The same motor-driven fan that pushed hot air through the ducts could also be used to push heavier cool air through them, making *central air conditioning* much cheaper and more common (see It's Not the Heat, It's the Humidity). Such a system also meant that, except for the fact that it burned coal and needed a coal bin, the furnace didn't even have to be in the basement, since heat flow no longer depended on the fact that warm air rose. If compact enough and burning gas or oil, a furnace could be in an attic, closet, or main floor utility room, the furnace then often not being called a furnace at all but a *heating unit*. This meant that houses no longer needed a basement to accommodate a furnace, so the basement could be dispensed with or, if there were one, the entire area could be devoted to extra living space or that rumpus room or family room.

Just as hot-water heating and steam-heating systems appeared at about the same time in the 1830s and 40s, oil and gas furnaces appeared at almost the same time in American homes in the 1920s and 30s (the Chinese had used oil and gas as fuels as early as the 11th century). Though the *oil stove* (1865, in the first U.S. patent for it) had appeared after the Civil War and the *kerosene heater* and *kerosene stove* had first been talked about and used in the 1870s, *fuel oil* (1893) was first used on a large scale in *oil burners* or *oil furnaces* to provide *oil heating* on the West Coast in the early 1920s and became fairly widespread in the 1930s. Most families then still used coal furnaces, but spoke longingly of installing *oil heat* if the Great Depression ever ended and they could afford it.

Oil was better than coal because it flowed directly from the oil truck through a hose into the home storage tank, from which it flowed to and burned in the furnace automatically, the oil furnace turning on and off by itself via a thermostat and *pilot light* (1890). Thus oil leaves no fine film of coal dust over the house, needs no dirty coal bin, no shoveling of coal, no banking of the fire at night or stirring it up in the morning, and it burns completely, leaving no ashes or clinkers. It was truly *automatic heating*, as oil burner manufacturers and heating oil suppliers kept reminding us in the 1930s and 40s.

Oil (via Middle English and Old French from Latin *oleum/olea*, oil, originally olive oil, olive tree, from Greek *elaía*, olive) has been in the English language since 1175 while *petroleum* (from the Latin, *petr/petra*, rock + *oleum*, oil) was first recorded as an English word in 1526. Originally, however, oil meant only mineral and vegetable oils, then also fish and whale oil, before coming to mean petroleum and some of its products in the mid 19th century.

By the time oil heating became popular, *oil* was a magic word conjuring up modern commerce and wealth. Everyone knew that oil came from an *oil well*, a term first recorded in 1847, twelve years before Edwin Drake brought in America's first one in Titusville, Pennsylvania, this well being 70 feet deep and pumping out an unprecedented 8 to 10 gallons of oil a day. We had long used the term *oil company* (1854, a company that owned an oil well and sold oil) and had talked excitedly about the first *oil fever* (1862), which attracted thousands to the Pennsylvania *oil region* or *oil district* (both terms 1862), where the *oil-bearing strata* (1863) was soon covered with *oil derricks* (also 1863) by those who had made an

The world's first oil well, at Titusville, Pennsylvania. It was drilled in 1859 by Edwin L. Drake (in the top hat) and pumped eight to ten gallons of oil a day.

oil strike (1864) or managed *to strike oil* (1866). By 1862 this Pennsylvania oil region was producing 3 million wooden barrels of oil a day, each barrel holding 42 gallons, which made Edwin Drake's 1859 oil well look puny in comparison. Much of this oil was used for kerosene for lighting, the oil stove not being invented until 1865 and there being little use for a dangerously inflammable byproduct which by 1865 was called *gasoline*. The oil was stored in an *oil tank* (also 1862, during the height of this first Pennsylvania oil boom) to be transported in a railroad *tank car* (1874, sometimes called an *oil car* by 1876), a train of such cars being called an *oil train* (1877). By the end of the 1870s the *oil industry* (1880) or *oil business* (1883), which produced and marketed petroleum products, was booming and the individual *oil prospector* (1885) soon hoped to become wealthy not only from drilling one well but by discovering an entire *oil field* (1894). Thus the romance of oil had made it part of American life and language some sixty years before it became a major household heating fuel.

Oil was soon rivaled by gas as a heating fuel. The term *gas heater* had appeared in 1866, *gas-heated* in 1877, and *gas furnace*, in England, in 1879, with the early gas heating fixture often being in the shape of a *gas log* (1885), a gas burner shaped to resemble a log and installed in the fireplace to create a *gas fire* (1910) that looked like a wood fire.

The first *gas well* in the U.S. had been drilled to a depth of 27 feet near a "burning spring" in Fredonia, New York, in 1821, though the term *natural gas* was not recorded until 1845. The Fredonia Gas Light and Water Work Co. was founded there in 1858, using the gas for lighting, as both natural and manufactured gas were used for lighting long before gas became a major heating fuel. In fact, it was actually the electric light that finally led to the upgrading of gas as a widespread household heating fuel—for as electricity began replacing gas for illuminating, many a local illuminating *gas company* (an 1817 English term) turned to promoting gas heating in order to stay in business. Despite early gas wells, most gas was manufactured in *gas works* (1828) until the discovery of large natural gas deposits in the southwestern United States in the 1920s, making gas heating in that region cheap. Then in 1925 electrically welded seamless steel pipe came into being, making economically possible the transportation of cheap natural gas (as well as oil) over long distances through a *pipe line* (1879, when it originally appeared as two words; the verb *to pipe*, meaning to transport through a pipeline, dates from 1889).

Many transcontinental pipelines were built before and especially during World War II, these pipelines then being used to bring natural gas to almost all areas of the country between the mid 1940s and the 1960s, putting almost all the gas works that manufactured gas from solid fuels out of business.

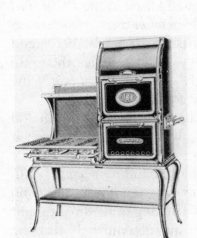

Black-enameled, nickel-plated gas ranges with four burners, a broiler, and a shoulder-high oven were once common household appliances. This 1912 Lindemann stove cost $57.

Gas furnaces began to replace coal and even oil furnaces in many homes after World War II because gas was cheaper and even easier and cleaner to use than oil, households using gas heat not even needing deliveries or storage tanks, since the gas is automatically piped into the house as needed, its delivery never delayed by bad weather or forgetfulness. Many people also liked the idea that one paid for the metered gas (*gas meter* was an 1815 English term) after it was used instead of having to pay for it beforehand. Thus by 1980 55 percent of all U.S. homes, some 44 million of them, were heated by natural gas; 20 percent, or about 16 million homes, by oil; 17 percent by electricity; and the remaining 8 percent, or 2 million, using coal, wood, propane gas, or solar heating.

The only future competition for gas seemed to be electric heating, the term *electric heater* having appeared in 1877 and *electric furnace* in 1885. However, most electric heating uses no furnace but electrical resistance coils or panels to provide *baseboard heating* or radiant *panel heating* (both 1954 terms, *baseboard* in this sense being an 1853 word), which heating had been developed in England around 1915. It was during the 1960s that such electric heating began to increase rapidly, being even easier to use and using even simpler apparatus than gas furnaces, though the cost of electric heating as compared to that of gas and *fossil fuels* (an 1835 English term, referring to coal and oil) was high, except in communities near *hydroelectric plants* (1909). Nevertheless, as family income grew after World War II, and we were willing to spend more for convenience, many upwardly mobile American families changed from coal to oil to gas to electricity between the early 1940s and the mid 1970s. Thus it seemed that electricity, gas, and oil, in that order, would serve the heating needs of the future and that wood and coal were certainly fuels whose day had passed.

Then suddenly in the late 1970s, as the U.S. imported more and more oil from the Middle East, people began to talk about a future *oil shortage*, and oil prices soared as the newly unified Arab dominated *Organization of Petroleum Exporting Countries* (*OPEC*, officially organized November 14, 1960) raised oil prices dramatically, with the cost of heating gas and electricity soon to follow the spiral of inflation upward. The oil shortage was indeed an *energy shortage:* our own *off-shore oil wells*, which had been developed since the early 1950s, seemed no longer sufficient; the *atomic power plants*, which since the late 1940s had promised such ready electricity, were now horribly expensive to build, required years to license, were increasingly considered too dangerous to control, and produced radioactive wastes, which could not be suitably disposed of. By 1978 many Americans who heated their homes with electricity and oil were telling horror tales of spending several hundred dollars a month for heating bills—and wondering if or when Middle Eastern politics would disrupt the world's oil sup-

Oil shortages and rapidly increasing prices of oil and gas doubled and tripled the cost of central heating in the late 1970s, leading many people to return to older ways of heating a room.

ply, or the depletion of oil and gas fields would leave them without heat or with fuels householders could no longer afford.

Thus, though a million Americans, mostly in poor rural areas, still heated their homes with wood, in the late 1970s many more affluent Americans talked of returning to wood-burning stoves, which were almost becoming a fad. Others talked of the future possibility of using newer, cleaner types of coal, such as *pulverized coal*, which could be delivered through pipelines, or of processing oil from *oil shales* (an 1877 English term). Still others spoke of using *windmills* (the word first recorded in English in the year 1297) to generate household electricity or using steam or *thermoheat* from the ground to generate electricity for cities and towns. The major newly popular term, however, was *solar heating*, though an experimental *solar boiler* had been talked about as early as 1884 and intensive modern research to develop heating from the sun's rays had begun in the late 1960s. The new widespread interest in solar heating had us talking about collecting *solar energy* in metal coils or in *solar panels* on the roof or the outside walls of a house to heat circulating water, such units beginning to appear in the late 1970s as more than just experimental curiosities.

Many Americans also turned down their central heating devices to conserve fuel and lower heating bills, such *energy conservation* considered not only the sensible and economical thing to do but also a patriotic way to "reduce our dependency on foreign oil." (For the first time since our widespread use of the stove, this made our homes cool enough for visiting Europeans to be comfortable in.) Turning the central heating down began to change our dress styles again and more Americans returned to wearing somewhat heavier clothing, or at least sweaters, indoors. To supplement the lowered central heating system various modernized types of oil, kerosene, and electric heaters came back into use, now called *space heaters* since they were used only to heat the area or space in a room actually occupied, leaving the rest of the room and house cool—just as fireplaces and stoves had once done.

Sometime in the future, the oil and gas will run out and we will be heating our homes by new man-made fuels, new natural fuels, windmills, some improved form of atomic power, solar energy, or chemical energy (*fuel cell* was a 1922 term, though it didn't become well known until fuel cells were used in space vehicles in the late 1960s). However, if none of these works we have coal for hundreds of years to come—and when that runs out there is still our traditional *renewable fuel*, man's old standby, wood.

may not have been America's most profound or original poet, but he has certainly been one of our most beloved and most quoted. His popular poems are lyrical and deal with basic American subjects, such as the Pilgrims (he was a descendant of John Alden), Indians, Paul Revere's ride (his maternal grandfather was a Revolutionary War general), blacksmiths (one of his paternal ancestors was a village blacksmith), children, shipwrecks, even the weather.

Both as a young poet and as an aged man of letters Henry Wadsworth Longfellow gave us many memorable and often-quoted phrases.

Under the spreading chestnut-tree
*   The village smithy stands;*
The smith a mighty man is he,
*   With large and sinewy hands.*
    "The Village Blacksmith," 1842.

Into each life some rain must fall,
*   Some days must be dark and dreary.*
    "The Rainy Day," 1842.

I shot an arrow into the air,
It fell to earth, I knew not where.
    "The Arrow and the Song," 1845.

This is the forest primeval. The murmuring pines and the hemlocks,
Bearded with moss, and in garments green, indistinct in the twilight
Stand like Druids of eld, with voices sad and prophetic.
    Evangeline, 1847.

Sail on, O Ship of State!
Sail on, O Union, strong and great!
Humanity with all its fears
With all the hopes of future years,
Is hanging breathless on thy fate!
    "The Building of the Ship," 1849.

By the shores of Gitche Gumee,
By the shining Big-Sea-Water,
Stood the wigwam of Nokomis,
Daughter of the Moon, Nokomis.
    The Song of Hiawatha, 1855.

Why don't you speak for yourself, John?
    The Courtship of Miles Standish, 1858.

A boy's will is the wind's will,
And the thoughts of youth are long, long thoughts.
    "My Lost Youth," 1858.

Footprints on the sands of time.
    "My Lost Youth," 1858.

Between the dark and the daylight,
*   When the night is beginning to lower,*
Comes a pause in the day's occupations,
*   That is known as the Children's Hour.*
    "The Children's Hour," 1860.

A Lady with a Lamp . . .
    "Santa Filomena," 1858, referring to Florence Nightingale.

Listen, my children, and you shall hear,
Of the midnight ride of Paul Revere,
On the eighteenth of April in seventy-five,
Hardly a man is now alive
Who remembers that famous day and year.
                . . .
One if by land and two if by sea;
And I on the opposite shore will be,
Ready to ride and spread the alarm
Through every Middlesex village and farm.
    "Paul Revere's Ride," 1863.

357

Born in Portland, Maine, Longfellow (1807–82) graduated from Bowdoin College in 1825, in the same class as Nathaniel Hawthorne, then studied French, Spanish, Italian, and German in Europe for three years before becoming a professor of modern languages, first a Bowdoin, then at Harvard. Tragically widowed twice, he lived the last forty-three years of his life at Cambridge, teaching for the first eighteen of them. He introduced thousands of students to European literature, was a respected literary essayist and translator, and even wrote and edited grammar and linguistic textbooks—but, most important, his popular poems created an audience for poetry in America.

Longfellow published his first volume of poetry in 1839; in 1841 his poem "The Wreck of the Hesperus" swept the country, as did *Evangeline* in 1847, *The Song of Hiawatha* in 1855, and "Paul Revere's Ride" (the first poem in his *Tales of a Wayside Inn*) in 1863. Not only was he the best-loved poet in America in the 19th century, but England loved him too: he received honorary degrees from both Oxford and Cambridge, has a memorial in Westminster Abbey, and his *The Courtship of Miles Standish* sold 10,000 copies the day it first appeared in London. Critics acclaimed him until lyric romanticism went out of style. But critical acclaim or not, ever since the 1840s we have heard his lines being cited and recited in homes and schools all over America.

Are You Boiling Mad?

The word *anger* entered English in the 13th century and *angry* in the 14th, both originally referring not to one's feeling of vexation but to that which caused the trouble or annoyance, as an "angry wound." *Anger* and *angry*, like *anguish* (literally a "tight place"), came to English via Latin *angor*, grief, from Latin *angere*, Greek *anchein*, to strangle. Thus the image of *choking with anger* (in use in English since at least the 16th century) or being *hot under the collar* (1910) is the very basis of our word *anger*.

In more modern times, however, the basic image behind our terms for anger seems not to be strangulation but boiling blood. The basic English expression *to make one's blood boil* dates from 1675, and the image of boiling, often as if the body is a steam boiler about to explode or blow a valve, is found in such terms as *to blow one's stack*, *boiling mad*, *hit the roof*, *pop off*, and *steamed up*, while the image of heat or fire is in such terms as *to flare up*, *go up in flames*, and *hot*. These and other American terms for anger, arousing and expressing anger, an outburst of rage, or for people who are ill-tempered or prone to anger, are heard often and include:

blow one's stack, to vent one's anger, 1847; *blow one's top*, 1929; *blow a fuse* (probably based on to "have a short fuse," see below, but changing the fuse to the entirely different protective "fuse" used in an electrical circuit), 1945; *blow a gasket*, 1953, based on to "blow a fuse" but returning to the image of being boiling mad, as a steam boiler about to explode.

boiling mad, 1906; *boiling*, 1937.

conniption fit, a fit of anger, 1833; *conniption(s)*, 1889 (from the English dialect *canapshus*, captious, ill-tempered).

crab, a cranky or irritable person, 1891; *crabby*, 1918.

cross has meant angry in English since 1588, from the meaning of *to cross*, to oppose. In America we have intensified this with such vivid expressions as *cross as a bear*, 1826; *cross as a bulldog*, 1849; and *cross as sin*, 1856. *Crosspatch* has meant an ill-tempered person, usually a woman, in English since 1700, with Sir Walter Scott being the first to use the word to refer to a man, in his 1818 novel *The Heart of Midlothian*. This English word *crosspatch* didn't seem to come to America until 1855 (the *patch* part means "fool," probably because fools or court jesters wore multicolored patchwork costumes—the nickname for Cardinal Wolsey's jester was Patch—though it could come from the Italian *pazzo*, fool).

crusty, ill-tempered, 1834.

cussedness, grouchiness, irritability, 1850s.

fit to be tied, nonplused with anger, 1924.

flare up, an outburst of anger, also a quarrel, 1839; *to flare up*, to become angry, 1940.

fly off the handle, become very angry, 1825. The image is of an ax head flying off its handle, a dangerous state of affairs.

get a rise out of (someone), arouse someone's anger, 1843.

get/have by the ear, cause to become angry, 1831; *set by the ears*, 1834; *on one's ear*, angry, 1871.

get/have one's dander up, to become or be angry, 1834 (perhaps *dander* is from Scottish *dunder*, to ferment); *get one's Ebenezer up/raise one's Ebenezer*, mid 1830s (*Ebenezer* was then also used by itself to mean anger or temper, the name being an implied nickname for the Devil); *get/have one's back up*, as a cat arches its back when angry, 1840s (this same image probably gives us the 1907 *humpy/humphy*, prone to anger, grumpy); *get/have one's Irish up*, 1880s; *get/have one's Indian up*, 1889. Such early "get" terms were so common that by 1867 *get* itself meant to annoy or anger, as in *that gets me*, that annoys or angers me.

get into one's hair, as lice do, hence to annoy, anger, 1880.

get one's goat, to annoy, to anger, 1904; *get one's nanny* (nanny goat), 1934.

get out (or *up*) *on the wrong side of (the) bed*, be irritable, about 1885.

get under one's skin, annoy to anger, 1915.

go up in flames, become enraged, 1924.

grouch, meaning both an irritable, grumpy person and a fit of ill temper, 1896 (from the Old French *grouch*, grumble); *have a grouch on*, also 1896; *grouchy*, 1902. A related form, *grouty*, ill-tempered, sullen, had appeared as early as 1833.

have a chip on one's shoulder, be angry, pugnacious, or sullen and looking for trouble, 1934. The literal putting of a wood chip on one's shoulder and challenging another to knock it off if he wanted to fight to settle an argument or a grudge was first

When angry count four: when very angry, swear.
Mark Twain, *Pudd'nhead Wilson's Calendar*, 1894.

recorded as common among schoolboys, in New York State, in 1830.

have a hemorrhage, to become enraged, 1932, usually in such sentences as, "He was so angry I thought he'd have a hemorrhage."

have a short fuse, be short-tempered, be quick to explode with anger (from the fuse of a bomb or a shell), World War II.

have kittens, become enraged, 1900.

hit the roof, become angry, 1882; *hit the ceiling*, 1923.

hopping mad, 1834; *hopping*, 1840.

horny, angry, 1834. By 1889 *horny* meant sexually excited, completely replacing its use to mean angry.

hot, angry, 1846 (*hot* has also meant sexually excited since the 1920s; as with *horny*, see above, this seems to imply a subconscious relation between sexual passion and anger). *Hot under the collar*, about 1910; *hot and bothered*, annoyed, upset, 1920s. *Het up*, angry, dates from 1886 (*het* has been a variant of heat, heated, since the 14th century); the standard form *heat up*, become angry, didn't appear until 1923.

in a huff, in a pique of anger or ill temper, breathing heavily, or huffing and puffing with anger or resentment, 1839; *huffy*, angry, sullen, 1848.

mad has meant "angry" in English since the 13th century, but because the British began to use it to mean "insane" in the 17th century, this original "angry" meaning was considered to be an American usage by 1778. *To mad*, to anger, exasperate, 1815; *get one's mad up*, 1847. *Mad as a wet hen*, 1821; *mad as a hornet*, 1833; *mad as a striped adder*, 1841; *mad as a meat ax*, 1855; *mad as fire*, 1899; *mad as hops*, 1900 (probably from the 1834 *hopping mad* rather than having anything to do with the plant used in brewing); *mad as Sam Hill*, 1902 (*Sam Hill* was a euphemism for hell); *mad as a rattler*, 1908 (*rattler* had meant *rattlesnake* since 1827); *mad as a bear with a sore head*, 1912; *mad as blazes*, 1947.

meat-ax disposition, irritable, mean, 1834.

miff, a fit of anger, sulking (the word is probably an imitation of a snort of disgust but could be from the German *muffen*, to sulk), 1832; *miffed*, mildly angered or offended, 1846.

old rip, an ill-tempered person, 1904, from the late-18th-century use of *rip* to mean a disreputable man and the Devil and the 19th-century *let rip* and *rip out* (1875), to utter a string of curses.

on the prod, on a rampage, prodding people with curses and criticism, 1903.

ornery, ill-tempered, mean, 1800. *Ornery* is just an informal pronunciation of *ordinary* and originally meant common, ill-mannered.

pee'd off, late 1930s; sometimes written *p'd off* since the 1950s. Though generally assumed to be a euphemism for *pissed off* (*pee* has been a euphemistic synonym or pronunciation abbreviation for *piss* since 1788 in America), *pee'd off* could very well be from *peeved off* (see below).

peevish, originally spelled *pevysh/pevish*, meant silly, foolish, in English in 1393, came to mean spiteful by 1468, and has meant angry since 1530. Since *peevish* sounds like an adjective based on the verb to peeve, we formed that hitherto nonexistent verb, and based verb forms, an adjective, and a noun on it, obtaining *peeved*, angry, 1905; *to peeve*, to annoy, anger, 1910; *peeve* and *pet peeve*, something that annoys and angers, 1918; and *peeved off*, angry, 1920s.

pissed off caused much comment when it appeared in Norman Mailer's 1948 novel about World War II, *The Naked and the Dead*, though it is certainly a much older term, one of many not recorded until the loosening of taboos against scatology and obscenity following the war. Even if the 1930s *pee'd off* actually came from *peeved off*, many people assumed it to come from *pissed off* and began to use this stronger form.

pop off, give vent to anger, about 1920; *pop one's cork*, to become enraged, 1940s.

rampant, in an ill humor, angry, 1906.

rile (up), to anger, 1825; *riley*, angry, 1843.

see red, become enraged, as a bull is supposed to do when it sees red, 1897.

shirty, angry, 1850, probably from the 1848 expression *to tear one's shirt*, to become enraged, as if tearing one's shirt in a rage of passion; the reverse expression, *to keep one's shirt on*, to keep calm, restrain one's anger, dates from 1854.

short as piecrust, extremely short-tempered, 1849 (*short* has meant quick to anger, easily provoked, in English since 1599, with the somewhat tautological *short in the temper* appearing in 1818 and *short-tempered* in the late 19th century).

sore, angry, 1886; *sore as a boil*, 1917; *sore as a crab*, 1920; *sore as hell*, 1928; *sore as blazes*, 1950.

steamed up, angry, 1923; *steamed*, 1924. The original image was, again, of a boiler about to explode or a person with steam coming out of his ears and nose, but the more modern image is of a person so hot with anger that his eyeglasses steam up.

stuffy, angry, sulking, 1889.

tantrum, a fit of anger, 1942.

throw a fit, have a fit of anger, 1825.

> *Thar ain't no sense in gettin' riled.*
> Bret Harte, "Jim," 1868.

President Lyndon Johnson expressing anger at his opponent Barry Goldwater's foreign policy views in a 1964 campaign speech.

ticked off, t'd off, tee'd off, angry, as a ticking bomb ready to explode, 1940s. The abbreviated forms *t'd off, tee'd off* evolved by analogy with *pee'd off, p'd off*.
wild, wild with anger, 1942.
wrathy, angry, full of wrath, 1828.

Anger, of course, can be expressed in many ways: some people *swear like a trooper* (1839), some merely *look daggers* (1845) at a person they are angry at, while other people tell someone they are angry at *to go jump in the lake* (1912) or that they *hate someone's guts* (1918).

Anger and angry people can also lead to an argument, a *fracas* (an English term of 1727, via the French from Italian *fracasso/ fracassare*, to smash, from Latin *cassare*, to break) or *tiff* (used in English since 1750 but of unknown origin) or to what we in America have also called a *spat* (1804), a *to-do* (1827), a *blow-up* (1831), a *falling out* (1848), a *scrap* (1874), a *mix-up* (1900), a *run-in* (1905), or *fireworks* (1923); especially when two angry people who have been *spoiling for a fight* (1860) or *have it in for* (1885) each other decide to *have it out* (1889) or *tangle with* (1934) each other.

Got a Match?

To the 17th-century colonists a *match* (Latin *myxa*, wick) was a fuse with which to fire a musket or a cannon; hemp was used for *slow matches*, cotton for *quick matches*. In the 18th century a *match* meant a *fire stick* for lighting pipes and fires; such a stick was set burning from *punk* (rotted sawdust) carried in a *tinderbox*, the initial spark being obtained from striking steel on flint.

In 1827, modern *matches* were invented in England, with *phosphorous matches* following in 1833, using yellow phosphorus (the first American patent on these was issued to Alonzo Dwight Phillips, of East Hartford, Connecticut, in 1836). These early matches were called *friction matches, scratch matches, splints*, and, less frequently, *instantaneous lights* (thus the question "Got a light?" goes back to the 1830s and 40s), *Congreves* (after the inventor), and *Lucifers* (early matches were tipped with sulfur, Lucifer's burning ingredient in hell). Early wax matches included *Vestas*, after the perpetual fire in the Temple of Vesta in ancient Rome, and *Vesuvians*, which produced a sputtering flame, like that of a small volcano. A popular cardboard match was called the *Fusee*. *Match maker* (an English term of 1643) had originally meant one who made matches or fuses for guns, but by 1851 in England it meant a person who made Lucifer matches (our other term *matchmaker*, one who negotiates or schemes for a marriage, is a 1639 English word and, of course, refers to a completely unrelated match, a match or pairing of a man and woman).

The *safety match* was invented in 1844. These replaced the unstable yellow phosphorus with safer red phosphorus and were sold in a box with a striking surface. By the time of the Civil War, household matches were often kept in *match safes* (1860), which were small, often decorative, metal, porcelain, or wooden matchboxes kept near gas brackets and in other convenient places. *Book matches* were an American invention and term of 1892, the year Joseph Pusey, a Philadelphia patent attorney, perfected them; the Diamond Match Company, which had experimented with such matches since the late 1880s, bought the patent and modernized the design around World War I—just in time for the cigarette boom. According to most accounts, World War I then gave us the expression *three on a match*, implying bad luck, because keeping a match lit long enough to light three cigarettes on the battlefield gave enemy snipers time to see the light, aim, and fire at it (reinforced by the much older superstition that bad luck, death, illness, etc., comes in threes).

Although there were many clumsy and dangerous early versions of the *cigarette lighter*, the item and term grew popular only with the success of the perfected Dunhill lighter of 1922 and Ronson's patented *quick-action lighter* in 1928. Our latest popular lighter, the inexpensive, nonrefillable *disposable lighter*, which is to be thrown away when the fuel is exhausted, appeared in the mid 1970s.

Three on a match *has been considered unlucky since World War I, as keeping a match lit long enough to light three cigarettes on the battlefield gave enemy snipers time to aim and fire at the light. Here Bette Davis watches as Joan Blondell holds the match for Ann Dvorak in a scene from the 1932 movie* Three on a Match.

Millionaire

A man who has a million dollars is as well off as if he were rich.

John Jacob Astor 4th, in the early 1890s. He went down with the *Titanic* in 1912, leaving a fortune of over $87 million.

The first American to be worth the equivalent of a million dollars was probably plantation owner and banker Robert "King" Carter, whose father arrived in Virginia in 1635 and began acquiring rich farmlands, the famous son then expanding these holdings and owning over 300,000 acres, 1,000 slaves, and Nomini Hall with its 28 fireplaces and a library of 1,500 volumes. But "King" Carter was not called a *millionaire*, because the word didn't enter English (from French *millionnaire*) until the 1820s. *Multimillionaire* is an American word, first recorded in the 1850s and then widely used in talking and writing about only one man—the recently deceased John Jacob Astor (1763–1848). He had arrived in New York from Germany at the age of twenty-one and, through his friendship and connections with Thomas Jefferson and other politicians and government officials who granted him exclusive trading rights, had amassed more than $20 million from his 1808 American Fur Company and his 1810 Pacific Fur Company, invested much of his money in real estate, and had long been known as "the richest man in America." His son, William Backhouse Astor, who owned or built over 700 stores and residences in New York City and was its largest landowner, was called "the Landlord of New York."

Billionaire appeared in 1861 and is used more often in America than in Great Britain, one reason being that it is easier to obtain that much money here, where a billion is a thousand million, while the British define a billion as a million million. The world's first billionaire was John D. Rockefeller (1839–1937), who, while still a young man, owned 90 percent of all American oil refineries, all the oil pipelines, and all the oil cars carried by the Pennsylvania Railroad, forming the basis of Standard Oil. Our next two billionaires were probably Andrew Mellon (1855–1937), the banker and aluminum industrialist; and Henry Ford (1863–1947), mass-producer of the Model T car. Thus during the first half of the 19th century some people were amassing millions and during the second half of the century a few were amassing billions. There are now several hundred thousand millionaires in America but only five to ten billionaires, most having made their initial fortunes from oil. *Trillionaire* is not yet used, but ingenuity, inflation, and oil cartels seem to make it a possible word of the future.

We have called a large sum of money a *windfall* (1464 in England, as trees and branches blown down, hence easy-to-obtain firewood, then used since 1542 in English to mean any unexpected acquisition or good fortune); a *mint* (1579 in England as a store of money, then used since 1655 in English to mean a fortune); a *pile* (1740, *to make one's pile* dates from 1850); *big money* (1876); and *megabucks* (1946 from Greek *megás*, large, powerful, especially as used in physics to mean a thousand times a given unit, as in *megacycle*, *megawatt*, etc.). Once multimillionaires and billionaires

John D. Rockefeller, the world's first billionaire.

appeared, fortunes could be large or small, with the somewhat contradictory term *small fortune* appearing in the 1890s. Incidentally, to *blow* (waste, spend) a fortune dates from 1880. *Gravy*, as money obtained without effort, especially political graft, appeared in 1900, while *on the gravy train* and *riding the gravy train* have been in use since the 1930s.

A person who has been able to *feather one's nest* (1862, originally meaning to provide for oneself at the expense of others) or to *strike it rich* (1869, originally as a gold- and silver-mining term) has been called or referred to as:

> *Nabob* (from Hindi *navab* or *nawwāb*, the plural of *nā'ib*, governor, viceroy), 1612, and *Mogul* (from Persian *mughul*, Mongol), 1613. A *Nabob* was a governor or deputy of a Mongol or Indian district or town; then the word came to mean a person of great wealth and rank in England by 1764, especially an Englishman who returned to England after acquiring great wealth in India. *The Mogul* was first used in England to refer to the Grand Mogul, Emperor of Delhi and Hindustan, then came to mean any great or autocratic personage by 1678. Thus these two words for a business tycoon came to America via the English experience in India and the Orient.
>
> *well fixed*, an American term first recorded in 1822. *Well-to-do* and *well off*, however, were both originally English terms (of 1825 and 1849 respectively).
>
> *monied, moneyed*, 1834, originally referring to wealthy corporations.
>
> *rich as* or *richer than Croesus, Astor*, etc. Such expressions first became popular in the 1840s with later variations, such as *rich as Rockefeller* and *rich as* other well-known rich people being coined to fit the times and locale from then until the present. *Croesus*, the 6th century B.C. Lydian king known for his wealth, and often considered to have been the first to issue gold and silver coins, has been a term for a wealthy man since the 1750s (originally in England). *Richer than God* was first recorded in 1945.
>
> *in the dimes*, 1843; *in clover*, 1847; *in the money*, 1902; *in the dough*, 1934 (*dough* has been slang for money since 1840); *in the chips*, 1938 (*chips* was a slang word for money in 1860, from the poker use).
>
> *tycoon* (via the Japanese *taikun*, shogun, military leader, from Chinese *ta kuin*, great prince). The word was brought back to America from Japan in the 1850s, either by Commodore Matthew C. Perry, whose naval squadrons peacefully "opened up" Japan to the West in 1853 and 1854, or by the man who soon followed him to Japan as our first consul there, Townsend Harris. *Tycoon* was then used from 1861 as an affectionate name for President Lincoln (probably from its meaning "military leader") during the Civil War by some of his cabinet members, secretaries, and close political friends. Beginning in the 1870s it was applied to such powerful and wealthy men as John D. Rockefeller and especially to those financiers who built, bought, and manipulated railroads, such as Jim Fiske, Jay Gould, Cornelius Vanderbilt, Leland Stanford, Mark Hopkins, Collis Potter Huntington, and Charles Crocker. Such *magnates* (a 1430 English

In the 1870s Cornelius Vanderbilt was one of the first wealthy men to be called a tycoon, *though the word had earlier been applied to Abraham Lincoln with its original meaning of "military leader" (from the Japanese* taikun) *in 1861.*

The title page of the 1867 Ben the Luggage Boy, *the first of Horatio Alger's* Ragged Dick *novels (as the illustration seems to indicate, it didn't matter whether the hero was a luggage boy or a shoeshine boy at the beginning of his rags-to-riches adventure).*

word) were also called *captains of industry* by the 1880s and sometimes *robber barons* by 1900.

heeled, 1880 as wealthy, from the 1867 use of the word to mean armed or equipped, probably referring to the razor-sharp spurs on the "heels" of fighting cocks. *Well heeled*, 1902.

high roller, 1881 as one who spends recklessly or can afford to (a dice term, literally, one who rolls the dice for high stakes); *to live high*, 1883, meaning to live luxuriously (the term *high living* wasn't recorded until 1934); *high stepper*, 1890s; *high flier*, 1904.

money bag, a wealthy person, 1896; it wasn't usually *moneybags* until the 1920s, when the post–World War I boom and soaring stock market prices seemed to give the rich more than just one bag of money.

on easy street, 1901.

money maker, 1905.

living the life of Riley. This expression was first popular around 1910 but probably comes from Pat Rooney's 1883 comic song *Is That Mr. Reilly?*, which tells what Mr. Reilly would do if he suddenly became rich, such as sleeping in the President's chair, owning hotels, etc.

sitting pretty has meant being in comfortable circumstances since 1910.

filthy with something has meant having plenty of it since 1929; *filthy rich* was first recorded in 1940.

an Horatio Alger story, a rags-to-riches life, a personal success story, 1935, from the poor but honest newsboys and bootblacks who by hard work and virtuous living overcome obstacles and achieve riches and success in the over 120 enormously successful boy's books written by the Unitarian clergyman Horatio Alger (1832–99), including the *Ragged Dick* (1867), *Luck and Pluck* (1869), and *Tattered Tom* (1871) series. Horatio Alger himself was the son of a clergyman and a graduate of Harvard and Harvard Divinity School but went to Paris as a rebellious bohemian before changing his ways and returning to America to become the chaplain of a Newsboys' Lodging House in 1866, where he met and cared for the poor boys he was to write about.

affluent has meant flowing in abundance in English since 1413 and flowing or abounding in wealth since 1769, but was not a common term for "wealthy" until John Kenneth Galbraith's 1958 best-selling book *The Affluent Society*.

Though we in America pride ourselves on having no rigid social classes, economic levels do divide us into such classes. Without inherited nobility, rank, or social position, we usually consider the wealthy as our highest class. In colonial days people of wealth, good family, and social position were called by the late-16th-century English terms *the gentry, gentle folk,* and *the quality.* Our 1787 term the *wellborn* was first used by John Adams in an article calling for the influential, "the rich, the wellborn, and the able," to support the newly drafted Constitution and was thus soon used as a derisive name for the Federalists who supported it. Though early Americans were not supposed to be proud of their family position or background, as early as 1770 a Philadelphia printer published

American genealogies—and by 1818 we were using the abbreviation *F.F.* to mean *First Family* (though at the time many of the First Families were not only wealthy and socially prominent but had actually been among the first families to settle their respective regions). By 1847 *F.F.V.* stood for First Families of Virginia and by the 1860s *F.F.T.* stood for First Families of Tennessee, though during the Civil War, Union soldiers humorously claimed *F.F.* stood for "fast-footed," and *F.F.V.* for the "Fast-Footed Virginians" who fled from their attacks.

Though the democratic term *self-made man* appeared in 1832 there was still such an undemocratic "class" as the *upper crust* (an Americanism of 1835, though England had its *upper ranks* in 1825 and was to have its *upper circles*, 1837, and *upper classes*, 1839, which last term gave English *upper class* by the 1890s). We even have our *blue bloods* (an 1863 English term for aristocrats) and our own *blue book* (originally the 1835 blue-bound Biennial Register of information about the U.S. government but by the late 1840s meaning a directory of socially prominent people) and our own *social register* (originally referring to the *New York Social Register*, first published in 1886).

That brings us back to America's first multimillionaire, John Jacob Astor. It was his daughter-in-law, Caroline Schermerhorn Astor (1792–1875), the first to be called "*The* Mrs. Astor," whose Fifth Avenue mansion had a ballroom that could comfortably hold 400 elite members of society. Lawyer and social leader (Samuel) Ward McAllister (1827–95) may have had this ballroom in mind when he coined the term *The Four Hundred* in 1888 (though since 1844 New York's elite had been called the *Upper 10,000*, shortened to the *Upper Ten* by 1848, the "ten" still referring to ten thousand).

Americans with wealth and social position have been accused of being arrogant or pretentious, of being *high and mighty* (1830), *on (one's) high horse* (1839 in the U.S. but dating back to a 1716 English term), *highfalutin* (also 1839), *high-toned* (1855), *high hat* (1920), of *putting on airs* (1820s, from the 1606 English *airy*, meaning affected or pretentious), and of being *stuck-up* (1829), *uppish* (1878), *uppity* (1880), a *stuffed shirt* (1913), and of being *ritzy* (1923), originally spelled *Ritzy*, from the palatial Ritz hotels built in New York, London, Paris, etc., by the Swiss hotelkeeper and restaurateur César Ritz (1850–1918), or of *ritzing* their inferiors by *putting on the Ritz* (both late 1920s terms). But no matter how *broke* (1820s, with *clean broke*, *dead broke*, and *flat broke* all appearing in the early 1840s, *stone broke* in 1887, and *go broke* in 1895) or *down and out* (1901) some of the rest of us might be, we have one overriding consolation: there's always the chance that one day we too might become millionaires.

There are only about four hundred people in fashionable New York society. If you go outside that number you strike people who are either not at ease in a ballroom or else make other people not at ease.

Ward McAllister, a retired lawyer and the social leader of New York City and Newport, Rhode Island, in an 1888 letter.

"The rich are different from us" is a line Edmund Wilson attributed to an awestruck F. Scott Fitzgerald (Hemingway was said to have re-buffed Fitzgerald with the laconic reply, "Yes, they have more money"). Here the rich are at the yacht club in 1905, in a Coaching Club photograph in 1906, and in Palm Beach in 1913.

Molasses, Honey, Maple Syrup, and Sugar,

meaning maple sugar, were the common sweeteners of early America. The first colonists brought the 16th-century English word *molasses* with them (via Portuguese *melaco* from Latin *mel*, honey) and also called this slow-pouring syrup *long-sweetening*. Late in the 17th century, British English dropped the word *molasses* and called it *treacle*, originally meaning an antidote for poison (from the Greek *antidotos thēriakē*, antidote for a poisonous beast), *treacle* then coming to mean molasses in Britain because so many antidotes and medicines were given with it to mask their taste. *Molasses*, however, continued to be the American word for the sweetener and gave us such terms as *molasses candy* (1809), *molasses cake* (1836), and *molasses cookie* (1887).

Honey bees were introduced into the Massachusetts Bay Colony around 1639, with the Indians soon calling them "the white man's flies." Honey was an important sweetener both in England and the colonies, and the colonists brought with them the 17th-century English term *to honey up*, to flatter, cajole; then by the 1840s we were using *to honey fuggle* to mean to flatter, cajole, or win with sweet promises. *Honey* had meant a sweetheart in England since the 14th century, became a term of endearment in America in the 1880s and by 1888 *a honey* meant any excellent person or thing. The slangier *honey bunch* appeared in 1904 but the southern *honey child* or *honey chile'* seems not to have been common until after World War I. The humorous euphemism *honey wagon* has been farm use for a manure wagon or manure spreader since about 1915, while *mind your own beeswax* and *none of your beeswax* were snappy ways to say "mind your own business, none of your business" around 1920.

But despite molasses and honey, it was *maple syrup* and *maple sugar*, both common in the colonies by 1720, that spawned a whole new industry in New England, especially after the British Molasses Act of 1733 and Sugar Act of 1764 imposed heavy duties on molasses and sugar imported from the French and Spanish West Indies. Soon after these acts were imposed, Americans were turning from these West Indies sugar cane products to the native *sugar maple* (1730) as the main source of sweeteners. Thus in the mid 18th century we began talking widely about such sweetened, flavored, or fermented products as *maple beer*, *maple candy*, *maple molasses*, *maple vinegar*, and *maple wine*.

Even after the Revolutionary War and the War of 1812 again gave us access to the West Indies sugar cane products, our own maple sugar products remained cheaper. Thus in the 1820s and 30s our maple sugar industry continued to grow with America, giving us many terms we still associate with New England, including:

> *sugar bush*, a grove of sugar maples reserved for tapping (it has also been a name for the sugar sumac since 1931).
>
> *sugar day* and *sugar weather*, when sugar maple sap flows freely. *Sugar month* and *sugar season* refer to the time for *sugaring* (see below).
>
> *sugar house*, a farm shed where maple syrup and sugar are made; also a sugar warehouse. New York City's windowless sugar houses became infamous during the Revolutionary War when the British used these dark, airless warehouses as prisons for captured American soldiers.
>
> *sugaring*, *sugaring off*, and *sugaring down*, boiling down the sap into syrup and crystallizing the syrup into sugar.
>
> *sugar snow*, a late spring snow prolonging the flow of the sap. Such snows, or the cold weather accompanying them, were a boon to the *sugarers*, increasing the amount of sap they could "catch," and giving them more time for their work.

The 1820s and 30s also saw the wide popularity of such terms as *sugar trough*, *sugar kettle*, *sugar chain* (to hold the large kettle of sap over the *sugar fire*), and *sugar ladle*, all used in collecting the sap and boiling the syrup. Gatherings to help collect and boil the sap and sample the new syrup and sugar were called *sugar frolics*, *sugar licks*, *sugar parties*, *sugar suppers*, and *sugaring offs*. Served at such gatherings were cornmeal mush with the new maple syrup, snow with the maple syrup poured over it, a variety of *maple cakes* and *maple pies*, and, mainly for the children, syrup frozen in the shape of *maple babies*.

Incidentally, a blend of maple and sugar cane syrups was developed by a St. Paul, Minnesota, grocer, P. J. Towle, in 1887 and named *Log Cabin Syrup* in honor of his boyhood hero, Abraham Lincoln (every child knows Lincoln was brought up in a log cabin). It became one of the most famous brand names in America and its original, distinctive can, shaped like a log cabin, was used until the World War II metal shortage made glass bottles easier to obtain.

Molasses, honey, and maple syrup were such common sweeteners in colonial America and sugar was so rare that the term *sugar bowl* didn't become common until the 1770s. Even then *sugar* usually meant the brown maple sugar, sometimes called *Indian sugar* (1784); it was for everyday use, the more expensive cane or "store-bought sugar" was reserved for special occasions, such as holidays or when company came to dinner. Not until the 1860s did *cane sugar* become as cheap as maple sugar and not until the 1880s was *beet sugar* generally available, with the new form and term *sugar cube* appearing in the late 1880s. Thus between the 1860s and 1880s the word *sugar* changed from meaning the common brown maple sugar to white sugar made from sugar cane or beets. Meanwhile, *sugar* had become a slang term for money around 1859; the term *sugar daddy* appeared in 1918 with post–World War I prosperity; and *sugar* became a widespread term of endearment in the 1920s.

Mom and Dad

From the 1770s to the 1930s, *mama* and *papa/poppa* were what most Americans called their parents. Both words are extremely widespread, with cognates in many languages, and probably derive from the cries babies have made since before the dawn of history. *MAma* and *PApa* were the common American pronunciations, though the British pronunciations of *maMa* and *paPA* were also heard on this side of the Atlantic. *Mama* also gave us *mum* and *mummy* in the 1820s, though these words were considered socially low until around 1900, when Americans heard them used by upper-class Englishmen. The form *mammy* appeared in the 1840s. *Papa/poppa* gave us *pappy* in the 1770s, *pap* in the first decade of the 1800s (primarily in Appalachia and the Mississippi valley), and *pop* in the 1830s, with *pop* also soon becoming a slang term for any elderly man (1844).

Ma and *pa* rivaled *mama* and *papa* in popularity from the 1780s to the 1860s. Thus the story about Washington chopping down the cherry tree, when first presented in the 1806 edition of Parson Weems's *The Life and Memorable Actions of George Washington*, has the young George saying, "I can't tell a lie, Pa. . . . I did cut it with my hatchet."

Today, however, *mama* and *papa* and *ma* and *pa* are seldom heard in urban America outside the South. Since the 1930s most Americans have called their parents *mom* and *dad*. *Mom* and *mommie* are both based on the old *mama* and first came into use in the 1900s, while *dad* and *daddy* entered English in the 16th century. *Mom and pop* has been used since the late 1950s to refer to a small store or business owned and operated by a married couple or a family.

Both *old woman* (since 1775) and *old lady* (1838) originally meant wife, as they still usually do; but they quickly came to mean mother also. On the other hand, *old man* originally did mean father (in the 1840s) and came to mean husband only 50 years later.

How about the basic words *mother* and *father* themselves? They have always been used in America, but until 1900 were primarily adult words, few children before then being so formal or educated as to use them. *Grandmother* and *grandfather* were also considered adult words until the 1900s—since colonial days most American children have called their grandparents *grandma* and *grandpa*, with *gramps* appearing in the 1860s.

Mother's Day and *Father's Day* also have their own stories. Some people were talking about setting aside "a day to commemorate mothers" in the early 1900s, including Frank Hering of South

MY MAMMY
THE SUN SHINES EAST — THE SUN SHINES WEST

AL JOLSON
in Sinbad

Words by
JOE YOUNG
and
SAM LEWIS

Music by
WALTER DONALDSON

Irving Berlin Inc
1507 Broadway N.Y.

Who ran to help me when I fell,
And would some pretty story tell,
Or kiss the place to make it well?
My Mother.

Bend, Indiana, who in 1904 began proposing that the Eagle lodges set aside such a day each year. However, it was Anna Jarvis of Philadelphia who in 1907 proposed the name *Mother's Day*, that it be the second Sunday of May, and that it be celebrated by wearing a red carnation if one's mother was alive and a white one if she was dead (a very popular custom well into the 1940s). Philadelphia adopted Miss Jarvis's plan and observed the first *Mother's Day* on May 10, 1908.

Father's Day is attributed to Mrs. John Bruce Dodd of Spokane, Washington, whose father, William Smart, had raised his children after his wife died. Thus Mrs. Dodd felt that fathers deserved a special day too. Prompted by her and by the new popularity of Mother's Day, Spokane ministers, newspapers, and stores promoted the acceptance of the idea—and Spokane celebrated the first *Father's Day* in 1910.

The Movies

Cave men probably made shadowgraphs on their cave walls at night. Later humans have continued to use this primitive form of casting pictures on a wall, using the light from a fireplace, candles, lanterns, and light bulbs. Beginning around 1645, Europeans began to marvel over an optical instrument that used a lens to throw onto a wall in a darkened room a magnified image of a transparent picture, painted or drawn on glass. A Dane exhibited such a device in Lyon, France, in 1665, the French calling it a *lanterne magique*, which was translated into *magic lantern* in England by 1696—magic-lantern shows, sometimes shown on a

special *screen* (1815 in this magic-lantern use), were used to entertain people from then until well into the early 20th century.

Beginning in the 1820s many devices appeared that created the illusion of moving figures or scenes by the rapid succession of still pictures or images. These devices used revolving, meshing, or rapidly flipping discs, cylinders, and rectangles carrying drawn, painted, or photographed pictures, paperdoll-like figures, or silhouettes. Though rather simple devices, usually handheld and with a peephole, they were given complicated names that were orgies of Greek words and word parts. In chronological order, they included the:

> *Panorama*, a box with a peephole or slit through which the viewer saw a scroll of pictures unreel from one cylinder to another. The word *panorama* (from the Greek words *pan*, all, every + *-hórāma*, view, sight) had been created by the Scottish painter Robert Barker in 1787 to name his own large *Panorama* device, which was a large cylinder with a scene painted on the inside, the spectator to stand in the center of the cylinder.
>
> *Thaumatrope*, Dr. William Fitton's 1827 device, named from the Greek *thauma/thaumato-*, miracle, and similar to the Phenakistoscope (see below).
>
> *Phenakistoscope*, a "scientific toy" invented and named in 1832 by the Belgian physicist Joseph Antoine Ferdinand Plateau. The name is from the Greek elements *phenakit/phenax*, deceiver + *skopein/-scope*, viewing instrument. More commonly called a *magic disc*, the *Phenakistoscope* contained two rotating discs, the "magic" one having drawn or painted pictures that seemed to move when they appeared through the slots of the second.
>
> *Stroboscope*, also called a *stroboscopic disc*, invented in 1836 and named from the Greek *strobos*, whirling, turning + *-scope*.
>
> *Kinematoscope*, invented by Coleman Sellers of Philadelphia in 1860 and named from the Greek *kinēma/kinētos*, motion, moving + *-scope*. This was the first such device to use actual photographs instead of drawings, paintings, or cutouts, the first to be said to present a *peep show* (1861)—and launched the word *kinema* on its movie career.

What was needed to improve such "scientific toys" were more realistic pictures, such as the photographs first used in the Kinematoscope, and, if these pictures were to be projected in an improved magic lantern, a bright, steady light source. Though the light source was not to be provided by Edison's electric light bulb until 1879, the more realistic pictures had been provided by development of the *Daguerreotype*, a word first recorded in English in January 1839, just a few days after the French painter and inventor Louis Daguerre had informed France's Academy of Science of his process. The words *photograph*, *photography*, and *photographic* (from the Greek elements *phôs/photo-*, light + *-graph*, drawn, written, one who or that which draws or writes) were then created by the renowned English astronomer and physicist Sir John Herschel, who introduced them into the language in a paper he read before the Royal Society on March 14, 1839, his paper being entitled: "Notes on the Act of Photography, or the Application of the Chemical Rays of Light to the Purpose of Pictorial Representation." In that paper Herschel used *photograph* only as a noun, but on the back of two of the 23 photographs he presented as supporting evidence and examples he had written, "Photographed Feb. 17/39," using *photograph* as a verb. Though Herschel may have gone directly to Greek for his word *photograph*, he may have taken the Greek *photo-* from William Henry Fox Talbot's term *photogenic drawing* (*photo-* + *genic*, produced, formed, hence literally light-produced drawing) for a picture produced by the chemical action of light on a sensitized surface, Talbot having used this term in a paper read before the Royal Society in January 1839. Herschel may have taken the Greek *-graph* from French physicist Joseph Niépce's word *heliograph* (Greek *hēlios*, sun + *-graph*, hence literally "sun drawing"), which Niépce had used for a photograph he achieved around 1824. As early as 1862 Herschel's word *photograph* was being shortened to *photo*.

In a paper read before the Royal Society in 1840, Herschel introduced the words *negative* and *positive* in their photographic senses, as well as the term "naturally *colored photograph*" (he, of course, spelled it the British way "coloured photograph"). The photographic use of the word *develop* came into use around 1845, then referring to the Daguerreotype process or to Talbot's own *Talbotype* process (patented in 1841), his process and a photograph taken by it also being called *calotype* (from the Greek words *kalôs*, beautiful + *typos*, impression, image).

Whatever their nationality, the men who invented early photographic processes probably knew the English use of the word *camera* (a Late Latin word for room, chamber, from Greek *kamara*, vault). It had appeared in the modern sense around 1730 as a shortened form of *camera obscura*, the viewing device, and had then first been used around 1826 to mean the box in which a heliograph could be made.

One photograph taken on a metal or glass plate, which had to be removed from the camera before the next one was inserted, is a long way from a series of pictures taken in rapid succession to convey the illusion of movement when passed before the viewer. In the 1860s and 70s various Americans and Europeans experimented with ways to take a series of photographs of moving objects in rapid succession. The most famous of these took place in California in the 1870s, at the Palo Alto stud farm of railroad tycoon Leland Stanford. To win a $25,000 bet that a running horse sometimes has all four hooves off the ground, Stanford asked railroad engineer John D. Isaacs and *photographer* (an 1847 word)

Eadweard Muybridge to record the motions of a running horse. Muybridge, who had been born Edward Muggeridge in England, was already known for his photographs of Alaska and Yosemite and had earlier been employed by various railroads to take pictures in Latin America—though some of the general public knew of him only because of his trial for and acquittal of murdering his young wife's lover. Isaacs and Muybridge set up a series of 24 cameras in a row, each *shutter* (a photography term since the 1850s) being tripped by a string as the horse ran past—sometimes with all four hooves off the ground. The two men also took similar successful sequential photographs of other animals and of humans. These earliest pictures of animals and man in motion became classics and were taken to Europe and shown as an early moving picture on existing mechanisms. After their success, Isaacs returned to designing and building railroads, and Muybridge devised his own means of projecting the pictures, eventually leading to his invention of one of the many early moving picture projectors, the *zoopraxiscope* (from the Greek elements *zōi/zôin*, life, living + *prâxis*, action + *-scope*).

Using a series of cameras in a row to take pictures of moving objects was, of course, impractical and the problem of moving a series of still photographs smoothly and quickly enough past the eye to give the illusion of continuous movement still existed. In 1887, Edison began to work on a device in which a series of pictures appeared to move when seen through a peephole. He soon realized that to take and show a continuous series of pictures quickly and smoothly he would need a flexible strip or roll of material. At the same time George Eastman of Rochester, New York, who since 1880 had been making *dry plates* (1859) and other photographic equipment, was seeking such a flexible material for the small *box camera* (originally an 1842 term for a camera obscura) and *roller photography* system he had been perfecting since 1884. In

Eadweard Muybridge's pictures of a horse in motion, the first series of motion in pictures.

1888 his Eastman Dry Plate and Film Company patented this camera and system under the name *Kodak*, Eastman coining the name purposely from no other known word and as having no other meaning, which avoided trademark problems, and because, he said, it was "short, vigorous," easy to identify, and he "favored" the letter *K*. His *Kodak camera* was then introduced in June 1888, selling for $25, including case and *shoulder strap* (1870 as meaning a carrying strap worn over the shoulder, from the 1688 use as a supporting strap on a woman's gown)—and each camera came fully loaded with a roll of Eastman's new opaque *stripping paper* that could take 100 *exposures* (*exposure* and *to expose* had been used in their photographic senses since 1839; the term *exposure meter* was first recorded in 1891). After taking the 100 pictures the owner would return the still fully loaded Kodak to the Eastman factory, which would remove the stripping paper, develop it, *print* the pictures (*print* had been used in photography as a verb since at least 1851 and as a noun since 1853), and return the pictures and the camera, with a new roll inserted, for $10. Photography for the masses had arrived. But Eastman and his customers weren't satisfied with that stripping paper; both Eastman and Edison needed a better flexible material to take pictures.

The original Kodak *camera of 1888.*

Hannibal Goodwin, a sixty-seven-year-old Episcopal clergyman, solved the problem on September 13, 1889, when he was granted a patent for a strong, flexible, transparent celluloid base coated with a "film" of photographic chemicals (he had applied for the patent for his *film* on May 2, 1887, but it took more than two years for him to fight off litigation by other inventors—the word *film* had been used since 1845 to refer to a film of photographic chemicals spread on glass). Eastman then manufactured the Goodwin film in inch-wide strips under the Eastman name, using it for his Kodak cameras. Edison obtained a 50-foot sample of this film for $1.50 and in a few weeks he, or perhaps his assistant, William Dickson, had invented the *Kinetograph* to take moving pictures and the *Kinetoscope* to show them. The Kinetoscope was first demonstrated at Edison's laboratory on October 6, 1889 (that it took only three weeks from the time Goodwin obtained his patent on transparent film until Edison got an Eastman sample and used it to invent the *Kinetoscope* shows that the three were merely waiting for the patent to be granted). Edison's *Kinetoscope*, whose name was strongly reminiscent of Coleman Seller's 1860 *Kinematoscope* (and also based on the Greek *kinēma/kinētos*, motion, moving + *-scope*), was merely an advanced peephole device with a 50-foot strip of film moving between a light and a revolving shutter.

Though Edison rushed to invent the *Kinetoscope* as soon as transparent roll film was available, he then lost interest in it and in the *motion picture* (1891). A battery of ten of his coin-operated "peep-show machines" were to be exhibited at the 1893 Columbia

A 1905 Mutascope.

Exposition in Chicago but were not ready in time, eventually being installed in two rows at the first *Kinetoscope Parlor*, which opened April 14, 1894, at 1155 Broadway in New York City, the machines showing bits of a prizefight and pieces of vaudeville acts. They immediately became the major attraction of dime museums and penny arcades all over the country and were also seen in London and Paris later that year.

Edison, always the practical inventor, seldom the visionary, thought of his Kinetoscope and its moving pictures merely as novelties the public would soon tire of. Thus he patented his Kinetoscope only in the U.S., not thinking it worth the additional $150 to patent it abroad—and for years he saw no need to couple it with a *projector* (1884 in this sense) to show his films to an audience rather than just one peephole viewer at a time. Thus the way was open for others, both in America and Europe, to develop improved versions of Edison's Kinetoscope and to convert it into a projecting machine. The Kinetoscope and Kinetoscope Parlor were soon rivaled by Herman Casler's 1897 *Mutascope* (from Latin *mutare*, to change + *-scope*) and *Mutascope Parlors*. The *Mutascope*, which snapped pictures on a rapidly revolving cylinder past the peephole, became one of the most popular *penny-in-the-slot machines* (a 1901 term). But it was those who rushed to turn the *Kinetoscope* into a device to project moving pictures on a screen or wall who were the most foresighted. Their first projecting motion picture machines were all invented and demonstrated in 1895 and included the:

> *Cinématographe*, invented by the French chemists and photographic manufacturers Louis and Auguste Lumière, brothers who had developed an early process for color photography and an earlier moving picture device (*Cinématographe*, of course, comes from the same Greek *kinēma/kinētos*, motion, moving, others had used + *-o-* + the Greek *-graph*, drawn, written, one who or that which draws or writes). After seeing Edison's Kinetoscope in Paris in 1894, the Lumières soon invented their Cinématographe, using it to give the first commercial presentation of a projected motion picture, at the Salon Indien in the basement of the Grand Café on the Boulevard des Capucines, in Paris on December 28, 1895.
>
> The Cinématographe was unique in that it was not only a projector but could serve as a camera and could even be used to make positive film prints from its negatives. Being the most versatile, compact, and portable of all the early motion picture machines, it became the basis not only of the French film industry but gained worldwide acceptance, dominating the early movie industry in many countries.
>
> *Cinématographe* seems to have lost both its accent mark and its final *e* in many American and British newspapers and magazines within a few months of its appearance, often being spelled *Cinematograph* in English by mid 1896. It made *cinema* (*cinéma* in French) a popular European term, the word appearing as a

shortened, usually adjectival, form of *Cinématographe* by 1899, the British then using *cinema* to mean any motion picture by 1909 and a motion picture theater by 1913 (the same year the British *cinema hall*, *cinema show*, and *cinema star* appeared), with *cinematic* appearing in 1927. Since the *Cinématographe* was more widely used in Europe than here, *cinema*, sometimes still spelled in our old way as *kinema*, didn't have any wide use in the U.S. until 1918, perhaps having been adopted from the British and French by American servicemen during World War I.

Theatrograph (from the English spelling *theatre* + -*o*- + -*graph*) was the name of the first British movie projecting machine, invented—in 1895, of course—by Robert Paul, who also started his work by trying to combine an Edison Kinetoscope with a projecting device. The Theatrograph was also called an *Animatograph* (from the Latin *animatus* or English *animate* + -*graph*) by 1896 and was the basis of the early British film industry.

Vitascope (from Latin *vita*, life + -*scope*, hence literally "machine for viewing life") was introduced—also in 1895—by the Washington, D.C., real estate investor Thomas Armat and originally used Edison Kinetoscope films, Armat calling the films *life portrayals*.

Similar devices followed by the next year, including the *Pantoptikon* (probably from *pantomime* or the Greek *pantomīnos* + the Greek *eikon*, image, figure), the *Eidoscope* (Greek *eidōlon/eidos*, image, shape + -*scope)*, and the much better known *Biograph* (from the Greek *bios*, life + -*graph*), which flickered and vibrated a lot but projected a large picture.

Thus the orgy of Greek words and word parts continued, often being the most classic element of the early movie industry. Words ending in -*scope*—*Animatoscope, Bioscope, Eidoscope, Kinematoscope, Kinetoscope, Magniscope, Mutascope, Phenakistoscope, Stroboscope, Vitascope*, and *Zoopraxiscope*—and in -*graph*—*Biograph* and *Cinématographe*—first referred to the viewing or projecting machines and systems, and then, both as nouns and adjectives, were soon used to refer to the pictures they displayed. Often, however, -*gram* (Greek for drawing, writing) was substituted as the last syllable to indicate the pictures displayed, so that one saw *Kinetograms* in a *Kinetoscope*.

Once Edison saw that projected motion picture machines were creating a sensation, he quickly adapted Armat's Vitascope as his own *projecting Kinetoscope* (*projector* was an 1884 word; *projection room* appeared in 1926) and presented the first American commercial exhibition of motion pictures projected on a screen, this show following the regular vaudeville show as an "added attraction" at Koster and Bial's Music Hall on the corner of 34th Street and Broadway on April 23, 1896 (a site later occupied by Macy's main department store). Called "mechanically reproduced theater entertainment," this first American movie show was a potpourri of a scene from a prizefight (always a favorite of Kinetoscope action fans), a few turns by a dancer, and a *shot* (1889 in photographic

The always interesting moving pictures in the biograph at Keith's will include this week four new scenes.
New York Tribune, Oct. 30, 1898

use, *to shoot* a picture dates from 1890) of waves rolling in on the beach at Dover, England. *The New York Times*, in what had to be its first movie review, said the films were "wonderfully real and singularly exhilarating." Koster and Bial didn't realize it at the time, but this "added attraction" to their vaudeville show would soon become the main attraction that would first push vaudeville into the background, often relying on it for a few "added acts," then kill it altogether.

For several years motion pictures were, indeed, only a novelty, impressing audiences with unrelated scenes of sports, pretty women at the beach, dancers, moving trains and cars, daredevil horseback riders, and some current events, filmed by the manufacturers of the projectors and shown as added attractions in vaudeville houses and music halls, or as the entire program in a *store show* (a small store serving as a motion picture theater by the addition of folding chairs) or *5¢ show* (one could see the entire performance of short pictures for 5¢). There were only three such *screen theaters* in the U.S. in 1897, one in New York, one in Chicago, and one in a black tent traveling as part of the Barnum and Bailey circus. It looked as if Edison had been right—that moving pictures were destined to be only novelties.

Then, beginning in 1899, the French magician Georges Méliès wrote, directed, designed, and acted in short movies that told fairy tales and science fiction tales, such as his 1902 *A Trip to the Moon:* moving pictures had begun telling stories. Others soon began making these new *story pictures*, including Edwin S. Porter, an Edison *camerist* (first recorded in 1890, then meaning a still photographer; the motion picture term *cameraman* didn't appear until around 1905).

Porter achieved fame with his third story picture, *The Great Train Robbery*, an 11-minute, 800-foot film containing 14 shots or scenes—in those days each step of the story was told in one scene, which one camera took in one continuous medium-long shot. This, the first movie western, was shot in Dover, New Jersey, and featured "Bronco Billy" Anderson (real name Max Aronson), making him the first actor given credit for a role in an American film. Telling the simple story of a train robbery and the pursuit and capture of the robbers, Porter used the film technique of the moving camera, which he had introduced in his earlier *Railroad Romance*, and the first low-angle shot (of a man being gunned down while trying to escape from the robbers), as well as a sensational spliced-in medium close-up of George Barnes, a New York stage actor, firing his gun directly into the camera, hence into the face of the audience, causing some members of the audience to duck, scream, or even faint. Porter, also for the first time, switched back and forth between several scenes (from the pursuing posse to the fleeing robbers and back again), filming all of each scene at once

The Great Train Robbery, *1903*.

and then splicing parts of them into the sequence he wanted in order to create suspense and tell the story.

Such sensational and dramatic devices made *The Great Train Robbery* a huge success by 1905 and suddenly many more screen theaters were opened to show such movies. One such 5¢ show was opened in a small theater on Smithfield Street in Pittsburgh, Pennsylvania, in 1905, by a local showman, John P. Harris, who renamed the theater the *Nickelodeon* and showed *The Great Train Robbery* that fall to sell-out crowds, though there were only 92 seats (others say it was Harry Davis who opened and named his motion picture theater the *Nickelodeon*, in McKeesport, Pennsylvania, in 1905 and still others that Harris and Davis were partners). *Nickelodeon* did become the most common word for any 5¢ show or store show; however, the word wasn't coined by any motion picture exhibitor in Pennsylvania; it had been used since 1888 as a name for the penny, nickel, and dime arcades where moving pictures were shown in peephole devices, change-in-the-slot Gramophones could be listened to, etc. (the word is from *nickel*, 5¢ piece + *-odeon* from *melodeon*, which had meant a music hall, as well as a type of accordion, and a small reed organ; following the association with change-in-the-slot Gramophones, *nickelodeon* also came to mean a juke box in 1938). A nickelodeon was also sometimes called a *nickelette* and a *nickel theater* (1912).

Five thousand motion-picture nickelodeons stretched across the U.S. by 1907, eight thousand by 1910, almost all being true to their name by charging a 5¢ admission. Many were located in small stores and storerooms converted into store shows by the addition of folding chairs—the chairs sometimes borrowed or rented from the local funeral parlor—most showing the films to piano accompaniment, the local pianist valiantly trying to match music to the mood of each scene. Many were in poor polyglot city neighborhoods where workingmen and newly arrived immigrants who understood English with difficulty, if at all, loved the silent, simple nickelodeon shows at which, for the same price as a tall glass of beer, they could escape to action and melodrama. Neighborhood entrepreneurs could open a nickelodeon for about $150, and a few would soon parlay that money to become major *exhibitors* (a 1613 English word), then Hollywood tycoons.

The first motion picture *studio* had been built by Edison in February 1892 on the grounds of his West Orange, New Jersey, laboratory to shoot Kinetoscope films. It was a true *studio* in the artist's and still photographer's sense, a building or room admitting much natural light and equipped with strong indoor lights and *flats* (1807 in theatrical use) on which background scenery was painted, these flats moved by men called *grips* (1888 in theatrical use, so called because they shifted the scenery by gripping it and shoving it around). It was not until 1913 that *studio* would mean not only

The first movie studio, *built by Edison on the grounds of his West Orange, New Jersey, laboratory in 1892. It was officially known as Edison's "Kinetographic theater" but unofficially called the* Black Maria *because it was covered with tar paper. It could be rotated so that sunlight would stream through the openings that could be made in the roof.*

Edison with one of his motion picture machines *(a projector) in 1905.*

the room or building where movies were shot but also the entire facilities, including film laboratories and offices, of a motion picture company, and not until around 1915 that the painted flats would be called a *set* by moviemakers (*set* was an 1861 theatrical term), and 1921 before the studio grounds were called a movie *lot*. That first movie "studio" cost Edison $635 to build; it was a large, flimsy shack that could be rotated to get the most sunlight and was known as the *Black Maria* because it was covered with tar paper.

After 1905 the suddenly popular nickelodeons and their audiences demanded a constant flow of new films, and studios sprang up in shacks, auditoriums, and lofts in New York City, nearby New Jersey, on Long Island, and even in Chicago. During the next ten years at such studios as Edison's, Biograph (founded by Edison's brilliant assistant, William Dickson), and Bison Life Motion Pictures, men such as D. W. (David Wark) Griffith and Mack Sennett learned their craft and created and expanded the form, techniques, and vocabulary of motion pictures. Most of the early techniques and terms came from the Biograph studios,

D. W. Griffith.

where D. W. Griffith perfected the dramatic use of the *close-up* and *long shot* and made them part of our consciousness and vocabulary, though he neither invented these techniques nor was the first to use the terms. Born in La Grange, Kentucky, he had given up his mediocre stock-company acting career and written an unsuccessful play before playing the leading role of the lumberjack in Edwin S. Porter's 1907 *Rescued from the Eagle's Nest*. He then "wrote some stories" for Biograph (not until after 1915, when movies became longer and more complicated, were the 1880s theatrical term *scenario* and the 1897 theatrical term *script*, from manu*script*, widely used in moviemaking) before going to work for that studio in New York City, directing hundreds of short Biograph films between 1908 and 1913.

Between 1905 and 1915, Griffith, Sennett, and other pioneers of *the silent drama* (a rather pretentious 1914 term for the movies) used and were responsible for the popularity of such terms as:

close-up, 1913. Before that a picture showing only the head and shoulders had usually been called a *bust photograph*, *bust shot*, or *bust* in both still and motion picture photography.

credit lines, 1914. By 1922 these were also simply called *credits* and, sometimes, *titles*. Most of the early short films didn't bother to list cast or contributors. Until 1915 most well-known stage actors felt it was degrading to appear in movies and many of the promising young stage actors who did appear in them preferred to remain anonymous, leaving the way open for theatrical cast-offs, the unsuccessful and the unpromising, to become movie stars. Not until the late 1920s were the names of the writer, art director, etc., always listed in the credits, as simple early films required few such people and, before strong movie guilds and unions, movie studios tended to ignore them.

director was a common movie term by 1911, with the verb *to direct* appearing in movie use in 1913 (both, of course, from the earlier stage use). Griffith and other early directors were much less specialized than modern ones, *casting* (1814 in theatrical use) their own films, suggesting or choosing sets and costumes, perhaps serving as their own cameramen or even filling in as actors.

dissolve and *fade*. Between 1905 and 1915 moviemakers learned to fade or dissolve the end of a scene in a chemical bath or *dissolver* (1912) for a *dissolving effect* (1915), later simply called a *dissolve* (1920), sometimes then using this process to make a *fade* or *fade-out* of one scene and a *fade-in* to the next (these last three terms all first recorded in 1918; such *chemical fades* are no longer necessary, dissolves and fades now more easily being produced in the camera).

dolly was a 1901 word for a flat platform on wheels, as used by movers, warehousemen, etc. Early directors experimented with putting camera on a *dolly* to move closer or farther from the actors while filming, but the movement of the camera and dolly was not called *trucking up* and *trucking back* or *moving in* and *moving back* until the late 1920s and the verb *to dolly* did not appear until 1939.

edit, *cut*, and *splice*. Sometime before 1903, Edwin S. Porter had become the first person *to splice* (a 1613 English word, originally applied only to ropes and cables) pieces of film to intersperse scenes and achieve dramatic effects. Within the next ten years directors had learned to give the audience just a *flash* (1913 as a brief scene flashed abruptly on the screen), *to cut* (1913 movie use) quickly to the next scene or *to cutback* (also 1913) to a previous scene, such a return to a previous scene first called a *switchback*, then a *cutback* (this noun use also 1913), and finally a *flashback* (1916). Directors didn't speak of examining or working with an individual *frame* until 1917, which was the same year splicing and cutting became known as *editing* and directors were said *to edit* their films (from the 1793 English publishing use).

long shot. Almost all very early films were made with a stationary camera at a fixed medium-long-shot distance from the actors. When Griffith and other early creative directors filmed action or actors at a longer distance they called the result a *distant view*, which wasn't completely replaced by the term *long shot* until 1922.

panning. Between 1905 and 1915 directors also developed the technique of pivoting the camera from one side of the scene to the other for dramatic effect or to follow the action, calling this *panning* by 1914.

Ready! Start Your Action! Early directors shouted *Ready!*, at which point the cameraman started cranking the camera and the actors froze in place, then *Start Your Action!*, at which point the actors started to move and emote. By 1923 the cameras didn't have to be cranked up ahead of time and many directors thought it more realistic to begin a scene with action already going on; thus the shout was often *Ready! Action! Camera! Go!*, the cry becoming *Lights! Camera! Action!* in the 1930s, though this was not as common as most movies about movies would have us believe. The "lights," of course, were the powerful carbon-arc *klieg lights* named for John and Anton Klieg, the brother-team lighting experts who invented them. Finally the equipment became so smoothly functional and casts and crews so professional that by the late 1950s the cry was merely *Action! Roll 'em!* Of course in the days of the silent films the director could shout instructions to cast and crew throughout the filming, calling out for more tears or a broader smile, a new gesture, expression, or action, creating the film as it was being made.

subtitles. Silent films required some dialogue or explanatory words, which, beginning around 1907, appeared on separate frames at appropriate places in the story. These were called *captions* until around 1913, then were called *screen titles* or *subtitles*.

Subtitles had to be short and easily read and understood by people with little education, while keeping the audiences' interest, often with sentimentality or humor. Thus, like greeting cards and comics, they catered to our love of the cliché and the wisecrack. Before 1913 they were not even written for individual movies but were often taken from a limited supply of stock rolls, so that certain subtitles were used over and over as, *That night*, *A year has passed*, and *Wedding bells*. At least two of these stock subtitles from silent films entered the general language as clichés and are still in use: *Comes the dawn* (originally written to be used

literally) and *Meanwhile back at the ranch* . . . The nickelodeon could also use such stock frames to make announcements to the audience, the best-remembered such line, thrown upon the screen before the movie started, being: *Ladies, we like your hats, but please remove them*, with the men being advised: *You would not spit on the floor at home. Do not do it here.*

Though New York and D. W. Griffith developed many early film techniques and terms, so did Hollywood and Mack Sennett. In 1907, the same year that the first house was built in *Beverly Hills* (named after Beverly, Massachusetts, which itself was named after the town of Beverley—with an extra *e*—in Yorkshire, England), the Selis Co. filmed the beach scenes for its *Count of Monte Cristo* on the beach of Santa Monica, California. Though not the first scenes filmed outdoors *on location* (a term not recorded until 1914), they were the first filmed in Southern California, whose good year-round weather and variety of scenery made it a perfect place for moviemaking. In 1909, Biograph sent Griffith on a trip west, where he set up a studio in Los Angeles, behind a tavern at the corner of Sunset Boulevard and Gower; and in 1911 the Nestor Co. built the first studio in a sleepy hamlet surrounded by farms and citrus groves but called *Hollywood* (a name the Wilcox family gave to its townsite there in 1887, though there had never been a true woods, or much holly growing in the region). It boasted one dirt thoroughfare, not yet called *Hollywood Boulevard*, and had been an official district of Los Angeles for less than a year. The man who was to make Hollywood famous soon arrived; he was Mack Sennett.

After an unsuccessful career in the circus and in burlesque, the Canadian-born Sennett had begun to work as a writer and actor, under D. W. Griffith at Biograph in New York from 1909 to 1911. Then, at the age of twenty-eight, he opened his Keystone Studio in the Los Angeles suburb of Glendale, in 1912. During the next dozen years he produced a flood of wildly creative slapstick comedies, the name *Keystone Comedy* entering the language in 1913 and soon meaning any frenetic slapstick comedy. Many featured his *Keystone Cops*, often then spelled *Keystone Kops* for humorous effect, who first appeared in 1912. This group, including "Fatty" (Roscoe) Arbuckle, Edgar Kennedy, Harry Langdon, and Slim Summerville, committed slapstick mayhem to the horror of their goatee-waggling, bug-eyed leader, played by Fred Sterling—and made *Keystone Cop* a term for any bungling policeman. Using the California beach to display his then daring Mack Sennett *Bathing Beauties* (see LET'S GO TO THE BEACH), Sennett introduced another term to the language. He also popularized the use of *trick photography* (1912) in the movies, especially using *stop motion* (1912), *fast motion*, and *slow motion* (an 1801 English theatrical term, referring then to the very slow movements of actors in "living portrait"

The Keystone Cops in a gripping comedy with Ben Turpin.

spectacles), which he used often for comic effects.

In addition to the famous Keystone Cops players mentioned above, Sennett also introduced or helped make famous such now well-known names as Wallace Beery, Charlie Chaplin, Charley Chase, W. C. Fields, Buster Keaton, Harold Lloyd, and Ben Turpin, as well as Marie Dressler, Gloria Swanson, and Mabel Normand (who, in a 1915 Keystone Comedy, threw the first movie custard pie, into the face of Ben Turpin).

Though Griffith is remembered as the early genius of the movies, millions first became regular moviegoers to watch Mack Sennett's comedies, made in Hollywood—for by 1915 Burbank, Culver City, Glendale, Santa Monica, any part of Los Angeles or Southern California where movies were made was *Hollywood*, and by 1918 *Hollywood* was another word for the American film industry.

The early, often foreign-born, nickelodeon moguls financed many early studios and, with their advertising men, exchanged many telegraph and telephone messages between New York and Hollywood, these terse long-distance messages perhaps contributing to the abbreviated, fast-talking brand of hyperbole later called *filmese*, which was then adopted and popularized by editor Joseph Dannenberg in the trade paper *Film Daily*. During this 1905–15 period, too, the moviemakers and the public firmly established the basic words *cinema*, *film*, *picture* and *motion picture*, *moving picture* and *movie*, as well as several lesser terms, for the new product, giving us:

> *cinema*, British use for a motion picture since 1909 (see *Cinématographe*, above, for more on *cinema* and the terms based on it).

film, as a motion picture, 1905; first used as a verb *to film*, 1899, in referring to making Mutascope moving pictures; *filming*, the act of making a motion picture, 1912; *the films*, the motion picture industry, 1920.

film studio, 1913; *film company*, 1918.

film rights, to a book, play, etc., 1913; *filmization*, the film version of a book, play, etc., 1918.

film land and *filmdom*, the world of motion pictures, both 1914.

film producer, 1914.

film star, 1914; *film actress*, 1919.

film maker, 1919.

film goer, 1919.

film editor, who, in the early days of moviemaking, also often wrote or edited the titles, 1921; *film splicer*, the person who spliced the bits and pieces of film into a movie, 1922.

film-struck, 1923 (based on the 1813 English stage-struck).

film music, 1927; *film composer*, 1948.

filmcraft, 1928.

film strip, as for educational use, 1930; the term *educational film* dates from 1910.

film critic, 1931.

film magazine, 1939.

film festival, referring to European ones, 1932.

filmography (*film* + biblio*graphy*), a list of films of an actor, director, producer, etc., 1962.

flicker, around 1910, when seventeen-year-old Mary Pickford said her job was making "flickers" (a motion picture was said to *flicker* annoyingly on the screen by 1899); *flick* has been English slang for motion picture since 1926.

moving picture, 1898 in the modern sense, but used since 1715 as the exhibition of moving cutouts and toylike objects and scenes, as a ship sailing on the sea, run by clockwork devices. *Movie*, 1906 as slang for a modern moving picture, and then also used since 1913 to mean a moving picture theater. *Movie show*, 1913; *movie picture*, 1916; *movie play*, 1917; *movie film*, 1922; the low slang or dialect pronunciation *mo'on pitcher* was first noted in 1929. As late as 1926 the motion picture industry opposed the word *movie* as slangy and degrading.

movie theater, 1907; *movie house*, *1914*; *movie palace*, an elaborate movie theater, 1917.

movie actor, 1913; *movie star*, for both a man and a woman, 1919; *movie actress*, 1924, with *movie queen* following in 1927 for a female movie star.

movie fan, 1913; *movie goer*, 1923, with *movie-going public* a 1938 term.

movie studio, 1913.

movie land, the film industry, especially Hollywood, 1914; *movie-dom*, 1916.

movie man, a projectionist or exhibitor, 1915.

movie business, 1916, which by 1928 was considered to have grown into the *movie industry*.

movie scenario, 1917.

movie camera, 1925.

movie cowboy, 1926.

movie hero, 1928.

movie magazine, 1929.

movie making, 1932; *movie maker*, 1957.

photoplay. In 1912 the Chicago motion picture company, Essanay, formed in 1907 by George Spoot and the star of *The Great Train Robbery*, Max Aronson (the "S and A" from their names), determined to stamp out that slangy, degrading word *movie* by offering a $25 prize for a new word for it, the prize going to a California musician, Edgar Strakosch, who was credited with coining the new name *photoplay*. *Photoplay Magazine* was founded, also in Chicago, later in 1912, using Essanay's prize-winning word in its name. An earlier word *pictureplay*, 1894, was popularized by Alexander Black, a writer and lecturer on the new art of taking *snapshots*, 1893, who used *pictureplay* to describe his stereopticon shows of dramatic action accompanied by his spoken lines. He considered the total performance a new art form (he later became a novelist).

picture show, 1881, and *motion picture*, 1891, both originally referring to items made for and seen in peephole devices, then used in the modern sense from 1896 on; *picture*, around 1900 as short for *motion picture*. The British have used *picture* where we would have used *movie*; they have formed such combinations as: *picturedom*, motion pictures collectively, the world of motion pictures, 1902; *picture playwright* and *picture dramatist*, both 1911; *picture palace*, a movie theater, 1912 (five years before our term *movie palace*); *picture house*, 1913 (recorded a year before our *movie house*); *picture theatre*, 1914 (three years before our *motion picture theater* and seven years before our *movie theater*); *picturedrome (picture + Hippodrome)*, a movie theater, 1914; *the pictures*, the motion picture industry, 1925; and *picture goer*, 1927 (four years before our *moviegoer*).

We, however, used *picture* first in the phrase *in the picture* (probably based on still photography rather than a motion picture frame), to be present, under consideration, or an influence, 1919, and *out of the picture*, 1929; and shortened *pictures* to *pix*, motion pictures, the motion picture industry, around 1930, then formed the singular *pic*, a motion picture, 1939.

release, a motion picture released for exhibition, 1912.

screen has been used as an adjective to mean motion picture or movie since 1915, as in *screen actor*, *screen-struck* (based on *stage-struck*), and *screen world*, the world of the movies, all first noted in 1915; *screen beauty*, a pretty movie actress, 1919; and *screen rights*, to a book, play, etc., 1920. *The screen* has meant the movies since 1928, sometimes more glamorously called *the silver screen* since 1931.

All these, of course, stem from the use of a screen on which to project pictures, *screen* having meant one on which magic lantern shows were shown since 1815, one on which still photographs were projected since 1891, and one on which moving pictures were projected since 1896. *To screen* has meant to project a motion picture for viewing since 1917, usually with the connotation that the viewers are a small, select group, a *screening* being a private showing of a film for friends, the cast, movie reviewers, etc.

In the above list note how frequently some of the similar, interchangeable terms appeared within a year or just a few years of one another; thus *film* appeared in 1905 and *movie* in 1906, both *film studio* and *movie studio* in 1913, *film goer* in 1919 and *movie goer* in 1923, which probably means only that those who wrote about the new industry were more apt to use *film* than *movie* and that *film*, *movie*, *motion picture*, and *picture* were often used completely interchangeably from the early days. Incidentally, *celluloid* appeared as a slang term for a movie in 1922, *Celluloid* (a trademark, from *cellulose* + *-oid)* having been invented by John W. Hyatt in 1871 and used as a film base as early as the 1890s.

Though we remember the creativity and entertainment of those early years, by 1910 the young film industry was a large, booming, cutthroat business. The studios originally sold each nickelodeon a *dupe* (an 1899 term for a duplicate copy of a film, the verb, *to dupe*, appeared in movie use in 1912) made from a *master print*. Soon, however, both legal and illegal systems of renting and exchanging films developed among the nickelodeon operators, as did the *pirating* of films (making and distributing unauthorized duplicates) by *film laboratories* (a 1907 term: before that they had been called *film factories)*. Fights for control of the various movie projector patents and of moviemaking and distribution went on in and out of court. In 1907 the failing Biograph (actually the combined American Mutascope and Biograph Co.), which Edison had sued, had been on the brink of being liquidated when its bank's financial consultant, Jeremiah J. Kennedy, persuaded Edison's company to license Biograph and six other movie production companies (Vitagraph, Essanay, Lubin, Selig, Pathé, and Méliès, the last two of which now produced in America), the eight then forming the immensely profitable Motion Picture Patents Co. and its monopolistic distribution arm, the General Film Co. The combine sought a monopoly over the entire industry, making and distributing films and providing the projecting machines—and woe be it to the nickelodeon operators who didn't agree or pay their weekly film, projector, and license fees. Led by William Fox, however, many of the larger nickelodeon operators did resist. Calling themselves *independents* (the first use of the term in the movie industry), they financed their own studios and produced and distributed films themselves, fighting both the trust's legal actions against them and its hired thugs, who sometimes tried to destroy the studios and films of the independents.

Not only did the independents finally win in court, when the by-then moribund combine was declared an unlawful monopoly and dissolved in 1917, but, before that, they had won with the movie audiences—by creating highly publicized longer movies and highly publicized movie stars. For maximum profit, the trust produced mainly short *one-reelers* and *two-reelers* (reel had meant a reel of movie film since 1901), also called *program movies* (1911, because it took four to six of them to make up an hour's program),

I have determined that there is no market for talking pictures.
Thomas Edison, 1926

388

with low-paid, unknown actors. Thus the combine paid a *lead actress* or *lead girl* $25 a day in 1908 and even the name of the famous *Biograph Girl*, Florence Lawrence, was kept secret until Biograph was forced to reveal it to counter a story that she had been killed by a streetcar in St. Louis (only to find that the story had been created as a publicity stunt by an independent to launch her as one of its own stars). To make their movies different from those of General Film, and probably because they were closer to the public and knew what it wanted, the independents began to produce longer multireel movies with more complex plots, exotic backgrounds, and publicized actors, advertising the actors' names and listing them on the screen from about 1910. Between 1910 and 1915 the independents produced many *three-reelers* and *four-reelers* (each reel containing 1,000 feet of film and taking about 15 minutes to show at the then-prevailing 16-frames-per-second silent-movie speed), the audience waiting patiently, or buying popcorn and candy from roving vendors, when the sign "One Moment While the Operator Changes Reels" was flashed on the screen.

The independents called their longer films *feature films* (1911), soon simply *features* (1913), and found the public willing to pay 10¢ or even 25¢ to see them.

The trust countered by calling each of its one- and two-reelers a *short feature*, 1913 (the word *featurette* didn't appear until 1942, then referring to a short educational or documentary film shown as a minor part of the bill with a regular, full-length movie). In 1913, too, both the trust and the independents began wide use of the term *first run* to refer to a brand-new picture, one being shown (or *run* through the projector) for the first time in any particular town. The three- and four-reel independent features created a strong interest in movie stories, with *Motion Picture Story Magazine* appearing in 1912 to publish the scenarios or plot outlines and summaries of the major movies, both for those who wanted to know what they were going to see and for those who didn't have the time or money to see all the movies that were now being so widely talked about.

Many of the most successful features were filled with adventure and romance in exotic settings, and it was during the 1910–14 period that many standard movie genres and names for them developed, the independents turning out many three- and four-reel *jungle movies* taking place "In Darkest Africa" (another silent title that entered the general language), *pirate movies*, *Canadian Royal Mountie movies*, *Arabian Nights movies*, *Egyptian Desert movies*, and *Bible movies*, as well as many melodramatic American *pioneer movies* (about pioneers), *Indian movies* (about Indians both noble and villainous), and *Civil War movies*. The longer, 45 minutes to an hour, movie could also present the classics and current novels and plays, with more than 600 novels and plays being made into

Pirate movies *were popular long before Douglas Fairbanks (left) and Errol Flynn (right) began to star in them.*

features between 1910 and 1914, including 15 works by Dickens, 13 by Shakespeare, 8 by Dumas, and 4 by Jules Verne. The longest movies of this period were actually melodramatic *serials* shown in weekly segments, each segment ending with the title "Continued next week" or "To be continued" just as the heroine was, most typically, about to lose her life or virtue, the audience having to return next week to see how she was saved, only to leave her in a similarly precarious situation that again was "Continued next week." Such serials went on for months and were later called *cliffhangers* (1937) because the heroines—such as played by Pathé's Pearl White, "the Queen of the Cliffhangers," in the 1915 *Perils of Pauline*—were left clinging to a cliff or in other dire peril at the end of each segment. But classics or corn, the public liked what it saw: by 1914 there were 17,000 movie theaters selling 10 million tickets a day and many lower- and middle-class families "went to the movies" once a week.

By then, both in America and Europe, the films were beginning to get even longer. Men like Adolph Zukor, a Hungarian immigrant from New York's Lower East Side, who had begun his financial rise as a furrier before becoming a penny-arcade and nickelodeon owner, felt that a single long movie, like a play or opera, could be a full evening's entertainment, even a cultural event. In 1911 the five-reel Italian film *Dante's Inferno* was brought to America and shown by itself as the sole attraction; in 1912 Zukor imported the French-made four-reel *Queen Elizabeth*, starring Sarah Bernhardt (whose appearance in this film was a major step in making movie acting respectable), and showed it as a single attraction. In 1913 two films made to be sole attractions were shown, the American-made *The Squaw Man*, featuring Dustin Farnum, directed by Cecil B. De Mille, and produced by him, Samuel Goldwyn, and Jesse Lasky (see *Metro-Goldwyn-Mayer* below), and the Italian import nine-reel spectacle *Quo Vadis*, which had cost all of $9,000 to make, was shown in 20 U.S. cities simultaneously—and was the first movie to cost $1.00 to see. In 1914, Mack Sennett's first full evening's movie, *Tillie's Punctured Romance*, was dwarfed by the twelve-reel Italian import *Cabiria*, which ran for almost three hours. Such films shown as the sole attraction were more than mere "features"; they were called *feature-length* (1914) films and *super features* (the word *super* had become something of a vogue word around 1910).

The film that established the feature-length movie, however, was D. W. Griffith's *The Birth of a Nation*. Based on Thomas Dixon's novel *The Clansman*, it was about the Civil War and the Reconstruction period in the South, showing the action through the eyes of two families, one northern, one southern, and using all the camera, lighting, and editing techniques Griffith, who had by now joined the independents, had acquired making his hundreds of short movies for Biograph. Costing a then record-breaking $110,000 to make, it opened in New York City in March 1915. Crowds flocked to see it because of its epic scope and spectacular battle scenes, and because it was controversial: Griffith, the son of a Confederate colonel, and the movie were accused of glorifying the Civil War South and the postwar Ku Klux Klan while denigrating "colored people." Thus, with justification, the young *National Association for the Advancement of Colored People* (the NAACP, founded in 1909) organized demonstrations against it. Twenty-eight copies of the film were distributed, many traveling from town to town with their own special sound-effects crews, orchestras, and publicity staffs: tickets cost $2.00—and *The Birth of a Nation* grossed $18 million during its first year. Thus the feature-length film was established as an art form and as popular commercial entertainment. Griffith never returned to the short film, making the even more ambitious *Intolerance* in 1916, a "film fugue" that wove together parables from four periods in history into a sermon against injustice. Other Griffith films included *Broken Blossoms* in 1919; *Way Down East* in 1920; and *Orphans of the Storm* in 1922, many of his films now starring the elfin Lillian Gish.

Full-length movies needed larger, more elaborate *movie theaters* (1907) than the nickelodeons. Zukor had leased a Broadway stage theater near New York City's Metropolitan Opera House to show *Queen Elizabeth* in 1912, calling the theater "the grand opera of motion pictures." In 1913 movie theater manager Samuel "Roxy" Rothafel, son of a Stillwater, Minnesota, pool-hall owner and

Lillian Gish in Birth of a Nation, *1915.*

Way Down East, 1920, with Lillian Gish.

Orphans of the Storm, 1922, with Lillian and Dorothy Gish.

showman, completely redecorated his Regent Theater in Harlem, adding luxurious seats, statues along the walls, and potted palms and gilded columns in the lobby. It was such a success that the following year he was hired to help architect Thomas Lamb design the first large, modern *movie house* (1914), New York City's Strand Theater. With its own even more luxurious seats and even more elaborate statues along the walls, potted palms and gilded columns, it opened, under Rothafel's management, with a 50-piece orchestra playing and an Italian tenor singing "O Sole Mio," to set the mood for a travelogue about Naples, followed by a newsreel of that very afternoon's Brooklyn baseball game, and the nine-reel feature *The Spoilers* (based on Rex Beach's story and play) shown on the first *multiple projectors* so that it ran continuously without having to be stopped while the projectionist changed reels.

"Roxy" Rothafel had served in the Marines before becoming a movie exhibitor and, remembering the Marine Corps, put well-disciplined *movie ushers* wearing impressive uniforms with polished buttons into the Strand theater and always began the show exactly on time, setting the pattern for many *movie palaces* (1917) that were to follow. The architect Thomas Lamb went on to design many more elaborate movie palaces in Chicago, Atlanta, and Los Angeles, while "Roxy" Rothafel stayed in New York to work his magic on the Rialto in 1915, the Rivoli in 1916, and finally in 1927 his own Roxy theater, costing $8 million and seating 6,250 people. The Roxy wasn't a mere palace but "the Cathedral of the Motion Pictures."

The independents succeeded not only because they made the longer feature movies but also because they created stars and attracted audiences with them. Despite little publicity, some early movie actors had become well known and well loved, as the beautiful Alice Joyce and the fat funnyman John Bunny. By 1912, Vitagraph would mail to all who sent in a dime, a picture of Lottie Pickford (Mary's sister), Maurice Costello, Norma Talmadge, or any of its thirty other featured players, including Eagle Eye, the Indian in many of its films, or even of its famous symbol, Jean, the Vitagraph Dog (such photographs weren't called *publicity stills* until 1918).

Despite such popular earlier favorites, the term *film star* was originally created to describe only one person—Mary Pickford. Born Gladys Smith in Toronto, Canada, she had begun her stage career at the age of five, under the management of her ambitious mother, and had become a successful young teenage actress, given the stage name *Mary Pickford* by New York theatrical producer David Belasco, before first being brought to the screen, at the age of sixteen, in D. W. Griffith's 1909 Biograph one-reelers, *Her First Biscuits* and *The Violin Maker of Cremona*. As had Belasco and stage audiences, Griffith and the movie audience loved her Victorian

Vachel Lindsay's poem to Mae Marsh as the star of the 1912 movie *A Girl of the Paris Streets*. Lindsay also was among the first to consider and review the movies as a serious art form, in his weekly column for the *New Republic*.

waiflike appeal. By 1911 many Griffith movies were built around her and she was soon known as *our Mary* and *little Mary* to the movie audience, and called *The Girl with a Curl* by reporters and *press agents* (an 1894 English term for those who worked for theaters to advertise their names and plays; the verb *to press agent* appeared in Hollywood in 1920). She played the American dream girl, a golden-haired but spunky, sometimes even mischievous, virgin: the poor girl who stayed good and made good, or the rich girl who understood the common man. The term *film star* was first used to refer to her in 1914, the same year that, as the star of *Tess of the Storm Country*, she became the first movie actress to "have her name up in lights" and was given the title *America's Sweetheart*, both on the marquee of Sid "Pop" Grauman's Egyptian Theater (soon replaced by the more opulent Grauman's Chinese Theater, where stars would be invited to immortalize their footprints in the pavement).

The simple name "Mary" and the titles of her major movies seemed to be on everyone's lips as the first generation of moviegoers grew up with her, crying over and proud of the girls and young women she played in such successes as *Stella Maris, Daddy Long Legs, Pollyanna, Poor Little Rich Girl,* and *Rebecca of Sunnybrook Farm*. In fact, many Americans began using the cliché *poor little rich girl* only after seeing Mary Pickford play the girl in the movie of that title and many started using the word *Pollyanna* (to mean an

Mae Marsh.

By 1912 Vitagraph would mail to anyone who sent in a dime a picture of one of its well-known actors, such as Norma Talmadge (left). Mary Pickford as Pollyanna, which popularized that word and the term poor little rich girl.

The twice-married thirty-four-year-old Mary Pickford finally got her first screen kiss in 1927 in My Best Girl. *"Buddy" Rogers gave her the kiss; he later became her third husband.*

irrepressible optimist) only after seeing Mary play the child heroine in that movie (from Eleanor H. Porter's 1913 novel, *Pollyanna*, which first launched the word). By 1916, the twenty-three-year-old veteran, who was an excellent businesswoman as well as a subtle, persuasive actress, was her own producer, her Mary Pickford Co. having a 50 percent partnership in all her films, but she continued to be *America's Sweetheart*. Her fans were happy for her when she married the screen's most swashbuckling hero, Douglas Fairbanks, in 1920, and even though this was her second marriage, they were still thrilled by her first romantic screen kiss in the 1927 *My Best Girl* (she was then thirty-four years old and that famous kiss was given her by Charles "Buddy" Rogers, the movie actor and bandleader who was to become her third husband ten years later).

The first major male star to approach Mary Pickford's popularity was Charlie Chaplin. He, too, was born outside the U.S., in London, and as the son of music hall performers (though he had sometimes lived in orphanages and on the London streets) had also been on the stage since childhood, from the age of seven. He came to the U.S. with a vaudeville troupe; Mack Sennett saw the act and signed the twenty-four-year-old Chaplin in 1913 to a $150-a-week movie contract. Chaplin assembled his famous costume of derby hat, tight suit jacket and baggy pants, oversized shoes, cane—and mustache—from the Keystone wardrobe and prop rooms and first wore it for his second Sennett comedy, the 1914 *Kid Auto Races at Venice*. He portrayed the endearing, humorous, pathetic *Little Tramp*, whom he always called "the little fellow," for the first time

When Mary Pickford and Douglas Fairbanks married in 1920 it seemed only natural that his estate overlooking Beverly Hills be renamed Pickfair. The main house was "the grandest in Hollywood" and, although the couple was divorced in 1936, Mary lived there from 1920 until her death in 1979 at the age of eighty-six, spending the last thirteen years there as a recluse and leaving a fortune estimated at $50 million, mainly from her continued financial interest in Universal Pictures.

Charlie Chaplin as The Little Tramp, *which he first played in 1915.*

in 1915 in *The Tramp*. After that, when people smiled and said "Charlie" they meant Chaplin, his name and the titles of his movies also becoming common terms as he soared to *stardom* (an 1865 theatrical term) with contracts with Essanay and Mutual, being guaranteed $670,000 for twelve two-reel comedies in 1915. Though Mary Pickford had been the first movie star to earn thousands a week, Chaplin's guarantee amazed the public and the movie industry and the race to see which performer could be "the highest-paid star" was on. In 1916 America's sweetheart went Charlie one better by obtaining a $675,000 guarantee, but then, in 1917, Chaplin topped her by signing Hollywood's first *million dollar contract*, for eight pictures with First National. Then, since no one else could afford him, he organized his own company in 1918, eventually starring in such silent classics as *The Kid*, 1921, in which he finds the four-year-old "kid," Jackie Coogan, in a trash can; *The Gold Rush*, 1925; *City Lights*, 1931; and *Modern Times*, 1936. Unlike Mary Pickford, Chaplin did not keep the public's love, he was not America's dream boy: his four marriages, a sensational divorce, a paternity suit, unpopular political views, nonpayment of U.S. taxes, and his refusal to become a U.S. citizen eventually turned much of the public against him and he left the U.S. in 1953.

Besides stars, movies also now had *extras* (1916 movie use, from 1772 English stage use), including those who played in *crowd scenes* (early 1900s theatrical use), especially in *costume pictures* (1921), and would eventually have *bit players* who played *bit parts* (both terms of the mid 1930s). Some movies also featured the *stunt actor*,

This 1926 movie would have been just another costume picture *but for Pola Negri's "hot-blooded" portrayal of Carmen (since this was, of course, a silent movie, it was based on "a stirring love tale of Old Spain," not on the opera).*

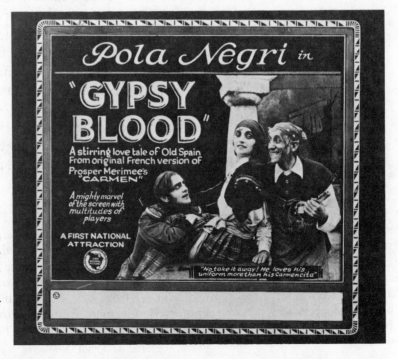

which, since 1904, had meant any actor who was known for his daredevil action feats on screen, such as Douglas Fairbanks, but around 1915 had also come to mean special actors who performed such feats for others, such men being called *stunt men* by the late 1920s. Most studios now also put each picture under the supervision of a *producer*, a 1909 theatrical term for a stage manager that was introduced into movie use in 1915 by Thomas Ince of Thomas Ince Pictures. Ince had begun to produce more films than he could supervise himself and hired supervisors he dubbed *producers*, each to have control over several pictures and each picture to fit into Ince's new *factory system* of making movies, in which each producer and movie was assigned a specific *shooting schedule* and times to use studio stages, editing equipment, etc., so that all facilities were used efficiently and a dozen or so movies could be in progress simultaneously. With such a system every producer and director soon needed an assistant, an assistant director in particular soon being called a *yes man* (1924 as movie use, the term from a 1913 T. A. "Tad" Dorgan cartoon in which the "yes men" were assistant newspaper editors praising the work of the editor). But important as the extras, bit players, and producers were, it was the stars who now brought audiences into movie houses. They made the *box office*, a term used since 1904 to mean the financial success or income from selling tickets to any kind of performance (from the 1786 English use of *box office* as the office where tickets could be purchased for a "box" in the theater).

Beginning in the 1920s, movie stars were true *celebs* (*celeb* was a 1913 shortening of *celeb*rity) who could defy directors and producers by missing a rehearsal or performance *call* (1780 in English theatrical use), relax while a *stand-in* stood in their place as lights and cameras were being focused, use a *double* to take their place in distant shots or scenes in which they needn't face the camera, and could demand another *take* (1926) if they felt they hadn't been shown to advantage in a scene. True stars had their own *fans* (1889, originally in sports use, then in theatrical use soon after), who would send them tons of *fan mail* (1924) or *fan letters* (1932), and buy *fan magazines* (1928, blended into the word *fanzine* by 1951)— while later stars would be pestered by *autograph hounds* (1937) and be the object of *fan clubs* (1941). Three of the most common terms popularized by early movie stars were:

Kiss me, my fool.
"Uttered" by Theda Bara as a subtitle in the silent movie *A Fool There Was*, 1914; it then became a mocking fad expression said by early flappers to their boyfriends.

vamp, a 1910 word popularized by Theda Bara's portrayal of the vamp in the 1914 *A Fool There Was*. This was the first movie in which Theodosia Goodman used her famous screen name, Theda Bara, and she kept the name as she and Pola Negri played many other vamps, keeping the word *vamp* before the public. It is, of course, from *vampire* (which entered English in the 17th century, via German, from the Tartar *ubyr*, witch). The verb *to vamp* also entered the language in 1910.

Theda Bara in Cleopatra, *1917.*

sheik (pronounced "sheek"), became the term for the flapper's typical Roaring 20s boyfriend, and for an irresistible romantic man, when the slim, black-haired Rudolph Valentino played the title role in the 1921 movie *The Sheik*. Having immigrated to the U.S. as Rodolpho d'Antonguolla in 1913, Valentino had been a gardener, cabaret dancer, and gigolo before his dark good looks made him a Hollywood star. He kept the word *sheik* before the public playing similar characters and, after some of the public had begun to mock him and the word, his timely death in 1926 assured the success of *The Son of the Sheik*, Paramount using his funeral as publicity by arranging a lying-in-state in New York City, helping to create a mob scene in front of the funeral home, holding a press conference in which Pola Negri announced she had been secretly engaged to him, and having an honor guard of black-shirted Fascisti around the coffin. Incidentally, *sheik* (sometimes spelled *sheikh* in earlier days, and increasingly pronounced "shayk" since the mid 1970s) entered English with its basic meaning of "Arab chief" in 1577.

it had been a euphemism for sexual intercourse in English since 1611; then Elinor Glyn's titillating and daring 1927 best-selling novel *It* made *it* a synonym for sex appeal, which the flapper idol Clara Bow popularized by starring in the 1928 movie based on the book. Clara Bow was widely advertised as the *It Girl* of the movie and carried the title "the It Girl" ever after.

Though Thomas Ince made the 1916 pacifist movie *Civilization*, while Erich Von Stroheim had become known as "the man you love to hate," playing sadistic Prussian officers, and many stars entertained our troops and led Liberty Bond and war relief drives and rallies, the American movie industry didn't even break stride during World War I. The major *war movies*, such as King Vidor's 1925 *The Big Parade*, the 1928 *Wings*, and Lewis Milestone's 1929 classic *All Quiet on the Western Front*, were made long after the war was over. But because American movie audiences were the largest in the world and most European studios had suspended or greatly curtailed production during the war, by war's end American movies dominated the world market. Silent movies needed only new sets of subtitles to be understood in any country, and American movies and American stars were now major movies and stars over much of the world.

With stars and feature films, large theater chains, and markets around the world, some of the early independent nickelodeon producers and studios who had fought a giant trust, the General Film Co., had grown, or merged, into giants themselves. By the mid 1920s Hollywood was turning out 700 films a year for an audience of over 55 million people a week; most of the major studios were in existence, and the public knew the names of:

Columbia Pictures, formed in 1924 by the crude but brilliant former song plugger and vaudevillian Harry Cohn. Its major asset was the director Frank Capra, whose warm, socially astute comedies—*It Happened One Night*, 1934; *Mr. Deeds Goes to Town*, 1936; *You Can't Take It With You*, 1938; and *Mr. Smith Goes to Washington*, 1939—created a special kind of movie which the public loved but which some later critics characterized as being full of *Capracorn* (a pun on Capricorn, of course, using *corn* to mean *corny*, which has meant hackneyed, sentimental, since 1937).

Metro-Goldwyn-Mayer (MGM) was formed by Marcus Loew of the Loew's theater chain in 1924 when he bought the *Metro* studio and united it with the *Goldwyn* Picture Corp. under Louis B. *Mayer*, hence the name, *Metro-Goldwyn-Mayer*.

Samuel Goldwyn, who had been born in Warsaw and whose Polish name had originally been translated to Saul Goldfish in America, had owned a successful glove agency, then, at the age of thirty-one, in 1913, he had joined his brother-in-law, who was vaudeville producer Jesse L. Lasky, and playwright Cecil B. De Mille to found the Jesse Lasky Feature Play Co., with De Mille its director. This company was most famous for producing the full-length 1913 *The Squaw Man*. Later, Goldwyn had formed the Goldwyn Picture Co. with Archibald and Edgar Selwyn and a young New York City advertising agency man and recent Columbia University graduate, Howard Dietz. Dietz chose Columbia University's football team mascot, *Leo the Lion*, as the symbol and trademark of the Goldwyn Picture Co., and MGM continued to use it (after all, Vitagraph had its dog, Pathé its rooster, and Bison its buffalo—and the Goldwyn lion seemed more dignified than Metro's symbol, which had been a parrot that presented the letters M-E-T-R-O one by one on the screen). Though the Goldwyn lion became part of Metro-Goldwyn-Mayer, Goldwyn, himself, never did; he didn't like the newly merged company and sold out for cash, never being part of the major company that bore his name.

Louis B. Mayer had his choice of having his name added to the company or not: Loew told him his pictures could carry the credit line, "Produced by Louis B. Mayer for the Metro-Goldwyn Corp." or "Produced by Metro-Goldwyn-Mayer," and Mayer chose the latter, giving us the full company name.

MGM was big and rich and best known for its *big-budget* costume dramas and musicals. It claimed "more stars than in the heavens." It did have the most, and the most glamorous, stars, including the Barrymores (John, "The Great Profile," Lionel, and Ethel), Leslie Caron, Ronald Colman (whom Goldwyn had originally discovered, as he had Pola Negri, Will Rogers, and Rudolph Valentino), and Clark Gable (whose handsome, easygoing masculinity in such movies as the 1935 *Mutiny on the Bounty* and the 1939 *Gone with the Wind* prompted gossip columnist Louella Parsons to dub him *The King*, meaning king of the box office). Other MGM stars included Greta Garbo, Judy Garland (whose first starring role was in the 1939 *Wizard of Oz*), Greer Garson, Myrna Loy, Jeanette MacDonald and Nelson Eddy, William Powell, Mickey Rooney, Norma Shearer, Elizabeth Taylor, Spencer Tracy, Lana Turner—and Lassie.

Paramount had its origins in the one-reeler nickelodeon days of 1912. Its major successes have included Cecil B. De Mille's epics and Ernst Lubitsch's sophisticated comedies, including the 1939 *Ninotchka*, which had what the critics called "the Lubitsch touch." For over 20 years it also featured the movie *crooner* (a 1930 term) Bing Crosby.

RKO (formed by the *R*adio Corporation of America, or *RCA*, and the *K*eith-*O*rpheum theater chain) was founded in 1921, in the early 1930s produced the first film starring Katharine Hepburn and paired Fred Astaire and Ginger Rogers for the first time (in the 1933 *Flying Down to Rio*), then brought Orson Welles to Hollywood and gave him a free hand to make the 1941 *Citizen*

MGM's Lassie (above) continued the line of canine stars going back to Rin Tin Tin (right) and Jean, the once-famous Vitagraph symbol.

Ginger Rogers and Fred Astaire were paired for the first time in RKO's 1933 Flying Down to Rio, *then moved to MGM by 1940.*

Kane. But Hepburn and Astaire and Rogers moved to MGM by 1940, the studio was sold to Howard Hughes in 1948, and produced its last film in 1953 (it was then sold to a former RKO chorus girl, comedienne Lucille Ball, and her bandleader husband, Desi Arnaz, who renamed it *Desilu, Desi + Lucille,* and produced their TV series "I Love Lucy" and many other TV shows there).

20th Century–Fox is the only major studio that was not in existence by the mid 1920s. It was formed when Joseph Schenck's *Twentieth Century* Pictures combined with William Fox's *Fox* Film Corp. in 1935. Its thrifty and popular early director and producer Darryl F. Zanuck kept it a major studio by creating such

Tyrone Power and Alice Faye, here in the 1938 In Old Chicago, *were stars for 20th Century–Fox.*

stars as Don Ameche, Dana Andrews, Linda Darnell, Alice Faye, Henry Fonda, Betty Grable (whose 1939 movie *Million Dollar Legs* helped make her a favorite *pin-up girl* of World War II), Victor Mature, John Payne, Tyrone Power, Gene Tierney, and Richard Widmark. Its earliest successes, however, were those featuring its best-known star, Shirley Temple, who gave the movies the term *child star* in the mid 1930s and eventually had everything from dolls to a nonalcoholic cocktail, the *Shirley Temple*, for little girls, named after her. It was also the studio where John Ford directed his early realistic dramas, the 1939 *Young Mr. Lincoln* and the 1940 *The Grapes of Wrath*, starring the youthful Henry Fonda.

Bill "Bojangles" Robinson, another 20th Century–Fox star, sometimes danced with Shirley Temple, shown here with Claudette Colbert, in her movies.

United Artists was exactly that, being formed by D. W. Griffith, Charlie Chaplin, Douglas Fairbanks, and Mary Pickford in 1919 to distribute their films and has continued to be known mainly as a distributor rather than a producer of films.

Universal was formed by the merging of several small studios in 1912 and became one of the most profitable studios, rivaling MGM in size and known best for its lavish spectacles.

Warner Brothers was the name the four brothers Albert, Harry, Jack, and Sam Warner gave the small studio they bought in 1923, the four having started as nickelodeon managers and then buying a chain of movie houses before entering the moviemaking business. They pioneered in early talkies, producing *The Jazz Singer* in 1927, and soon specialized in Depression Era gangster movies and musical extravaganzas, using the talkies to feature Busby

Douglas Fairbanks, first president of the Academy of Motion Picture Arts and Sciences, presents the first Academy Award *for "best actress" to Janet Gaynor in 1928.*

Berkeley's spectacular musical numbers, with such stars as Ruby Keeler and Dick Powell, as well as stars who seem to have been chosen for their distinctive, often hardboiled and nasal, voices, as Humphrey Bogart (who starred in *Casablanca* in 1943), James Cagney, Bette Davis (who starred in *Jezebel* in 1938), and Edward G. Robinson.

Stars, their fans, and their importance to the industry soon led to the giving of awards to "the best" and "most popular." *Photoplay Magazine* began giving popularity *Photoplay Awards* to the stars in 1921 and soon the Western Association of Motion Picture Advertisers (W.A.M.P.A. or *WAMPAs*) began giving *Wampas awards* to promising new stars, the recipients being called *Wampas babies* and including Clara Bow in 1924 (4 years before she became famous as "the It Girl"), hard-bitten heroine Joan Crawford in 1926 (5 years before her success in *Grand Hotel* and 19 years before her Academy Award for *Mildred Pierce*), and blond, bouncy musical star Joan Blondell in 1931.

Then, in 1928, Douglas Fairbanks, first president of the recently formed (1927) Academy of Motion Picture Arts and Sciences, presented its first annual *Academy Awards*, gold-plated statuettes designed by MGM's art director, Cedric Gibbon. The *Best Picture* award went to the 1928 *Wings*, the last great silent spectacle, known for its primitive color and carefully planned and expertly filmed aerial dogfights, with the *Best Director* award going to Frank Borzage for *Seventh Heaven* and Lewis Milestone for *Two Arabian Knights*. The first *Best Actress* award went to the demure ingenue Janet Gaynor for her performances in *Seventh Heaven*, *Street Angel*, and *Sunrise*, and the *Best Actor* award went to Emil Jannings for *The Way of All Flesh* and *The Last Command* (starting with the 1930 presentation for the 1929 films, the awards for the best acting went only for work in one film, not for the year's best work). *Best Supporting Actress* and *Best Supporting Actor* awards were not given until 1937, for movies made the preceding year. By 1936 an Academy Award was called an *Oscar*, the most likely of the various stories given for this name being that the statuettes looked like the Uncle Oscar of a secretary who worked in the Academy's office. For the first eleven years, the winners' names were given to the newspapers ahead of time, the papers pledging not to reveal the winners until they were announced from the stage. The *Los Angeles Times* broke this pledge in 1939, after which the names were kept secret and in sealed envelopes until opened and their contents read on stage during the Academy presentations, America hearing that fateful "The envelope, please" for the first time in 1940.

Besides seeing the emergence of bigger stars, bigger studios, and the Academy Awards, the 1920s saw the two most important and revolutionary developments since the invention of roll film—color and sound.

The "naturally colored photograph" mentioned in the paper Sir John Herschel had read before the Royal Society in 1840 was followed by the terms *color photography* (in 1872) and *color camera* (1893), and was then called a *color print* (also 1893, these terms, of course, originally applied only to still photography). The first *colored moving pictures* were a few Edison one-reelers that began to appear in 1896 (noncolored ones then being called *black-and-white*), but these were not "naturally colored" but hand-colored or tinted and thus also called *tinted moving pictures*. By 1905, studios could buy sepia and other tinted film stock tinted by the Pathé process, so that movies could be in shades of any one color, or night scenes could be in all blue, a scene of a fire all in red, etc. From 1908 to 1922, true photographic color movies were perfected with, in chronological order:

> *Kinemacolor*, invented by G. Albert Smith and first demonstrated in 1908 by Charles Urban, an American producer working in England. It was a *two-color process* using a red-orange and a blue-green filter on both camera and projector lenses. Initially used only for special news and cultural shorts, it gave many moviegoers in England and on the Continent their first glimpse of *color pictures* (1912) or *color films* (1914), as the English first called such movies. Despite the European success of a 1912 English production showing all the pomp and color of a 1911 royal visit to India, the American movie industry resisted Kinemacolor, fearing it would win audiences from their own black-and-white movies.
>
> *the Prizma process* was developed by another American, William Van Doren Kelley, during the second decade of the 20th century and was a two-color process using emulsions on the print, eliminating the need for color filters on the projector. In 1921 it was used for the first all-color story picture, the English *The Glorious Adventure*, starring Lady Diana Manners.
>
> *Technicolor* was invented by the Technicolor Motion Picture Corp. founded in 1915 by the Boston scientist Herbert T. Kalmus to carry on research and to perfect color movies. Dr. Kalmus said he based the corporation's *Technicolor* name on *Tech-* out of respect for his alma mater, the Massachusetts Institute of *Tech*nology; *Technicolor* was then first used to refer to the firm's color process in 1917. The process itself was originally a two-color, emulsion-on-the-film process, with the first *Technicolor movie* being *The Toll of the Sea*, which opened in New York City in 1922.

Technicolor demonstrated its full *three-color process*, natural color over the entire spectrum, in Walt Disney's 1932 animated cartoon *Flowers and Trees*, with the first full-length Technicolor movie being Pioneer Pictures' 1935 *Becky Sharp* (an adaptation of Thackeray's *Vanity Fair*), starring Miriam Hopkins. However, as in the 1939 *The Wizard of Oz*, in which the Kansas scenes were in black-and-white and the Land of Oz scenes in color, early color was often reserved for special effects and segments, with the all-color *Gone with the Wind* of that same year finally establishing the precedent that major films be all color.

Judy Garland, Ray Bolger, Bert Lahr, and Jack Haley (Dorothy, the Straw Man, the Cowardly Lion, and the Tin Woodsman) in the 1939 Wizard of Oz. *The Kansas scenes were in black-and-white, the Land of Oz scenes in color.*

As color was being perfected during the first decades of the 20th century, so was sound. Some of Edison's Kinetoscope Parlors of the 1890s had Kinetoscopes with earphones so one could hear accompanying Gramophone music or even dialogue with the peepshow pictures. Early movie houses were also seldom completely silent: the loud whir of the early projectors and the coughing and whispering of the audience were often accompanied by Gramophone music, and soon the film was usually accompanied by live piano music, or sometimes a three- or four-piece orchestra or, in the big movie palaces, by a full orchestra (the Roxy's had 70 pieces) or a "mighty" Wurlitzer organ producing full orchestral sounds plus 50 sound effects. In addition, some special movies, such as *The Birth of a Nation*, traveled with their own sound effects crews and orchestras, and some movie houses even provided live actors to read the titles and give groans, giggles, and shrieks to the mouthings of the silent actors on the screen. True sound movies, however, developed between 1912 and 1927 with the:

> *Speaking movies are impossible. When a century has passed, all thought of our so-called "talking pictures" will have been abandoned. It will never be possible to synchronize the voice with the picture.*
>
> D. W. Griffith, 1926

Kinetophone (from *Kineto*scope + Gramo*phone*), a 1912 Edison device combining a movie projector with separate recorded sound, though true synchronization of film and a record, moving at different speeds, was then impossible and the sound could not yet be amplified enough to fill a large theater. However, the Kinetophone movie was the first *talking moving picture* (1910), *talking picture* (1912), *talkie* (1913), *speaking film* (1918, the 1928 *speakie*, for *talkie*, never became popular), or *dialogue film* (1925).

Vitaphone. By the mid 1920s Bell Telephone Laboratories had

Al Jolson singing "Mammy" in blackface in The Jazz Singer, *1927.*

developed electrical recording and amplification so that Western Electric's *Vitaphone* could synchronize a film and a record disc and fill a movie theater with sound. Though movie companies had not pursued sound eagerly, by 1926 free radio, with its music and voices, was becoming competition (just as television would in the 1950s) and the financially ailing Warner Brothers took a desperate fling into Vitaphone movies, presenting a musical short subject and their silent feature *Don Juan* (starring John Barrymore) with music and sound effects added, at a special $10-a-ticket performance at their Warner Theater in New York City on August 6, 1926.

The Jazz Singer. Warner Brothers again used the Vitaphone synchronized disc-and-film method in this movie, which opened at their New York theater on the sultry evening of October 6, 1927, before a fashionable audience of flappers and their tuxedoed escorts. Unlike *Don Juan* with John Barrymore, *The Jazz Singer* was based on a popular melodrama and featured the vaudeville and follies star Al Jolson, who sang four songs, including his blackface rendition of "Mammy," in his unmistakable voice, and in one sequence actually spoke a few lines! As far as the public was concerned, this was the talkie that made talkies worthwhile; it grossed $3.5 million in its first six months and revolutionized the movie industry (George Jessel, who had starred in the stage version had wanted too much money to repeat his role in the movie; Jolson had taken the movie role for $75,000, refusing a smaller fee plus part of the profits because he didn't think the movie would be much of a success).

all-talking feature. The first "all-talking feature" was the 1928 *The Lights of New York*, produced and directed by Bryan Foy, who had grown up in vaudeville as one of "the Seven Little Foys." MGM's first picture with sound was its very successful 1928 *White Shadows in the South Seas*, originally filmed as a silent picture but then embellished with a musical score, sound effects, and one word of dialogue, "Hello," added later—as well as Leo the Lion's first roar.

Movietone. Although Dr. Lee De Forest had demonstrated his revolutionary *Phonofilm* sound-on-film process as an "extra added attraction" in theaters since 1923 in his Phonofilm shorts, he never contracted with a studio to produce major sound movies with it. It was Theodore Case, a former assistant of De Forest's, who developed a similar system for William Fox, the 1927 *Movietone* system. Like De Forest's Phonofilm, Movietone translated sound waves into electronic impulses which were recorded by light on the film itself—which meant there was complete synchronization of sight and sound and the film could truly talk (Fox immediately began to release sound-on-film shorts and, also in 1927, the *Movietone newsreel*). The *Movietone Cinematograph transparencies*, like the Phonofilm, thus used not a separate recording device but a *sound camera* (a concept and term first appearing in 1904) and film with a *sound path* (1921), later called a *sound track* (1929), to produce *sound on film* or *sound film* (both 1923 terms). Where silent film speed had been 16 frames per second, the sound film speed was 24 frames per second.

"Garbo talks!" was the ad for Greta Garbo's first talking picture, the 1930 Anna Christie, shown here playing at the Capitol in New York City.

Thus the commercial success of *The Jazz Singer* and the technical success of Movietone's sound-on-film truly turned movies into talkies and all earlier movies into *silent movies* (1929, the term *the silent screen* first appeared in 1930). In 1929: theater owners were rushing to install sound equipment; movie after movie was billed as "All Talking!" or "All Talking! All Singing!" and the public was so enthusiastic that movie attendance almost doubled, to a weekly 110 million; Mary Pickford, "The Girl with the Curl," cut off her golden curls and bobbed her hair flapper style for her first talkie, *Coquette,* for which she won the Academy Award as Best Actress; and since movies were so newly exciting again, Imperial Airways showed the first *in-flight movie,* a version of Arthur Conan Doyle's *The Lost World.*

The talkies led to many new movie terms and professions, such as *dialogue director, dubbing* (1929), *Movieola* (1929, the miniature projector with earphones for editing sound-on-film movies), *musical arranger, sound stage* (1931), and *voice coach.* Of course, the talkies found that some movie stars without stage training had never learned to memorize and deliver lines, some sultry screen sirens had chilling Brooklyn accents, some virile leading men (such as Douglas Fairbanks and John Gilbert) didn't have voices to match, and some foreign-born stars (as Emil Jannings) had too thick an accent to please American ears. While such silent stars lost their glow and soon disappeared, other silent screen actors, ranging from Ronald Colman, Gary Cooper, Greta Garbo, and Gloria Swanson to Laurel and Hardy, seemed to have voices or accents that matched their screen image and continued to flourish. A new generation of stars with memorable voices quickly rose to join them, the public soon recognizing the unique voices of Humphrey Bogart, James Cagney, Paul Muni, Edward G. Robinson, Cary Grant, and Mae West.

We'll never know how many immigrants improved their English by hearing the early talkies. There were some attempts in the 1930s at producing non-English talkies for foreign-born Americans, including about 100 *Yiddish films* starring the likes of Molly Picon, Moyshe Oysher, and Maurice Schwartz in sentimental folk tales and urban immigrant melodramas, many produced and directed by Joseph Seiden and filmed in Fort Lee, New Jersey— but such films had a limited and constantly shrinking audience as the immigrants were assimilated. More important, we'll never know how much the voices, speech patterns, and intonations of frequently heard, highly admired movie actors have influenced American ways of talking—how much, consciously or unconsciously, the voice, cockiness, or tough talk of actors such as Bogart, Cagney, and Robinson, the western drawl or slow speech of actors such as Gary Cooper, John Wayne, James Stewart, and Henry Fonda, the debonair accents or delivery of Ronald Colman and Cary Grant, or the voices and intonations of actresses such as Katharine Hepburn, Bette Davis, Lana Turner, and Marilyn Monroe have affected the way we speak. To many Americans and to most foreigners the voices of the movies, and of radio, television, and records, have truly become the voices of America.

Clark Gable and Vivien Leigh in Gone with the Wind, *1939.*

The 1930s began with the tidal wave of sound movies and ended with the first wave of major Technicolor movies (see above), the 1939 *Wizard of Oz* and David Selznick's *Gone with the Wind* (affectionately known as *GWTW* to Hollywood reporters), based on Margaret Mitchell's best-selling 1936 novel and starring Clark Gable and Vivien Leigh. In this Depression decade the studios explored and exploited the uses of voices, music, and sound effects to shock, thrill, and entertain audiences, producing fast-paced, sometimes violent movies full of the sound of screeching tires, gunfire, and sneering gangster voices, and new, babbling, light-hearted comedies and song-filled musicals. Americans stepped into the dark movie theaters to forget the harsh glare of the Depression and saw the:

gangster movie, a 1934 term (the word *gangster* itself dates only from 1896). Gangster movies were popular in the early 30s because this was the end of the Prohibition Era; for a decade the public had been reading daily newspaper accounts of bootleggers, speakeasies, and the mob. Warner Brothers led the way in gangster films with the 1930 *Little Caesar* and the 1932 *Scarface*, both starring Edward G. Robinson, and the 1931 *The Public Enemy*, starring James Cagney. These films made *tough-guy movies* (a mid-1930s term) popular and made stars out of actors who could play the *heavy* (1928 in movie use, from 1814 theatrical use, meaning both the villain's role and the actor who plays it).

horror movie, a 1937 term as meaning a movie made to send chills down our spines (but during World War II it was used to refer to documentaries and newsreels of wartime atrocities). These became a popular genre with the 1931 *Dracula* and *Frankenstein*, the latter starring Boris Karloff, and the 1932 *The Mummy*, with RKO's 1933 *King Kong* being the first to be called a *monster movie*.

musical, a new movie term that came in with sound movies, from the 1890 stage use, a shortening of the 1765 theatrical term

Gangster movie *was a term of the early 1930s, originally used to describe such films as the 1930* Little Caesar, *starring Edward G. Robinson.*

Horror movie *was also a new term of the 1930s, a genre made popular in 1931 by* Franken- stein, *starring Boris Karloff (left), and* Dracula, *starring Bela Lugosi (right).*

Monster movie *was a term first applied to the 1933* King Kong.

musical comedy. Warner Brothers also led the way in musicals, with its *42nd Street* (1933), *Gold Diggers of 1933*, and *Gold Diggers of 1935*, using such stars as Ruby Keeler, Dick Powell, and Adolphe Menjou, introducing such songs as "Lullaby of Broad-way," and including spectacular *musical numbers* (an 1885 English music-hall term) staged by dance director Busby Berkeley.

Music in movies was not, of course, limited to musicals. Background mood music was used in the early 30s but usually only behind major emotional scenes in major productions. After the unexpected success of the 1935 *The Informer* with a score by

Musical had been in theatrical use since 1890. It became a movie term in 1933 with such films as Gold Diggers of 1933. *One spectacular* musical number *staged by Busby Berkeley for that movie is shown here.*

Max Steiner, however, a full *musical score* throughout the entire picture became a mark of quality films.

newspaper movie was a term created to describe the 1931 *The Front Page*, which was so successful that other newspaper movies followed.

thriller was a 1920s movie term but was most often used to describe the films of Alfred Hitchcock in the 1930s. This English director came to the U.S. after directing the first British talkie, the 1931 *Blackmail*, then began making "Hitchcock thrillers" here, such as *The 39 Steps* (1935) and *The Lady Vanishes* (1938).

Margaret Lockwood and Dame May Whitty in the 1938 "Hitchcock thriller," The Lady Vanishes.

western appeared as a movie term in 1928, such a movie having earlier been called a *cowboy movie* (around 1920), *gun opera* (1921), and *horse opera* (1927). The noun *western* was not created by the movies, however; boys had been reading *penny westerns*, *half-dime* and *five-cent westerns*, and *dime westerns* such as *Denver Dan Jr. and His Band of Dead Shots* and *Arizona Joe, the Boy Pard of Texas Jack*, since the 1860s.

The first movie showing the Wild West had been the 1898 vignette *The Cripple Creek Barroom*, with the 1903 *The Great Train Robbery* (discussed earlier) being the first western story movie; its leading actor was "Bronco Billy" Anderson, the first cowboy star, who went on to appear in more than 500 one- and two-reel cowboy movies. In 1914 the forty-two-year-old William S. Hart, who had lived in the West and been a cowboy before becoming a successful stage actor, began acting in cowboy movies, starred in Thomas Ince's 1916 *The Aryan*, and became the best-known silent *cowboy actor* (a term not recorded until 1937).

The always popular western, however, had new life in the 1930s when, with talkies, the cowboy stars began to sing (real cowboys actually did sing occasionally, mainly to calm their herds at night, their cowboy songs being known as *Texas lullabies*). Singing authentic western songs, Tex Ritter became the first movie *singing cowboy*, though that term was first applied to Gene Autry, who was billed as "the Singing Cowboy" in the 1935 *In Old Santa Fe*, with Tom Mix and Roy Rogers also soon claiming that title.

Westerns, without the singing, have created, or added luster to, many stars, including Gabby Hayes, Walter Brennan, and Johnny Mack Brown in the early 1930s; Gary Cooper (who won a Best Actor Academy Award for the 1952 *High Noon*), Randolph Scott in the 1947 *The Gunfighter*, and Alan Ladd in the 1953 *Shane*. The best-known and best-loved actor who played in many westerns is, of course, John "Duke" Wayne (producer Raoul Walsh gave him the name John Wayne in 1929, the actor thus giving up his real name, Marion Morrison, for the movies but keeping his boyhood nickname, "Duke," given him because it was the name of his pet Airedale!) The big, strong college football star had worked at various jobs ranging from errand boy to prop man to stunt man before acting in John Ford's silent movies for $45 a week, then getting his first major role in Raoul Walsh's 1929 *The Big Trail*, which earned him not only his screen name but a $75-a-week five-year contract with Fox. He went on to star in scores of westerns, including such classics as the 1944 *Tall in the Saddle* and the 1952 *Red River*, and won the Academy Award for Best Actor in the 1969 *True Grit*.

Thus, despite the Depression, or perhaps because of it, the movies boomed in the 30s. Some theater owners and managers set aside special nights when the price of admission included canned goods for the needy; many held out the promise of quick fame or fortune by staging a weekly *amateur night* in which aspiring

Cowboy movie *was a term of around 1920, with such a movie being called a* western *by 1928. Gene Autry (upper left) was the first to be billed as a singing cowboy, in the 1935* In Old Santa Fe, *though the term was soon applied to Roy Rogers (upper right) and others. Gary Cooper (lower left) had his first talking role in the 1929* The Virginian, *and Alan Ladd (lower right) starred in the 1953* Shane, *here shown with Brandon de Wilde.*

singers, dancers, musicians, jugglers, and others from the audience could perform for cash prizes after the early evening movie; while still others had a weekly *bank night* (1936) drawing from the ticket stubs to dispense cash prizes or a *dish night* at which every patron received a free dish, cup, or bowl (it took many weeks and many movies for a family to complete a set, but getting something usable and free made everyone feel less guilty about spending money on movies).

When full-length features had proliferated after World War I, it seemed that multiple movie programs might disappear. But in competing for scarce Depression dollars, movies began to show two feature-length films, a *double feature* (1932) or *double bill*, for the price of one (*double bill* was originally an 1890s stage term for a bill featuring two stars or two short plays, *bill* having meant a list of acts or performers since 1851). The movie theaters couldn't afford to show two expensive pictures so they showed one expensive *A picture* coupled with a less expensive *B picture*, euphemistically called a *second feature* (all 1930 terms). The B picture was usually a *low-budget* quickly made *quickie* (a movie term of 1929) that the major studios put *in the can* (1930, meaning completed, the finished movie put in the film can ready to be distributed) as fast as they could. Such B pictures gave many promising and lower-paid movie actors experience and their chance to climb toward stardom. Thus, the irrepressible, klaxon-voiced Mickey Rooney and lovely Ann Rutherford appeared in MGM's *Andy Hardy* series, in which audiences also saw Judy Garland and Lana Turner for the first time; and Bryan Foy, who had produced that first all-talking feature in 1928, was to produce over 1,000 B pictures to become "the King of the B's." Most theaters got the same A and B pictures at about the same time, for the major studios now owned large chains of theaters and rented their pictures in a group (*block booking* it was called), often even before they were screened for the exhibitors (this was called *blind buying*). Thus, local movie houses showed what the studios sent them, feeling fairly sure it was what the public wanted (block bookings and blind buying were declared illegal in 1950).

In addition to the two movies, the program usually included such items as a:

> *preview* (1924 in movie use) of scenes from the next week's movie, or from the next several weeks' movies, these introduced as *previews of coming attractions*. The industry called this ad for next week's film a *trailer*, because it came after or trailed the feature.
>
> A *sneak preview* was not really a preview at all but the showing of a new film whose name had not been previously announced, often with the members of the audience being asked to fill out a form giving their opinions and comments. The term *sneak preview* comes from 19th-century newspaper use, then referring to a

preview of an interview, exposé, or other feature that was to appear later.

newsreel. The earliest projected films in 1896 showed current events, such as bits of a boxing match, a scene of New York's Easter parade on Fifth Avenue, and President McKinley's inauguration. The French motion picture pioneer Charles Pathé began making and distributing films of each week's major news events in France in 1909 (the French called such films *actualités*) and his *News of the Week* first appeared in the U.S. in 1910, such films becoming known as *newsreels* in America by 1916 (since they were reels of film devoted to news). Fox began to release the first sound-on-film newsreels in 1927, the *Movietone News*, and in 1935 Louis de Rochemont and Time Inc. originated *The March of Time* with news, news features, and interviews.

As political conditions grew more ominous in Europe in the early 1930s and war approached in the late 30s, newsreels became more important. As early as 1933 there were a few *newsreel theaters* or *news theaters* showing nothing but newsreels and shorts, the programs usually lasting about an hour, and by 1940 some of these theaters were showing full-length *news films* of the weekly progress of World War II.

selected short subjects or *selected shorts* could be just about anything: perhaps a short cultural film featuring a symphony orchestra; a "follow the bouncing ball," as it lights on the words, sing-along; a short about a baseball spring-training camp; a *travelogue*, which had first been a 1903 term for an illustrated lecture on travel to faraway places, the first famous travelogues having been given around that time by Burton Holmes, who may have coined the word (from *travel* + *-logue*, discourse, from Greek *-logos*, word, discourse); an *Our Gang Comedy* with the Little Rascals (the first of these was made in the silent days of 1922, the last in 1944); or, best of all, one or several *animated cartoons* (see below).

No double feature of the 1930s was complete without an animated cartoon. In 1906, Stuart Blackton drew a simple series of funny pictures, *Humorous Phases of Funny Faces* for Vitagraph and in 1909 Winsor McCay produced the first true American animated

A favorite selected short *was an* Our Gang Comedy *with the* Little Rascals. *The first* Our Gang Comedy *was made in 1922, the last in 1944.*

cartoon, *Gertie the Dinosaur*, by making 16 complete drawings for each second of action, the main action being Gertie drinking a lake, then regurgitating it when the reel was reversed, a rather spectacular device and one that saved McCay a lot of drawing. In 1911, McCay produced the *Little Nemo* series for Vitagraph, based on the Little Nemo character that had first appeared in the *New York Herald* in 1908. *Animated cartoon* had become a common term by 1912 (often shortened to *cartoon* by 1916), with *to animate* appearing as a movie term in 1916 and *animation* in 1919. By 1913, silent *cartoon series* were beginning to be a regular part of movie programs; by the early 1920s, Max Fleischer had developed the popular series *Ko-Ko the Clown*, which introduced the character Betty Boop, and Pat Sullivan had introduced *Felix the Cat*, these cartoons created by drawing the moving figures on *cels* (Celluloid sheets), which were laid over predrawn backgrounds, simplifying the time-consuming work.

Mickey Mouse, originally named Mortimer, and his girlfriend Minnie had been introduced by Walt Disney (who began making animated cartoons in 1923) in the silent *Plane Crazy* and *Gallopin' Gaucho* before becoming a success in Disney's first sound cartoon, the 1928 *Steamboat Willie*, in which Mickey's voice was that of Disney himself. Mickey became so popular that: twenty-one *Mickey Mouse cartoons* were produced in 1930–31; *Mickey Mouse movie* was the joking name our World War II servicemen gave to gruesome hand-to-hand combat training films and vivid anti-venereal-disease sex-hygiene films; *Mickey Mouse* was the Allies' password on D Day, June 6, 1944, beginning the invasion of

415

Snow White and the Seven Dwarfs, *1938*.

Hitler's Europe at Normandy; and since the 1950s *Mickey Mouse* has been used in American slang as an adjective meaning sentimental, corny, or cheaply insincere. After establishing Mickey Mouse, Disney produced his first *color cartoon* (and the first full-color *Technicolor* movie), *Flowers and Trees* in 1932, introduced Donald Duck in 1934, and made the first *feature-length animated movie*, his *Snow White and the Seven Dwarfs* in 1939 (the studio astutely refused to call it a *feature-length cartoon*, that term not appearing until 1956).

After Disney's success with Mickey Mouse, Warner Brothers opened a rival cartoon studio in 1930, featuring Leon Schlesinger's first *Merry Melodies* and *Looney Tunes*, the first always ending with the line *That's All Folks*, which became a popular expression, and the second introducing brash, irreverent humor into cartoons with the appearance of Porky Pig in 1935, Daffy Duck in 1937, and the fully evolved Bugs Bunny in 1940 (he had earlier appeared in various forms, originally in *Porky's Hare Hunt*), who gave us another catch phrase, *What's Up, Doc?* Terrytoon's Mighty Mouse and Heckle and Jeckle also became names every child and most adults knew in the 1930s and 40s, the murderous cat-and-mouse chases of Tom and Jerry and cat-and-bird chases of Sylvester and Tweety Pie became well known in the 1950s and 60s, with the lisping bird, Tweety Pie, giving us the catch phrase *I think I thee a puddy cat*.

Freer graphics and more-adult humor were provided by Stephen Bosustow's United Productions of America (UPA) studio with John Hubley's Mr. Magoo cartoons, beginning in 1949, and

Bob Cannon's Gerald McBoing Boing series, which began in 1950 and established the word *boing* as meaning the sound of a coiled spring popping out. By the mid 1950s both *boing-boing* and *boing* were male exclamations of appreciation or acknowledgment on seeing a sexually attractive woman (the cartoon had nothing to do with sex or erection but just made popular the humorous sounding *boing* and *boing-boing*). But such names and terms were in the future in the 1930s, when we first began to expect animated cartoons with our double features.

Despite the above movie terms of the 1930s, two others were to have greater impact on the general public: *home movie* and *drive-in*. Simple cameras and projectors had been developed so that movies could be taken and shown by the amateur in his own home by the mid 1930s. The term *drive-in* (for a movie theater) first appeared in the patent for a ramp system for a *drive-in*, granted to Richard M. Hollingshead, Jr., of Riverton, New Jersey, on May 16, 1933. Having experimented with showing outdoor movies at night on a screen in front of his garage, Hollingshead then opened the first movie *drive-in* in a 400-car parking lot on Wilson Boulevard in Camden, New Jersey, on June 6, 1933, offering a double feature every evening (the British didn't have their first drive-in movie, which they call an *open-air cinema*, until 1960, by which time there were 4,700 in the U.S.).

The movies remember 1941 as the year "the boy wonder" of radio and the stage, the twenty-four-year-old Orson Welles, produced, directed, and starred in *Citizen Kane*. His experiments with camera angles and dramatic lighting for that film required the development of new lenses and lighting and his introduction of an *off-screen narrator* or *off-screen voice* added these two terms to the movies' vocabulary.

The public, of course, remembers 1941 as the year Japan bombed Pearl Harbor and the U.S. entered World War II. During the war there were many *patriotic pictures*, including Gary Cooper in the 1941 *Sergeant York* (of World War I) and James Cagney in the 1942 *Yankee Doodle Dandy*; films of foreign intrigue, such as the 1943 *Casablanca* and *Watch on the Rhine*; and many *war movies* showing handsome Allied heroes laughing, loving, and fighting their way to victory against cruel Nazis and "dirty Japs"; as well as comedies about recruits, musicals with singing soldiers and WACS, etc. The real war was seen in newsreels and documentaries. The word *documentary* (from the French *documentaire*, factual film, travelogue) had first been used by the Scottish educator John Grierson in his February 8, 1926, *New York Sun* review of Robert Flaherty's film about Samoan life, *Moana*, this review written while Grierson was studying mass communications in the U.S. Flaherty is now known as "the Father of the Documentary," especially for his 1921 *Nanook of the North*, which used full motion

Nanook of the North, *1921.*

417

During World War II and after there were many patriotic pictures, war movies, and films of foreign intrigue. (Above left) Gary Cooper receiving the Academy Award for Best Actor in 1942 for the 1941 Sergeant York *(about the World War I hero) from Jimmy Stewart, then an air force lieutenant. (Above right) Ingrid Bergman and Humphrey Bogart in the 1943* Casablanca. *(Right) Frank Sinatra and Gene Kelly playing happy-go-lucky sailors in the 1949* On the Town.

picture creative technique to depict the fight for existence in the sub-Arctic of an Eskimo family, while Grierson, himself, later became a pioneer of the British documentary film.

Much of the World War II newsreel and documentary footage came from the millions of feet of *combat film* taken all over the world by *combat cameramen* to document the war and for use in educational and propaganda films. The best of these included Colonel Frank Capra's *Why We Fight*, army scenes which clearly and dramatically detailed the causes and progress of the war.

Most movies, however, had little to do with the war, except perhaps to help us escape it for a few hours. For the women there were the melodramatic, sentimental *women's pictures* starring noble women in tragic, or at least melancholy, situations, such as the 1942 *Mrs. Miniver* with Greer Garson. For youths there were slapstick B pictures such as those featuring a splinter group of "the Dead End Kids" called *the Bowery Boys* (see FIRE! for the origin of this term and the original Bowery Boys), who began the Bowery Boys series, featuring Leo Gorcey as Muggs and Huntz Hall as

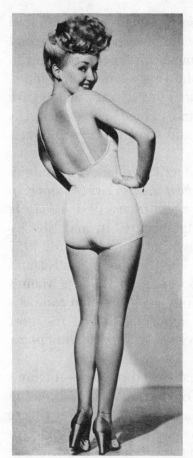

Pin-up girl *Betty Grable*.

Howard Hughes' 1943 The Out-law *featured Jane Russell and the contents of her* uplift bra.

Gimpy, in the 1941 *Pride of the Bowery* (showing the boys under Depression Era CCC camp discipline) and followed it with *Mr. Wise Guy* in 1942. After the war, movies seemed to get back to normal with Rita Hayworth in the 1946 *Gilda* and Broderick Crawford and Mercedes McCambridge in *All the King's Men* in 1949. However, the *pin-up girl* and the *sweater girl* of World War II, and relaxed moral attitudes after the war, led to increased publicity for movies starring any *oomph girl* (*oomph* had become a Hollywood term for sex appeal in 1939), *sex kitten* (1940), or *glamour girl* (1941), such as Rita Hayworth, Lana Turner, and Jane Russell, whose wearing of a special *uplift bra* designed for her by Howard Hughes for *The Outlaw* helped lead to the *breast fixation* of the movies, and of American males, of the late 40s and the 1950s.

Almost as soon as the war ended, European studios started making films showing the miseries of war and the problems of returning to the war-torn cities and mores of peacetime life. Although the Italian Luchino Visconti had combined a documentary style, natural backgrounds, and the use of nonprofessional actors into Italian neorealism, his films had not yet been shown outside Italy when his countryman Roberto Rossellini introduced *neorealism*, both as a cinematic approach and as a new movie term, to us with his 1945 *Open City*, starring the people and streets of Rome and showing the struggle of the Italian people under German domination. This was followed by Vittorio De Sica's 1946 *Shoe Shine* and 1948 *The Bicycle Thief*, starring the people and streets of Milan in a grim story of a father and his son trying to obtain a bicycle the man must have for a job. Such films opened the way for the success of other Italian directors, as Federico Fellini and Michelangelo Antonioni in the 50s and 60s. More important, they were the first *foreign-language films* (a newly popular term in the late 1940s) most Americans had ever seen or heard of. The term *subtitle* reappeared in movie use, now referring to the printed English translation, or summary, of the dialogue at the bottom of the frames.

British films imported after the war were also attracting favorable reviews and increasingly large audiences. We were again enjoying superbly acted British movies based on Dickens and Shakespeare, as the 1946 *Henry V* starring Laurence Olivier, and also seeing such British imports as David Lean's 1946 drama *Brief Encounter*, Carol Reed's 1947 *Odd Man Out* and 1949 *The Third Man*, and a delightful deluge of films with "British humor," such as Alec Guinness's many films of the period, including the 1950 *Kind Hearts and Coronets*.

By the late 1940s such imported Italian and British movies were called *foreign art films* or simply *foreign films* and had become something of a fad among some educated people who had never, with some good reasons, taken American movies seriously. These

The Bicycle Thief, *1948*.

Shelley Winters and Montgomery Clift in A Place in the Sun, *1951.*

foreign imports were seldom called *movies* but were usually referred to as *films*, which word then took on connotations of quality and artistic merit. Some smaller movie houses in larger cities and in college towns began specializing in showing such foreign films, often calling themselves not *movie theaters* but *cinemas*, which gave the word *cinema* a new connotation, too. Thus, soon Americans seemed to stop "going to the movies" and went to see a "film at a cinema" instead.

The 1950s had its share of good American movies, including: Joseph L. Mankiewicz's 1950 *All About Eve;* Gary Cooper in Stanley Kramer's 1952 *High Noon;* George Stevens' 1951 *A Place in the Sun,* with Elizabeth Taylor, Montgomery Clift, and Shelley Winters; Gene Kelly in the 1951 *An American in Paris* and the 1952 *Singin' in the Rain;* Marlon Brando and Lee J. Cobb in Elia Kazan's 1954 *On the Waterfront;* and Ernest Borgnine in Delbert Mann's 1955 *Marty*—but all was not well in Hollywood. Foreign competition was increasing and, much more important, in the 50s most Americans were buying their first television sets and staying home to watch them.

Italian imports were still of high quality and popular—Fellini's 1954 *La Strada* is an example—but French films were becoming more important in the world market and by the late 1950s were winning most of the awards at the major film festivals (the term *film festival* appeared in 1932 to refer to the very first one, held that year by the Italian film industry in Venice, that festival, under Mussolini's regime, having a strong nationalistic, propaganda undertone). The highly acclaimed new French movies were part of the French *nouvelle vague* (a term first used in 1958, soon translating into *new wave*) of films and filmmakers, often film critics turned directors, focusing on modern French life and its young people. These French films, such as François Truffaut's 1958 *The 400 Blows* and Jean-Luc Godard's 1959 *Breathless,* joined Italian and British films, and soon the films of Poland and other countries, to compete with Hollywood products at home and around the globe. By the late 1950s more than 600 U.S. movie theaters specialized in British and foreign-language films.

At the same time, the tightly controlled Hollywood studio system was breaking down. The Supreme Court had ruled that studios could not control moviemaking, distribution, and theaters, and during the early 1950s the studios had sold or closed their theaters and theater chains. American directors saw the greater artistic control European directors had over their films and demanded the same. The studios, feeling the squeeze of television more than that of foreign imports and losing their captive theaters, had to reduce overhead and salaries, releasing many of the stars, directors, writers, and producers they had under contract, eventually ending the contract *star system* (as it was now called), by which

Stars, such as Jane Fonda, shown here with her Academy Award for the 1971 Klute, *no longer work under the studio* star system *but choose and control many of the pictures they make.*

they had created, nurtured, and profited from so many stars. Some of the best directors, producers, and actors thus became a new breed of *independent*, making their own films and using the studios only as suppliers of equipment and stages, as financial backers, and as distributors.

Many moviemakers felt that the major advantage movies had over the small black-and-white TV screens of the 50s was being able to show larger-than-life full-color spectacles, full of vast scenes, thousands of actors, and "majestic grandeur," which the *small screen* or *home screen* (as television was now sometimes called to distinguish it from the movies) could not convey. The enormously expensive, ridiculously spectacular films they made, often based on tried and true subjects, included Cecil B. De Mille's 1956 *The Ten Commandments* (its "cast of thousands" needed more than 7,500 wigs and false beards), the 1959 *Ben Hur*, the 1962 *Mutiny on the Bounty* with Marlon Brando, and the 1963 *Cleopatra* with Elizabeth Taylor. Almost all such overblown spectacles were financial disasters.

Others sought to combat television not with individual movie spectacles but by developing even larger screens and realistic, three-dimensional effects, which no television set could match. Thus in rapid succession between 1952 and 1955 we had:

3-D, meaning *three-dimensional*, movies. They had been tried before, especially in 1935, when movie patrons were handed squarish cardboard glasses with red and green Cellophane lenses for viewing a few special movies shot through red and green lenses. Though some viewers had squealed and ducked as cars and trains and children on swings seemed to pop out of the screen at them, the glasses were annoying and most moviegoers preferred to lose themselves in a good movie rather than be aware of special effects.

In 1952 a more sophisticated *3-D* was developed, using light-polarizing lenses instead of colored ones. It provided a unique *sleeper* (1930s as an unexpected success) in the low-budget 1952 *Bwana Devil*, after which several other 3-D films were rushed into production, with MGM's *Kiss Me Kate*, featuring the tap-dancing star Ann Miller, being the "first 3-D musical." Although the original polarizing lens system had been improved and given the name *Natural Vision*, audiences did not flock to see 3-D (which had appeared a few months after Cinerama). By the end of 1953, the polarized light 3-D process had been relegated to use in a series of cheap horror films.

Cinerama. The first Cinerama movie, *This Is Cinerama*, opened at New York City's Broadway theater on October 1, 1952, and audiences thrilled at the spectacular "ride" on the Coney Island roller coaster, the large, almost three-dimensional, views of beautiful scenery, and all the other effects of large-screen, stereophonic reality.

The public also had some new terms: *Cinerama* (1951, from *Cine*ma + pan*orama*), and *wide-screen* and *wide-screen movie* (both

421

1952). *Wide-screen* also soon saw a little independent metaphorical use to mean "all encompassing" or "broad," as in asking someone to "take a wide-screen view" of a problem.

Cinerama, which was independently developed by Fred Waller, was not only the first *wide-screen process* but was the most complicated of all. It used three cameras and three projectors to get a huge three-piece picture on a wide, curved screen (about six times the size of a then normal movie screen)—and coupled the picture with Hazard Reeve's *seven-channel stereophonic sound* system, including a battery of speakers around the auditorium for multidirectional sound (Walt Disney's 1940 *Fantasia* had used a primitive form of stereophonic sound). Thus, the audience seemed surrounded with thrillingly realistic scenes and sound.

The three perfectly synchronized films (one could barely see them meet at the seams) not only showed large panoramic scenes and gave a 3-D effect on the curved screen, but could be used for special *split screen* (another 1952 Cinerama word) effects, projecting two or three different scenes side by side showing "now" and "then" or while-this-is-happening-here that-is-also-happening-there reality, or creating special montages (*montage* was originally a French moviemaking word of the 1920s, referring to film editing and editing effects in general before assuming its more specialized meaning in the 1930s).

-orama. In addition to giving us several new words, *Cinerama* gave us a new suffix, *-orama* (occasionally *-arama* or *-erama*), which was in wide fad use by the mid 1950s, especially to name or describe a usually cheap or flashy business establishment. Thus from the mid 50s into the 60s, one saw many a *dance-orama* (dance hall), *drinkorama* (bar), or *bookorama* (a bookstore or book sale), *-orama* vaguely used to mean offering a "panorama," or wide choice, exciting, or huge.

Though Cinerama was a huge success, taking, processing, and projecting the film was just too complex and expensive, even after a single-camera system was developed. Most theaters just couldn't afford the special projection and sound equipment needed and small theaters couldn't push back walls or remodel to accommodate the big screen or realize the system's full effects. Thus, although a few Cinerama movies were made into the early 1960s, Cinerama died, leaving many with fond memories and the language with *wide-screen*, *split-screen*, and *-orama*.

CinemaScope was introduced by Twentieth Century–Fox in 1953 with the religious epic *The Robe*, based on Lloyd C. Douglas's 1942 novel and starring Richard Burton. Much less complicated and less expensive than Cinerama, it became the most important wide-screen process. Based on a system first demonstrated in France by Henri Chrétien in 1928, it uses an *anamorphic lens* (a term most laymen hadn't heard of until CinemaScope appeared) to squeeze a wide panorama onto 35mm film, the projector lens then reversing the process onto a screen two and a half times as wide as it is high. Though called "the poor man's Cinerama" by some when it first appeared, CinemaScope was very good—and movie theaters could buy the lenses, screens, and sound equipment to show it for $20,000. Thus, by the mid 1960s, more than 30,000 theaters around the world were equipped to show CinemaScope movies.

VistaVision, Panavision, etc. Other systems as simple as Cinema-Scope were also developed. Paramount's 1954 *VistaVision* permitted greater magnification without graininess than CinemaScope, used a larger, squarer screen, and could be shown with standard projectors, although for full effect theaters would have to install new projectors to show 70mm contact prints. MGM's *Panavision* (*panorama* + *vision*) used 65mm film, and a later *CinemaScope 55* used 55.625mm film. Most theaters could not afford or didn't have room for all the different types of projectors and screens; thus the few movies made by these processes were usually reduced and shown on 35mm film, losing most of their advantages. Other systems, such as *SuperScope* and *WarnerScope*, were made for or adapted to the CinemaScope projectors and screens (the *-Scope* in their names means they are a part of the general *CinemaScope* system).

Todd-AO was developed for Mike *Todd* by Brian O'Brien of the *American Optical* Co. (hence, of course, the name *Todd-AO*) and introduced in the fall of 1955 with an adaptation of Rodgers and Hammerstein's musical *Oklahoma!*, followed by the better-known *Around the World in 80 Days*, based on Jules Verne's classic and starring David Niven as Phileas Fogg. Mike Todd's publicity for Todd-AO, his marriage to the beautiful Elizabeth Taylor, and soon his tragic death in an airplane crash, focused the public's attention on the process and its *Around the World in 80 Days*, but Todd-AO was doomed even before it was perfected, because it achieved its wide-screen effect with an ultrawide 70mm film and, as with VistaVision and Panavision, theaters could not afford the necessary variety of projecting equipment.

Though good for moviemakers and audiences alike, the wide screen didn't fill the movie theaters with patrons. In the 1960s and

Around the World in 80 Days, *1956, starring David Niven and Cantinflas, was made in* Todd-AO.

70s Americans were buying new color television sets and TV screens had gotten bigger. Also, America and the American family had changed: we weren't one big happy family anymore. There were fewer families with a mom, dad, and two children who went out together to the movies, or anywhere else, than there were in the 30s and 40s. Parking was becoming a problem and many large theaters were in midtown neighborhoods that had become unappealing or even unsafe at night. Audiences were fragmenting: some people went only to old-fashioned romantic and happy-ending movies, others enjoyed only "meaningful" movies with social or psychological messages, others wanted to see only artistic movies. Maybe it was a loss of national innocence or increased sophistication or cynicism, or maybe it was just a decade or two of television—but, somehow, movies just didn't seem that important any more. By the 1960s the movie audience, which had numbered 90 million a week in 1947, then 60 million a week in the 1950s, was down to 40 million a week, and the 20,000 movie theaters of 1947 had dwindled to 12,000. In the late 1960s and early 70s, 80 percent of all American movies lost money, almost every studio was in financial difficulties, and unemployment in the Hollywood craft unions was well over 65 percent.

Good movies were still being made. A new French style of neorealism, *cinéma vérité* (the term reached the U.S. in 1963 and we didn't feel it necessary to translate it into "cinema truth" or "truth-like movie") took its share of international awards and audiences. In America we had such happy and successful musicals as *My Fair Lady* and *Mary Poppins*, both 1964, and *The Sound of Music*, 1965; Stanley Kubrick's serious antiwar, anti-establishment comedy, the 1964 *Dr. Strangelove*; Mike Nichols' intelligent, dramatic shouting match, the 1966 *Who's Afraid of Virginia Woolf*, with Richard Burton and Elizabeth Taylor; the 1967 version of the love-conquers-all boy-girl love story (this time including the modern twist of boy sleeps with girl's mother), *The Graduate*, with one of the new, less glamorous, more talented breed of stars, Dustin Hoffman; and Arthur Penn's 1967 *Bonnie and Clyde* with its vivid slow-motion violence. Along with such successful movies, the wide screen, and the failing superspectacles, a new generation of movies was emerging, movies emphasizing more violence and sex accompanied by equally violent and obscene language. Movies need not be, and indeed could not be, for the entire family any more. As directors such as Russ Meyer and Sam Peckinpah knew, violence and sex were real and exciting in the modern world (and the FCC saw to it that the television networks couldn't compete with the movies in violence and sex). For America had also changed in its attitude toward what was and wasn't proper—or at least some Americans had.

Faye Dunaway and Warren Beatty in Bonnie and Clyde, *1967.*

We have had sexually titillating and even pornographic moving pictures—and censorship—since the early days of the peepshow. Though overshadowed by Little Egypt's exotic dancing of the coochie-coochie live, the peepshow screening of *Dolorita in the Passion Dance* brought publicity to the midway of the 1893 Chicago World's Columbian Exposition, this same peepshow later becoming the first to be banned by the police, when it was shown on the boardwalk in Atlantic City. After Mary Irwin and John Rice scandalized audiences with the first adult screen kiss in the 1896 *The Kiss* (actually just a short scene from the then current play *The Widow Jones*), many groups demanded screen censorship. Since then, efforts to avoid "morally objectionable" movies have given us such names and terms as:

the *National Board of Motion Pictures*, financed by the film companies in 1909 after New York City closed all its movie houses as being an "immoral influence." It created the *National Board of Censorship*, later replaced by the less honestly named *National Board of Review*, to police the industry. The censorship board outlawed the portrayal of "arson, poisoning, and suicide," except in movies based on the Bible, Shakespeare, or "other classics"; the "representation of crime, except with the object of conveying a moral lesson"; and, of course, all sex, nudity, and revealing costumes,

425

The movies changed as America and its attitudes changed; by the late 1960s sex and violence both in movie scenes and in dialogue were more explicit, even in good movies. (Above) From the silent days; (right) from the 1967 The Graduate.

"Fatty" Arbuckle as seen circa 1917.

though mermaids and harem girls were allowed to appear in tights. Such high-mindedness allayed much criticism and New York reopened its movie houses.

approved movies were those passed by the National Board of Censorship, which sent its list of such movies to theaters, local communities, and law enforcement agencies across the country.

Board of Movie Censors. Some states and cities didn't think the *National Board of Censorship* strict enough and had their own local *Board of Movie Censors.* They often forbade movies with those mermaids and harem girls in tights that the National Board accepted and usually forbade all romantic kissing except by engaged or married couples.

the Motion Picture Producers and Distributors of America, formed by the movie industry in 1922 to combat the public anger over the sex, drug, and booze orgies in Hollywood, as portrayed in Harry Leon Wilson's 1922 novel *Merton of the Movies* and seen in real life in two major 1921 scandals: the unsolved studio-lot murder of director William Desmond Taylor, which involved Mary Miles Minter, Mabel Normand, and drugs; and the San Francisco orgy of movie people in which "Fatty" Arbuckle was accused of killing a young woman by trying to rape her with a beer bottle.

morality clause. In 1922, the year after these scandals, the studios put a *morality clause* in their contracts, demanding seemly behavior from their employees (such clauses were still in effect during the McCarthy era of the early 1950s and used to ban suspected Communists, including the famous "blacklisted" *Hollywood ten*, from working in the movie industry).

the Czar of the movies. The movie industry chose Will H. Hays, who had been an attorney, a leading Republican congressman, and a postmaster general under Warren Harding, to organize and be president of the Motion Picture Producers and Distributors of America (MPPDA) and, hence, to codify and enforce movie morality. As president of the MPPDA for twenty-three years, from 1922 to his retirement in 1945, he became known as *the Czar of the movies* (see *the Hays code* and *the Hays office* below).

Central Casting. Hays immediately worked with the new Central Casting office to screen extras and would-be movie actresses and actors to keep out pimps, prostitutes, and drug sellers and users, so that every streetwalker stopped by the police could no longer claim she was an *out-of-work-actress*, which by 1922 had become a joking term for a prostitute. By 1924, movies also had a *casting director*, though some were said to choose actresses, not by their ability on the screen, but by their acquiescence on what was to become known as the *casting couch* (a term of the early 1940s).

the Hays code. Hays also created what came to be known as *the Hays code*, which, in its various incarnations, appeased the moral outrage of the clergy, temperance workers, ethnic groups, and others by stating that in the movies ministers were never to be treated as villains or as comic characters, that ethnic groups should be represented fairly, that the use of liquor was not to be shown unless "required by the plot or for proper characterization," that the "illegal drug traffic must never be presented," that no sympathy to crime be shown, that no how-to details be shown of murder, arson, safecracking, etc., that adultery was never to be "justified or presented attractively," that *scenes of passion . . . should be so treated that [they] do not stimulate the lower or baser element*," that seduction was "never the proper subject for comedy"—and that miscegenation was banned along with sex perversion, venereal disease, nudity, obscenity, and white slavery.

the Hays office. Despite the rather full Hays code, drinking scenes, glamorous gangsters, Blanche Sweet and Greta Garbo playing prostitutes and seductresses, a nearly nude Jacqueline Logan pining for Judas in De Mille's 1925 *King of Kings*, and some sultry films of platinum blonde Jean Harlow and the innuendos of Mae West in 1932 movies finally caused Hays to establish a *Production Code Administration* (PCA) in 1933 with a more detailed *code of decency*. Though Hays presided over the entire MPPDA, the PCA now became popularly known as *the Hays office* and the expression *Will it get by the Hays office?*—meaning "Is it moral, is it too sexy?"—soon entered popular fad use. The PCA's new code of decency forbade many things and elaborated on the fine points of the old code, including such items as forbidding *bedroom scenes* (1915) unless twin beds were shown or at least one of the occupants of the bed kept at least one foot firmly on the floor. Since major studios then owned about 70 percent of the first-run movie theaters and refused to distribute films that didn't have the PCA's approval, the Hays office was very important.

the National Legion of Decency. The U.S. Catholic Church wrote a moral code for movies and created this organization to enforce it

Will Hays in 1926.

Harness my zebras.
"Uttered" as a subtitle by Jacqueline Logan, playing the beautiful courtesan Mary Magdalene in Cecil B. De Mille's *King of Kings*, 1925; it then became a humorous fad expression meaning "Let's leave," and also, as *Well, harness my zebras!*, to express amazement.

Will it get by the Hays office? *This photograph mocked the movie code of decency by violating ten of its taboos.*

THOU SHALT NOT
1. LAW DEFEATED
2. INSIDE OF THIGH
3. LACE LINGERIE
4. DEAD MAN
5. NARCOTICS
6. DRINKING
7. EXPOSED BOSOM
8. GAMBLING
9. POINTING GUN
10. TOMMY GUN

Come up and see me sometime. Mae West in the play *Diamond Lil'*, 1932, and in the 1933 movie made from it, *She Done Him Wrong*.

in the early 1930s. The Legion and its code condemned movies for showing any hint of sex, nudity, brutality, or sympathy for sinners or evildoers, and for using objectional words (including the "damn" in *Gone with the Wind*). Until 1958 *the Legion of Decency,* as it was commonly called (later renamed the *Catholic Film Office*), used a somewhat complicated letter and number system to rate films (the British Film Censors had developed a *letter rating system* as early as 1912), then from 1958 until its closing in September 1980 used set phrases and critiques to rate movies. Between 1935 and 1980 the Catholic Film Office's bimonthly film *Review* carried ratings or critiques of over 16,000 films and millions of American Catholics saw and discussed such ratings and phrases as:

A-1 or *suitable for general patronage.*

A-2 or *morally unobjectionable for adults.* This was later merged into an *adults or adolescents* rating, as given to the 1962 *To Kill a Mockingbird,* considered objectionable for children because the ending seemed to justify the sin of lying.

A-3 and *A-4*, suitable for adults but with some specific reservations, which, after 1958, were spelled out.

B or *objectionable in part or all.* For example, the B rating was given to the 1947 *Miracle on 34th Street* because a major character was divorced and unrepentant.

Jean Harlow.

C or *condemned*, which rating truly condemned a movie since U.S. Catholics took a public pledge at Mass once a year to boycott such movies. From 1935 to 1968 the PCA and the Legion of Decency worked closely together, both often being consulted before a movie was shot or finally edited; in those thirty-three years the PCA gave its approval to only five movies the Legion of Decency condemned.

the Motion Picture Association of America (MPAA), the new name given the MPPDA by Eric Johnson when he succeeded Will Hays in 1945.

Throughout the 1950s and early 1960s, court rulings supporting wide interpretations of the constitutional guarantees of freedom of expression and suppressing the restraint of trade, competition among the studios and between movies and television, and the large number of independent directors and producers, combined with changing public attitudes concerning morality to make it increasingly difficult to enforce the PCA code of decency. Thus, in 1968 the MPAA stopped trying to control movies and turned to categorizing them with a *rating system*, giving us new terms we have used ever since:

G, general, all ages permitted.

PG, parental guidance suggested, though all ages permitted. By the 1980s this rating meant the movie might contain a few obscenities and perhaps a bit of not-too-explicit sex (children might think the couple were only kissing and hugging under the covers).

R, restricted, persons under seventeen must be accompanied by a parent or guardian. By the 1980s this rating often meant lots of obscenities or violence, some nudity, or rather obvious sex.

X, no one under seventeen admitted. Though legitimate first-run movies by major studios and producers are to carry the *X-rating* when they contain lots of violence, nudity, or explicit sex, such studios and producers usually try to avoid this rating by judicious rewrites and editing. With commercial pornographic movies and movie houses advertising or flaunting themselves as *X-rated,* however, since 1968 the term *X-rated* has entered the general language to mean "pornographic," "used for sex," and even "sexy," so we speak of *X-rated* books and records, *X-rated* motels, and even, jokingly, of *X-rated* (revealing, sexy) attire.

By the late 1960s, small, independent pornographic moviemakers and movie houses showing pornographic movies were proliferating, and *pornography* (an 1850 English word, from Greek *pornographos,* *pornē,* harlot + *-graphos,* writing, hence "writing about harlots") had become big business, often controlled by organized crime. We have called pornographic movies:

stag movies, since at least the early 1930s, then as relatively short pornographic movies shown at private parties for men, as at college fraternity and men's club parties and *stag parties* for men about to be married (from stag as meaning "for men only" since 1834).

adult movies, 1940s, usually then used only in referring to movies in peepshow arcades and in advertisements for pornographic movies that could be purchased through the mails for private viewing at home or for stag parties.

An "adults only" movie house, 1962.

blue movies, 1950s from the 1864 use of *blue* to refer to indecent or obscene talk.

skin flics, late 1960s, for commercial pornographic movies as shown at a *skin house* (movie theater openly showing pornographic movies, also a late 1960s term).

porn movies, *porno movies*, from the 1963 shortening of *porno*graphic, both as pornographic movies for private showing and as commercial ones shown in a *porn house* or *porno house* (both forms 1971).

As the above terms show, we have come a long way from the flickering nudity and mild passion of *Dolorita in the Passion Dance* and *The Kiss* of the 1890s, to the amateurish but truly pornographic short movies shown privately in the 1930s, 40s, and 50s, to the completely professional feature-length pornographic movies shown openly at certain commercial movie houses beginning in the late 1960s. Though the only true stars of porno movies are the prone woman and the standing male, Linda Lovelace was billed as the first *porno star* in the famous 1972 porno movie *Deep Throat*, which certainly paid more than mere lip service to explicit sex.

Porno movies, like prostitution and drugs, are widely talked about but otherwise generally ignored by the general public. Most American moviegoers of the 1970s and early 80s saw wide-screen, Technicolor movies that dealt with major themes, both old and new, and used modern, realistic editing techniques. Movies in old genres included the predictable and ultimate love story, the 1970 *Love Story*; spectacular, fast-paced violent gangster movies such as the 1971 *The French Connection* and Francis Ford Coppola's 1972 *The Godfather* and 1974 *The Godfather, Part II*; the "poor boy makes good" *prizefight movie* (a 1940s term) *Rocky*; excellent wide-screen musicals such as Bob Fosse's 1972 *Cabaret* and 1980 *All That Jazz*; and a new type of horror-thriller based on either the supernatural or on primitive nature, as the 1973 *The Exorcist* and the 1975 *Jaws*.

The Exorcist, *1973*.

Jaws, *1975*.

Rocky, *1976*.

Violent comedies with serious messages, usually that war is hell and society is crazy, appealed especially to younger audiences intellectually proud of being anti-establishment after the Vietnam War and included the 1970 *M*A*S*H* and *Catch-22* and the 1975 *One Flew Over the Cuckoo's Nest*, with Jack Nicholson.

In 1970 *Airport* had started a popular new trend that developed into the *disaster movie* (1974), basically an adventure movie purporting to show how the good, the bad, and the beautiful react to spectacular wide-screen disasters and including such movies as the 1972 *Poseidon Adventure* (an ocean liner turns upside down) and the 1974 *Earthquake*. The camera work, quick-cutting editing techniques, vivid color, and wide screen made many of these seem more realistic, or at least more vivid, than movies had been before. This new realism was also seen in some serious, exceptionally well acted and well directed movies about average, or at least believable or recognizable, people and families, such as Woody Allen's 1977 *Annie Hall* and the 1980 *Breaking Away*, *Kramer vs. Kramer*, starring Dustin Hoffman, and *Ordinary People*, directed by Robert Redford, one of several stars who had turned director.

The major success, however, was the innovative *space odyssey*, a term that first appeared in the title of Stanley Kubrick's 1968 *2001: A Space Odyssey*, and then was applied to George Lucas's 1977 *Star Wars* and its 1980 sequel *The Empire Strikes Back*, in which special effects entered a new dimension and which had millions of American children and adults talking about its intergalactic characters, Luke Skywalker, Princess Lea, the hairy creature Chewbacca, and the shiny robots R2D2 and C3PO, who, with cliffhanger action and the blessing *May the Force be with you*, which became a fad saying, fought the evil forces terrorizing the galaxy. Millions also

Chewbacca the Wookie, Luke Skywalker, Ben Kenobi and Han Solo contemplate the awesome size of the Death Star in Star Wars, *1977.*

Both old and new stars were bankable *by the mid 1970s: (left) John Travolta in* Grease, *1977; (above) Jack Lemmon in* Missing, *1982.*

bought toys, games, T-shirts, and paperback books based on or related to this first *space opera* (1979, based on *horse opera* for a western) and its characters. For movies that had once had commercial *tie-ups* (1920s) with the books on which they were based (meaning then that bookstores prominently displayed the books when the movie was shown and the movie ads mentioned the book titles) now could earn much money from the *tie-ins* they created (meaning TV shows, books, games, etc., based on them).

Thus there were fewer movies but more expensive and spectacular ones as moviemakers depended on *bankable* (early 1970s, meaning famous enough and having made enough successful movies to attract investors' money) stars, directors, and producers to provide spectacularly successful *blockbusters* (1950s, from the 1942 World War II use of *blockbuster* to mean a bomb large enough to destroy a city block). The factory system was no longer in effect on any wide scale, because profit could not be made by making and showing hundreds of run-of-the-mill movies; moviemakers had to concentrate on a few spectacular, and often very creative, films, such as the 1981 *Reds* and *Chariots of Fire* and the instant classic Steven Spielberg's 1982 *E.T.* By 1980 Universal produced only about 25 movies a year, Paramount and Warner Brothers about 15 each, Columbia and United Artists around 10 each, and MGM about half a dozen a year—a total considerably below 100 movies each year. The studios themselves were now often just divisions of large conglomerates that earned most of their money from other fields of communications or entertainment (radio and television stations, book publishing, resort hotels, etc.) or from

433

unrelated sources, such as oil and gas exploration and production.

Modern movies are not part of a booming industry, though the audience in the late 1970s and early 1980s seemed to have stabilized at about 25 million a week (though during certain weeks in 1981 only half that number of Americans went to a movie). The movies and movie stars aren't as glamorous as they once were, having now to share their pop glamour with stars from television and the record industry, and with celebrities created from many other fields by the modern mass media. Yet few things have influenced America and our way of looking at and talking about the world as have the movies. Many people saw their first, and perhaps only, car, ocean liner, woman in a revealing one-piece bathing suit, people drinking cocktails, passionate kiss, war, gangster, newspaper office, prizefight, murder, Oriental, foreign country, opera singer, surgeon, saint, in the movies. In the movies, too, many people heard their first foreign accent, western drawl, romantic voice, tough talk—and many words and expressions they were to use over and over until they had become an important part of our language.

Marilyn Monroe and Tony Curtis in Some Like It Hot, *1959.*

He Can't Cut the Mustard

Mustard came into English in the 13th century from the French (going back to Latin *mustum*, grape juice, originally used for mixing ground mustard seeds into a paste). By the War of 1812 *mustard seed shot* was an American term for small-gauge shot. Between 1900 and 1910, when commercially bottled mustard became popular, *mustard* appeared in several slang expressions that used the strength of the condiment as a metaphor: *to be the proper mustard* meant to be the genuine article, *to be all*

434

mustard meant to be excellent, and *to be up to the mustard* and *to cut the mustard* both meant to come up to expectations. Since World War I the last expression has been used almost exclusively in the negative—*he can't cut the mustard*—and among many men is used to mean unable to have an erection, to be unable to perform sexually.

Organized Crime was a term most Americans first heard in the 1920s, during Prohibition. Since then we've heard a lot about it in newspapers, books, movies, and television shows. Here are some other names we've known it by:

> *the underworld* (members of organized crime), 1920s. Since the 18th century *the underworld* had meant the world below moral society, the world of vice, prostitutes, pickpockets, etc. Before that it had meant both Hell and the terrestial world below Heaven, and in Greek and Roman mythology it was Hades, the abode of the dead.
> *Murder, Inc.*, 1930s.
> *the Syndicate, the Organization*, late 1930s.
> *the Mafia* (Sicilian dialect, "boldness," from Arabic *mahijah*, "boasting"), late 1950s; *Cosa Nostra* (Italian "our thing"), 1962.

Modern organized crime was started by Al Capone with bootlegging in Chicago in the 1920s, then spread to extortion, gambling, prostitution, narcotics, etc., with several large, well-organized groups controlling much of these illegal activities by the early 1930s. These organized gangs were loosely called *Murder, Inc.* (though the name is often used in fiction to mean organized crime's extermination squad). Its eight most talked-about leaders of the mid 1930s were Albert Anastasia, Louis "Lepke" Buchalter, Frank Costello, Vito Genovese, "Lucky" Luciano, "Dutch" Schultz, "Gurrah" Shapiro, and "Bugsy" Siegel. Luciano killed about forty other gang leaders and reorganized Murder, Inc., into specific territories, subsidiary and interlocking gangs, etc. This has been called *the Mafia* since the 1950s. The original Mafia was a secret Sicilian society started in the 15th century to settle vendettas. Similar organizations included *the Camorra*, the Neapolitan *Black Hand*, and *the Unione Siciliano*, all of which have also been used as synonyms for organized crime's Mafia. Today's American Mafia is related to the Sicilian one only in its tradition of violence, blackmail, and murder, and in emphasizing old-world family ties to solidify its membership. In 1962, Mafia informer Joe Valachi introduced the term *Cosa Nostra* to the general public in his testimony before a congressional committee investigating organized crime.

Organized crime has popularized many terms, including:

"Dutch" Schultz, one of the eight leaders of Murder, Inc., *was killed in a restaurant in 1935.*

stool pigeon, 1830 (from the fowler's use of a pigeon tied to a "stool" or perch to decoy other birds); *stoolie*, 1931. Other words for informer and informing include *to peach*, 1848 (from *impeach*); *squealer*, 1891 (*to squeal* has meant to inform or confess since 1859); *fink*, 1920s (originally a union term for a labor spy, from *Pink*, Pinkerton agent, see THE PINKERTONS AND THE MOLLY MAGUIRES); *canary*, 1940s (because he *sings*, informs, confesses, 1930); and *snitch*, a police informant, 1960s.

shake-down, 1840s; *extortion*, 1902.

graft, 1859, originally meaning to earn a living dishonestly as a con man or robber; *grafter*, 1896; the variants *grift* and *grifter* came a little later.

hoodlum, 1871; *hood*, 1930. Originally *hoodlum* was always "San Francisco hoodlum," an especially tough waterfront rowdy (from German Bavarian dialect *hodalum*, rowdy). *Thug* is a 19th-century British word, from the name of a religious organization of professional assassins in northern India (from Hindu *thagi*).

gangster, 1896, literally the member of a gang.

mobster, 1917; *the mob*, 1920s (*mob* entered English in the 19th century, from Latin *mobile vulgus*, the fickle crowd).

take for a ride, 1920s. Until the late 1930s the term was usually the full "take for a one-way ride."

racketeering and *racketeer*, 1928. *Racket* meant a swindle or fraud by 1892, from the 1840s *grabracket*, a confidence game in which a con man grabbed money and ran while his confederate(s) distracted the victim(s) by making a racket or commotion.

During the 1960s the Mafia gave us such terms as *family* (there are about twenty-six such close-knit gangs in the country, five of

Marlon Brando playing the title role in the 1972 movie The Godfather, *which helped popularize this term for the Mafia's chief* don. *James Caan is at the left.*

them in New York City); *button, button man,* and *soldier* for its low-ranking hoods (each Mafia family has from twenty to several hundred); *contract* for an agreement for a hired gunman to kill someone; and *hit,* the killing, to kill. A Mafia head is a *capo* (Latin, "chief, head") or *don* (a title of respect in Italian). The head don is the *capo di tutti capi* ("boss of bosses") or, since Mario Puzo's 1969 best-selling novel *The Godfather* (and the two popular movies made from it), the *godfather.*

Peanuts, Popcorn, and Crackerjack

Peanuts were brought to America from Africa in slave ships as cheap food for slaves. They were often called *ground nuts* by the early colonists, as they still are by the British, and later were sometimes called *ground peas,* 1769 (peanuts, which are related to the pea, are not true nuts, but do grow underground). *Peanut* became the most common name for them around 1800. By the 1830s most Americans also knew the popular southern word for peanut, *goober* (from Bantu *nguba*), with some southerners even using the combination *goober pea* (1833). Since peanuts are primarily a southern crop, by the 1850s backwoodsmen from Georgia and Alabama were derisively called *goobers* or *goober-grabbers,* with Georgia being known as *the Goober State* by 1877. Of course,

437

northerners ate peanuts too and by the 1850s the peanut vendor's call "Hot roasted peanuts! Hot peanuts!" was common on city streets.

Around 1890 a St. Louis doctor invented and named *peanut butter*, which he touted as a health food. It wasn't until the late 1920s that adults, and children, were asking for *peanut butter sandwiches*. These stuck to the roof of the mouth: it wasn't until the 1940s that specially treated *homogenized peanut butter* was developed, keeping the oil from separating and the mixture creamy, so that people could eat peanut butter without joking about how it glued their mouths shut. *Peanut butter cookie* first became a common term around 1940.

The word *peanuts* has meant something insignificant or of little value since the 1830s, which is when such expressions as "That's not worth peanuts" and "He'll work for peanuts" were first heard. *Peanut gallery* was in use in the 1880s, as a synonym for *nigger gallery* (1840s) or *nigger heaven* (1870s), the upper balcony where blacks sat, as in segregated theaters. Because *peanut* implied small size, it came to mean a small or insignificant person by 1919 and *peanut gallery* then gradually came to mean a section of seats reserved for children or an audience of children, which has been its only common meaning since the 1940s (especially since "the Peanut Gallery" became well known as the little grandstand where all the children sat on television's *Howdy Doody Show*, first broadcast in 1943). Charles Schulz's comic strip *Peanuts* first appeared in 1950, peopled only by small children and animals.

Popped corn was eaten at the first Thanksgiving in 1621, when Chief Massasoit's brother, Quadequina, brought bushels of it to the feast, amazing the Pilgrims (see THANKSGIVING, TURKEY, AND DRESSING). It was called *popped corn*, *parch corn*, and *rice corn* (a common variety used for popping) until the 1820s. Then it finally became a common treat, was sold widely by street vendors, and the name *popped corn* was shortened to *popcorn*. Molasses-coated *popcorn balls* didn't become widely known until the 1870s. In 1896, Americans were calling an exceptionally fine thing or person a *crackajack* or *crackerjack* (*crack* had meant excellent, expert, since the 1830s and, since the 1850s, *Jack* had been a breezy form of address

The peanut gallery *of television's* Howdy Doody Show.

to a man whose name was unknown). The same year *crackerjack* entered the language, the name *Cracker Jack* was given to the popcorn-peanuts-and-molasses confection made by the Chicago firm of F. W. Rueckheim and Brother, who had first sold it at Chicago's 1893 Columbian Exposition, but not by that name. Thus "Peanuts, popcorn, Cracker Jack!" has been a common cry of vendors at circuses, carnivals, fairs, and ball games since the early 1900s. Now, *Cracker Jack* is a trademark of the Borden Co. for its "candied popcorn and peanuts" mixture, and popcorn itself can be obtained from a *popcorn machine*, a term common by 1918, when the Butter-Kist popcorn machine was a fixture in many retail stores and store lobbies.

The Pinkertons and the Molly Maguires

Scottish immigrant Allan Pinkerton founded his Pinkerton National Detective Agency in Chicago in 1850. People were talking about it in 1861 when it foiled a plot to assassinate President Lincoln, during the Civil War when it served as a quasi-intelligence service for the Union's General George McClellan, and in 1866 when it solved the sensational $700,000 Adams Express Agency robbery. Thus everyone knew about *the Pinkertons* even before they brought an end to the Molly Maguires.

The Molly Maguires was a notorious secret organization of coal miners who terrorized mine operators and prevented miners who wished to do so from returning to work during "the long strike" of 1874–75, primarily in the Pennsylvania coal fields (it took its name

Allan Pinkerton, alias Major E. J. Allen, as an intelligence agent during the Civil War.

This woodcut of undercover detective James McParlan being sworn into the Molly Maguires appeared in Allan Pinkerton's 1877 book The Molly Maguires and the Detectives.

from a secret landlord-terrorizing organization in Ireland of the 1840s, led by and named for the widow Molly Maguire). The Philadelphia and Reading Railroad, which owned coal mines, placed an undercover agent of the Pinkertons, detective James McParlan, with the Molly Maguires during this long and bitter strike, and his testimony convicted 24 of its members in 1875, 10 of whom were hanged for murder. This ended the strike, the union, and the Molly Maguires—and gave the Pinkertons fame as strikebreakers.

The agency was widely talked about again in 1892 when 300 of its armed detectives were towed up the Monongahela River on barges to break the Homestead, Pennsylvania, *Homestead strike* against the Carnegie Steel Company works (they surrendered to the strikers after being beaten by them in a battle on shore, but the strike was broken later when 8,000 state militia allowed strike-breakers to work, delaying until 1930 the forming of a strong steelworkers' union).

Because of the Pinkertons' harsh attitude in guarding and protecting railroad property, and because of their labor spying and strikebreaking, hoboes and unionists grew to hate them, calling them *Pinks* and *Pinkies*, with labor especially protesting what it called *Pinkertonianism* (strikebreaking by violence) in the 1890s. Our word *fink*, meaning an informer (1902) or strikebreaker (1920s), probably came from this use of *Pink*.

Pirates, Privateers, and Buccaneers

Earlier Americans talked a great deal about the pirates and privateers who attacked our ships and plundered our towns along the Atlantic and Gulf coasts from 1623 until 1827, when the U.S. Navy finally drove the last pirates out of Puerto Rico and Cuba. For example, in the ten years from 1814 to 1824 alone, some 1,500 acts of piracy were reported against American ships, averaging about three a week. Since colonial days we had also talked about the scandalous dealings pirates had with some of our politicians and businessmen: in 1696 the famous British pirate John "Long Ben" Avery, who reigned as monarch of the pirate haven of Madagascar, visited Boston and bribed the colonial governor to allow him to dispose of his plunder there; several New England families became wealthy and famous selling shipbuilding materials and supplies to other Madagascar pirates; Captain Kidd started his career as a privateer for the colonial governor of New York; and Blackbeard made fortunes for several Carolina merchants.

One of N. C. (Newell Convers) Wyeth's famous 1911 illustrations for Treasure Island.

Pirates were talked of both as villains and heroes: pirate ships deprived early colonists of many needed supplies, but others smuggled in goods, subverting British blockades and taxes; some pirates helped us in the Revolutionary War and in the War of 1812, while others aided the British; and, later, privateers aided the South during the Civil War. At times it was hard to tell a patriotic shipowner or a privateer from a pirate—and some men were both. There were actually three types of men we now call "pirates"— true *pirates*, *privateers*, and *buccaneers*:

> *pirates* were first widely talked about in England in the late 14th century (the word first recorded in 1387, via Latin from Greek *peiratēs*, attacker). They were true outlaws, often ex-sailors who at the end of a war could find no work so took a ship and roamed

the high seas in search of booty. The English also called such true pirates *rovers* (1390) and *picaroons* (1629, from Spanish *picaron* via *picaro*, rogue, from *picar*, to prick, wound).

privateers originally meant privately owned warships (1646 in England) and then the commanders of such ships (1671 in England). In times of both war and peace such commanders held "letters of marque" authorizing them to attack the shipping and raid the ports of unfriendly, competing, or enemy nations, usually keeping 90 percent of the booty or plunder and turning in 10 percent to their sponsoring government, though governments also awarded privateers additional *prize money*. Some privateers stayed honest and served as an unofficial navy—but many didn't bother to bring their booty, plunder, and reports home and even attacked friendly ships, becoming pirates under the guise of being privateers. They claimed to be following in the wake of the 15th- and 16th-century English *sea dogs*, navigators and explorers like Drake and Hawkins, who had preyed on Spanish ships to further their own and their country's goals (by 1823 we Americans used *sea dog* to mean any seasoned sailor and also called the same man a *salt* by 1840).

As early as 1650 colonial governors in America employed privateers by granting them *privateering rights*, which is how Captain Kidd (see below) got his start. Though admiralty courts initially did the job, the colonies soon set up special *prize courts* to determine how much prize money should be awarded privateers. After 1789 the new United States turned this job over to its federal district courts. Regular naval crews also shared in booty or were awarded prizes for capturing enemy ships in time of war: such prizes were not abolished until 1904—when Admiral Dewey was refused prize money for capturing several small vessels at Manila Bay! Thus the difference between a country's navy and privateers could be very small, and privateers could be called glorious patriots or the most bloodthirsty pirates, depending on whose side they were on.

buccaneers were English, French, and Dutch adventurers who preyed on Spanish ships and pillaged Spanish colonies on the Spanish Main from about 1640 to 1689.

The English word *buccaneer* comes from French *boucanier*, hunter of wild oxen, literally "he who cures meat," from French *boucan*, a grill for smoking dried meat, and originally referred to European adventurers who had been hunters of wild cattle in Haiti. It was applied to this specific type of pirate because some of the same men were involved and because they provisioned their ships by hunting wild cattle on the Caribbean Islands, especially Santo Domingo (the French got the word *boucan* from the Tupi Indians of Brazil and Paraguay, from the Tupi word *mocaen*, barbecue frame; it is similar to the Spanish word *barbacoa*, which gives us the word *barbecue*).

The Dutch called these buccaneers *zeerovers*, from which English got *searovers*. The French also called them *flibustiers* (from Dutch *frij*, free + *buit*, booty), which gives English the word *freebooter* (and *filibuster*). The Spanish, whom they attacked, called them *corsarios* (from Latin *cursus*, plunder), meaning pirates, which gave English yet another word for them, *corsairs*.

The Welsh-born Sir Henry Morgan (1635-88) was chosen "admiral" of the buccaneers in 1666 and captured, ravaged, and sacked ports from Maracaibo to Gibraltar before being knighted and appointed lieutenant governor of Jamaica.

Edward Preble (1761-1807), commander of American warships sent to the Mediterranean in the first of the Barbary Wars.

The buccaneers themselves preferred the name *Brethren of the Coast*.

After Henry Morgan became the leader of the buccaneers they became a separate contender for wealth and power in the Caribbean, battling the English, French, Dutch, and Spanish for the treasures of the Spanish Main and establishing their own pirate republic on Tortuga. They could muster up to 30 ships and 4,000 men and from 1655 to 1671 alone sacked at least 57 Spanish towns around the Caribbean, some as many as eight times. At the outset of the War of the Grand Alliance in 1689 (France versus Spain, England, Holland, Sweden, and many German states), many of the buccaneers returned to their native lands and became legitimate privateers, ending the period of the true buccaneers.

All these pirates, privateers, and buccaneers had America talking for over 200 years after the Pilgrims landed, giving us and our children such now romantic terms and names as:

articles of agreement, a compact drawn up by buccaneers before every expedition, agreeing on which country's ships and towns could and could not be attacked and how the booty and plunder would be divided.

the Barbary Pirates, the Barbary Coast. The original *Barbary Pirates* served the Barbary States (named after *Berbers*, the chief magistrate of the region) of Algiers, Morocco, Tripoli, and Tunisia, attacking shipping off North Africa's *Barbary Coast* and exacting tribute from other nations. When the U.S. determined not to pay more tribute than stipulated in earlier treaties, we fought the *Tripolitan War* against them, in 1801–05, and the *Algerine War*, in 1815, the two wars together being called the *Barbary Wars*. All America was talking about Commander Edward Preble when he tried to blockade Tripoli and bottle up the pirates in 1803 and about Stephen Decatur in 1804 when he led an American expedition into the harbor of Tripoli to burn the captured U.S. frigate *Philadelphia* being held there. Tripoli then signed a treaty abolishing U.S. tribute payments in 1805 and the navy forced Algiers to renounce its tribute in 1815.

When San Francisco's waterfront district became infested with piratelike desperadoes, gangsters, gamblers, and prostitutes during the 1849 gold rush, it became known as *the Barbary Coast*, keeping this name and reputation until much of the area was destroyed in the 1906 San Francisco earthquake. Our word *shanghai* (1856) seems to have originated in this San Francisco district, where thugs were paid to drug men in the bars and brothels and deliver them to ship captains to serve as unwilling sailors on long voyages, as to Shanghai, China.

Blackbeard (real name Edward Teach or Thatch) was an English privateer before he became a pirate, terrorizing shipping in the Bahamas and off Virginia and the Carolinas with his 40-gun ship the *Queen Anne's Revenge* during 1713–18. This pirate, who tied up his large black beard into tails with colored ribbons, was successful and feared because he shared his booty with and was protected by Charles Eden, the corrupt colonial governor of

A 1736 drawing of Blackbeard, *showing his beard tied up into tails.*

North Carolina. Blackbeard gained additional protection by providing certain wealthy Carolina merchants with much of their wares (they also probably informed him of ship movements). Finally in 1718 Virginia governor Alexander Spotswood sent two sloops under Lieutenant Robert Maynard to stop Blackbeard: after a hard naval fight on the James River, Maynard boarded Blackbeard's ship and shot him dead.

booty originally meant items taken from the enemy in time of war; by the early 15th century, English pirates, many of them ex-sailors who had taken booty in wartime, were using the term for what they took from ships, their crews, and passengers. *Plunder* first appeared as an English verb in 1630 and was soon used also as a noun. Technically it means loot taken in pillaging during a time of war (from Dutch *plunderen,* to rob of household goods, Dutch *plunde* meaning household goods, clothing).

buried treasure has become part of pirate mythology because of Captain Kidd (see below). Most pirates weren't the kind of men to plan for their future financial security by burying treasure: when they had enough for a major spending binge or grew tired of sailing for a while, they divided the booty and spent it. However, since he always proclaimed his innocence and thought he would be pardoned, Captain Kidd feared being caught with booty on his ship and thus did bury some treasure (most of which was dug up soon after his imprisonment and hanging).

Captain Kidd (William Kidd, 1645–1701) was the Scottish-born son of a Calvinist minister who seems to have been a respectable family man and shipowner-captain in New York City before he became a privateer for New York's colonial governor Sir George Bellomont in 1689. By 1695, Kidd had a royal commission from London to protect East India Company shipping from pirates in the Red Sea and Indian Ocean, but he and his ship, the *Adventure Galley,* "disappeared" for long periods of time and he had definitely turned to piracy by 1697, though he always proclaimed his innocence. In 1699 he surrendered in New York City on promise of a pardon from Governor Bellomont, but the British took him to London, where he was tried and convicted for murder and piracy, and hanged in 1701.

to go on account, a buccaneer term meaning to become a buccaneer, take up piracy.

Jean Laffite (1780–1825) seemed to appear out of nowhere to become the leader of the Louisiana bayou smugglers and pirates known as the *Baratarian Pirates,* 1810–14 (so called because they lived on Barataria Bay, in the Mississippi Delta below New Orleans). During the War of 1812, Laffite refused a British bribe of a commission and $30,000 to join in the attack of New Orleans, warned the U.S. government of the British plans, and offered to help defend the city in return for full pardons for himself and his men. The pirates were put in charge of the artillery and were a major contribution to Andrew Jackson's victory at the Battle of New Orleans in 1815. Laffite and his men were then pardoned by President Madison, but by 1817 Laffite had returned to piracy, leading the *Galveston Pirates* and illegal slave traders who occupied Galveston Island, site of the future Galveston, Texas. Though he claimed to be a privateer for Mexico against Spain, when the U.S. threatened to move against him in 1821 he sailed

Buried treasure *became part of pirate mythology because of Captain William Kidd, shown here burying a treasure chest with his initials "W.K." on it.*

away in his favorite ship, *The Pride*, disappearing from history almost as mysteriously as he had arrived.

the Jolly Roger (an English term of 1785) was usually just called *the Roger* by sailors and often *the Skull and Crossbones* by others. We don't know how this flag or naval ensign came into being, but *Roger* had been thieves' cant for "rogue" since the 16th century and *jolly* wasn't used in our modern sense but in the 16th-century sense of "brave, gallant" (the song "For he's a jolly good fellow" really means "for he's a brave, good fellow"): thus *Jolly Roger* meant "brave rogue."

Millions for defense, but not a cent for tribute is supposed to have been said on October 26, 1797, by the American ambassador to France, Charles Pinckney, in answer to a demand for $250,000 made on behalf of the French foreign minister Talleyrand before he would allow Pinckney, John Marshall, and Elbridge Gerry to plead America's case with the French Directory to cease French attacks on our shipping. Although these words are inscribed on the cenotaph to Pinckney's memory in Charleston, South Carolina, he denied saying them, claiming he had simply said, "Not a penny, not a penny." The more dramatic saying originated as a toast given by South Carolina Congressman Robert Harper at a dinner given by Congress in Philadelphia on June 18, 1798, in honor of John Marshall when he returned from this mission to France. It was one of sixteen toasts to Marshall that evening, many of them defiant of France, its navy, and its privateers. Harper later explained that his toast did not refer to the bribe that had been asked for but merely meant that instead of permitting the French to plunder American merchant vessels of one cent he would spend millions in their defense.

the Spanish Main originally meant the Spanish-owned mainland of Central and South America, especially from the Isthmus of Panama to the mouth of the Orinoco River (*main* meant mainland by the 14th century). Soon, however, it came to mean the coastal waters off Spanish lands in Latin America and the Caribbean and by the 16th century meant the Caribbean itself, especially that part of it along Spanish trade routes.

swashbuckler was a 16th-century word for any flamboyant swordsman or adventurer (from *swash*, the noise of a strike or splash + *buckler*, a small round shield used in swordfights).

walk the plank is supposed to have been a common pirate term and practice, a way of getting rid of unwanted captives—but the term was first recorded in 1844, long after the most famous pirates, privateers, and buccaneers had been laid to rest.

Pirates and privateers are also responsible for three of the most illustrious names in American history: the *United States Coast Guard*, *United States Navy*, and *United States Marines*. The present-day navy and marines were both established by Congress in 1798 as separate armed services to protect our new nation against pirates, the navy to fight pirates and French privateers on the seas and the marines to stop piracy in the West Indies (*marine*, from Latin *marinus*, has meant "of the sea" in English since 1420 and was used as early as 1664 in England to refer to a specially trained corps of soldiers serving on warships). Earlier, in 1790, the first secretary of the treasury, Alexander Hamilton, recommended the establishing of a *Revenue Marine* to stamp out coastal smuggling and piracy and ten *cutters* were then built for this service (*cutter* is a 1745 English word for a warship's fast boat, used to carry dispatches, probably because such a fast boat "cuts" through the water). This Revenue Marine became the *Revenue Cutter Service* in 1863, was combined with the *Lifesaving Service* (created by Congress in 1871) and renamed the *United States Coast Guard* in 1915, then absorbed the *Federal Lighthouse Service* in 1939.

Potatoes and Rice

Potato (from the West Indian Taino word *batata*, sweet potato) meant only a sweet potato to the early colonists, who knew no other kind: thus the longer term *sweet potato* wasn't necessary or in use until the 1740s. Though native to the New World, what we call simply a *potato* today was first brought to Boston by the Irish about 1719—and for the next 100 years was used mainly for fodder, being considered by many unsophisticated people as a powerful aphrodisiac that could shorten one's life if eaten. Until the 1820s this potato was always called an *Irish potato* or a *white potato* to distinguish it from the more common sweet potato. Our word *spuds* has been around since the 1840s but didn't become popular until the 1890s (it comes from an old English word *spud*, a narrow-bladed or pronged spade used in digging up roots).

The Pennsylvania Dutch were not unsophisticated. They ate white potatoes, including *mashed potatoes*, which were first known as a Pennsylvania Dutch dish early in the 18th century and until the 1850s were often called *Dutch potatoes* or *German potatoes*. Thomas Jefferson wasn't unsophisticated either; he was one of the first to experiment with growing various varieties of white potatoes. He had learned about *French fried potatoes* while ambassador to France and served them at Monticello, but they didn't become a sought-after delicacy until the 1870s and weren't common until the 1900s. Their name wasn't shortened to *French frieds* until the late 1920s, which became *French fries* in the early 1930s and, increasingly, just *fries* or *frys* since the late 1960s (this shortest form popularized in the advertising of such large franchise hamburger chains as *McDonald's*). *Potato chips* (1840s) were originally much thicker than we know them today, closer to being thick, crisp slices of French fried potatoes (the British still use *potato chips* or *chips* to mean French fried potatoes, as in their *fish and chips*). The first modern-style thin potato chips were often called *Saratoga chips* or *Saratoga potatoes* in the 1870s and 80s, because they were invented by, and a specialty of, George Crum, an American Indian and chef at Moon's Lake Lodge at New York's fashionable

19th-century spa, Saratoga Springs. According to the story, he created these paper-thin chips in a rage in 1853, to satisfy a customer who kept returning orders of French fried potatoes, complaining they weren't thin enough.

Potato trap was slang for the mouth in the 1840s, and in the 1890s *hold your potatoes* was considered a clever synonym for the fifty-year-old expression *hold your horses*, be patient. In the late 1920s a *hot potato* meant a sexually appealing girl, which became the 1930s term *hot patootie*. *Potato* also meant a dollar in the 1930s, and *potato head* a clumsy dolt, in the 1950s.

True rice was first planted in America in 1671 by Dr. Henry Woodward in Virginia, but it was then talked about only as a local curiosity, as he didn't know how to clean it. Another variety was introduced into Charleston in 1694 from a Dutch brig out of Madagascar, and by 1787 was called *Carolina rice* or *golden rice*. *Piedmont rice*, important because it can be grown without irrigation, was introduced to America by Thomas Jefferson, who, according to the story, had stolen the seeds while traveling in Italy and brought them home in his pockets (Italy wanted a monopoly on this type of rice and the crime of stealing the seeds was punishable by death). *Wild rice* (1778) is not a true rice but the seed of an aquatic grass which the Indians grew and ate. Earlier Americans also called it *water oats* and *water rice* (both 1817 terms), *Indian rice* (1843), and *Meneninee*, the Chippewa name for wild rice and for a subtribe that grew it.

Prostitutes, Brothels, and Lewd Women

When the first colonists came to America, they brought with them such old English terms as the 12th century:

> *whore*, first recorded as *hōre* around the year 1100, from the Old Norse and Gothic *horr/hors*, adulterer. *Whoreson*, bastard, dates from the 13th century, *whoremonger* from the 16th. *Whore house* dates from the 16th century too, as do *bawdy house* and *brothel house* (see below).

the 13th century:

> *bad girl*, "bad" meant sexually immoral by the 13th century and "girl" then meant a young woman (it didn't come to mean a female child until the 16th century).
>
> *concubine*, from Latin *con*, with + *cubāre*, to lie down; hence a woman who "lies down" with a man.

the 14th century:

> *bawd*, procuress (probably from Old High German *bald*, bold). *Bawdy house* was first recorded in 1552.

447

paramour, from Old French *par amour*, by or through love.

strumpet, via Old French *strupe*, concubinage, from Latin *stuprum*, dishonor.

wanton, a lascivious woman. As an adjective it by then already meant lascivious, lewd; it has meant "undisciplined" since the 13th century.

wench, a wanton woman. It had meant a young woman or girl for a hundred years before this.

the 15th century:

harlot, 1430s. It had previously meant a rascal or vagabond, since the 13th century.

mistress. It had been a title of respect since the 14th century.

slut, an immoral woman. It had previously meant only a dirty or slovenly woman, since the 14th century.

the 16th century, which saw a flowering of Elizabethan lustiness and loose women, and the beginning of modern commercial sex, including streetwalkers and the modern urban whorehouse:

baggage, a worthless or immoral woman. It had originally meant portable property, especially packages, in the 15th century, then had also come to mean rubbish or refuse before coming to mean a woman who was "garbage."

bagnio, a brothel. The word also meant a Turkish bath (and comes from Italian *bagno*, bath); the change in meaning shows what many Turkish baths were known for during Elizabethan days.

bordello, 1598, as first recorded in Ben Jonson's comedy *Every Man in His Humour*, the first version of which used Italian names and places and hence may have introduced this Italian word into English (Italian from Old French *bordel*, meaning board hut, then small house, brothel).

brothel (from Old English *brēothan*, to deteriorate, go to ruin) had come to mean a prostitute by the 15th century, giving English the term *brothel house* in the early 16th century, with *brothel* itself then coming to mean such a house in the late 16th century. Thus *brothel* is a shortening of *brothel house*, prostitute's house.

doxy. It had previously been beggars' cant for a girl who traveled with them (perhaps from Dutch *docke*, doll).

jade, an immoral woman. It had previously meant a poor or worn-out horse, the kind to be ridden only when nothing better was available.

Jezebel, a shameless woman, after the infamous wife of Ahab, King of Israel, mentioned four times in *I Kings* beginning with *I Kings* 16:29–31.

prostitution and *to prostitute*, from Latin *prōstituere*, to offer for sale. *House of prostitution* also dates from the 16th century, but the noun a *prostitute* didn't appear until the 17th century.

street walker, 1592. *To solicit* was also now in use with its sexual meaning.

the 17th century:

easy, having easy morals, easy to seduce, first recorded in 1611 in Shakespeare's *Cymbeline*. *Lady of easy virtue* was first recorded in

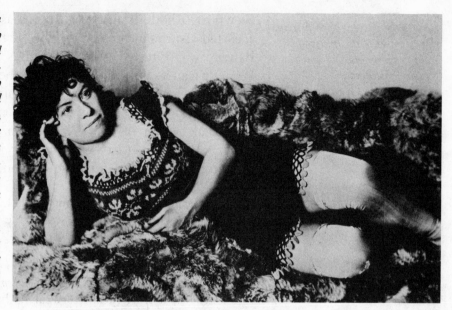

A *late-19th-century American* prostitute *known as "French Jenny." From our earliest colonial days we followed the British tradition of associating the French with sexual abandon. Syphilis was called the* French disease *and* French pox *in English beginning in the 16th century and* French gout *in the 17th century; an obscene picture was called a* French print *by 1850 and then widely known as a* French postcard *during and after World War I; the* French trick *referred to oral sex during the 19th century, with* French *used as both a noun and verb to refer to it during and after World War I.*

America, in 1809, in Washington Irving's *Knickerbocker's History of New York; easy woman* appeared in F. Scott Fitzgerald's 1920 *This Side of Paradise;* while *easy lay* dates from the 1930s (*a lay* first referred to a woman as a sex object around 1930; *to lay*, have coitus with, was first recorded in 1937).

hussy, huzzy, a bold or shameless woman. For a century before this the word had just meant housewife, another form of the earlier *huswif.*

pimp, first recorded in 1666 in Samuel Pepys's *Diary.* It may come via French *pimpant,* seductive, from Latin *pīpāre,* to chirp like a bird—this chirping concept, as to solicit a customer, is also found in *chippy* (see below). *Procurer* was first recorded in its special sexual sense in 1632, with *procuress* following in 1713. An older term is *pander,* dating from 1530.

trollop, perhaps from the old 14th-century word *troll,* to move back and forth, which did give English the word *trull,* a loose woman, in the 16th century.

Thus the early colonists had a solid English basis for talking about their prostitutes, brothels, and loose women. Since comparatively few of the English colonists were Puritans—some were Elizabethan-style adventurers, and about 40 percent had left England as convicts, drunkards, debtors, or runaways—such types as prostitutes, pimps, and their eager customers were not rare in early America.

For example: only 50 years after the Pilgrims landed, the port of Boston was talked about as being "filled with prostitutes"; in 1710, colonial Williamsburg was proud to report that it had only three brothels (none of which has been restored); and early Philadelphia was known for its low prostitutes who worked out of cavelike hovels built into the riverbanks along the Delaware. In the 1720s,

Newport, Rhode Island, was known as a city where streetwalkers accosted visitors in broad daylight; by the 1740s, New York City's Battery was infested with prostitutes; and in the Revolutionary War our leaders cursed the large number of *camp followers* (an older English term), who disrupted discipline and siphoned supplies from the Continental Army, as happened at Valley Forge during that bleak winter of 1777–78. Within 50 years after the Revolutionary War, America began adding its own terms referring to prostitutes, brothels, and loose women, which include:

house of assignation, an elegant brothel, 1834; *assignation house*, 1850s. At the other end of the scale were the low *floating brothels* of the 1830s, being flatboats docked along the Mississippi at many river towns.

sporting, the sporting life, having to do with gambling, drinking, and prostitution, 1845 (a *sporting gentleman* meant a gambler since the 1830s, *to sport* meant to wear flashy clothes by 1840); *a sport*, a gambler, drinker, and brothel frequenter, 1856; *sporting house*, a combination saloon, gambling house, and brothel, 1870s; *sporty*, 1896.

lady friend, mistress, 1848.

crib, 1848, a low saloon and brothel; by the 1870s it meant the small room used by a prostitute, especially one open to the street so she could sit in the doorway or window to display her wares; *crib house*, 1880s, in New Orleans.

hooker, 1845, originally referring to the prostitutes of "the Hook" (Corlear's Hook), a section of New York City having a large number of brothels. During the Civil War the many prostitutes in Washington, D.C., were humorously called *Hooker's Division*, a pun referring both to "hookers," prostitutes, and to their patronage by General "Fighting Joe" Hooker's Army of the

A New York City street scene of around 1850. The women were called whores, streetwalkers, *and in New York, by the new term* hookers.

450

Polly Adler was New York City's most famous **madam** *of the 1920s and 30s. Here she is on her way into court in 1935 after being charged with "maintaining a disorderly house,"* originally a *British legal term of 1877 referring to a brothel, gambling house, or other place "violating public order or morality."*

Potomac—but note that the term *hooker* predates the Civil War and General Hooker's troops.

stag party, 1854, as a bachelor's party, shortened to *stag* by 1904. Not until around 1910 did the connotation almost completely shift to such a party where prostitutes performed.

ponce, 1859, a man kept by a woman, a pimp (probably from the French name "Al*phonse*," French slang for a man supported by a woman, a pimp).

house, a brothel, whorehouse, 1860.

fancy lady, *madam*, *parlor house*, all became common terms during the Civil War. A *fancy lady* then meant a city prostitute in an elegant or at least homelike brothel, the *parlor house*, run by a *madam*. *Madam(e)* had been a polite title by which servants addressed the lady of a house since the 12th century; the brothel madam was also called a *landlady* and her girls *boarders*. *Madam* and *parlor house* may have been spread by Confederate troops from New Orleans, Charleston, etc., during the war, since parts of the South had retained a somewhat gallant and elegant concept of prostitutes and brothels, due in part to their Spanish and French traditions. Parlor houses flourished during the Civil War because they offered not only sex but also the elegance, or at least homelike comfort, that many homesick soldiers longed for during weary days on the battlefields. After the Civil War morality loosened and big cities continued to grow. As the language shows, casual sex, streetwalkers, and low dives proliferated: there were on the one hand more disrespectful terms for women; on the other hand, Victorian morality demanded more euphemisms for whores and brothels.

piece of dry goods, any girl or woman, 1869; *piece of calico*, 1880: these terms could be used to refer both to nice girls and to women as sex objects. *Piece*, a girl or woman as a sex object, 1891. *Piece of ass*, both as a girl or woman as a sex object and as coitus, not recorded until World War II, though the term is probably much older.

fallen women (fallen from grace), *menace to decent women*, *menace to society*, *lady of the night*, *lady of the evening*, *women of ill fame*, and *women of ill repute* were all popular 1870 euphemisms, though such euphemisms had flourished since the 1820s. In the 1870s, too, prostitution was called *the Social Evil* and brothels were first commonly known as *houses of ill fame* or *houses of ill repute*. Another popular euphemism for prostitute was *painted woman* or *painted lady*, though these had been used since the 1660s to refer to a woman considered immoral by Puritans because she wore makeup.

dance hall hostess was the western euphemism for a certain type of prostitute beginning in the 1870s. Western *dance halls* were the cowboy's equivalent of the eastern *sporting houses* (see above), combined saloons, gambling houses, and brothels. The most famous such dance hall was Dodge City's *Variety*, where Bat Masterson's brother, George, was bartender and where the famous, but not necessarily attractive, prostitutes included Big Nose Kate, the Galloping Cow, Hambone Jane, and Squirrel-Tooth Alice.

mack, a pimp, 1870s, originally spelled *mac* (probably from the

French *maquereau*, pimp, brothel keeper). From the 1870s to 1900 some men also used *mack* or *mac* to mean "bastard."

pick-up, 1871, when it meant a streetwalker. It was 1926 before the term meant a casual acquaintance, as met at a bar, who was willing to have sex.

chippy, *chippie*, 1880s, from *chip*, to chirp, hiss, as a streetwalker might do at a passing man.

tart, an immoral woman, 1880s; meaning a prostitute, 1908. Originally, in the 1860s, *tart* was used as an endearing reference to a girl, in the same way as "honey" or "sugar" is used; it, of course, comes from the dessert tart.

barrel house, 1880s. It originally meant a cheap dive selling beer from barrels, then a saloon where women were available, and finally a whorehouse and style of jazz played there.

white slave. This term was popularized by Barley Campbell's 1882 play *The White Slave*, which is set in the year 1857.

doss house, *bed house*, *joy house* were 1880s terms for a brothel; the first two had originally meant a flop house and always referred to cheap brothels.

the Tenderloin District was the name an obscure police officer named Williams gave to New York City's old 29th precinct (extending from 23rd Street to 42nd Street west of Broadway) about 1887. He said he was happy to be assigned to this vice-ridden, graft-filled precinct because its graft would enable him to stop eating cheap chuck steak and buy more expensive tenderloin. Within a few years *the tenderloin* came to mean any vice-filled neighborhood and soon, because of the connotation of "loin," to mean a city area where prostitutes abound.

gay woman, *gay lady*, a prostitute, 1890s, when "to be gay" meant to be familiar, take liberties.

In the late 1890s, New Orleans' Storyville was born and from then until World War I had a major influence on our image of prostitutes and houses and the words about them.

Storyville was the larger of two legalized brothel districts, and the birthplace of jazz, in New Orleans. Much to his consternation, it was called *Storyville* after alderman Sidney Story, who sponsored the ordinance limiting prostitution to these areas in 1896. Storyville opened in 1897, a 38-block area adjoining Canal Street and bounded by Basin, Iberville (Customhouse), Robertson, and St. Louis streets. The U.S. Navy closed the district just when it was most appreciated, in 1917, during World War I.

red light district, 1890s, assumedly from the red lights some brothels burned in their windows to announce their presence (though colored shades and covers had been used over candles, oil lamps, etc., in earlier days, the red light of this term was from Mr. Edison's electric light).

hustler, prostitute, 1900. *To hustle* had meant to be energetically aggressive, to move fast, since 1830, and by 1886 *hustler* had its general meaning of an aggressive person seeking business success.

grind, to rotate one's hips in coitus, about 1900; *grinder*, a prostitute, and *grind house*, a low brothel, both about 1910.

After the Civil War New Orleans' brothels became widely known and in 1896 the Storyville district was legally established. Many brothels printed advertising "souvenirs," and various guidebooks to the brothels in the district were available. The three shots (upstairs, downstairs, and in the room) advertised in this brochure refer not to whiskey but, for those in the know, to oral, anal, and vaginal sex; this sexual use of the term may have originated with Miss Lula White herself.

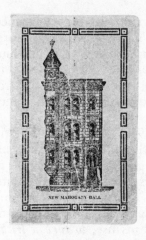

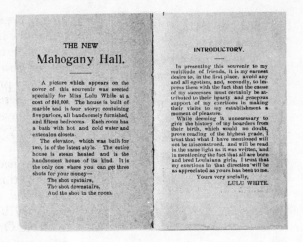

the badger game, this name first recorded in 1900 as a blackmailing confidence game (though used by prostitutes for at least 60 years before that) in which a woman entices the victim into bed and the couple is discovered there by her alleged husband, the victim having to pay to get out of the embarrassing situation or, if wealthy, famous, or married, to pay continuing blackmail. It is named after the victim, who has been called the *badger* since 1858, because he is trapped like a badger in its hole. Before becoming a confidence game it was worked in *panel houses* (1840s), brothels with secret panels through which customers could be robbed while otherwise engaged (smaller panels were also used as peepholes by other paying customers).

love nest, as the home of clandestine lovers, 1900.

cat house, became a popular term before World War I. However, it had been used long before that and *cat* has meant prostitute since the 17th century, probably from French *chat,* cat, French slang for the vagina (Americans are now beginning to use *cat* in this way too, but still prefer the 17th-century *pussy*).

This 1879 newspaper illustration purports to show how two young gentlemen from Chicago met, were entertained, and robbed by two "sharp damsels" in New York.

circus, a sex exhibition or performance, as in a brothel, 1905. One of Storyville's earliest attractions around the turn of the century was "Emma Johnson's Circus House."

floozie, floosey, 1909, both as a slovenly or vulgar woman and as a cheap prostitute. It's probably from the 1889 slang word *flossy*, ostentatious, showy, which comes from the word *floss*, a soft, silky material.

party girl, 1910, originally a prostitute, lewd dancer, etc., who provided the entertainment at a stag party; by the late 1920s the term had generally weakened to mean only a flapper who liked good times and going to uninhibited parties.

girl friend, as a man's mistress or paramour, 1910.

trick, 1910, as a prostitute's customer, may have originally been New Orleans use; *to turn a trick*, have a customer, engage in coitus for pay, 1930s. Incidentally, the term *that does the trick*, accomplishes the purpose, dates from 1812, and the general use of *trick* to mean a turn of duty or watch, as on a ship, dates from 1931.

fast, loose, promiscuous, around 1910 (*fast* had been used to mean dissipated since the 17th century). *Fast house*, a brothel, late 1920s. *Loose woman* also first became a common term around 1910.

pro, a professional prostitute, about 1914. *Pro* had been a short form for the general word "professional" since the 1880s.

World War I and the prosperity and mood of the Roaring 20s gave us many of our next terms for prostitutes, brothels, and lewd women. From this point on, the word *pimp* is still used but *madam* is disappearing: for all practical purposes, the prostitute and the pimp are now in ascendancy over the madam.

can house, a brothel, mainly World War I use (*can* was not a common word for buttocks until the early 1930s).

gold digger, 1915.

sugar daddy, 1918, originally for an elderly man lavishing gifts on a young woman (*sugar* had meant money since 1859); also sometimes *sugar papa* and *sweet man*.

call house, 1920, originally meaning any brothel because men could call on girls there. Due to confusion with the newer use of the term *call girl* (see below), by the 1950s some people used the term to mean a house or apartment building where call girls lived, received their telephone calls, and left to call on their customers.

quiff, a cheap prostitute or promiscuous girl, 1920s (originally British navy slang, spread to the U.S. during World War I); although the origin is uncertain, it may come from the British *coif*, coiffure, whig, *quiff*, then being British slang for a lock or curl of hair worn over the forehead by 1902.

on the make, looking for sex, available for sex, 1930s. In its general sense of willing to do anything to succeed, ruthlessly ambitious, the term dates from 1869.

hot pants, a very passionate woman, as one almost always willing to have sex, 1927 (*hot pants* were a style of very short shorts in the 1960s); *hot mama*, a daring flapper, 1929; *hot stuff*, 1930; *hot number*, 1932. Some of these women were merely *boy crazy* (1924)

454

*Most gentlemen don't like love,
    they just like to kick it
    around,*
*Most gentlemen don't like love,
    'cause most gentlemen can't
    be profound.*
*So just remember when you get
    that glance*
A romp and a quickie
Is all little Dickie
Means
When he mentions romance.
    Cole Porter, "Most Gentlemen Don't Like Love,"
    1938

girls and probably weren't really *hot* (1924, passionate) at all. Men who were after sex were said *to have hot pants* by the late 1920s too.

John, a prostitute's customer, 1930s, though it could be much older.

quickie, 1930s as a quick, nonemotional instance of coitus. *Quickie* originally meant a quickly produced, low-budget movie (1929), then in the 1940s *quick* became a popular adjective, as in *quick drink*, *quick snack*, etc.

call girl, 1935, as a prostitute who worked in a *call house* (see above), but not common until the 1950s, when it had come to mean a prostitute who is called on the telephone by her regular customers or by those given her number by friends, bartenders, etc., to meet with them in their hotel rooms, apartments, etc.

balling, mid 1930s, to mean "having a ball," having a wild good time drinking, dancing, having sex, etc. (this term was also influenced by the 1925 *balling the jack*, to move quickly, have a good time, and the railroaders' use of *highballing*, to go full speed). *To ball*, to have coitus, mid 1950s.

And, finally, World War II, our changing sexual mores and attitudes since the 1960s, and paperback novels, newspapers, newsmagazines, movies, and even TV shows have influenced and quickly disseminated our more recent sexual terms.

bar girl, 1938, a young woman who frequented bars to drink and talk with male customers, earning commissions on the drinks she helped sell, and often doubled as a prostitute; shortened to *B-girl* during World War II and by then meaning merely a prostitute who worked out of bars. Confused with the *B-girls* were the *V-girls* of World War II, who weren't prostitutes but were promiscuous or lonely young women willing to have sex with almost anyone in uniform.

round heels, a prostitute, because she spends so much time on her back, first recorded in 1943 in Raymond Chandler's *Lady in the Lake*.

shack job, 1945, as a man's live-in mistress, unmarried couples living together as man and wife being said to *shack up* since 1940 (originally probably a truckdriver's term but very common during World War II, especially for servicemen who lived off their military bases with their girlfriends).

zigzag, a prostitute, some World War II use, especially by servicemen for prostitutes in foreign countries. However, the term was usually used as a verb, meaning to have coitus, and seems to have been taken from 19th-century British military slang from troops stationed in the Near and Middle East and is probably a mispronunciation or reduplication of a native word.

working girl, a prostitute, late 1940s.

constant companion, a mistress or lover, 1960s, used as a euphemism in newspapers and newsmagazines in referring to the lovers of politicians, movie stars, etc.

swinger simply meant someone who was in rapport with modern, youthful attitudes and *life-styles* in the mid 1950s (from swing music use of the late 1930s and early 40s), but in the late 1950s and early 60s it came to mean a person of either sex, then especially a woman, who sought the uninhibited and often socially unacceptable sexual experiences then in the news, such as *wife swapping, group sex,* or *swinging both ways* (having both heterosexual and homosexual experiences). After the mid 1960s the word generally became more respectable again, referring to a single person of either sex (by then also called a *swinging single* or *single*) who pursued casual relationships with the opposite sex, as at *singles' bars* or on *singles' cruises,* which also catered to single people seeking more permanent relationships.

stable, a pimp's prostitutes, 1960s.

massage parlor, late 1960s. With call girls being increasingly expensive and streetwalkers being increasingly rough drug addicts, new types of brothels and sex shows opened in many downtown districts in the late 60s, ostensibly offering nude "models" to photograph, give massages, etc., but satisfying sexual desires for pay.

get it on, originally a prostitute's term for having coitus, mid 1970s, almost immediately followed by the term *get it off.*

go out, originally a prostitute's term for having coitus, 1977.

Quakers, Shakers, Mormons, Holy Rollers, Christian Scientists, and Jehovah's Witnesses

Religion, the Bible, and preaching have had a tremendous and profound influence on the American language, on its vocabulary, its speech rhythms, its intonations, etc. In addition, our (sometimes unobserved) tradition of freedom of religion has attracted and spawned a rich variety of religions and sects, each contributing not only its own name and terminology to our language but also, indirectly, the terms applied to it and its customs by outsiders.

QUAKERS. The first *Quakers* (an English name of 1650) arrived in America in 1656 but were persecuted and driven out of the Massachusetts Bay Colony by the Puritans. They found refuge in Rhode Island and, in 1681, were welcomed into Pennsylvania (Philadelphia eventually being called the *Quaker City*). Having a unique religion, customs, and dress, Quakers were talked about widely in early America, often with hatred or dislike. However, between the 1650s and 1690s most other colonists learned that Quakers believed people needed no clergy as spiritual intermediaries but could find guidance and understanding through an *inward light* supplied by the Holy Spirit, hence that *Quaker meetings* (1659) were primarily for silent meditation and were guided by a *clerk* (1688).

Justice Bennet of Derby was the first that called us Quakers, because I bid them tremble at the word of the Lord. This was in the year 1650.

George Fox, *Journal,* published posthumously in 1694

A Quaker meeting, 1790.

By 1679, Quakers were called *Friends* in America (because they refused to use titles, addressing each other as "Friend"), but it was almost another hundred years before the name the *(Religious) Society of Friends* was in use. Around 1680 they were also first known as *the plain people*, a general term also used to refer to any Pennsylvania Dutch, Mennonites, etc., who dressed, spoke, and lived plainly. By the American Revolution, *Quaker meeting* was also used humorously to mean any meeting or party where little was said. Also, since Quakers refused to bear arms, no guns or dummy guns were called *Quaker guns* and unarmed ships were called *Quaker ships*. By 1803, people called the plain, close-fitting hat that Quaker women wore a *Quaker bonnet*, the same item being called a *Quaker cap* by 1852.

But when Americans listened to Quakers talking they mainly remembered their use of *thou* and *thee*. Beginning in the 13th century, English-speaking people had begun to replace the nominative singular *thou* with the newer, Frenchified plural *you*, especially in the phrase "you are." By 1650 *thou* had almost disappeared, which is why the earliest Quakers then adopted it—as being an older, less sophisticated, and more humble word than *you*. They also used the objective form *thee*, and some soon used *thee* when the nominative *thou* would be expected. They retained these older uses, along with their traditional plain dress, well into the 20th century.

457

Incidentally, the *Quaker Oats* breakfast cereal trademark, with a picture of a man in Quaker dress, dates from 1877, chosen because Quakers were known for their frugality, orderliness, and integrity.

SHAKERS. The Shakers originated in a small 1688 French sect, *the Prophets*, whose members believed they received the gift of prophecy through "agitation of the body." The sect developed when members were forced to flee to England, where they joined with radical Quaker groups and turned their prophetic shaking into a ritualized, close-order shaking dance, with singing and handclapping. This English group was soon called the *Shaking Quakers*, then by 1747 *the Shakers (Sh*aking + Qu*akers)*. Its full official name was *The United Society of Believers in Christ's Second Appearance*.

America would never have heard of this sect if it hadn't been for Ann Lee (1736–84). The uneducated daughter of a Manchester, England, blacksmith, she became a Shaker at twenty-two, developed into a religious mystic, and at thirty-one declared herself "God the Mother." She preached God's dual sexual role—the masculine made manifest by Jesus Christ, the feminine by Ann Lee. By 1770 "Mother" Ann Lee led the Shakers. She then had a further revelation ordering her to establish the "Millennial Church" in the New World. She came to America in 1774 with eight followers, including her husband, brother, and niece, and settled in Watervliet, New York, in 1776. During the Revolutionary War (she was briefly arrested for treason) she converted several thousand Baptists, including entire congregations. Increasingly she made celibacy a cardinal principle of her sect (she had abandoned her husband), damning sex with obscene vividness and as a personal affront, asserting that since she, God the Mother, was now on earth the world would soon end and thus further propagation of the human species was unnecessary.

Although celibate Shaker colonies were established in Ann Lee's lifetime, it was only after her death in 1784 that living in neat, highly disciplined communal societies where all work and possessions were shared became a Shaker doctrine. The first such disciplined Shaker community was established in New Lebanon, New York, in 1787; by 1817 such communities were known as *Shaker communities*, by 1824 as *Shaker villages*, the population of each village being called a *Shaker family*. At the peak of the movement, from 1825 to the 1840s, there were 6,000 Shakers living in 18 Shaker villages in eight states (four New England states plus New York, Ohio, Indiana, and Kentucky). The admonition *Shaker your plate* (Clean your plate) was then well known to many children in New England and New York State: the Shakers believed that zestful eating glorified God but that not one morsel should be left or wasted. After the Civil War, religious fervor and Utopian societies dwindled, and by 1874 the Shakers were reduced to advertising in newspapers for members. Celibacy meant

[A consummated marriage is] *a covenant with death and an agreement with hell*.

"Mother" Ann Lee, founder of the Shakers in America

458

that the Shaker sect could survive only through an inflow of converts. It did not survive.

The Shakers contributed to American life and the American language out of all proportion to the sect's small size. Shaker farms, buildings, tools, clothing, and furniture had a strong influence on the rest of America. As farmers they invented the *rotary harrow*, developed the crossbred *Poland China* hog that became a staple on 19th-century farms, and had other farmers talking about their improved *threshing machine*. They became the largest producers of herbs and seeds in the country and were the first to sell garden seeds in small, labeled paper packets. Thus from the 1820s until the 1860s gardeners asked for *Shaker seeds*, and when we ask for a *packet of seeds* today we are using a Shaker term.

Besides greatly improving and thus popularizing the hand-powered *washing machine*, the Shakers invented the "flathead broom," which is what we mean by *broom* today (before the Shakers invented this, all brooms had cylindrical heads). They also invented the split-wooden *clothespin* and invented and named the *apple parer* (the term was first recorded in 1833). By the 1850s, *Shaker bonnets* and *Shaker straw bonnets* were something of a popular style, as were *Shaker cloaks*. By the 1860s householders who had never seen a Shaker were bragging about their *Shaker rocking chairs*, a style popular enough to be called simply *Shaker rockers* by the 1880s.

Antique collectors still talk about and haggle over Shaker items today. But we shouldn't forget the men who originally brought most of the Shaker clothes, gadgets, seeds, and furniture to the general public: the once well-known, eagerly awaited *Shaker pedlars*, who sold these wares to housewives and storekeepers during the middle fifty years of the 19th century.

MORMONS. Joseph Smith (1805–44) published the *Book of Mormon* and founded *the Church of Jesus Christ of Latter-Day Saints* in 1830, adding these two names to the American language. According to Smith, this was three years after the custodian angel *Moroni* had delivered to him the *golden plates* that had been hidden on Cumorah hill near the family farm near Palmyra, New York. On these golden tablets were written, in strange hieroglyphics, the *Book of Mormon*, which he translated with the aid of divine *magic stones* that accompanied them (the angel Moroni took the golden plates back after publication). Soon all America would be talking about Joseph Smith and his Church of Jesus Christ of Latter-Day Saints, and the words and the names associated with the Mormons would pass into our general vocabulary. These include:

The angel Moroni delivering the golden plates of the Book of Mormon to Joseph Smith on September 22, 1827.

Mormon, the name of the 4th-century American prophet-warrior who wrote the *Book of Mormon* (believers say his name is from Gaelic and a Teutonic dialect, *Mor*, more, great + *mon*, good). Members of the Church of Jesus Christ of Latter-Day Saints

459

were called *Mormons* from the beginning, in 1830, their church being called *the Mormon Church* since the mid 1830s.

the Book of Mormon, 1830, was called *the Mormon Bible* by the mid 1830s. It contains Mormon's sacred account of the pre-Columbian descendants of the lost tribes of Israel, how they came to the American continent via the Pacific in three migrations, and how their descendants (the American Indians) had their skins darkened by apostasy.

Saints and *gentiles*. Members of the Church of Jesus Christ of Latter-Day Saints were also simply called *Saints* from the beginning. They called non-Mormons *gentiles* from the early 1830s.

New Jerusalem or *Zion*. According to Mormons, this is the city that divine revelation told Joseph Smith to build on the borders of the *Lamanites* (the *Book of Mormon* word for American Indians). The Mormon mission was to convert the Indians so they could again become a "white and delightsome people" who could share in the millennium.

Smith gathered followers rapidly, but Zion was hard to establish. In 1831 the main body of believers settled in Kirtland, Ohio, and built the church's first *temple*. Mormon financial reverses during the Panic of 1837 and increasing conflicts with their gentile neighbors over land caused them to move to Jackson County, Missouri, joining a smaller group of Mormons who already were experiencing problems there. The troubles in Missouri in part concerned land and whether or not the Mormons would obey the local laws, but the Mormons were hated chiefly because they were abolitionists. When they refused to leave, the governor said they should be exterminated or driven off; mob violence increased, 17 Mormons were massacred, and soon 15,000 Mormon refugees were moving toward the next major name in Mormon history:

Nauvoo, Illinois. Smith and his followers moved to the small town of Commerce City, Illinois, on the Mississippi River, in 1838, Smith changing the name to *Nauvoo*. They built it into the largest city (20,000 population) in the state, and one of the most prosperous and attractive. Receiving a liberal charter, Nauvoo became a state within a state, the Mormons being responsible for many of the laws, with Joseph Smith the mayor and also lieutenant general of the Mormons' own 4,000-man militia, the *Nauvoo legion*.

In the 1840s in Nauvoo came the word that was to cause the death of Joseph Smith, to shape the history of the Mormons and the American West, and to cause millions of Americans to gossip about the Mormons for decades—the 1591 English word *polygamy* (Greek *poly*, many + *gamos*, marriage). Smith declared that God had revealed to him that polygamy was acceptable; he and the Mormons called it *plural marriage* and the extra wives *spiritual wives* (1843). His declaration shocked all the gentiles and many Mormons. A rival monogamous Mormon faction developed, and the

Joseph Smith, having declared that God accepted plural marriage or polygamy, was killed by a mob outside the Carthage, Illinois, jail on June 27, 1844.

first (and last) edition of its newspaper attacked Smith for polygamy and political ambitions. Smith and his municipal council had their Nauvoo police destroy the press, leading to charges of curtailing American freedom of the press, combining church and state, and—after Smith called out the Nauvoo legion—treason. Law officers from neighboring towns jailed him, his brother Hyrum, and other Mormon leaders in Carthage, Illinois. There, on the afternoon of June 27, 1844, a mob stormed the jail and shot Joseph and Hyrum Smith to death. Without the declaration of "plural marriage" and the charge of "polygamy" the Mormons might have had their Zion in Nauvoo, and we might never have talked about *Brigham Young* or *Salt Lake City*. The shout *Polygamy!* plagued the Mormons for decades, especially after Brigham Young made it a church doctrine in 1852. *Polygamy!* then caused Young to be removed as the first governor of the Territory of Utah, caused Congress to pass an *Anti-Bigamy* act in 1862, and prevented the admission of Utah into the Union until 1896, six years after a Mormon manifesto called for church members to respect U.S. marriage laws.

Brigham Young (1801–77), called "the Lion of the Lord," was the next famous Mormon name. He had been a farmer and journeyman carpenter-painter-glazier near Smith's home in New York State before being converted in 1831, to become a leading Mormon missionary and organizer. On Smith's death, Young, as senior member of *the Council of the Twelve Apostles*, became the Mormon leader.

the Mormon Wars, 1844–46, is the name of the often bloody conflict between the gentiles and the Saints in and around Nauvoo which followed Smith's murder and resulted in the Mormon evacuation. Historically, however, the term *Mormon Wars* was first used in 1833 for disturbances in Kirtland, Ohio. It was used again in the late 1850s when President Buchanan sent troops against the Mormons in Utah to ensure obedience—but Mormon guerrillas delayed the troops, Young won a moral victory and gained popular sympathy, and the expedition became known as *Buchanan's Blunder*.

the Mormon Trail. Brigham Young planned the mass exodus of his Mormons from Nauvoo and chose the Valley of the Great Salt Lake (still then technically part of Mexico) as the destination because its inaccessibility and unattractiveness would ensure that the Mormons be left in peace to establish their own commonwealth. They began to leave Nauvoo in subzero weather on February 4, 1846, following a 1,350-mile trail across Iowa, along the Platte River and part of the Oregon Trail to Wyoming, and on to Utah. In 1846–47, 15,000 Mormons with 3,000 wagons and 30,000 head of cattle started on the trail; 11,000 people made it to Utah. By 1850 their route was known as *the Mormon Road* or *the Mormon Trail*.

Salt Lake City. On July 24, 1847, Brigham Young first saw the Valley of the Great Salt Lake and said, "This is the place." A few

Inasmuch as laws have been enacted by Congress forbidding plural marriages, which laws have been pronounced constitutional by the court of last resort, I hereby declare my intention to submit to those laws, and to use my influence with the members of the Church over which I preside, to have them do likewise.

Manifesto from Wilford Woodruff, president of the Church of Jesus Christ of Latter-Day Saints, 1890, after the U.S. Supreme Court reaffirmed the constitutionality of the antipolygamy laws. The general conference of the church sustained this manifesto the same year, ending its sanction of plural marriages.

days later he laid out a two-mile-square city and named it *the City of the Great Salt Lake.* By 1849 outsiders also called it *Deseret City* and by 1878 *Mormon City.*

Deseret is the *Book of Mormon*'s word for honeybee, which the Mormons used as a symbol of their cooperative industriousness. They called the Great Basin, and sometimes Salt Lake City, *Deseret.* In 1849, a year after the transfer of the Southwest Territory from Mexico to the U.S., the Mormons modified their *theo-democracy* or "priestly government," established a provisional state government, and petitioned Congress for admission as the state of *Deseret.* This made the word well known and many Americans called the Mormon area around Salt Lake City *Deseret* well into the 1890s. But in 1850 Congress included the area in the Territory of Utah and in 1896, after the Mormons had renounced polygamy, it was not *Deseret* but *Utah* that was admitted as a state. (*Deseret* was also the name of a special 41-character "secret" alphabet that Brigham Young had George Watt, an English convert, design. Beginning around 1857, this alphabet was taught in all the Mormon schools.)

In addition to the above terms, some language historians believe the Mormons contributed a few curses to our vocabulary. Not taking the name of the Lord in vain or using obscenity, they substituted *hell* for taboo words in some oaths. Thus, *by hell!* and *son of hell* (for *by God!* and *son of a bitch*) were typical Mormon oaths. The 1845 word *hellion* is also said to have been popularized by Mormons.

HOLY ROLLERS. When I was a boy in Jacksonville, Illinois, I thought the Holy Rollers were a major widespread religious group that preferred to hold its meetings in tents. Now I know there is no such thing as an organized Holy Roller religion or religious group, that the term was a somewhat derogatory epithet applied to any fervent local sect or to any emotional revival meeting. The term *Holy Rollers* seems to have come into use around 1840 and may first have been used to refer to members of the Sweezyite sect in New York State, who did express their religious zeal by shouting, shaking, and even rolling on the floor.

CHRISTIAN SCIENTISTS. In frail health and afflicted with a spinal malady since her birth in 1821 in Bow, New Hampshire, Mary Baker, later known by her final married name of Mary Baker Eddy, tried various forms of physical and mental healing until she was temporarily cured in 1861 by Phineas Parkhurst Quimby of Portland, Maine. Quimby, an ex-clockmaker and hypnotist, was the father of the *New Thought* of "religio-metaphysical" healing; he believed that all illness was "a matter of the mind," due to "wrong thought," and practiced mental-suggestion healing. He was also the teacher of several famous *faith doctors* (an 1828 term), *faith curists* (1883) or *faith healers* (1885) and founder of various *faith cures* (1880s) and religious sects—as well as the creator of much of their

Mary Baker Eddy.

vocabulary. Quimby thought he had rediscovered Jesus's healing methods: the future founder of Christian Science agreed, studied his notes thoroughly, and wrote and lectured about his methods for religious audiences.

After Quimby's death in 1866, Mrs. Eddy's frail health returned. While recovering from a bad fall that same year, she read Biblical accounts of Jesus's healing, regained her full health, and discovered and named *Christian Science* (she considered the word *science* but another name for God's wisdom). Denying Quimby's influence, she claimed to have founded the religion on principles and divine laws formulated directly from the acts and sayings of Jesus. Mrs. Eddy began to write, supported herself by teaching students to be faith healers, and in 1875, using her then married name of Mary Baker Patterson, published *Science and Health*. In 1877 she married her third husband, Asa Gilbert Eddy, one of her followers, and has since been known as *Mrs. Eddy*.

She founded and named her *Mother Church*, or *First Church of Christ, Scientist*, in 1879, first in Lynn, then in Roxbury, Massachusetts. Its Boston edifice was completed in 1895. This church contained a *Christian Science Reading Room*, the prototype of similar rooms found today in most of the 2,500 Christian Science churches and in many other locations. In the 1880s and 90s, as Mrs. Eddy's religion grew, many people first began talking about *Christian Scientists*, its *readers* (the two who conduct the services, there being no clergy, one reading from the Scriptures, the other from *Science and Health*), and its *practitioners* (spiritual and healing guides). Another name that Mrs. Eddy added to the language is *The Christian Science Monitor*, the excellent newspaper she founded in 1908, two years before her death.

JEHOVAH'S WITNESSES. Charles Taze "Pastor" Russell (1852–1916) organized the *International Bible Student's Association* in 1872. This was the group from which *Jehovah's Witnesses* grew, but he never heard this name—his followers were known as *Russellites*. A wealthy unordained Congregationalist from Pittsburgh, Russell became "pastor" of his independent church there in 1877, preaching that the Second Coming of Christ had been an *invisible return* that had occurred in 1874, since which the world had been in the *Millennial Age*, which would end in 1914 with chaos, a resurrection of the dead, and the establishment of Christ's Kingdom on Earth. In 1879 Russell started a Bible journal that was later called the *Watchtower* (his wife disagreed on who should be editor, leading to their legal separation), then in 1884 founded the *Watchtower Bible and Tract Society*, a flourishing religious publishing house. He circulated 16 million copies of his own religious books and tracts and wrote a weekly sermon that appeared in 2,000 newspapers. Thus, if not widely talked about, he was certainly widely read.

On Russell's death Joseph Franklin "Judge" Rutherford (1869–1941) became the sect's leader. A Russellite convert and its former legal adviser, he de-emphasized the setting of any exact date of Christ's Second Coming and, in 1931, adopted the name *Jehovah's Witnesses* for the sect, along with the slogan "Millions now living will never die." The name *Jehovah's Witnesses* was taken not only to reaffirm the name Jehovah as the true God but also to identify those who witness in that name as His specially accredited followers. Thus the million worldwide *Witnesses* (headquartered in Brooklyn, New York) are all called *ministers* and keep Jehovah's command to preach the good news of the rapidly approaching God's Kingdom—at their *Kingdom Halls* (churches), by door-to-door evangelism, and by handing out the *Watchtower* and other religious tracts on street corners.

It's Raining Cats and Dogs

seems to be a good old-fashioned American expression. Here are some others we hear over and over:

> The *sight* of you is good *for sore eyes.*
> She's no chicken, she's on the wrong side of thirty, if she's a day.
> Fingers were made before forks.
> I thought you and he were *hand-in-glove.*
> She has more goodness in her little finger than he has in his whole body.

These are all familiar expressions, but none was originally American. They are all listed in English satirist Jonathan Swift's 1738 *Polite Conversations*—as examples of the banalities and clichés of polite British conversation! Swift also used another popular "American" expression in

> Hail fellow, well met,
> All dirty and wet;
> Find out if you can,
> Who's master, who's man.

"My Lady's Lamentation," 1765

It just goes to show that all our popular expressions don't originate in America.

During the last 200 years it seems it has almost literally been raining cats and dogs in America. Although American Indians kept pets, with dogs and beavers being the most common ones, the early colonists believed that keeping pets was a sign of witchcraft (two dogs were executed as witches in Salem, Massachusetts, in 1692). Keeping pets did become acceptable, however, during the mid 18th century, the habit spreading from European palaces and

Dear Miss: I lament with you most sincerely the unfortunate end of poor Mungo. Few squirrels were better accomplished for he had a good education, had travelled far, and seen much of the world. . . .

From Benjamin Franklin's only partially mocking letter to Miss Georgina Shipley, written in 1772 and including a mock epitaph epic poem to this squirrel who had escaped from its cage and been killed by a dog.

manor houses into the average home. Today there are at least 100 million cats and dogs in the United States—and each year more than a million people are bitten by dogs. Cats and dogs have given us such terms as:

to bark up the wrong tree, 1832, probably from hunting dogs thinking they had treed a raccoon.
cat burglar, 1907, when it first appeared in English.
catcry, a shout of displeasure or good-humored ridicule, 1898.
catfit, *catnip fit*, a fit of anger or frenzied excitement, 1905. If the original form was *catnip fit* it may have come into being merely as a corruption of or by confusion with *conniption fit*.
cat food, 1907.
cat nap, *cat's nap*, a short nap, 1820s.

In his 1944 Fala speech *President Franklin D. Roosevelt denied Republican charges that he had sent a naval destroyer to fetch his black Scottie Fala after a trip to the Aleutians and attacked his critics for attacking his dog. In his nationally televised* Checkers speech *in 1952 Vice Presidential candidate Richard Nixon denied receiving money from a secret political fund and claimed that the family's cocker spaniel Checkers was the only gift he had taken. President Lyndon Johnson never made a speech about his pet beagles but received much public criticism for being photographed picking up one of them by the tail.*

catnip, 1712, often called *cat mint* in bygone days; *catnip tea*, 1837. This aromatic mint plant, *Napeta cataria*, was named because of its attraction for cats; it has been widely used in cooking.

catty, given to spiteful remarks, around 1885.

copycat, 1915 as a noun, 1942 as a verb.

dog, an unsuccessful, ugly, or disliked person or thing, early 1930s.

dogcatcher, 1835, also euphemistically called a *humane officer*, 1939, and bureaucratically called a *canine control officer*, 1942.

dog eat dog, everyone for himself, 1834.

dog it, to shirk, 1920.

dog my cats!, an exclamation of surprise, 1839.

dognapper, 1940.

dog paddle, as a way to stay afloat or swim, 1904.

dog pound, 1875. Many pounds are now under the auspices of the *American Society for the Prevention of Cruelty to Animals (ASPCA)*, founded by Henry Bergh in 1866, when horses were often underfed, overworked, and cruelly treated.

look like the cat after it had eaten the canary, look guilty, 1871; *look like something the cat brought/dragged/drug in*, look bedraggled, late 1920s.

pooch, 1900 (the word is of unknown origin).

put on the dog, put on a display, dress up, etc., 1871.

see a man about a dog, to leave abruptly, especially in order to urinate, 1867 in English use.

The older English *it's raining cats and dogs* was joined by our *to rain pitchforks* in 1844, with the expression *right as rain*, meaning perfect, well, absolutely right, appearing in 1894.

Another old English expression dealing with a rainstorm is *to steal one's thunder*. The story behind this expression is that in 1709 English playwright John Dennis invented a new way to produce stage thunder for his play *Appius and Virginia*. Few people liked his tragedy and it soon closed, but not long after, Dennis was watching a new production of *Macbeth* and heard his thunder being used. He angrily got up from his theater seat and shouted to all the audience, "See how the rascals use me! They will not let my play run, and yet they steal my thunder!" So was born another popular American expression—in England. However, we Americans did add our own thunder terms, usually mild oaths or exclamations, as:

by thunder!, 1843.

go to thunder!, for "go to hell!," 1855.

like thunder, very quickly, greatly, 1835.

thunderation!, 1843.

thundering, damned, 1885.

who in thunder?, 1841; *what in thunder?*, 1844; *why in thunder*, 1863; *how in thunder*, 1895.

See Spot run!

Here, Flip, here!

Come and play, Sandy!

From children's typical first schoolbook readers, from the 1940s to well into the 1970s. Millions of American parents and teachers have heard these immortal lines as part of their children's first reading. "See Spot run" appeared in the Dick and Jane textbooks conceived by first-grade teacher Zerna Sharp of La Porte, Indiana, the books' simple stories built around an archetypical American family and its dog Spot and cat Puff.

Restaurants, Lunch Counters, Diners, and Drive-Ins

Colonial men might eat in *taverns* and *inns* when they were single, away from home, or wanted to meet and talk with other men. Traveling women were welcomed in many inns and hotel-like taverns too, though when away from home both men and women often took their meals with a family they knew or that had been recommended to them.

After the Revolutionary War our young nation loved its French ally and the French Revolution, and hence French customs, words, and food (which Thomas Jefferson, U.S. Minister to France from 1785 to 1789, helped popularize). Thus, from the time of Independence, fine American eating establishments have often had a French flavor and a French accent. As early as 1794, Bostonians were talking about Jean ("Julien") Baptiste Gilbert Payplat's fine eating establishment, Julien's Restorator. It helped make *restorator* (French, "restorer, resting place") an early American word both for restaurant and restaurant keeper. The French word *restaurant* ("restoring") was first used to mean an eating establishment in Paris in 1763, then recorded as being used in America in 1827, which was several years before it was used in England.

The new restaurants were unique in that they were not only for those who had to eat away from home but were also for those who wanted the treat of eating out. Such early restaurants were often expensive and still often associated with inns or hotels (the first American inn or tavern to be called a *hotel* was New York City's Corre's Hotel of 1790). They introduced many terms to America. In 1829, Bostonians were talking about their Tremont House (the first American hotel whose lobby was not a barroom and whose lavish restaurant could seat 200 people) and in 1855 about Harvey Parker's new Parker House, which introduced the term *à la carte* to America, serving any dish all day long and not just meals at fixed hours. Though this was then a revolutionary concept, this hotel and restaurant is best remembered today for another of its innovations, its soft, warm, folded *Parkerhouse rolls* (an item and a term most Americans knew by the 1870s).

Meantime, during the 1830s, American diners had begun to ask to see the *menu* or *menu card*, such written lists of available dishes being introduced during that decade. Since 1840, people had also been talking about New Orleans' Antoine's, which made *gumbo Creole* and, later, *oysters Rockefeller* famous, while New Yorkers boasted of their Taylor's and of the dining room at the St. Nicholas Hotel with its forty liveried waiters. Some dining rooms in resort hotels, such as Saratoga Springs' United States Hotel, were also fondly talked of. Such fancy eating places made the word *restaurant* a part of everyone's vocabulary between the late 1820s and 1855 and, during that same period, added such further French terms to America's restaurant vocabulary as *filet*, *bisque*, *table d'hôte*, *maître d'* and *à la* this or that, though the words, then as now, were often more French than the food or service.

After the Civil War lavish restaurants of all types flourished, to be called *eating palaces* and *lobster palaces* by 1900, and continued to introduce new concepts, dishes, and terms. Thus in the 1880s the British-financed Windsor Hotel in Denver introduced the *ladies ordinary*, the first dining room in the West to solicit the patronage of respectable, unescorted women (in the East all first-class hotels had separate *ladies dining rooms* until the 1870s). In 1897 New York City's ten-million-dollar Waldorf Astoria Hotel opened and its Palm Gardens, where patrons had to wear formal dress, became known for its maître d', Oscar Tschirky, better known as "Oscar of the Waldorf," who invented the *Waldorf salad* of cubed apples, nuts, and mayonnaise (others sometimes added celery and raisins).

But it was Delmonico's that was the best-loved, most-talked-about restaurant in America, still remembered as a beautifully supervised establishment that served the best food with the best service to more famous people over a longer period than any other. It was opened as Del's on New York City's William Street in 1827 by the brothers John and Peter Delmonico, immigrants from the vineyards of Switzerland, and originally served only wine, ices, and delicate cakes from a bilingual English and French menu. As the Delmonico family, the restaurant, and its menu grew, the full name Delmonico's was adopted. It became a mecca for gourmets, gourmands, and celebrities, constantly enlarging and moving through a dozen lavish locations, including Broadway at Bowling Green, where Jenny Lind and Louis Napoleon dined, and 14th Street and 5th Avenue, where Lincoln, Dickens, Thackeray, and just about every American and foreign visitor who could afford it ate at least once. It was from this Delmonico's that Samuel F. B. Morse sent the first transatlantic telegram over the new Atlantic cable while seated at his regular table. The last and most elaborate Delmonico's opened at 44th Street and 5th Avenue in 1897 and included a Gentleman's Elizabethan Café, a Ladies Restaurant, a Palm Garden, many private dining and banqueting rooms, a ballroom, and a rooftop conservatory. During its long history (1827–1923) Delmonico's created or popularized such dishes and terms as *Delmonico* steak, *Delmonico tomatoes* (stuffed with sweetbreads), *chicken à la King* (originally as *chicken à la Keene*, see A CHICKEN IN EVERY POT for this story), *lobster Newburg* and *pie à la mode*. *Lobster Newburg* was originally offered as *lobster Wenberg* in the 1890s, after customer Ben Wenberg, who had shown Delmonico's chef how a similar South American dish was prepared;

Delmonico's then renamed the dish *lobster Newburg* after it banned Mr. Wenberg from the restaurant, and its menu, for fighting. *Pie à la mode* had been a dessert and term since the 1880s but became widely known only after Delmonico's added it to its menu around 1918.

The development of fancy restaurants and food terms after the Revolutionary War was paralleled by the growth of less elaborate eating establishments and terms. Forty years after the Revolution some American businessmen and city workers were already forgoing large midday dinners (see DINNER OR SUPPER?) in favor of quick, convenient, and cheap lunches at *lunchrooms* or *lunches* (both terms of the 1820s), where one could get such filling meals as a slice of meat, mush, baked beans, and bread for one cent (by 1883 the average price of a complete meal in most taverns, hotels, and restaurants was already 25¢). Such cheaper eating places also flourished after the Civil War and were being called *hash houses* and *lunch stands* by the late 1860s, *lunch counters* by 1873, *lunch joints* by the 1880s, *snack bars* by 1895, and finally *luncheonettes* by the mid 1930s. A dishwasher or kitchen helper at a cheap restaurant had been called a *pot wrestler* as early as 1840 and a *pot-walloper* by 1860, and a waiter or waitress was called a *hash slinger* by 1868 and was said *to sling hash* by 1872. Even in fine restaurants a *short order* meant an *à la carte* serving of one dish by the 1890s, and by 1905 there were *short-order restaurants* and *short-order cooks*, and waiters yelling to cooks for an *order* of one dish or another. By 1910 some cheap eating establishments didn't bother to call themselves restaurants, lunchrooms, or anything else, but merely put up a sign advertising *EATS*. By 1912, cheap restaurants where customers ate

An Automat, *1903*.

in chairs off desklike armrests were called *one-arm lunch rooms* or *one-arm joints*.

Both *coffee shop* and *cafeteria* (Spanish-American for "coffee store") had meant a coffee house in America by the 1830s, and in many of them patrons poured their own coffee or carried it to their tables from a serving counter. By 1885, New York City had a complete self-service restaurant, for men only, but the modern *cafeteria* in which people choose from a variety of prepared foods from a long counter and carry it on trays to nearby tables seems to have originated in Chicago to feed hungry tourists quickly and cheaply during the 1893 World's Columbian Exposition. The spelling was often *caffeteria* then and such restaurants were also humorously called *conscience joints*, because the customers themselves added up the items on their trays and paid for what they said they had taken. Incidentally, the Horn and Hardart Baking Company opened its first *Automat* (Greek *automatos*, self-acting) in Philadelphia in 1902—but many people never used the name *Automat*, preferring to call the company's "nickel in the slot" restaurants *Horn and Hardart's*, and these vending-machine/cafeteria combinations became associated in many people's minds not with Philadelphia but with New York City, where they became not only a good cheap place to eat but also a tourist attraction.

Chuck wagons not only accompanied cowboys on the cattle drives of the 1860s and 70s but often followed them into the cow towns, such as Abilene, Kansas. These cowboy *chuck wagons* and the local *lunch stands* of the 1860s combined to give us the *lunch wagon* in the 1880s, some staying open until late at night and by the late 1880s being called *night owls* (*night owl* had meant a person who stays up late since 1846). These lunch wagons were usually made by local wagon-makers or blacksmiths, but Ruel Jones of Providence, Rhode Island, began making more elaborate wagons for sale in the late 1880s, and in 1891 Charles Palmer of Worcester, Massachusetts, applied for a patent on his specially designed lunch wagons, which he called *Night Owl Lunches*. Others, including T. H. Buckley, "The Lunch Wagon King," also created ever larger, more elaborate wagons, with nickel-plated coffee urns and stools, in the 1890s. Then in 1897, New York City, Boston, and Philadelphia sold many of their horse-drawn streetcars to replace them with electric ones, and local lunch-wagon owners bought many of the old streetcars for $15 to $20 apiece and converted them into *lunch cars*. Some cities and towns, such as Atlantic City, New Jersey, and Buffalo, New York, banned such lunch cars as unsightly or dirty or because they attracted undesirables, but Patrick Tierny gave them new respectability by designing and selling new lunch cars that included booths where ladies and families could sit (the ladies in their long dresses had found sitting on the stools awkward and unladylike) and were modeled on the designs of the elegant railroad dining cars, these becoming acceptable and sometimes called *diners* during the early 1900s. Such in-town diners did not become truly popular, however, until they were joined by *roadside diners* and could attract patrons who drove to them in the family car during the early 1930s.

Curb hopping, serving food to customers seated in their cars at the curb, seems to have originated in Miami during the Florida land boom of 1925 and by 1930 it had led to the terms *curb service* and *drive-in restaurant*.

Lunch-Counter Terms

Since the 1850s waiters and cooks have been communicating by verbal shorthand. Thus by the 1920s and 30s when lunch-counter waiters and waitresses called out their orders to short-order cooks and *soda jerks* (a 1915 term from the 1880s *soda jerker*) jerked soda but called out ice-cream and sandwich orders to *fountain men* they were drawing on an old tradition, using short, easily heard, and sometimes humorous codelike terms, many of them quite old, which some writers have dubbed *hashhouse Greek* (1930s). Since the 1950s such terms have been disappearing, because more and more lunch counters, coffee shops, and diners then began to have kitchens with cooks out of earshot, behind full partitions or closed doors, and found it more efficient to have waiters, waitresses, and soda jerks not call out the orders but to write them down on checks and to fill many beverage and side orders themselves. Since the

Serving lunch at New York City's old Fulton Fish Market.

471

1960s, too, fast-food chains offering only a few special items, often precooked or even prepackaged, have replaced many lunch counters.

Here are some of the most common and interesting lunch-counter and soda-fountain terms Americans have heard their waiters and waitresses shout out to the cook, fountain man, or each other.

AC, an *A*merican *c*heese sandwich.

Adam and Eve on a raft, two poached eggs on toast.

all the way (of a sandwich), with butter, mayonnaise, lettuce, onion, or everything on it. At soda fountains, however, *one all the way* meant an all-chocolate soda, with chocolate ice cream.

axle grease, *skid grease*, *salve*, butter.

baby, *cow juice*, *moo juice*, a glass of milk. After the 1940s a glass of milk was increasingly called a *grade A*. *Canned cow* is condensed milk; *one on the country* was buttermilk, which hasn't been popular enough to keep on lunch-counter menus for the last forty years.

belch water, a glass of seltzer or plain soda water.

black and white, a chocolate soda with vanilla ice cream. In some regions and periods this has also meant a chocolate malt and even black coffee with cream on the side.

black bottom, a chocolate sundae with chocolate ice cream.

black cow, a chocolate soda with chocolate ice cream (later, briefly, a plain root beer then a root beer with ice cream, vanilla ice cream unless otherwise specified). An all chocolate soda was also called a *mud fizz*; a chocolate milkshake a *mud shake*. In the 1920s and 30s, *Harlem* was sometimes used to mean chocolate, a *Harlem soda* a chocolate soda, *Harlem midget* a small chocolate soda.

blonde (of coffee), with cream; *brunette* meant "black" or without cream, as did *midnight* and *no cow*. *With sand* meant with sugar.

BLT, a *b*acon, *l*ettuce, and *t*omato sandwich, from the initial letters. A *BT* is a *b*acon and *t*omato sandwich, the New York City call once being a *BMT*, the M for "and" and a pun on the BMT (Brooklyn-Manhattan Transit Co.) subway initials. A plain *l*ettuce and *t*omato sandwich is an *LT*, but the New York City call was sometimes *IRT*, a pun on the IRT (Interborough Rapid Transit Co.) subway.

Bossy in a bowl, beef stew.

a bowl of bird seed, a bowl of cereal.

a bowl of red, a bowl of chili.

break it and shake it or *make it cackle*, put a raw egg in the drink, usually a milkshake.

a breath, *a slice*, *pin a rose on it*, with a slice of onion.

brown cow, chocolate milk (later advertised by cola manufacturers as cola with ice cream in it).

burn the British, a toasted English muffin (packaged *English muffins* for toasting in a toaster became popular in America in the late 1950s, the name catching on rapidly, even though they are neither English nor muffins).

burn one, a hamburger. Also *one on* ("put one on the grill") and *one in* ("I'm putting in one order for a hamburger"). *21* is two orders of "one," two hamburgers; *31* is three hamburgers, etc. In the early

part of the century *chewed fine* and *choke one* were also used to call out a hamburger or hamburger steak.

burn the pup, a bloodhound, a bow wow, Coney Island bloodhound, ground hog, a hot dog. Coney Island was considered a major home of the hot dog during the early part of this century, *Coney Island* itself being slang for a frankfurter by 1913; *ground hog* was, of course, a pun. As are many of the more breezy lunch-counter terms, these are as long as or longer than the common word: lunch-counter terms are not necessarily always efficient verbal shorthand but are often used merely to be breezy or to create an in-group camaraderie among coworkers.

a burnt one, a chocolate malt; *burn the van,* a vanilla malt.

carfare, subway, I got a tip; I'm putting a tip in the tip jar (really meaning "I'm not stealing the customer's change or keeping the tip for myself but am putting it in the jar of collective tips to be shared by all," preventing the boss or a coworker from asking why the waiter or waitress picked up change from the counter or table). The term stems from the fact that, until the late 1960s at least, the average lunch-counter tip was about equal to the cost of the worker's carfare to work.

cats' eyes, fish eyes, fish eggs, tapioca pudding.

CB, a cheeseburger. A *CB with* means cheeseburger with French fries.

Chicago, pineapple, as a *Chicago sundae,* or used by itself to mean a pineapple sundae or soda. This is a mid 1920s term, when Chicago meant Al Capone, gang wars, and *pineapples* (hand grenades or small throwable bombs).

CJ, a cream cheese and jelly sandwich. A *C and O* was a cream cheese and chopped olive sandwich, punning on the *C & O* (Chesapeake and Ohio) railroad.

clean up the kitchen; he'll take a chance; mystery; yesterday, today, and tomorrow, an order of hash.

clinkers, an order of biscuits, very old use.

coffee and, coffee and a doughnut or coffee and cake.

combo, a combination sandwich, the exact combination called out beforehand, as a *ham and cheese combo.*

cowboy, a western omelette or western-omelette sandwich.

a crowd, three of whatever is ordered, or three identical orders.

dog biscuits, crackers.

dough well done with cow to cover, buttered toast; before the mid 1930s this had simply meant an order of bread and butter.

down, toasted; *an order of down,* an order of toast. The term appeared after the advent of the modern electric toaster, on which a lever is pressed down to lower the bread into the toaster's slot and start the toasting. Before that an order of toast was called out as *stack one.*

down the garden, through the garden, with lettuce and tomato. *With leaves* or *with grass,* with lettuce; *keep off the grass,* without lettuce.

draw one, a cup of coffee; *a pair of drawers,* two cups of coffee. A cup of coffee is also a *(cup of) mud* or *java* or the alliterative *mug of murk.* At some later, more sophisticated lunch counters a cup of coffee is called a *44.*

Dusty Miller, a chocolate sundae with powdered malted milk topping, fairly common in the late 1920s and early 30s.

easy over (of fried eggs), turned over briefly while frying, so that the yolks are coated white and are not too soft; *flop 'em*, eggs to be fried on both sides; *sunny-side up* (1900) or *let the sun shine*, not turned over, so the yolks remain yellow and runny.

Eve with the lid on, apple pie.

first lady, spareribs. An old term and another, punning, reference to the Biblical Eve, who, of course, was made from Adam's "spare rib."

fly cake, *roach cake*, a slice of raisin cake. In times past, raisin loaf cake was more common than it is now, and owners and municipal health departments less concerned with cleanliness and jokes about it.

freeze one, a chocolate frosted.

Frenchman's delight, pea soup.

GAC, a grilled American cheese sandwich, from the initials; also *Jack*, from pronouncing *GAC*. A *Jack Benny* is a *Jack* with bacon, the *B* of *Benny* standing for *b*acon and the whole term using the name of comedian Jack Benny, whose popular Sunday evening radio show was in its heyday when the term was coined.

George Eddie, your customer is a nontipper, don't expect a tip.

graveyard stew, milk toast, also called *creamed goo* and *cream of goo* in the 1920s.

HC, ham and cheese sandwich.

high and dry (of a sandwich), with no butter, mayonnaise, mustard, etc.; plain.

Hoboken special, a chocolate and pineapple soda or sundae.

hold the hail (of a Coca-Cola or other soft drink), without ice.

hold the pickle, without pickle. *Hold* has become very common for "without" or "leave off," usually referring to an expected condiment, garnish, or side dish.

houseboat, a banana split, from its shape. *Split one* was an earlier term.

ice the rice, rice pudding with ice cream on top.

in the alley, à la carte, as a single dish or side order.

in the hay, or *shake one in the hay*, a strawberry milkshake, punning on "hay" as "straw."

Jew joints, *Hebrew enemies*, pork chops. Considered breezy and humorous until the 1930s.

looseners, a dish of stewed prunes.

mama, marmalade.

mayo, mayonnaise.

Mike and Ike, *the twins*, salt and pepper, the salt and pepper shakers.

Murphy, potatoes, thus *Noah's boy* (see below) *with Murphy carrying a wreath* is ham and potatoes with cabbage.

nervous pudding, *shimmy*, *shivering Liz*, Jell-O.

Noah's boy, a slice of ham, a ham steak (Ham was Noah's second son).

O.J., in the 1920s and 30s often *oh gee*, orange juice; *G.J.*, grapefruit juice; *T.J.*, tomato juice.

on the hoof or *let him chew it*, rare, as of a steak, hamburger, etc.

pig, pork or ham, as *sliced pig*, *pig sandwich* (also *pig between sheets*) or *pig on whiskey*, ham on rye.

Pittsburgh, the toast is burning, as a warning to the cook, referring to the smoke of Pittsburgh steel mills.

put out the lights and cry, liver and onions.

radio, a tuna fish salad sandwich on toast (a "tuna down," punning on "tune it down"; see *down* above).

red lead, ketchup, 1928.

red Merk, corned beef; *red Merk and violets* was corned beef and cabbage.

rush it, with *Russian* dressing.

seaboard, wrapped or packed to be taken out and eaten elsewhere, as in a c-board (card*board*) container. This is chiefly eastern and big-city use; in the West and in small towns *on wheels* is more common, having generally replaced the older *to walk*, *let it walk*, *walking*, *dressed*, *dress one*, and *runners*. The old term *to go* is still the most common.

spare, an empty glass.

spla, whipped cream, with whipped cream. Although this is probably a shortening of *splash* or *splay*, it could have been reinforced by the German "*mit schlag*," with whipped cream (*schlag* means "whipped" in German and is also a shortening of *schlag sahne*, whipped cream).

splash, soup, as *a splash of chicken* (chicken soup) or *a splash of red nose* (tomato soup).

a spot, a cup of tea; *a spot with a twist*, tea with lemon; *a cold spot*, a glass of ice tea. Until the 1930s a cup of tea was also *boiled leaves* and a *pot of tea* a *PT*.

a squeeze or *squeeze one*, limeade, lemonade, or orangeade, depending on the area or the house specialty. *Squeeze one* originally meant a glass of orange juice, in the days when orange juice was freshly squeezed.

a stack, an order of pancakes.

straw, strawberry, as a *straw shake*, strawberry milkshake.

stretch one, *a long one*, a large Coke; *shoot one*, *a shot*, *one shot*, a small Coke; *red stretch*, *stretch one—let it bleed*, *a virgin*, *virtue*, a cherry Coke. The "shot" and "stretch" refer to the time the Coke dispenser's handle is to be held down. "Virgin" means cherry because *cherry* has been a slang word for maidenhead or virginity since 1930. *Spike it* or *make it yellow* meant to add lemon flavoring to the Coke. *From the South* meant to make the Coke extra strong, and *western* meant a Coke with chocolate syrup. Later, *pop one* meant a bottle of Coca-Cola.

suds, a glass of root beer (*suds* has been slang for regular beer since 1904). At early lunch counters without soda fountains, *suds* once meant a cup of coffee, *sinker and suds* a doughnut and coffee.

a team, a pair, two of the same item. An old term from horse-and-buggy days.

van, vanilla, as a *van shake*, vanilla milkshake, or a *dish of van*, vanilla ice cream.

vanilla, a call to the cook or other workers to come see the pretty girl who just walked in. *87* meant come see the girl seated at a table with one leg resting over the other so you can get a good look, the sexy girl being the figure 8, her crossed leg the 7. *Fix the pumps* meant come see the girl with the large breasts.

Vermont, maple syrup.

warm (of a sandwich), serve it hot; thus *warm a beef* means a hot roast beef sandwich.

warts, olives, thus *cream cheese with warts* is a cream cheese and chopped olive sandwich.

whistle berries, bullets, repeaters, snappers, meant red, pinto, or kidney beans, but especially baked beans. Franks and beans were *hounds (hot dogs) on an island* in the 1920s and 30s.

white cow, a vanilla milkshake, sometimes a vanilla soda.

with blood, hemorrhage, with paint, paint it red, red lead, with ketchup.

with whiskey, on whiskey, with rye bread, on rye bread. An early and eastern term, when "whiskey" meant rye (see BOOZE AND BARS).

working, I've ordered this before, don't forget it (or the cook may call out or repeat the order and add "working" to mean "it's being prepared now").

wreck a pair, spoil a pair, two scrambled eggs.

5, a large glass, especially of milk. *2½* was a small glass of milk.

41, lemonade (though in some areas 41 means orangeade or even milk). This seems to have replaced the earlier *31*, meaning lemonade or orangeade, which had replaced *21!*

51, a cup of hot chocolate; *52* is two cups of hot chocolate, *53* is three cups, etc. Around 1930 *hot cha* was the breezy way to call out hot chocolate.

55, a glass of root beer.

80 or *81*, a glass of water; *82* is two glasses of water, *83* is three, etc. In earlier days a glass of water was also ordered by calling out *Adam's ale, dogsoup, on the city, city cocktail, on the house*, or *tin roof*. Water also had its local names as *Hudson River ale* and *Potomac phosphate*.

86, rhymes with and means "nix," usually called out from cook to waiter or waitress, meaning "we're all out of it, we don't have any." Also used to mean "no sale" and as a code meaning a person is not to be served, because he is broke, drunk, etc.

95, a customer is leaving without paying, stop him.

99, call or see the manager or owner, report to the boss. Some employees call *99, 13*, or *white bread* out to mean "be on your toes, the boss is here." Since *99* meant the boss or manager, one step below him was *98*, the assistant manager or person in charge when the boss was out.

The Sandwich and the Sandwich Islands

(former name of the Hawaiian Islands) were both named for John Montagu, the fourth Earl of Sandwich (1718–92), British First Lord of the Admiralty, notorious for his mismanagement, corruption, and gambling. The *sandwich* was so called by the 1760s, named after the earl, an inveterate gambler, because he often lunched on meat between two slices of bread while remaining at the poker table.

The first uniquely American sandwich we talked about was the *western sandwich*. It was created when pioneers crossing the hot western plains in covered wagons found their eggs quickly getting "high," so they mixed them with onions and served them on bread to cover up the strong flavor. The next widely discussed American sandwich was the *reception sandwich* accompanying the afternoon tea parties in vogue with American women in the 1870s. These reception sandwiches were dainty, British-style tea sandwiches that developed into our *finger sandwiches*, which accompanied *cocktail parties* when such events became popular in the 1920s (in spite of, or because of, Prohibition). Our American *club sandwich* (1903), sliced chicken breast, tomatoes and lettuce, sometimes with bacon, was also first widely popular in the 1920s and was then considered rather fancy and associated with country clubs. *Double-deckers* originally referred to double-decked riverboats in the 1830s, to double-decked railroad freight and cattle cars (carrying hogs) in the 1850s, then to double-decker horsecars and buses before referring to sandwiches in the 1920s (by the 1930s *double-decker* was another name for a double-dip ice cream cone). Such sandwiches became popular in the 1920s because soft, packaged *sandwich bread* was by then widely available.

The German contribution to the American sandwich is seen in hamburgers and hot dogs, as well as other sandwiches on rolls and buns. French and Italian bread loaves also contribute. In the late 19th century, New Orleans' tourists began to talk about the local *poor boy* sandwiches, hot or cold meat or fish, cheese, relishes, sometimes potatoes, vegetables, and just about anything and everything, making a complete meal on a small loaf of French bread split horizontally (some of these sandwiches even started with an appetizer at one end, had meat or another main dish in the middle, and ended with cheese or a sweet filling at the other, being a multicourse meal on bread). *Poor boys* are said to be named because they were made up to give to people begging for food. In 1921, brothers Clovis and Benjamin Marin opened a small café in New Orleans' French Market district selling their foot-long version of poor-boy sandwiches, crammed with meat and cheese, lettuce and tomato, for 10¢ each to dockworkers, sailors, farmers, and tourists—and made the *poor boy* truly famous.

Closely related to the New Orleans' poor boy is another heroic-sized sandwich, the *Italian Hero sandwich*, called simply a *hero* by the 1920s, especially in New York City. It's also called a *grinder*, especially in Boston and parts of the South and West; a *hoagie*, especially in Philadelphia, where it may have been invented in the Italian pushcart section of that city; a *submarine* or *sub*, especially in Pittsburgh and Los Angeles, from the sandwich's shape; a *torpedo*, also from its shape; a *wedgie* or *wedge*, especially in Connecticut, Rhode Island, and other areas with Portuguese neighborhoods; and a *Cuban sandwich* in Tampa, Florida.

Senior Citizens and the Social Security

Although we have generally talked with respect about our elders, we have had several disparaging terms for them, especially for old men. *Old codger* meant a crotchety, stubborn, or eccentric man by 1756 (from *cadger*, a chronic borrower); *old cock* dates from 1835; *old duffer* was in use by 1875 (a *duffer* is a clumsy or dull-witted person); and *old geezer* dates from 1896 (from *guiser*, a sport, one who makes sport). *Old fogey* was first used in the 1830s, but then meant an irritable old person rather than a staid one (from French *fougue*, quick-tempered). A person who hadn't accepted a new idea *since Adam was a boy* (1830s) was also known as a *back number* by 1882, while *old fuddy-duddy* became popular in the 1900s, coming from an English dialect word *fud*, the buttocks, hence a person who sits around on his duff doing nothing (the *-duddy* was added just to make the rhyme). On the other hand, we have spoken affectionately of an *old boy* or *old girl*, meaning an old man or woman, since the 1840s; called an elderly person an *oldster* since 1848; and used *old-timer* as a somewhat complimentary term since the Civil War.

In our lifetime our concept and words about the elderly have changed greatly, because their number, life, and place in society have changed greatly. *Senior citizen* has been a popular euphemism since the 1950s, when the number of older people suddenly seemed to have multiplied. It had: in 1900 the average life expectancy was forty-five, by 1950 the average life span was almost seventy years; the population had doubled but the number of people 65 and over had quadrupled to become 8 percent of the total. Meanwhile, *retirement* had become a common concept, a dream open to all. In 1920, two-thirds of the few men living past sixty-four years were still working, but by 1950 less than 25 percent of the men over sixty-four were working. Such mass retirement had been made possible by the initiation of union, state, and insurance pensions of the 1920s, by Social Security in 1935, and by company pensions to attract employees during the boom years after World War II. In the 1950s, for the first time, millions were reaching the age and had pensions to become *retirees*, a new American group, and a new word to most.

But by now pensions themselves, the small houses built quickly after World War II, and new postwar life-styles had destroyed the *extended family* in which the elderly lived with their children and grandchildren. People began talking about the new *retirement houses* in *retirement villages* and *apartments for seniors* where the elderly, according to the ads, could most happily spend their *golden years*. Warm places without the rigors of winter and expenses of furnaces and overcoats, such as Saint Petersburg, Florida, Orange County

478

in Southern California, and various specially built *Sun Cities*, were widely discussed.

Despite other pension plans, it was Social Security that made much of this talk possible. Many elderly and rural people still call this *the Social Security*, harking back to an older way of speaking when *the* was used more than it is today (young people are also apt to talk about "the invention of cars" rather than "the invention of the car," using plurals to avoid *the*). The added *the* to Social Security also comes from the many arguments in 1934–35 comparing *the* Townsend Plan with *the* Social Security Plan.

The Townsend Plan, initially called *the Townsend Recovery Plan*, was first advocated by California physician Dr. Francis Everett Townsend in 1934 and called for curing the ills of the Depression by a federal grant of $200 a month to all citizens over sixty so long as they refused employment, the money to be raised by a 2 percent national sales tax. Other widely talked about share-the-wealth plans of the period included Huey Long's *Share Our Wealth Clubs*, Father Coughlin's *National Union for Social Justice*, and Upton Sinclair's *EPIC (End Poverty in California)*. But it was the popular Townsend Plan that helped spur Congress into passing the New Deal's Social Security Act in 1935, and the Social Security has been a prime topic of conversation among the elderly ever since.

During 1963–65 a new portmanteau word, *Medicare (Medical + care)*, was the topic of heated debate, finally becoming part of Social Security in 1965, even though members of the American Medical Association had lobbied against it as *socialized medicine*. *Medicare* soon was joined by another new word, *Medicaid*, and eventually gave a new meaning to *nursing home*, as an institution for the old too sick or feeble to maintain their own home, while the once medical word *geriatrics* became known to us all.

Thus since the early 1950s we Americans have been talking about senior citizens, old age, and retirement a great deal and we have heard something else in America never generally heard before—the words, the wisdom and folly, the likes and dislikes, the joys and pains of people over sixty-five. The voice of America now includes the voices of the old.

Shut Your Fly Trap

was the 1830s way of saying "shut up," and the origin of our 1903 expression *shut your trap* (the mouth had also been called a *clam trap*, 1800, and a *potato trap*, 1843).

The fly trap referred to goes all the way back to at least 1790, being two blocks of wood hung over a table, one block spread with honey, molasses, etc. When a fly got caught on this primitive flypaper someone reached up and silenced the angry buzz by banging the two blocks of wood together, which was the early American way of shutting one's trap.

Having no screens, refrigeration, or insecticides, early Americans and their animals were plagued by flies and talked about and often cursed such pesky insects. In the 1790s a *fly flapper* was a humorous term for a woman's big, floppy hat and since about 1815 *fly time* has meant spring and early summer, an annoying time for farmers, stable keepers, etc. Fly traps began to give way to the *fly brush* or *fly whisk* in the 1820s (which grew into the *fly swatter* at the end of the century) and *flypaper* in the late 1840s, with outdoor types discussing the merits of the new *fly dope* in the 1890s. Before that, one had to keep moving or swatting to keep flies off, which is why since the 1850s *there are no flies on* (someone) has meant that person is alert and active.

From before the Revolutionary War until 1816 there was a famous Fly Market at the valley or foot of Maiden Lane in New York City. It wasn't called the *Fly Market* because of the flies but from its original name of the *Valley Market* or the *Vallie Market* which had been given the abbreviated Dutchlike name *Vly* or *Vlie Market*, pronounced as "Fly Market." Most people called this Vly or Vlie Market the Fly Market, to others Vlie Market became "Flea Market." Thus, the original American flea market was really the Valley or Vlie Market in New York City, with the term later applied to any open-air market of secondhand goods, the connotation now being that fleas may be in the used clothing, furniture, etc., purchased there (it was the 1920s before *flea market* became a common term, then a translation of the name of the famous Paris flea market or *marché aux puces*).

Even without flies and fly traps to shut, we Americans would still have many ways to tell people to be quiet or shut up, including:

button one's lip, 1926.
can it, 1906; *can the chatter*, 1918.
clam up, 1916.
dry up, 1852.
dummy up, 1920.
give us a rest, 1880.
hang up, 1900 (*hang up!* had been used as an interjection or command to stop what one was doing since 1854, long before its telephone use).
hush up, 1860.
knock it off, quit it, stop, stop talking, 1944.
not to open one's face, not to talk, 1896.
pipe down, speak softer, be quiet, mid 19th century, with the reverse term *pipe up*, to speak up, speak out, appearing in the 1880s.
save it, 1935.
shush, as a verb meaning to silence, to say "shush" or something else to silence someone, 1931.
shut up, 1860; *shut off*, 1892. *Put up or shut up*, to prove it, bet on it or

stop bragging, objecting, making claims, etc., dates from 1880.
shut your head, 1855; *shut your face*, 1928.
sign off, 1928, from the radio use.
stow it, 1919, from sailors' use.

Sissy! Crybaby! Yellowbelly! *Milksop* (1386)

and *quitter* (1611) are old English words and *coward* dates from the 13th century (Old French *couard*, Latin *cauda*, tail, referring to a dog with its tail between its legs). Suddenly in the 1830s and 40s, however, America had some new, mean words for cowardice, perhaps because life was now easy enough to admit weakness, or diverse and complex enough so that some could afford to claim that discretion was the better part of valor. Thus during this period we had such new terms as:

to back out, 1836; *back down*, 1849. *To back-pedal* came in 1901, after the bicycle craze of the 1890s. To *cop out* is from the 1960s.
chicken-hearted, 1848. *Chicken-livered* came in 1872; *chicken* wasn't popular until the 1930s.
yellow-bellied, 1847; *yellow*, 1856. *Yellow streak* didn't appear until 1900 and the noun a *yellow belly* wasn't common until the 1920s.

It doesn't seem to be until the 1850s that boys began to taunt each other with being timid, cowardly, or unmanly, perhaps because earlier frontier days had produced fewer such boys, or because now new diversity meant tough frontier and rural youths were meeting some milder boys. By the 1870s some of these words were being applied not only to boys but to young men; it was the same generation and some of the *crybabies* of the 1850s grew into the *goody-goodies* of the 70s. Thus we have:

crybaby, 1851.
you'll suck eggs!, 1860s.
'fraidy cat, *'fraid cat*, 1870.
goody-goody, *goody*, 1870s.
sissy had been a term of address to or nickname for a sister since the 1840s; by the 1880s it was a very common term for an unmanly or spoiled boy, with later variants such as the 1890s *sissy pants*.
mama's boy, 1896.
Willie boy, 1890s.
la(h)-de-da(h), around 1900. Note that as the years go by the connotation is shifting from timid or unmanly boy to effeminate youth (see also GAY MEN AND LESBIANS).
pussy-footer, 1903.
jellyfish (because he has no "backbone"), 1911.
panty-waist, 1920s, from the name of the children's underwear style, consisting of underpants buttoned to the undershirt or underwaist.

pretty boy, 1920s.

Casper Milquetoast, milquetoast, after 1924 when H. T. (Harold Tucker) Webster's newspaper cartoon, *The Timid Soul*, appeared, with its main character Casper Milquetoast.

Percy boy, Percy pants, 1930s.

cookie pusher, 1940, originally applied to politicians and intellectuals whom isolationists considered softhearted for wanting to aid the Allies before the U.S. entered World War II, later to members of the State Department considered to have too soft a policy (the implication being that such people conducted business by going to teas where cookies were served rather than doing hard work).

Small, Teeny, and Itsy-Bitsy

Small means not only little but inferior. *Small arms* (small caliber) was the first specialized "small" term used in America, in 1689. *Small beer*, however, doesn't mean a small serving but weak or inferior beer, and unimportant people were called *small beer* by 1705. *Small game* was in use by 1817 and *small change* by 1819. Insignificant things or people were called *small potatoes* by 1831 and unimportant people *small fry* by 1905 and *small timers* by the 1930s.

In the 1840s *teeny* became a variant of *tiny* and *taunty, teensy, teenty*, and *tointy* were also used, with such combinations as *teeny-weeny* and *teentsy-weentsy* appearing in the 1890s. These last two terms combined *teeny* with *wee*, and by 1915 *weeny* and *weensy* were used alone. Once *tiny* became *teensy* and *teentsy*, *bit* became *bitty* and *bittsy*, followed by *itty-bitty* and *itsy-bitsy*, all appearing in the 1890s.

Of course, we also call small people and things *shrimp*, 1891; *li'l* (little), 1908; *half pint*, 1926, and *pint-sized*, 1942; and *peewee*, 1942.

> *I will make it a felony to drink small beer.*
> William Shakespeare, *King Henry IV, Part II*, IV, 2 (1590–92)

> "Itsy Bitsy Teenie Weenie Yellow Polka Dot Bikini"
> Title of one of the most popular songs of 1960

A *Monarch* teenie weenie *sweet pickle ad of 1925.*

Mr. and Mrs. Smith: Common Last Names

Smith is the most common family name in the English-speaking world. There are well over 1¼ million Smiths in America today and Smith was the most common name on both the Army and Navy rosters in World War II (John Smith being by far the most common, and half of these Smiths had no distinguishing middle name or initial).

In the distant past a man was known only by one name (as is true in many primitive tribes); this name was often then made more personal and precise by combining it with his occupation, the place where he lived, or his father's name. Thus John the smith became John Smith—Smith is so common because originally it meant a worker not only in metal but also in wood and stone (later a lot of these Smiths would have been named *Carpenter* or *Mason*). The common *Miller* and *Taylor* are also occupational names. The son of a locally well-known John might also become *Johnson* or *Jones*, both meaning "son of John." Similarly, the common *Williamson* and *Wilson* mean "son of Will(iam)"; *Davis* and *Davidson* "son of David (or Davie)"; *Anderson* "son of Anders"; etc. Since names taken from places are more varied, they are not usually among the most common. However, a family who lived by a rose field might become *Roosevelt*, one who dwelt near the ford of a stream could become *Ford*, and people from Washington in Sussex or Durham (England) might be named *Washington*.

Captain John Smith (1580–1631), explorer and a leader of the Jamestown colony, bore the most common full name in America.

Here are the eighteen most common surnames heard in the United States:

Smith	Taylor
Johnson	Thomas
Williamson	Moore
Brown	White
Jones	Martin
Miller	Thompson
Davis	Jackson
Wilson	Harris
Anderson	Lewis

Sophia Smith (1796–1870) bequeathed her fortune for founding Smith College.

All these are English names—but only half of the people bearing them are of English descent! A lot of Smiths were once German *Schmidts* and Scandinavian *Smeds*, or perhaps *Goldsmiths* or *Smidnovics;* many Millers were once German *Mullers;* many Johnsons translated their names from Swedish *Johanson* or Dutch and Danish *Jensen* and *Janson* or Irish *McShanes;* and *Braunstine, Boronofsky* and *Addamic* and *Yutatamic* could become Brown and Adams, or just about anything else. An immigrant's name was what he told the immigration official it was (or what the official or friends and

Alfred E. Smith, four times governor of New York between 1919 and 1928, was the unsuccessful Democratic Presidential candidate in 1928.

neighbors in the New World thought they heard), or what he asked a judge to give him to help him melt into the melting pot. And these were almost always the familiar American-English names.

Though some slaves were given or known by their master's family name, most blacks weren't even accorded last names until they became free. Then they often took the family name of their master, overseer, or a famous or a common family name from the region in which they lived. Some took the last name of famous Americans, as Washington, Franklin, Jefferson, Jackson, Clay, etc., or from those who helped the black cause, as John Brown or especially the well-known Union general and head of the Freedmen's Bureau from 1865-74, General Oliver Otis Howard (who was also the founder and an early president of *Howard University*). So many blacks took General Howard's name that about a third of all *Howards* in the U.S. are black. The ten most common black family names in the U.S., in decreasing order of frequency, are:

Johnson, the most common black surname since 1830.
Brown
Smith
Jones
Williams
Jackson
Davis
Harris
Robinson
Thomas

These are certainly all American-English names and the list differs but little from that of the most common general American surnames. Beginning in 1931 a few Black Muslims began dropping their American surnames, which they regarded as "slave names," for Islamic names or a first name followed by X, resulting in such names as *Malcolm X* and *Herbert 3X* (the third Herbert in the group to take the X name) and, especially in the 1960s and 70s with the Civil Rights movement and growing black pride, in such widely talked about names as heavyweight boxing champion *Muhammad Ali* (originally Cassius Clay), basketball star Kareem Abdul-Jabbar (originally Lew Alcindor), and playwright Imamu Amiri Baraka (originally LeRoi Jones). Incidentally, adopting or emphasizing an ethnic name is not new: many prizefighters have done so in the past to attract an ethnic following (see BOXING, PRIZEFIGHTING, AND PUGILISM for examples).

However, the fact is that the 40 most common U.S. family names are English. The monotony is broken by the 41st most common—*Cohen*. The list of the 40 most common would, of

Kate Smith, the popular radio singer, in 1936.

course, be for all the country taken as a whole. In certain areas one would hear other names more often. Thus *Cohen* has been the most common surname in New York City; *Sullivan* and *Murphy* rank close to *Smith* in Boston; *LeBlanc* and *Boudreaux* are still common in New Orleans; *DeVries* and *Van Dyke* are among the most common in parts of Michigan; *Garcia, Lopez, Gomez, Gonzalez*, and *Rodriques* rank very high in some neighborhoods in the Southwest; and *Chan, Wong*, and *Lee* are about the only names found in certain neighborhoods in New York City and San Francisco. Such facts are fun if your name happens to be here—but the main fact is that the family name we have heard most and still hear most in America is *Smith*.

Sneak Thieves, Yeggs, and Muggers

Robber, thief, and *burglar* were in the English language before colonial days and by 1615 thieves were often called *hooks* (perhaps because some used long hooks to steal things through open windows). The 1870s American word *crook* also literally means "hook" (from Latin *croc*, hook). Since colonial days we have also added such words and uses as:

hook, to steal, 1840s; *lift*, 1848.
jimmy, a burglar's crowbar, 1848.
sneak thief, 1859.
mugger, a robber who leaves his victim helpless, 1863 (by 1910 it meant a robber who assaulted his victim from behind; by the late 1960s it meant any robber who confronted his victim). This comes from to *mug*, to hit in the face, *mug* having meant face since the 1840s (probably because drinking mugs were often made to resemble faces, as were the famous "Toby mugs"). *Mug* has meant a person since 1895 and a photograph of a face since 1896.
yegg man, a tramp, hobo, 1901 (probably from German *jäger*, hunter); *yegg*, a thief, especially a safecracker, 1926 (this probably comes from *yegg man*, but popular mythology has it coming from a John Yegg, said to be the first safecracker to use nitroglycerin).
caper, a robbery, 1925. The word had long meant a prank or spree (from the 16th-century *capriole*, a leap in dancing, though there was another, 17th-century, word *caper* meaning privateer, from the Frisian *kapeu*, to steal, plunder).
break in, breaking and entering, both late 1930s.
heist, a robbery, 1950s (a variant of "hoist").
'loid, a cellu*loid* strip for pushing back a lock's bolt, 1950s.
rip off, steal, 1960s (in thieves' slang to *rip* has meant to rummage through or search for something to steal since at least 1816).

To Spirit Away

was 17th-century slang for the enticing, or even shanghaiing, of British drunks, bums, runaways (husbands, wives, apprentices, and children), and those in trouble to the New World by professional recruiters, called *spirits* (1645 with this meaning), who worked for shipping companies or large colonial landowners. The fortunate or unfortunate victims—depending on how they fared in the New World—brought from four to eight pounds in the colonies as *indentured servants* (an English term of the 1670s). They worked from three to fourteen years to reimburse their new master for the money he had paid the ship's captain for their passage, which sum was considerably more than the ship's captain had paid the spirit who had *spirited* (enticed or shanghaiied) them aboard in England.

Our word *kidnapping* (1680s in England, from *kid*, child + *nap*, a variant of *nab*) also originated from this practice and at first referred specifically to children nabbed by such spirits and sent to the colonies.

Spiritualism, Mediums, and Ouija Boards

The original mediums, *the Fox sisters, Margaret (left), Catherine (center), and Leah (right).*

Spiritualism became a fad in England in the early 1830s and in the U.S. about 20 years later. The words *spiritualism*, meaning communicating with spirits of the dead through a living intermediary, and *spiritualist* were first recorded in America in 1853 when American spiritualists held their first convention, in Boston.

In America it all started with Andrew Jackson Davis's 1847 book *Nature's Divine Revelations*, about spirits and the possibility of communicating with them. Sure enough, the Fox sisters—Kate (Catherine), Margaret, and Leah—of Wayne County, New York, soon announced that Davis was right and that they had communicated with the spirit world. The Foxes, an immigrant Canadian family, had moved into a farmhouse known for its ghostly tappings and moanings, and Kate and Margaret claimed to have worked out a code of communication with the spirit through a system of rappings (yes, the spirit's first message was that its body had been murdered in that very house). The three sisters began to formulate spiritualism into a religion and, with Margaret as the leader, were soon giving séances and touring the U.S. and Europe, causing all America to talk about spiritualism. By 1852 the terms *medium* (also called *trance-medium* by 1878) and *(spiritual) rapping* were in the American language and America was also frequently using words like *séance* (used in England by 1845) and *clairvoyance* (used in England by 1842). Margaret Fox (1833–93) kept people talking about her and about spiritualism most of her life: she claimed to be the common-law wife of the famous Arctic explorer Dr. Elisha Kent Kane (1820–57), assumed the name Margaret Kane, and then in 1888 confessed she had never contacted the spirit world at all but was an imposter (she later retracted her confession).

After the Fox sisters made spiritualism popular and profitable in America, other mediums appeared by the score. The most famous was probably Daniel Dunglas Home (1833–84). Scottish-born, he was adopted by an American aunt, who threw him out of the house because of the mysterious rappings he caused. He made the word *levitation* popular in America, having been reported to have floated 70 feet above the ground. He performed before William Cullen Bryant, Robert Browning (who wrote a poem about him), and the crowned heads of France, Prussia, and the Netherlands.

Mystic communications were thus very much in the air during the 1880s. Then, first in England and soon after in America, F. W. Meyers popularized the terms *telepathy* (1882) and *thought transference* (1884), especially in his 1884 book *Phantasms Living*, leading to our term *mind reader* by 1887. *Fortune telling* (a 1557 English term) also had a resurgence with the term *on the cards* (1849) and then *in the cards* appearing, while *palmistry* (a 1420 English word) gave us our word *palmist* by 1886.

The *Ouija board* was patented as a toy by toy makers William and Isaac Field in 1892 and is a trademarked name (from French *oui*, yes + German *ja*, yes) now owned by Parker Brothers, the game manufacturers. It was a popular parlor game of the late 1890s, especially with courting couples, who balanced it between them on their knees, which some young men said had to touch. Not until 1919 did anyone claim that this toy was a serious means of communicating with the spirit world, but then Mrs. John Curran claimed she had done so with her Ouija board and gave public performances with it. A few people have claimed mystical powers for it ever since.

Square Deals, Meals, and People

Colonists were calling city blocks laid out on the grid plan *squares* by the 1760s (the term is often associated with Philadelphia but did not originate there). By 1832 men used *square* approvingly to refer to the natural, even gait of a good horse in such expressions as a *square-gaited* horse or a *square trotter*. By 1836 *square* meant full or complete, as a *square meal*, though people didn't talk about *three squares a day* until 1882. By the 1850s *to square* meant to put a matter straight and later to pay a debt.

As early as 1804, however, *square* had come to mean fair, honest, as in *square fight*, with *square talk* coming in 1860, *square deal* appearing as a card player's term in the 1880s, and *square shooter* in 1920. However, it was Theodore Roosevelt who popularized the term *square deal* in its general sense. He used it against business trusts soon after he succeeded the assassinated President McKinley in 1901, then made a *Square* Deal his slogan during his successful 1904 Presidential campaign. His use of the term made it the forerunner of Franklin D. Roosevelt's 1933–37 *New Deal* and Truman's 1949–52 *Fair Deal*.

In the late 1920s prostitutes, con men, and barkeeps started calling self-righteous suckers *square Johns*. By 1943 *square* was jazz musician use for those too old-fashioned or unsophisticated to appreciate their music. The term was spread by bop and cool musicians in the late 1940s and early 50s, and then by beatniks and hippies, who used it pejoratively to refer to old-fashioned people and conformists.

Steak, Ham, Barbecue, Scrapple, Jerky, and Pemmican

Steak, rather than the hamburger or the hot dog, is probably the most typical American food. *Steak* (from Old Norse *steik*, stick) has meant a strip of meat or fish cooked on a stick over a fire since the 15th century. From the earliest colonial times until the 1860s what you and I call a steak was called a *beefsteak*, to distinguish it from the often more common venison steaks, buffalo steaks, bear steaks, halibut steaks, etc., and the lesser-known *gopher steaks* (1856) and *mackerel steaks* (1859). By the 1760s some colonial inns and eating establishments were billing themselves as *beef steak houses*. Then around 1866 the first Texas longhorns reached New York via the Chisholm Trail and the railroads and soon the backyard cows, pigs, and chickens, and the wild deer and buffalo, had a competitor—beef raised solely for eating. Thus the modern steak and the cowboy were born together, and since the mid 1860s *steak* has meant beefsteak. By the end of the 1860s the *beef steak house* was simply called a *steak house*.

Various types of steaks have been in style over the years, depending on butchers' cuts and our changing tastes. We have talked about the:

> *porterhouse steak*, the first native American steak and steak name to become widely known. It was popularized as the "porterhouse beefsteak" around 1814 by Martin Harrison at his New York

porterhouse (an alehouse serving all malt liquors, including porter), which gave it its name. Years later, after the Civil War, Mark Twain said that steak and coffee was the most common American breakfast of his day and by "steak" he still meant porterhouse, his breakfast steak being an inch-and-a-half thick, pan-fried, and served with a creamed mushroom gravy.

tenderloin steak became popular soon after the porterhouse, and Americans were ordering it by name by 1828. It soon became the choice and most expensive cut, served in fancy restaurants.

T-bone steak appeared in 1928, after which many porterhouse steaks were called *T-bones*. It became the most popular steak until after World War II and was the steak men meant when they ordered *steak smothered with onions*.

sirloin steak became the favorite when steak re-emerged after the meat shortage of World War II. *Sirloin* is just a modern spelling of *surloyn* (Old French *surlonge*, *sur*, over + *longe*, loin, hip, hence "over the loin," a hip cut), which had been around since the 16th century. However, legend has it that the spelling was changed to *sir-* because this cut was knighted for its excellence.

Popular taste now demanded a *thick sirloin*, broiled over charcoal if possible. Thus in the late 1940s and 50s restaurants often advertised the mouth-watering *charcoal-broiled steaks*. Also, with the advent of the thick charcoal-broiled sirloin in the 1940s, *rare*, *medium*, and *well done* became a part of our steak language. *Rare* (Old English *hrēr*, half-cooked) and *well done* had been in the language of cooking a long time—but until the 1800s usually referred to eggs, *rare* meaning soft-boiled and *well done* meaning hard-boiled. Incidentally, it was Thomas Jefferson who introduced the combination of beefsteak and French fries to the colonies.

Pork products were a colonial staple and, from the first days of the Virginia Colony, were the most plentiful and the cheapest southern meats. This was because pork was the only meat improved by smoking (very important in the days before refrigeration) and because the imported European pigs had a population explosion in warm, lush colonial Virginia. Needing no care or milking, no fences or barns, pigs swarmed through the woods, fields, and streets, eating crops, wild plants, rattlesnakes, and garbage. Pigs were so common in Virginia that they weren't even counted as part of a dead man's estate.

Virginia hams, also then called *Tidewater hams*, were being exported to England under these names as early as the 1630s, though the names then meant any hams from Virginia or the tidewater region. Not until the 1820s did *Virginia ham* take on the specific meaning of a peanut- and corn-fed ham cured and smoked in a certain way.

Smithfield ham, from Smithfield, Virginia, an early colonial settlement, was talked about long before 1908, when the term came to mean only ham from the region's peanut-fed hogs, cured in

To devil *has meant to cook with hot spices or condiments since 1800. This is from a 1906 ad.*

hickory, oak, apple, and peanut-shell smoke, then aged for about a year.

sugar-cured ham was in the language by the 1830s, for a ham cured in brown sugar and smoked over green hickory. *Country cured ham* is merely a 1930s term for the common, saltier variety of smoked ham, black on the outside from hickory smoke. Today just plain *ham* (a 17th-century word from Old English *hamme*, hollow of the bent knee, later the thigh and buttock) can be "cured" by a quick injection of brine and smoked for a few days over sawdust.

Ham and greens was a common dish by the 1780s, but people didn't talk about *ham and eggs* in one breath, as one dish, until the 1830s. *Jambalaya* (from Spanish *jamón*, ham) was a 1700s Spanish dish of ham and rice that was later made popular in New Orleans as a Creole dish of rice, seafood, and fowl, most Americans not hearing of it until the 1870s. Ham gravy, made from ham drippings and water, often with a teaspoon of coffee added in the South, has been around for a long time, but the name *red ham gravy* and *redeye gravy* (from the small "eye" of gravy that forms in the center of the ham during cooking) were not common until the 1930s. Another pork product, *chitterlings*, which are usually spelled and pronounced *chittlins* and are pieces of batter-dipped small intestine fried in deep fat, seem very southern to us today; but the word is akin to the German *Kutteln* (entrails, tripe), and both the word and the dish were probably introduced into America by the Pennsylvania Dutch. We had been talking about *side bacon* since 1850 and *side meat* since 1873 (referring to the bacon or pork from the side of a hog), with the term *fat back* (the top of a side of pork, free of meat and bone) not appearing until the 1900s.

Barbecue has been popular in America since early colonial times. The word comes from the Spanish *barbacoa*, which Spanish explorers and adventurers of the 1660s got from the Taino tribe of Haiti, where it meant a framework of sticks on which to roast or smoke meat (it's related to the French *boucan*, which gives us the word *buccaneer*, see PIRATES, PRIVATEERS, AND BUCCANEERS). By 1709 in America *barbecue* meant a whole animal carcass roasted over an open fire, by 1733 a social gathering to roast and eat it, and by 1800 a political rally at which barbecue was served—a good way to attract and hold a large group of people through a long series of speeches. For example, William Henry Harrison, Whig candidate for President, held a mammoth political barbecue in 1840 at which party workers and prospective voters consumed eighteen tons of meat and pies (he won the election). The last such Presidential political barbecues were given by Lyndon Johnson at his Texas ranch, 1965–69.

Barbecues, however, are associated with cowboys in our mind and whole roasted steers were traditional for large cowboy gatherings: early recipes describe how to dig a pit ten feet deep, build a

A barbecue in Victoria, Texas, July 4, 1919.

special ladder for climbing into and out of it, etc. Railroad ties have been a favorite cooking fuel and a roll of wire fencing is still a favorite grill in Texas. Such gargantuan feasts are a far cry from the suburban *backyard barbecues* that became popular in the early 1950s, in which steak, chicken, or hamburgers were cooked over small *portable grills*. These replaced the *wienie roasts* of the 1920s and the *steak fries* of the 1930s in popularity and by the late 1950s were widely called *cookouts* (this word originating in the southwest U.S. around 1949). *Barbecue* also came to have a slang meaning in the 1920s, especially among blacks, of a mouth-watering girl, the general public being aware of this use mainly from the song "Struttin' with Some Barbecue."

Philadelphia scrapple (1817) has been a legendary mainstay of the upper-class Philadelphia breakfast for generations. It contains pork shoulder and neck meat while ordinary *scrapple* (literally "little scraps") is simply a Pennsylvania Dutch dish using scraps from hog butchering boiled with cornmeal, onions, herbs, and spices, and chilled into a loaf, then fried in slices. *Scrapple* was well known outside Pennsylvania Dutch regions by 1855 and was also called *pawnhaus* by the 1860s (a Pennsylvania Dutch term for finely chopped food or leftovers) and *poor-do* by the 1900s.

Since drying, salting, and smoking are the only ways to preserve meat without ice, refrigeration, or modern canning, early Americans talked about *salt horse*, *jerky*, and *pemmican*. In the 17th century large slabs of dried beef were called *jerkin beef*, and dried and salted meat, especially salt pork, was called *salt horse*, which was the meat carried on the *Mayflower*. We associate *jerky* with frontiersmen, soldiers, and westward-moving pioneers. It consisted of inch-thick strips of beef that were dried and then smoked. Sometimes we used the Spanish spelling *charqui*, the word coming from the Incan word *echarqui*, dried meat, which the Spanish got from the Quechua tribe of Peru and Ecuador.

Despite jerky and salt horse, the miracle food that allowed early explorers, trappers, and traders to survive in the wilderness for long periods was borrowed from the North American Indians, *pemmican* (Cree *pimekan*, based on Cree *pime*, fat). It consisted of strips of dried meat, usually deer meat in the East and buffalo in the West, or of jerky pounded into *beat meat*, and mixed with an almost equal quantity of fat. Dried berries and sometimes maple sugar were added to enhance the flavor, 25 to 100 pounds being made at a time and packed into skin bags or pressed into cakes. This food would last, and the meat-fat-berry combination was nourishing. In fact, without pemmican, jerky, and salt horse, America might never have been explored so that we can talk about steaks, ham, and barbecue today.

Sunday and Blue Laws

Sunday has always been widely talked about in America, first as the Sabbath, then increasingly after the Civil War as a day of recreation and family outings. Though *Sunday* is a pagan name (the pagan days of the week were named after the sun, moon, and the five visible planets), early accounts are full of the austerity of the Sabbath, which in colonial days began at sundown on Saturday.

As early as 1640 the General Court of New Haven passed strict puritanical laws making adultery, drunkenness, and failure to attend Sunday church services criminal offenses carrying severe punishment. The term *blue law* was first recorded in 1781 in *A General History of Connecticut* by Samuel Peters, a Loyalist clergyman who had fled the colonies seven years before. Full of hatred and anti-American exaggerations and inaccuracies, Peters's book claimed that in the New Haven area: Church of England clergymen were banned; citizens were forbidden to offer food, drink, or directions to Quakers; people were allowed to wear only those hair styles and clothing styles proper to their station in life; only clergymen were allowed to cross rivers on the Sabbath, and on the Sabbath, too, kissing, cooking, housecleaning, and shaving were forbidden to all. Some of these items were fact, some fiction, but *blue law*, often called *Connecticut blue law*, came to mean any such strict puritanical law (not just Sabbath ones), and by 1834 Connecticut was often called *the blue law state*.

Why *blue laws?* Because they were printed on blue paper (though some say the term comes from the blue bruises and dried blood brought forth from the punishment for failure to observe

GOING TO MEETING IN 1776.

these laws). By the 1880s, however, *blue laws* no longer meant any strict moral laws enacted by a state but only those regulating observance of the Sabbath, especially those limiting business and entertainment on Sundays.

Since such things as playing, cooking, and hitching up horses were forbidden on the Sabbath in early colonial days, talking about a "cold Sunday supper" is older than talking about a big, hot *Sunday dinner*, and a *Sunday walk* meant the walk to church long before it meant a pleasure stroll.

> *No one shall run on the Sabbath day or walk in his garden, or elsewhere, except reverently to and from meeting.*
> 17th-century General Court of New Haven, Connecticut law

Among themselves, children often spoke with dislike of the day when they were not allowed to run or play. They spent the Sabbath as did their parents, reading the Bible before and after the many hours spent in church (the separate *Sunday school* for children was a new American term in 1785). Young children might talk with excitement, however, about the toy wooden *Noah's arks*, complete with animals, they were allowed to "examine" on Sundays or the very popular *animal books* they were allowed to read, these being religious because they showed Adam naming all the animals.

The Sabbath was also responsible for the tradition and term *Saturday night bath* (which didn't become common until about the 1830s). It was also responsible for calling one's best clothes, the clothes one wore to "meetings" (a 17th-century English word for nonconformist church services), *meeting clothes* by 1775, *Sunday-go-to-meeting clothes* by 1831, and *Sunday best* by 1849. By the 1870s Sundays were much more relaxed for many Americans, baseball was already a Sunday game, and *Sunday stroll* and *Sunday picnic* were common terms. The pleasurable *Sunday drive* in the family car was a term already in wide use in the 1920s and those who

Colonial children were not to play with toys on the Sabbath but could "examine" Noah's arks.

493

drove slowly or with hesitation, as if the Sunday drives were their only driving experience, were already being called *Sunday drivers*. *Sunday punch* was first recorded in 1931, and again referred to one's best, but this time to a prizefighter's punch rather than to one's best clothes.

Supermarket

Grocer (Latin *grossus*, great) has been used in England since the 15th century to mean a wholesale trader in spices, fruits, sugar, whiskey, etc. Hence we have had the British *greengrocer* of fruits and vegetables and the American *liquor grocery*, a term still common in the mid 19th century. Americans have been calling such establishments *groceries* since the 1650s, when they were usually general stores, *trading houses* (1637), or *trading posts* (1796). The term *grocery store* appeared in the 1770s and by the 1840s enough American towns were laid out on the grid pattern for people to be talking about the *corner grocery*.

Tea merchant George Huntington Hartford (see COFFEE, TEA, AND MILK) opened his first retail tea store in 1859 at 31 Vesey Street, New York City, and in the next ten years it became one of the most successful *tea houses* (a 1689 British term) and mail order tea suppliers in the country. In 1869, now selling coffee and spices as well as tea, Hartford began adding more stores, naming his expanding company *The Great Atlantic and Pacific Tea Co.*, later known to millions as the *A&P*, to take advantage of the nationwide furor over the driving of the golden spike at Promontory Point, Utah, completing the nation's first transcontinental railroad (it was not until 1917, however, that the company actually spanned the nation by opening a store on the West Coast). Constantly increasing its line of groceries, the company grew to 29 stores by 1880 and to more than 200 stores in the 1890s, continuing to make good use of the transcontinental railroad by being the first to bring California oranges, Georgia peaches, and Texas grapefruit to middle-class American tables, then, as a major revolution in the 1890s, introducing the cash-and-carry policy—no deliveries and no charge accounts—to the grocery business. Thus the A&P formed the first *grocery chain*, though the term wasn't common until World War I. Many other grocery chains also grew from tea companies: the Jones Brothers Tea Co., established in Brooklyn in 1872, became the *Grand Union;* The Great Western Tea Company became *Kroger's* in 1902: and the Ginter Co., the John T. Conner Co., and the O'Keefe Co. joined in 1916 to become the *First National Stores*, often known by the acronym *FINAST* (FIrst NAtional STores).

Clarence Saunders is usually credited with having established the first self-service grocery in 1916, in Memphis, Tennessee, but there were several "wait on yourself" groceries established in

California around the same time, which were often called *groceterias* (after the self-service cafe*teria*). Saunders advertised and sold franchises under the name of *Piggly-Wiggly*, and walking through a Piggly-Wiggly turnstile was the first widely talked about experience many Americans had with self-service groceries. By 1929 there were 3,000 Piggly-Wiggly self-service grocery stores in 800 cities and towns serving 2.5 million customers every day. Many of these stores were eventually bought by other grocery chains and became the first *supermarkets*, a word that became popular in the 1920s in California—though the first *shopping cart* was not patented until 1930. By the end of World War II, the corner grocery had all but disappeared and when Americans said *grocery* we usually meant a large supermarket, an American word now known around the world.

Taxi!

Long before people were shouting for taxis they were shouting for *cabs*, an 1827 English shortening of *cabriolet*, a one-horse carriage with two seats and a folding top (early cars with folding tops were also called *cabriolets*). *Cabriolet* means "little leap" in French (from Latin *capreolus*, wild goat)—so *cabs* were supposed to be very fast. Another popular horse-drawn cab, especially in New York and Boston after the late 1850s, was the *hansom cab*, a two-wheeled one-

495

A hansom cab in Washington, D.C., in the early 1900s.

horse carriage with the driver seated behind and above the passenger compartment. It was named for English architect Joseph Hansom, who patented the *Hansom safety cab* in 1834.

The first *taximeter motor cab* appeared on the streets of New York on October 25, 1907. Soon people were calling them *taximeter cabs*, then *taxis* (all from *taximètre*, tariff meter, originally coined by a French company that made meters for horse-drawn cabs). By 1929 there were 29,000 taxis in New York (more than twice as many as today) and *taxi* had taken on the connotation of "hired"; thus *taxi dancer* was in the language by the mid 1930s.

Hack (1733) was originally short for *hackney* (Old French *haquenée*, Latin *equus*, horse), an ordinary horse for riding and driving, then by 1796 meant a horse and carriage for hire and later a person

A taxicab of the 1920s.

Sometimes jitney *is used to indicate a privately owned local bus service, even though the fare may be far more than five cents.*

who hires himself out for routine work, as a "literary hack." It was first applied to those taximeter motor cabs around 1912.

Jitney (French *jeton*, token, counter, coin) originally meant a coin in the U.S. (a *jitney bag* was a coin purse), then especially a nickel by 1903. The word, sometimes spelled *gitney*, seems to have spread from St. Louis and environs, when that area was still mainly French. It has meant a private car serving a buslike route since 1915, when jitneys or *jitney buses*, usually early Ford cars, began to compete with the streetcars in Los Angeles, charging passengers a *jitney*, a nickel, a ride.

The Telephone—The Li-on Is Busy

Mr. Watson, come here, I want you!
Alexander Graham Bell to Thomas A. Watson,
March 10, 1876, the first intelligible words
transmitted over a telephone

Alexander Graham Bell's gallows phone, *so called because of its shape, over which voice sounds were transmitted for the first time, on June 3, 1875.*

Alexander Graham Bell uttered these words just three days after he had received his patent on a *telephone* (Greek *tēle*, afar + *phōnē*, sound, voice). He had just spilled acid on his clothes and was calling for help.

Since then the telephone has changed our way of talking and living. It has helped make our language less formal, because the tone of phone conversations is less formal than that of letters. The phone also made possible a new type of communication, instant talk with anyone at anytime, impulsive business and personal talk in which we make, change, or cancel appointments, plans, reservations, purchases, opinions, and judgments, and spread news and gossip, without taking the time to write, wait for personal meetings—or have second thoughts. The telephone also broke the age-

497

The faculty and students of the Pemberton Avenue School for the Deaf, Boston, 1871. The young Alexander Graham Bell, teacher of the teachers, is at the right of the top row.

old isolation of the housewife—at a time when almost all women were housewives. Yet, the main change the telephone has made is simply this: it has greatly decreased the amount we write and increased the amount we talk. Today there are well over 430 million phones in the world, one-third of them in the United States—and Americans make more than 350 billion phone calls a year. The li-ons have indeed been busy—and the formal pen, spelling, punctuation, grammar, and syntax have given way to the informal voice.

The very first telephones were sold in pairs, with a direct wire between them; it wasn't until 1878 that Bell himself mentioned the possibility of *telephone cables* carrying many wires to *central offices,* so that any home or office could talk with any other. In 1878, too, a *call* already meant a telephone call and by 1882 *to call* meant to reach via telephone. Although telephone service was very expensive during its first decades ($240 a year in Manhattan) there were already 60,000 phones in the U.S. by 1880, about one-fifth of them Bell telephones. Then rate reductions led to widespread use of the telephone: by 1910 there were almost 6 million phones in the U.S. and by the end of World War I over 10 million—that's when you really would have begun to hear America talking by phone.

Since the telephone was developed to be part of telegraphy and used some of its equipment, it used many telegraph terms. Here are some important names and terms the telephone has added to our language:

> *telephone,* 1790s, when it meant both a megaphone and a speaking tube, as for the hard-of-hearing. Bell's invention was also called a

speaking telegraph in the 1870s. The shortened form *phone* has been in use since the 1880s.

Western Electric Manufacturing Co., founded in 1864 by two Western Union men and Elisha Gray (who invented the telephone about the same time Bell did but lost out in patents and law suits). It began making telephone equipment soon after 1876 and was acquired by the Bell Co. in 1882.

Alexander Graham Bell (1847–1922) was born in Edinburgh, Scotland, and moved to Canada with his parents in 1870. His father, a well-known speech teacher, had developed the Visual Speech Code, a diagram showing the position of the lips, tongue, etc., in making speech sounds. At the age of twenty-four Bell substituted for his father at the Boston School for the Deaf in teaching this code, and stayed to teach teachers of the deaf (he married a deaf girl and one of his early backers was the father of one of his deaf students). He also worked on developing a *harmonic telegraph*, which grew into the telephone. People began hearing about Bell in 1876–77 when he demonstrated his *telephone apparatus* in Providence, Boston, New York, etc., and when his telephone was exhibited at the 1876 Philadelphia Centennial Exposition, where Dom Pedro, Emperor of Brazil, exclaimed, "My word! It talks!" Incidentally, the telephone wasn't invented by an American: Bell became a citizen in 1882, six years after his patent was granted.

Thomas A. Watson (1854–1934), a Boston technician and machinist, made the apparatus for Bell's experiments, inventing the *telephone*

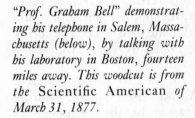

"Prof. Graham Bell" demonstrating his telephone in Salem, Massachusetts (below), by talking with his laboratory in Boston, fourteen miles away. This woodcut is from the Scientific American *of March 31, 1877.*

As this replica shows, the first telephone switchboard was indeed a board with switches.

bell and the *receiver hook*, as well as making the early phones, such as the *gallows type*, the *box telephone*, and the *head telephone*.

the Bell Telephone Co., formed in 1877 by Bell, his father-in-law, Watson, and three others; *the Bell System*, this name was first officially used in 1908; *Ma Bell*, an old familiar name for the Bell System, became widely known in 1947 when it was used derogatorily during a strike against the company.

telephone wire, 1877; *telephone pole*, early 1880s.

hand receiver, 1877; *wall set*, 1878, it had a crank to generate power to reach the operator.

operator, late 1870s (it had meant a telegraph operator since the 1840s); *hello girl*, mid 1880s, widely used, originally humorously; *telephone girl*, 1893. The first women operators were Emma M. Nutt and her sister Stella A. Nutt, employed by the Boston Telephone Dispatch Co. in 1878, both women having previously been telegraph operators. Many other women soon became telephone operators because they were considered to have more pleasing voices and nimbler fingers than men—and were also content to earn $10 a week.

switchboard, exchange, trunk line, central, late 1870s and early 1880s. When phone networks had few subscribers (New Haven, Connecticut, originally had 21), they could all be connected by one operator. Soon larger *switchboards* (an 1860s telegraph term) were needed and often *switchmen* (usually boys) were used to plug in the connections at the far ends of a switchboard-filled room. By 1878 the local phones and boards were called an *exchange;* in the 1880s *trunk lines* connected one exchange with another, so people could call out of their local area. By the late 1880s both a switchboard location and an operator were called *central*. Plugging in a caller to his exchange, that exchange to another one, and from there to the person being called made "We've been cut off" a common compliant until the early 1920s, by which time most switching was mechanized.

telephone number, Plaza-, Highland-, etc., early 1880s. *Telephone numbers* were first used in Lowell, Massachusetts, in 1879 during a measles epidemic, a local doctor fearing that the four operators might get sick and any substitutes would find it difficult to learn the names and connections of the subscribers. By the late 1880s *telephone number* was shortened to *number:* "Sorry, wrong number" became common by 1900. In the 1880s, too, some big-city exchanges began to have neighborhood or district names, such as *Nassau, Gramercy, Highland*, etc. In 1930, numbers were added to exchange names, so people began using such terms as *Plaza-1*, or *Butterfield-8* (which became the title of a 1935 John O'Hara novel).

the li-on is busy—this immortal intonation is said to have first been used at the Metropolitan Telephone and Telegraph Co.'s old Nassau exchange in New York City, by a Brooklyn-born operator around 1882.

American Telephone and Telegraph (abbreviated AT&T) was founded in 1885 to establish and operate long-distance lines; it was known as "the Long Distance Co." until it took over the Bell Co. in 1889. In 1908–13 it launched and pursued a policy of buying competing telephone services (at that time subscribers to one service

A telephone traffic operator at his switchboard in 1885.

A *telephone* operator *at her switchboard in 1920.*

could not be connected to those of another) with the slogan "One Policy, One System, Universal Service." This ownership of local companies lasted until 1982 when, in a settlement of an antitrust case, AT&T agreed to divest itself of local telephone companies in order to concentrate on manufacturing telephone and other communications equipment, to provide long-distance service, and to develop other electronic communications systems and services.

private line, party line. Although the first few lines of 1877 were all private, by the early 1880s almost all were shared, by as many as 20 subscribers: AT&T then first offered *private lines* in 1886 and the other, standard lines were called *party lines* by the early 1900s.

night rates, an 1887 term, when the Bell System began to offer lower rates at night over some of its lines. Such lower rates also became *Sunday rates* in 1936.

desk set, 1892, a stand-up phone, with the mouthpiece-transmitter on a vertical stalk that had a hook for the earpiece-receiver.

long distance became truly long distance in 1892, when a New York–Chicago line was inaugurated. Coast-to-coast service began in January 1915, over 13,600 miles of wire, a call taking 25 minutes to go through and costing a minimum of $20.70.

number please? In 1895, J. W. Thompson, city manager of the Chicago Telephone Co., wrote a letter to his chief operator, Miss Mesick, in which he said:

In answering calls the query "Number Please?" spoken in a pleasant tone of voice and with rising inflection must be invariably employed.

The entire Bell system followed this rule by 1904. Before that operators had usually asked "What number?" (Thomas Alva Edison had suggested we answer a telephone caller not with "hello" but by saying "ahoy.")

telephone directory, 1890s; *phone book*, 1900s. The first *listings* were in New Haven and New York City in 1878, giving only names and addresses, numbers not yet being used.

In large cities in the 1930s exchange numbers were added to the existing name, giving us such terms as Plaza-1 *and* Butterfield 8.

A desk set phone *adapted to public phone use in 1895; it could not be used without depositing a coin.*

A coin-operated telephone *of 1900.*

Howard G. Stokes, who coined the New York Telephone Co. slogan The Voice with the Smile *in 1912, shown here in the 1950s.*

telephone booth, late 1890s, when it was also called a *telephone box*. *Pay station* is a term dating from 1895. Though some enterprising men had gone into the business of charging others for use of their phone as early as 1878, the first practical public coin-operated telephone was installed in Hartford, Connecticut, in 1889. "It's your nickel—so talk" applied until 1951, when the 10-cent local call went into effect (some cities began charging 25 cents for local calls in the early 1980s).

yellow pages, 1906, when the Michigan State Telephone Co. of Detroit printed the first directory with classified advertising on yellow paper.

Information, 1906. Early operators served as Information and also would tell callers the time, give street directions, phone subscribers to wake them up, relay messages, and the like. By 1905–06 there were too many subscribers and calls for this, so many larger phone companies began training special Information operators.

give me a ring, I'll give you a buzz, by 1910 both *ring* and *buzz* meant a telephone call and to *ring up* someone meant to call him or her on the telephone.

The Voice with the Smile, a New York Telephone Co. slogan, first used in 1912.

radiotelephone, 1914, when used to connect Montauk Point, Long Island, with the mainland; a radiotelephone was first used aboard a ship in 1916 during a U.S. Navy mobilization test.

dial, as the circular plate with numbers and letters to be rotated by the finger to make a telephone connection, was used in the 1879 patent for the device. *Dial telephone* and *dial tone* were first used in

A *special long-distance* telephone booth *around 1900, with carved wood, stained glass, and carpeting.*

Automatic switching *had replaced almost all operators and switchboards when this picture was taken in 1941.*

the 1890s, though it wasn't until 1919 that these terms came into popular use—when new switching equipment and the large number of calls swamping the operators made dialing (and automatic switching) practical. The first *dial phones* went into general operation in Norfolk, Virginia, on November 8, 1919.

French phone, Continental phone, first available in the Bell system in 1927. As early as 1876 Bell had a wooden *Butterstamp phone* (so called because it looked like a dairy's butterstamp), which had a combined receiver-transmitter held in one hand. However, it was Robert Brown of Western Union who combined an Edison transmitter and a Gray receiver on one hand-held metal bar and introduced it in Paris, where he had been sent to open an exchange in 1879. This set, modernized and improved, had become popular in Europe and was thus known in the U.S. as the *French phone* or *Continental phone.*

At the tone the time will be . . . New York City established the first separate time-service number (MEridian 7-1212) in August, 1928.

an Ameche, slang for a telephone since the early 1940s, after movie actor Don Ameche played the lead in the 1939 movie *The Story of Alexander Graham Bell.*

red phone, mid 1950s. A special White House military phone the President is to use to signal an atomic warfare counterattack (to defend against or counter a surprise attack against the U.S.). Incidentally, the first telephone in the White House was installed for Grover Cleveland in the late 1880s and he always answered it himself.

colored phone, 1956. Before this date most phones were black.

the pipe, the horn, slang for telephone since the late 1950s.

Princess phone, 1959. A small, lightweight phone originally advertised as a private phone for teenage girls.

WATS line, 1961; an acronym for *Wide Area Telephone Service,* as provided to business or other customers placing many calls outside a local area so that each call is not handled or billed as a long-distance call.

Touch-tone telephone, 1963, when the dial began to be replaced by a panel of faster push-buttons, each button making a distinctive tone when pushed (however, the word *Touch-tone* was registered as a trademark, and the system tested, as early as 1960).

Picturephone, 1964, sometimes also called a *videophone;* the individual conversing parties could see each other on a small television-type screen (the Bell Telephone System began this service between New York, Washington, and Chicago in 1964, but it proved too expensive, was never expanded, and was discontinued in 1978). Since 1980, combinations of telephone lines and closed-circuit TV have been used by business firms for *videoconferences.*

hot line, mid 1960s, a special direct emergency line between the White House and the Kremlin so that the leaders of the two nations can communicate instantly to avoid an accidental atomic war (a Teletype is actually used for such emergency communications). By the late 1960s *hot line* meant any special direct telephone line, as one on which to ask for help or advice, take business orders, etc.

Early Bird, this first commercial communications satellite was launched in 1965, to hover over the Atlantic, providing 240 two-way telephone circuits between the U.S. and Europe.

911, the Bell system adopted this telephone number nationwide for police, fire, ambulance, and other emergency services in 1968.

Thanksgiving, Turkey, and Dressing

Thanksgiving was a familiar word to the early colonists, who often gave thanks to God. Local ministers and colonial governors proclaimed many a "day of thanksgiving" for the recovery of a sick person, the end of an epidemic, the safe arrival of a ship, an Indian truce, or a good harvest. Later, the Continental Congress declared several days of thanksgiving for various military victories and newly inaugurated President Washington proclaimed November 26, 1789, a day of thanksgiving to God for the establishment of our new nation. Thus our harvest-time *Thanksgiving* (1632) and *Thanksgiving Day* (1674) were not unique in early America.

The first *Thanksgiving* was celebrated in mid October, 1621, ten months after the Pilgrims landed in Plymouth. The first winter and its "General Sickness" (probably scurvy) had killed nearly half the original 102 Pilgrims. Then summer had given the survivors new hope and the harvest of their 20 acres of Indian corn brought them relief and rejoicing (their European crops had failed). This was the native corn that the Indian Squanto had taught them to plant, with fish as fertilizer. Governor Bradford thus decreed a day of "thanksgiving" for all to "rejoyce together" because they "had all things in good plenty." Four men were sent out to hunt wildfowl and brought back enough to last a week; there is no record of their bag, but it normally would have included the huge wild turkeys that were so plentiful. The Pilgrims' good friend, Chief Massasoit of the Wampanoags, was invited and came with 90 brightly painted braves: thus there were more Indians than Pilgrims at our first Thanksgiving.

Everyone did rejoice together: Captain Miles Standish paraded his men to the accompaniment of the one drummer and the one trumpeter, volleys were fired, a type of croquet called *stoneball* was played, and Pilgrim men and Indian braves competed in shooting, hand wrestling, throwing, running, and jumping contests (the women and girls mainly spent their time cooking, another Thanksgiving tradition). The gala occasion went on for three days. Everyone gorged on venison (Massasoit's braves had brought in five deer and other things to add to the feast), wild duck, goose, smoked eel, clams, oysters, lobster, greens such as leeks and watercress (and perhaps some root vegetables), corn, corn bread, pop corn, wild plums, and dried cherries, strawberries, and

The first Thanksgiving, celebrated in October 1621.

gooseberries, all washed down with strong sweet wine. Turkey was probably served, but cranberry sauce and pumpkin pie were not. Most of the cooking and eating was done outdoors, the game being roasted on spits and the shellfish in hot coals.

There is no record of a Thanksgiving in 1622, but many of our traditional trimmings appeared at the Pilgrims' next Thanksgiving, July 30, 1623. There, roasted wild turkey, cranberry sauce, and *pumpkin pudding* (pie without a top crust; our term *pumpkin pie* was first recorded in 1654) were definitely served. The turkey was probably served with dressing, as was all roast fowl at the time. Since 1621 the Pilgrim women had learned that cranberries not only went well with turkey but that they helped prevent scurvy. The cranberries weren't called *cranberries* but either *craneberries* (German *kraanbere*, because their stamens resembled cranes' beaks) or *bounceberries* (because they were bounced to see if they were ripe).

The Pilgrims' intermittent Thanksgivings grew into a New England tradition, becoming an annual day of celebration and thanksgiving to God in Connecticut in 1649, in Massachusetts Bay Colony by 1669, in Plymouth Colony itself in 1688, and in all of New England by the 1780s. New Englanders spread the tradition westward, but it meant nothing to the South; many governors outside New England resisted proclaiming Thanksgiving, because it was primarily a religious observance, and state and church were to be kept separate. In 1827, however, Mrs. Sarah Joseph Hall, first as the editor of Boston's *Ladies' Magazine* and later of its widely read successor, *Godey's Lady's Book* of Philadelphia, started a crusade to make Thanksgiving Day a nationwide observance. Her campaign eventually led to President Lincoln's proclaiming August 6 as a national Thanksgiving Day in 1863, then soon making another *Thanksgiving Day Proclamation* for 1864:

> *[I] invite my fellow citizens . . . to set apart and observe the last Thursday of November next as a day of thanksgiving and praise to our beneficent Father who dwelleth in the heavens.*
> Abraham Lincoln, October 3, 1863

Thus Lincoln established Thanksgiving as a national holiday and made it the fourth Thursday in November. Each year from 1864 to 1939 the President of the United States proclaimed Thanksgiving as the fourth Thursday of November. Then in 1939 President Franklin Roosevelt changed the date to the third Thursday in November, to help the economy by giving stores an extra week of Christmas business between Thanksgiving and Christmas. Americans really talked about that! Even though no one knows on which October days the Pilgrims' first 1621 Thanksgiving was held, even though their 1623 Thanksgiving was on July 30, even though Lincoln's first nationwide Thanksgiving of 1863 was on August 6, by 1939 the fourth Thursday of November seemed sacred to many Americans. There were so many cries of outrage during the next three "early" Thanksgivings that Congress passed a Joint Resolution in December 1941 changing it back to the last Thursday in November.

Now, how about that Thanksgiving *turkey*? Our North American bird was erroneously named *turkey* by European explorers as early as 1587, in confusion with the European turkey cock, a completely different bird (a mere guinea fowl, which got its name because it was introduced into Europe from Guinea through Turkey). Other stories, that our word *turkey* comes from some Indian word for it, or from the doctor on Columbus' ship shouting *Tukki!* (Hebrew for "big bird") when he first saw one, are not convincing. Our term *Thanksgiving turkey* didn't appear until 1829, and it wasn't called a *Thanksgiving bird* until 1870. Thanksgiving itself wasn't referred to as *Turkey Day* until 1916.

We called the southern brown vulture a *turkey buzzard* by 1672 and a *turkey vulture* by 1823. We were shooting turkeys for prizes at *turkey shoots* in the 1840s and calling fowling pieces *turkey busters* by the 1860s. New England colonists called salted cod *Cape Cod turkey*, and in the 1920s and 30s *Irish turkey* was a humorous term for corn beef and cabbage, as well as a hobo and army term for stew or hash with unidentifiable ingredients.

To talk turkey meant to speak plainly by 1830 (turkey gobbling was a distinct, natural sound on frontier farms) and the expression soon became *to talk cold turkey;* hence *cold turkey* came to mean cold facts, unpleasant truths. By the 1940s *cold turkey* was a drug addict's term for a sudden and complete withdrawal from drugs (reinforced by the addict's goose bumps, resembling uncooked turkey skin).

In 1908 everyone was talking about the new ragtime dance, the *turkey trot*, which resembled just that in the way the dancers moved, with a springing step on the balls of their feet while jerking their shoulders up and down. In 1873 *turkey* was recorded as meaning easy profits and soon meant a person easily duped, a victim, or a dumb or unsuspecting person, because such a person was easy to "catch" (this slang use came into vogue again in the late 1970s). By the late 1920s a *turkey* was a theatrical flop and within a few years meant any unsuccessful or useless thing.

When eating turkey or other fowl, early Americans were asked if they wanted a leg, thigh, or slice of breast. In the late 1850s, however, these words seemed immodest to Victorian sensibilities and the terms *white meat* and *dark meat* became common. How embarrassed our Victorian ancestors would be to learn that these genteel terms have come to be used sexually since the 1920s as slang terms referring to attractive or available white or black women. Such genteel uses also led Americans to call the filling cooked in a turkey or other fowl both *stuffing* and *dressing*. Although early American cookbooks gave recipes for *forcemeat* (a 17th-century word, from French *farcir*, to stuff), most Americans called it *stuffing* until the 1880s; then *dressing* somehow seemed more refined and slowly became our most common word for it.

The first Macy's Thanksgiving Day parade *was held in 1924, but* Thanksgiving Day processions, *as they were originally called, first became popular in the 1860s.*

507

Thar She Blows!

was not the usual shout of the masthead lookout on a whaling ship when he sighted the spouting of whales: he usually just yelled "She blows!" or "Blows!" The helmsman would shout back "Where away?" and, once he knew the course, the chase would begin. Most such whaling terms aren't American in origin: the Dutch and then the English began large-scale *whaling* in the very early 1600s, with English ships following *whales* (Old English *hweal*, large fish) across the Atlantic on *whaling ships*.

American whaling began with the Indians, who used canoes and stone weapons to pursue and kill porpoise and right whales from the New England coast (Indians often served on early American whaling ships and many were harpooners). The colonists started whaling on Long Island in the 1640s and by 1700 Nantucket Quakers were thriving from the sale of *whale oil* (a 1435 English term) and *whale bone* (a 17th-century English term). In fact, whale oil, for lamps, candles, soap, and lubricant, was soon called *Nantucket* or *Nantucket oil*. *Whale bone* was a newer word for *baleen* (14th-century English use, from Latin *ballaena*, whale): it's not bone at all but the hornlike elastic plate in the upper jaw of certain species of whales, called *whalebone whales*, used to filter plankton from the sea. Earlier Americans used it for corset stays, bustles, hoops in hoopskirts, and for shaping *whalebone bonnets* (1830s).

It was after the Revolutionary War that the ships called *Yankee whalers* took over the seas: by 1818, 80 percent of the world's whaling was in Yankee hands and New Bedford, Massachusetts, was the world's busiest whaling port. The words of whaling seem romantic to us today, but whaling was a tough, dirty job and only the toughest, most desperate sailors would sign on for the dangerous voyages that averaged three years and took them to the far reaches of the Atlantic, Pacific, Indian, and Arctic oceans.

Call me Ishmael.
First line of Herman Melville's *Moby Dick, or The Whale*, 1851. There really was a famous whale that sailors called Moby Dick in the 1840s. In the Bible, Ishmael (the name comes from Hebrew *Yishmā'ēl*, "God hears") was the son of Abraham by Sarah's Egyptian handmaid, Hagar. The angel of the Lord told Hagar to name the son this because the Lord had heard of her ill treatment at Sarah's hands. The angel of the Lord then told Hagar that Ishmael "shall be a man like the wild ass, his hand against every man and every man's hand against him; and he shall live at odds with all his kinsmen" (Genesis 16: 1–16).

508

When the whaling ship got close enough to its prey, the *whalermen* (1665) or *whalers* (1682, it also meant whaling ships by 1800) would let down the small double-ended *whale boats* (1670s) and row close enough for the *harpooner* (a 1605 English word) to "lay it on" or "let him have it," to throw his *harpoon* (an English word of about 1600, via French *harpon*, clamp, grappling iron, from Latin and Greek *harpe*, sickle). If the whale raced through the water in an attempt to dislodge the harpoon he would give the whalers in the attached whale boat a *Nantucket sleigh ride*. Later the *blubber* (a 1664 English word, from Old English *blober*, foam, bubble) was stripped from the whale by men called *flensers* (from Danish *flense*, to strip, skin a whale or seal), then boiled in a *copper* (kettle) or *tried out* (rendered) in a *trying pot* in a *try house* (1792). The oil was extruded and stored in a *whale house* (1640s) or *oil house* (1678), which was called an *oil factory* by 1841 (by which time whaling grounds were also called *oil fields* and whale oil called *liquid gold*).

When at home, a whaling ship owner or captain might scan the sea for returning vessels from his railed rooftop *captain's walk*. When the captain himself was at sea his wife might watch for his return from this captain's walk, which would then become her *widow's walk* (not because the husband had died at sea but because the wife was a *whaling widow*, one whose husband was away whaling).

One of the best-known whaling words is *scrimshaw/schrimshaw*, the elaborately carved contrivances sailors made out of whale ivory during their long whaling voyages. First recorded in the 1840s, the word comes from Dutch *schrimpen*, to wrinkle + *schrong*, carved. It was also called *scrimshandy*, *skrimshander* (as in Melville's 1851 *Moby Dick*), and *scrimshaw-work*. A sailor who carved it was called a *scrimshonger* and carving it was called *scrimshonging*.

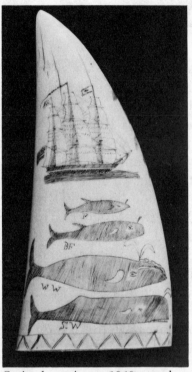

Scrimshaw *is an 1840s word,*
from the Dutch schrimpen, *to*
wrinkle + schrong, *carved*.

Whaling reached its peak in 1846, when 729 Yankee whalers were at sea. Old-fashioned whaling began to decline in the 1850s, with the introduction of the *whaling gun* (1852) and the *bomb harpoon* (1865) with its explosive head. During the Civil War many Yankee whalers were sunk by Confederate ships and after the war more modern methods of whaling had to be developed so that the whalers could compete with the new petroleum industry. Ever more modern methods of whaling have, however, proved self-defeating; larger, faster ships and modern methods of finding and killing whales have almost wiped out several species, and the question may well be which will become extinct first, whaling or whales?

ToMAYto or ToMAHto?

ToMAYto is the preferred and general American pronunciation. A hundred years ago, however, the fashion in America was to cultivate the broad *a* or *ah* sound as a mark of good breeding, so *toMAHto*, *AHnt* (for aunt), *poTAHto*, *vAHz* (for vase), etc., were heard. Today a few people still think such broad *a* pronunciations sound "high class"; but unless they are used by New Englanders and others as part of their natural accent, they just sound phony to the rest of us.

Tomatoes (from the Aztec Nahuatl *tomatl*) were originally thought to be as poisonous as their relative the nightshade, and thus were seldom eaten until the end of the 18th century, when such daring gourmets as Thomas Jefferson began to serve them. The general public, however, kept its distance until the 1860s, when tomatoes became common because of the ease with which they could be canned. In the 1880s *salads* finally became popular in America, and then so did the term *tomato patch*. *Tomato* has also been a somewhat contemptuous word for a girl since 1920: some lexicographers think it may first have been applied to any good-looking but nice girl who, like a tomato, didn't allow of pinching and handling, but the connotation is certainly more one of plump ripeness rather than moral goodness.

America's favorite condiment may be spelled *ketchup*, *catchup*, or *catsup* (in that order of preference). The differences exist because the English sailors who brought it from Singapore in the 17th century didn't know how this Malay word from Chinese *ke-tsiap* ("pickled fish sauce") should be spelled in English. No matter how it's spelled, its preferred and general pronunciation is *KETCH-up*, not *ket-sup*. The full term *tomato ketchup* (1831) is still heard in

You say ee-ther
And I say eye-ther,
You say nee-ther
And I say ny-ther;
Ee-ther, eye-ther,
Nee-ther, ny-ther,
Let's call the whole thing off!

You like po-ta-to
And I like po-tah-to,
You like to-ma-to
And I like to-mah-to;
Po-ta-to, po-tah-to,
To-ma-to, to-mah-to!
Let's call the whole thing off!

"Let's Call the Whole Thing Off," by George and Ira Gershwin for the 1937 Fred Astaire and Ginger Rogers movie *Shall We Dance?*

The term beefsteak tomato, *a large tomato often served in thick steaklike slices, was common by the late 1870s. This label is from a Campbell's can of around 1910.*

America, to distinguish it from ketchup using mushrooms or walnuts as a base; but since the late 19th century the "tomato" has been almost unnecessary because our common ketchup is tomato ketchup.

The F. & J. Heinz Co. and its first major product, *Heinz tomato ketchup*, both first appeared in 1876 (*F. & J. Heinz Co.* from a cousin, *Frederick*, and a brother, *John*, who advanced $1,600 of the $3,000 capital for the new business Henry J. Heinz started, though the company now goes under the H. J. Heinz name). The Heinz trademark *57 Varieties* was created by Henry in 1896 but was sometimes replaced by the slogan "57 good things for the table" in the early days, in case "varieties" was not plain or descriptive enough. This longer slogan appeared on New York City's very first electric sign, in 1900, which covered the side of a six-story building and used 1,200 lights. Even in 1896 the company produced more than 57 varieties—apple butter, peach butter, India relish, pepper sauce, sweet pickles, tomato ketchup, tomato soup, vinegars, etc.—but 57 sounded right for advertising and, no matter how many products were added or subtracted from the line, *57 Varieties* was used by the company until 1969.

Unions, Factories, and Strikes

The medieval craft *guild* (from Old Norse *gildi*, guild, payment, related to German *Geld*, money, and Old English *gield*, tribute) included not only the beginning *apprentice* (an English word of 1362, via Old French from Latin *apprendere*, to learn, apprehend) and experienced *journeyman* (an English word of 1463 for one who had served his apprenticeship and was thus qualified to receive wages for a day's work, from a 14th-century use of *journey* meaning a day's work), but also their masters and master craftsmen who owned their own shops. Thus the guilds were more trade associations than workers' unions, though some early unions were to be called a *guild* or a *brotherhood* (used in English as a synonym for *guild* since about the year 1340).

Until well into the 19th century, especially in rural areas and small towns in America, most families made as many of their own products as they could at home: so few items were manufactured by others in earlier days that the word *homemade* wasn't even necessary in English until 1689. Any item manufactured by others was made in a small *shop* (an English word of 1297 from the Old English *sceoppa*, booth, shed) from which the item was also sold— thus *shop* has come down to us to mean both a workshop or factory (*shop steward* is a 1915 term) and a small store where things are sold.

Later in English a shop where things were made was also called a *work(s)*, 1581; a *manufacture*, 1653, or *manufactury*, 1692 (both via Middle French from Latin *manū-/manus*, hand, plus *facere/factus*, to do, done, hence done or made by hand); and finally a *factory*, 1618 in this sense (from Middle French *facteur*, doer, commission merchant, which goes back to Latin *facere/factor*, to do, doer or maker).

One who did *work* (an Old English word of around the year 825 and originally spelled *weorc* or *worc*) in such a place was called a *worker*, 1382, or by 1638 a *workman* or *working man* (*working woman* was not recorded until 1853, all these terms first recorded in England). A shop's foremost or best worker, who thus might help or oversee others, was the *foreman*, 1574 in England (in this sense *forewoman* was an English term of the 1830s, but in America we often preferred the term *forelady* after 1889).

Then between 1750 and 1850 came the first phase of the *Industrial Revolution*, a term used only in retrospect, beginning in the 1870s. Large factories with power-driven machinery appeared and soon hundreds of items from shoes (*shoe factory*, 1835), clothing, and bricks to dishes and candy (*candy factory*, 1851) which had once been made by individuals working at home or in small shops were made in large quantities in factories. First in England and then in America *factory goods* (1793) appeared, goods made by the *factory system* (1830s), which employed not only the new *factory man* but many a *factory boy* and *factory girl* (all 1830 terms; *factory woman* appeared in 1858), every such *factory worker* (1840s) leading a *factory life* (1841), sometimes even in a *factory village* (1832), and all dependent for their livelihood on the mercies of the *factory owner* (an 1840s term).

Though some people did *piecework* (1830 in this sense) at home, the factories demanded huge numbers of workers, few of whom needed to be skilled craftsmen. The expensive machines needed for production gave the factory owners control over the workers, for a dissatisfied worker could not withdraw from or compete with the factory system by working for himself with a few hand tools. Now there was a new *working class* (1813) called *labor* (1830), and each worker was merely a part of the *labor market* (1830s). The individual factory worker had no power against the factory owner, who could offer the lowest survival wages and demand the longest hours in dangerous, dark, dirty factories, replacing workers with any cheaper ones he could find, reducing wages or demanding extra work as the need or whim struck him.

The workers had to gain some power, some control over their lives and work, by forming workers' organizations. Although the first local workers' organizations, of shoemakers, carpenters, and printers, began to appear in the late 18th century, the American *labor movement* (a term not widely used until the 1870s) did not truly begin until the 1820s and 30s when other skilled and

Workers of the world, unite!
Karl Marx and Friedrich Engels, *Manifesto of the Communist Party*, 1848

unskilled workers organized locally to obtain better pay, a ten-hour working day (it was then often twelve hours), the right to make liens against a factory owner for unpaid wages, and for such social reform as regulation of child labor and free public education. These early workers' organizations introduced such uses into English as (in chronological order):

strike. In 1768 a group of disgruntled British sailors refused to work by striking (taking down) their sails, *to strike* then immediately took on its labor meaning as, later that same year, a group of English hatters were said "to strike." Incidentally, those same British sailors were reported to have read a list of "grievances" before they struck their sails; thus *grievance* (used in English since 1481 to mean a complaint) was used in its labor sense on the same day *to strike* was first used.

The first American workers to be said *to strike* were the shoemakers, who won a new contract after staying off the job for ten weeks in 1799. We began using *strike* as a noun in 1809 (before that a strike had been called a *turnout*, one of the first such turnouts in America having been the 1741 New York City bakers' protest against the city's control of the price of bread). Other Americanisms include *general strike*, also 1809; *striker* and *on strike*, both 1850; and *to go out (on strike)*, 1878. The term *sit-down strike* was first used in the automotive industry in Detroit around 1935, during the United Automobile Workers Union organizing campaign, then gained national prominence during January 1936 when 1,000 workers *sat in* at the Firestone Tire and Rubber Co. plant.

scab (from Scandinavian *scab* and akin to Latin *scabies/scabere*, mange, to scratch) has referred to scabies and the crust over a wound in English since the 13th century, was English slang for a despicable person by 1590, meant a shirker by 1690 in America, and

"Lady shoemakers" from several Lynn, Massachusetts, shoe factories began a strike *in 1860 with this* strike *parade. Later they organized into the* Daughters of St. Crispin, *an offshoot of the* Knights of St. Crispin.

Children wearing anti-scab badges during New York City's streetcar employees' strike in 1916. Scab had taken on its special labor use by 1806.

then by 1806 came to mean a worker who replaced another by agreeing to work for lower wages or who refused to join a workers' organization. Thus, like *strike*, the labor use of the word *scab* is older than the labor *union* (see below). A *scab* was also said to *scab it*, also 1806, or later, *to scab on* fellow workers, 1917.

Blackleg was an early synonym for *scab*, first used in 1834, as an adjective, to refer to a craftsman who undersold others or a worker who replaced another for lower wages. Though this, like the labor use of *scab*, was originally an Americanism, it probably goes back to the 1771 English use of *blackleg* to mean a gambling swindler.

union didn't appear in its labor sense until 1833, long after *strike* and *scab* were established labor words. Like *unionist*, 1834, and *trade union*, 1835, it was first recorded in England. We added the terms *union man*, 1885; to *unionize*, 1890; and *craft union*, which was a popular early 1920s term for trade union. A union supporter or sympathizer was called a *laborite* by 1889.

The small, local labor organizations of the first half of the 19th century were most successful in calling attention to the extremely long working day. Philadelphia established the ten-hour working day for public servants in 1835, President Martin Van Buren established it for workers on all federal projects in 1840, and ten states then passed *ten-hour laws* in the 1840s and 50s allowing workers to *knock off* (1842 as meaning to stop work for the day) after ten hours—since the six-day work week was then standard, this meant that workers had to work only a 60-hour week!

Small, local unions restricted to one factory or town could not, of course, be very effective. Though there had been short-lived labor parties, a federation called the Mechanics Union and Trade Association in 1827, and even a National Trade Union from 1834 until the panic of 1837 and its following depression, nationwide unions truly developed in the 1850s and 60s, after an epoch-making 1842 Massachusetts Supreme Court decision on *Commonwealth* v. *Hunt* that ruled labor unions legal and not conspiracies under common law. This decision not only held that the Boston Journeymen Bootmakers Society was a legal organization but opened the door to all unions: one no longer need fear arrest for "conspiracy" with one's fellow workers when joining or organizing a union.

Thus the way was open for Philadelphia ironworker William H. Sylvis to form the National Union of Iron Molders in 1859 and, after the Civil War, in 1867, for boot and shoe workers to form the national Knights of St. Crispin, which soon had a membership of 50,000 workers and developed contracts whereby factories would employ only union shoemakers (the term *closed shop* was not recorded until 1904).

Successful nationwide unions of all workers, not just those in a specific trade, were also begun after the Civil War, these organizations often combining unionism with social reform and Utopian ideals. Having gained experience with his national iron molders' union, William Sylvis united several unions into the National Labor Union in 1866. It was open to both skilled and unskilled workers, men and women (women had formed an organization of "tailoresses" in New York City as early as 1826), even to farmers. Although the National Labor Union promoted the eight-hour day, it was best known for its grandiose program of social reforms; it created and sponsored the National Labor Reform party, and then, when its Presidential candidate, Supreme Court Justice David Davis, withdrew from its Presidential nomination, failed to survive the 1872 election.

More important, and longer lasting, was the Knights of Labor (1870), which a group of nine Philadelphia tailors, led by Uriah S. Stephens, had originally established as the secret Holy Order of the Knights of Labor in 1869 (many early labor groups were secret organizations). It, too, was successful because it was a combined labor and Utopian organization, as indicated by the word *Knights* in its title (for a discussion of the popularity of the word *knight* in America from the 1840s until after the Civil War, as in *Knights of Columbus*, *Knights of Pythias*, etc., see *knight of the road* at HOBOES, TRAMPS, AND BUMS). The Knights of Labor was open not only to manual, clerical, and professional workers, including women, but to merchants and farmers; it specifically excluded only bankers, lawyers, gamblers, and saloon keepers as equally undesirable. Its goals included not only the eight-hour workday, equal pay for equal work throughout every factory and town, the abolition of child labor, the establishment of workers' cooperatives, and a national Labor Day, but also a complete reorganization of the

Leaders of the Knights of Labor *grouped around a portrait of its founder, Uriah S. Stephens.*

currency and banking system. Helped by its all-encompassing idealism and the depression of 1873–78, which drove many workers to unions in desperation, the Knights of Labor was very successful. It got much of American labor to *organize* (1871 in the union sense) or at least to listen to the *union organizer* (1874) so that by 1885 Americans were talking about *organized labor*. It absorbed many smaller unions, including the members of the Knights of St. Crispin, in 1878, to become the "one big union" many had dreamed about. It reached its peak during the 1880s under its then *Grand Master Workman* (the Knights' official title for their president), the former railroad worker and machinist and the mayor of Scranton, Pennsylvania, Terence Vincent Powderly. It won major strikes against the Wabash and Missouri Pacific railroads, to prevent a wage reduction, in 1885 and by 1886 had grown to about 700,000 members.

By now unions and strikes had a powerful new weapon, *picketing* (first used in this sense in 1867, in England). *Picket* had appeared in English in 1761 as a noun, referring to a soldier or troops set out to watch for the enemy, troops being said *to picket* by 1775 (thus the Revolutionary War was the first in which soldiers picketed). By 1857 in England *to picket* also meant to set out union men around a factory being struck to watch those going to work and try to dissuade them from doing so, such a union watcher called a *picket* by 1867. But *management* (meaning the act of managing a business since 1598 in English and the people who govern or control an institution or business since 1739) was not without its weapons. As the unions had grown stronger from the 1850s to the 80s, factory owners had honed their old weapons and developed some new anti-union ones to control workers, including (in chronological order):

> *lockout*, 1854, as closing a factory during contract discussions to force the workers to come to terms. The general expression *to lock out* someone, as if locking a door to prevent entrance, was first recorded in England in 1590.
>
> *fire*. The easiest way to get rid of a union member was to fire that person. *Fire* has meant to dismiss from employment since 1885, with *to fire (out)* having meant to eject or throw a person out since 1871. Although *fire* has become the most common word, a boss could also *give (one) one's walking papers*, 1825, or *walking ticket*, 1835; *sack* someone, 1840, who is then said *to get the sack*, 1843 (from the 1825 English expression; the concept of being "sacked" had been widespread throughout Europe since the Middle Ages, some say because craftsmen were given back their tools in a sack when they were dismissed while others say it comes from the method of execution of being tied in a sack and drowned, a punishment used throughout Europe in the Middle Ages and going back to ancient Roman days when parricides were tied in a sack and drowned in the Tiber).
>
> Workers can also *get the bounce*, 1879; *get the boot*, 1888;

experience a *lay off*, 1889; be *shopped*, 1915, figuratively be thrown out of the shop; *get the blue envelope*, 1927; *get the pink slip*, 1930s; *get the skids*, 1936; or, in the case of an executive, *get the kiss off*, 1950s. The workers then, of course, have *to hit the asphalt*, 1909, or *pound the pavement*, 1923, to look for another job.

blacklist had been used as a noun in English since 1692 to refer to a list of people under suspicion or due for punishment or censure, with the verb *to blacklist* appearing in 1718. In America we have used *blacklist* since 1888 as a list of workers that management will not hire because they are union members, such lists being widely circulated from factory to factory during the late 19th and early 20th centuries.

raise. Of course the best way to keep an employee faithful is to give or offer a *raise*, 1888 (the English still call an increase in salary a *rise*), and factories often kept out unions by promising raises to workers who did not join them.

An employee not only "earns" money or pay, he can *rake down*, 1839, or *rake in*, 1882 (*rake off* meant illegal profit, an illegal share of the profits by 1888); *pull down*, 1917; *drag down*, also 1917; or *draw down*, 1928, his pay.

In addition to a raise a worker can also be rewarded by being given more status: workers traditionally earned hourly *wages*, professionals earned weekly *salaries;* but by the late 1850s some workers were earning *salaries* (in 1859 slang a salary was a *sal*) and a worker who had a secure position was said to have a *job*, 1858 (the term *job holder* appeared in 1904; *on the job* meant working hard and alertly by 1936).

yellow dog contract did not appear as a term until around 1920, when such contracts became widespread, but some employers used similar contracts from the 1870s on. The *yellow dog contract* was one the employer required an employee to sign promising that he would not join a union. *Yellow dog* had meant a worthless cur or mongrel by 1833 (*yellow* was first recorded as meaning cowardly in 1856) and a contemptible person by 1880; by 1894 a *yellow dog ticket* had meant a political ticket loyal party members were expected to support even though a contemptible person was on it.

Despite lockouts, blacklists, and firings the Knights of Labor and other unions were doing well by 1886 and called for May Day strikes and demonstrations to demand the eight-hour day. One of the 800 May Day strikes of 1886 was against the McCormick Harvesting Machine Company in Chicago, where fighting broke out along the picket lines and some strikers were injured when police entered the fray to restore order. A group of anarchists then called a May 4 meeting near Chicago's Haymarket Square, on Randolph between DesPlaines and Halsted streets, to protest this police action. Although inflammatory speeches were made, Mayor Carter Harrison saw that the meeting was peaceful so he sent the police reserves home and left himself. Then, as the meeting was ending, a police subordinate, angered by the speeches, ordered his men to move in and disperse the crowd. Someone then threw a

Samuel Fielden, on the speaker's platform, shouted "We are peaceable" to the police just before the dynamite bomb exploded at the Haymarket massacre *or* Haymarket Riot *in Chicago, May 4, 1886.*

bomb and in the ensuing *Haymarket massacre* (the anarchist and radical term for it) or *Haymarket Riot* (the police and general newspaper term for it) seven policemen and four workers died and about 120 police and workers were injured. The police charged eight anarchists and radical agitators with inciting the violence, though the bomb thrower was never found. These eight men were found guilty and four were hanged, one committed suicide, and the remaining three were eventually pardoned, in 1893, by Illinois Governor John Peter Altgeld. The Haymarket violence caused hatred to flare against the labor movement and unjustifiably blackened the reputation of the Knights of Labor, who had been a major sponsor of the May Day strikes. Thus, both because many held it accountable for the Haymarket Riot and because it lost a second strike to Jay Gould's railroads, the Knights of Labor's membership declined rapidly after 1886.

As the Knights of Labor declined, the leadership of the trade union movement passed to a younger federation of unions which New York cigar maker Samuel Gompers and others had organized in 1881 as the Federation of Organized Trade and Labor Unions of the United States and Canada and reorganized and renamed the American Federation of Labor (*AF of L*) in 1886. As its original name implied, it was a federation of already existing trade unions, each branch of which it called a *local* (1888, a local branch of a larger union had earlier been called a *branch* or *lodge*). It formed the locals of each industry into one overall *national union* or *international (union)* and oversaw them all—in American labor parlance *international* merely means that Canadian locals are included.

519

Samuel Gompers served as president of the American Federation of Labor *for all but one year from 1886 until his death in 1924.*

Under Samuel Gompers, who, with the exception of 1895, served as president from 1886 until his death in 1924, the AF of L had only one driving purpose: to organize skilled workers into trade unions to bargain collectively (*collective bargaining* was an 1891 term) for *higher wages, shorter hours,* and *better working conditions.* These were the ideas and words Gompers stressed over and over. Henceforth, the mainstream American labor movement was to be a labor movement only, dissociating itself from Utopian schemes, general social reforms, and any plans to form new political parties. As part of its contracts, Gompers' new AF of L had factories add union labels to goods made by its members and urged all shoppers to *look for the union label,* that is, buy union-made products (*union label* was an 1870s California term, such labels originally used by union workers there to distinguish their work from that of low-paid Chinese immigrants).

As the AF of L was being organized and began to grow, the Department of Labor and Labor Day were also becoming established. On June 27, 1884, Congress established a *Bureau of Labor* in the Department of Interior, then in 1888 gave this bureau independent status as the *Department of Labor* (in 1903 it became part of the *Department of Commerce and Labor,* then in 1913 became the separate Department of Labor again, this time with its head serving as a member of the President's cabinet as the *Secretary of Labor*). Thus William Sylvis' 1866 call for a Department of Labor was fulfilled. Meantime, the unrelated Matthew McGuire, a machinist from Paterson, New Jersey, and Peter J. McGuire, a New York City carpenter who had helped form the United Brotherhood of Carpenters and Joiners, played major roles in organizing the Central Labor Union's first *Labor Day Parade* in New York City, in September 1882; Oregon then becoming the first state to make *Labor Day* a legal holiday, in 1887; and President Grover Cleveland making it a national holiday, the first national one being held the first Monday in September, 1894. Thus, the Knights of Labor's call for a national Labor Day was also fulfilled.

All, however, was not sweetness and light. The Gay 90s was a violent decade for labor and *labor leaders* (1892), with bloody strikes at the Carnegie Steel Co. in Homestead, Pennsylvania, in the Pennsylvania coal fields, in western silver mines, in New York City's garment industry, in the nation's railway freight yards, and at the Pullman Palace Car Co.

In 1890, Congress passed the *Sherman Antitrust Act* (named for its author, Ohio Senator John Sherman, who had been chairman of the Senate Finance Committee and a secretary of the treasury), which was designed to prohibit trusts from restricting trade. Though not meant to be a *labor law* (1890s), it was soon used mainly against labor as manufacturers, railroads, and others would charge a striking union and its leaders with violating the law by interfering with trade and a judge would then issue an *injunction* (a 1533 English legal term) forbidding the offending strike.

In 1892 the Amalgamated Association of Iron, Steel, and Tin Workers struck the Carnegie Steel Co. in Homestead, Pennsylvania, after it reduced wages, and the strikebreaking Pinkerton thugs of this *Homestead strike* eventually gave labor the word *fink* (1902; see THE PINKERTONS AND THE MOLLY MAGUIRES; a strikebreaker was not called a *goon* or a *rat* until the 1930s, with the combination *rat fink* being, in general, nonunion use for a traitor or despicable person in the late 1960s).

In 1894, employees of the Pullman Palace Car Co. called the famous *Pullman strike*, also after the company cut wages, while refusing to reduce prices at its *company store* (an 1872 term) near Chicago. This strike was the first to be widely referred to as a *walk out*, its strikers the first to be said *to walk out*. Eugene V. Debs's newly formed American Railway Union declared a strike in support of the Pullman workers and refused to move the company's cars, this being the first *sympathy strike* to be given that name (though the term was not recorded until 1902). After hoodlums looted the Pullman Co.'s company stores as well as its idle railway cars, the government claimed that the Pullman strike and the Railway Union's sympathy strike interfered with mail trains, and a federal court issued a *blanket injunction* (the first time this term saw widespread common use) restraining all interference with the movement of the cars and the U.S. mail, and President Grover Cleveland sent troops to Chicago to end the strike. Debs, who had been a railroad shop worker and locomotive engineer before

Eugene Debs (1855-1926), leader of the American Railway Union during its sympathy strike with the Pullman Palace Car Co. employees in 1894, organized the Social Democratic party in 1897 and ran for President on the Socialist ticket five times.

521

becoming a union leader, and other strike leaders were sent to prison in contempt of court for defying the injunction. Six months later Debs emerged from prison a confirmed Socialist, later running for President on the Socialist ticket five times. His American Railway Union never recovered from its sympathy strike and dissolved within three years.

The injunctions and loss of the Homestead strike and Pullman strike in the early 1890s and further legal defeats and lost strikes in the late 1890s caused many of the nation's 800,000 union workers and their local leaders to feel that the AF of L was not militant enough and that its policy of trying to work within the capitalistic system was doomed to failure. Thus, led by the Western Federation of Miners, which had been formed in 1893 after the violent Coeur d'Alene lead and silver miners' strike in Idaho, some of the more radical workers and labor leaders formed the Industrial Workers of the World *(I.W.W.)* in Chicago in 1905. Its most famous founder and leader was an officer of the Western Federation of Miners, the outspoken Utah-born Socialist William Dudley "Big Bill" Haywood, who had been a miner since the age of fifteen. Its original members included many rugged western miners, seasonal lumberjacks, boxcar-riding migratory harvest workers, and footloose, often unemployed, Swedish, Finnish, and Polish immigrants. Some were anarchists, some Socialists, and some believed in *syndicalism*, a revolutionary movement of industrial workers to overthrow capitalism by a general strike, after which workers and their unions would own and manage industry (the movement had begun in France around 1864 as *syndicalisme*, meaning rule by the *chambre syndicale*, trade society, trade union).

Any I.W.W. member was soon called a *wobbly* or, in parts of the U.S. and in Canada, a *wobbie* or *wobby*. Though this is often said to be from the West Coast Chinese pronunciation of I.W.W. as "I Wobb(l)y Wobb(l)y," it is most probably from the pronunciation of the union's less frequently used abbreviation *W.O.W.* (Workers of the World) as *wow* + *-b(l)y*. Those who hated and feared the I.W.W. jokingly said the abbreviation stood for "I won't work." The union's members carried the I.W.W.'s small red *union card* (an 1874 term, when such cards were first issued to members of the International Typographical Union) or *union ticket* (1891), which some migratory workers and hoboes called a *pie card*, since showing it to a sympathetic housewife proved one was an honest, though out-of-work workingman worthy of a free meal (see HOBOES, TRAMPS, AND BUMS).

The I.W.W.'s best year was probably 1912, when it led a successful textile workers' strike in Lawrence, Massachusetts, this strike famous because as the striking workers ran out of money and food the strike leaders sent the workers' children to stay with labor sympathizers in other cities. However, after losing a series of

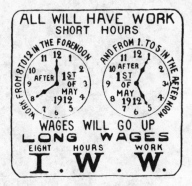

ALL WILL HAVE WORK
SHORT HOURS

WORK FROM 8 TO 12 IN THE FORENOON · AND FROM 1. TO 5 IN THE AFTERNOON
AFTER 1ST OF MAY 1912 · AFTER 1ST OF MAY 1912

WAGES WILL GO UP
LONG WAGES
EIGHT HOURS WORK
I.W.W.

COMPETITION IN THE LABOR MARKET IS THE MAIN CAUSE OF LOW WAGES! AGITATE · EDUCATE · ORGANIZE · IN THE INDUSTRIAL WORKERS OF THE WORLD, THE ONE BIG UNION OF ALL WAGE WORKERS
TAKE THE 8 HOUR DAY 1ST OF MAY 1912 · AND THE 8 HOUR DAY 1ST OF MAY 1912

Hallelujah, I'm a bum, bum, Hallelujah, bum again! Hallelujah, give us a handout, Revive us again!

"Hallelujah, I'm a Bum" was the best known of many I.W.W. *labor songs* (a 1921 term) about the labor movement and the poor, many of which became popular folk songs. Many were parodies of revival hymns, as was this one, which was sung to the tune of "Revive Us Again."

I WILL WIN

ONE BIG UNION OF ALL THE WORKERS
THE I.W.W.

MORE WAGES. BETTER WORKING CONDITIONS SHORTER HOURS EMANCIPATION W.I.W SOLIDARITY ABOLITION OF WAGE SYSTEM ABOLITION OF UNEMPLOYMENT SHOP DEMOCRACY GOOD PAY OR BUM WORK

THINK IT OVER JOIN THE
ONE BIG UNION
FIGHT FOR THE FULL PRODUCT OF YOUR LABOR

I.W.W.
WIN A WORLD
JOIN!

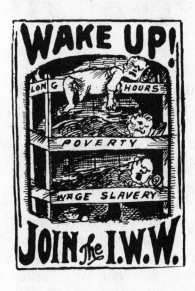

WAKE UP!
LONG HOURS
POVERTY
WAGE SLAVERY
JOIN the I.W.W.

I.W.W.
ONE BIG UNION OF ALL THE WORKERS
THE GREATEST THING ON EARTH

BETTER JOB
I W W UNIVERSAL
CONDITIONS

I.W.W. stickerettes such as these, plastered on fences, telephone poles, factory walls, and store windows, added to the fear and hatred many Americans had for the Wobblies.

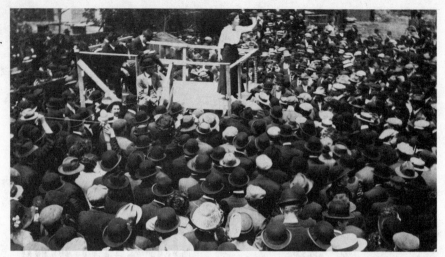

Elizabeth Gurley Flynn, the Joan of Arc of the I.W.W., speaking at a demonstration in support of striking Paterson, New Jersey, silk workers in 1913.

The petroleum industry strike of 1915.

strikes beginning with a silk workers' strike in Paterson, New Jersey, in 1913, then incurring the wrath of many for opposing U.S. participation in World War I and engaging in wartime strikes in such vital industries as copper and lumber, and with hundreds of its leaders and members convicted under the wartime Espionage Act, the I.W.W. membership dwindled rapidly. It still had 100,000 members in 1916 but had nearly disappeared by 1920, many of its few remaining activists soon joining the newly formed U.S. Communist movement. "Big Bill" Haywood, who had been acquitted in 1907 of having any part in the murder of a former Idaho governor, was arrested for sedition when the U.S. entered World War I, convicted and sentenced to twenty years' imprisonment in 1918, released on bail pending a new, postwar trial in 1919, but jumped bail and fled to Russia, where he died in 1928.

524

Cloak-makers on strike in New York City, 1916.

Under the full employment and prosperity during and immediately after World War I, union membership doubled, from 2.5 million in 1914 to 5 million in 1920. After the war, in 1919, the AF of L tried to gain a more militant image by organizing steel workers and leading their strike for higher pay but was forced to cancel the strike after the steel companies brought in swarms of strikebreakers, AF of L membership then dropping from 4 to 3 million during the 1920s after this embarrassing and costly failure. Many new unions were formed during the 1920s, however, including Philip Randolph's 1925 Brotherhood of Sleeping Car Porters.

Many factories still employed many a *company spotter* (1907) to spy out union organizers and union activists or created their own *company union* (a term of around 1915), led by a loyal *company man* (a term of around 1920), which they hoped would keep any independent workers' *outside union* (1921) at bay. Many companies also still found sources of cheap labor in child labor and newly arrived immigrant workers. A 10 percent excise tax had been levied on firms employing fourteen-year-olds beginning in 1914, and President Wilson had signed a Child Labor Act in 1916 forbidding some industries from employing those under sixteen years of age, but both these laws were stricken down by the Supreme Court within a few years (in 1905 the Supreme Court had also ruled minimum wage laws unconstitutional as depriving individuals of the *liberty of contract*). The cheap supply of immigrant labor was, however, greatly reduced by the Immigration Act of 1924, which limited the number of immigrants entering the U.S. each year.

Meantime, factory work was changing as constantly improving machines increased the rate of production and demanded fewer skilled and more unskilled workers. Although, soon after inventing the *cotton gin* in 1793, Eli Whitney had won a government contract by designing a system of manufacturing 10,000 guns made not individually but from mass-produced interchangeable parts and called this his *uniformity system* of production in 1798, the term *mass production* itself didn't appear until 1920. By then many factory workers were well used to having their *time* (1877 as the time or hours one worked per day or week) kept by a *time clock* (1887; see CLOCKS AND WATCHES) and *time card* (1891), though the terms *punch in* and *punch out*, on a recording time clock, didn't appear until the early 1920s, when *mass production* was still a new term.

Mass production was known best from Henry Ford's car company, which had introduced the terms *assembly line* and *profit sharing* in 1914. Henry Ford (1863–1947), "the man who put America on wheels," embraced or was associated with not only mass production but a variety of fads, detestable ideas, and high ideals, ranging from food fads, foot racing, and folk dancing, to anti-Semitism and pacifism, which kept his name in the news and added many terms to our language. Not only did his cars give us such names as the *Ford* (the first one was built in 1903), *Model T* (1909), *Tin Lizzie* (1915), and *Model A* (1927), but *Detroit* is synonymous with American cars because Ford, born in Greenfield, Michigan, lived in Detroit from 1887 and built his first cars there. He also gave history its *Ford Peace Ship*, the *Oscar II*, which he chartered in 1915–16 to take a group of pacifists to Europe in a futile attempt to organize a peace conference to end World War I and, of course, gave his name and money to the *Ford Foundation*, established in 1936. Though the factory term *assembly room* had been recorded in 1897, Ford's 1914 *assembly line* was a new concept, using an electric conveyor belt to move parts past a line of stationary workers who earned Ford's new $5 a day *minimum wage* and were eligible for a new *profit-sharing* plan in return for their pledge of sobriety and thrift. This was at a time when the average factory worker still earned $11 a week and few had even heard of the term *minimum wage*, much less *profit sharing* (though *minimum wage* had been first recorded in the 1860s from the 1810 English term *minimum rate of wage*). Not only was the Model T popular because it was a good, cheap, mass-produced car, but many bought it because it was made by a company that treated one's fellow workers properly.

In 1926 the Ford Motor Co. again made history when it established the *eight-hour day* and *five-day week* for its workers. These were neither new terms nor new concepts, but it was the first time a major company guaranteed them willingly to a large number of workers. *Working day* had meant one of the days one was required to work by a factory or store since around 1813; the term *eight hours' work*, as meaning the hours one worked per working day, appeared in English in 1849. Americans had been talking about labor's *eight-hour movement* and certain *eight-hour laws* since the 1860s, and using the term *eight-hour day* since 1899, when the term was still much more common than the practice. The carpenters' union had won an eight-hour day in 1888, the railroad unions in 1916, and the painters' union in 1920, after a strike for the *40–40*, $40 a week for 40 hours' work a week. But it was Ford's 1926 eight-hour day and five-day week that began to make these hours the standard for all workers, most unions then beginning to demand the *forty-hour week* (always then meaning five working days of eight hours each) in all new contracts. As standard hours developed, so did the concept of *overtime*, which had first been used to mean time worked over one's regular hours in England in 1858, and its amount and pay first mentioned as a labor grievance in 1861, when overtime didn't begin until after the standard 10-hour workday or 6-day, 60-hour work week.

Mr. [Henry] Ford has inaugurated the five-day working week. . . .
    The Saturday Review, October 2, 1926

The tube industry strike of 1933.

Though unemployment during the beginning of the Great Depression saw union membership sink to 3 million, in 1933, the Depression ultimately helped unions gain respectability, strength, and 8 million members by 1940, as many workers lost faith in business leaders and their political allies who could not solve the nation's problems and turned to organized labor and its political supporters as a way to maintain not only jobs and wages but hope and pride. To keep labor peace and help the economy and the workingman, Congress passed a major pro-labor law in 1932, the *Norris-La Guardia Act* (named for its sponsors, Senator George W. *Norris* of Nebraska and Representative Fiorello H. *La Guardia* of New York), which limited the power of federal courts to issue injunctions in labor disputes and made yellow-dog contracts unenforceable by declaring that workers could not be sued by their employers for breaking such contracts.

Then, beginning in 1933, President Franklin D. Roosevelt's New Deal programs to end the Depression did much to benefit labor. The National Industrial Recovery Act *(NIRA)* of June 1933 not only spent over $3 billion for public works but, with the National Recovery Administration (*NRA*, one of the early New Deal *alphabet agencies*, a 1933 term), guaranteed workers a minimum wage of 30–40 cents an hour (the Depression had dropped some wages to 25 cents an hour again), a 35–40-hour work week, and the "right to organize and bargain collectively" (*collective bargaining* was an 1891 term). Businessmen displayed the NRA *Blue Eagle* symbol with the slogan "We do our part" to indicate

"The Spirit of the New Deal,"
1933.

their acceptance of the NRA's *code of fair competition*, though many cursed and not a few subverted its 765 ineffective and often confusing codes. When the Supreme Court declared the National Industrial Recovery Act unconstitutional in 1935, the NIRA was replaced by the National Labor Relations Act, better known as the *Wagner Act* (because Senator Robert F. Wagner of New York led the fight for its passage), which also protected labor's right to organize and bargain collectively and established the National Labor Relations Board *(NLRB)*. Among its many tasks, the NLRB punished *unfair labor practices* and determined which unions should represent which workers when *union jurisdiction* was disputed—and the Supreme Court upheld the Wagner Act in a 1937 case brought against the NLRB by the Jones and Laughlin Steel Corp.

The Fair Labor Standards Act of 1938, also known as the *Wages and Hours Act*, supplemented the Wagner Act and contained some weakened provisions of the previous National Industrial Recovery Act. It established a 25-cent-an-hour minimum wage, with provisions to rise to the NIRA's 40 cents an hour within seven years; a 44-hour week, with provisions to reduce it to a 40-hour week in three years; prohibited the labor of children under sixteen; and established an overtime wage rate one and one-half times that of regular pay, giving us the common term *time and a half* for overtime pay.

The difficult times local unions had during the Depression helped the AF of L continue to grow and absorb large and small craft unions, such as the Amalgamated Clothing Workers of America in 1933. Although mass-production industries had grown rapidly since the beginning of the 20th century, the craft unions that dominated the AF of L, perhaps remembering the 1919 failure to organize the steel workers, did not want to organize unskilled mass-production workers into their federation. Though most of the AF of L leadership agreed that unskilled mass-production workers should be kept out of the federation, eight of the AF of L unions, led by John L. Lewis' United Mine Workers union (the *UMW*, founded in 1890), Sidney Hillman's Amalgamated Clothing Workers, and David Dubinsky's International Ladies' Garment Workers' Union *(ILGWU)*, established the Committee for Industrial Organization *(CIO)* in 1935 to "encourage and promote organizations of workers in the mass-production industries." With the help of experienced organizers from the recently dissolved Communist group, the Trade Union Unity League, the CIO quickly gained millions of members, especially among General Motors and Chrysler automotive workers (Ford Motor Co. workers were harder to organize), and the rubber and *big steel* companies (the CIO organized what it called *big steel* before turning to the smaller *little steel* companies). The success of the CIO under the AF of L only enlarged the dispute within the AF of L as to the direction it should take and who should control it. Thus, in 1936, the AF of L suspended and in 1938 expelled the CIO unions, the Committee for Industrial Organization then establishing its own federation and changing its name to the Congress of Industrial Organizations, which allowed it to keep its old initials, *CIO* (thus *CIO* stood for *C*ommittee for *I*ndustrial *O*rganization from 1935 to 1938 and for *C*ongress of *I*ndustrial *O*rganizations after 1938). The AF of L considered itself a federation of craft unions while the CIO became a federation of *industrial unions* (1923, as unions of all workers in a plant or industry rather than of workers in specific crafts or trades).

During the full employment and prosperity of World War II, union membership continued to grow, and by war's end one-third of the labor force were union members. Though the *wildcat strike* (1943, such an unauthorized strike having been called an *outlaw strike* since 1920) caused some problems, labor generally had good pay and improved working conditions during the war, especially when working in *defense plants* producing military planes, ships, tanks, trucks, arms, uniforms, etc., was considered patriotic and all labor shared in a one-for-all wartime camaraderie. Though general wage increases were prohibited during the war, workers could earn time-and-a-half working overtime or bonuses for working some of the unusual around-the-clock shifts, as the 4 P.M. to midnight *swing shift* (first recorded in 1944), which seemed to swing midway between a regular day shift and a full night shift (*shift* has meant work in English since 1572 and a relay of workers and span of working time since around 1810). Since wages were *frozen* (*to freeze* had first been used in this sense in 1937, the term *wage freeze* in 1942), unions concentrated on winning new *fringe benefits* for workers, including *paid vacations*, *paid holidays*, and company-paid *pension plans* and *hospital insurance* (these last four terms and practices were not new, but they became common during World War II).

The war was immediately followed by more economic growth and prosperity as millions of returning veterans and prosperous workers wanted the new homes, cars, appliances, clothing, etc., they had been denied during the war. Union membership soared, to 12 million in 1946, and there was a postwar wave of strikes as labor obtained large wage *hikes* (1931 as an increase in wages or prices) to make up for the wartime wage freeze, so that, to many, the unions seemed to be getting too powerful and to be responsible for high prices. Thus new laws to curb unions were enacted, the Republican-controlled 80th Congress passing the Labor-Management Relations Act of 1947, commonly called the *Taft-Hartley Act* (as it was sponsored by Senator Robert A. *Taft* of Ohio and Representative Fred A. *Hartley* of New Jersey), which not only banned union political contributions in national elections and

The CIO *was organized in 1935 and quickly gained millions of members, especially among auto workers. During and after World War II,* union *packages concentrated on higher wages, obtaining* company-paid *pension plans, hospital insurance, and other* fringe benefits, *as shown on these placards for the 1950 United Auto Workers' strike against Chrysler.*

established many restrictions on strikes but prohibited *jurisdictional strikes*, *sympathy strikes* (Eugene Debs's old weapon in the Pullman Palace Car Co. strike), and *secondary boycotts*, from the 1880 English word *boycott*, often spelled with the initial capital letter as *Boycott* until 1886, taken from the name of the English land agent Captain Charles C. Boycott, 1832–97, who was so harsh on the Irish tenants of his employer, Lord Erne, that his own neighbors refused to have anything to do with him or his family. Perhaps most important, however, the Taft-Hartley Act outlawed the *closed shop* (1904) in which unions had forbidden the employer to hire any but union members, although permitting the *union shop* (the employer may hire anyone, but the new employee must then join the union or pay the equivalent of union dues to it) where state law allows. This last led to the passage by many states, especially in the South, of *right-to-work* laws, which forbade the union shop, leaving only the *open shop* (1896, the English word *open* meant open or accessible to all by the 10th century), which can employ both union and nonunion workers and, of course, the shop which is completely *non-union* (an 1863 English term). The Taft-Hartley Act also established a 60-day grace period after the end of a contract during which no strike could be called, allowing additional time for the union and management to reach new contract agreements, to be followed by an additional 80-day injunction against striking if the President judged a strike as endangering the nation's health or safety or creating a national emergency. Even while the act was being passed in 1947, the 60-day grace period was called a *cooling-off period*, though later this term was also sometimes applied to the 80-day injunction period (*cooling-off period* had been used to refer to the weather since 1911 and by the early 1940s to *cool off* was used in the figurative sense of to calm down).

Faced with such growing opposition, to eliminate *raiding* between the two federations, and to increase effectiveness, the AF of L and the CIO merged in 1955, after the CIO expelled eleven of its unions that many felt were dominated by Communists or Communist sympathizers (who had been recruited into the unions by those experienced Trade Union Unity League members of the CIO's early days). Expelling the suspect Communist unions was necessary before the merger because the Taft-Hartley Act had included a provision requiring union officers to sign affidavits that they were not Communists. The name of the merged federation was just that, the American Federation of Labor and Congress of Industrial Organizations (abbreviated *AFL–CIO*, which meant that the old abbreviation *AF of L* lost its "of"). AF of L president George Meany, who had begun his career as a union plumber in the Bronx, New York, became the AFL–CIO's first president, and CIO president Walter Reuther, who led the United Automobile Workers *(UAW)*, became its first vice president and head of its industrial union department. (Meany and Reuther were too different in their political and social views to achieve a satisfactory working relationship, Reuther taking his UAW out of the AFL–CIO in 1968 and the UAW not rejoining the federation until 1981.) The combined AFL–CIO included 140 national and "international" unions comprising some 60,000 locals.

AF of L *president George Meany (left) and* CIO *president Walter Reuther discuss final plans to merge their unions into the* AFL-CIO, *1955.*

The AFL–CIO was not, of course, to be without its problems. Communists may have been eliminated, but *labor racketeers* were unearthed in the 1950s (a disliked labor leader had been called a *labor boss* since 1903), especially when a Senate Committee under Senator John L. McClellan of Arkansas revealed corruption and links to organized crime among some labor leaders, especially of the Teamsters Union (founded in the horse-drawn wagon days of 1899 as the International Brotherhood of Teamsters, Chauffeurs, Warehousemen, and Helpers of America). The AFL–CIO then expelled the Teamsters and two other unions, while Congress passed the Labor-Management Reporting and Disclosure Act of 1959 to guard workers against corrupt union leadership by regulating union elections, providing safeguards for union funds, and guaranteeing union members certain specific rights.

Union membership reached its peak of 17 million members around 1960. Since then it has declined steadily, now being somewhere between 20 and 25 percent of the labor force, owing to changes in the nation's population (there are fewer workers, more

Cesar Chavez (left), head of the United Farm Workers, *after signing the first union contract with grape growers in 1970, after nearly six years of strikes and boycotts.*

The new *municipal unions: Pittsburgh schoolteachers on strike in 1975.*

retired people), *automation* (a 1949 term, though as early as 1943 the railroad unions had been accused of *featherbedding*, demanding that unnecessary workers be kept on payroll, in that instance referring to their insisting that firemen be employed on locomotives that no longer ran on wood or coal), and the increase of the usually unorganized *white collar workers* (a 1929 term for office workers and professionals) over *blue collar workers* (1950s for those who work in factories, from the blue workshirts often worn).

In the 1960s Cesar Chavez began organizing migrant farm laborers and other agricultural workers in California and founded the United Farm Workers of America *(UFW)*. On January 17, 1962, President John F. Kennedy issued Executive Order 10988 recognizing the right of federal employees to organize and bargain collectively, but not to strike, and many states passed similar legislation, some allowing state and local employees to strike. This encouraged the rapid growth of the American Federation of State, County, and Municipal Employees and, during the 1970s, the first strikes by many police, teachers, sanitation workers, transit workers, and other employees of newly formed *municipal unions*. Those local government employees still forbidden to strike by local law during the 1970s and early 80s sometimes had a *work slowdown, job action* (following each rule meticulously so that little work was accomplished or the public was inconvenienced, as policemen devoting most of their time to giving out parking tickets), or a *sickout* (most union members staying home by claiming they were sick).

The U.S. Mail

The British still speak of *the post* and of *posting* a letter while we are more apt to talk about *the mail* and *mailing* a letter (*post* came into English via the 15th-century French *poste*, station, from Latin *positum*, positioned, placed; *mail* has been in English since the 13th century, from Old High German *malha*, satchel, bag). Our use of *post* and *postal* thus goes back to our British colonial days; *mail* came later, with *mail carrier* in 1790, *mail boat* in 1796, *mail pouch*, and *the mail*, the *U.S. Mail* in the 1840s, and *mail bag* in 1867. Here are the dates of the first American colonial use of some British postal terms:

postal system, 1639, in Massachusetts. This first system was simple: incoming overseas mail was to be left at the home of Richard Fairbanks in Boston and he transmitted it for a penny a letter.

postal service, 1672, when a monthly service was started between New York and Boston, over what in 1692 became the Boston *Post Road* (a road for transporting mail). By 1790 the U.S. had 20,000 miles of post roads.

post office, 1683, when the first American one was established in Philadelphia. It gave us our first colonial use of the word *postmaster*, being one Henry Waldy, whose main duty was to supply horses and riders.

postmaster general, 1694, when the British crown appointed Andrew Hamilton postmaster general of all the colonies, to establish intercolonial service. People were soon talking about his *post riders* and *post walkers* (poor roads made them faster than wagons or carriages).

These were the major British contributions to our postal language. Benjamin Franklin was appointed postmaster of Philadelphia in 1737 and served as "co-deputy postmaster general" of the colonies from 1753 to 1774, when he was dismissed by the crown for being too pro-American. He got even with the British by being appointed the first postmaster general of the *American postal system* by the Continental Congress in 1775. Now American mail terms slowly began to take over:

mail coach, late 1780s (a British term); *mail stage*, from 1792.

Post Office Department, Americans used this term from its beginnings in 1782 until 1971, when it became the *U.S. Postal Service*, an independent agency.

U.S. Postmaster General, 1789, when President Washington appointed Samuel Osgood as the first one, overseeing the nation's 75 post offices.

star route, 1820s, the route of a private contractor carrying mail for the post office where its own service didn't go (so called for the stars or asterisks printed next to such routes on the Post Office Department list).

post office box, 1833; *general delivery*, late 1830's.

"Motor cycle postman" of 1912.

Before 1847, U.S. postmasters printed their own postage stamps and supplied glue pots—the adhesive stamp wasn't invented until 1840, in England (the famous *penny black* being the first issue). Then on July 1, 1847, Congress authorized the first *U.S. Postage stamps:* a *5¢ Franklin* and a *10¢ Washington*. Within fifteen years all Americans were simply calling them *stamps* and calling their value *postage*. At first, some Americans humorously called such an adhesive stamp a *lick-and-stick*. Postage still covered only the carrying of mail from post office to post office; there was not free home delivery.

> *overland mail,* 1848, when the post office first started talking about a stagecoach mail service from Missouri to California, which *overland stage* service was begun in 1858.
>
> *mail car, mail train,* 1855; *post-office car,* 1857, as any railroad car or train on which mail was carried. Though the government began moving mail by train in 1832 to encourage railroad building, these three terms became popular only after the end of the Civil War when, in 1864, mail began to be sorted in special cars on moving trains, and *mail car, mail train,* and *post-office car* came to mean those on which mail was sorted in transit. Such mail trains reached their peak in the mid 1940s when 4,000 of them were in daily service: the last such train ran between Washington, D.C., and New York City on July 1, 1977, after which mail has been carried by truck, train, and buses but has no longer been sorted in transit.
>
> *mail robber,* 1855. He robbed the mail trains.
>
> *registered mail,* 1855, when the service began.
>
> *mail boy,* 1862, to distribute and collect mail in offices, which were now growing rapidly in size and number.

534

In 1863, when many families were writing to and receiving letters from their men who were fighting the Civil War, there were two big innovations in the Union's mail service: (1) mail was divided into classes and postage was based on the class rather than the distance it was carried; (2) mail service now began to include free home delivery in cities. Before this everyone had to pick up and deposit his own mail at the post office (or in a primitive letter box) or pay a *letter carrier* (an 1825 term) a 2-cent fee for each letter he delivered or picked up. Now we began to use the new terms:

first class (letters), *second class* (newspapers), *third class* (magazines and circulars), 1863. *Fourth class* (merchandise) wasn't added until 1879.

city delivery service, free city delivery, free delivery, 1863.

mailman soon became a common word after 1863, when he was employed and paid by the post office for free delivery. By the 1880s mailmen delivered as many as five times a day in commercial areas of New York and other major cities.

postal money order, 1864, originally created so Union soldiers could send money home safely during the Civil War.

postal card, post card, 1871, when the U.S. Post Office first issued a plain penny one, called a *penny post card* by 1873 (post cards had first been used by the Austrian post office in 1860).

branch post office, 1871.

mail box, 1872, two years after it was patented. Since the late 1850s people had been calling primitive types *letter boxes, street letter boxes,* and *street boxes,* but these were usually the brightly painted receiving boxes for independent carriers and express agencies. The patented U.S. *mailbox* did a lot to give the U.S. Post Office Department control of the business. They were also often called *letter drops* in the 1890s.

special delivery, 1885.

commemorative stamp, 1893, the first U.S. commemorative series being for the Chicago World's Columbian Exposition.

After having been discussed for several years, free delivery was extended to rural areas in 1896. Free rural delivery brought newspapers, magazines, and mail-order catalogs to farm families, breaking their isolation and "urbanizing" the outlook of rural America.

Rural Free Delivery, RFD, 1892; used in discussions four years before it went into effect.

mail order business, 1875; *mail order catalog,* 1883; *mail order house,* 1906. The mail order business mushroomed after RFD was introduced; Sears Roebuck entered the mail order business in 1895.

postal savings, 1911. This savings bank, operated by the U.S. Post Office Department for small accounts, was discontinued in 1961 when deposits dropped due to the low 2 percent interest limit.

parcel post, 1911; *C.O.D.* (Collect on Delivery), 1913, created to accompany parcel post, though business later used the term to mean Cash on Delivery.

Everyone was talking about the new airmail in 1917–18. It was a highly publicized joint venture of the post office and the War Department, using army planes and pilots, with President Wilson witnessing the departure of the first *airmail plane* from Washington to New York in 1918. In 1926 airmail was turned over to private airlines, encouraging the formation of many new ones, including *Pan American*.

> *airmail*, 1917.
> *airmail stamp*, 1918.
> *mail plane*, *mail pilot*, became romantic terms in the 1920s.
> *mail truck*, 1924.
> *certified mail*, 1955.
> *zip code* (*zone improvement plan*), 1963.

And last, but not least, people have been playing and giggling about the kissing game *post office* since 1851, just four years after they began "kissing" those new lick-and-stick adhesive stamps.

Vitamins

Early Americans warned each other of the debilitating aphrodisiac effect of white potatoes, argued whether or not tomatoes were poisonous, discussed the relative merits of graham crackers (see BREAKFAST FOOD) as a cure for dyspepsia, and of various grains, berries, fruits, vegetables, meats, and beverages as a cure for all the ailments of mankind. In the 1880s such national preoccupations led to the new term *health foods* and to widespread talk about *vegetarians*, *lacto-vegetarians* (who admitted dairy products to an otherwise vegetable diet), and even *fruitarians* (who usually suffered dietary deficiencies).

The word *nutrition* (Latin *nūtrire*, to nourish, as with mother's milk) has been in English since the 16th century and *protein* (Greek *prōtos*, first, chief) and *calorie* (Latin *calor*, heat) since the early 19th. But as late as 1895, Wilbur Atwater, chief of the Experiment Stations for the U.S. Department of Agriculture, published a food guide from which fruits and vegetables were eliminated because they have such low calorie content—vitamins had not yet been discovered.

Such an unknown substance was suspected and named *vitamine* (note the final *e*, from Latin *vīta*, life + *amine*, a class of organic compounds) in 1912 by biochemist Casimir Funk, who was on the track of an anti-beriberi substance that later became *vitamin B*. In 1913 people were talking about the first vitamin actually isolated, *vitamin A*, and its discoverer, physiological chemist Elmer McCollum, who also originated the general concept of health-protective foods. He had people talking again in 1922 when he discovered *vitamin D*, which was also the same year *vitamin E* was first in the news. Meanwhile, in 1920, the British scientist Drummond had changed the spelling of *vitamine* to *vitamin*, dropping the final *e* because most vitamins were not amines. That year he also named *vitamin C*, though it wasn't "discovered" until 1927, by Hungarian chemist Szent-Gyorgyi von Nagyrapolt, who named it *ascorbic acid* (from *antiscorbutic*, literally "anti-scurvy"). People were talking about *vitamin B* when it was finally isolated in 1926 and of the yellow B_2 when it was isolated in 1933 and named *riboflavin* (from *ribose*, a pentose sugar + *flavin*, a yellow pigment in organic tissues). The new vitamin term of 1934 was *vitamin K* and of 1937 *niacin* (an acronym on *nicotinic acid* + *-in*). By the 1940s the term *vitamin pill* was very popular.

No longer did that 1880s term *health foods* merely refer to fad foods laymen thought helped one toward good health; by the 1940s it also meant foods high in specific vitamins, minerals, protein, and other nutrients, and the term *balanced diet* now also had a scientific base. Beginning in 1948 publisher Jerome Rodale began to popularize in his *Organic Front* magazine the term *organic food*, foods grown untouched by chemical fertilizers or insecticides.

Wall Street

Though the first European stock exchange was established in 1531 in Antwerp, Belgium, not until the period of 1620–1700 did English merchants and bankers begin to develop our modern stock market terms. During those eighty years before 1700, *bond*, *broker*, *dividend*, *to hedge*, *securities*, *share*, *stock*, and *trader* took on their financial meanings. *Broker* appeared first, in 1622; it had originally meant *broacher* (from Vulgar Latin *broccātor*, tapster), wine retailer, one who broaches or taps wine casks; by the 14th century it had come to mean a middleman, one who doesn't grow or make something but who buys and sells it; then an agent; and finally an agent in financial transactions. *Securities* appeared last, around 1700, so called because they are the documents that prove or secure a creditor's or investor's rights and ownership.

By 1709, English brokers and investors were talking about *bears*, then added the expression *bears and bulls* by 1714, and by 1761 were using *bulls* as a separate word taken from that expression. Contrary to the popular belief, *bears and bulls* (those who expect the market to go down and those who expect it to go up) has nothing whatsoever to do with the fact that a bear attacks by sweeping its paws downward and a bull by tossing its head or horns upward. A *bear* was simply a speculator who agreed to sell shares he did not yet own, believing that the price would drop before he had to deliver them, so that he would profit by buying them at the lower future price while having already sold them at the present higher one. Since he was selling something he didn't yet have he was first

In this 1879 painting Bulls and Bears in the Market *the bulls are surging after a six-year depression in stock prices.*

called a *bear skin jobber*, then simply a *bear*, from the old proverb "Don't sell the bear skin before the bear is caught." *Bull* was then used to refer to the opposite of a bear, a bull being one who believes prices will go up and thus buys heavily in order to profit by selling when they do, because *bear* and *bull* went together from the then popular sport of bear and bull baiting, which had made *bear and bull* a common alliterative term. Later, in America, we would also call a bear, who sold stock before he owned it, a *short* (1849) and say he *sold short* (1852), and would call a bull, who bought heavily in expectation that a stock would go up, a *long* (also 1849).

London had a market called *the Stock(s) Exchange* since at least the 15th century, and a *Royal Exchange* since 1566, but neither of these was a stock exchange. *The Stock(s) Exchange* was a fish and poultry market said to have been given its name because it was on land where the city's *stocks* once stood (the wooden frame with holes to imprison the feet or hands of criminals or other offenders undergoing public punishment), while the *Royal Exchange*, named by Queen Elizabeth I, was a merchants' and banking exchange. The London financial brokers met and did much of their buying and selling in coffee houses until 1773, especially in one coffee house called New Jonathan's—which was on a narrow dirt street that had by then become known as *Exchange Alley* and was referred to in financial circles simply as *the Alley*. Then, in 1773, the brokers took over New Jonathan's completely and renamed it *the Stock Exchange*, putting that name on the door, this sign being the first recorded use of the term *stock exchange* as we know it today.

Some London bears and bulls who went bankrupt and "waddled" out of Exchange Alley in dejection were called *lame ducks* by

1761, a *lame duck* then coming to mean any bankrupt or person who had lost power and status. By 1863 *lame duck* was being used in American politics to refer to elected officeholders, especially Congressmen who had lost a November election but served out their old term until March, spending over three months as dejected, somewhat powerless lame ducks (in 1932 the *Lame Duck Amendment*, the Twentieth Amendment to the Constitution, was passed, calling for Congress and each new Presidential administration to take office in January instead of March and eliminating the *lame duck session* of Congress).

When the English established the Stock Exchange in 1773, our colonial merchants and bankers who dealt in securities were still meeting in New York City coffee houses and on the street in front of certain buildings and under specific trees around Wall Street. Though such leaders as Thomas Jefferson had complained bitterly about Revolutionary War *speculators* (a 1778 American use, born during the war boom) and urged people not to *speculate* (1785), American finances were simple. There was no need for a stock exchange until the first Secretary of the Treasury, Alexander Hamilton, began to consolidate and refinance our Revolutionary War debt through the sale of government bonds. Thus, on May 17, 1792, twenty-four merchants and auctioneers formed our first formal stock exchange by pledging to meet daily at regular hours under a large old buttonwood tree on Wall Street to buy and sell securities—and not to buy or sell for others at less than one-fourth of one percent *commission* (a term used by English brokers since about 1764). This group originally dealt in the new government bonds, in shares of Hamilton's First United States Bank, the Bank of North America, and the Bank of New York, and in shares of insurance companies. After a year under the buttonwood tree, the gentlemen moved indoors, originally into the Tontine Coffee House. By 1827, they and their successors were dealing in the stocks of 12 banks, 9 marine and fire insurance companies, and selected canal-building schemes, adding eight railroad companies to their list by 1837. This stock exchange, its rival that still conducted business on the curb, and America's overall stock and bond market were to have several names, in chronological order:

> *the stock market*, 1809. *Stock* had come to mean a business's capital in England early in that 1620–1700 period in which so many of our basic financial terms appeared. The other *stock market*, where livestock is sold, came later, in 1858.
>
> *the market*, 1830s. *Market* appeared in English in the 12th century, originally meaning both a gathering of people to transact business and the place where they met (via Old French from the Vulgar Latin *mercātus*, trade, market place, from *merc-/merx*, merchandise). By the mid 17th century it had its special financial use, with the term *market value* appearing in 1791, in England.

Never be a bear on the United States.

Attributed both to John Pierpont Morgan (1837–1913) and to his father, Junius Spencer Morgan (1813–90)

The market originally referred not to the entire securities market but, from the 1830s, to specific types of stocks, bonds, or commodities and their dealers; thus, at that time, one spoke only of the grain market, the cotton market, or the market in railroad shares. *Market man* meant a stock market expert by 1895.

the board meant a *board of brokers*, or stock exchange, by 1837. Such a board might also be a *board of trade*, the name for a board of brokers forming a *commodities exchange*, such as the *Chicago Board of Trade*, established in 1848 and growing into the world's largest grain exchange (*commodity* in this sense is an English use dating back to the 15th century).

Not until 1852 did *the board* also mean a blackboard where stocks and their prices were listed, with the New York Stock Exchange's quotation board called *the big board* since the 1920s (*quotation* has been in English stock market use since 1812, *to quote* since 1866).

Wall Street has been used to refer to New York's financial district and America's financial establishment and overall securities market since the mid 1830s (the term *Wall Street broker* was first used in 1836). Merchants, brokers, and bankers had met on the streets and in the coffee houses in the triangle formed by Wall, Broad, and New Streets in lower Manhattan for generations before the Revolutionary War or the organization of the first formal American stock market and, by the 1830s, many leading commercial houses and banks were located there.

Wall Street itself goes back to the days of New York's original Dutch settlers: in 1624 the Dutch West India Company sent the first settlers to what is now Manhattan, these settlers laying out a town and building Fort Amsterdam on the island's southern tip, naming the entire settlement *New Amsterdam*. Twenty-nine years later, in 1653, these Dutch settlers, then numbering about a thousand, had a wall built along the northern boundary of the settlement because they feared attacks from the Indians and the English. The Indians didn't attack, but the wall rotted and fell down in a few years and its outline became a short, narrow dirt road called *Wall Street* (the English fleet, under the Duke of York, did attack and capture New Amsterdam in 1664, the English changing the name of the settlement to *New York* and giving Wall Street its English, rather than its equivalent Dutch, name).

The Street. Wall Street and all of America's financial market was called *the Street* by 1863. This use echoes the English use of *the Alley* to refer to their Exchange Alley.

the New York Stock Exchange (NYSE). The original group that met under the buttonwood tree and at the Tontine Coffee House adopted the name *the New York Stock and Exchange Board* in 1817, then shortened this name to *the New York Stock Exchange* when it moved to its present location on Broad and Wall streets in 1863, during the financial boom period of the Civil War. Many Americans call it and its many branches and affiliates *the stock exchange*, though, of course, that had been the name of the original London one in 1773 and there are many other stock exchanges.

the American Stock Exchange (AMEX). Of course, many merchants, bankers, and brokers who traded in securities in lower Manhattan were not included in the formal group that was to become the New York Stock Exchange. These men were left outside on the

Wall Street in 1884, during a day of panic and frenzied activity.

street for a while longer and were called *curbstone brokers* (1848) and *street brokers* (1856). A group of them formed *the New York Curb Exchange* in 1842, simply called *the curb market* or *the curb* by 1890, and the members then called *curb brokers*, which became *the New York Curb Market Association* in 1911 and finally *the American Stock Exchange* in 1953.

Until 1871 the New York Stock Exchange was a *call market*, its president calling out the names of the securities in alphabetical order at each session as the brokers made their bids to buy and offers to sell from their seats, the transactions then being recorded in a *stock book* (1835). Only members had seats or were allowed to buy and sell; thus members literally had *a seat on the exchange*. Each member had equity in the building the exchange moved into in 1863; thus membership or a seat had real value and, beginning in 1868, was made saleable, giving us the expression *to buy a seat on the exchange* (the price of a seat has varied widely; it was $4,000 in 1876 and $515,000 in 1968, with neither of these being the high nor the low).

During the fifty-year period from about 1830 to 1880 speculators and unscrupulous merchants and brokers developed ways to "beat the market." The best way was to have advanced information on value, prices, and price fluctuations by being or knowing an *insider* (1830, the term *inside information* dates from 1888, *inside dope* from 1919). Another way was with the *wash sale* (1848), which originally meant any pretended sale, as to establish a false quotation (one established a high one and sold or a low one and bought) or to convince a seller his stock had been sold at a lower price than the broker had actually received for it. Other financiers and businessmen might try to *corner* (1836 in this sense) a rival, by manipulating stock prices to drive him out of the market or out of business, which soon led to trying to get a *corner* (this noun use 1841) on the market itself or trying *to corner the market* (1849). Financier and railroad tycoon Jay Gould and speculator James Fisk were masters at this and made these stock market terms well known to many when, on September 24, 1869, they tried to corner the market on gold. President Grant then had the U.S. Treasury put $4 million worth of gold on the market to *break the corner*, but not before the market and the country had their first *Black Friday* (that Friday, September 24, 1869) stock market *panic* (although *Black Friday* was a new American financial term, it was an old British use, based on various calamitous "Black Fridays" in British history and ultimately going back to *Black Friday* as an English designation for Good Friday, when clergymen wore black vestments. The financial use of *panic* as well as of *depression* had both first been used in America in 1819; see also LAISSEZ-FAIRE, INFLATION, AND BREAD RIOTS).

Another term unscrupulous financiers and businessmen added

Jay Gould was a master at ways to corner the market and helped make the term well known.

541

to the vocabulary in this same 1830–80 period was *to water* stock (1865, to dilute its value by issuing more shares initially than the total was worth or to dilute the value of existing shares by creating new ones). In the same period America's own bears and bulls were speculating by buying *long* or *short*, or combining both to *straddle* the market, especially in commodity *futures* bought on *margin* (these last three terms all from 1870). Dishonest brokers might open a *bucket shop* (1880 in financial use, from the original 1875 meaning as a low dive where one could buy questionable liquor cheaply by the pitcher or bucket), claiming it was a legitimate broker's office or stock exchange affiliate, where gullible investors became small-time speculators and stock market gamblers buying and selling small quantities of commodities or stocks quickly with each market fluctuation. By gambling on market fluctuations such people were trying to *scalp the market*, just as did big-time market *scalpers* (both terms 1886; *scalper* had meant one who took scalps from an enemy's head by 1760 and one who sold or resold theater tickets at exorbitant prices by 1869).

Such dealings were, of course, not the norm. Many people bought and held bonds and the new *common* and *preferred* stocks (both terms around 1850), though some preferred stocks were created only as a way to give insiders an advantage. Many people tried to avoid the *cats and dogs* (1879 as worthless or speculative stocks) and eventually hoped to become *coupon clippers* (1882, for wealthy people who live off their bonds by clipping coupons) or own a substantial number of *blue chips* (1904 as stocks of the largest, most reliable corporations, from the blue chips used in poker as the chips of the highest denomination).

The stock market also became much more reliable after the telegraph stock ticker and telephone became common, replacing the mails and messengers so that everyone would have access to the same information and quotations at the same time. The first stock ticker was installed in the New York Stock Exchange in 1867 and by the first half of the 1880s there were enough of them in service so that *stock ticker* and *ticker* were in the general language, with the term *ticker tape* following in 1902 (before that it had been called the stock ticker *ribbon*).

Though *market reports* (1866) had flooded the mails after the Civil War, many had been outdated and unreliable or, as are some similar reports today, merely enthusiastic recommendations of stocks the editors or their backers supported or gloomy condemnations of those they didn't. The telegraph, stock ticker, and telephone, however, also made it possible for publications to obtain and publish accurate information quickly. In 1882 financial statistician Charles Henry Dow and Edward D. Jones founded the publishing firm of *Dow Jones and Co.*, which pioneered in the compilation and dissemination of current and reliable securities

The public be damned! I'm working for my stockholders.
William H. Vanderbilt, to a *Chicago Tribune* reporter in 1883, when questioned about discontinuing an unprofitable New York Central Railroad New York-to-Chicago train that the public found useful.

information. The firm began to publish its first *Dow Jones Average*, the *Dow Jones Industrial Average* price of twelve selected industrial stocks, in 1884, then added other and more complex stock averages over the years (including its New York Stock Exchange *Common Stock Index* in 1966). It started publishing *The Wall Street Journal*, as a collection of day-by-day market and business news bulletins, in 1889 (Walker Barron, founder of several news bureaus and editor of *Barron's Financial Weekly*, acquired Dow Jones in 1909).

Thus by the 1890s anyone who wanted to be reasonably well informed about the stock market and its daily fluctuations and dealings could be, and an increasing number of Americans knew and talked about what went on on the *floor* (1903 as the trading floor of the stock exchange, especially the New York Stock Exchange) or knew that a *floor broker* or *floor man* (1912) assisted *commission house brokers* (floor brokers had been called *$2 brokers* since 1900, from their fee of $2 per transaction). Incidentally, the "floor" of a commodities exchange had been called the *pit* since 1886, this word earlier used to refer to an area on the trading floor where a specific commodity was traded and later used by insiders to refer to the commodities market itself.

As the country and its business grew, stocks proliferated and in 1910 the New York Stock Exchange limited its trading to securities that met certain minimum requirements as to capital assets, number of shareholders and publicly owned shares, etc., listing only these on its board. Such securities were called *listed securities*, all others being *unlisted*. The unlisted stocks were then not bought and sold on the exchange but *over the counter* and became *over-the-*

counter stocks (OTC), the term going back to the days before stock exchanges when various banks sold securities over their counters.

Thus the stock market and the dissemination of market information became more reliable and more Americans invested in the market to split the *melon* (1911 as total profits or dividends shared by stockholders in a company). Few people knew or cared that there had been a *stock market crash* in 1873 (the first time that term had been used; financial *boom* had been used for the first time to describe the recovery from it) or that there had been a *bust* in 1893 (the first time that term had been used to refer to economic conditions) or that many banks and businesses had failed during *the rich man's panic* of 1907. Thus the number of stock market investors and speculators increased, especially during the *Golden Twenties*, when making money in the market seemed like child's play, so that almost everyone seemed *to play the market* (an ominous 1927 term) and to talk about *good times* in 1928 as Montgomery Ward stock rose from 117 to 440 a share, RCA skyrocketed from 85 to 420, and, early in 1929, a seat on the New York Stock Exchange was sold for an all-time high of $625,000.

Then came the great stock market crash of 1929. On Wednesday, October 23, *Black Wednesday*, a selling wave developed and stock prices began to fall drastically; investors tried to save themselves and the selling wave swelled the next day, *Black Thursday*, the actual day of the crash; and on the following Tuesday, October 29, *Black Tuesday*, more than 16 million shares were traded. Three billion dollars in market value was lost as the market lost two-thirds of its value (some stocks fell to as little as one twenty-fifth of their previous value). The *panic*, as it was first called, had become a *crash*, as it was later called, and set off a *depression* that became the *Depression* or the *Great Depression* as the United States entered the deepest, longest economic depression in its history. One out of every four workers was out of work; business bankruptcies, bank failures, and factory closings were at an all-time high.

The Depression lasted ten years, until the outbreak of World War II in 1939. As one of the many aids to recovery, and so the stock market could be trusted again, President Franklin D. Roosevelt and his New Deal created the *Securities and Exchange Commission* (the *SEC*, one of Roosevelt's many *alphabet agencies*) in 1934 to regulate stock exchanges, license brokerage firms, and administer new federal laws governing the issuing, purchase, and sale of securities. Such laws were called *blue sky laws*, a term first recorded in 1912, when it was applied to laws a few states had passed to protect investors from fraud by preventing companies from promising or selling them "the sky" or "the blue sky."

By the time of our entry into World War II, in 1941, the country was stable again; a seat on the New York Stock Exchange was well worth its $17,000 price in 1942. Though the market had its ups

Ticker tape ain't spaghetti. Fiorello La Guardia in a March 29, 1946, speech to the United Nations Relief and Rehabilitation Administration, of which he was then director (he had been mayor of New York City from 1934–45). He meant that the poor of war-ravished Europe didn't share in our general prosperity, that one cannot eat good stock market news.

and downs, it generally prospered after the war and after a mild 1950s *recession* the 60s and early 70s saw the public invest in the *glamour stocks*, especially stocks of new electronics and aerospace firms that were part of a new technological industry. The same period saw the growth of *mutual funds* (*mutual fund* had been a 1798 term for an insurance company whose policy holders were also its shareholders), the first modern investment mutual fund, which pools the resources of individual investors to invest jointly in a variety of securities, having been established in Belgium in 1822. Mutual funds led to such new terms as *open-ended investment company* (a mutual fund in which an investor may buy additional shares at any time), *closed-end investment company* or *publicly traded investment fund* (having a fixed number of shares sold on a stock exchange), *load fund* (sold with a *load* or sales charge, including the dealer's commission), and *no-load fund* (investors buy directly from the fund and pay no sales charges or commissions). Those funds that were bought into quickly and with excitement were called *go-go funds* and those who handled them a *go-go manager*, *go-go broker*, or a golden *go-go boy* (from the early 1960s *go-go dancers*, scantily clad young women stage performers who went through the gyrations of the twist, frug, and other popular dances of the period for the patrons of a discothèque).

The early 1970s saw *stagflation* (a *stag*nant economy plus *inflation*) which gave way to *double-digit inflation* in the late 70s and early 80s. As inflation ran rampant many investors first put their money in bank *certificates of deposit (CDs)* and then in a new form of mutual fund, the *money market fund*. Thus, the stock market and its lure of appreciation and dividends found itself competing with the *money market* and its high interest rates as both large and small investors tried to keep pace with inflation. As always, some predicted that a stock market crash was imminent; others that the market would soon enter a boom period. The only thing that seems certain is that whatever happens there will always be new stock market terms to name and describe it.

We Wuz Robbed!

the immortal cry of the American sportsman, was first heard in thousands of homes on June 21, 1932, just after heavyweight boxer Jack Sharkey won the decision and title over Max Schmeling. Schmeling's manager, Joe Jacobs, shouted, "We wuz robbed!" into the radio microphone over which the fight had been broadcast—and people have been saying it ever since.

Joe Jacobs' other contribution to the American language is that favorite lament over a vain attempt, *I should of stood in bed*. Jacobs had left his sickbed in New York to go to Detroit to watch the 1935 World Series. He bet on Chicago; Detroit won. When he returned to New York he told the sports writers who came to interview him, "I should of stood in bed," which was printed in many papers the next day and has since been used widely to express our opinions about the sorry state of things.

Western Union

was a magic term in the first half of this century; it meant that a uniformed messenger boy, usually on a bicycle, or a telephone operator was delivering an important message: a baby had been born, a friend had arrived at a destination safely, or—during the World Wars—someone close had fallen in action. All young men knew that a *singing telegram* (introduced in 1933 not by Western Union but by the Postal Cable Co., of New York City) was the best way to wish a girlfriend happy birthday and that "What hath God wrought" was Samuel F. B. Morse's first successful telegraph message. This last wasn't true.

Samuel F. B. Morse patented the telegraph in 1832 and perfected Morse code in 1838.

Morse patented the *telegraph* (Greek *tēle*, afar + *graphein*, to write) in 1832, but it took him six more years to perfect his *Morse code* to go with it! Then in 1843 Congress gave him $30,000 to string wire (not called *telegraph wire* until 1852) between Washington and Baltimore, the first nationally important message being sent May 1, 1844, announcing Henry Clay's nomination for President. Not until twenty-three days later did Morse sit down at the sending device in the Supreme Court Chambers in Washington and finally get around to tapping out his famous "What hath God wrought."

The government owned the 44 miles of line between Washington and Baltimore and thought it would make the telegraph a government-run service, like the post office. However, since hardly anyone ever sent a message, even though the service was free at first, the line was turned over to the Magnetic Telegraph Co., operated by two of Morse's partners. In 1856 *Western Union* (Ezra Cornell suggested the name) was formed from the old New York and Mississippi Valley Printing Telegraph Co. and by 1861 extended its line from Omaha to California (the first transcontinental message being from California's Chief Justice Samuel J. Field to President Lincoln, declaring California's loyalty to the Union).

The communiqués were called *telegraphic dispatches, telegraphic communications,* or *telegraph messages* until about 1850, when they began to be called *telegrams;* then by the First World War they were beginning to be called *wires.* A telegram sent by underseas cable has been called a *cablegram* since the appearance of such a service in the 1860s, and the shorter form *cable* came into use in the 1870s. After 1901, transatlantic messages could also be sent via Marconi's *wireless telegraph* (1895) or *wireless* (1896) using radio

Postal telegraph messengers in the early 1900s. As the signs show, the terms cablegram *and* cable *are used interchangeably.*

waves, and these messages were called *Marconigrams* by many, *radiotelegrams* by the more technical, and simply *radiograms* by 1910.

By 1920, telegrams were no longer being sent by Morse code but by the new *teletype*. Teletype telegraphers were considered romantic figures in the 1920s and 30s and their lingo was popular: *glass arm* being the name for telegrapher's cramp and *mill* for his typewriter; *73* was telegraphers' code indicating "regards" or any standard closing to a message, and *88* meant "love and kisses." These terms never caught on but *30*, meaning the end of a message, did, and was eventually popularized by newspaper correspondents who used it to end dispatches and by Hollywood columnist Jimmy Fidler, who used it to end his columns and radio broadcasts beginning in 1934.

Wild Animals such as bear, elk, and deer, abounded in early America. But before the days of plentiful zoos and photographs most Americans had never seen or talked about wild animals from Africa, India, or other exotic places. It wasn't until enterprising sea captains imported exotic animals to sell to traveling showmen that words such as *lion* or *polar bear* had much vivid personal meaning. The first African *lion* was brought to America in 1721, the same year Bostonians were talking about seeing their first *camel*. The first *polar bear* came in 1733, the first *tiger* and

547

orangutan in 1789, the first *ostrich* in 1794, and the first *elephant* (a baby one) in 1796. You can be sure these strange creatures caused a lot of talk in their day.

In 1789 the first large collection of exotic wild animals, both alive and stuffed, was put on permanent exhibit in New York's Wall Street. By the 1830s most circuses had a collection of animals, which were generally under their own tent by the 1850s. These were called zoological *exhibitions* or *animal shows*, until the word *menagerie* became popular in the 1860s and 70s. Such circus collections included elephants, camels, lions, tigers, zebras, hippopotami, kangaroos, ostriches, etc., and served as traveling zoos where many Americans saw their first exotic wild animal.

Incidentally, our word *monkeyshines* dates from 1828. *To monkey around* and *monkey business* are expressions of the early 1800s and *to make a monkey out of someone* is from 1899, all being terms based on the increasing number of monkeys seen in circuses and zoos. A large or uncouth man was called a *big ape* by 1831 and *gorilla* was used to mean a hairy, tough man by the 1860s and a thug by 1926. These uses of *gorilla* weren't very imaginative or new, however. The ancient Greeks got their 5th century B.C. word *Gorillai* from the native name of a hairy African tribe and used it to mean any savage; our word *gorilla* was then first used in England in 1799 to mean a hairy aborigine. Only later was the name *gorilla* given to the largest of the anthropoid apes, by the American missionary and naturalist Thomas S. Savage, who on his return from Africa in 1849 was the first to describe and name it—thus *gorilla* actually meant a hairy, tough man before it meant the ape; the ape gets its name from the man and not vice versa as we might think.

Picture Credits

ABBREVIATIONS
LGC: The Lester Glassner Collection
MMA–FSA: Museum of Modern Art–Film Stills Archive
NYPL: New York Public Library
UPI: United Press International

page 16, Library of Congress. *page 17*, The Smithsonian Institution, top/Abby Aldrich Rockefeller Folk Art Collection, Williamsburg, VA, bottom. *page 18*, H. J. Heinz Company. *pages 19, 21*, Library of Congress. *pages 22, 23*, American Museum of Natural History. *pages 24, 26*, Library of Congress. *page 27*, Minnesota Historical Society. *page 28*, Free Library of Philadelphia, bottom. *page 30*, State Historical Society of Wisconsin. *page 31*, Minnesota Historical Society. *page 32*, Library of Congress. *pages 33, 35, 36, 37, 38, 39*, UPI. *page 40*, Library of Congress. *pages 41, 42, 43*, UPI. *page 44*, UPI, top/Library of Congress, bottom. *page 45*, Library of Congress, top center and top right/UPI, all others. *page 46*, UPI. *page 47*, UPI top/Wide World Photos, bottom. *page 48*, UPI. *page 51*, Library of Congress. *pages 53, 54, 55, 56, 57, 58*, UPI. *pages 59, 60*, Library of Congress, top/Miami Beach Visitor and Convention Authority, bottom. *page 61*, Library of Congress. *page 62*, UPI. *pages 63, 64*, Library of Congress. *page 65*, NYPL, top/Virga Archives, bottom. *page 67*, UPI. *page 68*, Minnesota Historical Society, top/UPI, bottom. *page 69*, Library of Congress. *page 70*, NYPL Picture Collection. *page 71*, Hanky Panky, Ltd. *page 72*, Library of Congress. *page 73*, Sealy, Inc. *page 75*, NYPL Picture Collection. *page 77*, National Gallery of Art. *page 79*, Free Library of Philadelphia. *pages 93, 94*, NYPL Picture Collection. *page 96*, UPI. *pages 99, 102*, Library of Congress. *pages 103, 106, 117, 121, 122, 123, 124, 125, 128, 129, 130*, UPI. *page 132*, NYPL Picture Collection. *page 134*, Land O'Lakes, Inc. *page 135*, Harper's Weekly, Nov. 29, 1862. *page 136*, Library of Congress, top/Leo Castelli Gallery, N.Y., bottom left/Campbell Soup Company, bottom right. *page 137*, BIRDS EYE (a registered trademark of General Foods Corporation), bottom. *page 138*, The Historic New Orleans Collection. *page 139*, Hershey Foods Corporation, top/Peter Paul Cadbury, Inc., bottom. *page 140*, Library of Congress. *page 141*, NYPL Picture Collection. *page 142*, Library of Congress. *page 144*, LGC. *page 146*, Library of Congress. *pages 148, 149, 150, 151*, NYPL Picture Collection. *page 152*, LGC. *pages 155, 157, 158, 161, 162*, The Mariners Museum, Newport News, VA. *page 163*, Harper's Weekly, Jan. 16, 1869. *page 165*, The Mariners Museum. *page 167*, Library of Congress. *page 168*, The Henry Ford Museum, Dearborn, Michigan, top. *page 169*, Seiko Time Corporation. *page 174*, Library of Congress. *page 175*, Thomas J. Lipton, Inc., top and bottom. *pages 176, 177*, Library of Congress. *page 178*, Borden, Inc. *page 180*, Library of Congress, top/Whitney Museum of American Art, NY, bottom. *pages 182, 183, 184, 188*, Chase Manhattan Archives. *page 189*, Library of Congress. *pages 191, 192, 194, 195, 196*, Chase Manhattan Archives. *page 197*, Chase Manhattan Archives, top/Coin World Photo-Lab, center/Chase Manhattan Archives, bottom. *pages 198, 199, 200, 201, 202*, Chase Manhattan Archives. *pages 213, 216*, Library of Congress. *page 217*, UPI, top/International Museum of Photography at George Eastman House, bottom. *page 218*, Library of Congress, top and bottom left/U.S. Dept. of Army, bottom right. *page 219*, Chicago Historical Society. *page 220*, Library of Congress. *page 222*, Library of Congress top/Index of American Design and Decorative Arts, bottom. *pages 223, 224, 225, 228, 229*, Library of Congress. *page 230*, UPI. *page 232*, The Art Institute of Chicago, top/Library of Congress, bottom. *page 235*, Harper's Weekly, July 15, 1865. *pages 237, 240, 242, 243, 245, 246, 248, 250, 251, 253, 254, 255*, UPI. *page 256*, ABC. *pages 258, 259, 260, 261*, UPI. *page 263*, Library of Congress. *page 267*, UPI. *page 270, 276*, UPI. *page 277*, UPI top, bottom center, bottom right/Library of Congress bottom left. *pages 278, 279*, UPI. *pages 280, 281, 282*, NYPL Picture Collection. *page 283*, Altermedia, Ltd., top/Avon, bottom. *pages 284, 285, 287, 288*, UPI. *page 291*, Free Library of Philadelphia. *pages 298, 299, 300, 301, 303*, Library of Congress. *page 304*, Jardine's Texas Foods, Austin, TX. *pages 305, 306*, Library of Congress. *page 307*, UPI. *pages 309, 311*, UPI. *pages 312, 313, 314, 315*, Library of Congress. *page 316*, Library of Congress, top and center/Harper's Weekly, Nov. 26, 1859, bottom. *page 318*, Ohio Historical Society. *page 319*, Library of Congress, top. *page 329*, Library of Congress, top and center left/UPI bottom left/The Metropolitan Museum of Art, Gift of Mr. and Mrs. Carl Stoeckil, 1897, bottom right. *page 331*, NYPL Picture Collection. *pages 335, 336, 342, 343*, Library of Congress. *page 345*, Brown-Sussman Archive, Shady, N.Y. *page 346*, Museum of the City of New York. *page 347*, Library of Congress, left/Colorado Historical Society, right. *pages 348, 349*, Library of Congress. *page 351*, UPI. *page 353*, Drake Well Museum. *pages 354, 356*, Library of Congress. *page 357*, Library of Congress, top/National Portrait Gallery, Smithsonian Institution, Washington, D.C. *page 358*, NYPL Picture Collection. *page 361*, UPI. *page 363*, LCG. *page 365*, UPI. *page 366*, National Archives, top/Library of Congress, bottom. *page 368*, Library of Congress. *page 371*, National Archives, top/Free Library of Philadelphia, bottom. *pages 372, 373*, Library of Congress. *page 375*, International Museum of Photography at George Eastman House. *page 376*, NYPL Picture Collection. *pages 377, 379*, Library of Congress. *page 381*, Henry Ford Museum, The Edison Institute. *page 382*, LGC. *page 383*, Library of Congress. *page 385*, LGC. *page 389*, Library of Congress. *pages 390, 391, 392*, LGC. *page 393*, MMA–FSA, left/LGC, bottom middle/UPI right. *page 394*, LGC top/UPI bottom. *page 395*, LGC top/Library of Congress, bottom. *pages 397, 398, 399, 400, 401, 402, 404, 405, 406*, LGC. *page 407*, Virga Archive. *page 408*, LGC. *page 409*, LGC, top/MMA–FSA, bottom. *pages 410, 412, 414*, LGC. *page 415*, Library of Congress. *pages 416, 417*, LGC. *page 418*, LGC, top left/MMA–FSA top right/Virga Archive, center. *pages 419, 420*, LGC. *page 421*, UPI. *pages 423, 425*, LGC. *page 426*, Library of Congress, top left/LGC, top right/MMA—FSA, bottom *pages 427, 428, 429*, LGC. *page 430*, UPI. *pages 431, 432*, LGC. *page 433*, LGC, left/Universal Pictures, right. *page 434*, NYPL Picture Collection. *page 436*, UPI. *page 437*, LGC. *page 438*, Borden, Inc., left/LGC, right. *page 439*, NYPL Picture Collection. *page 440*, National Portrait Gallery, Smithsonian Institution, top/Library of Congress, bottom. *page 441*, The New Britain Museum of American Art. *page 443*, Library of Congress. *pages 444, 447*, NYPL Picture Collection. *page 449*, Lane County Museum. *page 450*, Museum of the City of New York. *page 451*, UPI. *page 453*, The Historic New Orleans Collection, top/NYPL Picture Collection, bottom. *page 457*, Museum of Fine Arts, Boston, Bequest of Maxim Karolik. *pages 459, 461*, Library of Congress. *page 463*, First Church of Christ Scientist. *page 464*, Free Library of Philadelphia. *pages 465, 466*, UPI. *page 467*, "White Tower" by Ralph Goings, OK Harris Gallery, N.Y. *pages 469, 470*, Library of Congress. *page 471*, UPI. *page 473*, Library of Congress. *page 482*, NYPL Picture Collection. *page 483*, Library of Congress, top/Smith College Archives, bottom. *pages 484, 486, 487*, Library of Congress. *page 490*, Roger Fleming Estate, University of Texas, Institute of Texan Cultures. *page 492*, Library of Congress. *page 493*, Leslie Eisenberg Folk Art Gallery, N.Y. *pages 495, 496*, Library of Congress. *page 497*, Hampton Jitney, top/A.T.& T Photo Center. *page 498*, Library of Congress. *pages 499, 500, 501, 502, 503*, A.T.& T. Photo Center. *page 505*, Library of Congress. *page 507*, Macy*s Annual Thanksgiving Day Parade. *page 508*, Library of Congress. *page 509*, The Whaling Museum, New Bedford, MA. *page 510*, The Whaling Museum, New Bedford, MA, top/The Peabody Museum of Salem, left/Library of Congress, right. *page 511*, Campbell Soup Company. *pages 514, 515, 516, 519, 520, 521*, Library of Congress. *page 523*, The Archives of Labor and Urban Affairs, Wayne State University. *page 524*, The Archives of Labor and Urban Affairs, Wayne State University, top/Library of Congress, bottom. *pages 525, 527, 528, 530*, Library of Congress. *pages 531, 532*, UPI. *page 534*, Library of Congress. *page 538*, New York Historical Society. *pages 540, 541, 543*, Library of Congress. *pages 546, 547*, Library of Congress.

INDEX

This is a combined index of words and phrases (which appear in *italic* type)
and of subjects and names (which appear in regular type).

552

557

radiator, 348
radio, 203, 208, 475
radioactive wastes, 355
radio ad, 18
radiograms, 547
radiotelegrams, 547
radiotelephone, 502
(radio) tube, 208
rag, 82
rag, to, 76
ragged, 90
Ragged Dick (Alger), 366
ragging, 79, 82
Raiders, 260
raiding, 531
rail, 71
railroad, 203, 208
railroad, hoboes and, 311-12
Railroad Romance, 379
railroad stiff, 312
railroad time, 179
rails, 105, 208
Rail Splitter, the, 219
railway, 203, 208
Rain, 305
Rainbow, 156
raincheck, 38, 47
raincoat, 208
rain pitchforks, to, 466
"Rainy Day, The" (Longfellow), 357
raise, 518
raise Cain, 82
raise (in salary), 208
raise one's Ebenezer, 359
raising bees, 317
rake down, 518
rake in, 518
rake off, 518
rake over the coals, 82
Ralston, 133
Ralston's Health Club, 131
Ralston's Health Club Breakfast Food, 131
Rambouillet, France, 98
Ramillie wig, 67
Ramos, Henry, 172
Ramos gin fizz, 172
rampant, 361
Rams, 260
R and A, 263
Randolph, Philip, 525
rap, 82
rap, to, 82
rap, to beat the, 82
rap session, 82
rap (someone's) knuckles, to, 82
rare, 489
rare (meat), 208
raspberry, 38
rat, 521
rat cheese, 25
rates, 208
rat fink, 521
rating system, 429
rattle, 326
rattle away, 78
rattlebrain, 326
rattlebrained, 326
rattled, 91
rattlehead, 326
rattleheaded, 326
rattle off, 78
rattler, 295, 360
rattlesnake, 360
rattletrap, 78
rattle watch, 221
rattling, 295
rattrap cheese, 25
razor, 66
razor blades, 66
razor strop, 65
razz, 38

razzberry, 38
re-, 319
-re, 214
readers, 463
ready, the, 190
Ready! Action! Camera! Go!, 383
ready cash, 190
ready money, 190
ready pennies, 190
Ready! Start Your Action!, 383
ready-to-wear (clothes), 208
Reagan, Ronald, 254
real cool, 291, 310
real-estate agent, 208
real gone, 291, 310
reals, 185, 196
realtor, 210
Rebecca of Sunnybrook Farm, 393
Rebel, The (Camus), 310
rebel without a cause, 310
receiver, 246
receiver hook, 500
reception sandwich, 477
recess, 211
recession, 545
recompence, 214
recompense, 214
recruit, 39
recruiting, 245
red, 193, 257
Red, 216
red, see, 361
red barn, 31
red cent, 193
red dog, 257
red eye, 100
redeye gravy, 490
red-eye special, 100
Redford, Robert, 432
red ham gravy, 290
redhot monsters, 344
Red Ike, 218
red lead, 475, 476
red light district, 452
red Merk, 475
red Merk and violets, 475
Redneck Power: The Wit and Wisdom of Billy Carter, 286
red phone, 503
Red River, 411
Reds, 433
red shirts, 225, 228
Redskins, 260
Red Snapper, 173
Red Sox, 38, 261
red stretch, 475
Reed, Axton, 148
Reed, Carol, 419
reel of cotton, 209
reel off, 78
Reeve, Hazard, 422
reezon (reason), 213
referee, 51, 105
refrigerator, 318-20
refrigerator car, 319
regal, 185
registered mail, 534
register luggage, to, 203
registers, 348
Reid, John, 272
Reid, Mrs. John, 272
release, 387
religion:
    blue laws and, 492-94
    Sabbath observances in, 62-63, 142
religions, 456-64
religious conversion, 458-64
(Religious) Society of Friends, 457
renewable fuel, 356
rent, 206
repair area, 204
repairman, 208

repeaters, 476
Representative Men (Emerson), 309
Rescued from the Eagle's Nest, 382
research, 211
rest area, 204
restaurant, 467-71
Restaurants, Lunch Counters, Diners, and Drive-Ins, 467-76
restorator, 467
retard, 326
retirees, 478
retirement, 478
retirement houses, 478
retirement villages, 478
retiring a number, 247
return, 208
Reuther, Walter, 531
Revealing Secrets, 87-89
Revenue Cutter Service, 446
Revenue Marine, 446
reverse lamp, 204
reversible (overcoat), 208
reversing light, 204
Review (Catholic Film Office), 428
revolting, 298
Revolutionary era, 29, 31, 76
    alcohol in, 98-99
    camp followers in, 450
    cheese in, 25
    cocktails and, 169
    currency used in, 181-85, 196
    name-giving practices in, 331
    picketing in, 517
    religious conversion in, 458
    speculation in, 539
    sugar houses in, 370
    tea protests in, 174-75
    wigs in, 67
Reynolds, R. J., 147, 148
RFD, 535
Rhode Island chowder, 304
rhubarb, 44
rib, 86
ribber, 86
ribbing, 86
ribbon, 542
riboflavin, 537
ribose, 537
rice, 447
Rice, Grantland, 43, 251, 252, 253
Rice, John, 425
rice corn, 438
Rice Krispies, 133
Richard, 328, 330
Richard Roe, 327-28
rich as, 365
rich as Astor, 365
rich as Croesus, 365
rich as Rockefeller, 365
Richburg, Miss., 117
richer than Astor, 365
richer than Croesus, 365
richer than God, 365
rich man's panic, 544
Richmond, Bill, 108
Rickard, George Lewis "Tex," 124, 126, 127-29
Rickles, Don, 323
ride, 82, 258
riding, 82
riding blind baggage, 312
riding the gravy train, 365
riding the rails, 312
riding the rods, 312
riding wigs, 67
rifles, as symbol of victory, 337
Riggs, L. A. "Speed," 149
right, 34
right and left center guard, 239
right and left end rush, 239
right and left tackle, 239
right as a goose, to be, 287
right as rain, 466

right center, 34
right field, 34
right fielder, 34
right-hand, 270
right off the bat, 47
right of way, 208
right short, 36
right short fielder, 36
right shortstop, 36
right-to-work, 530
rile (up), 361
riley, 361
ring, 109, 502
ring, the, 109
ring around the collar, 95
ringside, 109
ringsiders, 109
Ring's Verbena Cream, 65
ring up, 502
ringworm, 92
rinse, 302
Rin Tin Tin, 399
rip, 360, 485
rip off, 485
rip out, 360
ripping, 295
riproaring, 295
riproarious, 295
ripsnorter, 295
rise, 208, 518
rising sun quilt, 71
risk, 214
risque, 214
Ritter, Tex, 411
Ritz, César, 367
ritzing, 367
ritzy, 367
Ritzy, 367
RKO, 399
roach cake, 474
Road, The (London), 315
road building bees, 317
roadie, 315
road kid, 315
road kids, 314
roadside diners, 471
road signs, 18
road sisters, 315
Road to Wellville, The (Post), 133
roarer, 295
Roaring 20s, 89, 205, 330
    cigarette smoking in, 150
    hairstyles in, 300-301
    sex in, 454-55
roast, 82
roasted, 82
robber, 485
robber barons, 366
robe, 73
Robe, The, 422
Robert, 330, 333, 334
Roberta, 332
Roberts, Arthur, 86
Robertson, Allan, 264
Robertson, Oscar, 57
Robinson, 484
Robinson, Bill "Bojangles," 291, 401
Robinson, Edward G., 402, 407, 408
Robinson, Jackie, 43
Robinson, Ray, 122, 123
Robinson, "Sugar Ray" (Walter Smith), 122-23
Rob Roy, 173
Rob Roy (Scott), 173
Rochemont, Louis de, 414
rock, 191
Rockefeller, John D., 364, 365, 366
Rockets, 260
rocking chair, 281
Rockne, Knute, 243, 246, 250, 254
rocks, to have a pocketful of, 191

About the Author

Stuart Berg Flexner is one of America's major linguists and social historians. After undergraduate work at the University of Louisville and graduate work at Cornell University, he was appointed professor of English Literature and Linguistics at Cornell; he subsequently pursued a varied and successful career in trade, textbook and reference publishing. He worked for six years in Mexico with the Mexican National Board of Education in its anti-illiteracy program, then became senior editor and Vice President at Random House, where he was a major editor of *The Random House Dictionary—The Unabridged Edition, The Random House College Dictionary*, and *The Random House School Dictionary*. After eight years as a publishing consultant, writer and lecturer, he rejoined Random House as an editor-in-chief of its dictionary department in 1980.

Mr. Flexner's own books include the landmark *Dictionary of American Slang, The Family Word Finder*, the highly successful *How to Increase Your Word Power*, and the widely acclaimed *I Hear America Talking*. His works on the American language and American social history have been translated into German, French, Japanese and Russian, and his articles have appeared in almost all major American magazines.

He lives with his wife and two children in Greenwich, Connecticut.